Affirmative Action in Antidiscrimination Law and Policy

Affirmative Action in Antidiscrimination Law and Policy

AN OVERVIEW AND SYNTHESIS

WILLIAM M. LEITER
SAMUEL LEITER

SECOND EDITION

Published by State University of New York Press, Albany

© 2011 State University of New York

For information, contact State University of New York Press, Albany, NY
www.sunypress.edu

Production by Ryan Morris
Marketing by Michael Campochiaro

Library of Congress Cataloging-in-Publication Data

Leiter, William M., 1934–
    Affirmative action in antidiscrimination law and policy : an overview and synthesis / William M. Leiter and Samuel Leiter. — 2nd ed.
        p. cm.
    Samuel Leiter name appears first on the earlier edition.
    Includes bibliographical references and index.
    ISBN 978-1-4384-3513-8 (hardcover : alk. paper)
    ISBN 978-1-4384-3514-5 (pbk: alk. paper)
    1. Affirmative action programs—Law and legislation—United States.
2. Discrimination in employment—Law and legislation—United States.
3. Discrimination—Law and legislation—United States. I. Leiter, Samuel, 1922– II. Title.

    KF4755.5.L45 2011
    344.7301'133—dc22   2010031921

10 9 8 7 6 5 4 3 2 1

Dedicated to Sheila Leiter—William's beloved wife and editor

Contents

Acknowledgments

Thanks are extended to FindLaw and Westlaw for permission to download and reproduce extended excerpts of U.S. Supreme Court opinions. Additionally, Sage Publications, Inc. granted the authors permission to reproduce a portion of their essay (see pages 114–19 herein) titled, *Affirmative Action and the Presidential Role in Modern Civil Rights Reform: A Sampler of Books of the 1990s*, 29 Presidential Studies Quarterly, 175, 184–88 (March, 1999)© Center for the Study of the Presidency.

Note on Citations

Citations used by courts have been incorporated in the opinions excerpted herein at the discretion of the authors/editors of this text. Where the footnotes of these opinions were reproduced, their numbers were changed to follow the order of this volume's citations.

The authors' text citations conform with the *The University of Chicago Manual of Legal Citation* (Bancroft-Whitney 1989). Where citations from other documents are reproduced in this volume, the style of the original was maintained.

Bracketed numbers located in excerpts from U.S. Supreme Court Opinions refer to page numbers in the reporter cited in the title. The 2009 U.S. statutory and regulatory dates cited herein are from the U.S. Government Printing Office web site of mid-summer, 2009.

One

Introduction

Introduction to Second Edition

Of Updates and Supplements

The purpose of the second edition is twofold: (1) to update the first edition published in 2002 to the onset of the Obama administration, particularly with respect to the nonremedial, diversity rationale which has been advanced to support preferences associated with traditionally practiced affirmative action; and (2) to supplement the first edition's primary focus on race/ethnic/gender discrimination by examining age, disability, sexual orientation, and criminal justice antidiscrimination initiatives. A new chapter—chapter 8—has been added to explore these initiatives and their affirmative action dimensions. Other supplements appear throughout the volume, including an examination of the impact of immigration and ethno-racial intermarriage on affirmative action; proposed affirmative action in the criminal justice arena; the U.S. Civil Rights Commission's critique of federal procurement programs; and previously uncovered efforts at housing integration.

The updating herein will review recent Supreme Court opinions on employment discrimination; educational admissions; the dilution of minority voting strength; electoral districting; and the statute of limitations in Title VII of the 1964 Civil Rights Act. Additional updating will focus on single-sex education; the treatment by the lower courts of the strict scrutiny requirement imposed on affirmative-action operations by the Supreme Court; the impact of English-immersion programs mandated by California for school children with limited English skills; programs designed to abolish state and local affirmative action; and recent statistics on employment patterns for groups protected by affirmative action.

Nonremedial, diversity affirmative action of central importance to the second edition involves an extremely controversial doctrine, which was enunciated at the Supreme Court level by Justice Powell in 1978[1] but remained

1

in limbo for twenty-five years due to the Supreme Court's refusal to treat the issue. Finally in 2003, the Court decided that the diversity rationale undergirding the University of Michigan's race/ethnic preferential admission program at its law school satisfied the dictates of the Equal Protection Clause. This decision legitimated the diversity rationale as an alternative to the traditional remedial basis of affirmative action in the area of public university admissions.

As described in the Introduction to the First Edition replicated in its essentials below, the traditional remedial rationale for affirmative action was to remedy prohibited discrimination, which was banned by law, and which had been cultivated by the nation's systemic mistreatment of minorities and females. Clearly, this remedial objective is furthered by diversity efforts—what we call nonremedial affirmative action because diversity advocacy calls for race/gender/ethnic preferences comparable to those in remedial affirmative action, and is doubtless driven by remediation objectives.[2] As presented by Justice Powell, though, and facially by diversity advocates, diversity affirmative action advocated that members from a wide variety of groups should be well represented in the nation's higher educational apparatus—not necessarily to correct illegal discrimination—but to expose differences in ideas among people, and to generate a robust exchange of ideas on campus. Currently, the diversity rationale is a dominant element in the ongoing debate over protected-group preferential treatment.

Introduction to First Edition, 2002

The Topic

The subject of this treatise/casebook is the legal and ideological controversy over the application of affirmative action policy to combat discrimination based on race, national origin/ethnicity, and gender. Racism, sexism, and ethnic discrimination have long represented a seemingly intractable problem. Affirmative action was conceived as an attack on this ingrained problem but today it is widely misunderstood. We feel the time is ripe to work toward a comprehensive review, which we attempt in this book.

Affirmative action differs from other antidiscrimination initiatives in that (1) it targets and seeks to remedy societal bias (as manifested in public and private illegal action), not individual malefactors; (2) it mandates race, ethnic, and gender-conscious remedies for the disproportionately adverse effects—the so-called *disparate impact*—of societal discrimination on protected groups, whether or not specific discriminatory intent on the part of individual defendants can be isolated; (3) it seeks to integrate institutions by race, ethnicity, and gender.[3] As will be seen, the doctrine of *disparate impact* is a particularly central reason for the quarrel over affirmative action, and thus a central theme of this book.

Affirmative action connotes remedial consideration of race, ethnicity, or sex as a factor, among others, in decision making about outreach, jobs, government contracting, K-12 student assignment, university admission, voting rights and housing. The goal of this process is to redress the disadvantage under which members of disparately impacted groups are said to labor. The relative weight accorded to the race, national origin/ethnicity, or sex-factor varies from program to program; thus, affirmative action remedies range from disseminating job information to preferential employment and admissions practices, classroom integration, the creation of majority-minority legislative districts, and court-ordered quotas in egregious discrimination cases.

Opponents of affirmative action generally portray it as a radical departure from equal opportunity's original goal. In their version, the founding fathers of modern civil rights reform conceived of racial, ethnic, and gender discrimination as *intentional* maltreatment—*disparate treatment*, so-called—and strictly limited the remedy to parity—*equal treatment*, as it became to be known. Affirmative action came into being by displacing these time-honored precepts with the revolutionary notion that the *group* effects of societal bias warrant government intervention, wholly apart from the question of intent. The upshot, according to the critics, has been the ascendancy of protected-group preferences and anti-meritocratic equality of *results*.

In this book, we endeavor to present an evenhanded account of these claims, and the counterclaims of affirmative action's advocates in the spheres of employment, contracting, education, voting rights, and housing. We focus on affirmative action as the remedy for the effects of *both* overtly neutral practices that disparately impact minorities and women; and government-sanctioned (*de jure*/ intentional) segregation of protected groups in education and housing.[4] In addition, we visit the alternative rationale of "diversity," that is, increased nonremedial inclusion of protected groups in the economy and education.

A Thumbnail History

Affirmative action came to the fore some half-century ago, at the beginning of a new era in civil rights reform. Prior reform initiatives had dealt mainly with intentional racial maltreatment of individuals and other traditional barriers to equal treatment. However, during our recent tumultuous confrontation with the nation's racist past, the ideology of reform took on a far more proactive cast. True equality, it was said, would be unattainable without some form of compensation for the inherited disadvantage of disparately impacted minorities and females.[5] Under the umbrella label of affirmative action, providing such special assistance on the basis of group membership—rather than individual victimization—displaced "equal treatment" as the hallmark of federal policy.

From the late 1960s, affirmative action fostered a nationwide torrent of court orders, government programs, and voluntary plans, which provided benefits ranging from outreach and special training; hiring goals and timetables; preferences in hiring, promotion, and university admission; public school integration; political representation; and ethno-racially "balanced" housing through the indirect means of subsidizing the movement of the poor to higher socioeconomic areas. More than any other recent experiment in social engineering, this profusion of minority and female privilege evoked public outcries against claimed overinclusiveness, violations of the merit principle, and "reverse discrimination." Nonetheless, with the spirited support of the courts until the end of the 1980s, affirmative action set the standard for equal opportunity in the public and private economies, and society as a whole. By the 1990s, the early limitation of "protected groups" to blacks had yielded to widespread coverage of Hispanics, women, American Indians, and Asians. Affirmative action represented the centerpiece of America's most ambitious, most promising, attempt to overcome the scourge of race, ethnic, and gender bias. (For a sampler of the extensive federal program, see Appendix One to this volume at 337–54.)

The promise has not been fulfilled. Affirmative action has surely worked important policy changes; but there is no avoiding the fact that antiminority discrimination and sexism remain forces to be reckoned with. Whether affirmative action is up to this task is open to increasingly serious question. A series of adverse court rulings and state referenda in the 1990s have raised doubts about its legality. Public opposition is great. One cannot discount the possibility that affirmative action will soon be discarded or emasculated. The day may come when we have learned how to handle our racial/ethnic differences; what the history of affirmative action teaches is that such a day is not yet upon us.

The Book

Affirmative action is indisputably the flashpoint of America's civil rights agenda. The book covers affirmative action's origins and growth; the reasons for its current predicament; its impact on American society; and its future antidiscrimination role, if any. We have immersed ourselves in the literature of discrete disciplines that deal with these subjects: law, history, economics, statistics, sociology, political science, urban studies, and criminology. Our text integrates the relevant legal materials (constitutional and statutory provisions, regulations, and case law) with analysis and commentary that draw upon the ranking specialists (academic and otherwise) in the cited fields of study. We are convinced that affirmative action would make an outstanding case study in constitutional law, and respectfully offer our treatment as a model for constitutional studies. Though the subject is intricate, our goal is simple: to further a better understanding of affirmative action's complexities through an evenhanded presentation of its roots, substantive operations and diverse applications, eye-crossing issues, and endlessly debated impact.

In chapter 2 of this interdisciplinary synthesis, we examine the government's abortive attempt to eradicate the effects of racial discrimination after the Civil War. We also examine the question of which groups should be covered by affirmative action. Chapter 3 deals with the genesis and operations of affirmative action in employment. Chapters 4 and 5 describe affirmative action's role in education. In chapter 6, we recount affirmative action's record in countering voting rights discrimination. Chapter 7 treats America's limited efforts to deploy affirmative action against residential segregation. The new chapter 8 treats age, disability, and sexual orientation discrimination. In chapter 9, we raise central legal questions and summarize primary ideological claims, including those made by a representative sample of distinguished disputants.

This book highlights affirmative action's legal dimensions. Here there has been no "separation of powers." Rather, the separate institutions of our national government—the courts, the bureaucracy, and the legislature—have all been involved in saying what law is. Often, the study of lawmaking is artificially truncated because our texts and courses focus on one branch to the neglect of others. Our study attempts to reduce this myopia. Further, it underscores the lack of guidance provided by Congress and the Supreme Court in critical areas. Thus, Congress—in equal employment opportunity (Title VII)[6]—did not formally adopt disparate-impact theory until some two decades after the courts and the administrators had nourished it into a flourishing concern. (And Congress has yet to define what it means by the concept.) Likewise, it was not until 1968 that the Supreme Court ruled that its 1954 decision to end racial segregation in the public schools also required racial integration. The merit of governmental ambiguity is a question that should also be explored in connection with the bureaucracy. At the heart of major affirmative action programs is the administrative requirement that good faith efforts be employed to provide compensatory benefits to protected groups. What constitutes good faith depends on the differing values of the scrutinizing bureaucrats who may impose serious sanctions for what are viewed as deviations from that slippery standard.

Our interdisciplinary approach argues that a central reason for affirmative action's current predicament is uncertainty over the objective of antidiscrimination law. Had Congress, in the beginning, defined *discrimination* in Title VII we might have been spared the fevered dispute over whether that law contemplates affirmative remediation (equal *results*) or only discrimination cessation (*equal treatment*). However, as we show in chapter 3, this fundamental substantive issue was left open. The concept of affirmative action as a remedy for disparate impact (what we call *disparate-impact* affirmative action) came into being as a court-sanctioned administrative interpretation of this legislative gap. In effect, the bureaucracy, with the courts' blessings, took it upon itself to complete Congress' unfinished business. It seems fair to say that Congress was primarily responsible for the legal muddle that is reflected in the conflicting rulings which the Supreme Court, over time, has issued in interpreting Title VII. For its part, as will be seen, the Supreme Court has magnified the legal muddle on the constitutional level by initially failing to muster a majority on the issue of the proper standard of affirmative action judicial review. Further, (as this volume goes to print) the Court has refused both to clarify critical aspects of that standard and determine the validity of nonremedial affirmative action.

We believe that this lamentable state of affairs is directly attributable to the government's consistent departures from constitutional norms. The repeated failure of both Congress and the Supreme Court to discharge their responsibilities, coupled with the bureaucracy's intrusion on the legislative sphere, have challenged the principle of separation of powers, and have deprived the public of sorely needed guidance. In our view, this perspective on affirmative action deserves greater emphasis.

Remembrance of Things Past

Affirmative action is not our first "equal opportunity" program. We see it as a revival of the ill-fated attempt to make citizens out of slaves after the Civil War. The past is prologue, and it is the past to which we will turn in chapter 2.

Two

The Roots of Affirmative Action; The Women's Movement; and Affirmative Action's Group Coverage

Reconstruction and the Origins of Affirmative Action

Reconstruction's Enduring Achievement

Affirmative action first cropped up in the modern era as a theory for advancing education, work, and voting opportunities for disadvantaged minorities. Affirmative action's initial agenda was to complete the task that post–Civil War Reconstruction had undertaken, but abandoned, a full century earlier, namely, the integration of America's black community into the economic and political mainstream. Affirmative action's operational concept was the achievement of nonracial civic equality—a notion that Reconstruction had inserted into our constitutional order. In this sense, affirmative action as a legal right originated in the Reconstruction era.[1]

Indeed, the inception of modern affirmative action might best be understood as a continuation or revival of Reconstruction. In the aftermath of the Civil War, as in recent history, the overriding antidiscrimination issue was whether to take "special action" in order to counteract the effects of historical discrimination. Then the specific problem was how to emancipate the slaves whom the Thirteenth Amendment had liberated in 1865. Should—the critical question was—these "freedmen" "be viewed as individuals ready to take their place as citizens and participants in the competitive marketplace, or . . . [should] their unique historical experience oblige the federal government to take *special action* on their behalf ?"[2] After a titanic struggle with President Andrew Johnson, the Republican majority in Congress opted for a form of federal intervention based on the principle of equal citizenship.[3]

This decision was one of the most significant events in our entire constitutional history. In contemporary constitutional theory, equality is a fundamental principle of our democracy. At the moment of birth, every American-born person is deemed the equal of every other American in civil rights and obligations. It is a given that civic equality—freedom as a universal entitlement—and the right to vote are the quintessential prerequisites of American freedom.

But, it was not ever thus. In fact, it was not until Reconstruction that the seminal notion of federally protected equality for whites and blacks entered the constitutional landscape. In drafting the Constitution, the Founding Fathers "left [many] important matters ambiguous, including . . . the constitutional status of slavery, and the issue of racial criteria for citizenship."[4] During infancy and adolescence, the new republic allowed white supremacy and a racial concept of citizenship to become its predominant institutional mode. For nominally "free" northern blacks, the antebellum years were a time of political disenfranchisement, social segregation, and severe economic privation.[5] And in the South, the plantation economy—long the epitome of institutionalized racial subordination—continued to flourish under the aegis of state "slave codes." On the eve of war, the system's four million black chattel slaves legally lived in servile bondage to their white owners, without personal freedom, or political democracy, and with only a much-attenuated opportunity for self-improvement.[6] In the words of the Chief Justice of the United States, Negro slaves and those who had slave ancestors were an "inferior" race, fit only for domination by whites, with no rights that the white man was bound to respect, and incapable of United States citizenship.[7]

To their everlasting credit, the makers of post–Civil War policy repudiated this view. In order to change the freedmen's legal status and integrate them, Congress installed civic equality as the explicit constitutional standard of citizenship.[8] The Thirteenth Amendment (1865) abolished slavery. The Fourteenth (1868) declared all American-born persons national and state citizens, and prohibited state violation of three general groupings of civil rights ("privileges and immunities," "equal protection," and "due process"). The Fifteenth (1869) prohibited federal and state violation of the right to vote "on account of race, color, or previous condition of servitude."

Congress enacted legislation to enforce the new constitutional mandates.[9] The prototypical civil rights statute of the period was the Civil Rights Act of 1866,[10] the enforcement statute for the Thirteenth Amendment, which declared any American-born person a citizen, regardless of race or color; provided that all citizens were entitled to "equal protection" of laws relating to persons or property, and had equal rights to sue, testify, contract, and own property; and authorized criminal prosecution of violators acting "under color of law," that is, the officers of the states and their subdivisions. Further, the Military and Reconstruction Act of 1867[11] placed the defeated South under military occupation pending readmission to the Union, and required the former secessionist states, as the price of readmission, to enact constitutional guarantees of black suffrage and to ratify the Fourteenth Amendment.[12] By 1870, the South complied and rejoined the fold.

There is no question that Reconstruction affected permanent constitutional and political change. By coupling a national commitment to color-blind ᵢbirthplace citizenship with a prohibition of invidious discrimination, it transformed the Constitution into a "vehicle through which members of vulnerable minorities could make a claim for substantive freedom and seek protection against misconduct by all levels of government."[13] Moreover, by endowing the federal government with the power to "define and protect citizens' rights,"[14] Reconstruction laid much of the groundwork for a later and "vast expansion of federal legislative power over matters which had been subject to state common law rules, including the law of employment,"[15] and voting.[16] It was in the exercise of this power—strengthened, starting in the late 1930s, by the Supreme Court's very liberal reading of the national commerce power under the Constitution—that the federal government produced the civil rights laws and regulations of the 1960s which outlawed various forms of invidious racial, national origin (ethnic/ancestral), and gender discrimination in the public and private sectors. Thus, the Civil Rights Act of 1964[17] prohibited race, color, and national origin discrimination in public facilities and accommodations (Title II);[18] in activities subsidized by federal funds (Title VI);[19] and in employment (Title VII).[20] Title VII also barred sex discrimination. President Lyndon Johnson's Executive Order 11246 of 1965 (EO 11246) prohibited discrimination in government contracting and federal employment on account of race, religion, or national origin. And the Voting Rights Act of 1965[21] was structured squarely on the Fifteenth Amendment. Early dimensions of affirmative action emerged as a legal theory for applying Title VII and EO 11246, and in implementing the Voting Rights Act. A later Civil Rights Act was enacted, in 1968, to battle racial discrimination in housing.[22] These statutes, and their associated administrative regulations, attempted to further Reconstruction's historic act of expunging racism from our legal edifice. The extent to which they have eradicated its real-world effects is a different matter. In this connection, it is appropriate to glance at the other side of the Reconstruction story.

Reconstruction's Tragic Failure

For all of Reconstruction's truly monumental long-term achievements, in its own time it proved unsuccessful. The program "promise[d] that the ideal of equal citizenship would be converted into a set of enforceable legal rights."[23] The South's quick return to the Union, and a concurrent flurry of black political and entrepreneurial activity,[24] seemed to augur well. But it was not to be. When the federal occupation force was withdrawn in 1877, thereby formally terminating Reconstruction,[25] its promise had not been fulfilled.

Notwithstanding their newly mandated franchise, the great mass of former slaves reverted to a status of political and economic dependency. This is considered Reconstruction's "greatest [short-term] failure."[26]

The debacle is attributable to an unusual combination of systemic policy flaws, reactionary Supreme Court rulings, the South's refusal to accept defeat, and the North's inability, or unwillingness, to stay the course. To begin, as Professor Foner has shown in his great study, the scheme of Congressional Reconstruction was "an incongruous mixture of idealism and political expediency."[27] Because "Republicans still believed the states retained rights beyond the scope of federal intervention,"[28] this potent states' rights lobby was able to impede the creation of constitutionally specific rights in the contemplated post–Civil War amendments,[29] and thus limit the national government's power to intervene directly against civil rights violations.[30] The Fourteenth and Fifteenth Amendments—the great exemplars of Reconstruction ideology—do not enumerate *specific* national rights, or otherwise challenge the states' claim of very extensive civil rights jurisdiction.[31] It may be, as some suggest, that the Framers deliberately opted for rhetorical effect over legalistic precision;[32] but, if so, they paid a heavy price indeed. Not only did their vagueness invite the nineteenth-century High Court to limit racial equality (see pp. 14–15), but it also raised serious doubts about the significance of the federal role. Some authorities suggest that Reconstruction's true purpose was to authorize the federal government to ensure that the states enforced their own laws.[33] Thus, in Professor Benedict's view, the framers opted to protect black rights in a way that preserved traditional states rights as much as possible.[34]

In any case, Congressional Reconstruction suffered from a far more serious defect. The policy "made no economic provisions for the freedmen."[35] The Republicans scorned public "economic underpinning," anticipating that "once accorded equal rights, the freedmen would find their social level and assume responsibility for their own fate."[36] This self-help scenario combined two elements. First, the then prevailing "free labor" model of *equal opportunity*: "a classless utopia (in which) industrious and frugal laborers could save money, purchase their own homes, and eventually acquire a farm or shop, thereby escaping the status of wage labor and assimilating into the republic of property holders."[37] Second, the sovereign power of the franchise: in Reconstruction theory, the right to vote *by itself* would enable the freedmen to market their occupational and vocational skills, and by diligent labor become independent, productive, self-respecting citizens and property holders.[38] Moreover, exercise of the franchise over time would ensure acquisition of self-sufficiency within the federal system.[39] In short, what Reconstruction's version of equal opportunity offered the freedmen focused upon a guarantee of political, but not economic autonomy.

In the end, neither was forthcoming. The prospect of political emancipation, seemingly at hand when the freedmen gained the vote, was a mirage.

The newly enfranchised freedmen came to be excluded from effective political activity by social and legal violence, fraud, and "structural discrimination" (poll taxes, literacy tests, gerrymanders, etc.).[40] By the turn of the century, their incipient political strength was neutralized, thanks in no small measure to the lack of timely Northern intervention.[41]

In addition, most of the former slaves never enjoyed any true employment or entrepreneurial opportunity, and for this the blame belongs equally to the North and the South. The "vast majority" of blacks emerged from slavery without the resources for acquiring land, "confronting a white community united in the refusal to advance credit or sell them property."[42] They yearned for economic independence[43] but they got little long-term assistance from their erstwhile liberators. Indeed, the architects of Reconstruction forfeited virtually every chance to help the freedmen become self-sufficient. For example, in 1867 Congress reneged on a wartime promise to settle the slaves on occupied Confederate land.[44]

Most freedmen were accordingly compelled to "enter . . . the world of free labor as wage or share workers on land owned by whites,"[45] under conditions dictated by their employers (often their former owners), and without bargaining rights or government protection.[46] In other words, the economic posture of the "emancipated" plantation slaves did not essentially change.[47] The fact that they were barred, on account of their race, from applying their considerable skills as craftsmen, farmers, and domestics in the open market[48] was proof positive of Reconstruction's failure.

The End of Reconstruction

Reconstruction's goal was to: "give the Negro [full citizenship, i.e.,] civil rights and the ballot, and get white men accustomed to treating Negroes as equals at least politically and legally . . . in effect, to revolutionize the relations of the two races."[49] By 1877, however, the country was in full "political and judicial retreat" from this goal.[50] And later in the century, it was apparent that the "program" had collapsed. Beyond the grant of citizenship and the paper right to vote, none of Reconstruction's equal opportunity goals had been achieved. No independent black workforce or property-holding class had come into being. On the contrary, the great mass of former slaves remained an impoverished, dependent, and disenfranchised rural proletariat. To be sure, they were now U.S. citizens; but this citizenship was legally unequal, due to the Supreme Court's myopic acknowledgment of it.[51]

For the North as well as the South, the great tragedy was not so much that a bold experiment in racial politics had failed, but that, notwithstanding the terrible carnage of the war, the time-hallowed primacy of racial subordination in our culture had been decisively reconfirmed. Racialization of the nation as a whole was well under way, on a hitherto unseen scale, and with retrograde cultural and political consequences that have persisted to this day.[52]

White Supremacy and the Origins of Disparate Impact

Definitions

The eye of the storm over affirmative action is the doctrine of *disparate impact*. This is the sophisticated, conceptual model of discrimination on which affirmative action has been centrally based. Disparate-impact theory demands legal relief for the effects of illegal societal bias on groups; the contrasting common law theory of "disparate treatment" restricts legal liability to cases of intentional discrimination against specific individuals. The contrast is most clearly visible in the area of legal proof. Disparate impact insists that (1) proof of discriminatory intent, and identification of victims, both requisite at common law, is *unnecessary* in cases of alleged group discrimination; (2) such allegations can be sustained by statistical demonstration that the complaining group has suffered from societal bias; (3) given such demonstration, compensatory remedies are in order for members of the impacted group solely on the basis of their membership; (4) employers and governing officials who do not take "good faith" steps, or other mandated requirements to remove the effects of disparate-impact discrimination may be responsible for violating antidiscrimination laws.[53]

Affirmative action's disparate-impact pillar has been under heavy fire from the moment of its advent in the 1950s. Detractors claim that the notions of group rights and compensatory relief (*equal results*) are unconstitutional, illegal, immoral, unfair, and counterproductive.[54] Proponents rebut these claims and assert that affirmative action is the only way to the "Promised Land."[55] The various manifestations of this controversy are treated throughout this volume.

Disparate-impact affirmative action, in legal parlance, is deemed remedial when it is designed to correct a legal wrong. The rationale behind nonremedial, ethno-racial, and gender-conscious programs—as postulated by Justice Powell in *Regents v. Bakke* (1978)[56] and much trumpeted by the higher education establishment[57]—seeks to seed higher education with students from many different groups, racial and ethnic being importantly among them. Powell insisted that the " 'Nation's future depends on leaders trained through wide exposure' to the ideas and mores of students as diverse as the Nation."[58] Business has chimed in with its "good for business" approach to diversity affirmative action. As the Court proclaimed in 2003, "[M]ajor American businesses have made clear that the skills needed in today's increasingly global marketplace can only be developed through exposure to widely diverse people, cultures, ideas and viewpoints."[59] These nonremedial objectives are, on the surface of things, analytically distinct from those associated with remedial affirmative action, although in practice the end results generally merge. Take, for example, a hypothetical plan for preferentially hiring blacks in a workplace from which they have previously been excluded as a consequence of historical/social discrimination. In the language of jurisprudence, this plan would be denominated "remedial" affirmative action if, as a consequence of litigation, it was to be a remedy for illegal discrimination. On the other hand, if black "underrepresentation" is not attributed to legally prohibited discrimination, a black preferential hiring plan to acquire different viewpoints, etc., would fall under the legal heading of "nonremedial" affirmative action. In either case, the number of blacks is increased. As of late, resort to nonremedial/diversity ethno-racial and gender-conscious programs has surged in the areas of employment and education.[60] And the Powell diversity rationale has gained Supreme Court sanction in connection with the race/ethnic preferential admission program of the University of Michigan law school.[61] But the Court in 2007 found race-conscious student assignment programs sponsored by the Louisville and Seattle school systems unconstitutional and unsupportable on diversity grounds since, unlike the Powell requirements, these programs were not designed to cultivate a broad variety of viewpoints beyond those associated with race.[62] (See 104–14 and 131–63 below for more extensive discussion of the Michigan, Seattle, and Louisville cases.)

University of Texas law professor Sanford Levinson has observed that diversity "has become the favorite catchword—indeed it would not be an exaggeration to say 'mantra'—of those defending the use of [affirmative action] racial or ethnic preferences."[63] To Levinson, what is substantially representative of university diversity policy was well understood by his colleague at the Yale law school, Professor Jack Balkin, who said: "In the context of educational affirmative action, I understand 'diversity' to be a code word for representation in enjoyment of social goods by major ethnic groups who have some claim to mistreatment."[64]

Levinson found the typical diversity arguments by law schools nothing short of disingenuous! How can diversity advocates be serious about cultivating ideational interaction through diversity when their diversity policy is typically limited to a small number of racial and ethnic groups and does not cover the multitude of others, including the variety of religious persuasions? Scorn is also heaped upon the business world's diversity devotees. How, Levinson asks, can manufacturers talk, as they do, about improving their products through diversity? What do race and ethnicity have to do with producing a better automobile, and the like?[65] Levinson does support disparate-impact affirmative action to overcome what Gunnar Myrdal labeled in the 1950s the American dilemma, that is, the systemic discrimination that has poisoned the well of American society.[66] Myrdal's theme was to bring excluded groups into the mainstream in order to cleanse our discriminatory environment.

While diversity affirmative action focuses on improving the lot of blacks, Asians, Hispanics, American Indians, and women, it nonetheless is part of the rich mosaic of diversity themes so prominent in American life. Professor Schuck finds that the United States is the most diverse nation on earth in terms of religious, cultural, and ethnic variety. It is but one of two nations (the other being Canada) actively seeking diversity in immigrant groups. He views the civil rights movement of the mid-twentieth century—with its wide acceptance of differences—as the antecedent of the nation's current diversity passion.[67]

Let us now turn to disparate impact's historical source. We believe that the plight of the black community during the peak period of white supremacy dramatically illustrates the invidious, systemic bias affirmative action was designed to correct.

The Apotheosis of White Supremacy

The nation's "retreat" from Reconstruction began even before its official demise, and was completed during the 1890s.[68] By the turn of the twentieth century, "the ideals of color-blind citizenship and freedom as a universal entitlement had been repudiated."[69] Through a stream of rulings, which culminated in the legendary *Plessy v. Ferguson* decision in 1896, the Supreme Court had displaced equality before the law for blacks with protection of business interests ("liberty of contract") as the basis for interpreting the Fourteenth Amendment.[70]

Plessy v. Ferguson is more than a century old, but remains one of the most controversial decisions in civil rights law. In this case involving state-mandated racial segregation of railroad passenger cars (a Jim Crow commonplace), the Court decided that the Equal Protection Clause does not outlaw segregation that equalizes separate facilities or services. The majority said that, while the Equal Protection Clause "was undoubtedly [intended] to enforce the absolute equality of the two races before the law . . . in the nature of things it could not have been intended to abolish distinctions based on color."[71] This celebrated statement of the "separate but equal" thesis evoked an equally famous rebuttal by Justice Harlan, whose dissent argued that segregation is discriminatory per se, because the Constitution is "color-blind, and neither knows nor tolerates classes among citizens."[72]

The majority's decision in *Plessy* conformed with a long line of cases in which the nineteenth-century High Court dampened Reconstruction's civil rights ideology: (1) The *Slaughterhouse Cases* (1873)[73]—held that the privileges and immunities protected by the Fourteenth Amendment do not include the "fundamental rights of citizenship," since these derive solely from the states; (2) *U.S. v. Cruikshank* (1876)[74] and *U.S. v. Reese* (1876)[75]—held that the Fifteenth Amendment does not confer a right to vote enforceable by criminal sanctions, but only "exemption" from discrimination in the exercise of that right under state law; (3) Jury Cases: so long as the exclusion of blacks from juries was not "open"—that is, not governmentally mandated—the Equal Protection Clause is not breached by *de facto* exclusion of blacks from jury service, *Virginia v. Rives* (1880).[76] However, jury exclusion officially imposed by government was unconstitutional. *Strauder v. West Virginia* (1880).[77] (4) The *Civil Rights Cases* (1883)[78]—held, the Civil Rights Act of 1875, desegregating privately owned public accommodations, violated the reservation of nondelegated powers to the states under the Tenth Amendment. The Fourteenth Amendment, which authorized that statute, applied only to *state* and not *private* action.[79]

Plessy was overruled by the High Court in the *Brown v. The Board* school segregation case in 1954.[80] Nonetheless, *Plessy* not only raised the most profound analytical questions about the meaning of "equality," but it also framed the unresolved civil rights disputes of our time. Some consider it a "betrayal" of our ideals, but, given the "vagueness" of the great amendments, one is tempted to wonder whether such demonizing begs the question.[81] In any case, the segregation thesis (i.e., that the races are "better off" apart) is still powerful, and it would be rash to discount the possibility that *Plessy* may yet rise from the dead and once again become the law of the land. As chapter 5 delineates (pp. 181–82), gender segregation in K-12 public schools has recently been trumpeted as pedagogically beneficial. Federal administrative regulations in the new millennium were changed to authorize this form of segregation to the chagrin of those who see it as contrary to federal antidiscrimination law.

Reconstruction's erosion went far beyond the mysterious realm of constitutional law.[82] Suffice it to say that the "polity and economy were more thoroughly racialized at the dawn of the twentieth century than at any other point in American history,"[83] and remained in that condition through the end of World War II.[84] It is an astonishing fact that an obsession with the superiority of whiteness helped define America for the seventy-five odd years during which it passed from the ghastly bloodletting of the Civil War through the convulsions of capitalist industrialization and the Armageddons of world war and economic depression, and became a troubled racial melting pot.

Jim Crow

In the post-Reconstruction South, white supremacy was practiced in the form of a quasi-religious, state-mandated caste system. The credo of the system was the thoroughgoing degradation of the black man, the annihilation of his personal autonomy. In Professor Litwack's apt summary: "To maintain and underscore its absolute supremacy, the white South systematically disenfranchised black men, imposed rigid patterns of racial segregation, manipulated the judicial system and sustained extraordinary levels of violence and brutality."[85]

These practices produced the classic forms of disparate impact. For example, because of educational segregation, generations of blacks were either illiterate or grossly undereducated, by comparison to their white counterparts. As a result of this socially imposed racial disparity, blacks as a class were frequently deprived of the right to vote, or the opportunity of finding desirable employment. Societal discrimination against blacks as a group was endemic in employment, education, voting, housing, administration of justice, and access to public facilities. It was in the areas of voting and employment that the Supreme Court, for the first time, accepted the notion of disparate-impact remediation for group discrimination.[86] And disparate-impact theory remained the main vehicle for affirmative action.

The Great Migration

Disparate-impact discrimination has by no means been confined to the South. The post–World War II industrial boom inspired a wave of black migration to the urban centers of the North and Mid-West which reached flood tide in the 1950s.[87] This was a period of massive social change for some two million black citizens, and the migration provided them with a higher standard of living and greater recognition of their civil rights. Nonetheless, barriers resulting from systemic racism prevailed throughout the nation. It should be emphasized that race discrimination was a fixture in the North long before the Civil War. The tremendous influx of Southern blacks in the twentieth century touched off an explosion of racial exclusion. For much of the twentieth century, Northern urban blacks were routinely excluded from higher-status jobs and training by racist employers and labor unions. Because of limited resources, they were unable to establish a significant number of small businesses.[88] Like their brethren in the South, they were often confined to inferior segregated schools and housing. The black influx produced an exodus of whites and good jobs. The central cities, inhabited, in large measure, by low-paid or unemployed blacks, developed the symptoms that have blossomed into the urban crisis of our own time: concentrated poverty and welfare dependency; dysfunctional families; drug addiction and high crime rates; inadequate health care and sanitation; inferior housing and education; and exploitative retail services.[89]

The Legacy of White Supremacy

Disparate-impact's discrimination curse has not been limited to slaves' descendants; women and various non-black minorities, too, have long suffered its "whips and scorns."[90] But it is undisputable that the black community's experience in discrimination's sad history was especially tragic.[91] In the words of a respected authority:

> [A]fter emancipation, as before the ending of slavery, the role of the black population remained different and separate from that of the rest of the population. . . . [U]nlike other groups the range of employment opportunities available to the black labor force was narrowly constrained. Freedom for African Americans therefore was subject to many more obstacles than . . . for other population subgroups. . . . While a free market ideology in principle is color-blind, the denial of employment to African Americans in the North, and the denial of full legal and civil rights in the South was the dominant reality experienced by the black population.[92]

In chapter 3, we will show that the original formulation of employment affirmative action policy was predicated on the disproportionate effects of white supremacy on the black population.

The Women's Movement: The First and Second "Waves"

It is a truism to note that minority and nonminority women have also been submerged by unique disparate-impact limitations. The cultural dominance of patriarchal thinking in our society pressured females into family maintenance undertakings, while greatly limiting their presence in the arts and sciences. The vast world of high and low jobs was left to be filled primarily by males.[93] Restrictions on females were much present in nineteenth-century law which regarded married women as "civilly dead," to use the language of that era's feminist movement.[94] The common law of that time considered spouses to be one, and that *one* was the husband. On their own, married women could not contract, own, and will property, or acquire guardianship over their children after divorce.[95] Exemplifying gender shackles was the prohibition on the right to vote.

Historians locate the inaugural of America's "first wave" women's rights movement in the 1840s when it focused on equalization of legal treatment. Some feminists of that day went farther by urging that females be allowed and encouraged to pursue careers other than homemaking and child rearing—a theme much trumpeted in feminism's "second wave" starting in the 1960s.[96]

In antebellum times, feminists served as "foot soldiers" for abolitionism, among other reasons, because freeing the slaves, it was thought, would help release women from their subordinate status. But females reaped few benefits as "Reconstruction left the law of marriage and conventions of gender relations largely intact."[97]

Between the 1870s and 1920s, feminist activism was roughly bifurcated: the single-issue "suffragists" who committed themselves almost solely to obtaining the vote; and the "social feminists" who (in addition to suffrage) were interested in social welfare reform, including protecting working females from exploitation.[98] While the suffragists were successful in removing gender barriers from voting through the Nineteenth Amendment, social feminists helped persuade the state legislatures to enact laws for women workers establishing minimum wages and maximum hours; excluding them from dangerous work (e.g., mining and foundry positions); and requiring that they be given rest periods at the workplace.[99]

After the 1920 ratification of the Nineteenth Amendment prohibiting gender discrimination in the right to vote, feminist fervor dissolved, leaving the movement largely moribund until the 1960s[100]—apparently, in part, a case of all passion spent after the vehement and exhausting battle for the vote. The absence of zealotry did not end disputes among women's organizations. Those peopled by the higher-income and college-educated tended to support earlier versions of the Equal Rights Amendment, which would have constitutionally imposed a strict ban on gender discrimination. Groups championing lower-income females opposed such equalization, fearing the undermining of protective labor codes.[101]

While feminism slept, the black rights cause—feeding on common grievances, and driven by an ideology that improvement was both essential and achievable—grew increasingly restive and robust. One result was the fusillade of 1960s rights legislation. The very robustness of the African American movement helped spark the birth of "second wave" feminism.[102] Of course, there were other reasons for the renaissance, including the writing of Betty Friedan, and the "consciousness raising" efforts of groups such as the National Organization of Women (NOW) which—at its inception—was headed by Friedan.[103] Some central points in her thinking are summarized in the following excerpt from her earlier "second wave" writing:

> Thanks to the early feminists, we who have mounted the second stage of the feminist revolution have grown up with the right to vote, . . . with the right to higher education and to employment, and with some, not all, of the legal right to equality. . . . [But] even those of us who have managed to achieve a precarious success in a given field still walk as freaks in "man's world" since every profession—politics, the church, teaching—is still structured as man's world. . . . Women, almost too visible as sex objects in this country today, are at the same time invisible people. As the Negro was the invisible man, so women are the invisible people

in America today. To be taken seriously as people, women have to share in the decisions of government, of politics, of the church—not just to cook the church supper, but to preach the sermon; not just to look up the zip codes and address the envelopes, but to make the political decisions; not just to do the housework of industry, but to make some of the executive decisions. . . . If we are going to address ourselves to the need for changing the social institutions that will permit women to be free and equal individuals, participating actively in their society and changing that society—with men—then we must talk in terms of what is possible, and not accept what is as what must be. . . . We need not accept marriage as it's currently structured with the implicit idea of man, the breadwinner, and woman, the housewife. There are many different ways we could posit marriage. To enable *all* women, not just the exceptional few, to participate in society we must confront the fact of life . . . that women do give birth to children. But we must challenge the idea that a woman is primarily responsible for raising children. Man and society have to be educated to accept their responsibility for that role as well. . . . If more than a very few women are to enjoy equality, we have an absolute responsibility to get serious political priority for childcare centers, to make it possible for women not to have to bow out of society for ten or fifteen years when they have children. Or else we are going to be talking of equal opportunities for a few.[104]

In chapter 3, we discuss feminist attitudes about affirmative action.

Which Groups Should Be Eligible for Affirmative Action Benefits?

The scope of affirmative action's coverage is the subject of persistent controversy. Since its inception in the mid-1950s as a remedy for discrimination against blacks, many of its programs have included women and a number of diverse racial and ethnic "minorities." Some critics maintain that the expanded coverage has been "overinclusive," that is, many of its group beneficiaries were not disparately impacted or disadvantaged, and hence not eligible to participate under a fairly administered equal opportunity standard.[105]

George R. La Noue and John C. Sullivan (L/S) have forcefully stated the overinclusion critique in their end-of-century reviews of presumptive eligibility determinations under federal "minority business enterprises" (MBE) programs.[106] In essence, these statutory programs set aside lucrative procurement and construction contracts for the benefit of firms owned by members of "socially and economically disadvantaged" groups.[107] The centerpiece of these programs is Section 8(a) of the Small Business Act,[108] which in 1978 conferred *presumptive eligibility* for such preferences on "Black Americans, Hispanic Americans, and Native Americans," and, prospectively, on *other groups* which the Small Business Administration might designate from time to time.[109] Under recent federal regulations, any citizen or legal resident who can identify with any of the following groups is presumptively eligible:

> Black Americans; Hispanic Americans; Native Americans (American Indians, Eskimos, Aleuts or Native Hawaiians); Asian-Pacific Americans (persons with origins from Burma, Thailand, Malaysia, Indonesia, Singapore, Brunei, Japan, China [including Hong Kong], Taiwan, Laos, Cambodia [Kampuchea], Vietnam, Korea, The Philippines, U.S. Trust Territory of the Pacific Islands [Republic of Palau], Republic of the Marshall Islands, Federated States of Micronesia, The Commonwealth of Northern Mariana Islands, Guam, Samoa, Macao, Fiji, Tonga, Kiribati, Tuvalu, or Nauru); Subcontinent-Asian Americans (persons with origins from India, Pakistan, Bangladesh, Sri Lanka, Bhutan, the Maldives Islands, or Nepal).[110]

The exponential growth of the eligibility list reflects a series of inclusion and exclusion determinations by SBA during the 1970s and 1980s.[111] L/S assert that Congress lacked both the "political will" and the "information to draw clear cut lines of inclusion/exclusion."[112] Moreover, in their view, SBA's decisions had not been based on objective measurement of "actual discrimination" or "comparative social disadvantage,"[113] but rather on bureaucratic convenience and political pressure.[114]

L/S offer a number of particulars in support of this indictment. First, while Section 8 articulates separate "social" (racial/ethnic bias) and "economic" (income limits) components for "disadvantage,"[115] SBA considered these definitions imprecise, indeed questions whether "a precise definition is appropriate."[116] SBA accepted applicants' "representations" of economic disadvantage, absent contrary evidence. In practice, the criteria of eligibility "for almost everyone are the racial and ethnic presumptions of social disadvantage."[117]

Second, SBA's inclusion decisions were not in keeping with objective socioeconomic data. Measured by the standard demographic indicators of business formation rates, education, and income, some groups on the presumptive eligibility list are at the socioeconomic bottom of our society, others at the top. Disparities of this kind and magnitude cannot be satisfactorily explained by any theory of discrimination or disadvantage. On the contrary, they clearly indicate unjustified overinclusiveness in preferential access to the highly prized benefits of MBE eligibility. A prime example is the "Asian-Pacific American" category, which contains groups deriving from twenty-five different counties and enormously different cultures. According to post-1990 census regression analysis of comparative business formation rates in affirmative action and non–affirmative action groups, Korean Americans stood at the very top of *all* groups surveyed, Laotian Americans at the very bottom, Chinese and Japanese Americans at the mean. These statistics show that treating Asian Americans as a single category is "clearly overinclusive." Similarly, in the "Hispanic-American" category, which contains distinct cultural differences between persons deriving from Spain and those from Central or Latin America, Cubans stood well above the mean in business formation, Central and Mexican Americans considerably below it.[118]

Third, there was no "principled basis" or "consistent rationale" for SBA's decisions.[119] In making racial and ethnic decisions to grant, or withhold, presumptive eligibility, the agency has not gathered any statistical data; sought any uniform measurement of educational or economic achievement; or supplied any consistent definition of group eligibility standards.[120] The agency did not require that a presumptively eligible person has suffered discrimination by the federal government, nor did it attempt to verify whether an applicant has actually suffered any form of discrimination.[121] Although many of SBA's inclusions are attributable to lobbying by politicians and advocacy groups, for example, the addition of the Asian American category to the presumptive list in 1979,[122] it has not conducted periodic reviews of social disadvantage. Once a person was identified with a group that is presumptively socially disadvantaged, he would always be deemed socially disadvantaged regardless of personal achievement.[123] The agency's policy has been *under*inclusive, as well as *over*inclusive, since, from time to time, it has failed to include, or has rejected, groups whose socioeconomic profiles were not significantly different from some included groups.[124]

To L/S, the MBE program has been the preeminent model for public and private sector affirmative action.[125] They conclude that SBA's administration of presumptive eligibility has been totally "political," based on racial and ethnic stereotypes which are out of touch with current demographic reality, and inconsistent with the past discrimination requirements of strict scrutiny established in *Croson* and *Adarand*[126] for affirmative action (these opinions are discussed at 60*ff*). They maintain that, in modern America, *any* group measure of social disadvantage will be "crude and overinclusive" and they call for replacement of presumptive eligibility with a policy "that targets aspiring entrepreneurs of any race or ethnicity who have endured measurable disadvantage."[127] One need not take L/S' assault on Congress and the bureaucracy, or their disavowal of disparate impact/ group remediation, or their view of strict scrutiny, at full face value in order to see that they have raised some troubling questions about race/ethnic-based affirmative action. They argue, in effect, that, as currently administered, MBE programs benefit many nondiscriminatees who had no valid claim to *any* preferences, much less presumptive entitlement. This contention cannot be dismissed out of hand. In casting doubt on the validity of group eligibility now available to many recently arrived immigrants,[128] L/S express widespread concern over this form of overinclusiveness. No less an authority than civil rights historian Professor Hugh Davis Graham shares this concern. He argues that millions of noncitizens can participate in affirmative action, and this operates to disadvantage African Americans whose welfare was the original purpose of affirmative action. This sad state has bred interminority conflict, and weakened affirmative action's moral imperative.[129]

L/S have made a powerful case for a complete evaluatory examination of affirmative action methodology. If SBA has been out of touch with socioeconomic reality, then what of the Equal Employment Opportunity Commission (EEOC), a major progenitor of affirmative action in employment, and now its major overseer? EEOC has prompted widespread adoption of its current affirmative action guidelines which require all "users" (e.g., covered employers and unions) to maintain records by sex, and the following races and ethnic groups: blacks (Negroes), American Indians (including Alaskan Natives), Asians (including Pacific Islanders), Hispanics (including persons of Mexican, Puerto Rican, Cuban, Central or South American, or other Spanish origin or culture regardless of race), whites (Caucasians) other than Hispanic.[130] On its face, this listing appears to replicate the gross overinclusiveness which L/S found in SBA practice. The records are meant to be and have been an important engine of employment affirmative action by encouraging the granting of employment opportunities to "underutilized" minorities and women. (See Appendices Two, Three, and Four of this volume for the EEOC regulations, and those of the Office of Federal Contract Compliance Programs, 355–73.)

That said, other views on this matter should be considered. Writing in the mid-1990s, Harvard Law Professor Christopher Edley argued that the case remains strong for designating blacks, Hispanics, and Asians as protected groups.[131] "Even the comparative 'success,' " he writes, "of Japanese Americans and many immigrants from the Indian subcontinent has not immunized from discrimination those subgroups, much less the diverse community of Asian and Pacific Islanders."[132] Thus, none of these groups—along with recent black immigrants from the Caribbean—should be excluded. Liberal inclusiveness should guide us. "We are whom we include."[133]

Nonetheless, Edley urged careful research in order to determine how much preferential treatment should be afforded various groups. Such study should concern itself with the following questions: Is it to be expected that a group will receive equal treatment without affirmative action? (Edley maintains, for example, that newly arrived Swedes will not be subject to discrimination, unlike Mexican immigrants.) How closely does economic need correlate with group membership? To what extent was coming to America voluntary? (Edley thinks that voluntary immigrants "have a lesser claim to our solicitude.")[134]

Questions of the Edley kind prompted his then Harvard colleague Orlando Patterson to propose an attenuated affirmative action policy. Patterson acknowledges that affirmative action has flaws, but would nevertheless maintain protected group preferences for the next fifteen years, phasing it out and ultimately replacing it with class-based preference[135] "for all American-born persons from poor families."[136]

This phaseout stance plainly reflects Patterson's internal struggle with the powerful pros and cons of the affirmative action controversy. On the one hand, he believes that affirmative action, because it has secured the inclusion of excluded groups, deserves major credit for black America's good fortune. Given that democracy is "quintessentially about inclusion,"[137] the circumstances argue for affirmative action's limited continuation notwithstanding its demonstrable flaws.[138] Patterson thus distances himself from the critics in this regard. He dismisses the "reverse discrimination" thesis as a "concoction,"[139] and scornfully decries the invocation of merit and color blindness by affirmative action's detractors.[140] By the same token, however, he forthrightly acknowledges both the necessity and the difficulty of reconciling group rights and individual rights in our ideological framework, which traditionally accented the latter, while the former is approached with great reluctance.[141] His final position, that affirmative action is defensible only as a "medium-term "solution,"[142] apparently represents an attempt to chart a middle course between the Scylla and Charybdis in the preferential affirmative action quarrel.

Patterson's proposal for phasing out affirmative action in fifteen years is studded with obvious administrative and equity issues. Initially, the only eligible Hispanics would be Puerto Ricans and Mexican Americans of second or later generations. First-generation black immigrants from anywhere are ineligible *except* for diversity purposes. All Asians are to be excluded save for the Chinese descended from the pre-1923 immigration. In five years, members of families with an annual income of more than $75,000 (in 1997 dollars) would no longer qualify. In ten years, only minorities and females from lower-class backgrounds would be eligible.[143] At the end of fifteen years, affirmative action would be restricted to "American-born persons from poor families."[144]

Among the significant issues in the above proposal left unaddressed by Patterson are: What is the justification for restricting the antipoverty program to native Americans to the presumed exclusion of naturalized citizens? Would

American Indians qualify? Patterson derides chauvinism,[145] but is there not a streak of that attitude in this proposal?

Immigration and Affirmative Action

Between 1965 and 2000, thirty-five million legal immigrants came to the United States (mainly from Mexico and Asia), and some twenty-six million of them could claim affirmative action benefits even though they had not been the victims of systemic discrimination affirmative action is designed to correct.[146] Why was this so? According to civil rights scholar Hugh Davis Graham, affirmative action coverage (other than for blacks) was not a product of public policymaking deliberation, but rather the outcome of closed bureaucratic determinations, which served agency needs first and foremost.[147] Graham found the extension of affirmative action to immigrants "strange" and a policy that weakened the logic[148] and its ethical fiber.[149] Graham questioned other dimensions of the protected-group categories: If the Asian category included Pakistan, why did the Asian boundary stop at Afghanistan? If Spaniards and Portuguese came to be included, why not Middle Easterners and North Africans?[150]

Graham concluded that employer hiring practices, both those focusing on affirmative action goals[151] and otherwise, have favored Hispanics and Asians in low-end restaurant, hotel, janitorial, and agricultural work.[152] The sociological research of Roger Waldinger and Michael Lichter in Los Angeles County supports the Graham position. They studied 228 restaurant, furniture-manufacturing, and hospital establishments and concluded that immigrant networking facilitated the acquisition of low-end jobs for nonblacks. Additionally, blacks were harassed by immigrant groups resulting in their frustration and encouraging their job loss. There was considerable intraethnic conflict, for example between Mexicans and Salvadorans.[153] Title VII of The Civil Rights Act of 1964, detailed in chapter 3, was meant to stop white work discrimination affecting blacks. Surely, this law covers discrimination by immigrants affecting blacks. Employers in L.A. County, moreover, tried to match the ethno-racial characteristics of their hirees with that of the customer base.[154] Is this diversification endeavor compatible with federal antidiscrimination law? Is it different from hiring whites to satisfy the "old Southern" white preference for white employees[155]—a practice that helped produce Title VII?

In her study of retailing in the black areas of New York and Philadelphia, sociologist Jennifer Lee reported that non-black store owners hired blacks as "cultural brokers" to reduce racial conflict and to adapt store practices to inner-city mores. Those blacks hired as "cultural brokers" in New York were typically West Indians or Caribbean and not U.S.-born.[156] Why are these immigrants favored? Is not this ethnic discrimination prohibited by employment law, or is it acceptable diversity practice?

The Multiracial Question

The native-born children of immigrants who came after 1965 increasingly married and had children outside their racial and ethnic groups. This was particularly true for Asians and Hispanics. For example, in 1990 more than half of young Asians (25–34) born in the United States married non-Asians, while that same year two-fifths of comparably aged Hispanics married non-Hispanics. In 1994, there were 1.3 million interracial/interethnic married couples (up from 310,000 in 1970), along with an additional one-half million interracial/interethnic unmarried unions.[157] Professor Graham opined that

> · [b]y 2150, intermarriage will have so thoroughly mixed the racial and ethnic ancestry of Americans that the old twentieth century distinctions between American Indians, Hispanics, Asians, and non-Latino whites will be meaningless. Black intermarriage rates, low in most of the twentieth century, but tripling after 1980, remain the demographic wild card.[158]

Professor Nathan Glazer echoed this Graham outlook regarding the erosion of strong racial/ethnic identity, but he argued that blacks experience a strong sense of inner and society-imposed separateness. Consequently, he would have government census enumerators count but two racial groups: blacks and others.[159]

The implementation of affirmative action (be it promoted by disparate-impact and/or diversity grounds) requires the determination of the specific racial/ethnic group populations to determine how well they are represented in education, employment, or government. To this end, the U.S. decennial census has of late required responders to self-identify as one of the following: White, Black (African American or Negro), American Indian or Alaskan Native, Asian, or some other "race."[160] Hispanics are not deemed a race, but Hispanic responders were to affiliate themselves with one of the aforementioned races.

In 2000, for the first time, the decennial census (and other federal census taking) allowed individuals to identify themselves as belonging to more than one race. One, for example could become Asian-White. For affirmative action purposes, though, where white and a minority status was cited, the minority population was increased in the 2000 census.[161] The new multicultural census taking (continued in 2010) was spurred by those who had intermarried. They argued that their children deserved the dignity to identify themselves as of mixed heritage, and to be proud of such inheritance rather by being boxed into bureaucratically/politically created single-race units. Fearing a reduction in their political cohesion and potency, black and Hispanic interest groups typically opposed multiracialism for the 2000 census, calling for the maintenance of single-race designations.[162] Multiracial responses (where white was one of the choices) actually increased minority counts for affirmative action, for example, by one million for blacks.[163] Nationwide, only 2.4 percent of the respondents chose a multiracial category. Only 5 percent of blacks did so. The groups making the most use of the new capacity were Asians (16%), and American Indians (66%).[164]

Given its capacity to weaken minority group cohesion and support, there are those who view multiracial census taking as capable of killing affirmative action.[165] If the rate of intermarriage operates to make race/ethnic distinctions meaningless for all but blacks, as Graham predicted, affirmative action's potency will be reduced radically. The U.S. Census Bureau forecasts that by mid-century the country will be a nation of minorities (see 225–28). If the Graham intermarriage prediction is correct, should not the Census restrict its count to blacks and non-blacks as Glazer suggests? In any event, census taking raises many difficult questions associated with affirmative action:

Who is really monoracial?

How much minority "blood" does a person need to eligible for affirmative action?

How much weight should be given to "white" responses in multiracial responses? How should the minority dimension of such responses be allocated? Given the allocation difficulty, should multiracial counting be undertaken at all?

White ethnics (e.g., the Irish, Poles, Italians) experienced periods where they were treated harshly by the socially dominant. Yet they have not been covered by affirmative action. Why not? In the view of a leading affirmative action scholar—John David Skrentny—policy elites excluded white ethnics because the histories were deemed insufficiently compelling to warrant inclusion.[166]

Three

The Career of
Affirmative Action in Employment

Prologue

The antidiscrimination ferment of the 1950s and 1960s sparked a radical shift in national policy, and the modern civil rights movement deserves a lion's share of credit for this change.

During the nineteenth century, American blacks generally refrained from organized civil resistance, preferring to cultivate various strategies of accommodation with the white majority. An example is Booker T. Washington's "self-help" regimen through vocational education and entrepreneurship.[1]

The modern movement began early in the twentieth century with a period of interracial lobbying, litigation, and public advocacy. The flagship of this phase was the National Association for the Advancement of Colored People, formed in 1910 to combat Jim Crow. Its Legal Defense Fund scored notable antisegregation victories in the 1930s and 1940s, then planned and won the legendary antisegregation *Brown v. The Board* case in 1954.[2] This period also witnessed the beginnings of presidential antidiscrimination politics conducted through executive order. To avert threatened black demonstrations during the labor crisis of World War II, President Roosevelt proclaimed a new policy of nondiscrimination in federal employment and defense contracting to be administered by a Fair Employment Practice Commission (FEPC).[3] Black protests over military segregation and exclusion from the phenomenal postwar boom drove President Truman to desegregate the armed forces in 1948, and brought about the creation of numerous state and local FEPCs.[4] The African American civil rights movement became part of the Washington "Beltway" establishment in 1949 with the formation of the Leadership Conference on Civil Rights, a permanent, Washington-based coalition of civil rights and labor activists.[5] These were the "little acorns" of modern civil rights reform.

The second phase of this civil rights movement was outright black insurgency, waged, in large measure, as Gandhiesque nonviolent civil disobedience.

27

This was a war of protest against the iron grip of Jim Crow in the South. After the celebrated 1955 bus boycott in Montgomery, Alabama, the tactics in this war ranged from "freedom rides," voter registration drives, and "sit-ins" to massive public demonstrations in the South's major cities. Not atypically, these were met with savage attacks by some local police; countless arrests and jail sentences; church burnings; assassinations; and race riots in the North as well as the South. By design, or otherwise, these protests dramatized the absurdity and inhumanity of racial discrimination, and the imperative need for federal intervention. In 1963, they culminated in King's bloody confrontation with the Birmingham, Alabama, police, followed by his storied march on Washington and "I Have a Dream" oration.[6]

The Shift In National Policy

In March 1961, President Kennedy issued an Executive Order directing federal contractors to refrain from discrimination, and to "take *affirmative action* to ensure that applicants are employed and that employees are treated . . . without regard to their race, creed, color, or national origin."[7]

In June 1963, in the wake of King's Birmingham march, Kennedy filed a bill to prohibit racial discrimination in public accommodations, education, voting, federally funded programs, and community relations. During hearings in the House, the Leadership Conference on Civil Rights secured insertion of a ban on employment and sex discrimination.[8] At that point, the campaign for equal employment opportunity legislation became the focus of the drive for civil rights reform.[9]

Congressional hearings on the bill lasted for more than a year, the longest such investigatory period in our history. On July 2, 1964, under President Johnson, it was enacted as the Civil Rights Act of 1964[10] (CRA 1964), effective July, 2, 1965, its Title VII provisions regarding equal employment opportunity to be administered by a newly created Equal Employment Opportunity Commission (EEOC).[11] The 1964 CRA was our first comprehensive legislative attack on the scourge of racism in the twentieth century.[12]

By August 1965, the pace of reform accelerated dramatically. In that month, following on the effective date of the new 1964 Civil Rights Act, Congress enacted a Voting Rights Act (VRA), which LBJ had filed only five months earlier. The act[13] prohibited race- or color-based denial of voting rights, and invalidated literary, character, or educational tests particularly in the South as preconditions for voting—an early example of remedial affirmative action meant to soften the longstanding, disparate denial of black voting rights. Responsibility for enforcing the 1965 voting law was assigned to the Office of Civil Rights in the Department of Justice. (See chapter 6 below.)

In September 1965, President Johnson reissued JFK's 1961 federal contracting order as Executive Order 11246. This order retained Kennedy's affirmative action mandate verbatim, added a ban on sex discrimination, and assigned its administration to the Office of Federal Contract Compliance Programs (OFCCP)—what was to become a key affirmative action enforcement branch of the Department of Labor.[14] The stage was now set for the emergence of employment affirmative action as an overriding issue in a climactic war over how to administer civil rights reform.

It is customary to characterize the war as a dispute over "goals." Should the goal be to end racial discrimination, or to ensure racial equality—to equalize "opportunity," or to equalize "results"? In our view, this characterization overlooks the problems faced by the working administrators. When the bureaucracies at EEOC and OFCCP began to implement their new mandates, the problem that surfaced immediately was not defining "goals." That job had already been done in the century that followed Reconstruction. In the view of the implementing bureaucrats, the disparity between blacks and whites in every walk of life was so enormous that—even by the most minimal standards of civic equality—the task of "ending" discrimination necessarily implied an obligation to ensure improvement. In other words, history had mandated the "goal" of equalizing both "opportunity" and "results." What confronted the administrators in 1965 was the daunting job of finding the right means to that end. As a general approach, they adopted the notion of race-, ethnic-, and gender-conscious compensatory remediation as the basis for allocating minority access to jobs, entrepreneurial opportunities, education, and electoral procedure reform. The bureaucrats' decision won initial court approval, and touched off an ideological war over constitutionality, fairness, and effectiveness. This war is still ongoing, its outcome uncertain. Lamentably, "the unifying moral vision of civil rights" has given way to a "divisive nightmare of race."[15]

Let us now explore the equal employment opportunity (EEO) front in greater detail.

Title VII and Employment Discrimination

Title VII

Title VII, *Equal Employment Opportunity*, is a central dimension of the 1964 CRA's eleven titles, reflecting the fact that employment discrimination has always been a prime target of civil rights advocacy.[16] It has "dwarfed all the other titles combined, frequently generating a huge backlog of cases in the . . . EEOC, and leading to thousands of judicial decisions."[17] Title VII has been judicially determined to be a permissible exercise of Congress' constitutional power to regulate commerce; thus, it reaches the enormous private sector labor market as well as public employment.[18]

The specific goal of this law was to eliminate the gross discrimination between whites and minorities, and between men and women, in employment, income, and types of work.[19] Currently, Title VII covers most private employers with fifteen or more employees; labor unions with fifteen or more members; employment agencies; and federal, state, and local governments. Under the caption *Unlawful Employment Practices* covered employers are forbidden to engage in the following "unfair employment practice(s)":

Section 703(a)(1)(2)

(1) to fail or refuse to hire or to discharge . . . or otherwise discriminate against any individual with respect to his compensation, terms, conditions, or privileges of employment because of race, color, religion, sex, or national origin.

(2) to limit, segregate, or classify . . . employees in any way which would deprive . . . any individual of employment opportunities or otherwise adversely affect his status as an employee because of race, color, religion, sex, or national origin. [20]

Two additional particularly controversial provisions in the Act are Sections 703 (j), and 706 (g):

Section 703 (j)

The "no preference" clause, providing in pertinent part that:

Nothing in this title shall be interpreted to require any employer . . . [or] labor organization . . . to grant preferential treatment to any individual or to any group on account of an imbalance which may exist with respect to the total number or percentage of persons of any race, color, religion, sex, or national origin employed by any employer . . . [or] admitted to membership . . . by any labor organization . . . in comparison with the total number or percentage of persons of such race, color, religion, sex, or national origin in any community, State, section, or other area, or in the available work force in any community, State, section, or other area.[21]

Section 706(g)

This is the enforcement clause, providing in pertinent part that:

If the court finds that the respondent has intentionally engaged in an unlawful employment practice . . . the court may enjoin the respondent from engaging in such . . . practice, and order such affirmative action as may be appropriate, which may include reinstatement or hiring of employees, with or without back pay.[22]

The Genesis of Employment Affirmative Action: The EEOC and Disparate-Impact Theory

When the EEOC opened for business on July 2, 1965, it enjoyed none of the quasi-judicial prerogatives that independent regulatory agencies normally exercise. It could not conduct adversary hearings; issue cease-and-desist orders; or seek court enforcement of such orders. It did not have the right to issue and enforce substantive rules and regulations. It did not even have the right to file and prosecute lawsuits on its own initiative. The entire package of enforcement and regulatory powers had been withheld by Congress in order to secure Title VII's passage. Thus, it came to pass that, apart from limited administrative functions, the new commission was restricted by statute to investigating, and attempting to conciliate, individual complaints.[23]

Over the years, EEOC has devoted the great bulk of its efforts to its prescribed task of treating individual complaints.[24] But it has always aspired to a role that transcended its initial statutory mandate. As Alfred Blumrosen, who held an important position on the early EEOC legal staff, has written, "From its inception, the EEOC attempted to develop a self-initiated program to investigate systemic discrimination independently of complaints."[25] If, as he believes, the commission has failed to develop "an effective program" for policing systemic discrimination in this country,[26] it has not been for lack of trying. By design or otherwise, much of the thrust of the operating policies the agency adopted in 1965 and 1966 was based on the notion that the discrimination affecting blacks was rampant (though often perpetrated unconsciously) in America—in short, it is systemic. It was in these policies that EEOC planted the seeds of employment affirmative action. Following is an itemized summary of these seed-policies, and of their underlying rationale, as set out by Blumrosen in his authoritative *Modern Law* treatise.

Title VII, Blumrosen argues, *was intended to improve the economic position of minorities in the workplace, not merely to provide "equal treatment" as a remedy for proven—intentional—discriminatory practices.*[27] The EEOC's task in interpreting Title VII was to determine the relationship between the language of the new law and the "desired alteration of existing behavior."[28] Title VII does not contain any statement of Congress' intent, nor does it define its key terms (e.g., *"discrimination"*) so as to permit reasonable inferences of that intent.[29] However, the legislative history of Congress' constant stress on the indicators underscoring the grossly inferior position of blacks in employment warrants the conclusion that: "In its broadest sense, the 'legislative purpose' was to improve the objective conditions of minority groups, as defined by these indicators."[30]

"*Discrimination*"—to continue the Blumrosen thesis—*under Title VII includes both adverse effects (disparate impacts) on groups and intentional maltreatment of individuals.*[31] Early on, in Blumrosen's view, the EEOC developed a policy of applying the concept of "group interest" in processing individual complaints based on employer practices with group-wide impact, for example, seniority systems and testing. Such complaints were treated as vehicles for group remedies. What the policy targeted were the "effects" of the practices on designated minorities and females. The EEOC could have interpreted the law as requiring proof of discriminatory intent, but chose not to do so, in order to avoid the difficult task of proving intent, and to prevent employers from relying on "good intent" in restricting minority opportunities. The "effects" test is in keeping with the sense in which *discrimination* was used during the debate over the enactment of the 1964 Civil Rights Act, and is aimed at maximizing the impact of the law on industrial practices[32]—*practices*—the EEOC concluded—*which adversely affect (have a disparate impact on) protected groups are illegal unless they can be justified.*[33]

In 1966, the EEOC initiated a national reporting system requiring covered employers, unions, and apprenticeship committees to file annual reports identifying the number of employees, union members, and apprentices by job category, and by race, sex, and national origin.[34] From the beginning, these data have been analyzed statistically in terms of the standard indicators of discrimination: relative occupational distribution, relative wage and salary income, and relative unemployment rate. Also, according to Blumrosen, from the beginning, the statistics confirmed widespread protected-group disparities of such magnitude as to compel the conclusion on the part of the EEOC that they could only have been caused by racial, ethnic, and gender discrimination. These data were used by EEOC and other agencies in their quest for remedial action, such as the establishment of minority hiring goals and timetables.[35] Absent justification, serious, statistically demonstrated racial, ethnic, and gender disparities, in and of themselves, were interpreted as violating Title VII and as requiring remediation.[36]

The Gospel According to *Griggs*

During the late 1960s, the seeds of employment affirmative action matured slowly. EEOC refined the emerging *adverse effects/disparate-impact* doctrine by incorporating it both in guidelines for interpreting the Title VII's testing provisions, and in supportive *amicus* briefs for court cases which it then lacked authority to prosecute on its own.[37] It worked in constant conjunction with the Leadership Conference on Civil Rights and its affiliates, if not, as some suggest, under their virtually direct tutelage.[38]

In 1971, it all came together in *Griggs v. Duke Power Co,* [39] which "lent blanket judicial approval to"[40] EEOC's disparate-impact interpretation of Title VII. As of the Act's 1965 effective date, the defendant-employer, a large electric utility, abandoned a longstanding practice of segregating black employees in low-paying laboring jobs. But it continued to implement a policy, initiated in 1955, under which access to high-paying "white" jobs was made available to all applicants, white or black, who held high school diplomas and/or passed two professionally developed general aptitude tests. The tests were not "job related" in the sense of the EEOC's testing guidelines.[41] The thirteen African American plaintiffs had been hired without diplomas into segregated jobs at various dates before and after 1955; all of them claimed that the requirements were discriminatory because they made it difficult to move from segregated jobs into previously white jobs.[42] An extended excerpt from *Griggs* follows:

Griggs v. Duke Power, 401 U.S. 424 (1971)

Mr. Chief Justice Burger delivered the opinion of the Court.

[428] The Court of Appeals was confronted with a question of first impression, as are we, concerning the meaning of Title VII. After careful analysis a majority of that court concluded that a subjective test of the employer's intent should govern, particularly in a close case, and that in this case there was no showing of a discriminatory purpose in the adoption of the diploma and test requirements. On this basis, the Court of Appeals concluded there was no violation of the Act.

[429] The Court of Appeals . . . noted . . . that the District Court was correct in its conclusion that there was no showing of a racial purpose or invidious intent in the adoption of the high school diploma requirement or general intelligence test and that these standards had been applied fairly to whites and Negroes alike. It held that, in the absence of a discriminatory purpose, use of such requirements was permitted by the Act. In so doing, the Court of Appeals rejected the claim that because these two requirements operated to render ineligible a markedly disproportionate number of Negroes, they were unlawful under Title VII unless shown to be job related. We granted the writ on these claims.

The objective of Congress in the enactment of Title VII is plain from the language of the statute. It was to achieve equality of employment opportunities and remove [430] barriers that have operated in the past to favor an identifiable group of white employees. Under the Act, practices, procedures, or tests neutral on their face, and even neutral in terms of intent, cannot be maintained if they operate to "freeze" the status quo of prior discriminatory employment practices.

The Court of Appeals' opinion, and the partial dissent, agreed that, on the record in the present case, "whites register far better on the Company's alternative requirements" than Negroes. This consequence would appear to be directly traceable to race. Basic intelligence must have the means of articulation to manifest itself fairly in a testing process. Because they are Negroes, petitioners have long received inferior education in segregated schools and this Court expressly recognized these differences in *Gaston County v. United States*, 395 U.S. 285 (1969). There, because of the inferior education received by Negroes in North Carolina, this Court barred the institution of a literacy test for voter registration on the ground that the test would abridge the right to vote indirectly on account of race. Congress did not intend by Title VII, however, to guarantee a job to every person regardless of qualifications. . . . [431] What is required by Congress is the removal of artificial, arbitrary, and unnecessary barriers to employment when the barriers operate invidiously to discriminate on the basis of racial or other impermissible classification. . . .

Congress has now provided that tests or criteria for employment or promotion may not provide equality of opportunity merely in the sense of the fabled offer of milk to the stork and the fox. On the contrary, Congress has now required that the posture and condition of the job-seeker be taken into account. It has—to resort again to the fable—provided that the vessel in which the milk is proffered be one all seekers can use. The Act proscribes not only overt discrimination but also practices that are fair in form, but discriminatory in operation. The touchstone is business necessity. If an employment practice which operates to exclude Negroes cannot be shown to be related to job performance, the practice is prohibited.

On the record before us, neither the high school completion requirement nor the general intelligence test is shown to bear a demonstrable relationship to successful performance of the jobs for which it was used. Both were adopted, as the Court of

Appeals noted, without meaningful study of their relationship to job-performance ability. . . .

[432] The Company's lack of discriminatory intent is suggested by special efforts to help the undereducated employees through Company financing of two-thirds the cost of tuition for high school training. But Congress directed the thrust of the Act to the consequences of employment practices, not simply the motivation. More than that, Congress has placed on the employer the burden of showing that any given requirement must have a manifest relationship to the employment in question.

[433] The facts of this case demonstrate the inadequacy of broad and general testing devices as well as the infirmity of using diplomas or degrees as fixed measures of capability. History is filled with examples of men and women who rendered highly effective performance without the conventional badges of accomplishment in terms of certificates, diplomas, or degrees. Diplomas and tests are useful servants, but Congress has mandated the common sense proposition that they are not to become masters of reality. . . .

[436] Nothing in the Act precludes the use of testing or measuring procedures; obviously they are useful. What Congress has forbidden is giving these devices and mechanisms controlling force unless they are demonstrably a reasonable measure of job performance. Congress has not commanded that the less qualified be preferred over the better qualified simply because of minority origins. Far from disparaging job qualifications as such, Congress has made such qualifications the controlling factor, so that race, religion, nationality, and sex become irrelevant. What Congress has commanded is that any tests used must measure the person for the job and not the person in the abstract.

The judgment of the Court of Appeals is, as to that portion of the judgment appealed from, reversed.

The Supreme Court's decision in *Griggs* is a Holy Writ of affirmative action: In Blumrosen's words:

The *Griggs* decision flows from an understanding of the legislative purpose. It constitutes a creative judicial interpretation in an area where Congress had not been clear as to the means to be used to improve the status of minorities. And it confirmed to some extent, the administrative agency judgments which sought to produce the maximum impact for the statute. . . . [T]hree different concepts of discrimination were used in *Griggs* as it worked its way through the courts. The district court applied an "intent to discriminate" concept, the court of appeals applied an "equal treatment" concept with respect to some of the black plaintiffs, and the Supreme Court developed the "adverse effect" or "disparate impact" concept.[43]

In the wake of *Griggs*, the EEOC encouraged private employers under its jurisdiction and other "users" (such as unions) to avoid costly lawsuits by using the racial, ethnic, and gender employment data they are required to keep[44] to engage in self-analysis so as to determine whether protected groups are underutilized. (The EEOC and its *Uniform Guidelines on Employee Selection* and its *Affirmative Action Guidelines* are excerpted in Appendices at the end of this volume, pp. 355–65.) The employee-selection guidelines note that where an employer or other user "has not maintained data on adverse [disparate] impact, . . . Federal enforcement agencies may draw an inference of adverse impact of the [employee] selection process from the failure of the user to maintain such data, if the user has an underutilization of a group in a job category, as compared to the group's representation in the relevant labor market, or, in the case of jobs filled from within, the applicable work force."[45] The same section of the guidelines contains the "four-fifths rule": "A selection rate for any race, sex, or ethnic group which is less than four-fifths (4/5) (or eighty percent) of the rate for the group with the highest rate will generally be regarded by Federal enforcement agencies as evidence of adverse impact." Adverse impacts are excusable if *validated* as being the result of job-related criteria consistent with business necessity. EEOC's guidelines relating to the validation of "selection procedures are intended to be consistent with generally accepted professional standards for evaluating standardized tests and other procedures"[46] such as those prepared by professional societies in psychology and education, as well as those contained in standard texts and journals in the area of personnel selection.[47] In *Albermarle Paper Co. v. Moody* (1975), the Supreme Court determined that even where an employer's practices (which disparately impacted protected groups) were job related and sanctioned by business necessity, they were still prohibited if there were less discriminatory procedures which equally met the business necessities of the employer.[48]

The Office of Federal Contract Compliance Programs (OFCCP)—as a condition of contract maintenance—requires larger federal contractors to engage in good faith efforts to remedy minority and female underutilization if required self-analysis exhibits deficiencies. OFCCP is subject to the *Uniform Guidelines on Employee Selection* noted above. Its affirmative action requirements for covered service and supply contractors are excerpted in Appendix Three at the end of this volume.

The employers' potential disparate-impact liability in connection with Title VII and its associated EEOC regulations prompted these words from Justice Scalia in his *Johnson v. Santa Clara* (1987)[49] dissent:

> This Court's prior interpretations of Title VII, especially the decision in *Griggs v. Duke Power Co.*, subject employers to a potential Title VII suit whenever there is a noticeable imbalance in the representation of minorities or women in the employer's work force. Even the employer who is confident of ultimately prevailing in such a suit must contemplate the expense and adverse publicity of a trial, because the extent of the imbalance, and the "job relatedness" of his selection criteria, are questions of fact to be explored through rebuttal and counterrebuttal of a "prima facie case" consisting of no more than the showing that the employer's selection process "selects those from the protected class at a 'significantly' lesser rate than their counterparts." If, however, employers are free to discriminate through affirmative action, without fear of "reverse discrimination" suits by their nonminority or male victims, they are offered a threshold defense against Title VII liability premised on numerical disparities. Thus, after today's decision the failure to engage in reverse discrimination is economic folly, and arguably a breach of duty to shareholders or taxpayers, wherever the cost of anticipated Title VII litigation exceeds the cost of hiring less capable (though still minimally capable) workers. . . . A statute designed to establish a color-blind and gender-blind workplace has thus been converted into a powerful engine of racism and sexism, not merely permitting intentional race- and sex-based discrimination, but often making it, through operation of the legal system, practically compelled.

Disparate-impact theory converted Title VII into a potential "double-edged sword" for employers as disparate-impact remediation through affirmative action could trigger disparate-treatment/reverse-discrimination suits by nonminorities. Scalia's dissent in *Johnson v. Santa Clara County* expressed the view that the majority opinion in that case suppressed the potentiality of reverse discrimination suits, thus facilitating affirmative action practice. This view was, in effect, corroborated by Justice Ginsburg who, dissenting in *Ricci v. DeStefano* (2009),[50] highlighted the historical encouragement by the Supreme Court and the EEOC of voluntary employment affirmative action meant to cure systemic discrimination.[51] Indeed, longstanding EEOC guidelines for employers state that the agency will not hold employers liable for reverse discrimination if they undertake "good faith" efforts to correct past discrimination.[52] Also, the Supreme Court has strongly supported employer efforts to mend disparate-impact burdens on protected groups. Once, however, in 1989 (*Wards Cove v. Atonio*[53]), and again in 2009 (*Ricci v. DeStefano*[54]) the Court attempted to restrain Title VII's affirmative action momentum. We address these matters in due course. (See 57–60 and 77–79.)

Office of Federal Contract Compliance Programs and Affirmative Action

Along with the EEOC, the Office of Federal Contract Compliance Programs (OFCCP) has been a leader in the development of employment affirmative action. Under OFCCP's administration in the late 1960s (arising from EO 11246), affirmative action became an authentic instrument of equal employment opportunity in the notoriously racist, federally funded construction industry for the first time since the term *affirmative action* was used in President Kennedy's 1961 federal contracting order. The prototype of the OFCCP's very expansive affirmative action efforts was the famous "Philadelphia Plan," a project which the OFCCP undertook in connection with the construction industry in the Philadelphia area in 1969, but which did not receive final approval until the Nixon administration in 1971. Basic elements of the plan were establishment by the OFCCP's "goals and timetables" for hiring specific percentages of "underutilized" minorities in each building trade, depending on their availability; and a required commitment by the covered contractors to use "good faith efforts" to achieve these goals.[55]

The Philadelphia Plan was upheld in a 1971 decision by the Third Circuit, which still controls.[56] The court held that the plan was constitutional, since it was based on an appropriate administrative determination that blacks were systematically excluded from the building trades on account of their race, and since inclusion of blacks in the building trades pursuant to the plan served the public interest by providing an adequate, integrated work force. The court also held that the plan did not violate the "no preference" provisions of Title VII (See Section 703 (j) at 30) since it did not arise under the statute, but rather was authorized by a presidential executive order (EO 11246).

Subsequently, the goals-and-timetables approach to equal employment opportunity was extended to all federal contracting and subsidized programs. The OFCCP undertaking is a major governmentally initiated vehicle of affirmative action in the country[57]—an exemplar of "big government." On their face, the OFCCP goals and timetables requirement (and comparable requirements such as those encouraged by the EEOC) do not mandate preferences for minorities or women. They require only that employers make "good faith" efforts to find qualified members of underutilized protected groups. However, if such good faith efforts are not evident to federal scrutinizers, the result could be a loss of federal contracts or other severe penalties. According to an appellate court, treating a Federal Communication Commission affirmative action goals requirement like that imposed by OFCCP, the potential of federal sanctions pressures employers to engage in preferential treatment. The court presented the following view:

> Nor can it be said that the Commission's parity goals do not pressure license holder to engage in race-conscious hiring. . . . It cannot be seriously argued that this [good faith scrutiny] screening device does not create a strong incentive to meet the numerical goals. No rational firm—particularly one holding a government-issued license—welcomes a government audit. Even DOJ [Department of Justice] argued . . . that they [the goals' guidelines] operated as "a *de facto* hiring quota," and that "broadcasters, in order to avoid the inconvenience and expense of being subjected to further review, will treat the guidelines as safe-harbors. . . ." [W]e do not think it matters whether a government hiring program imposes hard quotas, soft quotas, or goals. Any one of these techniques induces an employer to hire with an eye toward meeting the numerical target. As such, they can and surely will result in individuals being granted a preference because of their race.[58]

This view was disputed by OFCCP's senior trial attorney. She noted that the agency's regulations mandate only "good faith" efforts to achieve numerical hiring goals, and explicitly forbade "preferences" and "quotas." In her view, "goals and timetables" are "benchmarks," rather than rigid legal requirements.[59]

The Institutionalization of Employment Affirmative Action and Diversity Theory

The threat of litigation as a spur for the onset of much business and government affirmative action is doubtless a correct view.[60] Subsequent to their inauguration, affirmative action practices (particularly in large businesses) were installed as permanent operating modes in "human resources" personnel departments. Starting in the 1980s, "human resources" specialists "reframed" and "retheorized" their affirmative action *raison d'etre*, submerging remediation and latching on to the nonremedial concept of "diversity management,"[61] which insists that race/ethnic/gender-conscious employment practices are good for business.[62]

Why the shift to the diversity rationale? Organizational theorists maintain that organizations develop new ideological supports and theories to shore up their strength when it is threatened (i.e., to retheorize). And a number of anti–affirmative action threats emerged over the years. For one, the 1980s Reagan Administration expressed a distaste for traditional, remedial affirmative action and was regarded as capable of reducing its enforcement. Questions about remedial affirmative action's viability were raised by both the Bush I and Clinton administrations. The former, in 1990, vetoed a measure much sought after by affirmative action defenders; the latter proclaimed that affirmative action required mending. The Supreme Court, moreover, starting in 1989, delivered opinions that raised further doubts about remedial affirmative action's future.[63] (See pp. 57–68 and 77–79 for these Court decisions.) Thus, the birth and maturation of the diversity rationale as a tactic meant to enhance the potency of personnel departments already enlarged by affirmative action endeavors. It was presumed that "good for business" diversity, nonremedial arguments (e.g., sensitivity to an increasingly diverse customer base required a more diverse workforce) could withstand the growing criticisms of race/gender-conscious employment practices better than remedial insistencies.[64] To law professor Peter Schuck, diversity theory was a "Hail Mary" pass, an argument made in desperation in the wake of the threats to affirmative action. "Casting about for a safe harbor, defenders of preferences seized upon the diversity justification offered by Justice Powell in 1978."[65]

The Supreme Court and the Quarrel over Employment Affirmative Action, 1970–1989

A Parting of the Ways

A case can be made that 1971 was about the time the war over employment affirmative action began, at least in the sense of providing the *casus belli*. Disparate-impact analysis, at that date, was now an approved instrument of equal employment opportunity policy. Goals and timetables, to affirmative action's friends, seemed to be a way to promote aggressive hiring of females and other protected-group members without going against the American grain. The inner logic of both disparate impact and goals/timetables implied the need to use overt race/ethnic/gender-conscious devices to cure the evils of the historical and societal oppression against minorities and women. In short, the seeds of affirmative action had begun to mature.

The champions of reform saw this development as an opportunity to move the country away from the ominous racial divide which had been revealed by the urban riots of the late 1960s.[66] Others, however, viewed it with profound alarm. In their eyes, the emergence of disparate-impact theory and goals/timetables signaled the beginning of an "inner transformation of the civil rights vision," from "nondiscrimination" as required by Title VII to "preferential treatment for minorities."[67] As the traditionalists saw it, the logic of preference was that employment discrimination should be defined and attacked statistically as a differential, rather than traditionally as an invidious and injurious act of prejudice. Its measure was simply the gap between white and minority employment rates. This presumptive new definition in turn rested on an implicit normative theory of proportional representation in the workforce.[68]

The upshot, so the traditional school concluded, was no less than that by the early 1970s the legal majesty of the American state once again, as it had in the segregationist era between *Plessy* and *Brown*, ordained that citizens who had wronged no one must be denied important rights and benefits because of genetic attributes such as the color of their skin.[69]

Plainly, an ideological war over quotas and reverse discrimination was festering. The first skirmish took place in 1972 when the opponents of goals and timetables attempted—and failed—to amend the "no preference" clause in Title VII by inserting an explicit prohibition of "discrimination in reverse" through use of "fixed or variable numbers, proportions, percentages, quotas, goals, or ranges."[70] In addition to rejecting the proposed amendment, Congress extended Title VII's coverage, to federal and state employees, and granted EEOC power to sue private employers.[71] From that point it was relatively clear sailing for affirmative action until the late 1980s.

There is little quarrel in the employment arena about remedies for disparate treatment (intentional discrimination affecting individuals), and these remedies have at times been dubbed "affirmative action." Thus, Section 706 (g) of the 1964 Civil Rights Act reads: "If the court finds that the respondent has intentionally engaged in or is intentionally engaging in an unlawful employment practice. . . . [T]he court may enjoin . . . such unlawful employment practice, and order such *affirmative action* as may be appropriate"[72] (emphasis added).

However, the battle over affirmative action has largely concerned disparate-impact remedies. The principle of disparate-impact affirmative action posits that, by its very nature, systemic bias against protected groups requires a cure that goes "beyond compensation to individuals for direct individual injury"[73]—which remedy is provided by disparate treatment law. To the advocates of disparate-impact remediation, the injury systemic bias produces is a congenital handicap that every member of the impacted group inherits at the moment of birth, namely, an inability to compete deriving solely from the immutable fact of minority/gender status. It is both necessary and desirable that race, national origin, or gender-based disadvantage be redressed by a compensatory grant of race, ethnic or gender-based advantage, irrespective of whether intentional wrongdoing can be proven in law. "Special help" to be sure, but only as a benign offset to unfair detriment, not as a substitute for qualification, or as a predeterminant of outcomes. Since, moreover, disparate impact is a function of group membership, the remedial compensation must be available to every group member, regardless of the harm suffered by that member.

In theory, then, affirmative action is not an end in itself, but a tool for ensuring equitable distribution of America's bounty. Disparate-impact thinking has given rise to court-ordered and voluntary public and private plans meant to remedy the socially undesirable, disparate conditions affecting protected groups. Since the enactment of the 1991 Civil Rights Act,[74] disparate-impact affirmative action has been authorized by statute. Let us now consider what the Supreme Court has said about affirmative action, recognizing that its constitutional rulings as of late have helped trigger a nonremedial approach to affirmative action referred to as "diversity" theory. It is to be recalled that remedial affirmative action is meant to correct a legal wrong; nonremedial diversity theory facially seeks diversity for ideational pluralism and/or business improvement. These functions are analytically distinct, although in practice they have merged with the result being that more protected-group members acquire preferential treatment in the job market, and in admissions to colleges and universities.

In the 1970s and until 1989, the Supreme Court strongly supported affirmative action both in its statutory and constitutional interpretations. Two decisions in 1989—one statutory (*Wards Cove v. Atonio*);[75] the other constitutional (*Richmond v. Croson*)[76]—so flustered the civil rights/affirmative action advocacy groups that they successfully prodded Congress to statutorily legitimize the doctrine of disparate impact that *Wards Cove* threatened.[77] The Court's interpretation of the Constitution's Equal Protection Clause requirements in the aforementioned *Richmond v. Croson* also threatened the viability of disparate-impact affirmative action. Diversity theory, however, promised an alternative and potent reinforcement for race/ethnic/gender preferences. "[I]t ascribes no guilt, calls for no arguments about compensation. It seems to ask simply for rational, unbigoted judgement."[78] Consequently, affirmative action stalwarts strongly urged the Court to constitutionally sanction the notion that the quest for diversity enabled government to sponsor affirmative action–like policies.[79]

Let us consider the affirmative action decisions of the Court from the 1970s to *Wards Cove* and *Croson*. During this period, the Court was a main theater of operations in the "reverse discrimination" war. Between 1978 and 1989, all the Court's affirmative action decisions were split decisions, at times without majority support for the reasoning upholding the decisions, and with sharp differences among the justices. It is no wonder that this was so, given the novelty and difficulty of the issues, including the following questions: Is affirmative action a legitimate remedy? Should the burden of the remedy be imposed on innocent third parties? Is affirmative action compatible with the Equal Protection Clause of the Fourteenth Amendment? Are quotas permissible under law? In terms of Title VII, key questions included whether that Title banned disparate-impact discrimination, and how to interpret its Sections 703 (j) and 703 (g). The former forbade *requiring* employers or labor unions to grant preferential treatment to any group for the purpose of correcting racial/sexual/ethnic imbalances. The latter concerned the nature of judicial power to correct intentional discrimination. (For the critical texts of Title VII, see 29–31.)

At the constitutional level, the critical constitutional disputes have concerned the Equal Protection Clause of the Fourteenth Amendment (applicable to state government) and its "component" embedded[80] by Supreme Court decree in the Fifth Amendment's Due Process Clause, the latter clause applicable to the national government. The Equal Protection Clause prohibits any state government from depriving "any person within its jurisdiction the equal protection of the laws." An important affirmative action Equal Protection Clause question concerns the level of judicial scrutiny of government action that clause requires. Should it be *mid-tier* or "*strict*"? To survive mid-tier review, an affirmative action program must serve an *important* government interest, and employ means that are *substantially* related to that governmental end. On the other hand, strict scrutiny requires a *compelling* governmental interest, and means which are *narrowly tailored* to achieve that compelling interest. After years of inconclusive Supreme Court debate as to the merits of mid-tier versus strict judicial review, strict scrutiny was adopted by the High Court for racial/ethnic governmental classifications, first for state government in *Richmond v. Croson* (1989),[81] and later for the federal government in *Adarand v. Peña* (1995).[82]

Let us now turn to the Supreme Court's affirmative action opinions between 1971–1989. Initially, this review will cover the primary Title VII interpretations. The discussion merges into a survey of the primary equal protection/constitutional opinions that bear upon employment affirmative action. Where statutory and constitutional grounds were coupled, they will be examined as is appropriate to sort out the complicated workings of the Court. Italicized summaries of these decisions attempt to capture their essence.

Affirmative Action and the Supreme Court: The Title VII Decisions, 1970–1989

1.

Griggs v. Duke Power (1971)[83] has been treated at length above on 31–38. To briefly recapitulate, the Court in Griggs interpreted the coverage of Title VII of the 1964 Civil Rights Act as not only barring disparate-treatment (intentional) employment discrimination; it also prohibited disparate-impact discrimination arising from the historic/societal oppression of minorities, and reflected in their underrepresentation in the workplace. Employers are exempt from disparate-impact liability if job practices are job related and consistent with business necessity, and absent (as the Court, in 1975, concluded in Albermarle)[84] alternate employment practices—equally facilitative of business needs—which had a lesser disparate impact on protected groups.

2.

Title VII of the 1964 Civil Rights Act permits voluntary adoption of race/ ethnic-conscious affirmative action plans in the private employment sector for the purpose of eliminating racial imbalance in segregated job categories. Such plans need not be predicated on proven past intentional discrimination, and are permissible if they do not unnecessarily trammel the legitimate interests or expectations of nonbeneficiary employees, and are designed to achieve a balanced work force but not to maintain a permanent balance.

United Steelworkers of America v. Weber (1979) [85]—the first Title VII "reverse discrimination" case to reach the High Court—arose from a collective bargaining agreement which reserved for black employees at a Louisiana aluminum plant 50 percent of the openings in a newly created, in-plant training program. The purpose of the program was to train unskilled production workers to fill craftwork openings. At the time, only 1.83 percent (5 out of 273) of the plant's skilled craftworkers were blacks, even though the local labor force was about 39 percent black. Under the agreement, at least 50 percent of the training slots were to be awarded to black applicants until the percentage of in-plant, skilled black craftworkers approximated the percentage of blacks in the local labor force. Selection for training was to be by seniority within each racial group. Since the plant's unskilled production force was 90 percent white, relatively few blacks were available to bid for selection. It thus transpired that, in the group initially selected, the senior black workers had less plant-wide seniority than some rejected white bidders, including Weber the plaintiff. Weber claimed that the affirmative action plan resulted in a race-based preference for junior blacks over senior whites, and therefore violated the ban on discrimination in Title VII. Weber's claim was essentially that, even though he was junior to all of the successful white bidders, he was senior to all of the successful black bidders, and therefore, had he been black, his bid would have been accepted. This was the generic claim of reverse discrimination: race-based deprivation of a benefit due and owing to an innocent third party. The U.S. Fifth Circuit Court of Appeals upheld the claim, 2-1, holding that Title VII bars all race-based employment preferences, "including those preferences incidental to bona fide affirmative action plans."[86] In an opinion by Justice Brennan, the Supreme Court reversed, 5-2, saying that the provisions of Title VII do not prohibit all private, voluntary race-conscious affirmative action plans.[87] These provisions must be read against the background of legislative history and historical context:

Congress' primary concern was with "the plight of the Negro in our economy". . . . "[T]he relative position of the Negro worker [was] steadily worsening. . . ." Congress feared that the goals of the Civil Rights Act—the integration of blacks into the mainstream of American society—could not be achieved unless this trend was reversed. . . ." [T]he crux of the problem . . . [was] to open employment opportunities for Negroes in occupations which have traditionally been closed to them." . . . [I]t was to this problem that Title VII's prohibition against racial discrimination in employment was primarily addressed.[88]

It follows that Congress could not have intended to prohibit the private sector from taking effective steps to accomplish the goal that Congress designed Title VII to achieve. . . . It would be ironic indeed if a law triggered by a Nation's concern over centuries of racial injustice and intended to improve the lot of those who had "been excluded from the American dream for so long" . . . constituted the first legislative prohibition of all voluntary, private, race-conscious efforts to abolish traditional patterns of racial segregation and hierarchy.[89]

If Congress had intended to prohibit all race-conscious affirmative action, it could have provided that Title VII "would not require or *permit* racially preferential integration efforts."[90] However, the "no preference" clause in section 703(j)[91] provides only that preferential treatment is not *required*, thus leaving the "natural inference that Congress did not intend to forbid all voluntary race conscious" efforts to correct racial imbalances.[92]

The plan in the *Weber* case falls on the "permissible side" of the affirmative action line, since like the 1964 Civil Rights Act, it is designed to break down old patterns of racial segregation and hierarchy; it does not "unnecessarily trammel" the interests of the white employees, for instance, it does not require discharge of whites and their replacement with blacks, or absolutely bar their advancement; and it is a temporary measure, "not intended to maintain racial balance, but simply to eliminate a manifest racial imbalance."[93]

In articulating the "unduly trammeling" principle, the Court for the first time enunciated a standard for adjudicating the impact of affirmative action on nonminorities. Most of the Court's subsequent decisions in this period dealt with this issue.

The Rehnquist dissent in *Weber* was particularly vigorous, and it ended by saying:

There is perhaps no device more destructive to the notion of equality than the *numerus clausus*—the quota. Whether described as "benign discrimination" or "affirmative action," the racial quota is nonetheless a creator of castes, a two-edged sword that must demean one in order to prefer another. In passing Title VII, Congress outlawed *all* racial discrimination, recognizing that no discrimination based on race is benign, that no action disadvantaging a person because of his color is affirmative. With today's holding, the Court introduces into Title VII a tolerance for the very evil that the law was intended to eradicate, without offering even a clue as to what the limits on that tolerance may be. We are told simply that [the employer] Kaiser's racially discriminatory admission quota "falls on the permissible side of the line." By going not merely *beyond*, but directly *against* Title VII's language and legislative history, the Court has sown the wind. Later courts will face the impossible task of reaping the whirlwind.[94]

3.

Race-conscious, out-of-seniority layoffs of nonminority employees by public employers violate Title VII if they benefit nonvictims of discrimination. Court-ordered numerical union membership or promotion goals do not violate the "no-preference" to remedy imbalance clause of Title VII [703(j)] if they are necessary to remedy past discrimination, are flexibly implemented, and do not seek to maintain permanent racial balance in the work force.

The Supreme Court justices have felt it necessary to reaffirm the *Weber* holding that race-conscious affirmative action is not reverse discrimination per se. Thus, in *Wygant v. Jackson Board of Education* (1986),[95] Justice Powell's plurality opinion stressed the need for strict scrutiny of state-sponsored racial classifications, and then said:

> We have recognized, however, that, in order to remedy the effects of prior discrimination, it may be necessary to take race into account. As part of this Nation's dedication to eradicating racial discrimination, innocent persons may be called upon to bear some of the burden of the remedy. "When effectuating a limited and properly tailored remedy to cure the effects of prior discrimination, such a 'sharing of the burden' by innocent parties is not impermissible."[96]

The problem is to determine how much of the remedial burden the innocent party should be expected to bear—a process that necessarily works on a case-by-case basis. Still, some of the Court's decisions offer general guidelines. For example, in both of the layoff cases that came before the Court, the majority voted against affirmative action. In *Firefighters v. Stotts*

(1984),[97] the Court held, 5-4, that a federal district court judge violated Title VII by modifying a consent decree so as to permit layoff of senior white firefighters in order to retain junior blacks who had been hired pursuant to the decree. The asserted justification for this departure from the employer's longstanding seniority rules was the need to preserve the gains under the decree. The Court majority ruled that the district judge lacked authority under section 706(g) of the Act[98] to disregard the seniority system, since there was no finding that any of the retained blacks had "actually been a victim of illegal discrimination."[99] In *Wygant v. Jackson,* the Court reached a similar result but on constitutional grounds. (See 56.)

The results in *Stotts* and *Wygant* were the crest of the anti–affirmative action sentiment in the Court at the time, and of the Reagan Administration's largely abortive attempt to limit affirmative action.[100] In later cases, during the 1980s, the Court's most redoubtable champion of affirmative action, Justice Brennan, was able to muster majority support for his views. In *Sheet Metal Workers v. EEOC* (1986)[101] the Court upheld a court order requiring a local union, which had ignored prior orders to admit blacks, to increase its black membership by 29.23 percent. The Court held, 6-3 that section 706(g) of the act[102] authorizes the district courts to order preferential relief benefiting individuals who may not be the actual victims of discrimination.[103] The main problem in the case was that the 29.23 percent African American union membership requirement for blacks was arguably a quota-like, racial-balancing scheme prohibited by section 703 (j) of the 1964 Civil Rights Act.[104] Five members concluded that the goal did not violate either the equal protection component of the Fifth Amendment's Due Process Clause or Title VII.[105] No common standard of equal protection review was established, but the majority concluded that equal protection was not violated given the union's egregious racism.[106] Of this five-member majority, a four-member plurality, including Justice Brennan, held the following:

> [R]ace-conscious affirmative measures [may not be invoked under Title VII] simply to create a racially balanced work force.[107]

> [A] court should consider whether affirmative action is necessary [under Title VII] to remedy past discrimination in a particular case before imposing such measures, and . . . should also take care to tailor its orders to fit the nature of the violation it seeks to correct.[108]

The Brennan plurality—in an opinion that supported the widespread affirmative action effort to establish goals and timetables—continued by saying that the 29.23 percent requirement was necessary "to assure the equal employment opportunities guaranteed by Title VII," because of the union's "long continued and egregious" exclusion of blacks, and in order to combat "the lingering effects of [this] pervasive discrimination."[109] The plurality concluded that the 29.23 percent figure was a goal (and not a firm quota) because the lower court had been flexible in applying its previous requirements, and was likely to do so in the future. In short, the aforementioned numerical requirement was "not being used simply to achieve and maintain racial balance, but rather as a benchmark [for] measuring [the union's] compliance with [the court's] orders, rather than as a strict racial quota."[110] The goal was a temporary measure. It did not "unnecessarily trammel the interests of white employees": that is, no white union members were laid off, and there is no "absolute bar" to white applicants.[111]

Like union membership goals, race, ethnic, and gender-based hiring and promotion goals must pass muster under section 703(j). *Firefighters v. Cleveland* (1986)[112] arose from a court order approving a consent decree under which the employer agreed to promote one black firefighter for every white promoted until a stipulated level of black employment was reached. This formula was clearly much closer to the quota line than the one sanctioned in the *Sheet Metal* case, but it too was approved, this time 6-3. Justice Brennan's majority opinion concluded that the policy favoring voluntary compliance with the intent of the law overrode the arguable possibility that the evidence might not have justified a court order of such breadth.[113]

4.

Title VII permits voluntary adoption of sex-conscious affirmative action plans by public employers for the purpose of eliminating statistically demonstrated, manifest (disparate-impact) imbalances in traditionally segregated job categories. Such plans need not be predicated on past discrimination by the employers who undertake them, and are permissible if they do not unnecessarily trammel the legitimate interests or expectations of male employees, and are designed to achieve a balanced work force but not to maintain a permanent balance.

The National Organization for Women (NOW) was created to prompt EEOC to take the ban against employment sex discrimination in Title VII of the 1964 Civil Rights Act as seriously as that Title's ban against race discrimination. But as the EEOC was pursuing the acceptance of disparate-impact affirmative action for African Americans, its initial regulations permitted state-protective legislation for women in the workplace (e.g., mandatory rest periods, exclusion from dangerous work), and even gender-specific job advertisements. Lobbied by the burgeoning corps of "second-wave" feminists, the agency quickly shifted its regulatory gears, determining that the aforementioned gender bias ran afoul of Title VII.[114]

By the later 1960s, the feminist forces had resolved their long-standing differences over "equal rights" versus "special protection," in favor of a sex-blind version of the former. Concurrently, however, the black movement was moving from an equal rights, color-blind posture to one that emphasized affirmative action's race consciousness in hiring, educational opportunities, and the like—all for the achievement of "equal results." Thus, feminists did not initially march in lockstep with the African American civil rights movement.[115] But this soon changed. Women came to be classified as a protected group. In an early turnabout, feminist groups came to vociferously advocate affirmative action for women, and women soon gained a firm footing in the affirmative action mosaic.[116] Perhaps this reversal helps explain the defeat of the Equal Rights Amendment in 1982. As submitted to the states in 1972, its first section read: "Equality of Rights under the law shall not be denied or abridged by the United States or by any State on account of sex."[117]

The peak of Justice Brennan's influence came in *Johnson v. Transportation Agency of Santa Clara County* (1987),[118] where, for the first time, the Court was confronted with the issue of gender-conscious affirmative action. The Court held, 6-3, that a public employer's decision to promote a female to a skilled-craft job over a male applicant did not violate Title VII's prohibition of sex discrimination. The promotion was made pursuant to a voluntary affirmative action plan which was designed to move women into higher-ranking, traditionally male positions, and permitted consideration of qualified applicants' sex as one factor in promotional decisions. The rejected male had scored two points higher than the promoted female in a qualifying interview, and claimed that he had been denied promotion solely for the reason of sex.

In rejecting this claim, Justice Brennan's majority opinion ruled that the principle of *Steelworkers v. Weber* (1978)[119] applied to voluntary sex-conscious affirmative action designed to eliminate "a manifest imbalance that reflected under-representation of women in 'traditionally segregated job categories.' "[120] The majority concluded that the affirmative action plan at issue was valid under this principle, and that it was accordingly appropriate to give some weight to the promoted female's sex.

Pursuant to the rule in *Weber*, voluntary affirmative action plans are permissible under Title VII if designed to correct a "manifest imbalance" in a "traditionally segregated job category." In determining whether such an imbalance exists in a job that requires special training, it is appropriate to compare the percentage of minorities or women in the employer's workforce with those in the area workforce who possess the relevant qualifications.[121]

> The requirement that the "manifest imbalance" relate to a "traditionally segregated job category" provides assurance both that sex or race will be taken into account in a manner consistent with Title VII's purpose of eliminating the effects of employment discrimination, and that the interests of those employees not benefiting from the plan will not be unduly infringed.[122]

The only justification that Title VII requires of a voluntary affirmative action plan is conspicuous statistical imbalance (underrepresentation),[123] demonstrative of a disparate-societal/historical impact. Unlike the Equal Protection Clause, the 1964 Civil Rights Act does not require that a voluntary affirmative action plan, even one adopted by a public employer, *be predicated on the employer's prior discrimination*. Such a requirement "could inappropriately create a significant disincentive for employers to adopt an affirmative action plan," thereby running counter to Title VII's underlying purpose of encouraging "employer efforts to eliminate vestiges of discrimination."[124] Importantly, public employers when fulfilling the objectives of Title VII were not subject to the equal protection requirements of the Constitution. Answering Justice Scalia's insistence that these equal protection requirements were applicable (and consequently restricted affirmative action to curing the public employer's own unlawful discrimination),[125] the Court argued that Congress meant to free the states and their subdivisions from the constraints of the Equal Protection Clause. Title VII "was enacted pursuant to the commerce power . . . and was not intended to incorporate . . . the commands of the Fifth and Fourteenth Amendments. . . . Even when that Title was extended to public employers in 1972, 'Congress expressly indicated the intent that the same Title VII principles be applied to governmental and private employers alike.' "[126]

According to the Court, the Santa Clara plan at issue complied fully with the *Weber* standard: The employer's female employees were traditionally employed in "women's" work, namely, office and clerical positions, and "most egregiously underrepresented" in skilled-craft work (*zero* percent of 228 positions).[127] The plan did not set aside a specific number of jobs for women, but established hiring and promotional goals as guidelines for "statistically measurable" improvement.[128] The plan did not authorize "blind hiring" by the numbers to fulfill the goals, but required consideration of numerous factors, including the qualifications of female applicants for particular jobs.[129] Given the obvious imbalance in the skilled craft category, and the employer's commitment to eliminate such imbalances, "it was plainly not unreasonable for the . . . [employer] to determine that it was appropriate to consider . . . [sex] as one factor . . . in making its decision."[130] Further, the plan did not unnecessarily trammel the interests of male employees, or create an "absolute bar" to their advancement. No person is excluded from consideration. Sex may be taken into account, but only as one of a number of factors. Women must compete with all other qualified applicants. Since the plaintiff was only one of seven qualified applicants, any one of whom could have been chosen, he was not absolutely entitled to the promotion, and cannot claim the unsettling of any legitimate expectation.[131] Finally, the plan was a temporary measure designed to achieve a balanced work force, not to maintain a permanent sexual or racial balance.[132]

The *Johnson* case was a high water mark for employment affirmative action. It was the first time that a clear majority of the Supreme Court construed Title VII as a license for *public employers* to use "goals and time-tables" in order to remedy the effects of societal/historical employment discrimination, and without being concerned about the Equal Protection Clause criteria in the Fourteenth Amendment of the Constitution. It represented the triumph of the view originally propounded by Justice Brennan in *Weber*, that Title VII legitimates voluntary resort by employers to numerically based remediation in order to correct statistical imbalances without "unnecessarily" injuring nonminorities. Thus, it should be taken as a legal victory for disparate-impact theory.

The ascendancy of the disparate-impact school of antidiscrimination law in the employment arena was also apparent in the country at large. As noted, in 1979 and 1980, the EEOC had promulgated affirmative action and employee-selection guidelines, which effectively embodied the *Weber* principle.[133] The OFCCP went farther by requiring goals and timetables for federal contractors when they underutilized protected groups. By the late 1980s, affirmative action through employee-selection guidelines had taken root throughout the economy either voluntarily, or by court action, administrative regulation, or legislative dictate. The federal government's procurement policies extended substantial special considerations to minority and female entrepreneurs. Employment affirmative action was institutionalized in corporate America, in the apparatus of the government, including the military, and the educational establishment.[134] Affirmative action had a powerful lobby in Congress. All told, it seemed to be winning the war.

But in fact it had achieved only a temporary truce. In the High Court, after 1987, Justice Brennan was on his way to becoming a spent force. The dominant voices now were becoming Chief Justice Rehnquist and Justice Scalia, both archenemies of affirmative action. In their respective dissents in *Weber*,[135] and *Johnson*,[136] these justices contended that *all* race, ethnic, and sex-conscious employment remediation of the affirmative action variety constituted "discrimination" within the "plain meaning" of Title VII, and that *Weber* and its progeny were perversions of the law. The vehemence of their views virtually ensured that hostilities would resume.[137] And this is indeed what came to pass. As an antecedent to these hostilities, let us consider the Court's affirmative action constitutional law decisions in the 1970s up to *Richmond v. Croson*.

Additional Affirmative Action Constitutional Decisions by the Supreme Court before *Croson* (1989)

1.

Voluntary public affirmative action programs are not unconstitutional per se, but must undergo rigorous judicial review. State universities may consider race as a factor in admissions procedures, provided that no person may be excluded from consideration solely on grounds of racial or ethnic status.

Regents v. Bakke (1978)[138] was the Supreme Court's first attempt to define the standard of Equal Protection Clause judicial review in voluntary public affirmative action. This case arose from a decision by a state university's medical school faculty to reserve sixteen of the one hundred entering class seats for qualified African, Hispanic, Asian, and Native American applicants. Several black admittees scored lower on the standard Medical College Admission Test than some rejected whites, including Bakke, the plaintiff. Bakke claimed a violation of the Equal Protection Clause and Title VI of the 1964 Civil Rights Act,[139] contending that he would have been admitted if not for the set-aside. This is the classic "reverse-discrimination" claim: illegal and unfair race-based exclusion of a qualified, innocent third party from an important benefit in favor of a less-qualified minority. The university contended that its admission policy was justified as a remedy for past "societal discrimination," and an attempt to obtain the educational benefits that flow from an ethnically diverse student body.[140]

By different 5-4 majorities, in each of which Justice Powell cast the controlling vote, the High Court affirmed the lower court's order directing that Bakke be admitted and invalidating the university's admission policy, but reversed its order enjoining the university from considering race as a factor in future admissions decisions.[141]

Four members (Stevens, joined by Burger, Stewart, and Rehnquist) held whether race can ever be used as a factor in an admission decision, was not before the Court;[142] Bakke's rejection on account of his race violated the "plain language" of the 1964 CRA's Title VI;[143] and the lower court's judgment should be affirmed to the extent that it orders Bakke's admission.[144] In relevant part, Title VI of the 1964 Civil Rights Act provided: "No person . . . shall, on the ground of race . . . be excluded from participation in . . . any program . . . receiving Federal financial assistance."[145]

Four other Justices (Brennan, Marshall, White, and Blackmun) held that the set-aside was constitutional, and therefore the lower court' s judgment should be reversed in all respects:[146] Subject to the Equal Protection Clause of the Fourteenth Amendment, Title VI does not bar preferential treatment of racial minorities as a means of remedying past societal discrimination;[147] racial classifications are not per se invalid under Equal Protection;[148] this case is distinguishable from cases of invidious discrimination which are subject to strict scrutiny, since the set-aside does not stigmatize or disfavor any discrete group, but operates only for the purpose of helping disadvantaged minorities;[149] for such benign remedial racial classifications, the appropriate standard of review is intermediate scrutiny, which inquires whether the state has demonstrated an "important" purpose, and has used means which are "substantially" related to such purpose;[150] and the set-aside satisfied these requirements, since it reasonably addressed the important educational problem of correcting the societally discriminatory underrepresentation of minorities at the medical school.[151] (See 43, 300–301 for a discussion of the different types of judicial scrutiny under the Equal Protection Clause.)

Justice Powell agreed with the Brennan plurality that the Equal Protection Clause controlled and did not bar race-conscious remediation; therefore he voted with them to reverse the injunction of any future consideration of race for admissions.[152] However, he rejected their intermediate scrutiny standard, opting instead for "the most exacting judicial examination" of strict scrutiny. He concluded that the set-aside violated equal protection. Accordingly, he voted with the Stevens plurality to order Bakke admitted.[153]

Bakke decided only that a state university which receives federal funds may consider race as one factor, among others, in its admissions procedure, provided that it does not exclude any applicant from consideration on racial or ethnic grounds. Beyond that the decision sheds little light on the race, ethnic, gender-based preferences in employment, contracting, and voting that have engendered so much polarized controversy. Still, it remains a landmark case. It clearly enunciated the principle that the Constitution sanctions some forms of protected-group preference. And it previewed the main themes of the ensuing affirmative action controversy, in particular, the still-unresolved dispute over the concept of "quota" and its semantic cousin, "preference."[154]

Justice Powell's opinion in *Bakke* is required reading. With no support from any other justice, he took positions on the twin issues of strict scrutiny and nonremedial ethno-racial preferences, which today are the focus of critical legal issues facing protected-group compensatory programs. (See pages 74–75, 104–14, and 307–8.)

Following is a topical summary of the Powell opinion:

Title VI does not require color-blindness, but "proscribes only those racial classifications that would violate the Equal Protection Clause of the Fourteenth Amendment or its counterpart in the Fifth Amendment."[155]

[T]he voluminous legislative history of Title VI reveals a congressional intent to halt federal funding of entities that violate a prohibition of racial discrimination similar to that of the Constitution. Although isolated statements of various legislators, taken out of context, can be marshaled in support of the proposition that Sec. 601(of Title VI) enacted a purely color-blind scheme, without regard to the reach of the Equal Protection Clause, these comments must be read against the background of both the problem that Congress was addressing and the broader view of the statute that emerges from a full examination of the legislative debates.

The problem confronting Congress was discrimination against Negro citizens at the hands of recipients of federal moneys. . . . Over and over again, proponents of the bill detailed the plight of Negroes seeking equal treatment in (federally funded) programs. There simply was no reason for Congress to consider the validity of hypothetical preferences that might be accorded minority citizens; the legislators were dealing with the real and pressing problem of how to guarantee those citizens equal treatment.[156]

All racial or ethnic classifications are not per se invalid under the Fourteenth Amendment.[157] That is, the Constitution does not mandate color-blindness. But it does mandate "the most exacting judicial examination" of such classifications, since they are "inherently suspect."[158] In order to justify the use of a "suspect classification," "a State must show that its purpose or interest is both constitutionally permissible and substantial, and that its use of the classification is 'necessary . . . to the accomplishment' of its purpose or the safeguarding of its interest."[159]

Countering the "effects of societal discrimination," absent "judicial, legislative, or administrative findings of constitutional or statutory violations," does not qualify as a compelling interest. "Title VII principles support the proposition that findings of identified discrimination must precede the fashioning of remedial measures embodying racial classifications."[160]

Attaining a diverse student body is a clearly compelling interest. But ethnic diversity "is only one element in a range of factors a university properly may consider in attaining the goal of a heterogeneous student body," and must be "necessary to promote this goal."[161] The Davis set-aside in issue fails this test because it totally excludes nonminority applicants from a "specific percentage of seats . . . [n]o matter how strong their qualifications, quantitative and extracurricular, including their own potential for contribution to educational diversity." Absent any past discrimination findings, it violates their individual Fourteenth Amendment rights.[162]

In the evaluation of applications by disadvantaged minorities, race may properly be considered a positive factor in an admissions program flexible enough to consider "all pertinent elements" of educational diversity in light of the particular qualifications, and to place them on the same footing for consideration.[163]

2.

The Congress is not constitutionally barred from providing for "set-asides" of federal construction funding for the benefit of minority business enterprises (MBEs), where such measures lie within its constitutional powers and are, in its judgment, reasonably necessary to counteract discriminatory denial of access to contracting opportunities.

In the historic case of *Fullilove v. Klutznick* (1980),[164] the Court, 6-3, held that the Equal Protection Clause component of the Fifth Amendment's Due Process Clause did not invalidate a 1977 federal law which required that at least 10 percent of the federal funds granted for local public works projects be used to procure supplies or services from firms owned by minority group members. This was the first modern federal antidiscrimination statute to contain explicitly race/ethnic-based provisions. The lead opinion for the controlling Burger-White-Powell plurality deferred to Congress' judgment, since the set-asides derived from Congress' spending, commerce, and equal protection powers under the Constitution,[165] and, in Powell's view, were "a reasonably necessary means of furthering the compelling governmental interest in addressing the discrimination that affects minority contractors."[166]

Since 1980, *Fullilove* has fostered the creation of a host of federally funded MBE programs throughout the economy. Given that such programs are preeminent models[167] of race/ethnic-conscious federal affirmative action, it is fair to say that *Fullilove* and its progeny may have been affirmative action's greatest entrepreneurial achievement.

Presently, however, the case seems to be in legal limbo. The Court has so far failed to rule on whether *Fullilove's* outcome would meet the compelling-interest/narrow-tailoring requirement of the strict scrutiny standard which its 1995 *Adarand* decision imposed on federal affirmative action for the first time. (See 60–73.) In *Adarand*, the majority cast doubt on *Fullilove*, but said it was not necessary *today* to determine whether it would survive strict scrutiny.[168] That day has not arrived. This has left open such momentous questions as the scope of the Court's duty to defer to Congress, and whether the federal government is entitled to greater affirmative action leeway than the states and localities.

It is difficult to understand why the Court allows a cloud to linger over this trailblazing decision. No less an authority than Justice Powell—the "godfather" of affirmative-action strict scrutiny—acknowledged that the lead opinion in *Fullilove* incorporated the substance, if not the formal label, of strict scrutiny, and that the set-asides in issue effectively passed muster under that standard.[169]

3.

The impact of race-conscious affirmative action by public employers on innocent third parties does not violate their equal protection rights if it is necessary to remedy past discrimination and does not unnecessarily trammel their legitimate interests or expectations. Race-conscious, out-of-seniority layoffs of nonminority employees by public employers violate the equal protection clause absent prior discrimination. Court-ordered numerical union promotion goals do not violate the Equal Protection Clause if they are necessary to remedy past discrimination, are flexibly implemented, and do not seek to maintain permanent racial balance in the workforce.

In *Wygant v. Jackson Board of Education* (1986)[170] the Court rejected a disregard of a seniority system on varying constitutional grounds. The case arose from a collective bargaining agreement which allowed out-of-seniority layoffs of public school teachers where necessary to retain current levels of minority employment. Without the benefit of a single majority opinion, the Court held, 5-4, that the layoff provision violated the equal protection rights of senior white teachers who had been laid off in order to retain junior black teachers.[171] A four-member plurality held that the provision failed both prongs of strict scrutiny:

1. The "compelling interest" prong was not satisfied by the asserted goal of remedying "societal discrimination" by providing "role models" for minority school children. There must be "convincing evidence" of prior discrimination by the governmental unit involved.[172]

2. The layoff provision was insufficiently narrowly tailored. Though hiring goals may burden some innocent individuals they simply do not impose the same kind of injury that layoffs impose. Denial of a future employment opportunity is not as intrusive as loss of an existing job. "While hiring goals impose a diffuse burden [within society generally], often foreclosing only one of several opportunities, layoffs impose the entire burden of achieving racial equality on particular individuals, often resulting in serious disruption of their lives. That burden is too intrusive. . . . Other, less intrusive means . . . such as the adoption of hiring goals—are available."

In *United States v. Paradise* (1987),[173] a district court judge had ordered the State of Alabama to promote one black state trooper for every white trooper promoted until 25 percent of promoted troopers were black. For decades the state had engaged in open and pervasive racial discrimination in the hiring and promotion of troopers. The Court upheld the order, 5-4, ruling that the one-for-one requirement did not violate the Fourteenth Amendment's Equal Protection Clause.[174] A four-member plurality, including Justice Brennan, concluded that this arguable quota amply met the strict scrutiny test.[175] Brennan's opinion stated that the Court has not in all situations required remedial plans to be limited to the least restrictive means of implementation. We have recognized that the choice of remedies to redress racial discrimination is a "balancing process left, within appropriate constitutional or statutory limits, to the sound discretion of the trial judge." . . . There is no universal answer to the complex problem of desegregation; there is obviously no one plan that will do the job in every case. . . .

The remedy imposed here is an effective, temporary, and flexible measure. It applies only if qualified blacks are available, only if the [state] . . . has an objective need to make promotions, and only if the [state] . . . fails to implement a promotion procedure that does not have an adverse effect on blacks. The one-for-one requirement is the product of the considered judgment of the District Court, which, with its knowledge of the parties and their resources, properly determined that strong measures were required in light of the [state's] . . . long and shameful record of delay and resistance.[176]

Hostilities Continue

The Turn-Around

In 1989, the fortunes of war turned abruptly against affirmative action. The Supreme Court handed down no fewer than six decisions, which set off all the alarms in the civil rights camp.[177] For our purposes, the two most important were the *Wards Cove* and *Richmond v. Croson* cases.

In *Wards Cove v. Atonio* (1989),[178] a new anti–affirmative action majority on the Court undertook to reconsider the "proper application of Title VII's disparate-impact theory of liability."[179] The decision rattled so many cages that, as will be seen, Congress passed a law to overturn it. While now no longer part of case law, *Wards Cove* was symptomatic of a mindset that undoubtedly has lingered prominently in the Court to this day.

The case involved Title VII claims by nonwhite salmon cannery workers. These plaintiffs held low-paying, unskilled "cannery" jobs, and claimed that they had been excluded for racial reasons from higher-paying, skilled "non-cannery" work assigned to white employees. The basis for the claim was alleged "subjective" bias in the employer's hiring practices, as evidenced "solely . . . [by] statistics showing a high percentage of nonwhite workers in the cannery jobs and a low percentage of such workers in the noncannery positions."[180] The Court, 5-4, reversed judgment for the nonwhite plaintiffs. The majority opinion affirmed that subjective hiring practices may be analyzed under a disparate-impact model,[181] but held that the comparison between the racial composition of the cannery and non-cannery work forces failed to make a *prima facie* case of disparate impact.[182]

The proper basis for the initial inquiry in a disparate-impact case is:

> a comparison . . . between the racial composition of the qualified persons in the labor market and the persons holding at-issue jobs. . . . [W]here such . . . statistics . . . [are] difficult if not impossible to ascertain . . . certain other statistics—such as measures indicating the racial composition of "otherwise qualified applicants" for at-issue jobs . . . are equally probative for [disparate impact purposes].[183]

The main flaw in the comparison at issue is that the cannery work force did not reflect any pool of nonwhite applicants who were qualified for skilled noncannery positions:

> If the absence of minorities holding such skilled positions is due to a dearth of qualified nonwhite applicants (for reasons that are not . . . [the employers'] fault), the . . . [employers'] selection methods or employment practices cannot be said to have had "disparate impact" on nonwhites.[184]

The majority acknowledged that the result would be different if the employers "deterred" nonwhites from applying for noncannery jobs.[185] In any case, the majority's concerns ranged far beyond the outcome of this particular litigation. In their view, to permit disparate-impact suits to go forward solely on the basis of simple statistical disparity:

> at the very least, would mean that any employer who had a segment of his work force that was—for some reason—racially imbalanced could be hauled into court and forced to engage in the expensive and time-consuming task of defending the "business necessity" of the methods used to select the other members of his work force. The only practicable option for many employers would be to adopt racial quotas, insuring that no portion of their work forces deviated in racial composition from the other portions thereof; this is a result that Congress expressly rejected in drafting Title VII.[186]

In order to insulate employers from liability for " 'the myriad of innocent causes that may lead to statistical imbalances in the composition of their work forces,' "[187] the majority restated the legal standards that govern order, burden, and quantum of proof in Title VII disparate-impact litigation: As part of his *prima facie* burden, the plaintiff must show that "the application of a specific or particular employment practice" created the alleged disparate impact.[188] If a *prima facie* case has been made, the employer has the burden of "producing evidence of a business justification" for the challenged employment practice. This evidence must show that the practice significantly serves the employer's "legitimate employment goals," but need not show that it is " 'essential' " or " 'indispensable' " to the employer's business. This is a burden of production only. The burden of persuasion, that is, of proving that discrimination has occurred, is on the plaintiff.[189] If the plaintiff identifies alternate hiring practices that reduce disparate impact, while equally serving the employer's legitimate employment goals, and the employer refuses to adopt them, this would refute any claim that the existing practices are not discriminatory.[190]

It is to be recalled that *Griggs* held that employers could defend themselves against disparate-impact claims by establishing that the employment practice excluding minorities was required by business necessity—that is, related to job performance. Case law subsequent to *Griggs* fashioned the business necessity standard into one that was quite plaintiff-friendly. *Wards Cove* eased the judicial interpretation of what constitutes business necessity. Business necessity need not be something that was "indispensable" or "essential," but only a practice that promoted an employer's legitimate goals. In short, employer capacity to establish the business-necessity defense and defeat disparate-impact suits was much facilitated.[191] The civil rights lobby construed *Wards Cove* and its companion cases as a direct frontal assault on *Griggs*,[192] and, acting under the umbrella of the Leadership Conference on Civil Rights (LCCR), mobilized its supporters in Congress for a counter-attack. In 1990, the LCCR proposed a bill meant to overturn *Wards Cove* group of five, and added compensatory and punitive damages and jury trials to the "make whole" remedies available for intentional violations under the 1964 Civil Rights Act. With the cooperation of the Senate and House labor committee staffs, the LCCR pushed its bill through Congress and produced the Civil Rights Act of 1990. However, President Bush vetoed the law on the ground that the addition of punitive damages to the panoply of Title VII disparate-impact remedies unacceptably increased the risk of coerced quota hiring. The veto stood, and so did *Wards Cove*—until the next session of Congress. In 1991, a softened version of the 1990 act passed in the Congress and was signed by President Bush.[193] The Civil Rights Act of 1991 is now the law of the land.

The 1991 Civil Rights Act

Many disciples of *Griggs* believe that the enactment of this law[194] was a great, perhaps even a conclusive, victory for their cause.[195] Their rejoicing may have been premature. True, the act repudiated *Wards Cove*, and its companion decisions;[196] formally incorporated disparate impact into Title VII [Sections 3(3), 116]; and purported to adopt the principle of *Griggs*, and other pre–*Wards Cove* Supreme Court decisions, with respect to "business necessity" and "job related" burden of proof in disparate-impact cases and affirmative action.[197] But the act does not define key Title VII operative terms such as *discrimination* and *disparate impact*, or provide any fresh clues as to their intended meaning; indeed, it compounds the numerous unsettled questions that already exist on that score. It is a virtual certainty that the legal controversy over affirmative action as an instrument of equal employment opportunity will continue as long as the statute remains on the books in its present form. Unless, that is, disparate impact and affirmative action are declared unconstitutional under strict scrutiny—a prospect that cannot be summarily discounted, but which has not as yet occurred.

The Emergence of Strict Scrutiny: *Croson, Adarand*, and the Constitutionality of Government-Sponsored Affirmative Action

Before 1989, the Supreme Court failed to produce a majority on the question of what kind of judicial review was constitutionally mandated in affirmative action cases. Its first encounter with this all-important issue was the 1978 *Bakke* case, which only five justices saw fit to decide on constitutional grounds, and in which Justice Powell was joined only by Justice White in espousing the strict scrutiny test in Fourteenth Amendment cases. In the 1986 *Wygant* case, Justice Powell garnered only plurality support for his remedial restatement of this test, which required a "strong basis in evidence" of the requisite past or present discrimination by the government as a constitutionally required antecedent for publicly sponsored affirmative action. It was in the 1989 *Richmond v. Croson* case that, for the first time, a clear majority adopted Powell's reading of the Fourteenth Amendment's impact on state-sponsored affirmative action involving racial/ethnic classifications.[198]

The case involved a municipal "set-aside," that is, the earmarking of public funds for the benefit of disadvantaged minority entrepreneurs.[199] The specific question was whether the City of Richmond, Virginia, violated the Fourteenth Amendment's Equal Protection Clause by adopting a plan that required its prime contractors to subcontract at least 30 percent of their contracts to Minority Business Enterprises (MBE's).[200] The stated purpose of the plan was to promote wider MBE participation in public construction.[201] The *Croson* majority of five members found that Richmond failed to survive strict scrutiny because it failed to demonstrate that its "set-aside" served a "compelling government interest," and that it was "narrowly tailored" to meet that purpose.

Notwithstanding *Croson*, the Court initially declined to apply strict scrutiny to an affirmative action program sponsored by the national government. In *Metro Broadcasting Inc. v. FCC* (1990),[202] only a year after *Croson*, a 5-4 majority—on mid-tier scrutiny grounds—upheld Federal Communications Commission policies of awarding "enhancements" for minority ownership and management in radio and television broadcast licensing. The FCC policies were nonremedial attempts to comply with a statutory mandate to promote "diversification" in broadcast programming. The majority held that these policies did not violate the equal protection component of the Fifth Amendment.[203] In his opinion for the majority, Justice Brennan wrote:

> We hold that benign race-conscious measures mandated by Congress—even if those measures are not "remedial" in the sense of being designed to compensate victims of past governmental or societal discrimination—are constitutionally permissible to the extent that they serve important governmental objectives within the powers of Congress [e.g., the commerce, and general welfare powers] and are substantially related to achievement of those objectives. . . . Our decision . . . [in *Croson*] concerning a [municipal] minority set-aside program . . . does not prescribe the level of scrutiny to be applied to a benign racial classification employed by Congress. . . .
> We hold that the FCC minority ownership policies . . . serve the important governmental objective of broadcast diversity . . . [and] that they are substantially related to the achievement of that objective.[204]

After *Metro Broadcasting* the membership of the Court—and its balance of power—changed. In *Adarand Constructors, Inc. v. Peña* (1995),[205] a 5-4 majority of the members (Rehnquist, O'Connor, Scalia, Kennedy, and Thomas) held that all racial classifications—federal, state, or local—are subject to strict judicial scrutiny. The majority rejected the "intermediate scrutiny" which *Metro Broadcasting* had adopted for federal affirmative action, and overruled it on that point.

The *Adarand* case arose from the rejection of a white contractor's low bid for a construction job that was awarded to a minority contractor under a federal set-aside program. The opinion was confined to what should be the standard of constitutional review, necessitating a *Croson* revisit for more particulars as to the elements of that standard. As in *Croson*, Justice O'Connor delivered the majority opinion:

> [It is a] . . . basic principle that the Fifth and Fourteenth Amendments . . . protect *persons*, not *groups*. It follows from that principle that all governmental action based on race—a group classification long recognized as "in most circumstances irrelevant and therefore prohibited"—should be subjected to detailed judicial

inquiry to ensure that the *personal* right to equal protection of the laws has not been infringed. . . . [W]e hold today that all racial classifications, imposed by whatever federal, state, or local governmental actor, must be analyzed by a reviewing court under strict scrutiny. In other words, such classifications are constitutional only if they are narrowly tailored measures that further compelling governmental interests. To the extent that *Metro Broadcasting* is inconsistent with that holding, it is overruled.[206]

In Justice O'Connor's circumspect words, the *Adarand* decision "alter[ed] the playing field in some important respects."[207] Nevertheless, many questions remained unresolved. In the wake of the decision, President Clinton ordered a review of the entire federal affirmative action program. Based on the report of the review team,[208] the president announced on July 19, 1995, that he intended to continue the affirmative action program, modified so as to comply with the requirements of strict scrutiny.[209] Plainly, he was relying on the Justice Department's view that the *Adarand* court had not declared federal affirmative action unconstitutional.[210] While that was true, there was every reason to have believed that, insofar as remedial affirmative action is based on disparate impact, *Adarand* has placed its constitutionality at risk. Granted that, in her opinion, Justice O'Connor wrote:

[W]e wish to dispel the notion that strict scrutiny is "strict in theory, but fatal in fact." The unhappy persistence of both the practice and the lingering effects of racial discrimination against minority groups in this country is an unfortunate reality, and government is not disqualified from acting in response to it. . . . When race-based action is necessary to further a compelling interest, such action is within constitutional constraints if it satisfies the "narrow tailoring" test.[211]

However, this disclaimer should not cloud the fact that it is as plain as plain can be that, like every other member of the *Adarand* majority, Justice O'Connor harbored grave, deep-rooted doubts about the constitutionality of race/ethnic-based remediation for *group* discrimination.[212] As seen above, in the majority opinion, she explicitly derived the need for strict scrutiny from the principle that the Constitution protects *persons*, not *groups*, and that *all* race/ethnic-based government action is a "group classification" which is prohibited "in most circumstances."[213] Further, affirmative action, as we have defined it, and as it is generally understood, is indeed a group remedy. Consequently, it would appear that the function of strict scrutiny under *Adarand* is to determine whether there are any circumstances in which disparate-impact affirmative action is *not* prohibited. In *Adarand's* immediate aftermath, it would have been naive to pretend that the odds on an affirmative answer were overwhelmingly high. In the words of an eminent authority who wrote in the wake of *Adarand*:

> [A] Supreme Court comprised of its current members may set the bar against affirmative action so high that virtually no firm, university, or contract-letting agency can surmount it. After all, many members of the current Court (and, plausibly, new members over the next decade) are characterologically, if not ideologically, conservative. Affirmative action is, in the eyes of almost all who think hard about it, an anomaly, sitting uncomfortably between the 1964 Civil Rights Act, which ostensibly barred its use, and Americans' desire for real, not merely nominal, racial equality. Even proponents agree that it is a stop-gap temporary measure— although essential, in their eyes. It is not difficult to envision a cautious, centrist Court deciding that enough is enough, except in rare circumstances.[214]

The Scope of *Adarand* and *Croson*: The Meaning of Strict Scrutiny

How *Croson* and *Adarand* are interpreted is important; it would be difficult to overstate the stakes. Recall that *Adarand's* strict scrutiny net catches "all racial classifications, imposed by whatever federal, state, or local governmental actor."[215] What amounted to *racial* classifications was not defined by the *Adarand* majority. Clearly, they do not encompass gender discrimination. In *Craig v. Boren* (1976),[216] the high Court settled on a *mid-tier* equal protection test for sex discrimination claims: whether the disputed classification serves "important" government objectives and is substantially related to achieving them. This rule has taken on a broad perspective. In *United States v. Virginia* (1996),[217] the Supreme Court held, 7-1, that Virginia's maintenance of an exclusively male admissions policy at its storied military academy violated the Equal Protection Clause. The Court indicated that, in order to prevail, a mid-tier defendant must demonstrate a justification which is not only *extremely persuasive*, but also *genuine, not hypothesized*, and untainted by sexual stereotypes.[218] One must wonder how the "extremely persuasive" mid-tier rule in gender discrimination law differs from the strict scrutiny rule, which is supposed to govern race, and national origin discrimination cases. (See 178–81.)

While the concept *racial classifications* (to which strict scrutiny was to be applied) was not defined by the majority in *Adarand*, a plurality therein treated racial classifications as government action which imposed a burden on some or treated people unequally because of race. Using this distinction, lower courts have not found the gathering of racial/ethnic statistics a strict scrutiny topic. Nor, generally, have outreach efforts.[219]

But preferential contracting, promotion, hiring, layoffs, quotas, set-asides have been judicially treated under the strict scrutiny lens.[220] The foregoing are by no means the outside limits of possible federal exposure under *Adarand*. The Department of Justice held that strict scrutiny is not applicable to the affirmative action plans that are mandated for federal contractors by the Office of Federal Contract Compliance Programs. This contention is based on the premise that "race-based decision making is not used to achieve" minority hiring goals under such plans, inasmuch as these goals are not quotas, preferences, or set-asides.[221] This must be considered an open question at this time.[222] However, there is a small body of lower court strict scrutiny case law involving comparable "goals" affirmative action programs, and the courts have been split on the applicability of *Adarand*'s requirement of strict scrutiny.[223] If the government's position on Executive Order 11246 is ultimately disapproved, then all of the OFCCP's federal-contracting affirmative action programs involving at least one-third of the national work force[224] will fall under *Adarand*'s sway. Certainly this would be appropriate to those who regard the "goals and timetables" requirements of the OFCCP as forceful inducements for race and ethnic-based preferences.

Adarand threatened to broadly outlaw the public use of antidiscriminatory racial/ethnic preferences. Any public body—be it the U.S. Government or a local library board—that attacks systemic bias through preferences in employment or contracting runs the risk of potentially successful constitutional challenge. However, as President Clinton's constitutional analyst Professor Walter Dellinger correctly argued, *Adarand* was not necessarily "life threatening" because the opinion did not describe what the compelling governmental interest and narrow-tailoring prongs of strict scrutiny entailed.[225] For greater clarification, we must look to the *Croson* majority. With respect to the compelling government interest requirement, Justice O'Connor noted that government must have "a strong basis in the evidence" for its conclusion that remedial action was necessary.[226] An accepted "strong basis in the evidence" factual predicate was the lingering effects of past illegal government discrimination, or its ongoing manifestations.[227] And in this connection, Justice O'Connor notably promoted disparate-impact's theme that substantial statistical disparities between minority participation in a particular field and the applicable pool of minorities "could permit an inference of discrimination that would support the use of racial and ethnic classifications intended to correct those disparities."[228] But the *Croson* Court made it clear that "where particular qualifications are required to fill particular jobs, comparisons to the general population (rather than to the smaller group of individuals who may possess the necessary qualifications) may have little probative value."[229] Further to the Court, generalized assertions of historical/societal ethnoracial discrimination were insufficient to provide a strong evidentiary basis for remedial affirmative action.[230] A *Croson* excerpt follows:

Richmond v. Croson, 488 U.S. 469 (1989)

[498] We think it clear that the factual predicate offered in support of the Richmond Plan [requiring a 30 percent set-aside for minority contractors] suffers from the same two defects identified as fatal in *Wygant.* The District Court found the city council's "findings sufficient to ensure that, in adopting the Plan, it was remedying the present effects of past discrimination in the *construction industry.* . . ." (emphasis added) Like the "role model" theory employed in *Wygant,* a generalized assertion that there has been past discrimination in an entire industry provides no guidance for a legislative body to determine the precise scope of the injury it seeks to remedy. It "has no logical stopping point." "Relief" for such an ill-defined wrong could extend until the percentage of public contracts awarded to MBE's [minority business enterprises] in Richmond mirrored the percentage of minorities in the population as a whole. . . .

[499] While there is no doubt that the sorry history of both private and public discrimination in this country has contributed to a lack of opportunities for black entrepreneurs, this observation, standing alone, cannot justify a rigid racial quota in the awarding of public contracts in Richmond, Virginia. Like the claim that discrimination in primary and secondary schooling justifies a rigid racial preference in medical school admissions, an amorphous claim that there has been past discrimination in a particular industry cannot justify the use of an unyielding racial quota.

It is sheer speculation how many minority firms there would be in Richmond absent past societal discrimination, just as it was sheer speculation how many minority medical students would have been admitted to the medical school at Davis absent past discrimination in educational opportunities. Defining these sorts of injuries as "identified discrimination" would give local governments license to create a patchwork of racial preferences based on statistical generalizations about any particular field of endeavor.

These defects are readily apparent in this case. The 30% quota cannot in any realistic sense be tied to any injury suffered by anyone. The District Court relied upon five predicate "facts" in reaching its conclusion that there was an adequate basis for the 30% quota: (1) the ordinance declares itself to be remedial; (2) several proponents of the measure stated their views that there had been past discrimination in the construction industry; (3) minority businesses received 0.67% of prime contracts from the city while minorities constituted 50% of the city's population; (4) there were very few minority contractors in local and state contractors' associations; and (5) in 1977, Congress made a determination that the effects of past discrimination had stifled minority participation in the construction industry nationally.

[500] None of these "findings," singly or together, provide the city of Richmond with a "strong basis in evidence for its conclusion that remedial action was necessary." *Wygant,* 476 U.S., at 277 (plurality opinion). There is nothing approaching a prima facie case of a constitutional or statutory violation by anyone in the Richmond construction industry. *Id.,* at 274–275.

The District Court accorded great weight to the fact that the city council designated the Plan as "remedial." But the mere recitation of a "benign" or legitimate purpose for a racial classification is entitled to little or no weight. . . . Racial classifications are suspect, and that means that simple legislative assurances of good intention cannot suffice. . . .

A [501] governmental actor cannot render race a legitimate proxy for a particular condition merely by declaring that the condition exists. The history of racial classifications in this country suggests that blind judicial deference to legislative or executive pronouncements of necessity has no place in equal protection analysis.

Reliance on the disparity between the number of prime contracts awarded to minority firms and the minority population of the city of Richmond is similarly misplaced. There is no doubt that "[w]here gross statistical disparities can be shown, they alone in a proper case may constitute prima facie proof of a pattern or practice of discrimination" under Title VII. But it is equally clear that "[w]hen special qualifications are required to fill particular jobs, comparisons to the general population (rather than to the smaller group of individuals who possess the necessary qualifications) may have little probative value." . . .

[502] In this case, the city does not even know how many MBE's in the relevant market are qualified to undertake prime or sub-contracting work in public construction projects. . . . Nor does the city know what percentage of total city construction dollars

minority firms now receive as subcontractors on prime contracts let by the city. . . . Without any information [503] on minority participation in subcontracting, it is quite simply impossible to evaluate overall minority representation in the city's construction expenditures. . . .

[505] In sum, none of the evidence presented by the city points to any identified discrimination in the Richmond construction industry. We, therefore, hold that the city has failed to demonstrate a compelling interest in apportioning public contracting opportunities on the basis of race. . . .

[506]The foregoing analysis applies only to the inclusion of blacks within the Richmond set aside program. There is absolutely no evidence of past discrimination against Spanish-speaking, Oriental, Indian, Eskimo, or Aleut persons in any aspect of the Richmond construction industry. The District Court took judicial notice of the fact that the vast majority of "minority" persons in Richmond were black. It may well be that Richmond has never had an Aleut or Eskimo citizen. The random inclusion of racial groups that, as a practical matter, may never have suffered from discrimination in the construction industry in Richmond suggests that perhaps the city's purpose was not in fact to remedy past discrimination.

If a 30% set aside was "narrowly tailored" to compensate black contractors for past discrimination, one may legitimately ask why they are forced to share this "remedial relief" with an Aleut citizen who moves to Richmond tomorrow? The gross overinclusiveness of Richmond's racial preference strongly impugns the city's claim of remedial motivation. . . .

[507] As noted by the court below, it is almost impossible to assess whether the Richmond Plan is narrowly tailored to remedy prior discrimination since it is not linked to identified discrimination in any way. We limit ourselves to two observations in this regard.

First, there does not appear to have been any consideration of the use of race-neutral means to increase minority business participation in city contracting. . . . Second, the 30% quota cannot be said to be narrowly tailored to any goal, except perhaps outright racial balancing. It rests upon the "completely unrealistic" assumption that minorities will choose a particular trade in lockstep proportion to their representation in the local population. . . .

[508] [Further], . . . [u]nder Richmond's scheme, a successful black, Hispanic, or Oriental entrepreneur from anywhere in the country enjoys an absolute preference over other citizens based solely on their race. We think it obvious that such a program is not narrowly tailored to remedy the effects of prior discrimination. . . .

Strict Scrutiny, Government Contract Procurement, and Minority Enterprises

It was affirmative action in this government procurement realm which spawned both *Adarand* and *Croson*. We have reviewed Executive Order 11246 which requires those seeking federal contractors to engage in good faith efforts to reduce underrepresentation of minorities in performing work for the government. (See 38–39.) And government contract work looms large. Federal procurement outlays annually amount to some $300 billion.[231]

Lower federal court use of strict scrutiny in affirmative action cases concerned with minority business enterprises and government assistance in helping them acquire public contracts has produced a variegated pattern. After *Croson* and *Adarand,* states and localities tried to shore up their procurement assistance to minorities by sponsoring "disparity" studies designed to meet the dictates of strict scrutiny. Some 140 disparity studies (at a cost of $55 million) focused on the underutilization of minorities in public contracts were crafted. State/local assistance to minority firms was initiated, maintained, or expanded as a consequence of these studies. But they held up poorly when subject to strict scrutiny by the courts.[232]

While some nonfederal minority procurement-assistance programs survived, they were increasingly disallowed either because they were seen not to be supported by a compelling government interest, and/or were not narrowly tailored.[233] Judicial review in this connection has been quite demanding, insisting on "rigid statistical proof of disparities regarding the jurisdictions' utilization of minority firms, as compared to majority-owned firms."[234] A particular sticking point has been the alleged weakness of the evidence depicting the availability of qualified minority businesses.[235] Oft-cited, too, was a failure to narrowly tailor, as the preferences involved were not linked to the disparities presented in the studies.[236]

On the other hand, federal efforts to advance minority participation in government procurement through affirmative action benefits have generally passed strict scrutiny. (The courts, nonetheless, have been split on whether state/local efforts when coupled with federal programs have to be independently supported.) Federal efforts were typically upheld by relying on congressional hearings and reports on the disparity in minority utilization. One appellate court, however, appeared to impose a heavier burden on the national government. A mere listing of evidence presented to Congress was not enough. Detailed statistical information about discrimination was required.[237]

The Tenth Circuit deviated from the pattern of exacting judicial treatment of state and local minority enterprise affirmative action. In *Concrete Works of Colorado v. Denver*,[238] the court ruled that Denver did not have to show that the city was directly involved in discrimination for there to be a compelling reason for the city's preferential treatment of minorities in contracting for city needs. Passive acceptance of private discrimination was sufficient. Further, the city did not have to *prove* existence of private or governmental discrimination as required by the district court that heard the case initially; a strong basis in evidence was that empirical/statistical and anecdotal data which approached "a prima facie case of a constitutional or statutory violation; *not* irrefutable or definitive proof of discrimination." To prevail, Concrete Works had to show by a preponderance that Denver's plan did not support an inference of prior discrimination and thus a remedial purpose.[239] The Supreme Court majority refused to review this lenient approach to strict scrutiny. Justice Scalia, joined by Chief Justice Rehnquist, dissented, arguing that the evidence presented by Denver failed to show how many minority contractors were qualified to do the work Denver needed. Consequently, it was impossible to determine how much discrimination existed. To these dissenters, the Tenth Circuit accepted *possible* discrimination as a standard for strict scrutiny, which suggested that *Croson* was overruled. A more detailed presentation of this dissent[240] follows:

> [1027] Coming on the heels of our decision last Term in *Grutter* v. *Bollinger*, 539 U.S. 306, the Court's decision to let this plain disregard of *Croson* stand invites speculation that that case has effectively been overruled. . . .

> [1030] The Tenth Circuit interpreted the "strong basis in evidence" requirement in a miserly manner and ignored *Croson*'s requirement that the government *prove* that it is remedying identified discrimination. The District Court "believed Denver was required to *prove* the existence of discrimination." According to the Tenth Circuit, however, the District Court should only have asked "whether Denver had demonstrated strong evidence from which an inference of past or present discrimination *could* be drawn" (emphasis added). . . .

> The District Court was correct, and the Tenth Circuit mistaken. "While the States and their subdivisions may take remedial action when they possess evidence that their own spending practices are exacerbating a pattern of prior discrimination, *they must identify that discrimination*, public or private, *with some specificity* before they may use race-conscious relief." *Croson*, 488 U.S., at 504, 102 (emphasis added). Quite obviously, "discrimination . . . identif[ied]

with some specificity" is discrimination *that has been shown to have existed.* It is inconsistent with *Croson* to permit racial preferences as a remedy for mere "might-have-been" racial discrimination, established by nothing more than evidence "from which an inference of past or present discrimination *could* be drawn." . . .

[1031] With regard to the burden of proof, then, the Tenth Circuit got it exactly backwards. It is not enough for a discriminating governmental entity to identify statistical disparities, [to] *assume* (because it is a *possible* inference from the evidence) that these disparities were in fact caused by racial discrimination, implement racial preferences in public contracting on the basis of that assumption, and then require an injured contractor to demonstrate that the assumption of discrimination was *in*correct. Rather, when the injured contractor has established the government's use of racial preferences (a point conceded here), these preferences are presumed unconstitutional, and it then becomes the *government's* burden to prove that it is acting on the basis of a compelling interest in remedying racial discrimination. To be crystal clear: Denver *cannot* meet its burden without proving that there was pervasive racial discrimination in the Denver construction industry. . . .

[1034] One of the primary functions of the requirement that governmental entities identify discrimination with specificity before using racial preferences is to implement the demand of the Equal Protection Clause "that the deviation from the norm of equal treatment of all racial and ethnic groups [be] a temporary matter." *Croson*, [488 U.S.] at 510. Governmental use of racial preferences must be "limited in time" because "racial classifications, however compelling their goals, are potentially so dangerous that they may be employed no more broadly than the interest demands." *Grutter*, 539 U.S. at 342. Yet Denver has been using racial preferences in public contracting for a generation, and there is no indication that this will be anything other than business as usual for the foreseeable future.

Perhaps more than for any other reason, denial of certiorari in this case is important because of what it signals about this Court's ongoing commitment to exacting judicial review of race-conscious policies. If the evidence relied upon by governmental units to justify their use of racial classifications can be as inconclusive as Denver's evidence in this case, our former insistence upon a "strong basis in evidence" has been abandoned, to be replaced by what amounts to an "apparent-good-faith" requirement—that is, in the words of the Tenth Circuit, the existence of "evidence from which an inference of past or present discrimination *could* be drawn" (emphasis added). Some language in our recent racial-preferences-in-law-school-admissions case suggests a new willingness to rely upon good faith. See, e.g., *Grutter*, [539 U.S. at 342] "We take the Law School at its word that it would 'like nothing better than to find a race-neutral admissions formula' and will terminate its race-conscious admissions program as soon as practicable." We should grant certiorari to make clear that we stand by *Croson*'s insistence that "[r]acial classifications are suspect," that "simple legislative assurances of good [1035] intention cannot suffice," and that the courts will employ "searching judicial inquiry into the justification for such race-based measures . . . to 'smoke out' illegitimate uses of race." 488 U.S. at 500.

Narrow Tailoring and Government Procurement: The U.S. Civil Rights Commission Critique

A pertinent example of the impact of strict scrutiny under *Adarand* can be found in the September 2005 U.S. Civil Rights Commission's Report entitled *Federal Procurement After Adarand*. The report argues that the narrow-tailoring prong of strict scrutiny has been widely ignored in federal procurement and contracting programs. The commission reviewed the small, disadvantaged-business procurement programs of seven federal agencies (Departments of State, Defense, Transportation, Energy, Education, HUD, and the Small Business Administration) to determine whether they were in compliance with what the commission saw as *Adarand*'s requirement that federal agencies must seriously consider race-neutral alternatives to race-conscious procurement programs. This interpretation of *Adarand* was based on the following: (1) Justice O'Connor's statement in *Adarand* that courts must ask whether agencies have given "any consideration [to] the use of race-neutral means to increase minority participation in government contracting."[241] Relying on Department of Justice guidance, the commission found that this statement meant that *Adarand*'s narrow-tailoring aspect required agencies to explore race-neutral approaches to remedying discrimination and improving contracting opportunities for small and disadvantaged businesses before resorting to race-conscious measures; (2) Justice O'Connor's holding in *Grutter v. Bollinger* [242] that narrow tailoring requires "serious good faith consideration of workable race-neutral alternatives." Given these references, the commission found that *Adarand* requires agencies to consider and employ race-neutral strategies *before* resorting to a race-conscious one.[243] (The dissent to the majority commission report rejected this conclusion arguing that the requirement of serious, good-faith *consideration* is not a mandate to *employ* ethno-racial neutrality.)[244]

The result of the commission's review was a severe indictment of federal practice. Federal agencies disagreed about what factors render a program race-conscious or neutral. No reviewed agency engaged in the basic activities that are the hallmarks of serious consideration in their disadvantaged business programs, such as program evaluation, outcomes, measurement, reliable empirical research and data collection, and periodic review. Despite the Department of Justice's directive to consider race-neutral alternatives to the maximum extent practicable, the agencies failed to examine the viability of a wide range of race-neutral alternatives. Rather, they used only some race-neutral strategies, without measuring their impact, and without rigorously exploring the prospect that existing race-conscious programs could be replaced with an expanded array of race-neutral initiatives. Agencies did not communicate with one another about efforts to strengthen procurement practices, or engage in consistent information sharing or exchange of best race-neutral practices. Perhaps most alarming, the commission found no enforcement system for identifying and eliminating discrimination against minority or nonminority contractors or subcontractors, no comprehensive policies for filing or processing of complaints, and no remedial mechanisms.[245]

Two conclusions suggest themselves. First, the commission, relying on Department of Justice guidance, believes that the purpose of strict scrutiny under *Adarand* is to minimize, and ultimately eliminate, race-conscious affirmative action. "The end goal," the report states, "should be to eliminate reliance on race-conscious programs."[246] So much for Justice O'Connor's denial in *Adarand* that strict scrutiny is "strict in theory, but fatal in fact." (See 62.) Second, there was a wholesale lack of compliance with *Adarand* at the federal level. Due to the Department of Justice's failure to provide specific guidance as to what actions constitute serious consideration, agencies gave little thought to legal obligations, and disagreed both about what was required and about the legal ramifications of actions.[247]

For this lamentable situation, the commission prescribed an elaborate array of remedial recommendations. Congress was requested to enact an express prohibition of discrimination based on race, color, religion, sex, national origin, age, and disability in federal contracting and procurement. (The commission failed to clarify how such a law would comport with the continued testing of race-conscious programs that the commission insists upon in other recommendations.) Agencies were requested to develop and follow guidelines for ensuring serious consideration of race-neutral alternatives, subject to careful explanation by the Department of Justice of the circumstances under which agencies must seriously consider such alternatives in order to comply with *Adarand*. The commission recommended appointment of a White House task force to determine which race-neutral alternatives were effective; the [uncreated] task force was to report to Congress by March 2007. Agencies were requested to regularly review their race-conscious programs, evaluate whether alternatives could reasonably generate comparable outcomes, and implement such alternatives where the answer is yes. Agencies were requested to measure the race-neutral programs' effectiveness independently. Agencies were requested to conduct regular meetings with various interagency councils to share information, coordinate outreach, and discuss race-conscious and race-neutral strategies. Agencies were requested to develop comprehensive, up-to-date outreach programs to circulate information to all businesses about contracting opportunities; and to engage in other race-neutral programs which would provide educational and technical assistance; grant financial aid; expand contract opportunities; and enforce antidiscrimination.[248]

Given the vastness of federal procurement, it is obvious that the questions raised in the report bear directly on the future of affirmative action. It remains to be seen whether the commission's recommendations are carried out. But the general tenor of the report seems clear: *Adarand* is a tool for downgrading and perhaps ultimately abolishing, race-conscious affirmative action. This reading of *Adarand* is evidently predicated on the conviction that race-neutral alternatives are as effective as race-conscious programs in providing equality of opportunity. To advocates of affirmative action this reading is harsh and extreme. But it is not totally implausible. Whether it is the correct view has yet to be determined. But if the Supreme Court should adopt it, affirmative action's days are numbered.

In its quest for narrowly tailoring, the commission called for properly designed "benchmark/diversity" studies.[249] These would estimate the percentage level of minority firm participation in particular industries absent invidious discrimination. This percentage level would represent a "benchmark." The degree to which a federal agency conformed to that benchmark in its contracting would determine whether minority firms received preferential treatment. Thus, if agency minority contracting for a service exceeded the minority benchmark percentage participation in the industry providing that service, minority firms would not be entitled to affirmative action benefits in contracts associated with that industry.[250]

A benchmark scheme was central to the Clinton administration's "mend it, don't end it" reform promised after *Adarand*. The commission rejected this benchmarking mechanism as being based on obsolete and misleading data, noting that its criticism corresponded to that expressed by the National Research Council, which in turn relied on the work of Professor George La Noue.[251] The latter pointed out that Clinton-initiated benchmarking emerged from a 1999 Commerce Department study which was not only based on obsolete data, but which also grossly exaggerated minority capacity (e.g., minority firms constituted one-third of the wholesale trade–durable goods industry), and which erroneously assumed that all Section 8(a) designees (upon which benchmarking focused) were capable of performing and would bid for federal contracts.[252] Given the alleged ills of the 1999 Commerce Department benchmarking study, the commission maintained the "current data do not exist to demonstrate the necessity of race-conscious programs, and if, or why, race-neutral alternatives are insufficient for expanding contracting opportunities to all qualified firms."[253]

Diversity Theory and Its Potential Protection of Employment Affirmative Action

Nonremedial diversity doctrine, if sanctioned for the workplace under the Constitution and Title VII, would reduce strict scrutiny's capacity to undercut affirmative action because the diversity rationale relies on generalized assertions regarding the salutary effect of ideational pluralism, and avoids the need to prove legal wrongs. Strict scrutiny's threat to affirmative action served to cultivate diversity theory as a vehicle for affirmative action's support.[254] The thrust of diversity doctrine asks for no remedy for past racism, sexism, and the like; it focuses on proportional representation (and preferential treatment to achieve such) for groups now under the protective affirmative action umbrella because of the value associated with a better presentation of different viewpoints.[255] To anthropologist Peter Wood, diversity theory offered a "softer," less burdensome road to affirmative action.[256] Drawing from law professor, Eugene Volokh, Wood wrote:

> We can speak of diversity, [Volokh] says, without calling up theories of racial responsibility, group rights, compensation for past wrongs, or agreement about how much people in our society still suffer from discrimination. People *do*, of course, invoke all these grievances, but *diversity* offers a language for promoting racial togetherness that, on its face, is grievance-free. As Professor Volokh puts it, "Diversity is appealing because it's forward looking."[257]

Remedial affirmative action has a theoretical endpoint (when remedies are achieved). Not so for diversity affirmative action, as the value of diversity never ceases. The *Adarand* decision would obviously govern review of *Metro Broadcasting*'s nonremedial "diversity" holdings, but like *Croson*, *Adarand* involved "remedial" affirmative action, and did not explicitly address the issue of "whether and in what settings nonremedial objectives can constitute a compelling interest."[258] In *Grutter v. Bollinger* (2003),[259] which concerned race/ethnic admissions to the University of Michigan Law School, the Court asked, "Whether diversity is a compelling interest that can justify the narrowly tailored use of race in selecting applicants for admission to public universities."[260] The Court endorsed "Justice Powell's view that student body diversity is a compelling state interest that can justify the use of race in university admissions."[261] In so holding, Justice O'Connor, speaking for a five-member majority, accepted the law school's largely generalized assertions that student diversity provided substantial and praiseworthy educational benefits such as more spirited and enlightened discussion.[262] Business success was also enhanced by exposure to different "cultures, ideas, and viewpoints."[263] Diversifying the student body, according to the Court, also facilitated "cross-racial understanding [and] helps break down racial stereotypes."[264]

If applied to the workplace, *Grutter*'s notions as to the benefits of diversity would strongly challenge strict-scrutiny barriers to ethno-racial and gender preferences in that arena. As Justice Scalia aptly noted in his *Grutter* dissent, if the Michigan Law School was justified in using race-conscious techniques to advance socialization and good citizenship through better education, it was appropriate for the civil service and private employers to do the same.[265] Doubtless, champions of affirmative action in employment opportunities would err in not facilitating the migration of diversity doctrine to the workplace.[266]

A majority of the Court in 2007 (Roberts, Kennedy, Scalia, Thomas, Alito), in a case treating K-12 education, noted that the application of diversity theory to that educational level required emphasizing different ideas and cultures, and went beyond merely focusing on race.[267] In this way, diversity theory was restricted to the orthodox Powell position of advancing ideational pluralism. See *Parents Involved v. Seattle*.[268] Thus, diversity affirmative action might be accepted in employment if the diversification plan underscores a broad approach to diversification, and is not restricted to ethno-racial preferences. However, the *Parents Involved* justices were seen as showing their true conservative and civil-rights restraintist colors when they voted in *Ledbetter v. Goodyear* (2007)[269] to restrict the time frame in which plaintiffs may bring charges of disparate treatment (intentional discrimination) under Title VII. Such charges could be made, according to the Court's interpretation of Title VII, no later than 180 days after the alleged intentional mistreatment occurred for allowing suits outside that charging period could frustrate the determination of illegal intent. *Ledbetter* was criticized profusely by congressional Democrats as working to gut civil rights progress. They promised to annul the *Ledbetter* interpretation,[270] and this was accomplished in 2009 through amendments[271] that start the running of the statute of limitations when the plaintiffs are first subject to the alleged previously promulgated intentional employment discrimination, allowing them to attempt to prove that there are present applications of olden discriminatory policies. In 2010, the Supreme Court augmented the congressional disembowelment of *Ledbetter* by ruling that the time-limit restraints of that disparate-treatment case did not apply to Title VII's disparate-impact claims, each one of which was governed by a separate statute of limits, *Lewis v. Chicago,* Slip Opinion 08-974.

The Unresolved Issues of Affirmative Action in Employment

Clarifying the Law

Initially, we must ask whether *Grutter's* diversity theme will be applied to the workplace. If it is, the practice of affirmative action in employment will be much facilitated, leaving strict scrutiny a mere shadow of the potent force suggested by *Adarand.* But there is an avalanche of other questions. How does the reasoning in *Ledbetter* affect disparate-impact remediation? If intentional discrimination claims coming 180 days after they occur are unacceptable because of the difficulty in determining the facts of discrimination, why should adverse effects claims be allowed in disparate-impact cases where the root causes are alleged to have happened in history's mists? Additionally, there is much about civil rights law in employment that needs clarification. Neither Title VII, nor the Civil Rights Act of 1991 define key terms such as *discrimination, preferential treatment,* and *equal employment opportunity.* The question as to why Congress has not seen fit to shed light on these matters invites theorizing about congressional behavior. One view has it that legislators will commit themselves to popular measures while delegating problems to the administrators and the judges who then can be blamed when constituents complain.[272] This mode of legislative behavior opens the question of responsibility in a democratic society. How are the administrators and judges to be held accountable by a public that only dimly understands their activities and which cannot easily remove them?

The Supreme Court has delegated much affirmative action decision making to the subordinate courts, the legislatures, and the executive branches by requiring them to decipher the Court's puzzling affirmative action declarations. Questions abound in connection with strict scrutiny, including: What kind of affirmative action programs are subject to strict scrutiny? Are "goals and timetable" undertakings exempt as the Justice Department has insisted? Are "outreach" efforts to be excluded on the grounds that they, like goals and timetables, do not involve decisions on racial or ethnic grounds?

Law professor Michelle Adams argued that outreach/exhortation is nonpreferential, and as such should not be evaluated under the lens of strict scrutiny. In her view, other affirmative action devices do not involve preferences: the keeping and the analysis of protected-group statistical portraits by employers, school administrators, etc.; and the evaluation of whether affirmative action hiring and admission goals have been achieved.[273] Surely, though, the use of the aforementioned techniques will potentially induce and cultivate considerable preferential treatment. Given the potentiality of preferential treatment, should not strict scrutiny apply? Adams stresses that strict scrutiny might interfere with outreach activities, and this could "uneven the playing field" by denying the transmission of "opportunity" information to disadvantaged minorities.[274] One must inquire whether outreach is restricted to the truly disadvantaged? Should it be?

Aside from what affirmative action strict scrutiny covers, the elements of this form of judicial review are yet to be clarified by the Court. Government's own discrimination and its passive acquiescence in private discrimination have been cited at high federal levels as compelling reasons for affirmative action.[275] How should discrimination and passive acquiescence be defined?

As we have seen at 68–71, *Croson's* strong basis in evidence for a remedial action requirement has been interpreted differently by the lower courts: disparity representations by local governments supportive of preferences for minority businesses have been subject to rigid statistical review and often rejected. The Tenth Circuit, on the other hand, has determined that strong basis in evidence does not require conclusive evidence, but merely that which approaches a *prima facie* case, that is, sufficient evidence to require that those about whom one complains are required to produce evidence that may exonerate.

How should "strong basis in evidence" be defined? On the last day of its 2008–09 term, the Court, in *Ricci v. DeStefano*[276] shed some light on this problem, but it remains shrouded in vagueness. Ricci and other non-black New Haven firefighters sued New Haven, maintaining that the city had discarded exams taken by the plaintiffs for fire department promotion in violation of the ban against ethno-racial disparate treatment in Title VII of the 1964 Civil Rights Act. The city's defense was that the exams were not certified because promotions based on those exam scores would have produced a substantial minority underrepresentation in the promotional ranks, resulting in both a potential violation of Title VII's prohibition of disparate-impact discrimination, and a lawsuit against the city on that ground.

Justice Kennedy, writing for the majority and joined by Justices Scalia, Alito, Thomas, and Roberts, noted that the disparate treatment and impact dimensions of Title VII "point in different directions,"[277] creating dilemmas for employers. Thus, if an employer moved to mitigate the threat of a disparate-impact suit through race-conscious affirmative action, that employer could be charged with a disparate-treatment violation in a reverse discrimination suit as was the situation in *Ricci*. The Court's task was to "provide "guidance" to employers and courts for situations when these two prohibitions could be in conflict absent a rule to reconcile them."[278] There were "few, if any, precedents" available for this task.[279]

The guidance *Ricci* provided was that employers should not engage in disparate-impact remediation without a "strong basis in evidence" to believe that their employment practices would result in disparate-impact liability. Such liability would ensue if employment practices "were not job related and consistent with business necessity, or if there existed an equally valid, less-discriminatory alternative" that served business needs, and it was refused.[280]

There was, in the promotion exam results, a *"prima facie"* case of disparate-impact liability. But *prima facie* "evidence—essentially, a threshold showing of a significant statistical disparity and nothing more—is far from a strong basis in evidence that the City would have been liable under Title VII had it certified the [exam] results."[281] "Good faith" belief that a disparate-impact suit will be forthcoming is insufficient to warrant employer affirmative action avoidance. A good faith rule "would encourage race-based action at the slightest hint of disparate impact . . . even where there is little if any evidence of disparate impact. That would amount to a *de facto* quota system in which a 'focus on statistics . . . could put undue pressure on employers to adopt appropriate prophylactic measures.' "[282] Alternatively, the Court's opinion refused to accept the plaintiffs' position that "avoiding unintentional discrimination cannot justify intentional discrimination."[283] That would violate *Griggs* and the congressional determination (in the 1991 Civil Rights Act) that Title VII recognize and implement disparate-impact liability.

The Court concluded by ruling that New Haven failed to demonstrate that it had a strong basis in evidence that the test certification would produce disparate-impact liability. Consequently, throwing out the exams constituted disparate treatment in violation of Title VII.[284]

Justice Ginsburg's spirited dissent (joined by Justices Souter, Breyer, and Stevens) argued that employers should be exempt from disparate-treatment liability where they have "good cause" or "reasonable" grounds to believe that their affirmative action measures are needed to correct job practices having a disparate impact on protected groups.[285] The city had ample grounds to believe that the tests at issue were not job related in that they appeared to measure the capacity to memorize texts, and not firefighting skill.[286]

The "good cause" test, to Ginsburg, conformed well with the guidelines given to employers by the EEOC, and which had historically been given "respectful consideration" by the Court. These guidelines stated that "Congress did not intend to expose those who comply with the Act [Title VII] to charges that they are violating the very statute they are seeking to implement."[287]

The "strong basis in evidence" test, to the dissent, was "enigmatic,"[288] and contrary to the Court's repeated emphasis that Title VII " 'should not be read to thwart' " efforts at voluntary compliance. Such compliance, we have explained, is 'the preferred means of achieving [Title VII's] objectives.' "[289] If Santa Clara County could, she argued, engage in affirmative action to redress the underrepresentation of females in the public service, why should New Haven be prevented from correcting racial/ethnic imbalances? The Court in *Johnson v. Santa Clara County* (1987), Ginsburg continued, found the preferential treatment practiced by Santa Clara to be " 'fully consistent with Title VII' " since "plans of that order can aid 'in eliminating the vestiges of discrimination in the workplace.' "[290]

What will be the impact of *Ricci*? It may be that *Ricci* will suffer the same fate as *Wards Cove*: civil rights advocates could generate a statutory amendment that will emasculate the strong basis in evidence test as Title VII was amended to stop the *Wards Cove* (1989) potential to interfere with disparate-impact affirmative action. (See 57–60.) Employer perplexity over *Ricci*'s strong basis in evidence would be very understandable. The standard is indeed "enigmatic." How is business necessity to be defined? What are the equally valid alternatives that have less of a discriminatory impact? What is a *prima facie* case of statistical underrepresentation of protected groups? Rather than litigate these difficult questions (probably for long periods of time and at great expense), employers may opt to continue or adopt affirmative action measures and use pretextual explanations to ward off disparate-treatment claims. Surely, there will be strong pressure from civil rights groups to maintain affirmative action measures. On the other hand, *Ricci*'s perplexities may encourage employers not to undertake affirmative action until matters are clarified. One *Ricci* certitude is that the Court refused to treat the question of whether disparate-impact affirmative action is permitted by the Equal Protection Clause, a question the Court has "ducked" for close to half a century.

A critical issue in disparate-impact analysis is not the mere *fact* of disparity, but its comparative *extent* or *degree*. It follows that proof of disparate impact is primarily, if not entirely, a process of statistical measurement and inference. This is, in any event, the view of professional statisticians versed in Title VII litigation. Indeed, *Griggs* came to the High Court because black applicants for hire and promotion by the defendant employer were failing its standard IQ tests "at a *substantially* higher rate than white applicants."[291] The Court attributed this disparity to the "inferior education" which African Americans as a class had long received in the State's traditionally segregated public schools. Notwithstanding the absence of any discriminatory intent on the employer's part, the Court concluded that the disparity created by use of the tests was "directly traceable to race," and would therefore violate Title VII's ban on discrimination unless justified by business necessity.[292] Three leading academic statisticians analyze *Griggs* in the following way:

> The present use of statistical evidence in employment discrimination cases stems in large part from *Griggs* . . . where the Supreme Court established "disparate impact" as a basis for challenging employment selection procedures under Title VII. . . . Under *Griggs*, use of a qualifications test for which the pass rate for

black applicants is "substantially" less than that of whites is illegal unless the employer can show that the use of the test is a business necessity. The burden of demonstrating business necessity being onerous . . . and proof of discriminatory intent being unnecessary, the prima facie showing of disparate (or "adverse") impact may often be sufficient for the plaintiff to prevail. *Disparate impact cases are thus uniquely statistical, with much depending on the interpretation given to the word "substantial" and on how large a disparity must be to be judged substantial.*[293]

In this light, it is quite remarkable that the High Court has never defined "substantial," nor has it squarely adopted a statistical formula for quantifying it. In the *Griggs* opinion, the Court characterized, but did not specifically identify, the disparity; nor did it cite any evidence in support of its finding that the black applicants' failure rate was "substantially higher," or the related finding that it was "markedly disproportionate."[294] Moreover, the Court has not attempted to fill this conceptual hole in any subsequent disparate-impact decisions, or, for that matter, in any of its disparate-treatment cases concerned with the intentional discrimination of individuals, where the meaning of "substantial" is no less decisive.

The closest that the Supreme Court has come to statistical precision in this connection was in *Hazelwood School District v. U.S.* (1977)[295]—a case involving the low number of blacks on the appellant's teaching staff. There, the Court said, with reference to the disparity, that "a fluctuation of two or three standard deviations [from random hiring rates] would undercut the hypothesis that decisions were being made randomly with respect to race."[296] While "standard deviation" and "random sampling" are well-established mechanisms of statistical inference, the court did not identify a disparity of "two or three standard deviations" as "substantial." On this crucial point, it said only that "where gross statistical disparities can be shown, they alone may in a proper case constitute prima facie proof of . . . discrimination."[297]

Given the absence of an explicit Supreme Court statistical standard in disparate-impact and treatment theory, "a flood of statistical tests (since *Griggs*) has . . . thundered forth from the lower courts" in Title VII litigation, but members of the statistical fraternity insist that the need for a "*quantitative criterion of substantiality is undiminished.*"[298]

Absent such a criterion, the law of employment discrimination remains a statistical enigma. This fact leaves us on the horns of a dilemma. As seen above, disparate impact is a creature of measurement by numbers. If, as some suggest,[299] we forego inferential statistics altogether, enforcement of the law becomes a game of chance. On the other hand, statistics by themselves are clearly not a panacea. A number of leading statisticians feel that "statistical analysis of employment patterns is highly questionable and of limited utility."[300]

For example, reliance on "random sampling" procedures in hiring discrimination cases may be illusory, because it overlooks the fact that "the employment process is necessarily highly non-random,"[301] and because random sampling procedure is based "on the implicit . . . and highly questionable assumption that, in the absence of discrimination, the percentage of (alleged discriminatees) hired would not differ substantially from the percentage of . . . (such persons) in . . . (the relevant occupational) population."[302] Harvard's constitutional law expert, Professor Lawrence Tribe, has gone farther, insisting that the use of statistical inference hides unstated assumptions and often focuses on those areas of legal controversy that are quantifiable but not necessarily the most important. Indeed, to Tribe, quantification efforts make manifest the vagueness of legal analysis, and thus weaken the edifice of the law by lessening respect for it.[303]

The statistical standard dilemma has been hanging fire since the day that *Griggs* was handed down in 1971. If disparate-impact affirmative action is to have any claim to conceptual specificity, its proponents must, once and for all, demonstrate whether a meaningful quantitative criterion of "disparity" can be worked out;[304] and, if not, whether, like other legal coin of the realm (such as "reasonable"), "substantial" is a term that can never be defined in the abstract, but which is nonetheless indispensable.

The compelling government interest prong (i.e., a strong basis in the evidence of discrimination) of strict scrutiny invites different interpretations. (See 68–74.) What does the narrow tailoring prong of strict scrutiny involve? In this connection, the Clinton administration's associate attorney general instructed the government's top lawyers as follows:

> In determining whether race-based employment action is narrowly tailored to serve a compelling interest, the courts have usually considered the following factors: 1) whether the government considered race-neutral alternatives before using the racial or ethnic criteria, 2) the manner in which race or ethnicity is used in making decisions—*e.g.*, is it one of many factors to be considered, or is it the sole or dominant factor, 3) the comparison of any numerical target to the number of qualified minorities in the labor pool, 4) the scope of the program, 5) the duration of the program, and 6) the impact of the program on nonminorities.[305]

This instruction raises numerous questions: What neutral methods can adequately replace race and ethnic consciousness? Is socioeconomic disadvantage an appropriate substitute? To the Department of Justice, race and ethnicity, where employed as criteria, should be but one of many factors to be considered. But how is one to determine whether multidimensionalism guided decision making? Also, the Justice Department noted that narrow tailoring prohibits burdens on nonminority employees which are too "oner-ous,"[306] leaving the problem of how to define onerousness.

To dissenting Justice Rehnquist in *Grutter v. Bollinger* (2003) [See 131–63 and 104–14 for further commentary on this case], previous cases had established that where public institutions use ethno-racial criteria, narrow tailoring required a "fit" between the use of race/ethnicity and a compelling state interest that was marked by "greater precision than any alternative means."[307] The University of Michigan Law School claimed that its compel-ling interest in its race/ethnic preferential admissions program was to acquire a "critical mass" of underrepresented students—critical mass defined as that number needed both to prevent minority students from feeling isolated and enabling the furtherance of a diverse exchange of ideas.[308]

To Rehnquist, the critical mass rationale was a "sham."[309] If the law school was true to the critical mass objective, it would have offered admission to about the same number of blacks, Hispanics, and Native Americans—the three groups that were the focus of Michigan's preferential admissions program. Actually, between 1995–2000, black admittees numbered twice the number of Hispanics. American Indians in that period numbered between thirteen and nineteen, about one-sixth the size of the black admission group. How could this number of Native Americans constitute a critical mass?

What then really lurked behind the critical mass posture? To Rehnquist, the Michigan scheme was just an exercise in crude proportional-representation racial balancing, an undertaking that annually selected about the same percent-age of minorities as existed in the entire applicant pool. Thus, for example, in 1995, when 9.7 percent of the applicants were black, 9.4 percent of the admittees were African American.[310] Rehnquist reminded the Court major-ity in *Grutter* that its own opinion in that case made clear that ensuring a particular number of students would be admitted merely because of race would be "patently"[311] unconstitutional. Justice Kennedy was equally blunt in his dissent by referring to the Michigan preferential admissions program as no different than an unconstitutional "quota."[312]

Affirmative Action's Economic Impact and Its Puzzles

During the 1970s and 1980s, race, ethnic, and gender-conscious affirmative action programs became a fixture in public and private employment and contracting. What impact have these federal initiatives had? Surveys indicate that protected-group affirmative action programs were widely adopted by America's large corporations, whose executives cultivated them, numerical goals and all. Of the 128 chief executives in America's largest (by net income) industrial corporations who were interviewed about their affirmative action plans, 95 percent insisted that they would continue using numerical goals and guidelines for the promotion of minority and female occupational prog-ress. Affirmative action became part of big business's organizational culture, nurtured by an entrenched affirmative action bureaucracy.[313] No comparable commitment has been reported for the nation's small businesses.

For all that blacks and Hispanics have begun to climb the job ladder, their economic status is quite mixed. The number of blacks and Hispanics in management, professional, and related jobs are not proportionate to their share in the population.[314] In 1980, the black unemployment rate (in percent) was 14.3; in 2005 it had been reduced to 10. Hispanic unemployment for the same years was 10.1 and 6.0, while that of whites was 6.3 and 4.4.[315] Still, 26 percent of the black population fell beneath the poverty level in 2004, as did 22 percent of Hispanics, and 8.8 percent of whites.[316]

African Americans have experienced recent income gains. Black males earned but 61 percent of white male median income in 1990; in 2004 the percentage was 72 percent. Black females did even better when compared to white female median income—rising from 81 percent (1990) to 98 percent (2004). Again using median income as the standard, Hispanic males went from 63 percent of white males (1990) to 68 percent. Hispanic females (when compared to white female median income) went from 73 percent (1990) to 82 percent (2004).[317]

By many measures, recent U.S. history has witnessed impressive gains by women in education, salaries, and participation in traditionally male occupations such as business, medicine, and law. In 1979, full-time women's earnings were 62 percent of their male counterparts; in 2005, the percentage was 81.[318] In that year, females held in excess of "half of all professional, and related positions."[319] Facilitating the movement of women into higher pay-ing jobs has been their increased college attendance.[320] In 1970, 10 percent of females in the workforce had four years of college, but in 2005, at least one-third had earned baccalaureate degrees.

There has also been an extraordinary growth in female workforce participation. Labor force participation of women sixteen or older was 43 percent in 1970; by 2000, it was 60 percent. Participation by mothers was more dramatic. Presence in the labor force by those females with children under eighteen rose from 47 percent 1975 to 71 percent in 2000.[321] Con-tributing to this phenomenon—and the enhanced status of women in the workplace—were such factors as improved education; birthrate decline; the rise in divorce; the reduction in housework burdens because of modern appli-ances; the reduction in male-dominated heavy industry and manufacturing jobs; and the concomitant rise in "service job" opportunities more accessible by women;[322] changes in public assistance standards requiring mothers on welfare to work,[323] and, of course, second-wave feminism itself was successful in its battle to incorporate females in affirmative action programs providing more work opportunities.[324]

The increased movement of women to the workplace has not been an unmixed blessing. Helping to generate its momentum was the large army of "deadbeat" former husbands who have not met their alimony and child-support responsibilities.[325] Moreover, analysts insist that the nation is suffering from a child care crisis. In 2005, some 74 percent of children between ages one and five were in nonparental childcare,[326] and—allegedly—most nonparental childcare is mediocre or worse. Attendants at child care centers are paid salaries that hover around the minimum wage level; and about one-third leave their jobs annually, creating much instability. Providers who care for children in their own homes earn less than those who are center-based.[327]

Initially, second-wave feminism was a strong proponent of governmental augmentation of group child care facilities. But this advocacy has been muted, as women of higher economic status and power often choose "nannies" to care for their young. Nannies work for little, and have no job security. All of which replicates the oppressive foreign countries they often come from. Arguably, the nanny industry reinforces these long-standing inequalities in order to "liberate" more fortunate women.[328] The solution to the child care "crisis" is, to many, a kind of "reverse feminism": encourage females to stay at home, caring for their young there. Others still insist on urging greater governmental, nonparental child care subsidization and regulation.[329]

Why are female salaries still a substantial distance away from those of men? Why do they seem stuck in middling managerial positions or lower?[330] Why are only 14.7 percent of the Fortune 500 board memberships held by women?[331] By 1987, females constituted 36 percent of the new admittees to state bars. But in 1991, 67 percent of all law firms remained totally male?[332] Why? In 1990, women represented 23 percent of the medical profession, but made only 87 percent of the income earned by their male counterparts.[333]

Critics argue that the feminist objective is to give women a bigger share of jobs held by men—jobs structured in accordance with the male situation. Females are not similarly situated to males in the labor market. Females, by our culture, have been allocated the primary child care and home maintenance functions. These demands, plus the biological restriction of birthing to females, often make women less than ideal workers. They are absent more than men caring for their children; they cannot travel as much as men; they need time off to give birth; and they do not have the leisure and comfort men garner from the care of doting wives. Further, women are impeded by a culture that subordinates them to male domination.[334] Gender equality, to some, requires a substantial reallocation of child care and other household duties to males.[335] Others call for government sponsored child day care programs, on a national basis, which would allow females to fulfill their potential, and which would correct the deficiencies in the current system.[336]

Male-female wage differentials are also likely to reflect invidious discrimination. In 2006, two policy researchers—Harry Holzer and David Neumark—reported on studies that

find that even within narrowly defined occupations within establishments in which workers are likely to be very similar (at least in terms of what matters on the job), there is a sex gap in wages. . . . And limited evidence from audit studies points to hiring discrimination against women. . . . Of course, some of the apparently discriminatory behavior of employers toward women may reflect employer expectations of differences in women's behavior because of future childbearing, although such statistical discrimination is illegal. Differences in managerial pay within occupations also likely reflect a combination of current/past discrimination in promotion opportunities as well as choices of career tracks with the exact mix not well understood.[337]

Despite the variety of clashing claims, some commentators maintain that racial/ethnic/gender disparities have largely been overcome;[338] others insist that, in many important respects, these disparities have not only widened, but are "demonstrably intractable."[339] What is plainly lacking is a standard of judgment that will enable us to evaluate these claims. At present, it is an open question whether equal employment opportunity is at hand.

This brings us up against an overriding question: Assuming that we have made significant progress toward equal employment opportunity, does affirmative action deserve any credit? From the start, our macroeconomic theorists have been embroiled in doctrinal warfare. One school vehemently maintains that enforcement of Title VII impairs efficiency, and negates the market's inherent antidiscrimination mechanisms.[340] But, contrary to this "neo-classical" free market dogma, a different camp insists that Title VII enhances the market's efficiency and its ability to end discrimination.[341] There is no basis for resolving this conflict. Indeed, a comprehensive economic review written by Holzer and Neumark at the start of the new millennium concluded that "the theoretical literature from labor economics generates ambiguous results on whether or not affirmative action programs result in efficiency gains or losses."[342]

Some outstanding scholars insist that affirmative action has been critical to the recent expansion of the black middle class.[343] Indeed, the increase in the percentage of black families earning between $50,000 and $75,000 annually is noteworthy, rising from 11.7 percent in 1975 to 14.4 percent in 1996, and to 17 percent in 2004. During the same time frame, Hispanic families experienced an increase from 11.2 percent to 13 pecent, and to 17.5 percent in 2004.[344] On the other hand, Abigail and Stephan Thernstrom emphasize that middle-class African America was growing rapidly prior to affirmative action's inaugural. It does not follow, then, that affirmative action was the *sine qua non* of black middle class growth.[345] What then was responsible? Those who have performed the most careful of statistical surveys disagree with each other. Thus, James Smith and Finis Welch claim that equal employment opportunity law produced a sharp increase in black male income starting in 1967. But subsequent to 1972, this was followed by a downturn to more traditional levels when compared to whites. To them, equal employment opportunity (EEO) laws had little long-term effect;[346] the driving force behind the rapid economic advance experienced by blacks between 1940–1970 was improved education.[347] John Donohue and James Heckman, however, suggest that the governmental changes brought by the civil rights movement of the 1960s constituted the major contributor to black progress between 1965–1975.[348] But even they feel that EEO laws have not had a detectable impact since 1975.[349]

Another straddle is plainly visible even in the Holzer-Neumark essay published in the September 2000 issue of the *Journal of Economic Literature.* The piece is an exhaustive technical survey of the economic literature, focused primarily, though not exclusively, on whether race/ethnic/gender-based affirmative action "improves or impedes efficiency or performance." Its arcane methodology may be largely unintelligible to noneconomists. But that said, the following "empirical" "inferences"[350] are instructive: (1) "significant" labor market discrimination and "societal disadvantage" persist;[351] (2) to an extent that "may not be large," affirmative action "redistributes" jobs and government business from white males to minorities and women, thereby definitely increasing employment and contracting opportunity;[352] (3) "redistribution" has resulted in a reduction of about 10–15 percent in white male employment in "affirmative action establishments,"[353] and may have achieved "near proportional representation" for minority-owned businesses in public procurement and contracting awards;[354] (4) wages for minorities and women are about 10 percent higher in affirmative action establishments;[355] (5) affirmative action does not materially impair efficiency or performance.[356] But these are *inferences.* The authors stress that "it is impossible to assess the overall efficiency or welfare effects of affirmative action from [available] evidence."[357] Moreover, "it seems very unlikely" that such evidence will ever be unearthed![358]

The estimate of white replacement as a consequence of affirmative action was raised to 15–20 percent in a 2006 update by Holzer and Neumark of their year 2000 article just reviewed.[359] To them, in 2006—continuing a theme of the year 2000 article—affirmative action's costs to employers "in the form of lower productivity also appear quite limited."[360] The last inference is muted when the authors note that "the existing research finds clear evidence of weaker credentials, but more limited evidence of weaker labor market performance among the beneficiaries of affirmative action."[361]

Conclusion: Equal Employment Opportunity and Affirmative Action

In the 1960s, we set out on the road to mandated equality of employment opportunity. Clearly, we are not at journey's end. Discrimination is still among us, and we cannot agree on how far we have come. We believe that many have benefited, but we are not sure of how much, or at what cost to others. We are particularly unclear on whether affirmative action has helped or hurt. When its most ardent advocates equivocate,[362] one must wonder if their cause may have been oversold.

It remains to be seen whether we will ever reach our destination.

Four

Affirmative Action and the Primary and Secondary Schools

Prologue

In this chapter, we deal with affirmative action's troubled role in countering racial discrimination in the nation's elementary and secondary schools. Segregation has afflicted public classrooms throughout the country since long before the Civil War. At the turn of the last century, although grossly unjust, it gained a measure of constitutional respectability under the "separate but equal" umbrella of *Plessy v. Ferguson* (1896).[1] Thereafter, it continued to flourish, *de jure* (by law) in the South; *de facto* in the North and West as a by-product of segregated housing.

Plessy's separate but equal formula was the constitutional linchpin for Jim Crow segregationism in America.[2] The formula was extended to legitimate black/white segregation in public parks, schools, prisons, courtrooms, and swimming areas.[3] Jim Crow was not restricted to the South where its practice was most pervasive. The separate but equal doctrine itself emerged from an 1849 Massachusetts high court opinion (*Roberts v. City of Boston*)[4] which upheld a law requiring school segregation in the City of Boston—the very citadel of abolitionism. In that case, Chief Justice Lemuel Shaw opined that the segregation requirement was aligned with sociological conditions and attitudes; would help maintain peace and calm; and was not violative of equal protection so long as blacks had a right to attend public schools.[5] Blacks in the North and West, moreover, were either excluded from public accommodations (hotels, theaters, and the like), or restricted to particular areas. Some states even barred the immigration of African Americans to their jurisdictions.[6]

Segregation reflected a racist belief in the inferiority of African Americans. They were regarded as a lesser people, incapable of participating in civic affairs as full citizens. In the South, they were disenfranchised, prohibited from jury service, and were the recipients of inferior public services.[7] Sadly, during the late nineteenth and early twentieth centuries, the U.S. Supreme Court

89

was an important bulwark of black "lesser citizenship." *Plessy* is illustrative. Moreover, in the *Civil Rights Cases* (1883),[8] the Court determined that the Fourteenth Amendment only applied to state and not private action, thus frustrating Congress' Reconstruction effort at abolishing segregation in public accommodations. Yet, even at this time the Supreme Court did provide some victories, limited as they were, for black civil rights. Legally imposed racial zoning in housing was nullified.[9] Here the Court determined that property rights were superior to the segregation rights sanctioned by *Plessy*. Further, the Court took some steps to enforce the Fifteenth Amendment by barring both an Oklahoma literacy test for voting (which exempted most whites from testing, but included most blacks),[10] and a Texas ban on black participation in the Democratic primaries.[11] And from the depression years of the 1930s, the Court increased its support for the African American freedoms embedded in Reconstruction's principles.

In the epochal *Brown v. Board* (1954),[12] the Court struck down public school segregation imposed by government. The opinion (excerpted below) was a critical event in the abolition of Jim Crow. Soon after *Brown*, and relying entirely on *Brown* precedents, the Court extensively abolished other state-sponsored segregation.[13] To constitutional scholar Kenneth Karst, *Brown* was both a culmination of an effort to eliminate segregation, and "the catalyst for a political movement that . . . encouraged challenges to other systems of domination and dependency: systems affecting women, aliens, illegitimate children, the handicapped, homosexuals."[14]

For all its merit, *Brown* was evasive. It mandated the remedy of "desegregation," but left unclear the question of whether this meant merely the abolition of racial bars, or required, in addition, active mixing of the races. *Brown*'s implementation was left to unguided case-by-case rulings by the federal district courts. (See *Brown v. Board* [*Brown II*] [1955].)[15] In Title VI of the 1964 Civil Rights Act, Congress banned racial discrimination in federally subsidized education (and other programs), and provided that violators be denied federal funds.[16] But it was not until the late 1960s and early 1970s that the High Court established "integration" as the legal standard of desegregation in constitutional litigation: "dual" systems of governmentally segregated schools were to be totally and rapidly dismantled and permanently replaced by "unitary" systems of racially balanced classrooms, facilities, faculties, curriculums, and support services.[17] The irony of *Brown* is that while it constitutionally barred racial (and later ethnic) segregation in the classroom, big-city schools, prominently in the northeast and midwest where antisegregation themes were enunciated most vociferously, are overwhelmingly African American and Hispanic. Ironically too, many states in the South where the battle for segregation was vehement now harbor more black children going to white majority schools than most states.[18]

Brown has been read by many (but not all) as resting on the theory that segregation psychologically and academically burdened black children by cultivating hobbling inferiority complexes. Social scientists, at the time of *Brown,* were much unified in the belief that only integrated schools could smother that sense of inferiority and improve African American educational attainment.[19] In this chapter, we review more recent considerations regarding the value of school integration—opinions by Justices Marshall, Breyer, Kennedy, and Thomas; and studies by a number of academics identified immediately below. Marshall's dissent in *Board of Education v. Dowell* (1991)[20] reflects the previously mentioned "social scientist" point of view, and argues that the *Brown* opinion was based on it. As will be summarized, a latter-day version of it is presented by Gary Orfield in his *Dismantling Desegregation,* where he argues that the psychic and academic disadvantages of segregated schools are produced by their impoverished student bodies and disillusioned teaching staffs. Justice Thomas's concurrence in *Missouri v. Jenkins* (1995)[21] insists that *Brown's* prohibition of segregation is attributable solely to the dictates of the Equal Protection Clause as properly interpreted, and was not rooted in the psychic damage theory.[22] This view is compatible with the black pride and Afrocentrist viewpoint advocated in tandem with the inferiority complex school of school integration. Briefly, to Thomas, blacks cannot constitutionally be barred from attending "white schools" on the basis of their race, but black schools could be just as educationally sound as those that were integrated. Thomas also insisted that *Brown* barred only state-mandated—*de jure*—segregation (not that which is generated by *de facto* housing patterns); and that *Brown* did not require integration save as a remedy for *de jure* governmental discrimination. These *Missouri v. Jenkins* views are forcefully reiterated in Thomas's forceful concurrence in *Parents Involved v. Seattle* (2007)[23] penned in response to Justice Breyer's equally impassioned dissent presented here. In that case, Breyer conceptualized racial integration in K-12 as a public need compelled by educational, societal, and democratic necessities, and there was no need to find *de jure* segregation. *Parents Involved* is extensively excerpted below as it dramatically illustrates the policy battleground over school segregation/integration—a battleground where diversity theory has come to loom large.

Stephen Halpern's work accepts the Thomas view that minority schools can be the equal of nonminority institutions, but he calls for compensatory funding for minority schools. Some even insist that white majorities at school impede African American intellectual progress, and that blacks would do better in single-race environments inhabited by members of their own race who could help purge feelings of dependency and inadequacy cultivated by past and existing white racism.[24] Ethnocentrism is also on display in the affirmative action battle over bilingualism, another topic covered herein. This chapter additionally analyzes David Armor's *Forced Justice*, a book that challenges the view that integrated schools improve minority academic performance, a view subscribed to by Stephan and Abigail Thernstrom's *No Excuses*, also reviewed herein. The Thernstrom volume argues that non-Asian minority children are woefully behind whites and Asians in basic academic skills, and that racial integration in the classroom does not positively affect the academic skills of African American children. Finally, we present the scholarship of Peter Edelman, Harry Holzer, and Paul Offner who maintain—in *Reconnecting Disadvantaged Young Men* (2006)[25]—that millions of the young in the United States (including an abundance of black and Hispanic males) have not been affected by efforts to integrate education and the economy. These young are conspicuously disconnected from educational and economic pursuits. As we shall see, these authors, like the Thernstroms, do not look to traditional affirmative action preference programs in their prescriptions for solutions.

In fact, if not in name, public school integration conceptually overlapped affirmative action thinking in employment, voting rights, and housing. This thinking applied racial/ethnic consciousness and attempted group remedies for minorities. The objective was to employ proportional representation guideposts to remedy past group discrimination, eradicate its lingering effects, and prevent its recurrence. There has been a technical, legal distinction—though much watered-down in school desegregation cases outside of the South—which has served as a barrier to big city/suburban integration. Traditional constitutional law has it that *Brown's* requirements only apply to *de jure/intentional* segregation perpetrated by government, and not *de facto* segregation caused by such factors as residential patterns. If followed to its logical conclusion, *de jure* theory did not permit the presumption, in law, of discrimination when gross disproportionalities existed, as disparate-impact law has in the areas of employment and political representation. Of course, *de jure* theory was not a barrier to the abolition of segregation in the South where government required racial separation. Further, the *de jure* limit was softened for northern and western schools in *Keyes v. School District # 1, Denver* (1973)[26] where it was ruled that if *de jure* segregation is found in one portion of a school district, the entire district is presumed *de jure* segregated. Many northern and western districts have been subject to comprehensive desegregation through this presumption doctrine.[27] The Supreme Court rejected Denver's argument that the concentration of races in the schools was the function not of racism, but of the district's neighborhood student placement policy. To education specialist Diane Ravitch: "Denver's experience showed . . . [that] sufficient evidence could be assembled to prove that almost any *de facto* segregated school system was actually an unconstitutional *de jure* system. While school officials claimed that racial concentrations reflected residential patterns, over which the schools had no controls, civil rights lawyers contended that school policies and other state actions were responsible for creating and maintaining segregated schools."[28]

Nonetheless, the *de jure/de facto* distinction did have an important impact on the integration of urban and suburban schools. After finding *de jure* segregation in the Detroit public schools, the district court ordered a remedy, which required transport of students from a number of suburban Detroit areas to Detroit proper. In opposition, the Supreme Court ruled in *Milliken v. Bradley* (1974)[29] that school districts could be ordered to participate in curing *de jure* segregation elsewhere only if they helped cause that segregation, or were guilty of segregating their own districts. The expense and time consuming nature of meeting the *Milliken* challenge resulted in attenuating cross-district remedies. The school population patterns evident today are significantly the function of *Milliken*: minority schools are concentrated in the core cities of metropolitan areas surrounded by predominantly white suburban schools.

As of 2007, a five-member majority of the Supreme Court maintained the *de jure/de facto* distinction in *Parents Involved v. Seattle*,[30] but it emerged from that case in an even more weakened state. Four members found the distinction lacking in merit. Justice Kennedy of the majority insisted on maintaining the distinction, but he also concluded that school districts that had not violated antisegregation law could seek integration on diversity grounds by using race as a factor in the student admissions process.[31]

Many school districts have undertaken integration efforts on a voluntary, nonremedial basis, that is, without a determination that intentional governmental segregation has occurred. The need for student diversity has been used to support such voluntarism, but this thesis has met with considerable constitutional difficulty. Key appellate cases concern the Boston Latin School as well as magnet programs in Virginia. The courts in these cases concluded that the involved schools were operating racial-balancing/diversity programs in opposition to the Equal Protection Clause. In the Boston case, it was determined that racial/ethnic balancing was not shown to be "either a legitimate or necessary means of advancing" diversity, even assuming that diversity was a compelling state interest.[32] Virginia's racial balancing was found in violation of the narrow-tailoring prong of strict scrutiny. There, the precedent-setting case was *Tuttle v. Arlington County School Board* (1999),[33] where the court determined that narrow tailoring was frustrated because innocent, third-party children were excessively burdened by the racial-balancing program. The court said: "The innocent third parties in this case are your kindergarten-age children like the applicants who do not meet any of the [racial-balancing] policy diversity criteria. We find it ironic that a Policy that seeks to teach young children to view people as individuals rather than members of certain racial groups classifies these same children as members of certain racial and ethnic groups."[34] The capstone of this rejection of voluntary, diversity affirmative action came in *Parents Involved v. Seattle* (2007).[35]

The school integration movement is now "sputtering" along in "troubled waters." In 1995, the Supreme Court ruled that a primary goal in desegregation cases was restoration of local control, irrespective of whether integration goals have been fulfilled.[36] Several large districts have resegregated, in part, after going to court and winning a declaration that they have achieved "unitary" (i.e., integrated) status, thus freeing them from court-ordered integration plans.[37] Additionally, the advocacy for racial/ethnic balancing in the schools has become much muted (where voiced at all), smothered, in part, by other educational reform crusades such as the charter school and voucher movements. The former are public schools that have been granted a state charter to operate independently of the regular school system. Charter seekers hope to produce an alternate and improved teaching environment, which is supposedly not realized in the existing public school system.[38] Vouchers are cash grants to parents, permitting them to send children to schools of their choice. Both charters and vouchers could be vehicles for integration, but, charters educated only 627,000 of the some 47 million K-12 youngsters in 2004, and only about 150,000 use vouchers.[39] Their growth may be much limited by the public school establishment, which insists that vouchers and charter schools are academically unsound because they drain funds and good students from the regular schools. Moreover, it is charged, voucher undertakings could be found to violate the constitutionally mandated separation between church and state since the private schools involved are often parochial. Vouchers are also challenged on the grounds that state constitutions require that the allocation of public monies be restricted to public schools.

Passionate defenders of public school integration remain, but even to some of these, that objective has become increasingly irrelevant,[40] for it is widely agreed that a major progress toward that goal rests on the doubtful realization of housing integration.

The Epochal Brown Ruling

Affirmative action has not been confined to the workplace. During the same year as *Griggs v. Duke Power* (1971), the Supreme Court—in *Swann v. Charlotte-Mecklenburg*—sanctioned racial-balancing integration as an appropriate remedy for the evils of segregated public education.[41] During the ensuing generation, in tandem with equal employment opportunity, court-ordered classroom integration and busing swept through our society. This process can be seen as a variant of affirmative action, disparate-impact remediation that calls for cures designed to overcome societal discrimination affecting minorities irrespective of whether nefarious intent can be proven. In legal theory, K-12 educational integration is mandated only in intentional (*de jure*) discrimination. This "intent" requirement, however, has been much softened.

As noted above, if a portion of a district was found to have been intentionally segregated, the remainder of the district is *presumed* to have suffered the same fate.[42] Beyond that, the remedial rationale for school desegregation is generically the same as that offered for disparate-impact affirmative action in employment, voting rights, and housing: racial segregation and other abuses have imprinted generations of minority children with deep-rooted feelings of inferiority, apart from robbing them of the intellectual benefits of adequate schooling. Merely to condemn segregation, and order that it cease, as was done in *Brown v. Board of Education* (1954), does not begin to repair the damage. Only if proportionately sized groups of African American and/or Hispanic children are placed in the same classrooms as their white peers, through busing and other devices as necessary, can the scourge of educational inequality be expunged. In short, a theory of compensatory group relief for discrimination imposed on groups.[43]

Let us now turn to the legendary *Brown v. The Board* (1954):

Brown v. Board of Education, 347 U.S. 483 (1954)

Chief Justice Warren delivered the opinion of the Court.

[486] These cases come to us from the States of Kansas, South Carolina, Virginia, and Delaware. . . .

[487] In each of the cases, minors of the Negro race, through their legal representatives, seek the aid of the courts in obtaining admission to the public schools of their community on a nonsegregated basis. In each instance, [488] they had been denied admission to schools attended by white children under laws requiring or permitting segregation according to race. This segregation was alleged to deprive the plaintiffs of the equal protection of the laws under the Fourteenth Amendment. In each of the cases other than the Delaware case, a three-judge federal district court denied relief to the plaintiffs on the so-called "separate but equal" doctrine announced by this Court in *Plessy v. Ferguson*, 163 U.S. 537 [1896]. Under that doctrine, equality of treatment is accorded when the races are provided substantially equal facilities, even though these facilities be separate. In the Delaware case, the Supreme Court of Delaware adhered to that doctrine, but ordered that the plaintiffs be admitted to the white schools because of their superiority to the Negro schools.

The plaintiffs contend that segregated public schools are not "equal" and cannot be made "equal," and that hence they are deprived of the equal protection of the laws. . . .

[490] In the first cases in this Court construing the Fourteenth Amendment, decided shortly after its adoption, the Court interpreted it as proscribing all state-imposed discriminations against the Negro race. The doctrine of [491] "separate but equal" did not make its appearance in this Court until 1896 in the case of *Plessy v. Ferguson*, involving not education but transportation. American courts have since labored with the doctrine for over half a century. In this Court, there have been six cases involving the "separate but equal" doctrine in the field of public education. In *Cumming v. County Board of Education*, 175 U.S. 528 [1899], and *Gong Lum v. Rice*, 275 U.S. 78 [1927] the validity of the doctrine itself was not challenged. In more recent cases, all on the graduate school [492] level, inequality was found in that specific benefits enjoyed by white students were denied to Negro students of the same educational qualifications. *Missouri ex rel. Gaines v. Canada*, 305 U.S. 337 [1938]; *Sipuel v. Oklahoma*, 332 U.S. 631 [1948]; *Sweatt v. Painter*, 339 U.S. 629 [1950]; *McLaurin v. Oklahoma State Regents*, 339 U.S. 637 [1950]. In none of these cases was it necessary to re-examine the doctrine to grant relief to the Negro plaintiff. And in *Sweatt v. Painter*, the Court expressly reserved decision on the question whether *Plessy v. Ferguson* should be held inapplicable to public education.

In the instant cases, that question is directly presented. Here, unlike *Sweatt v. Painter*, there are findings below that the Negro and white schools involved have been equalized, or are being equalized, with respect to buildings, curricula, qualifications and salaries of teachers, and other "tangible" factors. Our decision, therefore, cannot turn on merely a comparison of these tangible factors in the Negro and white schools involved in each of the cases. We must look instead to the effect of segregation itself on public education. . . .

[493] Today, education is perhaps the most important function of state and local governments. Compulsory school attendance laws and the great expenditures for education both demonstrate our recognition of the importance of education to our democratic society. It is required in the performance of our most basic public responsibilities, even service in the armed forces. It is the very foundation of good citizenship. Today it is a principal instrument in awakening the child to cultural values, in preparing him for later professional training, and in helping him to adjust normally to his environment. In these days, it is doubtful that any child

may reasonably be expected to succeed in life if he is denied the opportunity of an education. Such an opportunity, where the state has undertaken to provide it, is a right which must be made available to all on equal terms.

We come then to the question presented: Does segregation of children in public schools solely on the basis of race, even though the physical facilities and other "tangible" factors may be equal, deprive the children of the minority group of equal educational opportunities? We believe that it does.

In *Sweatt v. Painter*, in finding that a segregated law school for Negroes could not provide them equal educational opportunities, this Court relied in large part on "those qualities which are incapable of objective measurement but which make for greatness in a law school." In *McLaurin v. Oklahoma State Regents*, the Court, in requiring that a Negro admitted to a white graduate school be treated like all other students, again resorted to intangible considerations: ". . . his ability to study, to engage in discussions and exchange views with other students, and, in general, to learn his profession." [494] Such considerations apply with added force to children in grade and high schools. To separate them from others of similar age and qualifications solely because of their race generates a feeling of inferiority as to their status in the community that may affect their hearts and minds in a way unlikely ever to be undone. The effect of this separation on their educational opportunities was well stated by a finding in the Kansas case by a court which nevertheless felt compelled to rule against the Negro plaintiffs:

"Segregation of white and colored children in public schools has a detrimental effect upon the colored children. The impact is greater when it has the sanction of the law; for the policy of separating the races is usually interpreted as denoting the inferiority of the [N]egro group. A sense of inferiority affects the motivation of a child to learn. Segregation with the sanction of law, therefore, has a tendency to [retard] the educational and mental development of [Negro] children and to deprive them of some of the benefits they would receive in a racial[ly] integrated school system."

Whatever may have been the extent of psychological knowledge at the time of *Plessy v. Ferguson*, this finding is amply supported by modern authority.[44] Any language [495] in *Plessy v. Ferguson* contrary to this finding is rejected.

We conclude that in the field of public education the doctrine of "separate but equal" has no place. Separate educational facilities are inherently unequal. Therefore, we hold that the plaintiffs and others similarly situated for whom the actions have been brought are, by reason of the segregation complained of, deprived of the equal protection of the laws guaranteed by the Fourteenth Amendment. . . .

The Meaning of *Brown I*

The concept of psychic stigma arising from segregation was a central construct in *Brown I*. Further, social scientists were once nearly unanimous in agreement that single-race schools would continue cultivating inferiority feelings among black youngsters, interfering with their learning capabilities. It followed that racially balanced schools were essential both to the elimination of such stigma, and in the achievement of black intellectual progress.[45] Justice Marshall's 1991 dissent in *Board v. Dowell* fully honors the view that *Brown I* should be interpreted as requiring integration to alleviate the psychic damage of segregation. On the other hand, Justice Thomas's 1995 concurrence in *Missouri v. Jenkins* maintains that *Brown I* only mandated that state *de jure* segregation end. This would permit the extensive continuation of single-race schools. These opinions leave the question of how *Brown I* should be interpreted.

Missouri v. Jenkins, 515 U.S. 70 (1995)

Justice Thomas, concurring.

[114] It never ceases to amaze me that the courts are so willing to assume that anything that is predominantly black must be inferior. Instead of focusing on remedying the harm done to those black schoolchildren injured by segregation, the District Court here sought to convert the Kansas City, Missouri, School District (KCMSD) into a "magnet district" that would reverse the "white flight" caused by *de*segregation. . . .

[T]he [district] court has read our cases to support the theory that black students suffer an unspecified psychological harm from segregation that retards their mental and educational development. This approach not only relies upon questionable social science research rather than constitutional principle, but it also rests on an assumption of black inferiority. . . .

[115] The mere fact that a school is black does not mean that it is the product of a constitutional violation. . . . Instead, in order to find unconstitutional segregation, we require that plaintiffs "prove all of the essential elements of *de jure* segregation—that is, stated simply, a current condition of segregation resulting from *intentional state action directed specifically* to the [segregated] schools." (emphasis added). "The differentiating factor between *de jure* segregation and so-called *de facto* segregation . . . is *purpose or intent to segregate*." (emphasis in original). . . .

[116] It should by now be clear that the existence of one-race schools is not by itself an indication that the State is practicing segregation. The continuing "racial isolation" of schools after *de jure* segregation has ended may well reflect voluntary housing choices or other private decisions. Here, for instance, the demography of the entire KCMSD has changed considerably since 1954. Though blacks accounted for only 18.9% of KCMSD's enrollment in 1954, by 1983–1984 the school district was 67.7% black. That certain schools are overwhelmingly black in a district that is now more than two-thirds black is hardly a sure sign of intentional state action. . . .

Without a basis in any real finding of intentional government action, the District Court's imposition of liability upon the State of Missouri improperly rests upon a theory that racial imbalances are unconstitutional. . . . [119] This position appears to rest upon the idea that any school that is black is inferior, and that blacks cannot succeed without the benefit of the company of whites. . . .

Such assumptions and any social science research upon which they rely [120] certainly cannot form the basis upon which we decide matters of constitutional principle.[46]

It is clear that the District Court misunderstood the meaning of *Brown I*. *Brown I* did not say that "racially isolated" schools were inherently inferior; the harm that it identified was tied purely to *de jure* segregation, not *de facto* segregation. Indeed, *Brown I* itself did not need to rely upon any psychological or social-science research in order to announce the simple, yet fundamental, truth that the government cannot discriminate among its citizens on the basis of race. See McConnell, *Originalism and the Desegregation Decisions*, 81 Va. L. Rev. 947 (1995). As the Court's unanimous opinion indicated: "In the field of public education the doctrine of 'separate but equal' has no place. Separate educational facilities are inherently unequal." At the heart of this interpretation of the Equal Protection Clause lies the principle that the government must treat [121] citizens as individuals, and not as members of racial, ethnic, or religious groups. It is for this reason that we must subject all racial classifications to the strictest of scrutiny, which (aside from two decisions rendered in the midst of wartime, see *Hirabayashi v. United States*, 320 U.S. 81, (1943), *Korematsu v. United States*, 323 U.S. 214 (1944)) has proven automatically fatal.

Segregation was not unconstitutional because it might have caused psychological feelings of inferiority. Public school systems that separated blacks and provided them with superior educational resources—making blacks "feel" superior to whites sent to lesser schools—would violate the Fourteenth Amendment, whether or not the white students felt stigmatized, just as do school systems in which the positions of the races are reversed. Psychological injury or benefit is irrelevant to the question whether state actors have engaged in intentional discrimination—the critical inquiry for ascertaining violations of the Equal Protection Clause. The judiciary is fully competent to make independent determinations concerning the existence of state action without the unnecessary and misleading assistance of the social sciences. . . .

Given that desegregation has not produced the predicted leaps forward in black educational achievement, there is [122] no reason to think that black students cannot learn as well when surrounded by members of their own race as when they are in an integrated environment. Indeed, it may very well be that what has been true for historically black colleges is true for black middle and high schools. Despite their origins in "the shameful history of state-enforced segregation," these institutions can be " 'both a source of pride to blacks who have attended them and a source of hope to black families who want the benefits of . . . learning for their children.' " . . . Because of their "distinctive histories and traditions," . . . black schools can function as the center and symbol of black communities, and provide examples of independent black leadership, success, and achievement.

Board of Education of Oklahoma City v. Dowell, 498 U.S. 237 (1991)

Justice Marshall with whom Justice Blackmun and Justice Stevens join dissenting.

[251] Oklahoma gained statehood in 1907. For the next 65 years, the Oklahoma City School Board (Board) maintained segregated schools—initially relying on laws requiring dual school systems; thereafter, by exploiting residential segregation that had been created by legally enforced restrictive covenants. In 1972—18 years after this Court first found segregated schools unconstitutional—a federal court finally interrupted this cycle, enjoining the Board to implement a specific plan for achieving actual desegregation of its schools.

The practical question now before us is whether, 13 years after that injunction was imposed, the same Board should have been allowed to return many of its elementary schools to their former one-race status. The majority today suggests that 13 years of desegregation was enough. . . .

In my view, the standard for dissolution of a school desegregation decree must reflect the central aim of our school desegregation precedents. In *Brown v. Board of Education*, (1954), a unanimous Court declared that racially "[s]eparate educational facilities are inherently [252] unequal." This holding rested on the Court's recognition that state-sponsored segregation conveys a message of "inferiority as to th[e] status [of Afro-American school children] in the community that may affect their hearts and minds in a way unlikely ever to be undone." Remedying this evil and preventing its recurrence were the motivations animating our requirement that formerly *de jure* segregated school districts take all feasible steps to *eliminate* racially identifiable schools.

I believe a desegregation decree cannot be lifted so long as conditions likely to inflict the stigmatic injury condemned in *Brown I* persist and there remain feasible methods of eliminating such conditions. Because the record here shows, and the Court of Appeals found, that feasible steps could be taken to avoid one-race schools, it is clear that the purposes of the decree have not yet been achieved, and the Court of Appeals' reinstatement of the decree should be affirmed. I therefore dissent. . . .

[257] Our pointed focus in *Brown I* upon the stigmatic injury caused by segregated schools explains our unflagging insistence that formerly *de jure* segregated school districts extinguish all vestiges of school segregation. The concept of stigma also gives us guidance as to what conditions must be eliminated before a decree can be deemed to have served its purpose. . . .

[258] Remedying and avoiding the recurrence of this stigmatizing injury have been the guiding objectives of this Court's desegregation jurisprudence ever since. . . .

Brown's Progeny

The above 1954 opinion—often called *Brown I*—was followed by *Brown v. The Board, II* (1955),[47] where the High Court allocated the initial primary responsibility for fulfilling the requirements of *Brown I* to the federal district courts in order to encourage sensitivity to local conditions. In doing so, the district courts were directed to proceed "with all deliberate speed," and to use their very expansive equity powers to advance justice.[48]

Whether *Brown I* required the states to go beyond the abolition of *de jure* segregation was left unclear by that case. In any event, Southern states (the initial focus of concern) widely resisted integration efforts. The latter were pursued by the Office for Civil Rights (OCR), now in the Department of Education. OCR threatened the cutoff of federal education funds where integration was not actively pursued on the theory that such failure violated *Brown I*, as well as Title VI[49] of the 1964 Civil Rights Act which prohibits racial and national-origin discrimination in educational programs subsidized with federal funds.

Initially, federal education officials allowed jurisdictions with *de jure* segregation histories to use "freedom of choice" plans, enabling parents to choose the schools their children were to attend in a school district. This scheme proved unsatisfactorily slow to federal officials who then sought more rapid integration. This quest gave rise to *Green v. County School Board* (1968)[50] where the Supreme Court decided (fourteen years after *Brown I*!) that school districts that had practiced *de jure* segregation were required by *Brown I* to adopt plans which realistically promised to promptly convert school systems into ones "without a 'white' school and a 'Negro' school but just schools."[51] A year later, the Court reaffirmed its *Green* doctrine as follows:

> The question presented is one of paramount importance, involving as it does the denial of fundamental rights to many thousands of school children, who are presently attending Mississippi schools under segregated conditions contrary to the applicable decisions of this Court. Against this background the Court of Appeals should have denied all motions for additional time because continued operation of segregated schools under a standard of allowing 'all deliberate speed' for desegregation is no longer constitutionally permissible. . . . [T]he obligation of every school district is to terminate dual school systems at once and to operate now and hereafter only unitary schools.[52]

The Court in 1971 continued its *Green* activist stance in *Swann v. Charlotte-Mecklenburg* by recognizing judicial enforcement of "racial balancing" formulas and busing as among the equity powers granted the lower courts in *Brown II* to combat segregation. The *Swann* ruling directed school authorities to "make every effort to achieve actual desegregation."[53] This command was generally interpreted by the lower courts to require racial-balancing/proportional- representation schemes.[54] The impact of this new requirement in the "Old South" was quite dramatic. Although that area had fought bitterly to maintain segregation, federal education officials threatening fund cutoffs under Title VI prompted a considerable degree of race-conscious student assignment. By *Swann*'s date of 1972, most Southern blacks went to school with whites. Still many predominantly or all-black schools remained, but later racial balancing in the South reduced that considerably.[55]

The causes of Northern and Western *de jure* segregation were more subtle and obscure than the open and blatant racism of the South. We have already emphasized that the Supreme Court facilitated the process of finding actionable discrimination in those areas by presuming the existence of *de jure* discrimination in an entire district where it was found to exist in any part of it.[56] Further, artful (but very expensive, and time-consuming) legal maneuvering could produce the needed *de jure* evidence. In the words of Diane Ravitch:

> A permissive transfer policy was one such . . . piece of evidence. School officials claimed that they adopted it to minimize white flight, but civil rights lawyers argued that white students used such policies to escape schools that were growing blacker; conversely, a nonpermissive transfer policy could be characterized as evidence of intent to lock blacks into their neighborhood schools. A school board's decision to build a school in a minority community could be construed as a tacit effort to contain blacks; conversely, refusal to build in a minority community caused black students to attend antiquated and inferior schools.[57]

In the 1974 case of *Milliken v. Bradley*,[58] the Court overruled a district court order requiring numerous Detroit suburbs to engage in cross-district busing to help desegregate Detroit's predominantly minority schools. School districts, the Supreme Court ruled, could be required to participate in remedying another district's segregation only if they helped create it or were guilty of their own *de jure* segregation. *Milliken* dealt a severe blow to metropolitan integration so important to segregation's demise. In the words of desegregation scholar Gary Orfield: "No longer was the most severe segregation found among schools within the same community; the starkest racial separations occurred between urban and suburban school districts within a metropolitan area."[59]

The above-cited cases concern themselves with court-ordered desegregation where *de jure* violations were found to exist. Many communities initiated school integration programs voluntarily, without court orders. The Supreme Court in 2007 evaluated two such voluntary efforts by school districts in the cities of Seattle and Louisville. These districts defended their programs on diversity, nonremedial grounds. Extended excerpts of the majority opinion written by Chief Justice Roberts and joined by Scalia, Alito, Thomas, and Kennedy follow:

Parents Involved v. Seattle School District; *Jefferson County Board of Education,*

127 S. Ct. 2738 (2007)

[2746] The school districts in these cases voluntarily adopted student assignment plans that rely upon race to determine which public schools certain children may attend . . . so that the racial balance at the school falls within a predetermined range based on the racial composition of the school district as a whole. . . .

It is well established that when the government distributes burdens or benefits on the basis of individual racial classifications, that action is reviewed under strict scrutiny. [2752] As the Court recently reaffirmed, " 'racial classifications are simply too pernicious to permit any but the most exact connection between justification and classification.' " In order to satisfy this searching standard of review, the school districts must demonstrate that the use of individual racial classifications in the assignment plans here under review is "narrowly tailored" to achieve a "compelling" government interest.

Without attempting in these cases to set forth all the interests a school district might assert, it suffices to note that our prior cases, in evaluating the use of racial classifications in the school context, have recognized two interests that qualify as compelling. The first is the compelling interest of remedying the effects of past intentional discrimination. Yet the Seattle public schools have not shown that they were ever segregated by law. . . . The Jefferson County public schools were previously segregated by law and were subject to a desegregation decree entered in 1975. In 2000, the District Court that entered that decree dissolved it, finding that Jefferson County had "eliminated the vestiges associated with the former policy of segregation and its pernicious effects," and thus had achieved "unitary" status. Jefferson County accordingly does not rely upon an interest in remedying the effects of past intentional discrimination in defending its present use of race in assigning students.

Nor could it. We have emphasized that the harm being remedied by mandatory desegregation plans is the harm that is traceable to segregation, and that "the Constitution is not violated by racial imbalance in the schools, without more." Once Jefferson County achieved unitary status, it had remedied the constitutional wrong that allowed race-based assignments. Any continued use of race must be justified on some other basis.

[2753] The second government interest we have recognized as compelling for purposes of strict scrutiny is the interest in diversity in higher education upheld in *Grutter*, 539 U.S., at 328. The specific interest found compelling in *Grutter* was student body diversity "in the context of higher education." *Ibid.* The diversity interest was not focused on race alone but encompassed "all factors that may contribute to student body diversity." *Id.*, at 337. We described the various types of diversity that the law school sought:

"The law school's policy makes clear there are many possible bases for diversity admissions, and provides examples of admittees who have lived or traveled widely abroad, are fluent in several languages, have overcome personal adversity and family hardship, have exceptional records of extensive community service, and have had successful careers in other fields." *Id.*, at 338. . . .

The entire gist of the analysis in *Grutter* was that the admissions program at issue there focused on each applicant as an individual, and not simply as a member of a particular racial group. The classification of applicants by race upheld in *Grutter* was only as part of a "highly individualized, holistic review," 539 U.S., at 337. As the Court explained, "[t]he importance of this individualized consideration in the context of a race-conscious admissions program is paramount." *Ibid.* The point of the narrow tailoring analysis in which the *Grutter* Court engaged was to ensure that the use of racial classifications was indeed part of a broader assessment of diversity, and not simply an effort to achieve racial balance, which the Court explained would be "patently unconstitutional." *Id.*, at 330.

In the present cases, by contrast, race is not considered as part of a broader effort to achieve "exposure to widely diverse people, cultures, ideas, and viewpoints," *ibid.*; race, for some students, is determinative standing alone. The districts argue that other factors, such as student preferences, affect assignment decisions under their plans, but under each plan when race comes into play, it is decisive by itself. It is not simply one factor weighed with others in reaching a decision, as in *Grutter*; it is *the* factor. Like the University of Michigan undergraduate plan struck down in *Gratz*, 539 U.S., at 275, the plans here "do not [2754] provide for a meaningful individualized review of applicants" but instead rely on racial classifications in a "nonindividualized, mechanical way." *Id.*, at 276, 280 (O'Connor, J., concurring).

Even when it comes to race, the plans here employ only a limited notion of diversity, viewing race exclusively in white/nonwhite terms in Seattle and black/ "other" terms in Jefferson County. But see *Metro Broadcasting, Inc. v. FCC,* 497 U.S. 547, 610 (1990). ("We are a Nation not of black and white alone, but one teeming with divergent communities knitted together with various traditions and carried forth, above all, by individuals") (O'Connor, J., dissenting). . . .

In upholding the admissions plan in *Grutter,* though, this Court relied upon considerations unique to institutions of higher education, noting that in light of "the expansive freedoms of speech and thought associated with the university environment, universities occupy a special niche in our constitutional tradition." 539 U.S., at 329. . . . The Court in *Grutter* expressly articulated key limitations on its holding—defining a specific type of broad-based diversity and noting the unique context of higher education—but these limitations were largely disregarded by the lower courts in extending *Grutter* to uphold race-based assignments in elementary and secondary schools. The present cases are not governed by *Grutter*. . . .

[2760] The districts have also failed to show that they considered methods other than explicit racial classifications to achieve their stated goals. Narrow tailoring requires "serious, good faith consideration of workable race-neutral alternatives," *Grutter, supra,* at 339, 123, and yet in Seattle several alternative assignment plans—many of which would not have used express racial classifications—were rejected with little or no consideration.

Jefferson County has failed to present any evidence that it considered alternatives, even though the district already claims that its goals are achieved primarily through means other than the racial classifications. . . .

In his *Parents Involved* concurrence, Justice Kennedy asserted the need for avoiding racial isolation by implementing diversity policies. But these should not include racially classifying students (as was done by Seattle and Louisville) unless the demands of strict scrutiny could be met. Kennedy joined the above-cited opinion in its finding that the school districts failed strict-scrutiny surveillance.[60]

To Kennedy, racial classifications were used by the school districts because each student was treated "in a different fashion solely on the basis of race." Racial diversity could be encouraged by means "unlikely to require strict scrutiny."[61] The supposed nonracial classification procedures cited by Kennedy were presented by him as "race conscious," but "facially neutral" mechanisms: "strategic site selection for new schools; drawing attendance zones with general recognition of the demographics of neighborhoods; allocating resources for special programs; recruiting students and faculty in a targeted fashion; and tracking enrollments, performance, and statistics by race." These "facially neutral' means could be supplemented "if necessary, [by] a more nuanced, individual evaluation of school needs and student characteristics that might include race as a component. The latter would be informed by *Grutter,* though of course the criteria relevant to student placement would differ based on the age of the students, the needs of the parents, and the role of the schools."[62]

One must wonder how any of the diversity techniques suggested by Kennedy could avoid the label of racial classification and strict scrutiny? Would not each one of these potentially give rise to the notion that students were being (or could be) treated differently because of race?

Kennedy objected to the following antiracial balancing observations penned by Roberts and joined by Justices Scalia, Thomas, and Alito. These sentiments were, in Kennedy's view, contrary to "history, meaning, and reach of the Equal Protection Clause":[63]

[2755] . . . In design and operation, the [school districts'] plans are directed only to racial balance, pure and simple, an objective this Court has repeatedly condemned as illegitimate. . . . [2757]

Accepting racial balancing as a compelling state interest would justify the imposition of racial proportionality throughout American society, contrary to our repeated recognition that "[a]t the heart of the Constitution's guarantee of equal protection lies the simple command that the Government must treat citizens as individuals, not as simply components of a racial, religious, sexual or national class." *Miller v. Johnson*, 515 U.S. 900, 911 (1995). [2758] Allowing racial balancing as a compelling end in itself would "effectively assur[e] that race will always be relevant in American life, and that the 'ultimate goal' of eliminating entirely from governmental decisionmaking such irrelevant factors as a human being's race' will never be achieved." *Richmond v. Croson*, 488 U.S. 469, 495 (1989). An interest "linked to nothing other than proportional representation of various races . . . would support indefinite use of racial classifications, employed first to obtain the appropriate mixture of racial views and then to ensure that the [program] continues to reflect that mixture." *Metro Broadcasting*, [497 U.S.] 547, at 614, (O'Connor, J., dissenting).

The validity of our concern that racial balancing has "no logical stopping point," *Croson, supra,* at 498, is demonstrated here by the degree to which the districts tie their racial guidelines to their demographics. As the districts' demographics shift, so too will their definition of racial diversity. . . .

[2767] If the need for the racial classifications embraced by the school districts is unclear, even on the districts' own terms, the costs are undeniable. "[D]istinctions between citizens solely because of their ancestry are by their very nature odious to a free people whose institutions are founded upon the doctrine of equality." *Adarand,* 515 U.S., at 214. Government action dividing us by race is inherently suspect because such classifications promote "notions of racial inferiority and lead to a politics of racial hostility," *Croson, supra,* at 493 "reinforce the belief, held by too many for too much of our history, that individuals should be judged by the color of their skin," *Shaw v. Reno,* 509 U.S. 630, 657 (1993), and "endorse race-based reasoning and the conception of a Nation divided into racial blocs, thus contributing to an escalation of racial hostility and conflict." *Metro Broadcasting,* 497 U.S., at 603 (O'Connor, J., dissenting). As the Court explained in *Rice v. Cayetano,* 528 U.S. 495, 517 (2000), "[o]ne of the principal reasons race is treated as a forbidden classification is that it demeans the dignity and worth of a person to be judged by ancestry instead of by his or her own merit and essential qualities."

All this is true enough in the contexts in which these statements were made—government contracting, voting districts, allocation of broadcast licenses, and electing state officers—but when it comes to using race to assign children to schools, history will be heard. . . .

[2768] Before *Brown*, schoolchildren were told where they could and could not go to school based on the color of their skin. The school districts in these cases have not carried the heavy burden of demonstrating that we should allow this once again—even for very different reasons. For schools that never segregated on the basis of race, such as Seattle, or that have removed the vestiges of past segregation, such as Jefferson County, the way "to achieve a system of determining admission to the public schools on a nonracial basis," *Brown II*, 349 U.S., at 300–301, is to stop assigning students on a racial basis. The way to stop discrimination on the basis of race is to stop discriminating on the basis of race. . . .

In dissent, Justice Breyer (joined by Justices Ginsburg, Souter, and Stevens) asked why Seattle and Louisville could not engage in race-conscious efforts to integrate their students when public entities, on a widespread basis, employed race-conscious affirmative action programs to improve racial conditions. "In fact," he wrote, without being exhaustive, I have counted 51 federal statutes that use racial classifications. I have counted well over 1,000 state statutes that similarly employ racial classifications."[64] Breyer continued by arguing that both school district plans passed strict scrutiny:

[2820] The principal interest advanced in these cases to justify the use of race-based criteria goes by various names. Sometimes a court refers to it as an interest in achieving racial "diversity." Other times a court, like the plurality here, refers to it as an interest in racial "balancing." I have used more general terms to signify that interest, describing it, for example, as an interest in promoting or preserving greater racial "integration" of public schools. By this term, I mean the school districts' interest in eliminating school-by-school racial isolation and increasing the degree to which racial mixture characterizes each of the district's schools and each individual student's public school experience.

Regardless of its name, however, the interest at stake possesses three essential elements. First, there is a historical and remedial element: an interest in setting right the consequences of prior conditions of segregation. This refers back to a time when public schools were highly segregated, often as a result of legal or administrative policies that facilitated racial segregation in public schools. It is an interest in continuing to combat the remnants of segregation caused in whole or in part by these school-related policies, which have often affected not only schools, but also housing patterns, employment practices, economic conditions, and social attitudes. It is an interest in maintaining hard-won gains. And it has its roots in preventing what gradually may become the *de facto* resegregation of America's public schools.

Second, there is an educational element: an interest in overcoming the adverse educational effects produced by and associated with highly segregated schools. Studies suggest that children taken from those schools and placed in integrated settings often show positive academic gains. See, *e.g.*, Powell, Living and Learning: Linking Housing and Education, in Pursuit of a Dream Deferred: Linking Housing and Education Policy 15, 35 (J. Powell, G. Kearney, & V. Kay eds.2001) (hereinafter Powell); Hallinan, Diversity Effects on Student Outcomes: Social Science Evidence, 59 Ohio St. L.J. 733, 741-742 (1998) (hereinafter Hallinan).

[2821] Other studies reach different conclusions. See, *e.g.*, D. Armor, Forced Justice (1995). See also *ante*, at 2776–2777 (THOMAS, J., concurring). But the evidence supporting an educational interest in racially integrated schools is well established and strong enough to permit a democratically elected school board reasonably to determine that this interest is a compelling one.

Research suggests, for example, that black children from segregated educational environments significantly increase their achievement levels once they are placed in a more integrated setting. Indeed in Louisville itself the achievement gap between black and white elementary school students grew substantially smaller (by seven percentage points) after the integration plan was implemented in 1975. See Powell 35. Conversely, to take another example, evidence from a district in Norfolk, Virginia, shows that resegregated schools led to a decline in the achievement test scores of children of all races. *Ibid.*

One commentator, reviewing dozens of studies of the educational benefits of desegregated schooling, found that the studies have provided remarkably consistent results, showing that: (1) black students' educational achievement is improved in integrated schools as compared to racially isolated schools, (2) black students' educational achievement is improved in integrated classes, and (3) the earlier that black students are removed from racial isolation, the better their educational outcomes. See Hallinan 741–742. Multiple studies also indicate that black alumni of integrated schools are more likely to move into occupations traditionally closed to African-Americans, and to earn more money in those fields. See, *e.g.,* Schofield, Review of Research on School Desegregation's Impact on Elementary and Secondary School Students, in Handbook of Research on Multicultural Education 597, 606–607 (J. Banks & C. Banks eds.1995). Cf. W. Bowen & D. Bok, The Shape of the River 118 (1998) (hereinafter Bowen & Bok).

Third, there is a democratic element: an interest in producing an educational environment that reflects the pluralistic society in which our children will live. *Swann,* 402 U.S., at 16, 91 S.Ct. 1267. It is an interest in helping our children learn to work and play together with children of different racial backgrounds. It is an interest in teaching children to engage in the kind of cooperation among Americans of all races that is necessary to make a land of three hundred million people one Nation.

Again, data support this insight. See, *e.g.,* Hallinan 745; Quillian & Campbell, Beyond Black and White: The Present and Future of Multiracial Friendship Segregation, 68 Am. Sociological Rev. 540, 541 (2003) (hereinafter Quillian & Campbell); Dawkins & Braddock, The Continuing Significance of Desegregation: School Racial Composition and African American Inclusion in American Society, 63 J. Negro Ed. 394, 401–403 (1994) (hereinafter Dawkins & Braddock); Wells & Crain, Perpetuation Theory and the Long-Term Effects of School Desegregation, 64 Rev. Educational Research 531, 550 (1994) (hereinafter Wells & Crain).

There are again studies that offer contrary conclusions. See, *e.g.,* Schofield, School Desegregation and Intergroup Relations, in 17 Review of Research in Education 356 (G. Grant ed.1991). See also *ante,* at 2780–2781 (THOMAS, J., concurring). Again, however, the evidence supporting a democratic interest in racially integrated schools is firmly established and sufficiently strong to permit a school board to determine, as this Court has itself often found, that this interest is compelling.

[2822] For example, one study documented that "black and white students in desegregated schools are less racially prejudiced than

those in segregated schools," and that "interracial contact in desegregated schools leads to an increase in interracial sociability
and friendship." Hallinan 745. See also Quillian & Campbell
541. Cf. Bowen & Bok 155. Other studies have found that
both black and white students who attend integrated schools are
more likely to work in desegregated companies after graduation
than students who attended racially isolated schools. Dawkins
& Braddock 401–403; Wells & Crain 550. Further research has
shown that the desegregation of schools can help bring adult
communities together by reducing segregated housing. Cities
that have implemented successful school desegregation plans have
witnessed increased interracial contact and neighborhoods that
tend to become less racially segregated. Dawkins & Braddock
403. These effects not only reinforce the prior gains of integrated
primary and secondary education; they also foresee a time when
there is less need to use race-conscious criteria.

Moreover, this Court from *Swann* to *Grutter* has treated these civic
effects as an important virtue of racially diverse education. See,
e.g., Swann, supra, at 16; *Seattle School Dist. No. 1,* 458 U.S., at
472–473. In *Grutter,* in the context of law school admissions, we
found that these types of interests were, constitutionally speaking,
"compelling." See 539 U.S., at 330, 123 S.Ct. 2325 (recognizing
that Michigan Law School's race-conscious admissions policy
"promotes cross-racial understanding, helps to break down racial
stereotypes, and enables [students] to better understand persons
of different races," and pointing out that "the skills needed in
today's increasingly global marketplace can only be developed
through exposure to widely diverse people, cultures, ideas, and
viewpoints." . . .

[2823] The compelling interest at issue here, then, includes an
effort to eradicate the remnants, not of general "societal discrimination," *ante,* at 2758 (plurality opinion), but of primary
and secondary school segregation, see *supra,* at 2803, 2807; it
includes an effort to create school environments that provide better educational opportunities for all children; it includes an effort
to help create citizens better prepared to know, to understand,
and to work with people of all races and backgrounds, thereby
furthering the kind of democratic government our Constitution
foresees. If an educational interest that combines these three
elements is not "compelling," what is? . . .

The plurality tries to draw a distinction by reference to the well-established conceptual difference between *de jure* segregation ("segregation by state action") and *de facto* segregation ("racial imbalance caused by other factors"). *Ante,* at 2815. But that distinction concerns what the Constitution *requires* school boards to do, not what it *permits* them to do. . . .

[2824] I next ask whether the plans before us are "narrowly tailored" to achieve these "compelling" objectives. I shall not accept the school board's assurances on faith, and I shall subject the "tailoring" of their plans to "rigorous judicial review." Several factors, taken together, nonetheless lead me to conclude that the boards' use of race-conscious criteria in these plans passes even the strictest "tailoring" test.

First, the race-conscious criteria at issue only help set the outer bounds of *broad* ranges. They constitute but one part of plans that depend primarily upon other, nonracial elements. To use race in this way is not to set a forbidden "quota." [2825]. . . .

In fact, the defining feature of both plans is greater emphasis upon student choice. In Seattle, for example, in more than 80% of all cases, that choice alone determines which high schools Seattle's ninth graders will attend. After ninth grade, students can decide voluntarily to transfer to a preferred district high school (without any consideration of race-conscious criteria). *Choice,* therefore, is the "predominant factor "in these plans. *Race* is not. . . .

[T]he manner in which the school boards developed these plans itself reflects "narrow tailoring." Each plan was devised to overcome a history of segregated public [2826] schools. Each plan embodies the results of local experience and community consultation. Each plan is the product of a process that has sought to enhance student choice, while diminishing the need for mandatory busing. And each plan's use of race-conscious elements is *diminished* compared to the use of race in preceding integration plans. . . .

[2836] Finally, what of the hope and promise of *Brown?* For much of this Nation's history, the races remained divided. It was not long ago that people of different races drank from separate fountains, rode on separate buses, and studied in separate schools. In this Court's finest hour, *Brown v. Board of Education* challenged this history and helped to change it. For *Brown* held out a promise. It was a promise embodied in three Amendments designed to make citizens of slaves. It was the promise of true racial equality—not as a matter of fine words on paper, but as a matter of everyday life in the Nation's cities and schools. It was about the nature of a democracy that must work for all Americans. It sought one law, one Nation, one people, not simply as a matter of legal principle but in terms of how we actually live.

Not everyone welcomed this Court's decision in *Brown*. Three years after that decision was handed down, the Governor of Arkansas ordered state militia to block the doors of a white schoolhouse so that black children could not enter. The President of the United States dispatched the 101st Airborne Division to Little Rock, Arkansas, and federal troops were needed to enforce a desegregation decree. Today, almost 50 years later, attitudes toward race in this [2837] Nation have changed dramatically. Many parents, white and black alike, want their children to attend schools with children of different races. Indeed, the very school districts that once spurned integration now strive for it. The long history of their efforts reveals the complexities and difficulties they have faced. And in light of those challenges, they have asked us not to take from their hands the instruments they have used to rid their schools of racial segregation, instruments that they believe are needed to overcome the problems of cities divided by race and poverty. The plurality would decline their modest request.

The plurality is wrong to do so. The last half-century has witnessed great strides toward racial equality, but we have not yet realized the promise of *Brown*. To invalidate the plans under review is to threaten the promise of *Brown*. The plurality's position, I fear, would break that promise. This is a decision that the Court and the Nation will come to regret.

I must dissent.

Academic Scholarship on School Integration and Education Deprivation: A Variety of Views

Here we supplement the bibliographical research on minority K-12 education supplied by Justice Breyer in his just presented *Parents Involved* dissent, and that offered by Justice Thomas in his *Missouri* v. *Jenkins* concurrence, at 98–100.[65]

Stephen Halpern's volume, *On the Limits of the Law* argues that racial-ethnic balancing and its associated legalistic efforts to move children from school to school have concentrated civil rights concern on a matter of lesser importance, to the neglect of improving educational opportunities for black children.[66] This improvement requires not the physical shifting of bodies that the "legal rights" strategy of school integration involves (although that strategy may be of some help), but a channeling of educational resources to poor children so that they might be given the same advantages as wealthier students. The enriched backgrounds of the latter enable them to do better in school.[67] Remarkably enough, Halpern paid no attention to government's long-standing inventory of social welfare, compensatory education, and economic improvement programs. Likewise, while warning of the threat that integration poses for our historically black colleges and universities,[68] he passed over the question of whether African Americans might fare as well in an integrated collegiate milieu as on largely black campuses.

The bulk of Halpern's book deals with Title VI of the 1964 Civil Rights Act,[69] which prohibits racial, national origin, and color discrimination in the conduct of any federally subsidized educational program. Administrative enforcement was in large measure the province of the Office for Civil Rights now in the Department of Education. OCR's ultimate statutory sanction is the withholding of funds.

Halpern claims that OCR was originally the vanguard for advancing the educational opportunities of African Americans through Title VI, but it surrendered this role to the courts during the Nixon administration. He claims further that the courts have compromised the mission of aiding African American education by concentrating on physical integration, and not on educational and fiscal resources. Halpern supplements his integration-questioning brief with an unsparing critique of the OCR and the Justice Department. In this Halpern scenario, Nixon decides to emasculate the vigorous enforcement program that began under LBJ. His motives were crassly political: to shore up his Southern support by ensuring that OCR would not withhold funds on a broad scale. To advance this scheme, he transferred the initiative in integration policy from OCR to the courts, where the hapless bureaucrats are overwhelmed by the lawyers of the civil rights lobby. Oddly, the latter are less committed to the substance of civil rights than one might expect; they use the courts as arenas for purely procedural wrangles over time limits and similar lawyers' games. In any case, during the post-Nixon presidency (at least to the end of the first Bush administration), OCR and the Department of Justice had become "paper tigers," habitually declining to commit their substantial resources to advance minority education through Title VI.[70] One advocacy group (Citizens' Commission on Civil Rights) emphasized that the

Clinton OCR has been particularly vigorous, not in the realm of interschool integration, but in the effort to reduce racial and ethnic bias in intraschool student placement and ability grouping.[71] The second Bush Administration can be remembered as one that attempted to change the focus of federal K-12 policy from integration and improved funding to one that sought to ensure improved literacy, math, and science skills by mandating state standards, testing, and responsibility (No Child Left Behind).[72]

There is no passion for racially balanced school integration in Halpern's book; the opposite is the case for the 1996 volume by Gary Orfield et al., *Dismantling Desegregation*.[73] "Research shows," Orfield writes,

> that desegregation opens richer opportunity networks for minority children, but without any loss for whites. Part of the benefit for minority students comes from learning how to function in white middle-class settings, since most of the society's best opportunities are in these settings. . . . [T]he theory is not one of white racial superiority but a theory about the opportunity networks that historic discrimination has attached to white middle-class schools and about the advantages that come from breaking into those mobility networks.[74]

Orfield notes that studies of four school districts undertaken by the Harvard Project on School Desegregation found no evidence that compensatory education efforts (e.g., extra funds) undertaken in segregated settings cured educational deficiencies,[75] and while better-designed compensatory programs may work they cannot replace integration as the means for improving minority education.[76] Moreover, rather than find fault with school integration's complicated legalistic forays as Halpern does, Orfield calls for even more sophisticated lawyering to stem what he saw as a clear trend by the Supreme Court to remove districts found guilty of *de jure* segregation from judicial supervision.[77]

Dismantling Desegregation is a compilation of case studies, framed by a legal and political history of *Brown v. Board*'s "quiet reversal" (to quote from the book's subtitle) in the years since 1954. To Orfield, the reversal is a veritable counterrevolution. Simply put, the Supreme Court, he argues, has gradually, if not formally, disavowed *Brown* and *Charlotte-Mecklenburg*. This sorry process began in *Milliken I* (1974)[78] where the Court forbade interdistrict, urban-suburban integration as a remedy for urban segregation, save for those districts guilty of intentionally fostering segregation. With this decision, as Orfield puts it, "the impetus of *Brown* and the civil rights movement for desegregating American schools hit a stone wall,"[79] since mandatory suburban/inner city integration was much hobbled as a consequence. Seemingly to compensate for the damage done by *Milliken*

I, the High Court in *Milliken II* (1977)[80] permitted lower courts in heavily minority and segregated areas (subject to *Milliken I* restraints) to allow the allocation of disproportionate benefits to schools there as a way of equalizing integrated and nonintegrated education. But even here the Court, in Orfield's view is dismantling desegregation. He points to *Missouri v. Jenkins* (1995),[81] holding that programs for equalizing segregated and integrated education must be limited in time and scope, and that the sponsoring school districts cannot even be required to show that any improvement in the segregated children's educational status has actually been achieved. In Orfield's words, "[The] rapid restoration of local control [had become] the primary [Supreme Court] goal in desegregation cases."[82] And local control, to Orfield, invites resegregation.[83] If this is so, and if the studies assembled by Orfield reflect the national attitude, then integration may be truly doomed, since, as these studies suggest, most of the local communities—all over the country—have never been reconciled to the integration vision of *Brown* found in *Green* and *Swann*. Orfield bitterly lamented this state of affairs, and he urged that *Brown* be revived through (among other ways) the extraordinarily contentious policy of cross-town and metropolitan busing. Orfield argues that GOP Presidents have been primary villains in the gutting of *Brown*, particularly through their choice of conservative judges.[84]

Orfield correctly notes that the greatest advances in school integration have come in the South.[85] What he does not assess are reports that Nixon—after he failed to slow Southern integration in the courts—personally encouraged Southern school officials to integrate their schools, participating in what became the largest school integration experienced in the nation.[86] Orfield also neglects to note the marked decline in the zeal for public school integration in the liberal camp.

David Armor's *Forced Justice,* complements the Halpern and Orfield volumes in that it incisively details what the judiciary came to mean by school desegregation; the techniques used to achieve these judicial standards; and some of the results of these efforts.[87] The author is a seasoned academic, with an impressive command of the specialized school integration literature. He clearly supported the goal of desegregation, but felt that the system now in place was failing to achieve that goal, and ought to be reconsidered. He offered a concrete alternative.

The book contains an exceptionally clear, concise, and comprehensive review of the judicial requirements regarding school integration from *Brown* to the close of the century. This is no mean accomplishment, considering that the Supreme Court never promulgated any uniform standards for implementing its mandates in *Charlotte-Mecklenburg*. For this dicey job, the states and localities were given broad discretion (subject to judicial guidance), with the result that a bewildering variety of proportional representation schemes have sprung up. Commonly, they performed matches, by grade level and with prescribed deviations, between the racial/ethnic composition of a given student body and the corresponding composition of the school district as a whole. For example, Boston allowed a deviation of plus or minus 10 percent; Denver, 15 percent: and even greater deviations have emerged recently as many communities struggled with the problem. Where minority students comprised a large majority of the student population, the courts customarily imposed an absolute numerical standard: for example, in St. Louis and Detroit, where the school populations were 75 percent African American, the desegregation goals called for a 50/50 racial split.[88] Here, Professor Christine H. Rossell's scholarship adds an important point. During the 1970s, judges imposed *mandatory* reassignment plans to achieve racial balancing goals. By 1981, new judicially spawned, racial-balance integration plans focused on *voluntary* student reassignment induced at most by enticing "magnet" schools. We have, in short, returned "full-circle" to "freedom of choice" (a 1965 emphasis)[89] because the courts—faced with "white flight" and other rejections of mandatory mechanisms—have come to view voluntarism as a more effective integration tool.[90]

Armor argues that involuntary desegregation has not brought about significant educational improvement. In his view, the stress on impairment of minority self-esteem, as per *Brown v. Board*, is exaggerated. The socioeconomic condition of the African American family, and federal compensatory undertakings, seem to be considerably more important to African American educational achievement than is desegregation. Armor was also alarmed by the urban population shift which headline writers are wont to call "white flight." He noted that white flight is related to desegregation, but argues that it occurs to a lesser degree in communities that adopt voluntary plans.[91]

As a measure of educational pathology, Armor relied on a so-called index of exposure. This is said to express the degree to which minority students are "exposed" to whites in school settings. By his account, in his base year of 1968, the "typical" African American student attended schools that averaged 43 percent white in the country's large school districts. In 1972, the exposure rose to 54 percent, only to fall by 1989 to 47 percent, a mere 4 percent above the base. For the "average" Hispanic student the index stood at 70 percent in 1968, but fell dramatically to 51 percent in 1989. Armor contends that the decline in these numbers reflects white flight.[92]

What to do? Armor proposed to replace existing policy with a decentralized program of voluntary integration based on magnet schools and a voucher system. This would significantly reduce white flight and ensure freedom of parental choice. Public subsidies were to be provided, as necessary, to give poor parents meaningful options. Armor opined that freedom of choice will bring about a deeper understanding of minority concerns and a greater willingness to strive for educational equality.[93]

Some parts of this disturbing book are open to question. Is the index of exposure conceptually valid? If "exposure" means mere physical proximity, what exactly is the educational significance of Armor's numbers? If it is also supposed to measure intellectual and social interchange, how can such intangibles be quantified? Is Armor's negative appraisal of integration as evenhanded as it might be? Is he too quick to write off the issue of self-esteem? Has he given adequate weight to Orfield's claim[94] that there has been a rise in minority test scores, and a decrease in minority dropout rates in integrated systems? Would his proposed voucher system unjustifiably deprive less favored public schools of active, concerned parents and promising students?

Be all that as it may, there can be no question that Armor has made a powerful case for reexamining affirmative action in the schools, and this reexamination should take into account the strong feelings that quality education can occur in nonintegrated settings.

Stephan and Abigail Thernstrom's volume *No Excuses: Closing the Racial Gap in Learning*[95] maintains that measuring integration by determining the exposure of minorities to whites is shortsighted. To them, the more appropriate measure is racial balance. In their scheme, if each school replicated the racial distribution of the district as a whole, the index would be zero; and where *de jure* segregation prevailed the index would be 100. In the last thirty years, they claim, the index has fallen from 60 to 30 nationwide meaning that schools are approximating the racial distribution in their districts more than ever before.[96]

The Thernstroms argue that increased black-white togetherness in the classroom has not improved black academic achievement. That the impact on African American children of school integration is much disputed has not deterred these authors from insisting that there has been a huge social science research effort in this connection, and that there is not a single example in the published literature of a comprehensive racial plan that has improved black achievement, or that has reduced the black-white achievement gap significantly.[97] And black and Hispanic academic achievement in K-12 has been woeful if one relies on the National Assessment of Educational Progress (NAEP) tests as the Thernstroms do. The NAEP testing mechanism was inaugurated by Congress in 1969, and periodically provides nationally representative samples of fourth, eighth, and twelfth-grade students who are tested in math, reading, civics, U.S. History, science, writing, and geography.[98] Generally, by the twelfth grade, blacks are four years behind whites and Asians, with Hispanics performing somewhat better than blacks. For five of the seven categories tested, the majority of blacks scored below basic,[99] that is, they were unable to display "a partial mastery of the perquisite knowledge and skills that are fundamental for proficient work."[100]

The Thernstroms insist, fairly enough, that there can be no true racial equality until the academic racial gap is erased.[101] They dispute the notion that minority educational deficiencies are the result of underfunding of minority-heavy schools. Public school spending per capita has nearly doubled in the last thirty years, but the educational strengths of America's young have not improved. In truth, urban schools that are overwhelmingly minority receive somewhat less financial assistance, but that small difference cannot explain the large racial/ethnic gap in educational achievement.[102] *No Excuses* also notes that substantial equality in school funding is nothing new. James Coleman in his 1966 iconic and massive *Report* concluded that contrary to his initial assumptions black and white schools were largely equal in school resources, and that student achievement was not dependant on whether students attended schools with good or bad resources.[103]

Black income and educational status do not eliminate the achievement gap. Shaker Heights—the model for the Thernstrom view here—is a wealthy community in Ohio. African Americans are typically well-to-do and educated. The community is committed to racial integration, and the schools reflect the community demography as a whole. School spending is 50 percent above the national average, and school staffs are dedicated to assisting struggling students. Still, the white-black educational achievement gap is dramatic.[104]

The key to black educational problems, the Thernstroms assert, is a cultural deficiency—habits of the mind, and not the capacity of the mind itself. There is insufficient emphasis on those qualities of scholarly effort and concern needed for high educational progress.[105] There needs to be better schools designed to provide a cultural change—schools that reject the inertia of the existing public school bureaucracy and teacher unions. The hope lies in the development of schools untethered to the regular public school machinery, e.g., charter schools funded by public vouchers and dedicated to traditional learning and values.[106]

For all their emphasis on rigorous statistical analysis in their book, the Thernstroms were unable to support their charter school theme with empirical evidence. They explain in a footnote that "[c]harter schools are a relatively new addition to the educational scene, and few have been subjected to careful scholarly evaluation. None, in fact, has been examined with the use of control groups as in the voucher studies."[107] However, the voucher studies they refer to have been subject to withering criticisms because, allegedly, 292 voucher students were not counted. Had they been counted, the critics maintain, it would be made clear that the voucher students (all of whom went to private schools) did not do better than the control group non-voucher students who remained in public schools.[108]

Underscoring the failure of schools while calling for their reform and extensive expansion, the authors of *Reconnecting Disadvantaged Young Men*[109] (Peter Edelman, Harry Holzer, and Paul Offner) present a disturbing portrait of an American malaise involving two to three million sixteen to twenty-four-year-olds who are disconnected from both work and schooling. Aside from frequent criminality, these young experience long periods of unemployment in the legitimate market place. They are lesser educated, holding a high school diploma at most. Young black males (who are often non-custodial fathers) are central to this American tragedy, while African American females have recently experienced marked success in escaping the nether world of "disconnectedness." This male/female differentiation reflects the efficacy of recent welfare reforms designed to encourage single-mother employment—black or otherwise.[110] The authors complain that we heavily subsidize single mothers (e. g., tax credits, child-care assistance), while imposing the equivalent of a heavy tax (i.e., child-support payments) on young non-custodial fathers.[111]

The figures for young noninstitutionalized black males are particularly disturbing as some 17.1 percent have been unemployed for at least a year. The percentages of unemployed for a similar period in other groupings are: white males, 4.2; Hispanic males, 11.9; white females, 7.1; black females 9.9; Hispanic females, 10.4.[112] Very troubling additionally, is that while unemployment for African American young men lagged behind whites and Hispanics by 20 percent at the end of the 1980s, it increased to 30 percent at the conclusion of the 1990s, a decade of dynamic economic surge.[113]

What is wrong? How can the disadvantaged young males, particularly young black males, be "reconnected"? The authors delineate a parade of woes responsible for disconnectedness: schools have failed; there is a spatial mismatch between residence and job opportunity; networking skills of the disconnected are weak; blue-collar job availability has experienced a dramatic decline; criminal activity among young males is high; low minimum wages and high child-support payments operate as disincentives; and the young males at issue have not been adequately supervised by their parents.[114] Amelioration requires higher minimum wages, wage subsidization, and less burdensome child support requirements.[115] Centrally, school reform should incorporate improved education/vocational training[116] supplemented by comprehensive afterschool and/or post-school mentoring and training by which at-risk disadvantaged young persons would be prompted to achieve purposeful, crime-free, self-sufficient lives. One model suggested by the authors is the ASM program (After School Matters) in Chicago—a collaborate undertaking of the city government, the school system, the public library, the park district, and local businesses. The objective is to offer disadvantaged youngsters an integrated program of afterschool recreation, role models, safe areas, and training for marketable skills in technology, the arts, sports, and communications.[117] Another proffered model is the Job Corps created during the Great Society's 1960s War on Poverty. Currently, the Corps services some 72,000 at-risk young by providing educational, occupational training. The goal is to provide the educational/vocational skills required for steady employment, and needed for self-sufficiency.[118]

Ethnocentrism, Affirmative Action, and Bilingual Education

The modern civil rights movement for integration was supplemented in the later 1960s with both the ethnocentric themes of black, brown, and red power, as well as the value of nurturing distinct forms of cultural expression. And so the flames of today's diversity mantra were fed and fanned. One dimension of ethnocentrism was the insistence that the training of "limited English proficient" students (LEPs also referred to as ELLs or English Language Learners) in their native language and culture (so-called bilingual education) was important to their development. Denial of "native" learning was and is pictured as cognitively damaging. This quest to foster ethnicity commitment was an important impetus behind congressional subsidization of bilingual education starting in 1968. Members of Congress and some bilingual advocates, however, viewed bilingualism as a way of facilitating the learning of English. Antagonists are quick to note, though, that many bilingual advocates pursue the objective of preserving the native language and culture of LEP students.[119] Thus, the fear of the "disuniting" of America.

Commonly, advocates of bilingual education support it as a necessary affirmative action measure—as a form of remedial group compensation for the societal discrimination suffered by those with limited English skills. As guardians of Title VI of the 1964 Civil Rights Act, The Department of Education's Office for Civil Rights (OCR) championed this dimension of affirmative action. The criticism of OCR's language training role by those who question the bilingual education format sharply contrasts with Stephen Halpern's critique of that agency's role in school integration. OCR is faulted not for laggardness as it is in Halpern's brief regarding public school racial integration, but for aggressively pursuing the *segregation* of students with limited English skills.[120]

Linda Chavez's indictment of the OCR in this regard is particularly severe. As president of the Center for Equal Opportunity, an organization devoted to the abolition of bilingual education, she wrote in 1998 that:

> OCR has repeatedly made clear its bias in favor of bilingual education in meetings and conversations with numerous school districts. OCR has been staffed with ideologues more interested in the politics of bilingual education than its effectiveness. Using the threat of a cut-off of funding, a dozen states and hundreds of school districts have been blackmailed into instituting bilingual programs. Bilingual education . . . is now harming over a million Hispanic children in American public schools.[121]

Bilingual education, as most widely understood, teaches academic subjects to LEPs in their native tongue. Training in English, so it is maintained, is gradually provided so that students can transfer to mainstream classes where the language of instruction is English.[122] Linda Chavez argued that bilingual education is largely restricted to Hispanics who are segregated from other students, even in their English instruction. In the Chavez scenario, some other language minorities are taken from the regular classes for only part of the day to get special "English as a Second Language" instruction in classrooms that have students from a variety of nationality backgrounds. Still other LEPs with different ancestries are gathered together for all or most of the day in sheltered/structured English "immersion" programs. Consequently, non-Hispanic minorities have a far more integrated educational experience. To Chavez, OCR's promotion of bilingual education was discriminatory and very much prohibited by Title VI of the 1964 Civil Rights Act.[123] She argued further that the bilingual educational mode was nourished by Hispanic organizations to thwart the assimilative process so that their constituencies and power are preserved. Assimilation was frustrated because bilingual training typically lasted five to seven years, was restricted almost entirely to Spanish-language instruction, and often was associated with an Hispanic "cultural maintenance" emphasis.[124]

Nine states mandate bilingual education, and most others have permitted its use. Congress has helped finance its operations.[125] To its backers, bilingualism is the appropriate vehicle in that students—while learning English—are not denied an education in the arts and sciences accessible to them in their native languages. The executive director of the League of Latin American Citizens (LULAC) insisted that bilingualism did not nurture separatism. "Our purpose," he said, "in supporting these [bilingual] programs is precisely that of helping students be better contributors to mainstream American society. Those who insist on relegating minority-language students to an inferior status by placing them in situations where they are doomed to lag behind or fail are those who are actually promoting a continued separation due to lack of achievement."[126]

This was nonsense to former Congressman Robert Livingston, who, in a 1998 congressional hearing, claimed that the United States was the only nation in the world that cultivated the view that a national language is best taught if it is withheld and parceled out in small doses. The less time you spend in teaching English, the longer it takes to learn it. Teachers, he continued, are forced to watch multitudes of Hispanic children denied meaningful English instruction when they could learn English within a year. This must end, he demanded. The denial of English relegates Hispanic children to jobs as busboys when they could be doctors. In 1998, There were 3.2 million LEPs (up from 1.5 million in 1985), and the number is growing. The problem goes beyond economics; there is a threat of national disunity, as the use of English serves to bond us. What is more, the vast majority of valid studies demonstrate that bilingual education is worse than doing nothing for the growing LEP population.[127]

The supposed segregative impact of bilingualism has added fuel to the already furious—and unresolved—combat over how best to teach LEPs. One widely discussed 1977 study (financed by the U.S. Government) reviewed thirty-eight bilingual projects and studied 286 bilingual classrooms. It concluded that most bilingual students were Hispanic, but that only one-third were English-deficient. In short, bilingualism barred those proficient in the English language from participating in integrated, mainstream classrooms.[128]

This report prompted Gary Orfield, a former friend of bilingual education and consistent champion of school integration, to say: "As now operated, I believe that the grants [for bilingualism from the national government] often provide for expensive, highly segregated programs of no proven educational value to children."[129] However, the studies on the matter vary, for example, a later Government Accounting Office investigation determined that bilingualism was indeed effective in English language training.[130]

In a 1970 memorandum, the Office for Civil Rights fashioned Title VI of the 1964 Civil Rights Act into an affirmative action vehicle for language minorities. This directive declared that "where inability to speak and understand the English language excludes national origin-minority group children from effective participation in the educational program offered by a school district, the district must take affirmative steps to rectify the language deficiency in order to open its instructional program to these students."[131]

The OCR memorandum, while requiring affirmative action, did not insist on any particular approach to curing language deficiencies. The Supreme Court assumed the same latitudinarian standard when it upheld OCR's interpretation of Title VI's requirements in *Lau v. Nichols* (1974).[132] That case involved a class action suit brought under Title VI for the purpose of requiring that the San Francisco school system increase its efforts to help LEP students of Chinese ancestry overcome their English language shortcomings. To the court of appeals, which assumed a "sink or swim" attitude, the students did not have a cause of action as, "every student brings to the starting line of his education career different advantages and disadvantages caused in part by social, economic and cultural background, created and continued completely apart from any contribution by the school system."[133] The class action students did not claim intentional mistreatment by the school system. Rather, they relied on Department of Health, Education, and Welfare guidelines which barred disparate-impact discrimination in educational institutions receiving federal monies. In finding for the students, the Supreme Court approved these guidelines as appropriate for implementing Title VI of the 1964 Civil Rights Act. In so doing, the Court quoted from the administrative regulations as follows:

> [The] discrimination among students on account of race or national origin that is prohibited includes "discrimination . . . in

the availability or use of any academic . . . or other facilities of the grantee [educational institution]. . . ."

Discrimination is barred which has that *effect* [of restricting students in the use of educational resources] even though no purposeful design is present: a recipient [of federal money] "may not . . . utilize criteria or methods of administration which have the effect of subjecting individuals to discrimination" or have "the effect of defeating or substantially impairing accomplishment of the objectives of the program as respect individuals of a particular race, color, or national origin."[134]

In *Lau*, the Court offered no specific regimen for treating language deficiency. "Teaching English to the students of Chinese ancestry . . . is one choice. Giving instructions to this group in Chinese is another. There may be others. Petitioners ask only that the Board of Education be directed to apply its expertise to the problem and rectify the situation."[135]

Subsequent to *Lau*, OCR, in 1975, published what came to be called the *Lau* Guidelines, implementing the Court's ruling. But the latitudinarianism of that ruling vanished in that these new guidelines construed as acceptable only LEP training which emphasized native language instruction. The *Lau* Guidelines resulted in some five hundred consent agreements devised by OCR with the school districts.[136] To one former senior OCR official: "These plans were in a very real sense coerced agreements, since OCR threatened to cut off federal funds if a school did not implement a bilingual education program."[137]

The *Lau* Guidelines were not formulated in accord with the formal administrative law requirement that regulations from the bureaucracy be subject to public comment prior to implementation. When challenged on this ground in court, the guidelines were withdrawn. In 1985, the Reagan administration OCR notified the school districts with *Lau* Guidelines–approved plans that bilingualism was no longer required. Schools were to conform with the standards of the widely cited Fifth Circuit Court of Appeals opinion in *Casteneda v. Pickard* (1989).[138] That opinion ruled the *Lau* assistance requirement could be met by using any technique judged educationally sound by at least *some* expert educators, so long as that technique was periodically evaluated and changed if found wanting. Reportedly, however, the *Casteneda* flexibility did not impede the Clinton administration OCR from strongly reemphasizing bilingualism.[139]

One language policy student has written that bilingualism advocacy involved both a Hispanic ethnocentric status quest, and one that generated a "status backlash" by English-only/English-first movements. These latter movements found bilingual education threatening to their notion of the American way of life. The backlash has mobilized public opinion sufficiently to have

English declared as the official language in at least eight states and numerous localities. Both bilingual and English-first/only advocates view language as critical to cultural identity and allegiance. Consequently, the debate has been acrimonious, involving fevered charges and denials of racism, immigrant bashing, and anti-Americanism.[140]

Doubtless, this status conflict fueled the furious confrontation over California's Proposition 227 (1998), which established a requirement that the English-deficient students be subject to sheltered English immersion in their schooling—an immersion "not normally intended to exceed one year." Once English learners have acquired a good working knowledge of English, they were to be transferred to mainstream English classrooms. " 'Sheltered English immersion' means an English language acquisition process for young children in which nearly all classroom instruction is in English but with curriculum and presentation designed for children who are learning the language." Waivers, good for one year, from English immersion, and permitting the continuation of bilingualism can be obtained by parents for one of the following reasons: children demonstrate good English skills by standardized tests; where children are ten or older, and the school educators feel that an alternative to immersion is appropriate; and where there are children under ten with special needs, that is, those who educators feel would do better with an alternative to English immersion. Written descriptions of these special needs are required to support these waivers, and these descriptions are subject to review and approval by local school superintendents who are to operate under guidelines created by local and state boards of education.[141]

Proposition 227 was ratified by a 61 percent majority, with fewer than four out of ten Hispanics supporting it.[142] Claims of prejudice, racism, and discrimination were passionately voiced in postreferendum interviews, despite the efforts made by leading proponents of 227 to portray the measure as necessary for Hispanic upward mobility.[143] The Clinton administration attacked 227 as too rigid, impeding the flexibility needed for English training.[144] In fact, however, the proposition allowed for a flexible waiver policy outlined above. At the onset of 227's implementation, the granting of waivers varied from jurisdiction to jurisdiction. Some 40 percent of Oakland and Hayward's LEP's were given waivers. In Berkeley, 14 percent were; but in Oceanside, only five of the 150 requests were allowed.[145]

At least initially, some school administrators fashioned "flexible" approaches in connection with the "nearly all in English" requirement in 227's immersion scheme. Many LEPs have experienced much Spanish instruction in their "English immersion."[146] Some districts used a 60-40 percent English-foreign language formula in their "immersion" programs; other formulas included 80-20; and 70-30 distributions.[147]

In her 2002 extensive study of 227's implementation, political scientist Christine Rossell regarded the 70-30 English/Spanish standard as a violation of 227's command that immersion classes be conducted nearly all in

English. She also determined that other violations existed. To her, San Diego schools improperly conducted its "English immersion" essentially in Spanish; the California State Board of Education wrongly permitted students to stay in English immersion beyond the one year intended by the Initiative; and teachers/administrators controlled the immersion waiver process by adjusting their encouragement of opting out of English immersion to conform with the availability of bilingual teachers. Nonetheless, Rossell concluded that the number of bilingual students declined greatly in the wake of 227—from some 410,000 in 1997–98 to 167,000 in 2000–01.[148]

Initiatives similar to 227 were ratified in Massachusetts and Arizona.[149] But the practice of bilingual education is very much alive. Most states provide bilingual education programs,[150] agitating the question of whether national unity is threatened by this pedagogy and its blood kin, namely, the diversity/multiculturalism mantra honoring cultural variety. One essayist suggests that both the proponents and opponents of bilingual education could fashion a positive compromise in K-12 policy since language activists, in his view, broadly recognize the need for social unity, the free exchange of differing viewpoints, and the broad-based inclusion of residents in the economic and political life of the United States.[151] One hopes that this view is correct.

Both sheltered immersion and bilingualism are very much affirmative action programs. Both involve group remedies for the purpose of helping protected minorities achieve full-measure participation in American life by avoiding the negative impact imposed on LEPs by an English language society. And overcoming this societal/systemic disparate impact is a committed objective of the language activists on all sides. Their bickering and cries of conspiracy indeed reflect the intensity of that commitment. Despite the race and ethnic consciousness associated with LEP affirmative action, it has escaped strict judicial scrutiny. In light of *Croson* and *Adarand*, should this exemption continue? Can a compelling case be made for any approach to the training of LEPs? Professor Peter Schuck's policy proposal deserves consideration. To him, existing evaluation research on how to teach English to LEPs does not support firm conclusions. Better provide the parents of LEPs with government vouchers enabling them to select a private or public English-training pedagogy that seems to fit their children best. Parents who choose to place the children in public school mainstream classes could use their voucher funds to acquire supplementary English tutoring.[152]

The Twilight of School Racial/Ethnic Balancing, and the Continuing Quest for Reform

Racial/ethnic integration in the schools as a vehicle for improving minority performance has lost much of its vitality. It has been overshadowed by other quests to improve the allegedly flawed public and secondary school system for all students. In the last half century, the nation has been agitated by numerous education reform proposals and policies. After the Soviets launched a space missile (Sputnik) in 1957, many were "up in arms" over the need to improve science and technology training. This concern led to such developments as the "new math," now largely abandoned to the relief of many parents and teachers. During the post-Sputnik era, there was a particular focus on "open education" with its emphasis on increasing "self-directed" child learning. Teachers were to act more as facilitators, rather than as transmitters of book learning through formal lecturing, memorization, and the like.[153] At the opening of the new millennium, voucher subsidization, and charter schools are very much in vogue. Existing voucher programs are meant to incorporate the minority poor and their children, but the criteria are economic, or (in the case of Florida) academic performance, and not race or ethnicity.[154]

Political scientist Patrick McGuinn sees this new millennium as ushering in the national government's first major effort at establishing academic performance standards for K-12 through its No Child Left Behind Statute[155] sponsored by the George W. Bush administration. That statute called for performance exams beginning with state-devised examination in reading and mathematical skills annually for grades 3–8, and once during high school. Science exams were to be added later. Schools making inadequate student achievement progress for two consecutive years were to receive additional assistance from their school district governments. The latter are also to offer the parents of children in low-performance schools these options for their children: transfer to a higher performing school; free tutoring; afterschool programs. Four years of inadequate student performance requires schools to replace certain staff or adopt a new curriculum; and five years of failure was to be grounds for new governance structures such as the creation of charter schools, or transfer of school governance to the state. This emphasis on performance and choice, to McGuinn, represents a radical innovation in federal educational policy. Previous federal educational policy, he feels, was primarily concerned with promoting the equitable treatment of all students.[156]

Recent reform efforts have not been restricted to those discussed above. Few pedagogical areas have been spared. A more comprehensive list of reform policies would include: early childhood undertakings meant to overcome cultural deprivations (e.g., Head Start); higher graduation standards; curriculum reform in every subject; and the redesign of teacher preparation.[157] Nonetheless—in the view of student-performance experts—"only a portion of the achievement gap between the advantaged and disadvantaged students and between majority and minority students" has been closed, and remains dramatically wide." "Moreover, most of the documented achievement gains have been in the form of fewer students achieving at very low levels" Societal forces largely uncontrollable by educators hinder reform: poverty;

unstable communities, and the schools therein; high mobility rates among disadvantaged students which are "often mirrored by the high turnover of principals and teachers. . . . Even if reforms are successfully implemented in a school, highly mobile students will not be able to attend long enough for the school to make a difference to them." It may be that school reform is of secondary importance for the disadvantaged young. "[I]ncreasing the supply of adequately paying jobs for their low-skilled parents may be more pressing than school improvement. . . . All this suggests that a much more broadly conceived educational and social reform agenda may be required to respond effectively to the needs of our increasingly diverse student population, and its most disadvantaged segments."[158]

Five

Affirmative Action in
Higher Education

Prologue

Access to higher learning is one of the most esteemed prizes in our society. In this chapter, we survey the intense legal and scholarly controversy over remedial and nonremedial (diversity) affirmative action as a vehicle of eligibility for this benefit.

Does the Equal Protection Clause countenance race, ethnicity, or sex as criteria of admission to our colleges and universities? Does this depend entirely on proof of past discrimination; or may the need for more "diverse" student bodies also justify a resort to affirmative action? What is the capacity of state government and its referendum process to limit affirmative action in education and elsewhere? Manifestly, these are bedrock issues.

Here we confront a bedlam of conflicting opinions about the value of affirmative action and the quest for student body diversification in admissions policy; the substitution of "class preference" for race/ethnic preference; and the value of a testing meritocracy—that is, the benefit of standardized testing such as the SAT versus grades and other indicia of competence.

Other major concerns surveyed in this chapter include efforts to integrate the formerly *de jure*-segregated Historically Black Colleges and Universities (HBCUs) and their white counterparts, the Traditionally White Institutions (TWIs); the constitutional status of single-sex schools; and considerations related to the prohibition of sex discrimination in Title IX of the Education Act of 1972.[1]

Affirmative Action and Student Admissions: The Scholarly Debate

Our universities and graduate schools are a separate battleground in the war against discrimination. In the past, they too often restricted or excluded

131

minorities. Nevertheless, resistance to preference affirmative action in admissions policies has been a constant theme. For those seeking reasonable promptness and certainty in the law, the scenario is regrettable and saddening. To escape loss of federal funding under Title VI of the Civil Rights Act of 1964,[2] and prodded by the civil rights upheaval of the 1960s and the attendant desire "to develop interracial leadership for the future good of society"[3] state-sponsored institutions devise preferential schemes for admitting, and/or awarding scholarships to, assertedly deserving minority applicants. The devices have ranged from fixed quotas to weighted considerations of race, ethnicity, gender, and the like. These devices are supported either as group remedies for past systemic discrimination, in accordance with orthodox affirmative action compensatory theory, and/or as attempts to ensure the diversity of the student body. (Particularly since *Croson/Adarand* and its strict scrutiny requirement, the dominant theme has come to be diversity.) Application of the preferential formulas results in rejection of some nonminority applicants in favor of arguably less qualified minorities. Suits claiming violation of constitutional guarantees and charging reverse discrimination follow. The issues reached the Supreme Court in 1974, producing a plethora of opinions and culminating thus far in two important 2003 cases concerned with preferential admissions as vehicles for diversity.

The Supreme Court's first encounter with reverse discrimination in university admissions ended in a 5-4 refusal to decide the merits of the case, on the disingenuous grounds that the issue had become moot! *DeFunis v. Odegaard* (1974).[4] The second time around was the watershed case of *Regents v. Bakke* (1978),[5] the High Court' s first attempt to define the standard of judicial review for voluntary public affirmative action. (See the discussion of *Bakke* at 51–54.) The decision came to stand for the proposition that state-supported universities may apply race/ethnicity/gender as a criterion, among others, of admission.[6] Some viewed *Bakke* as representing the Court's first nonremedial application of strict scrutiny in that it was widely taken to mean that preferential admissions for diversity purposes could conform to the dictates of compelling government interest and narrow tailoring. In 1996, however, that view was rejected by the Fifth Circuit in *Hopwood v. Texas*.[7] Whether diversity concerns can support preferential admissions under strict scrutiny has since become a most controversial issue in civil rights law. *Hopwood* held that diversity can *never* be a "compelling interest" for strict scrutiny purposes, and that the University of Texas Law School violated the Equal Protection Clause by lowering Law School Aptitude Test (LSAT) and grade requirements for minority applicants.[8] In *Grutter v. Bollinger* (2003),[9] the nation's High Court determined in a long-awaited pronouncement that the University of Michigan Law School's policy of seeking student body diversity through affirmative action did meet the standards of strict scrutiny. On the same day, the Court held that the University of Michigan's College of Literature, Science, and Arts failed that test in its diversity affirmative action program. *Gratz v. Bollinger* (2003).[10]

The impact of *Bakke* on medical and law schools was the concern of Susan Welch and John Gruhl's 1998 volume *Affirmative Action and Minority Enrollments*.[11] To this end, the authors studied minority enrollment trends over the twenty-year periods before and after *Bakke*. Additionally, the volume relies on a survey of medical and law school admissions officers taken in 1989.

Welch and Gruhl concluded that most medical and law schools practiced preferential minority admissions before and after *Bakke*, and that *Bakke* prompted an even greater emphasis on racial considerations in the admissions process. They cite Professor Bernard Schwartz's *Behind Bakke*[12] in their conclusion:

> "Virtually all universities and professional schools (after *Bakke*) have maintained their program for minority admissions and have operated them to secure roughly the same percentage of minority students each year" (B. Schwartz 1988, 155). An admissions official responding to our survey was only slightly more circumspect. ". . . *Bakke* taught me that I should be careful not to think or express myself in terms of quotas. I think too that it vindicated what most law schools had been doing for a long time, i.e., bending over backwards to give minorities a chance."[13]

Welch and Gruhl argue that by legitimating affirmative action, *Bakke* set the stage for dramatic increases in the number of blacks and Hispanics at the undergraduate level and in professional schools. Black college enrollment increased 30 percent between 1986–1994. In that time, African American acquisition of undergraduate degrees rose by 34 percent; master's by 40 percent. For the same period, Hispanic enrollment and the earning of bachelor's degrees surged by 50 percent. And Hispanics experienced almost the same increase in the winning of master's diplomas. Minority progress in medical and law schools has been equally impressive.[14]

Welch and Gruhl's coupling of *Bakke* with the rise in minority undergraduate enrollment is questionable. Stephan Thernstrom may very well be correct in his view that "[t]he vast majority of blacks and Hispanics [like other college students] then and now attend basically non-selective schools at which there are no racial double standards in admissions; there are hardly any standards at all."[15] In any event, the percentage of minorities surveyed by National Center for Educational Statistics who received bachelor's degrees rose every year from 1990 to 2005—the time frame of the survey. The rise in percent in that span of years was: African Americans, 6.8 percent to 12.5 percent; Hispanics, 5.5 to 8.5 percent; Asian/Pacific Islanders, 24.2 to 31.8percent; and American Indian/Alaskan Native, 5.9 to 10.3 percent.

Between 1995 and 2005, moreover, there was an increase in the number of graduate and first professional degrees: Blacks, 3.6 percent to 5.2 percent; Hispanics, 2.8 to 3.5 percent; Asian/Pacific Islanders, 12.9 to 17.4 percent; American Indian/Alaskan Native, 2.7 to 4.2 percent.[16]

Thernstrom also takes Welch and Gruhl to task for failing to "even mention the academic difficulties of preferentially-admitted medical students and the huge and shocking racial differential in rates of passing Part I of the Medical Boards and in qualifying as board-certified physicians in their specialty."[17] Thernstrom accentuated the failure rate among minority law students in his critique of Linda Wightman's influential 1997 New York Law Review article, *Threat to Diversity in Legal Education.*[18] There—relying on a formidable data base which included the 1990–91 applicants and admittees to the American Bar Association (ABA)–approved law schools—she concluded that preferential admissions played a very significant role in minority admissions. So much so that if admission relied solely on LSAT scores and grades the result would have been "a law school student body that mirrored the ethnic makeup of law schools of thirty years ago."[19] Further, the data suggested that there is "little to no difference" between preferential admittees and those accepted on grades and LSAT scores in terms of bar exam passage.[20] Stephan Thernstrom used Wightman's data to underscore black failure in law school. He wrote that "wash out" (by failing to graduate or pass the bar) for blacks "who entered law school as a result of racial preference—the vast majority of them—was a horrendous 43.2 percent."[21] Thus, some four out of ten African Americans who entered ABA-approved law schools never became attorneys.[22] Of course, this Thernstrom challenge leaves important issues: Were the "wash outs" really "wash outs?" Did they not gain much from the law school experience? Has America benefited from their experience?

In the polemics over minority admissions, the proponents of class-based preference are particularly vociferous. For instance, Richard Kahlenberg, in *The Remedy,*[23] maintains that the substantial black-white gap in SAT scores is essentially a function of differences in economic status, rather than race, and therefore that race should be supplanted by consideration of class status as a criterion of admission. Contrary to this view, Appiah and Gutmann contend that the SAT gap statistics tend to support both race and class as admission criteria.[24] In other words, the statistics warrant an inference of both race disadvantage and class disadvantage, and class advocates have not adduced any independent basis for differentiating between the two. Therefore, it is inconsistent and unfair to exclude racial preference from the remedial picture. If this analysis has merit, it argues for retention of race-based affirmative action in higher education, in order to ensure the inclusion of meritorious blacks.[25]

An impassioned case for continuing race-based affirmative action in higher learning has been made by Ronald Dworkin in a *New York Review of*

Books essay, *Affirming Affirmative Action*.[26] Dworkin reviews William Bowen and Derek Bok's *The Shape of the River: Long-Term Consequences of Considering Race in College and University Admissions*,[27] and uses that review as a springboard for a moral and practical defense of preference affirmative action at the university level, and for antidiscrimination policy generally.

According to Dworkin, the Bowen and Bok book, written by two scions of the Ivy League, is a comprehensive and statistically sophisticated study of the impact of affirmative action in higher education. It analyzes the undergraduate and post-university careers of more than eighty thousand matriculants at the twenty-eight "most selective" universities that used preference affirmative action.[28] It attempts to chart affirmative action's consequences for the individual students and graduates, their universities, and race relations in the country as a whole.[29] Bowen and Bok conclude that:

> [T]he most selective colleges and universities have succeeded in educating sizable numbers of minority students who have already achieved considerable success and seem likely in time to occupy positions of leadership throughout society . . . [and] that academically selective colleges and universities have been highly successful in using race-sensitive admission policies to advance educational goals important to everyone.[30]

Dworkin maintains that Bowen and Bok's underlying findings are the best evidence yet available that affirmative action "seems impressively successful . . . violates no individual rights and compromises no moral principles."[31] In defending this position, he surveys the affirmative action controversy in university admissions. This survey would strike liberals as a tour de force of succinct substantive exposition. Dworkin's contentions follow in summary form:

Affirmative action does not accept unqualified blacks.[32]

Blacks do not waste the opportunities offered by affirmative action.[33]

Affirmative action has produced, as hoped, more African American businessmen, professionals, and community leaders. According to Bowen and Bok, black elite school graduates earn considerably greater incomes than the typical black with a bachelor's degree, and are "strikingly" more likely to participate in black community activities.[34]

Racial diversity in a university student body helps to break down stereotypes and hostility among students; the benefit endures in post-university life.

Affirmative action does not stigmatize blacks.[35]

Replacement of affirmative action by race-neutral standards would greatly reduce the proportion of blacks in prestigious institutions. Dworkin cites Bowen and Bok's estimate of a 50 to 75 percent drop in elite schools, and a calamitous drop in law and medical schools. Dworkin rejects the contention that these drops would not take place if preferences were confined to low-income applicants, given that so many African American applicants are poor. Dworkin considers it a fallacy, because poor applicants are still predominantly white, so that even race-neutral tests aimed at economic diversity would greatly reduce the numbers of blacks.[36]

Affirmative action does not unfairly violate the rights of rejected white applicants.[37]

It is not the case that race-sensitive admissions policies judge applicants only as members of large groups, not as individuals.[38]

It is not the case that racial classifications are always wrong in principle.[39]

Race has a special psychological character as racial discrimination expresses contempt and wholly destroys the victims' lives. Racial classifications can inflict a special form of injury, but "it would . . . be perverse to disallow . . . [their use] to help combat the racism that is the true and continuing cause of that injury."[40]

Dworkin castigates Stephan and Abigail Thernstrom for their allegedly misleading and shoddy material,[41] which emphasizes that the high rate of black university dropouts is evidence of affirmative action's "disappointing even counterproductive results."[42] The Thernstroms argued that African Americans would not have so high a failure rate, and thus would have experienced a better growth experience, if more had attended less selective and competitive schools.[43] In Dworkin's view, Bowen and Bok's work was far more scholarly, and it demonstrated that the black dropout rate at the very elite schools was small "by national standards," although it was 11 percent higher than the white rate.[44]

However, the Thernstroms did note that at the very elite schools (the subjects of Bok and Bowen's book) pretty much all students graduate, given the high caliber of the admittees. But even here (save for Harvard and Princeton) blacks were at least twice as likely to drop out.[45]

UCLA law professor Richard Sander challenged the Bowen and Bok thesis in an iconoclastic and provocative 2004 essay[46] analyzing affirmative action for blacks in American law schools. "Affirmative action, as currently practiced by the nation's law schools," he asserts, "does not . . . pass even the easiest test one can set. In systemic, objective terms, it hurts the group it is most designed to help."[47] The preferential treatment afforded blacks by affirmative action is "very large,"[48] resulting in admitting them to schools where the teaching pace and content exceed their academic preparation.[49] This academic mismatch produces poor law school and bar exam grade performance.[50] Placed in less competitive schools, blacks could thrive "because the pace would be slower, the theoretical nuances would be less involved and the student would stay on top of the material. The student would thus perform better."[51] But affirmative action admission practices and their "cascade effect" undermine both the placement of blacks in schools where they could blossom, and facilitate the admission of students who have no business in law school.[52]

The late 1960s, Sander reports, witnessed a dramatic increase in law school affirmative action, and this for the purpose of reducing African American civil disobedience, and to help compensate them for past and present ill treatment. Race-conscious preferential treatment took the form of admitting blacks with academic records (college grades and Law School Aptitude Test scores) considerably inferior to those submitted by whites. Black student populations in law schools rose. The number of first-year black students (outside the historically black institutions) in 1964–65 was about two hundred. It rose to 800 in 1969–70; and to 1,700 in 1973–74. In 2001, 3,400 African Americans began their law training in accredited law schools, or 7.7 percent of the student body, closely matching the African American college graduate population percentage of 8.9 percent. Until *Bakke*, the determination that the Davis medical school preferential admission program was unconstitutional, law schools were quite open about preferences granted blacks. Given African American victimization—so the argument ran—lenient treatment was deserved. But it was difficult to distinguish Davis's unconstitutional policy from that operative at the law schools. Justice Powell offered the veil of diversity, or better yet the veil of duplicity. Pressured by faculty and students to admit more blacks, admissions officers now disguised their efforts to correct historic wrongs through the diversity veil. Powell's diversity (all applicants had to be individually assessed to determine how they would augment a diverse education) was no standard at all. Admissions could do as it pleased with the fig leaf of diversity.[53] "Viewing Powell's holding as hypocritical, law school deans joined the hypocrisy. For most, this probably seemed a small price to pay in the cause of an apparently greater good."[54]

Relying on his observations as a UCLA law professor as to the practices at that school, and on an extensive analysis of law school admissions at the University of Michigan (for 1999–2000) and seven other law schools (for 2002–04), Sander concluded that the Powell thesis of painstaking individual assessment for diversity assets was not practiced to any substantial degree. Admissions are driven largely by college grade point average (GPA), LSAT scores, and in some cases residency. Nonracial diversity factors such as overcoming hardship, leadership skills, and work experience are given short shrift. Blacks are admitted at the same rates as whites. This statistical solidity would not exist if there was a careful weighing and balancing of nonracial assets and how they would contribute to a bountifully diverse educational experience.[55]

Sander constructed a one thousand point, academic index scale using the formula LSAT-120+UNGPA (undergrad grade point average).[56] The preferences afforded African American applicants are displayed in the following chart,[57] which Sander derived from 1991 data provided by Law School Aptitude Council and covering 95 percent of the nation's accredited law schools:

Black-White Academic Index Gap in Six Groups of American Law Schools, 1991 Matriculants

Law School Group	Median Academic Index		Black-White Gap	Standard Deviation in Index for Whites
	Blacks	Whites		
Group 1: Very Elite Schools (n=14)	705	875	170	74
Group 2: Other "National" Schools (n=16)	631	805	174	89
Group 3: Midrange Public Schools (n=50)	586	788	202	75
Group 4: Midrange Private Schools (n=50)	560	725	165	75
Group 5: Low-Range Private Law Schools (n=18)	493	665	172	73
Group 6: Historically "Minority" Schools (n=7)	516	641	125	103

The failure of affirmative action to serve blacks in law school is attributed to a combination of preference and leniency in admission and its cascading effect. The most prestigious (top-tier) schools offer admission to many who are not prepared for that level of competition. Lower-tier schools are then restricted to accepting even less qualified, and this process of taking the less and less qualified cascades downward, resulting in the lowest status schools taking students who are not qualified at all (some 14 percent of admittees in Sander's estimate). Often academically mismatched at each level, African Americans struggle and often fail. "Entering black law students are 135% more likely than whites to not get a law degree." "Close to half of black law students end up in the bottom tenth of their classes," and this negatively affects job opportunities. "Blacks are nearly six times as likely as whites to not pass state bar exams after multiple attempts."[58]

A race-blind admission system, to Sander, would not produce an "unthinkable Armageddon."[59] Some 86 percent of black applicants would still be eligible, albeit, in many cases, for lesser status schools. The widespread notion that race-blindness would decimate the black law student ranks is nonsense. If this 86 percent went to schools appropriate to their preparation, there would be more and better-trained black lawyers.[60] As a middle ground, and catering to those wedded to the virtues of educational diversity, Sander proposed race preferences designed to achieve a 4 percent black presence. This would reduce the mismatch problem, but its quota-specificity is, he admits, constitutionally suspect.[61]

Sander's voluminous (116 pages) and explosive effort to capture the "goings-on" in the mystery world of university admissions warrants attention and evaluation, as should his scathing challenge to affirmative action orthodoxy. The essay directly contradicts Bowen and Bok, and it has been assailed. Law and sociology professor Richard Lempert of the University of Michigan scoffs at the notion that blacks will attend less prestigious schools, as these schools may be inconveniently located.[62] (Sander recognizes that black willingness to transfer to the scholastic trenches is debatable.)[63] Lempert also charged that Sander both neglected the positive dimensions of black law school attendance, and the role of "stereotype threat" in black underachievement—that is, the acceptance by African Americans of the very inferiority which racist thinking has mercilessly insisted exists. Dean Christopher Edley, now of Boalt Hall, opines that even if Sander is correct, the answer is more mentoring and tutoring.[64] Sander's solution (encouraging greater black attendance at less prestigious law schools) rests on his notion that law schools can be differentiated by the pace of their teaching and their emphasis on theoretical nuance, with the elite schools marked by the greatest speed and theoretical complexity. This gradation thesis is not supported by evidence that Sander provides, is speculative, and represents stereotypical thinking, but, nonetheless, may be common thinking at the prestigious schools.

At this juncture, we return to the year 2000 Holzer-Neumark survey on affirmative action[65] (discussed previously at 85–87) and again couple it to its 2006 Supplement,[66] which allocates prominent attention to Professor Sander's thesis. These surveys of affirmative action literature deal with the impact of affirmative action on university admissions as well as employment. With respect to the former, we learn that the "theoretical literature" is "ambiguous,"[67] but the following "empirical" findings are offered: affirmative action programs have played a "major role" in bringing about the "striking increase" in African American and Hispanic undergraduate and graduate enrollments since the 1970s;[68] lower average minority SAT scores are not reliable indicators of preferential treatment, or are poor predictors of college success;[69] minority college students on average perform less well, but not more so at the most selective schools;[70] both black and white students benefit from attending selective schools;[71] there is some evidence that underperforming minority medical school students are ultimately more likely than nonminority MDs to treat minority or low-income patients;[72] and there is only a little evidence that minority and female beneficiaries act as role models or mentors.[73]

The 2006 supplement informs the reader that evidence from the learned literature "suggests" that "opportunities and outcomes" for students are improved by affirmative action,[74] but that minority performance in colleges and universities "clearly lags behind that of whites and their dropout rates are substantially higher."[75] New evidence has emerged regarding the positive educational benefits attributed to diverse ethno-racial student bodies. Gurin's positive conclusions (at 142–43) seem "plausible,"[76] but no "firm conclusions"[77] can as yet be made, and more study should be undertaken, particularly with respect to the question of whether diversity appears to lead to employees who are more valued in the labor market.[78]

Holzer and Neumark viewed Sander's "academic mismatch" thesis as "interesting" and "provocative," but "there is more work to be done to address issues of the impact of affirmative action on minority law students and graduate students more generally."[79] They were disappointed and found it "striking" that Sander did not run a regression with bar passage or graduation as the dependent variable, and LSAT scores, college grades, and law school quality as independent variables.[80] How such an analysis would undercut Sander's dismal conclusions about affirmative action and law schools is not clarified by Holzer and Neumark.

What comfort will affirmative action disputants derive from these findings? Holzer and Neumark strongly question some of the criticisms, for example, that affirmative action at selective law schools presents minority students with challenges they are not equipped to handle. On the other hand, diversity proponents will obviously be dismayed by their failure to fully accept the thesis of diversity's asserted educational benefits. All told, it is clear that the authors consider affirmative action at the university level a topic that requires much further study. It should be noted that they do not address the merit of diversifying the Historically Black Colleges and Universities as was required (through means which are academically appropriate) by the Supreme Court in *U.S. v. Fordice* (1992).[81] (See 170–78.) Nor do they make an effort, at least in the surveys covered here, to survey the literature on the state of our primary and secondary schools.

There are those who question the supposed educational benefit of diversity's race/ethnic-conscious admissions policies. A senior writer for the *Chronicle of Higher Education*—Peter Schmidt—editorialized in a 2008 *Wall Street Journal* article that "*America's Universities Are Living A Diversity Lie.*"[82] According to Schmidt, before the Powell opinion in *Bakke*, most universities had never considered, and still do not believe, that race/ethnic-conscious admissions lead to better education for all students. The affirmative action admissions policies practiced prior to *Bakke* were supported by invoking *remedial* justifications: the mitigation of past and present unlawful discrimination. Tellingly, the University of California, in its defense of the Davis sixteen-seat set-aside, said nothing about diversity's educational virtues. But Powell's diversity opinion in *Bakke* encouraged admissions officials to express an abiding commitment to diversity's pedagogical benefits to avoid losing reverse discrimination suits charging them with practicing race discrimination without the requisite tie between their universities and illegal race discrimination—a tie required for the lawful practice of remedial affirmative action. Few colleges have even tried to support their newfound diversity enthusiasm with social science data. The studies that exist are so weak that even strong advocates of diversity affirmative action admit that social science is not on their side.[83]

A penetrating critique of ethno-racial diversity benefits in higher education was authored by Stanley Rothman, Seymour Martin Lipset, and Neil Nevitte.[84] They tell the reader that existing research on this subject relies heavily on surveys of students responding to questions about the educational merits of diversity. Very large majorities respond positively in these surveys, but questions asked of students, they argue, involve "valence" issues—propositions that garner almost universal support, such as whether one supports freedom of speech. There are also indoctrination problems. Faculty tell students that diversity affirmative action is good; students parrot back positive responses.[85]

The Rothman, Lipset, and Nevitte study relied on a 1999–2000 survey covering 140 colleges, 4,088 students, 1,632 faculty, and 808 administrators. An effort was made to acquire a representative sample of the nation's colleges in terms of their size and quality. Historically black colleges were not included. Students were asked how well colleges educated, and how hard students worked. There were no questions about the value of diverse student bodies and the like. The answers were then correlated with the number of black, Asian, and Hispanic students on campus. The results were controlled (through multiple regression analysis) for such traits as race, gender, religion, college selectivity, public/private status, student-faculty ratio. The results were clear to the authors: the greater race/ethnic diversity in student body populations, the greater dissatisfaction expressed by students regarding their educational experience. Also, the greater the student body diversity, the greater was the dissatisfaction expressed by the faculty and administrators as to student preparedness.[86]

The University of Michigan's race/ethnic-conscious preferential admissions policies at issue in *Grutter v. Bollinger*[87] and *Gratz v. Bollinger*[88] were defended by the university as facilitative of a better education for all students.[89] Researchers at the university who supplied expert testimony during the court evaluation of these diversity policies maintained that in previous court cases arguments linking better education to diversity affirmative action were not well grounded in theory and empirical evidence. Michigan's researchers claimed that they had filled that gap, providing information important to the Supreme Court's recognition of the constitutional legitimacy of diversity affirmative action in *Grutter*,[90] as well as information important to the *amici* briefs (some seventy-five) in *Grutter* and *Gratz* which supported the university's position that student body diversity affirmative action represented a compelling government interest. The number of *amici* briefs was extraordinary, and were sponsored by a large number of universities, educational associations, state governments, civil rights groups, retired military officers, and law school students.[91] Indeed, the Supreme Court majority cited "the expert studies and reports entered into evidence at trial" as bolstering its constitutional conclusion that the law school diversity admissions program passed strict scrutiny.[92] The Michigan research was one of these expert reports.[93] The central findings of this research were outlined in *Defending Diversity: Affirmative Action at the University of Michigan* published by that university's press in 2004.

The Michigan research tapped two data sources: (1) A national survey provided by the Cooperative Institutional Research Program, and the UCLA Higher Education Research Institute involving 11,382 students from 184 colleges who were surveyed in 1984 when they entered college; interviewed when they were seniors; and, finally, interviewed again five years after graduation; (2) entrance and fourth-year data culled from a questionnaire covering 1,582 University of Michigan students, consisting of all students of color and a large representation of whites.[94] For both the national and Michigan surveys, efforts were made to statistically control for such things as race, gender, high school grades, SAT scores, and ethnic diversity in high school.[95] *Defending Diversity's* use of the national study was restricted to reporting on its findings regarding informal interaction "measured by the frequency with which students socialized with a person of a different race, discussed racial issues, or attended cultural awareness workshops over four years of college."[96] A variety of student experiences were examined in connection with the Michigan student survey: how much students were exposed to classes focused on understanding other races/ethnicities; whether they had taken a course that had an important effect on their racial, ethnic, informal contacts with diverse peers; and the extent to which students participated in multicultural events such as Asian Awareness week.[97] Throughout, student self-assessment was relied upon by the analysts.

The results to the Michigan analysts were clear: the greater the diverse experiences of students, the greater were their intellectual energy and democratic competencies. The former concerned motivation and academic skills.[98] Democratic competencies included a desire to improve communities and work with people to that end,[99] as well as recognizing commonalities in basic values such as those concerned with work and family.[100] Blacks, Asians, and whites in the Michigan survey with the greatest diversity experiences expressed the highest degree of commonality values.[101] The Michigan researchers added that their research conformed with traditional social psychology theory and research confirming that "positive and equal" interracial contact diminishes negative stereotypical thinking,[102] and that it was manifest to the researchers that race/ethnic interactions stemming from increased diversity experiences help reduce the "segregation which threatens the fabric of our pluralistic society."[103]

Assuming no "valence-issue" infection of student self-assessment and no student "brainwashing" by faculty, the Michigan research still raises questions. Since whites and Asians were important to the diversity benefits cited by the study, should they have received the same preferences as blacks, Hispanics, and American Indians? Also, did the intellectual and democratic benefits provided by the preference beneficiaries warrant the pain suffered by those rejected as a consequence of those preferences?

As the body of the Michigan study makes clear, the reduction of negative stereotyping and the increase in racial/ethnic integration were central concerns to the Michigan scholars and the university as a whole. Of course, these are traditional objectives of remedial affirmative action. There is then a coupling in the Michigan diversity advocacy of remedial and nonremedial affirmative action themes, an overlap that is quite evident in the O'Connor opinion of the Court in *Grutter*, which we shall examine shortly.

Traditional affirmative action remedies were urged by others in their support of Michigan's affirmative action admissions policy. An illustration is the *amicus* brief of the Association of American Medical Colleges, which maintained that admissions diversity and its attendant affirmative action preferences were required to produce more black and Hispanic doctors. These were more likely to serve downtrodden minority populations and research the treatment of their unique medical problems. On the other hand, sixty corporations supported Michigan in order to promote better business and economic gain. America's diverse peoples and the increased emphasis on global business necessitated the presence of students familiarized with the cultures of different people.[104] One skeptical editorialist opined that the true objective of corporate America in its support of Michigan was the acquisition of college-educated minorities as a barrier against disparate-impact suits.[105]

A pro-diversity brief submitted by thirty top-ranking retired military officers supporting Michigan reportedly was of particular interest to Supreme Court members. The retired officers observed that nearly 40 percent of the current military was minority. The relative absence of minority officers during the Vietnam conflict produced much dissension in the minority ranks, gravely impeding our war effort there. To improve our warmaking capacity, the service academies had come to aggressively recruit minorities for officer training, providing them with substantial preferential treatment in admissions (e.g., lower test scores for admissions, and lower grade point averages in high school). Prep schools had also been established by the academies focused, in large measure, on improving the academic skills of minorities. ROTC also aggressively recruits minorities, providing scholarships to minorities, the barriers to which are less burdensome than those applied to whites.[106]

At the *Grutter/Gratz* oral argument stage—when a huge crowd of five thousand demonstrators milled around the steps of the Supreme Court— Theodore Olson, U.S. Solicitor General, was responsible for presenting the Bush administration's policy of seeking student diversity through allegedly race-neutral means such as admitting top-ranking high school graduates from all race/ethnic areas. He was challenged by Justices Breyer and Souter who asked for the reasoning behind the administration's opposition to race/ethnic-conscious admission practices by state colleges when the U.S. service academies were doing so. Justice Ginsburg asked whether the practices of the academies were unconstitutional. Justice Stevens wanted to know whether these practices at the academies were necessary and valuable. Olson replied that "we don't accept the position that black soldiers will only fight for black officers."[107] He added that the administration had not taken a position on the race/ethnic admissions practices of the academies.[108]

Strict Scrutiny, Diversity, and University Admissions: The *Hopwood, Grutter,* and *Gratz* Cases

Both remedial and nonremedial (diversity) arguments have been advanced to support affirmative action in college and university admissions. But supporting remedial affirmative action—that is, affirmative action needed to remedy past or present unlawful discrimination—has become particularly difficult for select universities. Select universities and colleges compete very vigorously to attract qualified minorities and most have not had a history of official segregation. In some cases, where universities had historically engaged in *de jure* segregation, arguments for remedial-affirmative action to cure the lingering effects of such discrimination were rejected by some courts at the federal appellate level. See *Podberesky v. Kirwan*, (1994)[109] where race-exclusive scholarships were rejected; and *Hopwood v. Texas*, (1996),[110] where a preferential admissions program at the University of Texas Law School was outlawed. However, on other formerly *de jure* campuses, affirmative action is judicially and/or administratively required to help remedy that discrimination. (See 170–78.)

At the time of *Grutter/Gratz* (2003), the constitutional status of the use of ethno-racial admissions preferences to promote collegiate diversity was unclear. Conflicting approaches had been taken by the federal circuits as to whether such practices were compelling government interests as required by strict scrutiny under the Equal Protection Clause. For example, *Hopwood v. Texas*,(1996)[111] said that they were not; while *Smith v. University of Washington Law* School (2000)[112] said that they were. *Hopwood's* reasoning on diversity theory stands in stark contrast to that expressed in *Grutter*.

In *Hopwood v Texas*,[113] the court expressed its opposition vigorously:

> Within the general principles of the Fourteenth Amendment, the use of race in admissions for diversity in higher education contradicts, rather than furthers, the aims of equal protection. Diversity fosters, rather than minimizes, the use of race. It treats minorities as a group, rather than as individuals. It may further remedial purposes but, just as likely, may promote improper racial stereotypes, thus fueling racial hostility.

> The use of race, in and of itself, to choose students simply achieves a student body that looks different. Such a criterion is no more rational on its own terms than would be choices based upon the physical size or blood type of applicants. . . .[114]

> To believe that a person's race controls his point of view is to stereotype him.[115] . . . Finally, the use of race to achieve diversity undercuts the ultimate goal of the Fourteenth Amendment: the end of racially-motivated state action.[116]

Contrary to *Hopwood*, the Ninth Circuit—in *Smith v. University of Washington Law School* (2000)[117]—upheld the race/ethnic-conscious, preferential admissions program of that school, holding that the Powell opinion accepting diversity objectives under strict scrutiny was *implicitly* accepted by four additional justices (the Brennan plurality).[118] This despite the fact that the Brennan plurality *explicitly* relied on the *remedial* thesis that the Davis plan served the important governmental interest of remedying the present effects of past discrimination [119]

The "implicit-majority" thesis of *Smith* was not accepted by the district court charged with ruling on the diversity/preference admission scheme operative at the University of Michigan's College of Literature, Science, and Arts. *Gratz v. Bollinger* (2000).[120] When the Supreme Court later in *Grutter v. Bollinger* (2003) endorsed the Powell diversity view, it pointedly declared that it did not find it " 'useful' " to pursue the *implicit-acceptance* methodology " 'when it has so obviously baffled and divided the lower courts that have considered it.' "[121] As interpreted by the *Gratz* district court, however, the *Bakke* majority did not *prohibit* the diversity rationale as a basis for admission preferences. And the *Gratz* district court went on to conclude that preferential treatment for the purposes of diversification served a compelling governmental interest because there was "solid evidence" that educational benefits flow from racially and ethnically diverse student bodies, including intellectual growth, better understanding of multiple perspectives, and more creative solutions to problem solving.[122] This district court stressed that "over 360 institutions, represented by the Association of American Law Schools assert that they have learned through their extensive experience . . . that the quality of education is greatly enhanced when student bodies include persons of diverse backgrounds, interests, and experiences, including racial and ethnic makeups."[123] Further, the Michigan undergraduate preference plan was narrowly tailored as it treated minority status as only one factor, among many, in the admission process.[124]

Another district court—ruling on protected-group preference admissions at the University of Georgia—rejected the diversity argument as totally speculative and intellectually bankrupt. To that court, there was no hard evidence that persons from a "homogeneous" background could not work well with members of other groups. *Johnson v. University of Georgia* (2000).[125]

Confusion about the constitutionality of preferential diversity admissions was augmented by a district court determination that the University of Michigan Law School race/ethnic-conscious program was unconstitutional. In that case, Judge Feinberg found that the Supreme Court in *Croson* and *Adarand* (among other cases) had concluded that race classifications were unconstitutional unless they were "intended to remedy carefully documented effects of past discrimination."[126] It was clear to Judge Feinberg that the Supreme Court has rejected broad-gauged benign defenses for race classification—defenses such as providing minority role models; societal discrimination; and diversity.[127] But even if diversity was a compelling interest—and the judge pointedly noted that the law on the matter was murky[128]—the law school admissions system was, in effect, a quota system, which frustrated the narrow-tailoring prong of strict scrutiny.[129] The Supreme Court saw things differently in *Grutter v. Bollinger* (2003) when it dealt with the constitutionality of the Michigan Law School race/ethnic-conscious admissions policy.

Grutter v. Bollinger, **539 U.S. 306 (2003)**

[311] Justice O'CONNOR delivered the opinion of the Court.

This case requires us to decide whether the use of race as a factor in student admissions by the University of Michigan Law School (Law School) is unlawful. . . .

[315] The hallmark of that policy is its focus on academic ability coupled with a flexible assessment of applicants' talents, experiences, and potential "to contribute to the learning of those around them." The policy requires admissions officials to evaluate each applicant based on all the information available in the file, including a personal statement, letters of recommendation, and an essay describing the ways in which the applicant will contribute to the life and diversity of the Law School. In reviewing an applicant's file, admissions officials must consider the applicant's undergraduate grade point average (GPA) and Law School Admission Test (LSAT) score because they are important (if imperfect) predictors of academic success in law school. The policy stresses that "no applicant should be admitted unless we expect that applicant to do well enough to graduate with no serious academic problems." . . .

The policy aspires to "achieve that diversity which has the potential to enrich everyone's education and thus make a law school class stronger than the sum of its parts." [316] The policy does not restrict the types of diversity contributions eligible for "substantial weight" in the admissions process, but instead recognizes "many possible bases for diversity admissions." The policy does, however, reaffirm the Law School's longstanding commitment to "one particular type of diversity," that is, "racial and ethnic diversity with special reference to the inclusion of students from groups which have been historically discriminated against, like African-Americans, Hispanics and Native Americans, who without this commitment might not be represented in our student body in meaningful numbers." By enrolling a " 'critical mass' of [underrepresented] minority students," the Law School seeks to "ensur[e] their ability to make unique contributions to the character of the Law School."

The policy does not define diversity "solely in terms of racial and ethnic status." Nor is the policy "insensitive to the competition among all students for admission to the [L]aw [S]chool."

Rather, the policy seeks to guide admissions officers in "producing classes both diverse and academically outstanding, classes made up of students who promise to continue the tradition of outstanding contribution by Michigan Graduates to the legal profession." . . .

[322] We granted certiorari, to resolve the disagreement among the Courts of Appeals on a question of national importance: Whether diversity is a compelling interest that can justify the narrowly tailored use of race in selecting applicants for admission to public universities. Compare *Hopwood v. Texas*, 78 F.3d 932 (C.A.5 1996)*(Hopwood I)* (holding that diversity is not a compelling state interest), with *Smith v. University of Wash. Law School*, 233 F.3d 1188 (C.A.9 2000) (holding that it is).

We last addressed the use of race in public higher education over 25 years ago. In the landmark *Bakke* case, we reviewed a racial set-aside program that reserved 16 out of 100 seats in a medical school class for members of certain minority groups. 438 U.S. 265 (1978). . . .

[323] Since this Court's splintered decision in *Bakke*, Justice Powell's opinion announcing the judgment of the Court has served as the touchstone for constitutional analysis of race-conscious admissions policies. Public and private universities across the Nation have modeled their own admissions programs on Justice Powell's views on permissible race-conscious policies. . . . We therefore discuss Justice Powell's opinion in some detail. . . .

[324] Justice Powell approved the university's use of race to further only one interest: "the attainment of a diverse student body." *Id.*, at 311. With the important proviso that "constitutional limitations protecting individual rights may not be disregarded," Justice Powell grounded his analysis in the academic freedom that "long has been viewed as a special concern of the First Amendment." *Id.*, at 312. Justice Powell emphasized that nothing less than the " 'nation's future depends upon leaders trained through wide exposure' to the ideas and mores of students as diverse as this Nation of many peoples." *Id.*, at 313. In seeking the "right to select those students who will contribute the most to the 'robust exchange of ideas,' " a university seeks "to achieve a goal that is of paramount importance in the fulfillment of its mission." 438 U.S. at 313. Both "tradition and experience lend support to the view that the contribution of diversity is substantial." *Ibid.*

Justice Powell was, however, careful to emphasize that in his view race "is only one element in a range of factors a university properly may consider in attaining the goal of a heterogeneous student body." *Id.,* at 314. For Justice Powell, "[i]t is not an interest in simple ethnic diversity, in which a specified percentage of the student body is in effect guaranteed to be members of selected ethnic groups," that [325] can justify the use of race. *Id.,* at 315. Rather, "[t]he diversity that furthers a compelling state interest encompasses a far broader array of qualifications and characteristics of which racial or ethnic origin is but a single though important element." *Ibid. . . .*

[F]or the reasons set out below, today we endorse Justice Powell's view that student body diversity is a compelling state interest that can justify the use of race in university admissions.

[326] The Equal Protection Clause provides that no State shall "deny to any person within its jurisdiction the equal protection of the laws." U.S. Const., Amdt. 14, § 2. Because the Fourteenth Amendment "protect[s] *persons,* not *groups,*" all "governmental action based on race—a *group* classification long recognized as in most circumstances irrelevant and therefore prohibited—should be subjected to detailed judicial inquiry to ensure that the *personal* right to equal protection of the laws has not been infringed." *Adarand Constructors, Inc. v. Peña,* 515 U.S. 200, 227 (1995). We are a "free people whose institutions are founded upon the doctrine of equality." *Loving v. Virginia,* 388 U.S. 1, 11(1967). It follows from that principle that "government may treat people differently because of their race only for the most compelling reasons." *Adarand Constructors, Inc. v. Peña,* 515 U.S. at 227.

We have held that all racial classifications imposed by government "must be analyzed by a reviewing court under strict scrutiny." This means that such classifications are constitutional only if they are narrowly tailored to further compelling governmental interests. . . . We apply strict scrutiny to all racial classifications to " 'smoke out' illegitimate uses of race by assuring that [government] is pursuing a goal important enough to warrant use of a highly suspect tool." . . .

[327] With these principles in mind, we turn to the question whether the Law School's use of race is justified by a compelling state interest. Before this Court, as they have [328] throughout this litigation, respondents assert only one justification for their

use of race in the admissions process: obtaining "the educational benefits that flow from a diverse student body." In other words, the Law School asks us to recognize, in the context of higher education, a compelling state interest in student body diversity.

We first wish to dispel the notion that the Law School's argument has been foreclosed, either expressly or implicitly, by our affirmative-action cases decided since *Bakke*. It is true that some language in those opinions might be read to suggest that remedying past discrimination is the only permissible justification for race-based governmental action. But we have never held that the only governmental use of race that can survive strict scrutiny is remedying past discrimination. Nor, since *Bakke*, have we directly addressed the use of race in the context of public higher education. Today, we hold that the Law School has a compelling interest in attaining a diverse student body.

The Law School's educational judgment that such diversity is essential to its educational mission is one to which we defer. The Law School's assessment that diversity will, in fact, yield educational benefits is substantiated by respondents and their *amici*. Our scrutiny of the interest asserted by the Law School is no less strict for taking into account complex educational judgments in an area that lies primarily within the expertise of the university. Our holding today is in keeping with our tradition of giving a degree of deference to a university's academic decisions, within constitutionally prescribed limits.

[329] We have long recognized that, given the important purpose of public education and the expansive freedoms of speech and thought associated with the university environment, universities occupy a special niche in our constitutional tradition. In announcing the principle of student body diversity as a compelling state interest, Justice Powell invoked our cases recognizing a constitutional dimension, grounded in the First Amendment, of educational autonomy: "The freedom of a university to make its own judgments as to education includes the selection of its student body." *Bakke, supra,* at 312. From this premise, Justice Powell reasoned that by claiming "the right to select those students who will contribute the most to the 'robust exchange of ideas,' " a university "seek[s] to achieve a goal that is of paramount importance in the fulfillment of its mission." 438 U.S., at 313. Our conclusion that the Law School has a compelling interest

in a diverse student body is informed by our view that attaining a diverse student body is at the heart of the Law School's proper institutional mission, and that "good faith" on the part of a university is "presumed" absent "a showing to the contrary." 438 U.S., at 318–319.

As part of its goal of "assembling a class that is both exceptionally academically qualified and broadly diverse," the Law School seeks to "enroll a 'critical mass' of minority students." The Law School's interest is not simply "to assure within its student body some specified percentage of a particular group merely because of its race or ethnic origin." [330] *Bakke*, 438 U.S., at 307 (opinion of Powell, J.). That would amount to outright racial balancing, which is patently unconstitutional. *Ibid.* Rather, the Law School's concept of critical mass is defined by reference to the educational benefits that diversity is designed to produce.

These benefits are substantial. As the District Court emphasized, the Law School's admissions policy promotes "cross-racial understanding," helps to break down racial stereotypes, and "enables [students] to better understand persons of different races." These benefits are "important and laudable," because "classroom discussion is livelier, more spirited, and simply more enlightening and interesting" when the students have "the greatest possible variety of backgrounds."

The Law School's claim of a compelling interest is further bolstered by its *amici*, who point to the educational benefits that flow from student body diversity. In addition to the expert studies and reports entered into evidence at trial, numerous studies show that student body diversity promotes learning outcomes, and "better prepares students for an increasingly diverse workforce and society, and better prepares them as professionals." Brief for American Educational Research Association et al. as *Amici Curiae* 3; see, *e.g.,* W. Bowen & D. Bok, The Shape of the River (1998); Diversity Challenged: Evidence on the Impact of Affirmative Action (G. Orfield & M. Kurlaender eds.2001); Compelling Interest: Examining the Evidence on Racial Dynamics in Colleges and Universities (M. Chang, D. Witt, J. Jones, & K. Hakuta eds.2003).

These benefits are not theoretical but real, as major American businesses have made clear that the skills needed in today's increasingly global marketplace can only be developed through exposure to widely diverse people, cultures, ideas, and viewpoints. Brief for 3M et al. as *Amici Curiae* [331] 5; Brief for General Motors Corp. as *Amicus Curiae* 3–4. What is more, high-ranking retired officers and civilian leaders of the United States military assert that, "[b]ased on [their] decades of experience," a "highly qualified, racially diverse officer corps . . . is essential to the military's ability to fulfill its principle mission to provide national security." Brief for Julius W. Becton, Jr., et al. as *Amici Curiae* 5. The primary sources for the Nation's officer corps are the service academies and the Reserve Officers Training Corps (ROTC), the latter comprising students already admitted to participating colleges and universities. *Ibid.* At present, "the military cannot achieve an officer corps that is *both* highly qualified *and* racially diverse unless the service academies and the ROTC used limited race-conscious recruiting and admissions policies." *Ibid.* (emphasis in original). To fulfill its mission, the military "must be selective in admissions for training and education for the officer corps, *and* it must train and educate a highly qualified, racially diverse officer corps in a racially diverse educational setting." *Id.*, at 29 (emphasis in original). We agree that "[i]t requires only a small step from this analysis to conclude that our country's other most selective institutions must remain both diverse and selective." *Ibid.* . . .

We have repeatedly acknowledged the overriding importance of preparing students for work and citizenship, describing education as pivotal to "sustaining our political and cultural heritage" with a fundamental role in maintaining the fabric of society. . . . This Court has long recognized that "education . . . is the very foundation of good citizenship." For this reason, the diffusion of knowledge and opportunity through public institutions of higher education must be accessible to all individuals regardless of race or ethnicity. The United States, as *amicus curiae,* affirms that "[e]nsuring that public institutions are open and available to all segments of American [332] society, including people of all races and ethnicities, represents a paramount government objective." Brief for United States as *Amicus Curiae* 13. And, "[n]owhere is the importance of such openness more acute than in the context of higher education." *Ibid.* Effective participation by members of all racial and ethnic groups in the civic life of our Nation is essential if the dream of one Nation, indivisible, is to be realized.

Moreover, universities, and in particular, law schools, represent the training ground for a large number of our Nation's leaders. . . .

In order to cultivate a set of leaders with legitimacy in the eyes of the citizenry, it is necessary that the path to leadership be visibly open to talented and qualified individuals of every race and ethnicity. All members of our heterogeneous society must have confidence in the openness and integrity of the educational institutions that provide this training. As we have recognized, law schools "cannot be effective in isolation from the individuals and institutions with which the law interacts." Access to legal education (and thus the legal profession) must be inclusive of talented and qualified individuals of every race and ethnicity, so that all members of our heterogeneous society [333] may participate in the educational institutions that provide the training and education necessary to succeed in America.

The Law School does not premise its need for critical mass on "any belief that minority students always (or even consistently) express some characteristic minority viewpoint on any issue." To the contrary, diminishing the force of such stereotypes is both a crucial part of the Law School's mission, and one that it cannot accomplish with only token numbers of minority students. Just as growing up in a particular region or having particular professional experiences is likely to affect an individual's views, so too is one's own, unique experience of being a racial minority in a society, like our own, in which race unfortunately still matters. The Law School has determined, based on its experience and expertise, that a "critical mass" of underrepresented minorities is necessary to further its compelling interest in securing the educational benefits of a diverse student body. . . .

To be narrowly tailored, a race-conscious admissions program cannot use a quota system—it cannot "insulat[e] each category of applicants with certain desired qualifications from competition with all other applicants." *Bakke*, 438 U.S., at 315 (opinion of Powell, J.). Instead, a university may consider race or ethnicity only as a " 'plus' in a particular applicant's file," without "insulat[ing] the individual from comparison with all other candidates for the available seats." *Id.*, at 317. In other words, an admissions program must be "flexible enough to consider all pertinent elements of diversity in light of the particular qualifications of each applicant, and to place them on the same footing for consideration, although not necessarily according them the same weight." *Ibid.* . . . [334]

We find that the Law School's admissions program bears the hallmarks of a narrowly tailored plan. As Justice Powell made clear in *Bakke,* truly individualized consideration demands that race be used in a flexible, nonmechanical way. It follows from this mandate that universities cannot establish quotas for members of certain racial groups or put members of those groups on separate admissions tracks. See *id.,* at 315–316. Nor can universities insulate applicants who belong to certain racial or ethnic groups from the competition for admission. *Ibid.* Universities can, however, consider race or ethnicity more flexibly as a "plus" factor in the context of individualized consideration of each and every applicant. *Ibid.*

[335] We are satisfied that the Law School's admissions program, like the Harvard plan described by Justice Powell, does not operate as a quota. Properly understood, a "quota" is a program in which a certain fixed number or proportion of opportunities are "reserved exclusively for certain minority groups." . . .

[336] That a race-conscious admissions program does not operate as a quota does not, by itself, satisfy the requirement of individualized consideration. When using race as a "plus" [337] factor in university admissions, a university's admissions program must remain flexible enough to ensure that each applicant is evaluated as an individual and not in a way that makes an applicant's race or ethnicity the defining feature of his or her application. The importance of this individualized consideration in the context of a race-conscious admissions program is paramount. See *Bakke,* 438 U.S., at 318, n. 52.

Here, the Law School engages in a highly individualized, holistic review of each applicant's file, giving serious consideration to all the ways an applicant might contribute to a diverse educational environment. The Law School affords this individualized consideration to applicants of all races. . . .

[338] What is more, the Law School actually gives substantial weight to diversity factors besides race. The Law School frequently accepts nonminority applicants with grades and test scores lower than underrepresented minority applicants (and other nonminority applicants) who are rejected. See Brief for Respondent Bollinger et al. 10. This shows that the Law School seriously weighs many other diversity factors besides race that can make a real and dispositive difference for nonminority applicants as well. By this [339] flexible approach, the Law School sufficiently

takes into account, in practice as well as in theory, a wide variety of characteristics besides race and ethnicity that contribute to a diverse student body. . . .

Petitioner and the United States argue that the Law School's plan is not narrowly tailored because race-neutral means exist to obtain the educational benefits of student body diversity that the Law School seeks. We disagree. Narrow tailoring does not require exhaustion of every conceivable race-neutral alternative. Nor does it require a university to choose between maintaining a reputation for excellence or fulfilling a commitment to provide educational opportunities to members of all racial groups. Narrow tailoring does, however, require serious, good faith consideration of workable race-neutral alternatives that will achieve the diversity the university seeks.

[340] We agree with the Court of Appeals that the Law School sufficiently considered workable race-neutral alternatives. The District Court took the Law School to task for failing to consider race-neutral alternatives such as "using a lottery system" or "decreasing the emphasis for all applicants on undergraduate GPA and LSAT scores." But these alternatives would require a dramatic sacrifice of diversity, the academic quality of all admitted students, or both.

The Law School's current admissions program considers race as one factor among many, in an effort to assemble a student body that is diverse in ways broader than race. Because a lottery would make that kind of nuanced judgment impossible, it would effectively sacrifice all other educational values, not to mention every other kind of diversity. So too with the suggestion that the Law School simply lower admissions standards for all students, a drastic remedy that would require the Law School to become a much different institution and sacrifice a vital component of its educational mission. The United States advocates "percentage plans," recently adopted by public undergraduate institutions in Texas, Florida, and California, to guarantee admission to all students above a certain class-rank threshold in every high school in the State. The United States does not, however, explain how such plans could work for graduate and professional schools. Moreover, even assuming such plans are race-neutral, they may preclude the university from conducting the individualized assessments necessary to assemble a student body that is not just racially diverse, but diverse along all the qualities valued by the university. We are satisfied that the Law School adequately considered race-neutral alternatives currently capable of producing a critical mass without forcing the Law School to abandon the academic selectivity that is the cornerstone of its educational mission.

[341] We acknowledge that "there are serious problems of justice connected with the idea of preference itself." *Bakke,* 438 U.S., at 298. Narrow tailoring, therefore, requires that a race-conscious admissions program not unduly harm members of any racial group. Even remedial race-based governmental action generally "remains subject to continuing oversight to assure that it will work the least harm possible to other innocent persons competing for the benefit." *Id.,* at 308. To be narrowly tailored, a race-conscious admissions program must not "unduly burden individuals who are not members of the favored racial and ethnic groups."

We are satisfied that the Law School's admissions program does not. Because the Law School considers "all pertinent elements of diversity," it can (and does) select nonminority applicants who have greater potential to enhance student body diversity over underrepresented minority applicants. . . .

We agree that, in the context of its individualized inquiry into the possible diversity contributions of all applicants, the Law School's race-conscious admissions program does not unduly harm nonminority applicants.

We are mindful, however, that "[a] core purpose of the Fourteenth Amendment was to do away with all governmentally imposed discrimination based on race." [342] Accordingly, race-conscious admissions policies must be limited in time. This requirement reflects that racial classifications, however compelling their goals, are potentially so dangerous that they may be employed no more broadly than the interest demands. Enshrining a permanent justification for racial preferences would offend this fundamental equal protection principle. We see no reason to exempt race-conscious admissions programs from the requirement that all governmental use of race must have a logical end point. The Law School, too, concedes that all "race-conscious programs must have reasonable durational limits." . . .

[343] We take the Law School at its word that it would "like nothing better than to find a race-neutral admissions formula"

and will terminate its race-conscious admissions program as soon as practicable. It has been 25 years since Justice Powell first approved the use of race to further an interest in student body diversity in the context of public higher education. Since that time, the number of minority applicants with high grades and test scores has indeed increased. We expect that 25 years from now, the use of racial preferences will no longer be necessary to further the interest approved today.

In summary, the Equal Protection Clause does not prohibit the Law School's narrowly tailored use of race in admissions decisions to further a compelling interest in obtaining the educational benefits that flow from a diverse student body. Consequently, petitioner's statutory claims based on Title VI and 42 U.S.C. § 1981 also fail. . . .

Justice Thomas, in his *Grutter* [130]dissent joined by Justice Scalia, challenged the Michigan diversity policy in a provocative fashion:

[349–50] Frederick Douglass, speaking to a group of abolitionists almost 140 years ago, delivered a message lost on today's majority:

"In regard to the colored people, there is always more that is benevolent, I perceive, than just, manifested towards us. What I ask for the negro is not benevolence, not pity, not sympathy, but simply *justice*. The American people have always been anxious to know what they shall do with us. . . . I have had but one answer from the beginning. Do nothing with us! Your doing has already played the mischief with us. Do nothing with us! If the apples will not remain on the tree of their own strength, if they are worm-eaten at the core, if they are early ripe and disposed to fall, let them fall! . . . And if the negro cannot stand on his own legs, let him fall also. All I ask is, give him a chance to stand on his own legs! Let him alone! . . . Your interference is doing him positive injury." . . .

[364] The Court's deference to the Law School's conclusion that its racial experimentation leads to educational benefits will, if adhered to, have serious collateral consequences. The Court relies heavily on social science evidence to justify its deference. [B]ut see also Rothman, Lipset, & Nevitte, Racial Diversity Reconsidered, 151 Public Interest 25 (2003) (finding that the racial mix of a student body produced by racial discrimination of the type practiced by the Law School in fact hinders students'

perception of academic quality). The Court never acknowledges, however, the growing evidence that racial (and other sorts) of heterogeneity actually impairs learning among black students. See, *e.g.,* Flowers & Pascarella, Cognitive Effects of College Racial Composition on African American Students After 3 Years of College, 40 J. of College Student Development 669, 674 (1999) (concluding that black students experience superior cognitive development at Historically Black Colleges (HBCs) and that, even among blacks, "a substantial diversity moderates the cognitive effects of attending an HBC"); Allen, The Color of Success: African-American College Student Outcomes at Predominantly White and Historically Black Public Colleges and Universities, 62 Harv. Educ. Rev. 26, 35 (1992) (finding that black students attending HBCs report higher academic achievement than those attending predominantly white colleges). . . .

[372] The Law School tantalizes unprepared students with the promise of a University of Michigan degree and all of the opportunities that it offers. These overmatched students take the bait, only to find that they cannot succeed in the cauldron of competition. And this mismatch crisis is not restricted to elite institutions. See T. Sowell, Race and Culture 176–177 (1994) ("Even if most minority students are able to meet the normal standards at the 'average' range of colleges and universities, the systematic mismatching of minority students begun at the top can mean that such students are generally overmatched throughout all levels of higher education"). Indeed, to cover the tracks of the aestheticists, this cruel farce of racial discrimination must continue—in selection for the Michigan Law Review, see University of Michigan Law School Student Handbook 2002–2003, pp. 39–40 (noting the presence of a "diversity plan" for admission to the review), and in hiring at law firms and for judicial clerkships—until the "beneficiaries" are no longer tolerated. While these students may graduate with law degrees, there is no evidence that they have received a qualitatively better legal education (or become better lawyers) than if they had gone to a less "elite" law school for which they were better prepared. And the aestheticists will never address the real problems facing "underrepresented minorities," instead continuing their social experiments on other people's children.

[373] Beyond the harm the Law School's racial discrimination visits upon its test subjects, no social science has disproved the notion that this discrimination "engender[s] attitudes of superiority

or, alternatively, provoke[s] resentment among those who believe that they have been wronged by the government's use of race." "These programs stamp minorities with a badge of inferiority and may cause them to develop dependencies or to adopt an attitude that they are 'entitled' to preferences."

It is uncontested that each year, the Law School admits a handful of blacks who would be admitted in the absence of racial discrimination. Who can differentiate between those who belong and those who do not? The majority of blacks are admitted to the Law School because of discrimination, and because of this policy all are tarred as undeserving. This problem of stigma does not depend on determinacy as to whether those stigmatized are actually the "beneficiaries" of racial discrimination. When blacks take positions in the highest places of government, industry, or academia, it is an open question today whether their skin color played a part in their advancement. The question itself is the stigma—because either racial discrimination did play a role, in which case the person may be deemed "otherwise unqualified," or it did not, in which case asking the question itself unfairly marks those blacks who would succeed without discrimination. Is this what the Court means by "visibly open"? . . .

[377–78] Indeed, the very existence of racial discrimination of the type practiced by the Law School may impede the narrowing of the LSAT testing gap. An applicant's LSAT score can improve dramatically with preparation, but such preparation is a cost, and there must be sufficient benefits attached to an improved score to justify additional study. Whites scoring between 163 and 167 on the LSAT are routinely rejected by the Law School, and thus whites aspiring to admission at the Law School have every incentive to improve their score to levels above that range. Blacks, on the other hand, are nearly guaranteed admission if they score above 155. As admission prospects approach certainty, there is no incentive for the black applicant to continue to prepare for the LSAT once he is reasonably assured of achieving the requisite score. It is far from certain that the LSAT test-taker's behavior is responsive to the Law School's admissions policies. Nevertheless, the possibility remains that this racial discrimination will help fulfill the bigot's prophecy about black underperformance—just as it confirms the conspiracy theorist's belief that "institutional racism" is at fault for every racial disparity in our society [378]. . . .

For the immediate future . . . the majority has placed its *imprima-tur* on a practice that can only weaken the principle of equality embodied in the Declaration of Independence and the Equal Protection Clause. "Our Constitution is color-blind, and neither knows nor tolerates classes among citizens." *Plessy v. Ferguson*, 163 U.S. 537, 559 (1896) (Harlan, J., dissenting). It has been nearly 140 years since Frederick Douglass asked the intellectual ancestors of the Law School to "[d]o nothing with us!" and the Nation adopted the Fourteenth Amendment. Now we must wait another 25 years to see this principle of equality vindicated. I therefore respectfully dissent.

Dissenting, and joined by Justices Kennedy, Thomas, and Scalia, Chief Justice Rehnquist rejected the Law School preference policy as one that did not extend individual consideration to each applicant. Rather, "the Law School has managed its admissions . . . to extend offers of admission to members of selected minority groups in proportion to their statistical representation in the applicant pool. But this is precisely the type of racial balancing that the Court itself calls 'patently unconstitutional.' "[131] In support of this view, Justice Kennedy offered the following[132]:

There was little deviation among admitted minority students during the years from 1995 to 1998. The percentage of enrolled minorities fluctuated only by 0.3%, from 13.5% to 13.8%. The number of minority students to whom offers were extended varied by just a slightly greater magnitude of 2.2%, from the high of 15.6% in 1995 to the low of 13.4% in 1998.

[390] The District Court relied on this uncontested fact to draw an inference that the Law School's pursuit of critical mass mutated into the equivalent of a quota. 137 F. Supp. 2d 821, 851 (ED Mich. 2001). Admittedly, there were greater fluctuations among enrolled minorities in the preceding years, 1987–1994, by as much as 5 or 6%. The percentage of minority offers, however, at no point fell below 12%, historically defined by the Law School as the bottom of its critical mass range. The greater variance during the earlier years, in any event, does not dispel suspicion that the school engaged in racial balancing. The data would be consistent with an inference that the Law School modified its target only twice, in 1991 (from 13% to 19%), and then again in 1995 (back from 20% to 13%). The intervening year, 1993, when the percentage dropped to 14.5%, could be an aberration, caused by the school's miscalculation as to how many applicants with offers

would accept or by its redefinition, made in April 1992, of which minority groups were entitled to race-based preference. . . .

The narrow fluctuation band raises an inference that the Law School subverted individual determination, and strict scrutiny requires the Law School to overcome the inference.

In a companion case, *Gratz v. Bollinger*(2003),[133] Chief Justice Rehnquist contributed the majority opinion regarding the Michigan undergraduate admission practice of granting twenty points to underrepresented minority applicants to the College of Literature, Science, and the Arts (LSA). That opinion concluded that the twenty-point policy failed strict scrutiny's narrow tailoring test[134] in that it frustrated the individual consideration required by the Powell doctrine:

> The current LSA policy does not provide such individualized consideration. The LSA's policy automatically distributes 20 points to every single applicant from an "underrepresented minority" group, as defined by the University. The only consideration that accompanies this distribution of points is a factual review of an application to determine whether an individual is a member of one of these minority groups. Moreover, unlike Justice Powell's example, where the race of a "particular black applicant" could be considered without being decisive, see *Bakke*, 438 U.S., at 317, the LSA's automatic distribution of 20 points has the effect of making "the factor of race . . . decisive" for virtually every minimally qualified underrepresented minority applicant.[135]

Justice Souter disagreed, arguing that the twenty-point augmentation was a procedure that fell acceptably in the family of *Grutter* requirements:[136]

> The record does not describe a system with a quota like the one struck down in *Bakke*, which "insulate[d]" all nonminority candidates from competition from certain seats. The *Bakke* plan "focused *solely* on ethnic diversity" and effectively told nonminority applicants that "[n]o matter how strong their qualifications, quantitative and extracurricular, including their own potential for contribution to educational diversity, they are never afforded the chance to compete with applicants from the preferred groups for the [set-aside] special admissions seats." . . .

The plan here, in contrast, lets all applicants compete for all places and values an applicant's offering for any place not only on grounds of race, but on grades, test scores, strength of high school, quality of course of study, residence, alumni relationships, leadership, personal character, socioeconomic disadvantage, athletic ability, and quality of a personal essay. *Ante*, at 6. A nonminority applicant who scores highly in these other categories can readily garner a selection index exceeding that of a minority applicant who gets the 20-point bonus. . . .

On the face of things, however, this assignment of specific points does not set race apart from all other weighted considerations. Nonminority students may receive 20 points for athletic ability, socioeconomic disadvantage, attendance at a socioeconomically disadvantaged or predominantly minority high school, or at the Provost's discretion; they may also receive 10 points for being residents of Michigan, 6 for residence in an underrepresented Michigan county, 5 for leadership and service, and so on. . . .

The very nature of a college's permissible practice of awarding value to racial diversity means that race must be considered in a way that increases some applicants' chances for admission. Since college admission is not left entirely to inarticulate intuition, it is hard to see what is inappropriate in assigning some stated value to a relevant characteristic, whether it be reasoning ability, writing style, running speed, or minority race. Justice Powell's plus factors necessarily are assigned some values. The college simply does by a numbered scale what the law school accomplishes in its "holistic review," the distinction does not imply that applicants to the undergraduate college are denied individualized consideration or a fair chance to compete on the basis of all the various merits their applications may disclose. . . .

Drawing on admissions systems used at public universities in California, Florida, and Texas, the United States contends that Michigan could get student diversity in satisfaction of its compelling interest by guaranteeing admission to a fixed percentage of the top students from each high school in Michigan. Brief for United States as *Amicus Curiae* 18.

While there is nothing unconstitutional about such a practice, it nonetheless suffers from a serious disadvantage. It is the disadvantage of deliberate obfuscation. The "percentage plans" are just as race conscious as the point scheme (and fairly so), but they get their racially diverse results without saying directly what they are doing or why they are doing it. In contrast, Michigan states its purpose directly and, if this were a doubtful case for me, I would be tempted to give Michigan an extra point of its own for its frankness. Equal protection cannot become an exercise in which the winners are the ones who hide the ball.

Diversity on Campus Continued

In 1997, the Supreme Court was presented the opportunity to rule on the constitutionality of nonremedial diversity policy when it accepted *certiorari* in *Piscataway v. Taxman*,[137] where the Third Circuit Court of Appeals ruled that Title VII of the 1964 Civil Rights Act prohibited the nonremedial layoff of a white public school teacher and the retention in the same job of a black teacher. Since the teachers were equal in seniority and qualification, and since the sole reason for layoff was racial preference, the case seemed to furnish a definitive, long-overdue vehicle for adjudicating nonremedial affirmative action. But it was not to be. After *certiorari* was granted, the parties settled the litigation by agreement, thereby thwarting the Court's apparent desire to clarify the law. The onset of this High Court clarification in *Grutter/Gratz* was to take another five years. Nevertheless, the Clinton administration's *Piscataway* brief should be studied and compared with the Fifth Circuit's position on diversity in *Hopwood*.

The brief argued that a public employer could constitutionally take race into account for nonremedial purposes if race consciousness was narrowly tailored to meet a compelling governmental purpose.[138] This document went on to say:

> There are some circumstances . . . in which an employer should be permitted to demonstrate that taking race into account for nonremedial purposes is narrowly tailored to further a compelling interest. For example, if an undercover officer is needed to infiltrate a racially homogeneous gang, a law enforcement agency must have the flexibility to assign an officer of the same race to that task. Against the backdrop of racial unrest, a diverse police force may be essential to secure the public support and cooperation that is necessary for preventing and solving crime. Prison institutions may find it impossible to cope with racial tensions without an integrated work force. And school districts may responsibly conclude that a diverse faculty is essential to dispel students' stereotypes and promote mutual understanding and respect. The careful, tailored use of race to serve similarly compelling goals would satisfy the Constitution's strict scrutiny standard.[139]

The brief is surely correct in its stress on the need "to dispel students' stereotypes and promote mutual understanding and respect," a traditional, affirmative action remedial goal subscribed to by the High Court in *Grutter*.[140]

The preferential admissions controversy has focused primarily on the practices of selective/competitive colleges and universities. Some argue that "[m]ore selective schools rely on preferences to a greater degree, but even second and third-tier schools discriminate on the basis of race."[141] To others, race/ethnic-based admissions decisions do not seem to be factors in entrance policies at the bulk of the nation's colleges, given the relative ease of admission.[142] The most persuasive evidence to Holzer and Neumark informed them that for the majority of colleges, the impact of race/ethnic preferences is quite small. The impact of affirmative action preferences is greatest at elite schools.[143] They wrote as follows:

> Thus, while the aggregate effect of affirmative action in university admissions seems quite small, its effect in generating the highly educated graduates of elite colleges/universities and graduate programs is quite substantial. But these findings also suggest that the displacement of white applicants by minorities, even at the elite schools, is not very large—because blacks and Hispanics still account for only 10–15% of all students at these schools, even with affirmative action.[144]

Attendance at elite schools is regarded by minority advocates as an important avenue for individual and protected-group progress. Some scoff at this view. Thus, Martin Trow, emeritus professor at Berkeley, wrote: "The notion that you have to go to one of the most selective universities to fulfill your potential, or to become a leader in America, betrays an elitist conception of American life."[145]

Abigail Thernstrom, in her critique of Bowen and Bok's *The Shape of the River*, wrote that those authors argue "that affirmative action in the highly selective institutions created the black middle class. It's an . . . [h]istorical point; blacks made impressive and rapid gains in the decades before preferences. Moreover, where did they get the notion that in our wonderfully open and fluid society, degrees from certain colleges are make-or-break? . . . In fact, as they surely know, the economically and professionally successful of all races started out in a wide variety of schools."[146]

Strident administrative support for university affirmative action, and the fog of professorial silence about it are not unique. It appears that many academics would at least silently concur with a Berkeley professor's assertion that there is an "unwritten compact" at selective schools not to discuss affirmative action.[147] But significant opposition to affirmative action in higher education does exist. The appellate opinions in *Hopwood, Johnson,* cited above are important legal manifestations of that opposition, as are the Supreme Court dissents in *Grutter*. California's constitutional amendment (Proposition 209) is another. Similar referenda were ratified by the people in the states of Washington[148] and Nebraska[149] as statutes, and in Michigan as a constitutional amendment,[150] that is, the 209 states. What follows are excerpts from California's Proposition 209:[151]

California Proposition 209 (1996)

The state shall not discriminate against, or grant preferential treatment to any individual or group on the basis of race, sex, color, ethnicity, or national origin in the operation of public employment, public education, or public contracting. . . .

Nothing in this section shall be interpreted as prohibiting bona fide qualifications based on sex which are reasonably necessary to the normal operations of public employment, public education, or public contracting.

Nothing in this section shall be interpreted as invalidating any court order or consent decree which is in force as of the effective date of this section.

Nothing in this section shall be interpreted as prohibiting action which must be taken to establish or maintain eligibility for any federal program where ineligibility would result in a loss of federal funds to the state. . . .

This section shall be self-executing. If any part or parts of this section are found to be in conflict with federal law or the United States Constitution, the section shall be implemented to the maximum extent that federal law and the United States Constitution permit. Any provision held invalid shall be separable from the remaining portions of the section.

Faced with the difficulties presented by *Hopwood*, Proposition 209, and similar views, diversity advocates have adopted measures meant to facilitate the presence of underrepresented minorities without seeming to violate bans on race or ethnic preferences.[152] Thus, after *Hopwood*, the Texas Legislature mandated that those high school graduates who rank within the upper 10 percent of their classes be admitted to Texas public colleges.[153] In Florida, the Board of Regents endorsed the governor's proposal allowing those who fell within the upper 20 percent of their high school classes a guaranteed place within the ten public universities of that State.[154] The University of California Regents also adopted a high school class-standing plan guaranteeing those students who fall within the upper 4 percent of their high school class a seat at one of the University of California (UC) campuses. Do these state percentage plans—racially motivated as they seem to be—conform with *Grutter*'s requirement of individual/multidimensional assessment where race is used as a factor? Left unclarified in the California plan is the issue of which students are to be restricted to the less-prestigious UC schools and what difference it makes. Also left hanging is whether the California outreach efforts (referenced below) can pass muster under Proposition 209.

Recent studies concerned with admissions to "flagship" universities, report that in Florida, California, and Texas—states with class-standing percentage plans—the primary beneficiaries have been Asian Americans who have been long considered to be central losers in race/ethnic-conscious practices at selective public universities. In a study published in a 2008 edition of *Interactions: UCLA Journal of Education and Informational Studies*, researchers tracked freshman enrollment from1990 through 2005 at the University of Texas (Austin); the University of Florida; and the University of California (Los Angeles, Berkeley, San Diego). The black share of enrollment at the cited schools generally declined. The Hispanic enrollment pattern was mixed, and white enrollment declined slightly. Asian Americans filled the gap left by blacks and Hispanics at these flagships. Examples: Asian American freshman enrollment rose from 37.30 percent in 1995 to 46.59 percent in 2004 at UC-Berkeley. Similar large Asian American increases occurred at UC-San Diego and UCLA. At U Florida, the Asian American presence grew from 7.50 percent (2000) to 8.65 percent (2005); at Texas, in the same time frame, from 14.26 to 17.33 percent.[155]

What kind of affirmative action ban is imposed in the 209 states? One interpretation is that 209 prohibits race/ethnic/gender-conscious behavior which is the sole or dominant reason for a particular result such as being admitted to a college. This was the position of affirmative action advocates in Michigan in connection with the 209 version adopted in that state. University of Michigan officials insisted, however, that race/ethnicity would no longer be a factor in their decisions.[156] If Proposition 209 imposed a comprehensive race/ethnic consciousness ban, does the California 4 percent plan—meant to channel more minorities to the University of California—pass muster?

The "loss of federal funds" exemption in 209 warrants attention. It reads: "Nothing in this section shall be interpreted as prohibiting action which must be undertaken to establish or maintain eligibility for any federal program where ineligibility would result in a loss of federal funds to the state." The City/County of San Francisco and a few other public entities have sought to safeguard their affirmative action efforts through this exemption.[157] The vehicle that could result in the loss of federal funds for the abolition of ethno-racial affirmative action at universities is the Education Department's administrative regulations, which, implementing Title VI of the 1964 Civil Rights Act,[158] bar the recipients of federal funds (e.g., public universities) from disparately impacting racial and ethnic minorities.[159] The legal question of whether the 209 states can suffer financial loss stemming from Title VI's regulations is an open one. These regulations coexist with a *Bakke* majority which ruled that Title VI limited only intentional/disparate-treatment discrimination.[160] Even if the regulations apply to public universities in the 209 states, how is the disparate impacting of minority students to be determined? Unexplored territory indeed!

It is claimed that affirmative action bans can be easily thwarted. Professor Richard Sander, whose work has been discussed (see 136–39), wrote that Justice O'Connor was either "naïve" or "cynical" in calling for painstaking individual assessment in *Grutter* when admissions takes race into account. Nothing is easier than presenting *Gratz*-like point schemes and even quotas as individual assessment plans, and such disguises can be anticipated.[161] When *Gratz* banned the point scheme at Michigan, other campuses using automatic point augmentation (e.g., UMass and Ohio State), announced that they had switched to "holistic" individual assessment analysis conforming to *Grutter*.[162] "Holism" is extensively practiced at the UC system. Holism surely permits disguises.

Holistic review at the University of California takes into account grades, scores on standardized tests, leadership ability, life's challenges, and the like.[163] Thus, when first confronted with 209's barrier against using race, ethnicity, and gender, UC Irvine developed a most elaborate applicant review system involving (in addition to grades and SAT performance) considerations about leadership/initiative; honors/awards; personal challenges; geographic challenges (which incorporated the quality of the geographically available educational resources); self and civic awareness, and specialized knowledge.[164] These "expanded criteria" "resulted in significant admissions gains for underrepresented ethnic groups—particularly African Americans, American Indians, and Chicanos."[165] Admissions officers reported that "we learned . . . that it is possible for a selective university to admit an academically well-prepared and diverse freshman class without the use of race or ethnicity as a factor in the review process."[166] Reportedly, deft "fiddling" of this sort also enabled Berkeley, in 1999, to admit 305 more undergraduate minorities than it had a year before when 209 was inaugurated. A similar increase occurred at Boalt Hall, the Berkeley law school.[167] Most undergraduate minorities who were denied admission to Berkeley in 1998 "cascaded" to the less-prestigious UC campuses.[168] According to one federal judge's extensive review, between 1995–2000 the numbers of minorities in the UC system as a whole declined only 1 percent. And there was an increased minority population at three campuses.[169] The most elite UC schools experienced significant declines in minority populations which would have been greater had not intense drives been undertaken to recruit qualified blacks and Hispanics. At UCLA, for example, more than two hundred new, need/merit scholarships were created, and these helped recruit minorities.[170]

The UCLA need/merit scholarships were not enough to prevent a self-described crisis in 2006 when only 103 blacks said that they would attend that campus as freshmen, that is, only 2 percent of the incoming class—the lowest number in thirty years. The next year's percentage figure was 4.5. Producing this change was a very vigorous outreach effort; phone-a-thons; hosting fifty black admittees, flying them to the university for a whirlwind of activities; taking into account life's challenges, and special circumstances along with grades; and the raising of private donations of $1.75 million guaranteeing each black freshman at least $1,000.[171] Was not the connection between the private donors and the state such as to make the process in reality state action banned by 209?

If the entire University of California is considered, the role of holistic admissions seems impressive. In the year before 209, blacks, Hispanics, and American Indians made up 18.8 percent of the UC student body.[172] Twenty-three percent of those admitted in 2007 were members of those minority groups.[173] As of 2006, however, the black and Hispanic presence at the elite UC schools had not regained the level that existed prior to 209's implementation.[174]

Access to top schools is a concern to both minority advocates and those who find the small numbers of poorer students at those places troublesome. Affirmative action based on family income and background, together with race, would—to some researchers—benefit both the white poor and minority students at the expense of wealthier whites. Others regard "fusion" affirmative action as certain to reduce minorities in selective schools, given the larger number of white poor with the grades and test scores permitting access to academe's best.[175]

Some scholars have concluded that increasing the numbers of minorities and low-income students at elite campuses could be accomplished by giving less weight to standardized test scores and more weight to such things as high school class ranking.[176] At one time, the Educational Testing Service (ETS)—the creator of the Scholastic Aptitude Test (SAT)—itself reportedly planned to confront the minority performance issue. ETS calculated expected SAT scores based on fourteen different categories including family income, parental education, high school socioeconomic mix. It concluded that Hispanics and African Americans will, as groups, score lower than whites or Asians. However, blacks and Hispanics who score 200 or more points higher than expected were to be dubbed "strivers," and this status, so ETS suggested, could be used by admissions officers as a positive, equity promoting, race/ethnic-blind eligibility factor.[177] Obviously, the "striver" scheme is hardly race/ethnic-blind. Further, and questionably enough, it fosters group stereotyping. Perhaps these dimensions helped ETS to shelve the plan.

A novel (Bial-Dale) "Adaptability" test was experimentally employed by a number of universities, and "could provide one answer if we lose affirmative action,"[178] opined Gary Orfield, who helped oversee the test's implementation. The Bial-Dale analysis tested what its promoters call "non-cognitive" skills such as the ability to participate in the group construction of "Lego" models. These "non-cognitive" tests were supplemented with extensive interviews focusing on how students solve problems, to wit, how poor grades can be remedied. This pilot scheme was slated for use in seven hundred New York public high schools where the majority of (but not all) students were African American or Hispanic.[179] One must wonder whether the Bial-Dale approach was administered on a race/ethnic-blind basis. Also, is performance in a group an appropriate admissions measuring device?

The quest for minority students has indeed been intense. When *Hopwood* ended overt race/ethnic preferences by public universities in Texas, many universities from other states outside of the Fifth Circuit's jurisdiction, increased their efforts to recruit minorities in Texas. Some schools (Indiana University, the University of Iowa, Tulane, and Washington University) either opened recruiting offices in Texas, or sent representatives to reside in that state for extended periods. Financial aid has been a primary "raiding" tool. The University of Oklahoma awarded about $3 million in financial aid to Texas students in 1999, some 16 percent of its total student aid budget. The average Oklahoma award for a Texas minority student was $4,052; that for Texas whites, $3,207. The University of Iowa offered $5,000 annual scholarships for meritorious minority students. Affirmative action opponents saw their efforts frustrated by out-of-state raiders who practiced what Texas officials were forbidden to do. Uniform rules were demanded.[180] "National law should be, in fact, national," argued one law professor from the University of Georgia, "the Constitution shouldn't mean one thing in Texas and another in Georgia. The solution to that is for the United States Supreme Court to clarify what national constitutional law is."[181] That Court did not speak until *Grutter/Gratz* in 2003.

Financial aid has been an important weapon in the affirmative action arsenal. California and Texas schools have responded with new financial aid packages. Mention has already been made of the two hundred new merit/need scholarships at UCLA, and the privately raised contributions to confront the low black enrollment crisis of 2006. The University of Texas at Austin and Texas A&M have developed race/ethnic-blind Adversity Index scholarships which award aid to poorer students who come from low-achieving high schools. Blacks and Hispanics—only 11 percent of the total number admitted to these schools in 1999—were awarded 61 percent of the adversity scholarships.[182]

During the 1990s, the U.S. Education Department's interpretation of the legitimacy of race/ethnic-exclusive financial aid had a frenzied history, and one that reflected the unsettled nature of affirmative action law. Late in 1990, that department's head of the Office for Civil Rights (OCR) insisted that the department viewed race/ethnic exclusivity in financial aid as generally illegal. Stormy outcries followed, as did a departmental directive allowing public colleges to use private or state funds for minority-only financial aid so long as they did not use university-targeted, public appropriations for that purpose. However, when a new secretary was installed in March 1991, a new policy was announced: the 1990 directives could be ignored, and—pending a review of the issue—universities could revert to their traditional affirmative action ways in the distribution of financial aid. The Bush administration ended before final regulations were issued on the matter. New rules were issued by Secretary Riley of the Clinton administration in February 1994. These guidelines permitted public university aid reserved for minorities in order to either remedy past discrimination or promote diversity. Shortly thereafter, the Fourth Circuit in *Podberesky v. Kirwan* (1994),[183] declared unconstitutional the University of Maryland's Banaker scholarships available only for blacks.[184]

OCR's chief explained why the department did not change its guidelines after *Podberesky*. She argued that OCR and the Fourth Circuit agreed that minority aid targeting was permissible to remedy the present effects of past discrimination; the difference was over what kind of "present effects" are to be cured, and who is responsible—key disparate-impact issues indeed. In any event, the department would not challenge aid exclusivity, leaving that burden to private plaintiffs.[185] The former (Bush administration) OCR head regarded this non-challenge posture as "irresponsible." "It's allowing," he said, "discrimination to take place unless a private individual sues."[186] To him, the OCR's duty was to enforce the law, not ignore it.[187] *Grutter/Gratz*—with their emphasis that race could be but one factor in collegiate awards—clearly made race/ethnic-exclusivity financial aid constitutionally suspect. Accordingly, many colleges opened their minority scholarships to all races. Williams, Indiana University, and Carnegie Mellon were among them.[188]

The Formerly *De Jure* Segregated Universities: The Historically Black Colleges and the Traditionally White Institutions

At one time, nineteen states racially segregated higher educational institutions, creating the "Historically Black Colleges and Universities (HBCUs)," and the "Traditionally White Institutions (TWIs)." HBCU expansion was facilitated by Congress in 1890 when it authorized the creation of separate black institutions under the land-grant college program.[189] Discrimination against African Americans by land-grant institutions was prohibited by that statute. But that law—antedating the comparable *Plessey* doctrine—stipulated that "the establishment of such colleges separately for white and colored students will be held in compliance with the provisions of this Act if the funds received be equitably divided."[190]

There are now 103 HBCUs with fourteen thousand faculty members, and they are located largely in the "Old South." Roughly one-fifth of college-bound blacks (300,000) choose to attend these institutions which award 22 percent of the bachelor degrees earned by African Americans.[191] While HBCU students are no longer exclusively black, these campuses remain "racially identifiable," with a student body generally well over 80 percent black. To many of their supporters, these colleges have the unique capacity to and the primary mission of serving the educational needs of black youth. The Thernstroms find it "remarkable" that HBCUs grant 40 percent of undergraduate degrees in the physical sciences and 38 percent of the bachelors in math and biological sciences to African Americans. To them, there is something about these campuses that, more than others, encourages blacks to accept the burdens of the most difficult of subjects. We should not, they tell us, be concerned about black clustering at the HBCUs for such "sticking together" accords well with the precepts of democratic pluralism. Who worries about too many Catholics attending Notre Dame, or too many Jews at Yeshiva U ?[192] Ward Connerly, California's Prop 209 champion, viewed things differently:

> The American people have a decision to make. Two different ideals, both popular but mutually exclusive of each other, are at war in our colleges and universities. The first is that racial diversity is an intrinsic good that should be promoted at every opportunity on every campus. This is the position of the federal government, after the Supreme Court ruled last summer that states have a "compelling interest" in fostering diversity. It is also the position of the overwhelming majority of college and university administrators, many of which submitted briefs to the court supporting this idea. And polls show that a sizable number of Americans agree with them.

> But directly opposed to the diversity ideal are historically black colleges and universities (HBCUs). An HBCU's entire reason for being is to not be diverse. Yet Americans support HBCUs as well, understandably so given their historic origins. We show our support by channeling federal funds to HBCUs every year. Here lies the dilemma.

Very few would call for a halt in federal funds to HBCUs. Just as very few would like to see publicly funded universities cease to exist. But it is hypocritical to support the public funding of HBCUs and then turn around and criticize a "lack of diversity" at other public colleges and universities, since HBCUs, by their very nature, draw away many black students who would otherwise attend racially mixed schools and affect their "diversity."[193]

While the national government does indeed subsidize HBCUs, it has concurrently attempted, with limited success, and in the face of much HBCU supporter opposition, to change the reason for HBCU existence: from institutions serving blacks to those with diverse student bodies. *De jure* racial separateness was declared unconstitutional in *Brown v. The Board* (1954), but the national administrative apparatus did not promote university integration in the formerly *de jure* segregation states until the late 1960s.[194] The initial effort was regarded as so weak that private civil rights advocacy groups sued to spur greater OCR integration efforts.[195] By 1977, this private plaintiff suit resulted in the creation of the following OCR "dismantling segregation" regulations applicable to the former *de jure* segregated states.[196] As in the case of K-12 desegregation, the regulations were meant to alleviate group wrongs through proportionality remedies:

> The mission of the TWIs and HBCUs was to be defined in nonracial terms.
>
> The HBCUs were to be academically strengthened so as to become attractive to non-blacks. But, importantly, the HBCUs were not subject to numerical goals for the increase in white students.
>
> Each of the states was to establish the goal of achieving in its public higher education system that proportion of black high school graduates which would at least be equal to the proportion of white high school graduates.
>
> The states were to adopt as a goal the reduction of the disparity between the proportion of white and black high school graduates entering TWIs.
>
> Each state was to take all reasonable steps to reduce any disparity between black and white higher education graduation rates.
>
> The states were to adopt as a goal—for academic positions requiring the doctorate—the employment of that proportion of blacks which would be coequal with the proportion of blacks in the relevant labor market who held the doctorate.
>
> The states were to adopt as a goal—for college/university positions not requiring the doctoral degree—the hiring of

that proportion of blacks for those positions which would at least equal: (1) the proportion of blacks with M.A.s in the appropriate discipline from schools in the state system; or (2) the proportion of blacks in the relevant labor market with the necessary training, whichever was the greater.

Bedeviling the integration question in the formerly *de jure* states was the question of whether *Green v. New Kent County* (1968)[197] was applicable to higher education. That ruling, for the K-12 level, interpreted the Equal Protection Clause as requiring school integration ("just schools") as contrasted with the mere abolition of racial attendance barriers. To the OCR, *Green* was surely applicable to higher education. That agency's rules, as noted, established numerical goals for black attendance at TWIs, and HBCUs were to be made more attractive to white students. For two writers on the subject, this was a profoundly mistaken policy.[198] To them, colleges are clearly different than grade schools. In the latter, the state commands attendance; college students choose whether to participate in higher education. The efforts to enhance HBCUs to attract whites has largely failed, and the pressure on TWIs to obtain more African Americans has siphoned needed intellectual talent from the HBCUs. HBCU enhancement encouraged more blacks to attend them, rather than attracting whites. Besides, there are African American educational leaders who insist on maintaining HBCUs as essentially black institutions because such an environment is more conducive for African American educational advancement. One leader maintained that the "historically white colleges are not capable of addressing the needs of black students because whites are socially and culturally deprived of understanding the needs, desires, abilities, and mores of black students."[199] Moreover, the HBCUs have such strong political support that the effort to convert them to "just schools" is not politically feasible.[200]

In the capstone case of *U.S. v. Fordice* (1992),[201] the Supreme Court did not impose the "radical" remedy of student reassignment as a route to HBCU integration—a remedy subscribed to in the wake of *Green v. New Kent County*. The Court did, however, order—where educationally practicable—the dismantlement of policies that lead to segregated higher education.[202] The overriding issue in *Fordice* was the scope of Mississippi's "affirmative" duty to dismantle its dual system of publicly funded higher learning: five "traditionally white institutions" (TWIs) and three historically black colleges and universities (HBCUs), all at one time *totally* segregated by law. The Court set aside a decision by the Fifth Circuit that the state had indeed complied with its duty by implementing race-neutral admissions standards at all of its campuses. The High Court held that the dispositive question was "whether Mississippi ha[d] left in place certain aspects of its prior dual system that perpetuate[d] the racially segregated higher education system."[203] The majority opinion framed the applicable standard as follows:

If the State perpetuates policies and practices traceable to its prior system that continue to have segregative effects—whether by influencing student enrollment decisions or by fostering segregation in other facets of the university system—and such policies are without sound educational justification and can be practicably eliminated, the State has not satisfied its burden of proving that it has dismantled its prior system. Such policies run afoul of the Equal Protection Clause, even though the State has abolished the legal requirement that whites and blacks be educated separately and has established racially neutral policies not animated by a discriminatory purpose.[204]

The Court held that the lower courts had applied the wrong standard, and, in so doing, had ignored the "readily apparent" evidence that "certain remnants" of the prior system were, or might be, unconstitutional under the standard that should have been applied. Accordingly, the Court remanded the entire matter for a full-scale examination of such remnants, including, but not limited to, four continuing practices which the Court itself chose to identify for "highlighting" purposes: (1) requiring "significantly higher" test scores for admission to TWIs than to HBCUs; (2) duplication of BA and MA programs at both TWIs and HBCUs; (3) classifying the eight schools by rank-ordered educational "mission" for funding purposes; and (4) operating all eight schools without consideration of waste or inefficiency. The Court held that these vestiges of the old regime tended to compromise students' freedom of choice and perpetuate segregation, and directed the remand courts to determine whether it would be "practicable and consistent with sound education practices "to eliminate or modify them.[205]

The *Fordice* decision initiated a remand process which has run for years, and the indefiniteness of the *Fordice* standard invites further controversy. What is the educationally sound way of abolishing the vestiges of segregation? Obviously, this indefiniteness relegates the Mississippi HBCUs, and by extension their counterparts in other states, to an indefinite limbo. Champions of HBCUs have indignantly denounced the *Fordice* "educationally practicable" straddle; but it is possible to forgive. More perhaps than any other type of desegregation case, the *Fordice* model requires government to craft a reconciliation of the seemingly irreconcilable. To order that publicly funded HBCUs be allowed to continue both as racially identifiable and as equally endowed would fly in the teeth of *Brown* and *Green*, and rouse the ghost of *Plessy*. But is there a tenable alternative? HBCUs have traditionally been—and may still be—the only effective means for many African Americans of countering racist exclusion from mainstream learning; if they represent educational apartheid, the onus is on the segregators. To let them die in the name of desegregation would work the ultimate in cruel irony—the sacrifice of the resisting victim in order to punish his oppressor. In this light, it is perhaps understandable that the *Fordice* Court resorted to quasi-Solomonic finesse.

Eventually, the issue will have to be sorted out. What will be the way out of the dilemma? Will the day be carried by the anguished pleas of the HBCU advocates? Will the Supreme Court determine that the integrationist impulse of *Brown* and *Green* should be replaced, in our public institutions of higher learning, by some variant form of the "separate but equal" heresy? Will the Court try to preserve integration by redefining "racial identifiability" so that black institutions will have to admit more white students in order to preserve a substantial measure of separate identity? Will the black colleges die out because the conditions that created them no longer prevail? And when will we know?

The last question should be underscored given the refusal of the Supreme Court to review the post-*Fordice* arrangements that have been crafted either by the federal courts, or by the Education Department's Office for Civil Rights (OCR) which office claims it still employs the "ingredients" of its previously listed guidelines.[206] These arrangements have involved all or a number of the following components: (1) efforts to enhance the operations of HBCUs through change of admission requirements and/or the increase of public funding; (2) commitments of TWIs and HBCUs to seek "other-race" students; (3) the avoidance of unnecessary duplication and/or the creation of special educational missions for the two sets of colleges.[207]

Post-*Fordice* district and appellate court decisions (*Ayers v. Fordice*) mandated the establishment of equal admission standards for Mississippi's system of higher education, despite the claim that these would decimate the state's HBCUs.[208] Admission to the HBCUs has been less difficult than acceptance at the TWIs, and the apparent objective of the court in *Ayers* was to reduce the stigma of lesser competence associated with the HBCUs—making them more attractive to white students. Likewise, the application of *Fordice* in Alabama focused on improving HBCU reputation. There, the state was ordered by the court to both provide at least $100 million over the next fifteen years for the improvement of HBCU academic quality, and to finance scholarships reserved for whites who attended HBCUs.[209] Both of these requirements became the subject of new suits: one brought by an African American who challenged the "whites only" scholarship plan as unconstitutional discrimination against blacks.[210] In Mississippi, state authorities agreed to spend $500 million (over seventeen years) to improve HBCUs there. To acquire full control of some $105 million, the black colleges are required to achieve a 10 percent non-black student population in the upcoming years.[211] The federal judge presiding over the Mississippi case has insisted that the whites be given first priority in distributing the scholarship money.[212]

Critics argue that more HBCU funding will just expand the poison of "separate but equal." Others do not understand why it is necessary to attract whites to institutions created as a response to white racism. Of interest is that the TWI quest for black students has prompted HBCUs to seek out Hispanics as an enrollment-growing tactic.[213]

Other dimensions of post-*Fordice* planned arrangements adhered to by federal officials include:[214]

> Maryland's higher education officials committed themselves to spend more money for HBCUs; to diligently avoid duplication in degree offerings; to better prepare teachers for increasingly diverse classrooms; and increase the state's efforts to recruit and retain black students.
>
> Tennessee was to spend $75 million to desegregate higher education and improve black opportunities. Most of the aforementioned funds was to be allocated to Tennessee State (the HBCU) to enhance its academic capacities. The University of Tennessee (TWI) and Tennessee State were to jointly plan to increase their populations of other-race students; and Tennessee State was to raise its admission standards.
>
> In Louisiana, an agreement was reached enabling Southern University (an HBCU) to specialize in nutrition science. That university was to receive more state aid to otherwise improve its curriculum.

Researchers at the Southern Education Foundation reported at the end of the old millennium that *Fordice* had yet to prompt an acceptable level of desegregation. HBCUs remain overwhelmingly black; TWIs remain the preserve of whites. To be sure, TWIs have adopted race-conscious affirmative action admission programs as a result of either negotiation with OCR or court action. And, (except for Texas) these programs were operative throughout the "Old South"—even in Mississippi and Louisiana, which were covered by the Fifth Circuit's *Hopwood* opinion. Still, in 1996, only 8.6 percent of first-year students at the TWI "flagship" southern campuses were black, while about 20 percent of the population between 18–24 years in the South was black. A major objective for the Southern Education Foundation was to obtain an African American population at the flagship campuses which much more closely approximated the percentage of young blacks in the population covered by these campuses. In short, an emphasis on proportional representation integration, and to this end, the Foundation urged that state colleges expand their outreach efforts in the minority communities, helping the young there prepare for college.[215]

Justice Thomas's concurrence in *Fordice* described how the rule in *Fordice* is quite different from that of *Green*. The latter required thoroughgoing integration, and assumed that integration was educationally advantageous; the former requires the adoption of integrative mechanisms only when it would be educationally sound, and Justice Thomas feels that there is much to be said for the educational soundness of the HBCUs as predominately one-race schools. An excerpt from his *Fordice* concurrence follows:

> [748] In particular, we do not foreclose the possibility that there exists "sound educational justification" for maintaining historically black colleges as such. Despite the shameful history of state-enforced segregation, these institutions have survived and flourished. Indeed, they have expanded as opportunities for blacks to enter historically white institutions have expanded. . . . These accomplishments have not gone unnoticed: "The colleges founded for Negroes are both a source of pride to blacks who have attended them and a source of hope to black families who want the benefits of higher learning for their children. They have exercised leadership in developing educational opportunities for young blacks at all levels of instruction, and, especially in the South, they are still regarded as key institutions for enhancing the general quality of the lives of black Americans." Carnegie Commission on Higher Education, From Isolation to Mainstream: Problems of the Colleges Founded for Negroes 11 (1971).
>
> I think it indisputable that these institutions have succeeded in part because of their distinctive histories and traditions; for many, historically black colleges have become "a symbol of the highest attainments of black culture." J. Preer, Lawyers v. Educators: Black Colleges and Desegregation in Public Higher Education 2 (1982). Obviously, a [749] State cannot maintain such traditions by closing particular institutions, historically white or historically black, to particular racial groups. Nonetheless, it hardly follows that a State cannot operate a diverse assortment of institutions—including historically black institutions—open to all on a race-neutral basis, but with established traditions and programs that might disproportionately appeal to one race or another. No one, I imagine, would argue that such institutional *diversity* is without "sound educational justification," or that it is even remotely akin to program duplication, which is designed to separate the races for the sake of separating the races. . . . It would be ironic, to say the least, if the institutions that sustained blacks during segregation were themselves destroyed in an effort to combat its vestiges.[216]

Scalia's dissent in *Fordice* asserted his view that *Brown I* barred *de jure* segregation because of its capacity to impose psychic harm on blacks.

To him, however, "[l]egacies of the dual system"—that is, the HBCU and TWI state institutions—"that permit (or even incidentally facilitate) free choice of racially identifiable schools—while still assuring each individual student the right to attend *whatever* school he wishes" are not associated with these negative psychic consequences.[217] Is the justice correct? Recall that to the typical social scientist at the time of *Brown v. The Board* (1954), school integration was needed to alleviate segregation's stigmatic affliction hobbling African Americans.[218]

Gender Discrimination and Education

We are here concerned with Title IX of the Education Act of 1972,[219] which prohibits sex-based discrimination in the administration of any educational undertaking financially assisted by the federal government. The bar against governmental sex discrimination in the Constitution's equal protection guarantees is also a focus. Both the statute, which has been interpreted as requiring remedies for disparate-impact gender discrimination, and the Constitution are primary tools in combating sex discrimination in our educational institutions. Our initial focus is on equal protection doctrine.

Constitutional Sanctions and Single-Sex Schools

Sexual classification has long been the subject of equal protection litigation. Over the last few decades, the U.S. Supreme Court gradually assimilated changing societal attitudes about the role of women in social and domestic relations, employment, and personal conduct. In the modern era, the High Court has been active in using the Fifth and Fourteenth Amendments to emancipate women from age-old sexist stereotyping and harassment.

The statutory universe of the early 1960s contained much in the way of gender classification and discrimination. Work-protection legislation limited the number of hours women could work, the weight they could lift, and even the type of work (such as night work) they could undertake. Such protectionism—regarded as running afoul of Title VII of the 1964 Civil Rights Act—has been invalidated.[220] Title VII is not applicable, though, to the broad spectrum of sex-specific legislation, which, among many other things, mandates that mothers in divorce situations be given preference in issues related to child custody; that fathers bear the primary burden for child support after divorce; that female prostitutes be subject to criminal punishment that was not imposed on their male customers; and that in statutory rape cases only men be subject to punishment.[221] To what extent do the aforementioned, and other existing sex-specific classifications, conform with the equal protection guarantees of the Constitution?

Before 1971, prevailing constitutional doctrine had it that state gender discrimination did not violate equal protection if such discrimination met the requirement of "mere rationality"—that is, if there was *any* basis in reason to support it. Given this lowest tier of equal protection judicial scrutiny, the Supreme Court did not bar a sex discrimination statute until 1971.[222] Even as late as 1948, the Court accepted Michigan's statute denying bartender licenses to females unless they were the wives or daughters of male (not female) tavern owners.[223]

The High Court began changing its gender discrimination, equal protection tack in *Reed v. Reed* (1971),[224] when it declared unconstitutional an Idaho statute providing that males be preferred as administrators of decedents' estates. The preferential treatment afforded males was deemed arbitrary, and thus not rational. Justice Ginsburg was involved in *Reed* as an attorney, and in that role she advocated the adoption of a strict scrutiny standard for sex discrimination statutes.[225] Strict scrutiny was not adopted by the Court in *Reed*, but in *Frontiero v. Richardson* (1973),[226] a four-member plurality did champion the highest of standards.

In *Craig v. Boren* (1976),[227] the High Court settled on a "mid-tier," equal protection test for sex discrimination claims: whether the disputed classification serves "important" government objectives and is substantially related to achieving them. Arguably, this rule has now been broadened. In *United States v. Virginia* (1996),[228] the Supreme Court held, 7-1, in an opinion written by the now Justice Ginsburg, that Virginia's commitment to an exclusively male admissions policy at its storied military academy violated the Equal Protection Clause. This decision not only toppled a major citadel of state-supported male exclusivity, but also teaches a lesson in the dynamics of antidiscrimination law.

The Court indicated that, in order to prevail, a mid-tier defendant must demonstrate a justification that is not only "exceedingly persuasive," but also "genuine, not hypothesized," and untainted by sexual stereotypes.[229] In the Court's no-nonsense view, Virginia's defenses fell far short of clearing this bar. The contention that the Virginia Military Institute's males-only program furthers educational "diversity" was caustically dismissed as a lawyer's concoction, and the argument that the program is too rigorous for females was found to be emptyheaded.[230]

There is a learned dispute over whether the "exceedingly persuasive" concept expands, or merely restates, mid-tier law.[231] Also, it remains to be seen whether the seemingly broadened mid-tier rule in gender discrimination law differs from the strict scrutiny rule which governs public race/ethnic-discrimination. And important here is the question as to why strict scrutiny should not be applicable to gender discrimination. What is more, the *Virginia* majority left open the issue as to the equal protection legitimacy of "separate but equal" single-sex schools. That majority insisted that it was not addressing the question; however it noted that "[s]everal *amici* have urged that diversity in educational opportunities is altogether an appropriate governmental pursuit and that single-sex schools can contribute to such diversity. Indeed, it is the mission of some single-sex schools 'to dissipate, rather than perpetuate traditional gender classifications.' We do not question the Commonwealth's prerogative evenhandedly to support diverse educational opportunities."[232] Later, the Court went to great lengths to insist that Virginia had not—as it claimed it did—remedied its equal protection violation by establishing the Virginia Women's Institute of Leadership (VWIL) at Mary Baldwin College, a private women's college geographically close to VMI. The majority concluded its exhaustive review of the VWIL's shortcomings relative to VMI, with the following written by Justice Ginsburg.[233]

U.S. v. Virginia, 518 U.S. 515 (1996)

[553] Virginia's VWIL solution is reminiscent of the remedy Texas proposed 50 years ago, in response to a state trial court's 1946 ruling that, given the equal protection guarantee, African Americans could not be denied a legal education at a state facility. See *Sweatt v. Painter*, 339 U.S. 629 (1950). Reluctant to admit African Americans to its flagship University of Texas Law School, the State set up a separate school for Herman Sweatt and other black law students. As originally opened, the new school had no independent faculty or library, and it lacked accreditation. Nevertheless, the state trial and appellate courts were satisfied that the new school offered Sweatt opportunities for the study of law "substantially equivalent to those offered by the State to white students at the University of Texas." . . .

Before this Court considered the case, the new school had gained "a faculty of five full-time professors; a student body of 23; a library of some 16,500 volumes serviced by a full-time staff; a practice court and legal aid association; and one alumnus who ha[d] become a member of the Texas Bar." This Court contrasted resources at the new school with those at the school from which Sweatt had been excluded. The University of Texas Law School had a full-time faculty of 16, a student body of 850, a library containing over [554] 65,000 volumes, scholarship funds, a law review, and moot court facilities.

More important than the tangible features, the Court emphasized, are "those qualities which are incapable of objective measurement but which make for greatness" in a school, including "reputation of the faculty, experience of the administration, position and influence of the alumni, standing in the community, traditions and prestige." Facing the marked differences reported in the *Sweatt* opinion, the Court unanimously ruled that Texas had not shown "substantial equality in the [separate] educational opportunities" the State offered. Accordingly, the Court held, the Equal Protection Clause required Texas to admit African Americans to the University of Texas Law School. In line with *Sweatt*, we rule here that Virginia has not shown substantial equality in the separate educational opportunities the State supports at VWIL and VMI. . . .

[557] VMI, too, offers an educational opportunity no other Virginia institution provides, and the school's "prestige"—associated with its success in developing "citizen-soldiers"—is unequaled. Virginia has closed this facility to its daughters and, instead, has devised for them a "parallel program," with a faculty less impressively credentialed and less well paid, more limited course offerings, fewer opportunities for military training and for scientific specialization. VMI, beyond question, "possesses to a far greater degree" than the VWIL program "those qualities which are incapable of objective measurement but which make for greatness in a . . . school," including "position and influence of the alumni, standing in the community, traditions and prestige." Women seeking and fit for a VMI-quality education cannot be offered anything less, under the State's obligation to afford them genuinely equal protection. . . .

The decade of the 1990s witnessed a considerable interest in the expansion of single-gender public schooling long prominent in private and parochial schools. Current gender separation advocates argue, for example, that all-male minority academies would improve academic performance by eliminating female distractions, and by improving self-esteem through an emphasis on minority role models such as the Reverend King, Marcus Garvey, and Paul Robeson. There are some studies indicating that minority males in single-gender school environments do achieve higher test scores than their coeducational counterparts. But the single-sex schools emphasize discipline and parental involvement, and it may be that the latter two variables operate without sexual segregation to improve scholarship.[234]

Support for all-female classes rests on notions that girls tend to be overawed and stifled in the presence of males, particularly in the areas of science and math; that they are both more harshly treated and ignored by teachers than are boys; and that exams are too often "gender biased."

Graduates of women's colleges, moreover, are far better represented in high-status positions than females who went to coeducational institutions.[235] A study that was often cited to support all-female schools was published in 1992 by the American Association of University Women (AAUW) and was titled, *How Schools Shortchange Girls*. But the Educational Foundation of that same organization published a later study in 1998, *Separated by Sex: A Critical Look at Single-Sex Education for Girls*. This report grew out of an extensive review of the empirical literature on the subject. Key points in that 1998 report concluded that there is no evidence that single-sex education is superior to coeducation; that some students prospered in a single-sex setting, but it was unclear whether coeducation could not produce the same results; that the long-term effect of single-gender learning was unknown; and that more scholarly attention had to be devoted to determining the components of a good education.[236]

There is another dimension of support for single-sex learning called the "essential difference" point of view, which regards the learning capacities of boys and girls as biologically different, and that these differences would be mitigated through separate classes. Among other things, females hear better, and are more adept at distinguishing "nuance of color and texture." Boys are more competent in "seeing action."[237]

In 1995, two single-sex public schools functioned in the entire nation; at the end of 2007, there were forty-nine, with many more anticipated.[238] One education academic whose research on the topic is far-reaching, concluded that "research evidence on the relative benefits of publicly supported single-sex schooling is undeniably inadequate," and that "findings to date are concededly inconclusive."[239] Nevertheless, the Bush administration Secretary of Education announced in October 2006 that Title IX regulations would be changed to make single-sex education easier to implement. Previously, these regulations permitted single-sex education only in very limited circumstances such as contact sports and sex education classes. The new rules would permit voluntary separate-gender (nonvocational) education where it was substantially related to an important government interest, and where substantially equal coeducation was provided to those who did not participate in separate-sex education.[240] The reader should note that the "exceedingly persuasive" standard of *U.S. v. Virginia Military Institute* was not cited by the Bush education secretary. Even so, given the "inadequate" nature of the research on single-sex schooling, how can it be supported by an important governmental interest? Further, is "separate but equal" an important governmental interest?

Title IX and Education

Title IX of the Education Act of 1972 reads in part: "No person . . . shall, on the basis of sex, be excluded from participating in, be denied benefits of, or be subjected to discrimination under any education program or activity receiving Federal financial assistance."[241] In education, Title IX has been prominent as a tool for curbing sexual harassment, and for increasing female educational and athletic opportunities. The women's rights movement has seized upon this title to reduce educational obstacles affecting females as a result of societal mores and intentional discrimination. The title's impact in this regard is reportedly impressive. Thus, in 2002, a high-level official at the education department's Office for Civil Rights (OCR) associated the 1972 Title with the following developments:[242]

> A majority of college students were women.
>
> Forty-three percent of medical degrees were given to females as compared to 9 percent in 1972.
>
> Forty percent of dental degrees are given to women as compared to 1 percent in 1972.
>
> The percentage of female engineering graduates rose from 1 to 17 percent.
>
> Female grads in the physical sciences rose from 15 to 37 percent.
>
> One-half the zoology grads at the turn of the millennium were female as compared with 22 percent in 1972.

Women's rights advocates, nonetheless, fiercely challenged the notion that matters were acceptable in the realm of mathematics and the sciences because there was a distressing trend in female computer graduation rates. More distressing was the paucity of bachelors, masters, and doctorates in engineering. While females were approaching parity at the bachelor and masters level in math and the physical sciences, they received only one-fourth of the PhDs in those areas.[243] Various corrective affirmative action remedies have been urged: gender preferences should be employed in the distribution of educational aid and faculty jobs; academic jobs should be structured to accommodate the family responsibilities of females; and math/science departments at all levels should investigate the reasons for female underrepresentation and take corrective action.[244]

Intercollegiate Athletics

Title IX's ban on educational gender discrimination helped engender a sizeable enlargement in female athletic programs: the number of women participating in collegiate athletics has grown from 30,000 in 1971 to some 135,000 in the mid-1990s.[245] In 1972, one girl in 27 played high school sports; currently, it is one in 2.5.[246] At the college level, the female share of athletes was 15 percent in 1972. In 2006, it was some 42 percent.[247] Feminist thinkers regard

Title IX as a mechanism for eliminating restrictions on female participation in areas dominated by males, and as a vehicle for females to demonstrate their talents and differing perspectives. To the more radical among feminist thinkers, Title IX helps reduce male domination in our society.[248]

The dispute at Brown University over the meaning of Title IX in connection with female athletics has been important to the law affecting intercollegiate athletics. At a congressional committee hearing, Brown's then-president Gregorian expressed his frustration with Title IX's administrative regulations: "These [OCR administrative] rules and guidelines are so ambiguous, so inconsistent, and so imprecise that they leave judges with total discretion."[249] He concluded by saying that "proportionality . . . is the (judiciary's) paramount test."[250] Here, Gregorian was correct. The courts have widely imposed a proportionality test at the collegiate level for intercollegiate athletics. That is, either that the numerical proportion of males and females participating in sports conforms with (or has a history of substantially moving toward) their proportions in the student body; or that the interests of the proportionately underrepresented sex are fully and effectively accommodated so that proportionate-interest representation is achieved. Should that test be extended to the other areas of university life?

Gender segregation is the accepted norm in intercollegiate sport. Title IX athletics discrimination claims accordingly pose unique analytical problems. In *Cohen v. Brown* (1996),[251] (the illustrative appellate opinion in this area and one that involved the dispute President Gregorian was discussing above), a 2-1 majority of a First Circuit review panel reaffirmed the lower court's conclusion that the defendant Brown University, which experienced a significant numerical disparity between female participation in its sports program and its female student enrollment, violated Title IX by cutting off funding for certain female teams. Given the statistical disparity, the majority held that the cutoff demonstrated the university's failure to comply with its duty, under applicable federal administrative regulations, "effectively to accommodate" its female students. Thus, the numerical disparity finding was critical in the analytical process.[252] In short, disparate-impact analysis and the need for proportional affirmative action relief is the keystone of *Cohen*, and of the four other circuit court decisions on which the majority relied.

The *Cohen* majority's rationale is open to question. It held that the lower court's female/male proportionality ruling did not create an impermissible gender "preference" barred by Title IX. This was so, the majority said, because the remedial "gender-conscious" reallocation of funds mandated by the ruling would affect only resources for athletic programs that were *already* gender-segregated. Accordingly, the appropriate way to correct disproportionalities in an existing gender-segregated milieu was to impose gender quotas! But this reasoning seemingly runs contrary to a segment of Title IX requiring that the prohibition against educational sexual discrimination in that statute shall not "be interpreted to require any educational institution to grant preferential treatment or disparate treatment to the members of one sex on account of an imbalance which may exist with respect to the total number or percentage of persons of that sex participating in or receiving the benefits of any federally supported program or activity, in comparison with the total number or percentage of persons of that sex in any community, State, section or other area."[253]

The *Cohen* majority grappled with the above-cited Title IX prohibition by arguing that, since colleges allocate monies for male and female programs separately, gender discrimination claims *must* compare the participation opportunities provided for both in order to follow Title IX's requirement that allocations for athletics disadvantage neither sex.[254]

The *Cohen* decision placed great weight on its understanding of the Office for Civil Rights' (OCR) *Policy Interpretation* of Title IX's administrative regulations. According to the *Policy Interpretation*, college athletics programs conformed with Title IX if: (1) Intercollegiate-level participation opportunities for male and female students are provided in numbers substantially proportionate to their respective enrollments; or (2) Where the members of one sex have been and are underrepresented among intercollegiate athletes, whether the institution can show a history and continuing practice of program expansion which is demonstrably responsive to the developing interest and abilities of the members of that sex; or (3) Where the members of one sex are underrepresented among intercollegiate athletes, and the institution cannot show a continuing practice of program expansion such as that cited above, whether it can be demonstrated that the interests and abilities of the members of that sex have been fully and effectively accommodated by the present program.[255]

The *Cohen* majority ruled that Brown University had failed to conform to these administrative regulations because the proportion of female athletes (13.1 percent of all athletes) was not substantially proportionate to the total school female population, and because Brown did not otherwise appropriately cater to female interests. The university insisted that it provided athletic opportunities consistent with levels relative to interest, and that, as its statistics attempted to demonstrate, females were less interested in sports.[256] To which the majority replied:

> Thus, there exists the danger that, rather than providing a true measure of women's interest in sports, statistical evidence purporting to reflect women's interest instead provides only a measure of the very discrimination that is and has been the basis for women's lack of opportunity to participate in sports. . . . [T]o allow a numbers-based lack-of-interest defense to become the instrument of further discrimination against the underrepresented

gender would pervert the remedial purpose of Title IX. We conclude that, even if it can be empirically demonstrated that, at a particular time, women have less interest in sports than do men, such evidence, standing alone, cannot justify providing fewer athletics opportunities for women than for men.[257]

Brown also argued that the proportional representation scheme imposed upon it would not pass the strict scrutiny test required by *Adarand v. Peña* (1995),[258] and that, as a result, Brown's equal protection rights under the Fifth Amendment were violated. The court accurately noted [259] that "[i]t is well settled that the reach of the equal protection guarantee of the Fifth Amendment Due Process Clause—the basis for Brown's equal protection claim—is coextensive with that of the Fourteenth Amendment Equal Protection Clause." However, the court majority ruled that intermediate scrutiny (and not strict scrutiny) was the appropriate standard for gender discrimination, and that *U.S. v. Virginia* changed nothing.[260] While the *Cohen* court defined intermediate scrutiny as requiring an "exceedingly persuasive justification," it maintained that the Supreme Court had used that standard for intermediate scrutiny in cases other than *U.S. v. Virginia.* It also insisted that the proportionality requirement required of Brown measured up to the dictates of intermediate review because such balancing was needed to implement a federal statute.[261]

The provocative dissent in *Cohen* argued that the majority, by rejecting Brown's effort to prove that females had a lesser interest in sports, paralyzed the university's capacity to prove that it complied with the third prong of the *Policy Interpretation* cited above. Thus, the issue, in this case, was effectively restricted to crude numerical proportionality, though the majority incongruously asserted that the determination of female "interests" rather than mere numbers was central to its resolution, and that statistical balancing was not mandated by its opinion.[262] This majority claim that its opinion did not mandate statistical balancing was scathingly rejected. To the dissent, the first prong of the *Policy Interpretation* delineated above surely requires statistical balancing. The second prong is "essentially a test that requires the school to show that it is moving in the direction of satisfying the first prong," and that can only be done by showing an improvement in statistical balancing.[263] Finally, the third prong, interpreted as the majority does, dispenses with statistical balancing only because it chose to accord zero weight to one side of the balance by adopting a severe form of proportional-interest recognition. Even a single person with a reasonable unmet interest defeats compliance.[264]

The dissent contended that the "exceedingly persuasive justification" requirement of *U.S. v. Virginia* elevated the test applicable to sex discrimination cases, and that test was surely not met here. Congress expressly disavowed the kind of quota scheme accepted by the majority.[265] In addition, "The majority has put the power to control athletics and the provision of athletic resources in the hands of the underrepresented gender. Virtually every other aspect of college life is entrusted to the institution, but athletics has now been carved out as an exception and the university is no longer in full control of its program. Unless the two genders participate equally in athletics, members of the underrepresented sex would have the ability to demand a varsity level team at any time if they can show sufficient interest. Apparently no weight is given to the sustainability of the interest, the cost of the sport, the university's view on the desirability of the sport, and so on."[266]

The federal appellate courts were not alone in emphasizing numerical proportionality as the way for college athletics to conform with Title IX. The Clinton administration director of OCR informed college administrators that numerical proportionality was the "safe harbor" route to adherence.[267] The George W. Bush Administration OCR director reported that this was a mistaken policy which "led many schools to believe, erroneously, that they must take measures to ensure strict proportionality between the sexes. In fact each of the three prongs of the test is an equally sufficient means of complying with Title IX, and no one prong is favored."[268] OCR, during the Bush II years, provided schools with a model questionnaire, suggesting that it be used to survey female students as to interest in sports.[269]

Two Title IX scholars note that a 2004–05 survey of 1,895 institutions indicates the average female share of the undergrad population was 55.8 percent, but the female share of athletes was 41.7 percent. The large majority of the colleges had a proportionality gap of more than 3 percent. In their view, the gap meant that—despite the judicial emphasis on proportionality—most colleges, in the structuring of athletic commitments, really relied on their understanding of female interest in sports.[270] How this administrative-judicial disconnect plays out remains to be seen.

Extensive praise has been granted Title IX for reducing barriers to female athletic participation. Two critics though, tell us that while they support more female participation in sports, the implementation of Title IX—because it typically involves creating gender-segregated teams—has only reinforced the stereotype that females are athletically inferior to men. Separate but equal, they insist, does not work for womanhood in sports. What is needed are unisex teams, enabling females to voluntarily seek to earn places on any team. Many women, they note, can creditably compete with men in athletics.[271]

Sexual Harassment on Campus

The law of sexual harassment, like antidiscrimination law generally, seeks to protect against the disparate treatment of individuals. Punishing what is regarded as the sexual maltreatment of females is also viewed as a way of reducing the charged sexual atmosphere resulting from male lust, which systemically operates to disparately impact female well-being. However, one authority, discussed below, sees sexual harassment regulations on American college campuses as having an unfair disparate impact on the *male* student body.

In the school setting, Title IX litigation closely tracks the sexual harassment law of Title VII. The lead appellate case of *Lipsett v. University of Puerto Rico* (1988)[272] expounds the substantive elements of the sexual harassment violation under Title IX: either "quid pro quo" harassment—a demand for sexual favors in return for workplace benefits, or punishment for refusing the demand; and/or "hostile environment" harassment—a continuing display of sexual hostility or verbal abuse so severe or pervasive as to poison the workplace for its targets. The threshold fact question is always whether the demands, gestures, or expressions involved are "unwelcome" or "poisonous"—a tricky eye-of-the-beholder riddle for the conscientious fact-finder. Title VII of the 1964 Civil Rights Act has also been interpreted by the Supreme Court as prohibiting "hostile environment" sexual harassment (including that of the same-sex variety) for *all* workplaces covered by the act.[273]

The Supreme Court has additionally held that a school district would be liable for damages under Title IX for being deliberately indifferent to teacher-student and student-on-student sexual harassment. In the latter case, the successful plaintiff must prove that the harassment is so severe and pervasive as to undermine the victim's education. *Davis v. Monroe County Board of Education* (1999).[274]

The Foundation for Individual Rights in Education (Fire) contends that many campus sexual harassment codes (along with their racial, ethnic, and disability counterparts) deviate egregiously from the *Davis v. Monroe* harassment standard. That rule, to Fire, prohibits conduct that goes far beyond the "dirty joke" and the offensive op-ed. "Harassment is extreme and usually repetitive behavior—behavior so serious that it would interfere with a reasonable person's capacity to get his or her education."[275] The culture of extreme gender, ethnic, and racial sensitivity exhibited in these codes threatens to disparately impact and undermine the constitutionally protected robust exchange of ideas on campus.[276] The abuse of harassment regulations became so widespread that it prompted a 2003 letter (often unheeded)[277] from director of OCR, a portion of which follows:

> Some colleges and universities have interpreted OCR's prohibition of "harassment" as encompassing all offensive speech regarding sex, disability, race, or other classifications. Harassment, however, to be prohibited by the statutes within OCR's jurisdiction, must include something beyond the mere expression of views, words, symbols or thoughts that some person finds offensive.[278]

Gender harassment regulations are often preferentially female in objective in that they are meant to protect women against the allegedly more sexually aggressive and sexually disrespectful males.[279] In her book *Heterophobia*, Daphne Patai argues that these rules are cudgels used by academic feminists to rid the universities of male domination and male oppressiveness. To Patai, the view of males as the oppressors is unsound. Females are just as oppressive and offensive, sexually and otherwise. But the harassment rules—particularly those emanating from the "hostile environment" mold—routinely sacrifice the rights of the accused male in favor of the alleged female victims. Patai, in effect, argues that males have become the victims of disparate-impact discrimination as a consequence of campus societal norms generated by radical feminists. As a result, male due process is sacrificed, male freedom of speech chilled, and interpersonal paranoia is generated at the universities.[280]

A different view of sex harassment regulation is found in Stephen Schulhofer's *Unwanted Sex*. To him, millions of women face sexual harassment on campus, the workplace, and in professional relationships. Federal law is biased in favor of males in that females, in a federal harassment lawsuit, have to prove that sexual advances are unwelcome, and this requirement has proved to be notoriously ambiguous and subjective. Better law would require males to prove that their advances were welcome.[281]

Six

Affirmative Action and the Political Representation of Minorities

Prologue

In this chapter we review affirmative action's record in securing fair representation for America's racial/ethnic minorities and women.

The initial object of the Voting Rights Act (VRA) of 1965[1] was the enfranchisement of minority groups who had been denied the ballot through the governmental use of literacy, educational, or character tests. The act banned such tests according to a prescribed formula; it did not require a showing of intentional discrimination before the ban took effect. The test ban was triggered by low voting or low voter registration figures in the states and their subdivisions. The assumption of the act was that such data reflected the oppressive societal burdens (such as poor schools) imposed on African Americans and other minorities—burdens that resulted in greatly limiting their voting. The act's objective was to remove or reduce these discriminatory voting restraints. In brief, the Voting Rights Act was an affirmative action measure initially focused on several Southern states where impediments to black voting were particularly egregious. Not much later, literacy tests for voting were totally banished nationwide on the obviously correct assumption that the South had no monopoly on the mistreatment of people of color.

Thus, affirmative action in voting test abolition began its work contemporaneously with affirmative action in employment and education. From the beginning, enforcement of the act focused on securing access of protected minority groups to the polls. Early too, a primary target of the act became "dilution," the claimed weakening of minority voting power through state and local election laws and practices. The government's antidilution program has included strong support for the creation of "majority-minority" voting districts by state and local redistricting authorities. These districts, in which protected minorities comprise effective voting majorities, are designed to further the election of minority-preferred candidates for office.

In the 1990s decade, racial/ethnic districting encountered serious legal difficulties. The Supreme Court has invalidated a number of majority-minority districts on constitutional grounds, and has disapproved the policy of maximizing the number of such districts. Affirmative action's future voting rights role is uncertain.

This chapter is much concerned with the rancorous dispute over electoral affirmative action in redistricting. Is the VRA intended only to prevent racial/ethnic disenfranchisement, or also to assist in the election of minority-preferred candidates? Does fair representation require proportionality in the election of minority officeholders? Are racial/ethnic minorities underrepresented? Is *partisan* gerrymandering entitled to greater deference than *racial/ethnic* districting? Is the VRA intended to provide remedies for vote dilution? Does a numerical majority in districts actually help minorities to attain their electoral goals? If not, what are the alternative methods for safeguarding their interests? These questions are main themes in the ideological war over affirmative action as we face the decennial census. Adding to the complexity are the revolutionary demographic shifts which are now under way throughout the country.

The 1965 Voting Rights Act and Its Amendments

The Central Portions of the 1965 Voting Rights Act

The right to vote epitomizes the shared functions of our federal system. Federal law *protects* this right,[2] but does not *create* it. Instead of a single national suffrage law, we must contend with a bewildering multiplicity of state and local systems. On the one hand, federal law imposes substantial constraints on the states' electoral prerogatives. On the other, the states, in large measure, control voter eligibility, districting, and the rules and procedures for *all* elections, federal as well as state. At bottom, the history of suffrage reform is the record of a never-ending federal-state battle for the upper hand in this tempestuous relationship.[3]

It is a twice-told tale that VRA came into being only when Congress finally realized that drastic federal intervention would be needed to end the almost century-old disenfranchisement of Southern blacks.[4] In *South Carolina v. Katzenbach* (1966), the Supreme Court, 8-1, upheld the constitutionality of VRA's Sections 4 and 5 as appropriate enforcement of the Fifteenth Amendment.[5] In his opinion for the Court, Chief Justice Warren wrote:

> The Voting Rights Act was designed by Congress to banish the blight of racial discrimination in voting which has infected the electoral process in parts of our country for nearly a century.

The Act creates stringent new remedies for voting discrimination where it persists on a pervasive scale, and . . . [it] strengthens
existing remedies for pockets of voting discrimination elsewhere
in the country. . . . Congress felt itself confronted by an insidious
and pervasive evil which had been perpetrated in certain parts
of our country through unremitting and ingenious defiance of
the Constitution. . . . Congress concluded that the unsuccessful
remedies which it had prescribed in the past would have to be
replaced by sterner and more elaborate measures in order to satisfy
the clear commands of the Fifteenth Amendment.[6]

Initially, Section 5 of the VRA mandated that political jurisdictions—which by the VRA Section 4 were required to end their literacy tests
because of the low number of voters or registrants in the 1964 presidential
election—were to be prohibited from imposing new voting procedures unless
the U.S. attorney general registers no objection to them, or a special three-judge
District of Columbia District Court authorizes them as not discriminatorily
affecting protected groups. A covered (so-called preclearance) jurisdiction
may petition the District Court for the District of Columbia for a ruling
that its proposed change neither "has the purpose nor will have the *effect* of
denying or abridging the right to vote on account of race or color."[7] Or a
"preclearance" jurisdiction may first seek *administrative* preclearance from the
attorney general under the previously cited, purpose/effect test, and thereafter
appeal to the District Court if approval is refused. The act also authorizes
private lawsuits to compel preclearance.[8] The 2006 reauthorization of the
VRA[9] maintained the preclearance feature, and its coverage formulas, which
have been amended to include low voter registration and turnout in the
1968 and 1972 presidential elections.[10] In 1965, preclearance was applicable
to the states of Alabama, Mississippi, South Carolina, Virginia, Louisiana,
Georgia, their political subdivisions, and parts of North Carolina.[11] Because
of coverage formula amendments extending the determination of low voter
turnout/registration to the 1968 and 1972 presidential election years, other
preclearance states and/or their subdivisions were added, bringing the current
number to more than twelve thousand.[12]

Section 2 of the original act barred states and their subdivisions from
denying or abridging the right to vote on the basis of race or color. When
Section 2 was amended in 1982, it took on a decidedly disparate-impact and
antidilutionist cast. (More of this at 205–10.)

Section 4 and Disparate Impact

Section 4[13] created a major affirmative action program. Once an important weapon in preventing blacks from voting, literacy tests, by that Section, can

no longer be employed to bar suffrage and work a disproportionate impact on the voting patterns of racial and ethnic minorities as they have in the past. To its everlasting credit, the VRA has expansively opened America's voting booths to blacks, Latinos, and other minorities. It has significantly improved their ability to participate in the affairs of government.

The results of Section 4's implementation are impressive. Shortly after the act was passed, most voting-age African Americans were authorized to vote across the entire South, including the seven states originally targeted by the act. This was a dramatic change. In 1960, only 5.2 percent of Mississippi blacks were registered to vote; in Alabama and South Carolina, some 14 percent. Only in Tennessee was a black majority registered to vote (50.9). Black officeholding rose greatly nationwide and in the South. The Old Confederacy experienced a tenfold increase in the number of African American publicly elected officials (565 to 5,579 from 1970 to 2000), but it was not until the 1990s that black representation in the Southern legislatures began to approximate their percentage in the population. One dimension of the VRA impact was its correlation with a large movement of whites from their "solid" Democratic Party commitment to the GOP, leaving voting in the South quite racially polarized—blacks voting Democratic and whites generally backing Republicans.[14]

VRA amendments abolished the literacy test nationwide (1970) and extended the preclearance mechanism to cover various boroughs in New York and counties in Arizona and California (1970). Additional counties in California, as well as counties in New York, Florida, Michigan, New Hampshire, and the entire states of Texas and Arizona were added to the preclearance roster by VRA amendments in 1975. These amendments enhanced the voting capacities of Hispanic, Asian, and Native Americans, as did VRA §203 (1975), providing bilingual ballots to language minorities.[15] Section 203 was reauthorized for twenty-five years in 2006[16] and provides that where Hispanic, Asian, and Native Americans constitute more than 5 percent of the population in a state, and if they experience an illiteracy rate higher than the national average (as measured by the number of people who do not complete the fifth grade), they are to be given voting materials both in English and their native tongues in the political subdivision where they are more than 5 percent of the population. Section 203 is applicable in all of California and Texas, as well as in several hundred political subdivisions in twenty-six other states.[17]

Officeholding by Hispanics and Asians has increased strongly as the literacy test was abolished, and with the operations of §203 and the creation of VRA-induced majority-minority districts—that is, voting districts where a majority of the population is minority. Seven of ten of the 5,049 non-black minority office holders (2003) come from districts covered by §203, and many of these also reside in majority-minority districts.[18]

When the act was inaugurated in 1965, there were fewer than one hundred elected black officeholders in the seven targeted states, and less than two hundred nationwide. By 1990, these numbers had soared to 3,394 in the targeted jurisdictions, and 7,370 nationally.[19] In the six states with the greatest Hispanic populations—Arizona, California, Florida, New Mexico, New York, and Texas—the number of elected Latino officials rose from 1,280 in 1973 to 3,592 in 1990.[20] Nationwide, the number of such officials increased from 3,063 to nearly 5,000 between 1984 and 1990 alone.[21] In 1965, when the VRA was passed, there were five African Americans and three Hispanics in Congress. In 1996, there were seventeen Hispanics and thirty-eight blacks, a six and sevenfold increase.[22] In the 2008 presidential nomination races, African Americans overwhelmingly supported the Obama candidacy, helping him win a number of nomination races, while Clinton was favored by Hispanic voters.[23] In the general election, both of these groupings coalesced strongly behind Obama.[24] No presidential candidate since Lyndon Johnson in 1964 received a majority of the white votes. This was true for Obama, but clearly a large white vote was necessary for his presidential win.[25]

These remarkable increases in minority officeholding can be attributed, in large measure, to the operation of the VRA as a whole: abolition of discriminatory voting tests; preclearance requirements; and expanded minority registrations; followed by increased minority voter turnout. But it is abundantly clear that a critical factor in the entire mix has been the adoption of majority-minority congressional and other legislative districts by state redistricting authorities.[26] For example, when fourteen blacks and six Latinos came to Congress in 1992—the greatest absolute increase in black representation ever in a single year—almost all of them were elected from majority-minority districts drawn under Sections 2 and 5.[27] Hispanics and blacks have rarely won in majority-white congressional districts. In 1996, for example, of the thirty-eight blacks in the House, thirty-one came from majority-black districts, and five of the remaining came from majority-minority districts where Hispanics made up most of the non-black population. All the 1996 Hispanic House members were from majority-minority districts.[28]

Creation of Majority-Minority Districts: Section 5 of the Voting Rights Act

As Section 4's implementation produced an explosive jump in registration and voting by Southern blacks,[29] many of the affected Jim Crow jurisdictions countered with a campaign of "massive resistance" which some authorities liken to their attempts to evade *Brown v. The Board's*[30] 1954 school desegregation requirement.[31] While not designed to *deny* the vote to the newly enfranchised blacks, these schemes ran the vote-*dilution* gamut, ranging from blatantly discriminatory shifts to at-large or multimember elections in which black voters would be submerged in a sea of their white brethren, to racial gerrymanders, changing offices from elective to appointive status, majority instead of plurality runoffs, and so on.[32] Congress had enacted Section 5 for the specific purpose of dealing with such attempts to circumvent the new law,[33] but the preclearance provisions were not invoked to address dilution through redistricting until the aftermath of *Allen v. State Board of Elections* (1969).[34]

In *Allen*, the Supreme Court interpreted Section 5 (the preclearance section) to protect not only the right to vote, but also the right to an *effective* vote.[35] That case involved Mississippi's effort to change the mode of electing county supervisors from a ward (district) mechanism to an at-large system. Critics regarded this change as an effort to smother the potency of new black voters by submerging them in mainly white, at-large voting areas.[36] Mississippi contended that Section 5 was restricted to registration for voting, and had no bearing on voting as such. The Court rejected this claim, and held that the change was preclearable because of its potential dilutive effect on African American voting power. In so ruling, the Court said:

> The right to vote can be affected by a dilution of voting power as well as by an absolute prohibition on casting a ballot. Voters who are members of a racial minority might well be in the majority in one district, but in a decided minority in [a larger voting unit]. . . . This type of change could therefore nullify their ability to elect the candidate of their choice just as would prohibiting some of them from voting.[37]

In holding that redistricting was preclearable, the *Allen* Court relied on *Reynolds v. Sims*,[38] which ruled that the Equal Protection Clause required voters to be weighted equally in the construction of legislative districts ("one man, one vote"), thus barring vote dilution because of geographical location. *Reynolds* was a victory for *majority* rights; *Allen*'s linkage of minority rights to *Reynolds* consequently wedded majoritarian and minority theories of vote dilution.

Allen's extremely broad ruling established beyond question that *all* arguable electoral changes must be submitted for preclearance. In administering the "effect" prong of Section 5's purpose/effect test, the U.S. Department of Justice (DOJ) acted on the affirmative action premise that the Voting Rights Act's ultimate objective was not merely to pry open the doors of the voting booth, but also to help minorities elect minority candidates, and that race/ethnic-based districting was the sine qua non of fair minority representation. This premise was based, among other things, on the African American historic inability to elect black officials from white-majority districts.[39] Early on, DOJ's preclearance policy was to withhold approval of potentially discriminatory redistricting plans unless the redistricters agreed to include some form of majority-minority districting.[40] By the mid-70s, it was common practice to include one or more "super" majority-minority districts (65 percent or more) in new districting plans in order to pass preclearance scrutiny.[41] Although this antidilution program was initiated under the preclearance provisions of VRA Section 5, since 1982 it has been conducted, in large measure, under amended VRA Section 2 (see 205–10). From the beginning, race-based districting has applied to Latino groups as well as African Americans.[42]

For the most part, the courts initially approved DOJ's activist preclearance policy for redistricting.[43] The main reason for racial districting's ascendancy was the impetus the *Allen* decision lent to DOJ's activist reading of its Section 5 preclearance power. Subsequently, however, the Supreme Court drastically curtailed its support for majority-minority districting under Section 5. In 1976, the Supreme Court refused to sanction DOJ's policy of attempting to compel covered jurisdictions to maximize the number of majority-minority districts. The lead 1976 *Beer* case [44] arose from a plan for reapportioning New Orleans' five city council districts in order to accommodate a population increase. The city's population ratio was 55 percent white, 45 percent black, and its registered voter ratio was 65 percent white, 35 percent black. The redistricting plan called for five new districts arranged in the existing north-to-south pattern, with black *population* majorities in two districts, and a registered black *voter* majority in a third.[45]

The U.S. attorney general denied the city's Section 5 request for several reasons, including the claim that, since the black neighborhoods were generally located in an "east to west progression," using north-to-south districts "almost inevitably would have the *effect* of diluting the *maximum potential impact* of the Negro vote."[46]

On the city's appeal, the district court concluded that given the opportunity to elect councilmen in proportion to their share of the city's registered voters, or of the city's population, the city's African Americans would have been able to elect at least two or three. However, under the disputed plan, given the long history of racial bloc voting in the city, "Negroes would probably be able to elect only one, . . . the candidate from the one . . . district in which a majority of the voters were Negroes."[47] Therefore, the plan would have the effect of abridging the right to vote on account of race or color, and was not entitled to preclearance.[48]

The Supreme Court reversed, declaring that:

> [T]he purpose of Section 5 has always been to insure that no voting-procedure changes would be made that would lead to a retrogression in the position of racial minorities with respect to their effective exercise of the electoral franchise. . . .

[A] legislative reapportionment that enhances the position of racial minorities with respect to their effective exercise of the electoral franchise can hardly have the "effect" of diluting or abridging the right to vote on account of race or color within the meaning of Section 5.[49]

The Supreme Court majority found that, under the previous reapportionment, none of the five city council districts had a black voting majority, and no black was ever elected to the council. By contrast, under the disputed plan, in addition to the above-mentioned black voter majority district, two would have black population majorities. Accordingly, the majority held that there was "every reason to predict, upon the . . . hypothesis of bloc voting, that at least one and perhaps two Negroes [might] . . . well be elected to the council under [the disputed plan]" Therefore the plan could not have a dilutive "effect" in the sense of Section 5.[50]

The *Beer* retrogression doctrine limits Section 5 preclearance review of proposed redistricting plans to the question of whether they would impermissibly reduce minority voting strength. This notion suggests a seemingly simple, objective standard for resolving redistricting disputes: Will affected minorities be better, or worse off, in terms of their ability to elect? Apart, however, from the fact that this "nonretrogression" standard is not as simple as it may seem,[51] it has not been widely adopted as a definitive criterion of minority representation. It is not available for measuring unchanged rules and procedures in jurisdictions covered by Section 5, dating in some cases back to the end of Reconstruction, or rules and procedures of any kind in uncovered jurisdictions. Furthermore, in the mainstream liberal view, by mandating preclearance in nonretrogression cases, the *Beer* ruling precludes consideration of whether more "might be accomplished in terms of increasing minority representation."[52] In effect, the status quo has become a ceiling rather than a floor, and Section 5's function has been reduced to preventing erosion rather than sustaining the momentum of civil rights reform.[53] Thus, even though majority-minority districts first emerged as antidilution remedies from Section 5, preclearance law offers little help in defining dilution or evaluating race/ethnic-based districting.[54]

Beer confirmed that the Court's post-*Allen* view of antidilution and race-based districting was not invariably supportive. But in Abigail Thernstrom's persuasive view, the voting-rights arm of the Department of Justice continued to seek Section 5's assistance to acquire the creation of the maximum number of safe majority-minority districts, that is, that number that corresponded to the department's view of proportional racial fairness.[55] Supreme Court opinions, in the *Beer* decade of the 1970s, sometimes were supportive of this quest, sometimes not. Shortly after VRA's enactment, while refusing to rule that multimember districts inherently diluted minority voting power, the Court allowed that they *might* be unconstitutional if operated "*designedly or otherwise* . . . to minimize or cancel out the voting strength of racial or political elements of the voting population."[56] However, in *Whitcomb v. Chavis* (1971), the Court, 5-4, rejected a constitutional equal protection claim based on the chronic inability of black ghetto residents in a multimember legislative district to elect proportionate numbers of their preferred candidates.[57] Since the Constitution does not mandate proportional representation, and since there was no evidence that the claimants had been discriminatorily denied an equal opportunity to participate in the political process, their underrepresentation, in the majority's view, did not result from dilution.[58] However, in *White v. Regester* (1973),[59] involving a similar claim, the Court, 5-4, reached the opposite conclusion. The majority held that the minority claimants had been deprived of the requisite opportunity by the "totality of the circumstances," including discriminatory voting rules and invidious maltreatment, and it upheld the district court's order to create new single-member legislative districts as the remedy for the unconstitutional dilution.[60] *White's* criteria did not include discriminatory intent.[61]

Just one year after *Beer,* the Court did provide constitutional support for the creation of majority-minority districts in *United Jewish Organizations [UJO] of Williamsburg, Inc. v. Carey* (1977).[62] The Supreme Court, in that case, upheld a redistricting plan which, based on preclearance negotiations with DOJ, created a 65 percent "nonwhite" (black and Puerto Rican) supermajority in one district, and assigned part of the district's thirty thousand–member Hasidic Jewish community to another district. The reason for the reassignment was to ensure that the population of the nonwhite district did not exceed the applicable limit of one person, one vote. The Hasidim claimed that the dispersal violated their Fourteenth and Fifteenth Amendment rights by diluting their power to elect one of their own members to office.

The Court rejected this claim, 7-1. Justice White announced the judgment. Writing for himself and Justices Brennan, Blackmun, and Stevens, he concluded that the plan's use of racial criteria in attempting to comply with Section 5 and to secure the attorney general's approval did not violate the Fourteenth or Fifteenth Amendments.

> [C]ompliance with the [VRA] Act in reapportionment cases, . . . often necessitate[s] the use of racial considerations in drawing district lines. . . . [T]he Constitution does not prevent a State subject to the . . . Act from deliberately creating or preserving black majorities in particular districts in order to ensure that its reapportionment plan complies with Section 5.[63] The permissible use of racial criteria is not confined to eliminating the effects of past discriminatory districting or apportionment. . . .
>
> [I]n the process of drawing black majority districts in order to comply with [Section] 5, the State must decide how substantial

those majorities must be in order to satisfy the . . . Act. . . . But whatever the specific percentage [of majority], the State will inevitably arrive at it as a necessary means to ensure the opportunity for the election of a black representative and to obtain approval of its reapportionment plan. . . . [A] reapportionment plan does not violate the Fourteenth or the Fifteenth Amendment merely because a State uses specific numerical quotas in establishing a certain number of black majority districts.[64]

In Part IV of his opinion, writing for himself, and Justices Stevens and Rehnquist, Justice White concluded that, entirely apart from the need to comply with Section 5 of the statute, the state's "deliberately . . . purposeful"[65] use of race did not violate the Constitution:

[The] plan represented no racial slur or stigma with respect to whites or any other race, and [therefore] no discrimination violative of the Fourteenth Amendment. . . .[66] [N]or [was there] any abridgment of the right to vote on account of race within the meaning of the Fifteenth Amendment. . . .

[Even though] New York deliberately increased the nonwhite majorities in certain districts in order to enhance the opportunity for the election of nonwhite representatives from those districts . . . there was no fencing out of the white population from participation in the political processes of the county, and the plan did not minimize or unfairly cancel out white voting strength.

UJO stands for the proposition that the Constitution permits the use of racial criteria and numerical quotas in drawing district lines, absent proof of collateral damage. Chief Justice Burger filed a dissent, which foreshadowed the racial gerrymander decisions of the 1990s. He wrote:

The result reached by the Court today in the name of the Voting Rights Act is ironic. The use of a mathematical formula tends to sustain the existence of ghettos by promoting the notion that political clout is to be gained or maintained by marshaling particular racial, ethnic, or religious groups in enclaves. It suggests to the voter that only a candidate of the same race, religion, or ethnic origin can properly represent that voter's interests, and that such candidate can be elected only from a district with a sufficient minority concentration. The device employed by the State of New York, and endorsed by the Court today, moves us one step farther away from a truly homogeneous society. This retreat from the ideal of the American "melting pot" is curiously out of step with recent political history—and indeed with what the Court has said and done for more than a decade. The notion that Americans vote in firm blocs has been repudiated in the election of minority members as mayors and legislators in numerous American cities and districts overwhelmingly white. Since I cannot square the mechanical racial gerrymandering in this case with the mandate of the Constitution, I respectfully dissent.[67]

In pursuing Section 5's preclearance assistance in obtaining the maximum majority-minority districts, the voting rights officialdom claimed that failure by covered jurisdictions to meet that objective was in and of itself the "retrogression" prohibited by *Beer*.[68] This entailed taking that section's 1965 requirement that an electoral rule change "does not have the purpose and will not have the effect of denying or abridging the right to vote on account of race or color," and separating "purpose" and "effect." Thus, the reading went, failure to create the appropriate number of majority-minority districts manifested the purpose of abridging or denying the right to vote. This reading was rejected by the Court in *Reno v. Bossier Parrish* (2000)[69] although the Court admitted that one of its opinions in 1975 lent credence to the Department of Justice's interpretation. Writing for the majority, Justice Scalia said:

> When considered in light of our longstanding interpretation of the "effect" prong of §5 in its application to vote dilution claims, the language of §5 leads to the conclusion that the "purpose" prong of §5 covers only retrogressive dilution. . . . As we have repeatedly noted, in vote-dilution cases §5 prevents nothing but backsliding, and preclearance under §5 affirms nothing but the absence of backsliding. . . .

> [B]y suggesting that §5 extends to discriminatory, but nonretrogressive vote-dilutive purposes, appellant . . . would also exacerbate the "substantial" federalism costs that the preclearance procedure already exacts perhaps to the extent of raising concerns about §5's constitutionality.[70]

Another blow to the voting rights officialdom safe, majority-minority district quest came in *Georgia v. Ashcroft* (2003).[71] In a reapportionment plan, Georgia Democratic state legislators had reduced the black majorities in a number of districts (e.g., 60.58 to 50.31 percent; 55.43 to 50.66 percent; 62.45 to 50.80 percent) to "unpack" them, and spread African Americans in sizable numbers to white districts where they could be potent participants in political coalitions with whites. The Department of Justice denied Section 5 preclearance viewing black majority size reduction as an "abridgement" of the right to vote on the basis of color or race.[72] The Supreme Court majority disagreed, ruling that the determination of retrogression required an investigation of the totality of circumstances. O'Connor, for the majority wrote:[73]

Georgia v. Ashcroft, 539 U.S. 461 (2003)

[A]ny assessment of the retrogression of a minority group's effective exercise of the electoral franchise depends on an examination of all the relevant circumstances, such as the ability of minority voters to elect their candidate of choice, the extent of the minority group's opportunity to participate in the political process, and the feasibility of creating a nonretrogressive plan. [480] "No single statistic provides courts with a shortcut to determine whether" a voting change retrogresses from the benchmark. *Johnson v. DeGrandy*, 512 U.S. 997, at 1020–1021.

In assessing the totality of the circumstances, a court should not focus solely on the comparative ability of a minority group to elect a candidate of its choice. While this factor is an important one in the § 5 retrogression inquiry, it cannot be dispositive or exclusive. The standard in § 5 is simple—whether the new plan "would lead to a retrogression in the position of racial minorities with respect to their effective exercise of the electoral franchise." *Beer v. U.S.*, 425 U.S. 130, at 141.

The ability of minority voters to elect a candidate of their choice is important but often complex in practice to determine. In order to maximize the electoral success of a minority group, a State may choose to create a certain number of "safe" districts, in which it is highly likely that minority voters will be able to elect the candidate of their choice. Alternatively, a State may choose to create a greater number of districts in which it is likely—although perhaps not quite as likely as under the benchmark plan—that minority voters will be able to elect candidates of their choice.

Section 5 does not dictate that a State must pick one of these methods of redistricting over another. Either option "will present the minority group with its own array of electoral risks and benefits," and presents "hard choices about what would truly 'maximize' minority electoral success." *Thornburg v. Gingles*, 478 U.S. 30, at 89. On one hand, a smaller number of safe [481] majority-minority districts may virtually guarantee the election of a minority group's preferred candidate in those districts. Yet even if this concentration of minority voters in a few districts does not constitute the unlawful packing of minority voters, such a plan risks isolating minority voters from the rest of the State, and risks narrowing political influence to only a fraction of political districts. And while such districts may result in more "descriptive representation" because the representatives of choice are more likely to mirror the race of the majority of voters in that district, the representation may be limited to fewer areas.

On the other hand, spreading out minority voters over a greater number of districts creates more districts in which minority voters may have the opportunity to elect a candidate of their choice. Such a strategy has the potential to increase "substantive representation" in more districts, by creating coalitions of voters who together will help to achieve the electoral aspirations of the minority group. It also, however, creates the risk that the minority group's preferred candidate may lose. Yet as we stated in *Johnson v. De Grandy*, 512 U.S. at 1020.

"There are communities in which minority citizens are able to form coalitions with voters from other racial and ethnic groups, having no need to be a majority within a single district in order to elect candidates of their choice. Those candidates may not represent perfection to every minority voter, but minority voters are not immune from the obligation to pull, haul, and trade to find common political ground, the virtue of which is not to be slighted in applying a statute meant to hasten the waning of racism in American politics."

[482] Section 5 gives States the flexibility to choose one theory of effective representation over the other.

Section 5 of the VRA was amended in 2006 in a fashion that supported the longtime objectives of the Department of Justice, and those civil rights advocates who regarded *Bossier* and *Ashcroft* as major threats.[74] Note the separation of *purpose* and *effect* in the amended statute, as the department has urged for years, and the amendment appears to annul *Bossier*. Note, too, the prohibition against diminishing the capacity of any citizen to elect their preferred candidate on the basis of race or color. This provision denies what *Ashcroft* permitted: reducing the size of the majority in majority-minority districts. The words of the amendment follow:

Public Law 109-246—July 27, 2006 120 STAT 577

Section 5 of the Voting Rights Act of 1965 (42 USC 1973c) is amended . . .

(2) by striking "does not have the purpose and will not have the effect" and inserting "neither has the purpose nor will have the effect"; and

(3) by adding at the end the following:

"(b) Any voting qualification or prerequisite to voting, or standard, practice, or procedure with respect to voting that has the purpose of or will have the effect of diminishing the ability of any citizens of the United States on account of race or color, . . . to elect their preferred candidates of choice denies or abridges the right to vote. . . .

"(c) The term 'purpose' in subsections (a) and (b) of this section shall include any discriminatory purpose.

(d) The purpose of subsection (b) of this section is to protect the ability of such citizens to elect their preferred candidates of choice."

In *Northwest Austin Municipal Utility District v. Holder* (2009),[75] Chief Justice Roberts writing for an eight-member majority concluded that Section 5, and its preclearance requirements and coverage formula, raised "serious constitutional questions" because states were treated differently under these provisions, resulting in a deviation from the "fundamental principle" that states share "equal sovereignty." Departure from that principle requires that disparate treatment is warranted by the problem.[76]

Roberts noted that the antiminority voting discrimination may no longer be geographically concentrated as it was at the birth of the VRA. Impressively enough, the racial gap in voter registration and turnout is lower in the original preclearance states than in the nation at large. With respect to these suffrage matters, the evidence points to "more similarity than difference." Additionally, according to equal protection dictates and VRA's Section 2, race cannot be the predominant factor in legislative districting. What is doomed under the Fourteenth Amendment and Section 2, enables jurisdictions to be precleared under Section 5.[77]

Despite these constitutional misgivings, the Court decided not to rule on Section 5's constitutional problems. Rather, the Court concluded that relief could be granted the petitioners (i.e., eligibility to "bail out" of the preclearance requirements) through statutory interpretation of Section 5.[78] The Chief Justice asserted that previous interpretations by the Department of Justice as to which political subdivisions were eligible to apply for bailout were too "limited." This narrowness was, in part, responsible for the small number of bailouts—only seventeen since 1982 of the twelve tnousand preclearance jurisdictions. To ease bailing out, the Court read the VRA as allowing the preclearance states and all their political subdivisions, including Northwestern Austin Municipal Utility, to apply.[79] As Justice Thomas pointed out, however, acquiring bailout status presented challenges, so much so, he believes, that "[b]ailout eligibility is a distant prospect for most covered jurisdictions."[80] Applicants are required among other things, to show that for the last ten years there had been no test or device, in their jurisdictions, which had the purpose and effect of denying voting rights for racial purposes; that no final federal court judgments finding that denial or abridging voting on account of race or color had occurred in any part of the applicant's jurisdiction; and that the U.S. Attorney General did not object. Applicant jurisdictions, moreover, have to present information about minority electoral participation, minority voting registration over time, and disparities between minority and nonminority voting participation.[81]

Antidilution Under the Amended Section 2

In *City of Mobile v. Bolden* (1980)[82] a Supreme Court plurality decided that, "in order to establish a violation either of Section 2 or of the Fourteenth, or Fifteenth Amendments, a minority voter must prove that a contested electoral mechanism was *intentionally* adopted or maintained by a state official for a discriminatory purpose."[83] This ruling caused a furor in the voting rights lobby because it appeared to vitiate minority rights—such as the ability to formulate majority-minority districts—under existing case law.[84] In 1982, "Congress substantially revised Section 2 to make clear that a violation could be proved by showing discriminatory *effect* alone and to establish as the relevant legal standard the 'results test' applied by this Court in *White v. Regester* and by other federal courts before *Bolden*."[85]

As amended in 1982, Section 2 prohibits the imposition of any voting rule or procedure "which *results* in denial or abridgement of the right to vote on account of race, color, or membership in a language minority."[86] A violation of the aforementioned occurs where the "totality of circumstances" discloses that:

> [T]he political processes leading to nomination or election . . . are not equally open to participation by members of a . . . [protected] class . . . in that its members have less opportunity than other

members of the electorate to participate in the political process and to elect representatives of their choice. The extent to which members of a protected class have been elected to office . . . is one circumstance which may be considered: *Provided*, that nothing in this Section establishes a right to have members of a protected class elected in numbers equal to their proportion in the population.[87]

The statutory language and its history[88] underscore the primary features of the 1982 amendments:

> That the adoption of the "results" test in Section 2(a) "squarely decoupled" Section 2 from the presumed Supreme Court's holding in *City of Mobile v. Bolden* (1980).[89] *Bolden's* plurality ruled that statutory-dilution claims under the original Section 2 required proof of discriminatory purpose.[90]
> The "totality of circumstances" provisions of Section 2 incorporated the constitutional dilution test which the Supreme Court formulated in *White v. Register* (see 199), and which did not include an intent requirement.[91]
> Section 2 is violated if "plaintiffs do not have an equal opportunity to participate in the political processes and to elect candidates of their choice." Proof of a violation could include a "variety of factors," depending on the rule, practice, or procedure called into question. There is no requirement that any particular number of factors be proved, or that a majority of them point one way or the other.[92]

The new Section 2 has displaced Section 5 as the primary, federal-statutory guardian of minority voting rights.[93] As the Supreme Court has explained:

> [M]anipulation of district lines can dilute the voting strength of politically cohesive minority group members, [either] by *fragmenting* the minority voters among several districts where a bloc-voting majority can routinely out-vote them, or by *packing* them into one or a small number to minimize their influence in the districts next door. Section 2 prohibits either sort of line-drawing where its result, " 'interact[ing] with social and historical conditions,' impairs the ability of a protected class to elect its candidate of choice on an equal basis with other voters." [94]

Given that the rationale of the "results" test is the mirror image of the "effects" test, which is enshrined in equal employment opportunity (and approximated in education) law as disparate-impact affirmative action,[95] Section 2 plainly functions as a vehicle of race/ethnic-conscious antidilution remedies.[96] In this respect, it is subject only to the disclaimer, which provides, in essence, that the statute does not *mandate* proportional representation. However, it is not clear whether the quest for such proportionality is constitutionally *permissible.* By design or otherwise, this circumstance has left open a most fundamental unresolved voting rights issue: Is it a legitimate social goal to foster election of minority-preferred candidates in numbers that approximate the minorities' shares of the population? [97]

By far the most troubling question about Section 2 is whether the application of the results test, which it codified, has produced an acceptable standard of fair representation. On this point, the lead case is *Thornburg v. Gingles* (1986).[98]

Since 1982, the great bulk of affirmative action, racial/ethnic-dilution litigation has taken place under Section 2.[99] The contours of this litigation were defined in *Gingles* (1986), where the Supreme Court for the first time construed amended Section 2.

The black plaintiffs in this landmark case were residents of several multimember districts in North Carolina which had been established under a legislative redistricting plan. They claimed that the state's choice of the multimember districts diluted their votes by "submerging them" in white majorities. Specifically, the plaintiffs contended that the multimember districts contained several contiguous concentrations of black citizens large enough to function as effective voting *majorities* in single-member districts. The Court upheld the dilution claim with respect to four of the disputed districts, but rejected it in a fifth, where the minority-preferred candidate had won in six successive elections.[100]

As the primary basis for its judgment, the Court majority employed two standards: the level of minority electoral success, and the extent of racial bloc voting.[101] These factors were embodied in the evidentiary test which Justice Brennan set out in his opinion for the majority:

> The essence of a Section 2 claim is that a certain electoral law, practice or structure interacts with social and historical conditions to cause an inequality in the opportunities enjoyed by black and white voters to elect their preferred representatives. . . . [M]ultimember districts and at-large voting schemes "may operate to minimize or cancel out the voting strength of racial [minorities]." . . . The theoretical basis for this type of impairment is that where minority and majority voters consistently prefer different candidates, the majority, by virtue of its numerical superiority, will regularly defeat the choices of minority voters. Multimember districts and at-large voting schemes, however, are not *per se* violative of minority voters' rights. . . . Minority voters

who contend that the multimember form of districting violates Section 2 must prove that the use of a multimember electoral structure operates to minimize or cancel out their ability to elect their preferred candidates. . . .[102]

First, the minority group must be able to demonstrate that it is sufficiently large and geographically compact to constitute a majority in a single-member district. . . . *Second*, the minority group must be able to show that it is politically cohesive. . . . *Third*, the minority must be able to demonstrate that the white majority votes sufficiently as a bloc as to enable it—in the absence of special circumstances, such as the minority candidate running unopposed—usually to defeat the minority's preferred candidate.[103]

Under *Gingles*, the results test was established as the expansive foundation of dilution law. In true disparate-impact fashion, what counted for Justice Brennan was whether—not why—racial bloc voting diluted minority votes.[104] *Gingles* established the rule that, regardless of the lawmakers' intent, a voting district that has the effect of impermissibly diluting the voting strength of an identifiable minority group violates Section 2 and warrants affirmative relief. The three-part test is not restricted to cases arising from the electoral impotence of minorities submerged in multimember systems, as in *Gingles* itself. It applies also in single-member cases where the plaintiffs have achieved some representation, but claim that their ability to gain the maximum has been diluted.[105]

Even though *Gingles* unequivocally embraced the results test, it left behind considerable confusion and uncertainty about its scope. The Court did not define the decision's basic terms, namely, *geographical compactness, cohesive, usually,* or *majority.* It failed to make clear whether the three-prong test supplants the nine factors enumerated in the Congressional description of "totality of the circumstances."[106] It did not address the extremely controversial issue of whether Section 2's reference to "representatives of choice" impliedly contains a same-race limitation. Most significantly, the Court indicated that, in a dilution case, difficulty in electing minority-preferred candidates and the extent of racially polarized voting outweigh geographical compactness in importance.[107] This ruling led many states to ignore compactness in creating new majority-minority districts, thus setting the stage for the racial gerrymander litigation of the 1990s. In short, *Gingles* exemplifies the support/opposition syndrome in dilution case law; on the one hand, the Court enshrined the results test, but on the other hand, it laid down the basis for the greatest challenge to its application.[108]

Justice Brennan's ruling that "the single-member district is generally the appropriate standard" of minority representation[109] encouraged the lower courts and DOJ to promote creation of single-member, majority-minority districts in preclearance jurisdictions during the redistricting round of the 1990s. By triggering this explosion of new majority-minority districts, the ruling provided the raw material for the current constitutional dilemmas over racial gerrymandering.[110] By the same token, it provoked an ideological clash in the Court. In her *Gingles* concurrence, Justice O'Connor rejected the rationale of the ruling on the ground that it was tantamount to an endorsement of "rough" proportionality, which while "not quite the same as a right to strict proportionality . . . [is] inconsistent with Section 2's disclaimer and with the results test that is codified in Section 2."[111] Later racial gerrymander cases make clear that the rift over this crucial issue remains to this day.

As noted, the initial standard that must be met to establish a majority-minority district under Section 2 reads: "*First*, the minority group must be able to demonstrate that it is sufficiently large . . . to constitute a majority in a single-member district." Did Section 2 and the first *Gingles* standard require redistricting that enhanced minority political opportunity where the minority did not constitute a majority? This was the asserted position of North Carolina's redistricting authorities in *Bartlett v. Strickland* (2009).[112] These authorities had grafted the African American population in Pender County (where blacks were 35.3 percent of the voting age population) to a new congressional district where they were 39.6 percent of the voting age population. This new district, it was claimed, would give blacks the opportunity to elect representatives of their choice with the anticipated help of nonminority votes. Blacks in the new district would be an "effective" majority, as contemplated by *Gingles*.

The Supreme Court rejected the "effective" majority thesis. *Gingles* was applicable only when the protected group was an actual voting age majority, insisted Justice Kennedy's plurality opinion. The effective-majority view would require courts to speculate as to when there were sufficient crossover nonminority votes to enable the minority group to acquire a desired candidate. This was a "bridge too far." Section 2 was designed to prevent racist interference with existing protected-group majoritarian will, and not *require* (although it *permitted*) the creation of special opportunities for the augmentation of minority political power either through "crossover" or "influence" districts. The latter, already rejected by the Court as a Section 2 requirement, involve moving minorities to districts in a way so as to enhance their influence. As for the constitutional status of majority-minority, Justice Kennedy warned that VRA statutory interpretation did not constitutionally entrench majority-minority districts. Kennedy referenced his majority opinion in *Miller v. Johnson* (1995)[113] as to what the Constitution requires in connection with majority-minority districts. *Miller* will be discussed starting at 210.

Justice Thomas (joined by Justice Scalia) concurred with the Court's judgment that Section 2 did not require minority opportunity districting.

He referenced his opinion in *Holder v. Hall* (1994),[114] which argued that the VRA prohibited only state denial of the franchise for racial/ethnic reasons. By pursuing the objective of reducing minority vote dilution through the creation of majority-minority districts, "we have devised a remedial mechanism that encourages federal courts to segregate voters into racially designated districts to ensure minority electoral success. In doing so, we have collaborated in what may aptly be termed the racial "balkanization" of the Nation."[115]

Gingles and its racial gerrymandering progeny have prompted apprehensions about judicial furtherance of "racial essentialism," that is, that the courts had in Voting Rights Act cases accepted the doctrine that people of one race and ethnicity think alike and take the same approach to matters.[116] A majority in *LULAC v. Perry* (2006)[117]—in an opinion written by Justice Kennedy—ruled that the majority-of-the-protected-group dimension of *Gingles* required not only a numerical racial/ethnic majority, but also a similar socioeconomic identity within that number. This was a significant departure from the *essentialist* position in traditional affirmative action advocacy that race/ethnicity alone was sufficient for affirmative action assistance, and a departure antedated in Kennedy's *Miller v. Johnson* opinion.

LULAC concerned a Texas reapportionment plan (Plan 1374) which reduced the Hispanic citizen, voting-age population in one district (#23) from 57.5 percent to 46 percent. A sizeable Hispanic population in that district had demonstrated a strong, cohesive social/political ideology over the years in opposing a conservative congressional incumbent. To prevent Section 2 voter-dilution liability, the reapportionment plan crated a new district (#25) consisting of a 55 percent Hispanic citizen, voting-age population. The new district stretched three hundred miles in a north-south fashion from the middle of the state (Austin) to the Mexican border. This elongated vertical route incorporated the populations of numerous counties. The Court majority found that the northern Hispanic portion of #25 consisted of people sociologically/economically quite different from the Hispanics in the southern portion. Consequently, the new district (#25) did not compensate for dismemberment and the dilution of the Hispanic majority-minority in old district #23, and thus violated Section 5.[118]

The "Racial Gerrymander" Cases of the 1990s and the Constitutional Requirements of the Equal Protection Clause

Background

The Court's VRA interpretations in the new millennium posed challenges to the practice of majority-minority districting: *Bossier II*[119] rejected DOJ's quest to maximize such districting through preclearance; *Georgia v. Ashcroft*[120] accepted the lessening of their majoritarian strength; and *LULAC v. Perry*[121] rejected "racial essentialism" as the rationale for majority-minority districting. (See 210.) However, the greatest threat to this districting dimension of affirmative action came with the *Shaw/Miller* equal protection cases of the 1990s. Equal protection constitutional law is of vital concern to affirmative action, but ironically the Court has not clarified its *Shaw/Miller* "race-predominant" standard, leaving the question of how it is to be applied, and its very existence, in doubt since the Court concluded in *Hunt v. Cromartie* (2001)[122] that political gerrymandering was a defense against the charge of illicit racial gerrymandering.

In the *Shaw/Miller* cases, the Supreme Court established the rule that majority-minority districts drawn with race as the "predominant" factor are presumptively unconstitutional racial gerrymanders under the Equal Protection Clause—a presumption that can be overcome only if the districting at issue survives strict judicial scrutiny.[123] In these decisions, the Court, 5-4, invalidated majority black districts which had been created in North Carolina, Georgia, and Texas during the post-1990 census redistricting round.

With these actions, the Court opened a new chapter in the controversy over the appropriate remedy for voting discrimination, though its standards remain murky. Nonetheless, these decisions have called into question the government's race/ethnic-based antidilution program.

Strictly speaking, "gerrymandering" is synonymous with "dilution." Both terms connote drawing district lines in a way that arbitrarily limits the voting power of identifiable groups. In general usage, these terms imply distortion, political favoritism, or racial bias. In fact, both are forms of "districting," which "*always* involves choices among competing apportionment schemes that may favor one or another political party, incumbent official, regional interest, minority group, etc."[124] In this sense, " '*all districting is gerrymandering.*' "[125]

Generically, "racial gerrymanders" result from " 'the deliberate and arbitrary distortion of [voting] district boundaries . . . for . . . [racial] purposes.' "[126] They were the stock in trade of racial segregation in the post–Civil War South.[127] They have "come in various shades": at-large schemes that submerge minority groups in nonminority-majority multimember districts; "cracking," dispersing minorities among various districts where they will always be in the minority; "stacking," a large minority concentration within a larger nonminority population; and concentrating minority voters into districts where they constitute supermajorities.[128]

The 1990s Decisions

Between 1990 and 1992, during the post-1990 redistricting cycle, fourteen states created fifteen new black-majority districts and ten new Latino-majority districts. These dramatic changes were attributable to pressure by the U.S.

Department of Justice in preclearance negotiations; fear of government and private "Section 2" suits in the wake of *Gingles*; and the agitation for increased minority representation. Through the use of enhanced computer technology, many of the new districts were drawn with convoluted lines that completely obliterated long-standing county and city boundaries.[129]

Shaw v. Reno (1993) and its progeny through the end of the millennium represent the cutting edge of a reignited anti–affirmative action counterrevolution, which challenges the efficacy, the legality, and the morality of majority-minority districting.[130] These cases emerged from the crucible of preclearance negotiations. They were brought by white plaintiffs who did not claim dilution of their own voting rights. They were all decided, 5-4, by the same bloc: Justices Rehnquist, Scalia, O'Connor, Kennedy, and Thomas. It remains to be seen whether the "predominance-of-race" doctrine—which emerged from these decisions—is, in fact, a mechanism for declaring majority-minority districts unconstitutional in the future.

However this plays out, there is inflamed controversy over the VRA's role, and this will not abate. As we experience the redistricting of the new millennium, the time has come to reevaluate the Voting Rights Act. This evaluation should consider the thinking of the Court majority on racial gerrymandering as well as the views of the justices who have dissented from it.

Shaw v. Reno (1993)[131] was the Court's first brush with North Carolina's Twelfth Congressional District, a single-member majority-black district, which the state created in order to meet the Department of Justice's (DOJ) preclearance demand for a *second* new majority-black district in the state's post-1990 reapportionment plan.[132] The district consisted of a narrow, bizarrely shaped band of linked black-population concentrations, traversing several counties and cities, plainly designed to elect a black congressman.[133] The case held that the plaintiffs stated an equal protection claim for relief by alleging that the district was an unconstitutional racial gerrymander, since its shape showed that it *must* have been drawn solely to ensure election of black officeholders.[134] Following is an excerpt from Justice O'Connor's opinion for the Court, effectively expressing the "race-as-predominant-factor" principle.

> [The district] . . . is so extremely irregular on its face that it rationally can be viewed only as an effort to segregate the races for purposes of voting, without regard to traditional districting principles and without sufficiently compelling justification.[135] . . .

> When a district is obviously created solely to effectuate the perceived common interests of one racial group, elected officials are more likely to believe that their primary obligation is to represent only members of that group, rather than their constituency as a whole. This is altogether antithetical to our system of representative democracy.[136]

The dissenting Justices contended that the Equal Protection Clause bars racial districting only if it denies access to the polls or dilutes voting strength, citing *UJO v. Carey* (1977)[137] (see 199–201), where the Court rejected an equal protection attack on a majority-minority district, since the white plaintiffs had not been harmed in the dissenters' view. Consequently, *UJO* was indistinguishable from *Shaw*.[138]

Miller v. Johnson, 515 U.S. 900 (1995)

[In this case the Court applied the rule of *Shaw v. Reno* in striking down a majority-black district in Georgia, which the state drew in order to comply with DOJ's preclearance demand for a *third* such district. Justice Kennedy's opinion for the Court is the definitive statement of the rule. His opinion was unguided by *UJO v. Carey's* support of majority-minority districting. Following is an extended excerpt.]

Justice Kennedy delivered the opinion of the Court:

[903] The constitutionality of Georgia's congressional redistricting plan is at issue here. In *Shaw v. Reno*, 509 U.S. 630 (1993), we held that a plaintiff states a claim under the Equal Protection Clause by alleging that a state redistricting plan, on its face, has no rational explanation save as an effort to separate voters on the basis of race. The question we now decide is whether Georgia's new Eleventh District gives rise to a valid equal protection claim under the principles announced in [904] *Shaw*, and, if so, whether it can be sustained nonetheless as narrowly tailored to serve a compelling governmental interest.

The Equal Protection Clause of the Fourteenth Amendment provides that no State shall "deny to any person within its jurisdiction the equal protection of the laws." Its central mandate is racial neutrality in governmental decision making. . . .

[905] In 1965, the Attorney General designated Georgia a covered jurisdiction under [Section] 4(b) of the Voting Rights Act. In consequence, [Section] 5 of the Act requires Georgia to obtain either administrative preclearance by the Attorney General or approval by the United States District Court for the District of Columbia of any change in a "standard, practice, or procedure with respect to voting" made after November 1, 1964. The preclearance mechanism applies to [906] congressional redistricting plans, and requires that the proposed change "not have the purpose and will not have the effect of denying or abridging the

right to vote on account of race or color." . . . A special session opened in August 1991, and the General Assembly submitted a congressional redistricting plan to the Attorney General for preclearance on October 1, 1991. . . . [907] The Department's objection letter noted a concern that Georgia had created only two majority-minority districts. . . .

The General Assembly returned to the drawing board. A new plan was enacted and submitted for preclearance. This second attempt . . . increased the black populations in the Eleventh, Fifth and Second Districts. The Justice Department refused preclearance again, relying on alternative plans proposing three majority-minority districts. . . .

Twice spurned, the General Assembly set out to create three majority-minority districts to gain preclearance. Using the ACLU's [American Civil Liberties Union] "max-black" plan as its benchmark, the General Assembly enacted a plan that [included the newly designed Eleventh District at issue in this case]. . . .

[909] The Almanac of American Politics has this to say about the Eleventh District: "Geographically, it is a monstrosity, stretching from Atlanta to Savannah. Its core is the plantation country in the center of the state, lightly populated, but heavily black. It links by narrow corridors the black neighborhoods in Augusta, Savannah and southern DeKalb County." Georgia's plan included three majority-black districts, though, and received Justice Department preclearance on April 2, 1992. . . .

[The plaintiffs], five white voters from the Eleventh District, filed this action against various state officials . . . (Miller Appellants) in the United States District Court. . . . Their suit alleged that Georgia's Eleventh District was a racial gerrymander and so a violation of the Equal Protection Clause as interpreted in *Shaw v. Reno*. . . .

[911] Just as the State may not, absent extraordinary justification, segregate citizens on the basis of race in its public parks, buses, golf courses, beaches, and schools, so did we recognize in *Shaw* that it may not separate its citizens into different voting districts on the basis of race. The idea is a simple one: "At the heart of the Constitution's guarantee of equal protection lies the simple command that the Government must treat citizens as individuals,

not as simply components of a racial, religious, sexual or national class." . . . When the State assigns voters on the basis of race, it engages in [912] the offensive and demeaning assumption that voters of a particular race, because of their race, "think alike, share the same political interests, and will prefer the same candidates at the polls." Race-based assignments "embody stereotypes that treat individuals as the product of their race, evaluating their thoughts and efforts—their very worth as citizens—according to a criterion barred to the Government by history and the Constitution." . . . They also cause society serious harm. As we concluded in *Shaw*: "Racial classifications with respect to voting carry particular dangers. Racial gerrymandering, even for remedial purposes, may balkanize us into competing racial factions; it threatens to carry us further from the goal of a political system in which race no longer matters." . . .

[914] It is true that redistricting in most cases will implicate a political calculus in which various interests compete for recognition, but it does not follow from this that individuals of the same race share a single political interest. The view that they do is "based on the demeaning notion that members of the defined racial groups ascribe to certain 'minority views' that must be different from those of other citizens," the precise use of race as a proxy the Constitution prohibits. . . .

[916] Redistricting legislatures will, for example, almost always be aware of racial demographics; but it does not follow that race predominates in the redistricting process. . . . The distinction between being aware of racial considerations and being motivated by them may be difficult to make. This evidentiary difficulty, together with the sensitive nature of redistricting and the presumption of good faith that must be accorded legislative enactments, requires courts to exercise extraordinary caution in adjudicating claims that a state has drawn district lines on the basis of race. The plaintiff's burden is to show, either through circumstantial evidence of a district's shape and demographics or more direct evidence going to legislative purpose, that race was the predominant factor motivating the legislature's decision to place a significant number of voters within or without a particular district. To make this showing, a plaintiff must prove that the legislature subordinated traditional race-neutral districting principles, including but not limited to compactness, contiguity, respect for political subdivisions or communities defined by actual

shared interests, to racial considerations. Where these or other race-neutral considerations are the basis for redistricting legislation, and are not subordinated to race, a state can "defeat a claim that a district has been gerrymandered on racial lines." . . .

[917] In our view, the District Court applied the correct analysis, and its finding that race was the predominant factor motivating the drawing of the Eleventh District was not clearly erroneous. The court found it was "exceedingly obvious" from the shape of the Eleventh District, together with the relevant racial demographics, that the drawing of narrow land bridges to incorporate within the District outlying appendages containing nearly 80% of the district's total black population was a deliberate attempt to bring black populations into the district. . . . The court found that "it became obvious," both from the Justice Department's objection letters and the three preclearance rounds in general, "that [the Justice Department] would accept nothing less than abject surrender to its maximization agenda." . . . [918] It further found that the General Assembly acquiesced and as a consequence was driven by its overriding desire to comply with the Department's maximization demands. . . . And in its brief to this Court, the State concedes that "[i]t is undisputed that Georgia's eleventh is the product of a desire by the General Assembly to create a majority black district." Hence the trial court had little difficulty concluding that the Justice Department "spent months demanding purely race-based revisions to Georgia's redistricting plans, and that Georgia spent months attempting to comply." On this record, we fail to see how the District Court could have reached any conclusion other than that race was the predominant factor in drawing Georgia's Eleventh District; and in any event we conclude the court's finding is not clearly erroneous. . . .

[920] Race was, as the District Court found, the predominant, overriding factor explaining the General Assembly's decision to attach to the Eleventh District various appendages containing dense majority-black populations. As a result, Georgia's congressional redistricting plan cannot be upheld unless it satisfies strict scrutiny, our most rigorous and exacting standard of constitutional review.

To satisfy strict scrutiny, the State must demonstrate that its districting legislation is narrowly tailored to achieve a compelling interest. There is a "significant state interest in eradicating the effects of past racial discrimination." The State does not argue, however, that it created the Eleventh District to remedy past discrimination, and with good [921] reason: there is little doubt that the State's true interest in designing the Eleventh District was creating a third majority-black district to satisfy the Justice Department's preclearance demands. . . .

[924] Instead of grounding its objections on evidence of a discriminatory purpose, it would appear the Government was driven by its policy of maximizing majority-black districts. . . .

[925] In utilizing [Section] 5 to require States to create majority-minority districts wherever possible, the Department of Justice expanded its authority under the statute beyond what Congress intended and we have upheld. . . .

[926] Based on this historical understanding, we recognized in *Beer* that "the purpose of [Section] 5 has always been to insure that no voting-procedure changes would be made that would lead to a retrogression in the position of racial minorities with respect to their effective exercise of the electoral franchise." 425 U.S., at 141. The Justice Department's maximization policy seems quite far removed from this purpose. . . .

[927] The end [the eradication of invidious discrimination] is neither assured nor well served, however, by carving electorates into racial blocs. "If our society is to continue to progress as a multiracial democracy, it must recognize that the automatic invocation of race stereotypes retards that progress and causes continued hurt and injury." It takes a shortsighted and unauthorized view of the Voting Rights Act to invoke that statute, which has played a decisive role in redressing some of our worst forms of discrimination, to demand the very racial stereotyping the Fourteenth Amendment forbids. . . .

Following *Miller*, in 1996, the Court ruled that a number of congressional districts were shaped predominantly by racial considerations and would not pass strict scrutiny. One of these was the redistricting plan involved in *Shaw v. Reno* (1993).[139] In *Shaw v. Hunt*, (1996)[140] the Court invalidated North Carolina's Twelfth Congressional District, once again maintaining as it had done in *Miller v. Johnson* (1996),[141] that strict scrutiny was not satisfied despite the fact that the district was created to conform with the Section 5 preclearance requirements imposed by DOJ. That department was bluntly reminded by the Court that the national government was not authorized to require the states to maximize the number of majority-minority districts.

In *Bush v. Vera* (1996),[142] three Texas majority-minority districts were also struck down in 1996 as unconstitutional under the *Miller* rule. Six separate opinions were filed, none joined by more than three justices. The principal opinion in support of the judgment was delivered by Justice O'Connor, writing for herself, Chief Justice Rehnquist, and Justice Kennedy. In restating the *Miller* [143] rule, Justice O'Connor said: [Strict scrutiny does not] "apply to all cases of intentional creation of majority-minority districts, . . . [but only upon a showing] . . . that other, legitimate districting principles were 'subordinated' to race."[144] Justice Thomas, joined by Scalia, did not accept O'Connor's nonacceptance of strict scrutiny with regard to some intentionally created majority-minority districts. In a caustic vein, he wrote that: "Only last Term, in *Adarand Constructors v. Peña*, we vigorously asserted that all government racial classifications must be strictly scrutinized."[145]

Shaw v. Reno and its progeny cases in the 1990s evoked a number of harsh dissents from Justices Stevens, Souter, Ginsberg, and Breyer. The dissenters expressed their commitment to enhancing minority voting power as a legal and moral imperative. In their view, the *Shaw* doctrine is constitutional heresy, impossible to apply, and should be repealed. A representative sample is the following excerpt from the *Bush v. Vera* dissent filed by Justice Souter, normally the Court's most dedicated guardian of *stare decisis*:

> [The predominance test is inherently flawed because many] . . . traditional districting principles cannot be applied without taking race into account and are thus, as a practical matter, inseparable from the supposedly illegitimate racial considerations.[146]

> [In continuing to adhere to this doctrine, the Court fails] . . . to provide a coherent concept of equal protection injury . . . [or a coherent test for determining its existence.][147] [It is impossible to comply with *Miller's*] . . . obligation to untangle racial considerations from so-called "race-neutral" objectives (such as according respect to community integrity and protecting the seats of incumbents) when the racial composition of a district and voter behavior bar any practical chance of separating them.[148]

> [The Court's options for dealing with *Shaw's* unworkability are] . . . to confine the cause of action by adopting a quantifiable shape test or to eliminate the cause of action entirely. . . . [T]here is presently no good reason that the Court's withdrawal from the presently untenable state of the law should not be complete.[149]

Redistricting in the Post-2000 Era

The *Shaw/Miller* cases of the 1990s pose extraordinary redistricting puzzles. Among other matters, how does one determine whether race/ethnicity predominates in legislative district construction? As a way of thwarting the "predominance" barrier, one analyst suggests that districts be constructed with sizeable minority-voting populations; but not a majority. His thesis is that in such districts minorities, though politically strong, will have to cooperate with whites to achieve their legislative objectives, and that such districting will be regarded by the Court as promotive not of segregation but of integration. Consequently, that kind of racial/ethnic ("minority-interest") gerrymandering will be accepted by the Supreme Court, as that tribunal has never rejected that districting species.[150]

The Court may have been affected by such a "less-than-a-majority" thesis in the first major *Shaw/Miller* case of the new millennium—*Hunt v. Cromartie* (2001).[151] Once again, that high tribunal visited the Twelfth North Carolina Congressional District, which it had struck down in 1996 in *Shaw v. Hunt*.[152] Thereafter, the state redrew the district, reducing the number of split counties and cities, and reducing its former black voting majority to 47 percent, but essentially retaining its irregular shape. On a challenge that the new district violated the *Shaw/Miller* doctrine, the district court found that the state's motivation had been predominantly racial, and held the new district unconstitutional. However, in the *Cromartie* case, the Supreme Court in yet another 5-4 ruling, reversed, holding that the plaintiffs had failed to sustain their burden of proving racial considerations were "dominant and controlling," and that the district court's findings were "clearly erroneous."[153] The decision turned on the undisputed evidence that the district's black voters registered and voted Democratic between 95 and 97 percent of the time.[154] In his opinion for the majority, joined by Justices O'Connor, Stevens, Souter, and Ginsberg, Justice Breyer held that this evidence warranted a finding that "race in this case correlates closely with political behavior."[155] In accordance with prior declarations by the Court, this correlation sufficed to refute the district court's conclusion.[156]

Cromartie, in effect, upheld the constitutionality of District 12, thereby marking the first time that the Court actually applied the "political affiliation" (political gerrymandering) defense in a racial gerrymandering case. Moreover, the defense is available, under Justice Breyer's rationale, in any case "where majority-minority districts (or the *approximate* equivalent) are at issue and where racial identification correlates highly with political affiliation."[157] *Hunt v. Cromartie* thus legitimates creation of largely or mostly black, Hispanic, or Asian districts, if shown to be motivated by traditional political considerations.

The 2006 VRA amendments prohibit the reduction of the size of the majority in majority-minority preclearance districts. Even in districts where it is available, however, the scope of the *Cromartie* political affiliation defense is not clear at this time. *Cromartie* applied, but did not clarify, the distinction between the Court's prior decisions concerning strict scrutiny of the motivation for race-dominant districting, and the right to engage in "constitutional-political gerrymandering."[158] It is unknown whether the requisite political motivation must be shown in accordance with stipulated substantive and evidentiary guidelines or whether the outcome in each case will depend entirely on its specific facts, as construed by individual justices.[159] Furthermore, the Court has yet to elucidate the difference between "constitutional" and "unconstitutional" *political* gerrymandering *or* the difference, if any, between racial and political gerrymanders. These overriding issues implicate complex policy considerations, but the Court has failed to promulgate standards of adjudication.[160]

In short, *Hunt v. Cromartie* notwithstanding, the controversy over racial districting is far from over. In the light of the currently ongoing demographic revolution, one may expect a large increase in Hispanic and Asian-controlled voting districts and a tidal wave of resultant equal protection litigation. In this connection, it must be borne in mind that *Cromartie* did not repeal the *Shaw/Miller* doctrine; on the contrary, all nine justices apparently agree that the doctrine of applying strict scrutiny to districting where racial/ethnic considerations are predominant is still the law of the land. Therefore, if a race/ethnic-conscious redistricting fails to give due weight to traditional districting principles, then it must either assert and substantiate a political affiliation defense, or else withstand strict scrutiny. Given the continuing lack of guidelines, many redistricters may be unable to sustain these burdens.[161]

One must conclude, then, that, even as liberalized by *Hunt v. Cromartie*, *Shaw/Miller* has cast an ominous cloud over race/ethnic-conscious remedies for dilution. Whether the end is nigh depends on the orientation of the Court's old-time, recent, and future membership. As we await equal protection clarification, the merits of majority-minority districting should be pondered. Surely, they have increased the number of minority representatives. But has the *descriptive* (nominal and physical) increase been matched by *substantive* advance? One view, as expressed by law professor Grant Hayden, submits that the packing of minorities "appears" to increase the number of Republican legislators by reducing the number of minorities in districts abutting majority-minority enclaves, and this "seems" to result in policies antithetical to minority views. A partial solution, to him, is the amelioration of the strict enforcement of the one-man, one-vote rule of *Reynolds v. Sims*,[162] enabling the creation of majority-minority districts smaller than that required by strict numerical equality.[163] In this way, minorities could be shifted from smaller majority-minority districts to "white" areas where they could coalesce in politically advantageous ways. Of course, Hayden admits, the "true electoral effect of redistricting is unclear,"[164] and that reducing the mathematical rigors of *Reynolds* might give rise to a successful *Shaw/Miller* challenge.[165]

There are other serious questions raised in the political science literature concerning majority-minority districts: Are representatives in these districts so secure that they are insensitive to constituent needs? Is the strength of incumbency so strong in these districts that it cultivates a politically somniferous citizenry?[166]

Women and Electoral Politics

Gender discrimination is not prohibited in the VRA as it is in Title VII of the 1964 Civil Rights Act and Title IX of the 1972 Education Act. The great struggle to abolish the "dilution" of female voting power came in the suffrage struggle of the Nineteenth and early Twentieth Centuries. A decade after the ratification of the Nineteenth Amendment (1920)—which barred the denial or abridgement of the right to vote on the grounds of sex—the vibrancy of the feminist movement evaporated politically, to be born again with the second-wave feminism of the 1960s and thereafter.[167] The dream of some suffragettes that female voting and political participation would end war and produce social harmony and justice was obviously not realized.[168] Even after gaining suffrage, the bias against females in elected positions was "strong enough to make female candidacies almost irrelevant."[169] But the feminist movement of recent vintage helped produce a remarkable turnabout. Prejudice against females running for office has markedly declined. Political science professor Kathleen Dolan, relying on extensive poll data (and perhaps too optimistically) reports that:

> [B]y 2000, a remarkable shift has taken place when fully 57 percent of people surveyed said more women in government would be a positive for our country. . . . At a time when women's participation in elected office is at an all-time high, it is clear that the public sees this trend as positive. . . .[170] Yet this is not to suggest that there is no bias among the public, only that levels of bias are low enough to no longer provide a significant impediment to women's chances of election. . . .[171] Clearly, given the opposition women candidates in earlier times faced, the relationship between the public and women who seek elected office has changed tremendously. Gone are the days when the most significant thing about a woman candidate was her sex, which was seen, depending on the time, as a disqualifying characteristic, or a charming curiosity. Today, women who run for office are

likely to do as well as similarly situated men whether in gaining party nominations, raising campaign funds, or winning votes from the public.[172]

Party leaders have come to pursue the goal of increasing female political participation seriously, and they have come to aggressively seek out viable women candidates.[173] Specialized funds have been created to encourage female candidacies, e.g., EMILY's List (which, when operative, was reserved for women Democrats), and the WISH List (for Republicans).

The increase in female elected officeholding has been steady, rising since 1979 to 2009 from 8 percent of the state legislative seats to 24 percent; from 11 percent of statewide elective positions to 23 percent; and from 3 percent of Congress to 17.[174] Why are the figures not more in harmony with the fact that females constitute more than half of the population? Incumbency strength is part of the answer. The strength exercised by incumbents makes it difficult for them to be unseated. For example, a very large majority of members of Congress are reelected.[175] In this connection, women (given their later emergence in electoral politics) are not "similarly situated" as men as societal expectations allotting females primary child care responsibility restrict their political participation time.[176]

What difference would getting more women in office make? As reported by Professor Reingold, there is much in the scholarly literature asserting that women treat the issues concerned with females and children with greater sensitivity than do men. Some evidence suggests, too, that women office-holders were more responsive to their constituents' needs.[177] From her own studies including in-depth surveys of the California and Arizona Legislatures, Reingold concluded (admittedly in an "ambiguous, complicated, and conditional" way)[178] that: "In short, the behavior of public officials is by no means completely or even primarily a function of sex or sex ratios, even when it concerns the representation of women's policy and policymaking preferences."[179] Possible reasons for this "genderless" phenomenon include the more or less equal gender distributions in the populations of the governmental districts served; partisan/ideological affiliation, which overrides gender orientation; and institutional norms of reciprocity, collegiality, and courtesy.[180] She finds little evidence to support the view that female/male outlook similarities are a function of male dominance working in the legislative process to generate servile female submission to the male agenda.[181]

The Rutgers Center for American Women and Politics has sponsored a study of the impact of women in public office. Its head—in contrast to Reingold—reported that her study of state legislators led her to conclude that gender does have an impact. Among other things, women legislators augment the capacity of poorer people to gain access to government decision making. Women give greater priority than men to health care, child and family welfare questions, and to women's issues.[182] Another contributor to the Rutgers study—Kathlene Lyn aligning herself with Carol Gilligan's theory—found that women are "contextual" in their policymaking in that they rely on a broader range of people and groups than do men, whose narrower focus is called "instrumental."[183]

Indicative of the lack of agreement in this area, another women's politics academic summarizes her view by saying that "women's issues" are approached differently by different women and men, and that there is no guaranteed link between gender and public performance.[184]

Epilogue

Differing Schools of Thought on the Voting Rights Act

VRA began America's long-delayed attempt to fully achieve voting rights for minorities. Over the past thirty-five years, affirmative action has indisputably provided our racial, ethnic, and gender groups with a considerable measure of political opportunity. Yet, as we enter the twenty-first century, there is much harsh debate over minority voting rights.

What many see, overall, is incomplete voting rights reform. To them, despite the substantial progress, race remains at the faultline of American politics. Racially polarized voting remains a salient characteristic of our system; King's vision of multiracial coalitions is a utopian fantasy.[185] Relative to their share of the electorate, minorities are grossly underrepresented in terms of officeholding.[186] But even if proportional representation is reached in officeholding, voter turnout, and registration, minorities numerically would be but a small grouping subject to white dominance in many state and local legislatures, and surely in the Congress.[187] In short, minorities, according to this view, have a long way to go before they enter the Promised Land of political equality.

Nonetheless, another school of thought holds that the VRA has overprotected minorities. In this view, affirmative action has grafted racial preference onto a law which was designed to protect access—and nothing more.[188] "Equal treatment alone," that is, guaranteed access, so the argument goes, has been "deemed insufficient to compensate" for centuries of exclusion. Accordingly, just as in the case of employment discrimination,

> minority preference [has been] required to produce the proportionally equal results that would have been expected in the absence of discrimination. In voting rights law, affirmative action policy has taken the form of giving preference to selected minorities in electoral districting arrangements. The potential power of these

minorities, most notably blacks and Hispanics, is protected from dilution, while all other groups and interests are denied such protection.[189]

Moreover,

the logic of affirmative action in voting rights . . . extend[s] beyond equal access to the ballot box and reach[es] toward minority representation in elective office that approximates the demographic profile of protected classes.[190]

To this school, application of the "results" test and the concept of "dilution" under amended Sections 2 and 5 have conferred on protected minorities a privilege which no other citizens can claim: namely, the *legal right* to elect preferred candidates in numbers that are proportional to population share. Racial proportionality is now the legal standard of fair minority representation.

Exhibit A in this brief are the numerous single-member, majority-minority districts that have come into being in Section 2 litigation, or Section 5 preclearance negotiations. To the extent that such units have brought about "safe" minority seats, they prove that the VRA has been turned into a racial quota system. This is anathema. It breeds backlash and resegregation. Furthermore, as a growing segment of minority opinion now reflects, it is inimical to long-range minority interests. Political affirmative action stigmatizes and ghettoizes its supposed beneficiaries; it impedes the coalition building without which we can never have true civil rights reform.

It follows that the Voting Rights Act must be purged. The sole statutory voting right should be the right to cast secret ballots and have them fairly counted, and the statutory mechanisms limited to enforcement of that right. The "results" test and the doctrine of dilution should be abolished, the doctrine of intentional discrimination restored; and the range of the attorney general's discretionary preclearance authority sharply curtailed. If these changes should decrease the number of minority officeholders, or their influence on policy, so be it. No group should have the right to elect by the numbers. As long as they enjoy equal access and equal procedural rights, minorities should be content to take their chances in the political arena, just like everybody else.[191]

Black civil rights leader, Congressman John Lewis of Georgia has provided ammunition for VRA critics. In his deposition regarding the *Georgia v. Ashcroft* litigation, Congressman Lewis focused on VRA successes:

[I]n the American South . . . in 1965, there [were fewer] than a hundred elected black officials. Today, there are several thousand.

The Voting Rights Act of 1965 has literally transformed not just southern politics, but American politics. . . .

[D]uring the past 25 years, you have seen a maturity on the part of the electorate and on the part of many candidates. I think many voters, white and black voters, in metro Atlanta and elsewhere in Georgia, have been able to see black candidates get out and campaign and work hard for all voters. . . .

So there has been a transformation. It's a different state, it's a different political climate, it's a different political environment. It's a different world that we live in. . . . The state is not the same state it was. It's not the same state that it was in 1965 or in 1975, or even in 1980 or 1990. We have changed. We've come a great distance. . . . [I]t's not just in Georgia, but in the American South, I think people are preparing to lay down the burden of race.[192]

Needless to say, these views critical of the VRA have been scathingly denounced by pro–affirmative action elements of the civil rights community.[193] However, to one degree or another, they apparently resonate with the Supreme Court majority's treatment of the *Shaw/Miller* cases of the 1990s, as well as with the growing segment of the public at large which opposes affirmative action in employment and education. Nonetheless, the Congress in its 2006 VRA reauthorization found that the evidence compiled by that body "demonstrates that without the continuation of the Voting Rights Act of 1965 protections, racial and language minority citizens will be deprived of the opportunity to exercise their right to vote, or will have their votes diluted, undermining the significant gains made by minorities in the last 40 years."[194]

Reevaluating the Voting Rights Act

These warring schools of thought confirm that there is an urgent need to reevaluate the voting rights program. This is bound to be an extremely difficult undertaking. At present the politics of race and ethnicity are vibrant in this country, and promise to be a central dimension of the continual redistricting disputes in the years to come.[195] Furthermore, the upcoming redistricting round must deal with a radical transformation in the country's racial and ethnic makeup. The states are much engaged with the problems of population growth;[196] reapportionment's one-person, one-vote requirement; competition for federal dollars; conflicting political demands; and Section 5's preclearance negotiations. In addition, they will be confronted with the host of unfamiliar demographic phenomena which the 2000 census disclosed, including the explosive nationwide growth of the Hispanic minority and its ascendancy over African Americans, and the decline of the non-Hispanic white population.[197] It stands to reason that redistricting and the promotion of minority rights will be far more difficult than ever.

In our opinion, the advance of minority rights should be guided by the demographic changes facing the nation. The U.S. Bureau of the Census, in 2008, reported that the entrenched "non-Hispanic white" majorities have been dethroned by seismic population shifts in California, Texas, Florida, Hawaii, New Mexico, and the District of Columbia. These entities have become majority-minority places. On the verge of being placed in that category are Maryland, Georgia, and Nevada, each with a minority population of 42 percent.[198] According to Census projections, by 2042, the majority in the United States will be minorities: blacks, Hispanics, Asians, Native Hawaiians, and Pacific Islanders. Non-Hispanic, single-race whites will comprise 46 percent of the U.S. population in 2050.[199] The question becomes how to advance ethno-racial rights where no group is a majority and the racial and ethnic groups we have been concerned with are all minorities.

Take California, where the non-Hispanic white population has fallen from nearly 56 percent of the State total in 1990 to less than one-half, while the Hispanic and Asian shares soared to nearly 35 and 13 percent respectively.[200] Among many other things, these changes mean that the voting strength of all three minorities must be rethought, in order to determine whether any of them might be entitled to protection against dilution, and what type of districting and voting mechanisms would provide such protection.

To repeat, it is expected that racial and ethnic diversification a la California will spread nationwide within the next half-century; "[t]hen everyone will be a minority."[201] There is no way of predicting the ultimate impact on minority voting rights, but we feel that even with the high degree of cultural homogeneity in this country of increasing "minoritization," a first priority is a minority voting rights reform that encourages harmonious intergroup relations.

Granted that fair legislative representation is a centerpiece of our democracy, to what extent does its efficacy depend on the racial/ethnic identity of legislators? A seemingly intractable controversy over "descriptive" versus "substantive" representation has spawned a plethora of conflicting views. Some insist,[202] others deny,[203] that a minority influences the policy process only to the extent that it elects fellow group members to office. Descriptive representation normally can serve as a mechanism for gaining substantive representation, because, rightly or wrongly, the minority expects one of its own to be more responsive to its needs than a nonminority legislator. To be sure, such expectations are not always fulfilled; the incidence of such failures should be factored into any policy review. Moreover, a minority might not *need* descriptive representation if its bloc voting power is critical to the reelection of its nonminority representatives, for instance, Southern white Democrats. All told, experience suggests that the desirability of descriptive or substantive representation must be assessed on a case-by-case basis.

There is considerable doubt that majority-minority districting has advanced fair minority representation very much.[204] This suggests a policy under which single-member districts with bare majorities or the presence of a minority group in substantial numbers can provide minorities with much opportunity to influence the political process and elect candidates of their choice. In such districts, minorities would require the assistance of nonminority voters, requiring the development of harmonious coalitions. The majority opinions in *Georgia v. Ashcroft* (2003)[205] and *Hunt v. Cromartie* (2001)[206] provide support for the creation of such crossover and influence districts. In formulating this coalition-districting policy, a primary problem requiring great political sophistication would be to prescribe the requisite level of minority voting strength needed to maintain minority power.[207]

For multimember districts, other minority-empowering electoral policies have been suggested:

> *Cumulative Voting:* Each voter has as many votes as the at-large seats to be filled, and may distribute them as one sees fit. A cohesive minority could elect its candidate even in the face of a hostile majority by concentrating its votes.
>
> *Limited Voting:* Each voter has fewer votes than the at-large seats to be filled. Theoretically, the majority cannot capture every seat even by voting a straight ticket, but a cohesive minority with enough votes can control at least one.
>
> *Lowering the 50% plus 1 margin of victory in at-large elections.*

These are all, as noted, at-large, multimember district remedies. Proponents maintain that they can be implemented without recourse to controversial single-member districting while producing reasonably equivalent electoral outcomes. [208]

Advocates of minority power also urge the embrace of various legislative mechanisms, including: minority vetoes; supermajority requirements for certain legislative enactments; cumulative voting by legislators by presenting legislative alternatives in multiples of three or more. These are forms of "proportionate interest representation." A leading advocate offers it as "[a] normative directive to reinvigorate the basic motivation for . . . [the VRA] by attempting to . . . move the process of governmental decision-making away from a majoritarian model toward one of proportional power."[209]

Most of the controversy over minority voting rights would be mooted by amendment of VRA. For example, Congress could state in clear language whether the act is intended only to provide access to the polls, or, in addition, to foster election of minority representatives. Similarly, it could tell us whether, and how, the act is supposed to protect the right to vote against dilution. By taking such long overdue steps, Congress would put a welcome stop to all the quarrelsome speculation about its presumed intent.

The Supreme Court should elucidate the relationship between VRA and the equipopulation rule in *Reynolds v. Sims*,[210] which postulates that population is the "controlling criterion" of districting disputes. To what extent does the rule permit deviations for race/ethnic-based or partisan districting? To put it somewhat differently, if there is a conflict between one-person, one-vote and a racial or partisan district, which prevails? What are the standards of constitutionality of political gerrymanders? If these differ from the standards for racial gerrymanders, why the difference? The Supreme Court should make clear what the Equal Protection Clause permits in the way of partisan gerrymanders. *Hunt v. Cromartie* (2001)[211] permitted partisan gerrymanders as a potential defense against *Miller v. Johnson*'s (1996)[212] prohibition of districting primarily motivated by racial objectives. In *Davis v. Bandemer*, (1986),[213] the Court ruled that disputes over the constitutionality of partisan gerrymanders are justiciable, but declined to set any standards for determining such disputes. Given the pivotal role of political gerrymanders under *Hunt v. Cromartie* (2001), it seems pertinent to inquire what these standards are, and how they differ from those governing racial/ethnic gerrymandering.

Surely too, the issue of proportional representation must be dealt with. As one commentator has astutely remarked: "The debate over voting rights is a . . . variant of a long-standing issue in political science—the relative merits of . . . proportional representational systems. . . . [P]roportionality is something of a dirty word in the Anglo-American tradition. Americans prefer to use terms such as *fairness* and *nondilution* . . . without explicitly defining them."[214]

The specific issue is the propriety of the long-standing ban on the maintenance of a ratio between racial minorities' population share and the number of their descriptive representatives. (See disclaimer in VRA Section 2(b).) In our view, the Supreme Court's muddled treatment of the problem indicates the need for reconsideration. As seen in the 1971 *Whitcomb* case, and again in the 1980 *Bolden* case (at 199, 205), the Court ruled that proportional representation is not a legitimate dilution remedy. But it seems to us that the Court's actions in other dilution cases are not consistent with that conclusion. For example, the Court's repeated failures to formulate broadly acceptable representational baselines bespeak a tacit refusal to acknowledge that rough proportionality is an obvious standard.[215] By the same token, majority-minority districting is analytically a form of proportionality.[216] By approving it in the 1986 *Gingles* case, the Court in effect created a right to that form. The time has come to determine once and for all whether proportional representation should be recognized as the appropriate measure.

To conclude: In 1966, Chief Justice Warren said of VRA: "Hopefully, millions of nonwhite Americans will now be able to participate for the first time on an equal basis in the government under which they live."[217] Has this hope been realized? If voting rights affirmative action should be declared off-limits, what will take its place fifty years from now when all Americans have become minorities?

Seven

Affirmative Action and Fair Housing

Prologue

Residential separateness is at the heart of educational segregation as well as operating as a barrier to the elimination of inner city poverty. Nevertheless, substantial residential segregation has survived all attempts at public regulation, including that provided by the Fair Housing Act (FHA/Title VIII) of 1968.[1]

The FHA was the Great Society's last major civil rights initiative. It prohibits public and private discrimination in the sale or rental of residential housing on account of race, color, religion, sex, national origin, disability, or family status. FHA's implementation by the Department of Housing and Urban Development (HUD) has focused on mitigating forbidden, intentional discrimination in real estate matters. HUD's enforcement of the 1866 Civil Rights Act[2] has also been important in this connection. In implementing these statutes and in its nonfederal subsidy programs, HUD has not attempted to require suburbia to create housing attractive to lower-income minorities, and thus has largely failed to provide that antidote to the segregative force of societal/systemic discrimination as manifested in white flight to the suburbs and exclusionary zoning.[3]

At the birth of the FHA, civil libertarians believed that the dismemberment of intentionally imposed discriminatory residential barriers would result in widespread black/white racial integration. HUD's reluctance to extend its enforcement of the FHA beyond forbidden intentional discrimination, and proactively cultivate racial/ethnic balancing through that statute, is attributable to such diverse factors as the lack of controlling Supreme Court precedent regarding disparate impact in the housing area; antipathy to housing affirmative action within the civil rights community; and administrative foot-dragging. Whatever the correct explanation, HUD's FHA implementation—and that department's substantial affirmative action effort (albeit indirect) to move minorities and other poor into higher socioeconomic areas as an inducement to present or future integration—have not overcome residential segregation. Neither have state/local integrative policies.

Housing Segregation

Times change, it is said. But not, it seems, generally, in our neighborhoods. The decline in black/white separateness has been painfully slow, remaining high in urban areas where large numbers of blacks live. The Urban Institute's expert, Margery Turner, reports that on a scale of zero to 100 (with 100 being complete segregation), most large metropolitan areas registered above 70 percent in 1968 when the Fair Housing Act was passed. In 2000, that dissimilarity index stood at 65 percent.[4] Generally, Asians and Hispanics are less residentially segregated from non-Hispanic whites than are blacks. Nonetheless, the average Hispanic/white dissimilarity index was 51 percent in 1980, rising to 51.6 percent in 2000. Average Asian/white segregation stood at 42.2 percent in 2000, up from 41.8 percent in 1980.[5] According to housing scholar James Kushner, between 1990 and 2008, America experienced "hyper-segregation."[6] For the first time in U.S. history, most city centers during the 1990s became majority-minority. The divide between the minority population located in the cities and older suburbs, and the predominantly white newer suburbs was more emphatic than ever.[7]

The war for civil rights has been waged. Open housing advocates have had their say. "Fair housing" laws adorn national, state, and local statute books. Here and there, racial frontiers are being crossed—at least temporarily. Yet, we remain a nation of segregated enclaves. Virtually every metropolitan area in the land includes ghettos of blacks (and increasingly Latinos), ringed by affluent white neighborhoods or suburbs. The central city black ghettos are studies in urban decay, mired in poor jobs, poor schools, and poor public services, breeders of an American underclass. The outlying neighborhoods and suburbs (though some of them have become extensions of the black city ghetto) often remain bastions of white exclusivity, and racial exclusion. One wonders how long these explosive ingredients can be kept from once again erupting into destructive upheavals.

During the first half-century after the Civil War, African Americans remained primarily a rural people congregated in the South. Shortly before World War I, blacks began a major migration to American cities. Today, they are predominantly urban.[8]

In the cities, African Americans have been concentrated in ghetto areas in large measure as a consequence of white racism abetted by governmental support. The latter included police acceptance of white harassment directed at blacks moving into non-ghetto areas; judicially enforced, racially restrictive covenants; and local governments that were steadfast in the maintenance of apartheid through such devices as regulations governing where blacks could reside.[9] For some time, the federal government shamefully facilitated segregation. The Federal Housing Administration greatly assisted home purchasing by whites by guaranteeing mortgages requiring low down payments and long periods of amortization. But this aid was not (until the 1970s) available for older housing in the central cities where blacks were forced to live. It is not surprising, then, that blacks remain far behind whites in real property wealth accumulation.[10] Further, the massive development of the "lily-white" suburban America immediately after World War II is partially attributable to restrictive racial covenants required (until 1950) by the Federal Housing Administration for new suburban developments. Federally supported urban renewal and highway construction in postwar America also uprooted African American communities, necessitating an even greater concentration of blacks in the ghettos that remained.[11]

The Urban Institute's Margery Turner has not been alone in reporting the continued high incidence of residential segregation. Using measurement that differed from Turner's, a report on the 1990 and 2000 Census by the Mumford Center at the State University of New York-Albany[12] reported the following: The typical metropolitan-area white person lived in a neighborhood (defined as a census tract of four to six thousand people) that was 86 percent white in 1990, and 80 percent white in 2000. The average metropolitan-area black person lived in a neighborhood that was 56 percent black in 1990, and 51 percent black in 2000. While some progress in black/white integration was evident in the 2000 census,[13] Hispanics and Asians have become more "isolated" in the large majority of metropolitan areas.[14] Further, while adult blacks and whites were living in more integrated areas than in 1990, their children are not, particularly in the major metropolitan areas of the Midwest and Northeast. Typically, minority children are raised in an area where they are a majority.[15]

The negativity of residential segregation is stark. To Gary Orfield:

[I]n a white-dominated society, separate is inevitably unequal both in terms of resources that go into a community and in terms of the way in which society values that community, its institutions, and its people. . . . [T]he basic problem that integration addresses is the problem of white prejudice and the fact of institutional and individual discrimination in favor of whites and white communities.[16]

A National Advisory Commission on Civil Disorders (The Kerner Commission) was appointed by President Johnson in 1967 to report on the reasons for, and the cure for, the racial disorders convulsing the nation during the 1960s. In its report, the commission highlighted urban residential segregation, arguing that its continuation would greatly limit black access to good jobs as these were rapidly becoming suburbanized. Continued exclusion of blacks from good jobs would have other catastrophic effects. Poverty would increase; families would be torn asunder because male breadwinners—overwhelmed with feelings of inadequacy—would abandon their family responsibilities; and social order would be threatened.[17]

Writing in the 1990s, Harvard professor William Julius Wilson adopted a theme similar to that of the Kerner Commission when he argued that a "new urban poverty" has emerged in the nation's inner city ghettos marked by far more pervasive impoverishment than had existed there in the 1950s. The cause, primarily, has been the movement of jobs to the distant suburbs, and the "spatial mismatch" between the residencies of the very poor African Americans and employment availability.[18]

In its review of residential segregation, the Kerner Commission also warned that "[w]hen disadvantaged children are racially isolated in the schools, they are deprived of one of the significant ingredients of quality education: exposure to others with strong educational backgrounds. [Important studies] . . . establish that the predominant social/ economic background in a school exerts a powerful impact on achievement."[19] This educational thesis is still emphasized.[20]

One scholar summarized the impact of residential segregation in the following way:

> *A complex, interlinked cycle of racial discrimination and economic disparity continues to keep many African Americans from experiencing equal opportunities in the suburbs, and the effects are likely to impede meaningful residential integration in the immediate future.* Economic, educational and social disparity has resulted from intractable patterns of segregation. As a result of this disparity, it is difficult for many blacks to afford suburban housing. This absence of African Americans from suburban locales feeds white prejudice, which in turn motivates continuing subtle discrimination. Core resistance to integration in the suburbs runs deep and is unlikely to be overcome by increased contact between whites and blacks when strong social and economic disincentives also exist, not the least of which is the lowering of status and property values that may be associated with integration. Faced with these impediments, many African Americans reasonably may choose to live in predominantly black areas in which a sense of community exists and a decent life is available.[21]

Integration proponents vociferously demand sweeping, affirmative action cures: broad-scale, race-conscious governmental mandates, and incentives that will racially diversify the segregated neighborhoods.[22] By contrast, champions of race neutrality maintain that the true causes of residential segregation are ingrained segregationist "attitudes" in *both* black and white households, and economic barriers. In other words, both blacks and whites either *prefer* segregated living or cannot afford anything else. In this view, emphasis on housing integration affirmative action is pointless: it will not ameliorate the attitudinal and economic problems, but most likely will exacerbate them.[23] In its most radical formulation—by some expounders of "critical race theory"—we are presented with a view that rejects racial integration as a current social goal,[24] on the grounds that it accepts "the underlying system" of white domination, rather than operating to achieve a radical change in black status.[25] Various minority politicians have also opposed pro-integrative housing measures, fearing reductions in their power base.[26] Skepticism among blacks about pro-integrative measures (beyond the abolition of intentional discrimination) is nourished—among other reasons—because of their capacity to interfere with black housing choice.[27] For example, integrative techniques seeking racial balance could be associated with restraints on black access to prevent the onset of the tipping point provoking "white flight."

Residential separatist thinking has supported a "gilding the ghetto" thesis (also called "community development"), which has competed with the prointegration effort for support.[28] Integrationists/diversifiers have surely derived "cold comfort" from the Glaeser and Gyourko study, which suggests that greater ethnic diversity in the United States as compared to European countries has resulted in lower social welfare spending in America than in Europe; and from Robert Putnam's thesis that diversity negatively affects social cohesiveness in the short run.[29]

The Putnam U.S survey-study[30] was carried out in 2000 and had these features according to its author: a total sample size of some thirty thousand; smaller representative samples covering the nation and forty-one "very different" communities in the country ranging from large metropolitan areas (e.g., Chicago) to small towns and agricultural areas (e.g., Yakima, Washington, rural South Dakota); and great variety in ethnic diversity (95 percent white in South Dakota, 30–40 percent white in Los Angeles). The survey was undertaken at the time of the 2000 U.S. Census so that the demographics (race, education, income, etc.) of the census tracts were known and taken into account. The neighborhoods studied ranged from very homogeneous to very diverse in all respects. Hispanic, non-Hispanic white, non-Hispanic black, and Asian were the ethno-racial categories used to measure diversity.[31] The Putnam conclusions follow:

> Ethnic diversity is increasing in most advanced countries, driven mostly by sharp increases in immigration. In the long run immigration and diversity are likely to have important cultural, economic, fiscal, and developmental benefits. In the short run, however, immigration and ethnic diversity tend to reduce social solidarity and social capital. New evidence from the US suggests that in ethnically diverse neighbourhoods residents of all races

tend to 'hunker down.' Trust (even of one's own race) is lower, altruism and community cooperation rarer, friends fewer. In the long run, however, successful immigrant societies have overcome such fragmentation by creating new, cross-cutting forms of social solidarity and more encompassing identities. Illustrations of becoming comfortable with diversity are drawn from the US military, religious institutions, and earlier waves of American immigrants.[32]

Federal Antidiscrimination Law Affecting Housing: The 1968 Fair Housing Act

A centerpiece of modern housing reform is the Fair Housing Act. This Statute comprises Title VIII of the Civil Rights Act of 1968, as amended.[33] The act targets discrimination in the ownership, sale, lease, and rental of residential dwellings, together with the cluster of related activities: advertising, brokerage, financing, and property insurance. The declared goal is "affirmatively" to provide national "fair housing."[34] A portion of the Act's central prohibitions follow:

United States Code, TITLE 42 (2009)

Sec 3604—Discrimination in the sale or rental of housing and other prohibited practices as made applicable by section 3603 of this title and except as exempted by sections 3603(b) and 3607 of this title, it shall be unlawful—

(a) To refuse to sell or rent after the making of a bona fide offer, or to refuse to negotiate for the sale or rental of, or otherwise make unavailable or deny, a dwelling to any person because of race, color, religion, sex, familial status, or national origin. (b) To discriminate against any person in the terms, conditions, or privileges of sale or rental of a dwelling, or in the provision of services or facilities in connection therewith, because of race, color, religion, sex, familial status, or national origin. (c) To make, print, or publish, or cause to be made, printed, or published any notice, statement, or advertisement, with respect to the sale or rental of a dwelling that indicates any preference, limitation, or discrimination based on race, color, religion, sex, handicap, familial status, or national origin, or an intention to make any such preference, limitation, or discrimination. (d) To represent to any person because of race, color, religion, sex, handicap, familial status, or national origin that any dwelling is not available for inspection, sale, or rental when such dwelling is in fact so available. (e) For profit, to induce or attempt to induce any person to sell or rent any dwelling by representations regarding the entry or prospective entry into the neighborhood of a person or persons of a particular race, color, religion, sex, handicap, familial status, or national origin.

The Fair Housing Act of 1968 (which a number of circuit courts of appeal concluded was rooted in the Thirteenth Amendment)[35] sought to eliminate the "badges of slavery" for blacks in residential transactions. But the 1968 Act is not restricted to African Americans. The 1968 Act empowers the federal officials to assist aggrieved parties and prohibits specific practices such as discrimination based on race, color, religion, national origin, and family status in advertising, financing, and brokerage services. The focus of the housing integrationists, in the 1968 era, was on removing those racially motivated government and private real estate barriers that frustrated rentals and home purchases by blacks. These barriers, so the thinking had it at that time, imprisoned African Americans in the ghetto; their elimination promised substantial integration.[36] This assumption proved faulty despite the decline of these impediments, and the associated expansion of black housing opportunities. To one commentator:

> Despite the hope that outlawing housing discrimination would result in desegregation, African Americans in metropolitan areas continue to live in neighborhoods that are composed predominantly of members of their own race. In particular, the replication of this segregation in the suburbs to which African Americans are moving in large numbers, seems to contradict the assumptions of 1968, at which time it was argued that blacks were trapped in central city ghettos due to discrimination by the housing industry, hostile white suburbs, and timid government.[37]

The 1968 Act does not explicitly limit its reach to *intentional* violations. Moreover, it directs the U.S. Attorney General to combat discrimination by bringing "pattern or practice" suits which have "general public importance."[38] To some, this suggests that the act was intended to encompass both the "effects" (irrespective of intent), that is, disparate-impact standard of proof, as well as the "intent," standard, just as under Title VII of the 1964 Civil Rights Act. A number of federal circuit courts of appeal have so held. To these courts, a protected minority complainant can establish a *prima facie* case by presenting evidence that a facially race-neutral policy has had a disparate/adverse impact on his minority. For example, the grievant can offer statistical evidence that his minority has had a much greater rate of rental or purchase rejection than whites. The burden would then shift: in order to escape liability, the defendant would have to prove a "business necessity," that is, a legitimate, nondiscriminatory business reason for its conduct.[39] In short, to these courts, the 1968 Act incorporates disparate-impact theory, allowing its use to provide affirmative action, group remedies as a cure for societal, historical discrimination affecting protected groups without the need to prove that the discrimination was intentional.

In 1994, the Department of Justice and HUD solemnly pledged to apply disparate-impact theory under Title VIII where appropriate.[40] It would appear, then, that Title VIII tracks the equal employment opportunity modus operandi of Title VII of the 1964 Civil Rights Act, and Section 2 of the Voting Rights Act with respect to disparate impact, and that the federal government is involved in achieving racially balanced communities through this statute, just as it has sought proportional representation in employment, and majority-minority legislative districts by employing other enactments. But this is misleading. The Supreme Court has yet to address the question of disparate impact under FHA's Title VIII. In fact, even though the act became law in 1968, the Court has not formally decided either its constitutionality or *any* of its standards of evidence. There is no *Griggs, Gingles,* or *Charlotte-Mecklenburg* in housing discrimination law. This is remarkable, not to say extraordinary, given that housing discrimination is so intimately interwoven with discrimination in employment and public education that a Justice Department spokesperson considered it to be the "root" of the latter.[41] In any event, the classic fair housing cases that the Supreme Court has so far decided on the merits are not related to Title VIII. *Buchanan v. Warley* (1917)[42] nullified intentional racial residential zoning as contrary to the Equal Protection Clause. *Shelley v. Kraemer* (1948)[43] ruled that judicial enforcement of intentionally imposed, racially restrictive covenants constituted forbidden "state action" under the Fourteenth Amendment. In *Jones v. Mayer* (1968),[44] the issue was the constitutionality of 42 U.S.C. § 1982, the codification of a Reconstruction statute that provided that all citizens had the same rights as whites to buy, sell, and lease property. Designed to protect blacks in their real estate transactions, the act was upheld by the Court on the grounds that the Thirteenth Amendment authorized Congress to ban the "badges and incidents of slavery."[45] And in the more recent Title VIII case of *United States v. Starrett City Associates,* the Court denied *certiorari* for a Second Circuit Court of Appeal holding that the management of a privately owned apartment building violated the Fair Housing Act by basing rental decisions on explicit racial quotas for the purpose of achieving racial integration.[46]

While the Supreme Court has pointedly refused to decide whether Title VIII incorporates disparate-impact theory,[47] it accepted the judicial ruling that a remedy for HUD's intentional segregation of public housing in Chicago was the requirement that HUD spread its subsidized housing around the Chicago metropolitan area.[48] Further, in its focus on Title VIII's prohibition of intentional real estate discrimination, the Court has been liberal, finding that the act prohibited "blockbusting" and "redlining," and that the act's "standing to sue" provision was sufficiently broad to permit whites to sue landlords on the grounds that they were denied the right to live in an integrated environment.[49]

The High Court's failure to rule on whether Title VIII incorporates disparate-impact theory has been only one bar to direct federal race/ethnic-conscious, aggressively pro-integrative efforts in housing. A major impediment has been federal administrative foot-dragging,[50] congressional ambiguity, and lack of enthusiasm—if not hostility—in the civil rights community.[51] We are then witness to a major exception in recent civil rights law and policy. Whereas, in the areas of voting, employment, and education, *direct* race/ethnic-conscious, integrative/proportional representation affirmative action has been a very prominent feature of federal action, this has not been the case in the housing realm. While there has been some direct affirmative action in housing on the part of government, the primary government format has focused on indirectness. One close observer reported in 1998 that the national government has been so hesitant in applying disparate-impact theory in establishing Title VIII violations that it has never brought a housing disparate-impact claim in a lawsuit. He wrote further that it was not until 1980 that the federal government began using "testers" (minorities and whites who claim to have similar economic and social backgrounds when seeking housing) to determine whether landlords are intentionally discriminating in an unlawful way, though that device had proven to be effective for some time before.[52] Even federally subsidized "public housing," remains pervasively racially segregated.[53] That said, the federal government has undertaken significant affirmative action steps to move minority and other poor into higher economic areas, as have numerous localities. But this use of economic integration as an indirect cultivator of racial/ethnic integration has still left America's residential apartheid very much intact.[54]

Given the present-day absence of a broad *political* constituency for direct race/ethnic-conscious housing affirmative action,[55] it is safe to assume that the eradication of forbidden intentional discrimination will continue to be the mainstay of Title VIII enforcement.[56] The continuation of segregation; the phenomenon of resegregation; and the "expansion of the ghetto" to the suburbs underscores a primary dilemma: Is residential segregation compatible with the education, employment, and public service needs of blacks? If not, what pro-integrative techniques has government employed in the housing realm? These crucial questions bring us to policies aimed at achieving and maintaining residential integration. Their dominant theme has been the movement of the poor to a better economic environment. Such a policy was advocated by President Nixon who referred to the federal government as "the biggest slumlord in history"[57] in its administration of the nation's public housing projects. Nixon recognized that American history and society had dealt harshly with the dominant group in the "family" (nonelderly)[58] public housing units, namely African Americans. They, the president said, "are often strangers to one another—with little sense of belonging. And because so many poor people are so heavily concentrated in these projects, they often feel cut off from the mainstream of American life."[59] Direct cash rental aid should be available to these minority project dwellers and other poor people to help alleviate the baneful effects of poverty concentration, promote beneficial economic integration (a stepping stone to racial/ethnic integration), and give "the poor the freedom and responsibility to make their own choices about housing."[60] Nixon, thus, espoused the same policy ideology that led to the creation of the federal "economic-class," affirmative action housing "voucher" program, enabling the impoverished among blacks and other groups to rent housing in private dwellings where owners could voluntarily admit them or not. Primary beneficiaries were meant to be the minority poor who are concentrated in public housing.[61] By the early years of the new millennium, vouchers aided more than 1.8 million households—a greater number than any other federal housing program.[62]

One civil rights scholar, Charles Lamb, remembers Nixon in a different light—as a primary impediment to suburban racial integration. Nixon, unlike his first secretary of Housing and Urban Development (HUD), George Romney, opposed cutting off HUD grants (such as water and sewer subsidies) to pressure suburban localities into accepting the development of low-rent housing which would be both attractive to racial minorities and facilitative of much-needed suburban racial/ethnic integration.[63] To Professor Lamb, Nixon "established a powerful precedent that no subsequent chief executive overturned. The core reasoning of Nixon's 1971 policy statement remains the status quo for federal policy on suburban housing integration to this day."[64] The policy was not to impose "economic integration upon existing local jurisdictions."[65] The Nixon policy is excerpted below:

> This Administration will not attempt to impose federally assisted housing upon any community.
>
> We will encourage communities to discharge their responsibility for helping to provide decent housing opportunities to the Americans of low- and moderate-income who live or work within their boundaries.
>
> We will encourage communities to seek and accept well-conceived, well-designed, well-managed housing developments—always

within the community's capacity to assimilate the families who will live in them.

We will carry out our programs in a way that will be as helpful as possible to communities which are receptive to the expansion of housing opportunities for all of our people . . . without disrupting the community. In other ways as well, we are and will be working to promote better and more open housing opportunities. . . .

In speaking of "desegregation" or "integration," we often lose sight of what these mean within the context of a free, open, pluralistic society. We cannot be free, and at the same time be required to fit our lives into prescribed places on a racial grid—whether segregated or integrated, and whether by some mathematical formula or by automatic assignment. Neither can we be free, and at the same time be denied—because of race—the right to associate with our fellow citizens on a basis of human equality.[66]

Affirmative Action and Residential Integration

Even without federal imposition of required ethno-racial housing integration, there has been a substantial degree of affirmative action designed to advance housing integration. What clearly drives the housing affirmative action integration measures is the objective of helping minorities and other poor by placing at least a portion of them in improved socioeconomic environments.[67]

Measures meant to implement this demographic transfer include: vouchers; a program titled Hope VI; the Quality Housing Act; affirmative marketing/special mobility; inclusionary zoning/fair share; the regulation of real estate advertising; and financing assistance for the purchase of homes. These policies have resident and dwelling site selection dimensions aimed at encouraging residential integration.

Vouchers

Voucher rental assistance has been regarded as an important siting device for the deconcentration of poverty. Enabling low-income groups to acquire housing in privately owned units, this rental assistance program has become the major form of federal housing aid to such people, currently providing some 1.8 million dwellings—outdistancing the 1.3 million public housing dwellings owned and operated by government.[68] Vouchers, once called Section 8 aid (after Section 8[69] of the 1974 Housing Act[70]) now fall under the Housing Choice Voucher program of the Quality Housing and Work

Responsibility Act of 1998.[71] These certificates allow the qualified (initially, households with incomes up to 80 percent of a particular area's median) to rent privately owned units with government generally paying the difference (in vouchers) between 30 percent of adjusted income and fair market rent—defined as the median of the rent charged in the most expensive markets for various sized apartments.[72]

Vouchers were to empower the poor to move to higher income areas where they could better adopt the habits of the self-sufficient, and hopefully experience more racial/ethnic mingling.[73] Studies have shown that those who rent with vouchers tend to live in areas that are far more similar to those lived in by unsubsidized renters than are the areas inhabited by public housing dwellers. More than 50 percent of public housing is located in census tracts with a poverty rate of 30 percent or more. Fifteen percent of voucher holders live in such poverty-impacted areas as do 13 percent of unsubsidized renters. Further, only 21 percent of public housing exists in tracts where minorities are less than 10 percent of the population; while 44 percent of voucher renters and 48 percent of all rental dwellings are found in such areas. Though minority voucher recipients live in areas that are less racially segregated than minorities living in public housing, a substantial number of voucher beneficiaries have neighbors who are predominantly minority, Likewise, these minority voucher beneficiaries are far more likely than their white counterparts to reside in neighborhoods characterized by high concentrations of poverty.[74]

Hope VI

The congressionally authorized Hope VI program[75] is helping to change the face of public housing. Between 1993 and 2004, Hope VI has financed the demolition of 150,000 public housing units, replacing them with new, mixed-income developments with improved physical amenities (e.g., lower density, central air conditioning, washer/dryers) intended to attract ethno-racial and socioeconomic integration and better living conditions than are available in the destroyed properties. Residents of the condemned units were given a number of options: seek apartments in private developments with voucher assistance; leave subsidized housing; move to a vacant public housing unit in another development; obtain one of the limited number of public housing units in the new Hope VI mixed-income developments. The public housing segment of the Hope VI mixed-income units are planned to replace some 78 percent of those condemned units that were occupied prior to demolition.[76]

Hope VI has generally eliminated only a small portion of public housing in particular locales. Not so for Chicago. There, Hope VI and funds from other programs have been involved in an undertaking to demolish nearly the entire Chicago stock of public housing, replacing it with new or rehabilitated dwellings. Only one-third of these will be public housing units; and much of the remainder slated for higher-income households including those that can afford market rents. Administrators of Hope VI units are given considerable latitude in devising resident eligibility standards higher than those generally applicable to public housing. Chicago's requirements (work, school enrollment, credit histories) are such that authorities there estimated that only about one-half of existing residents of public housing would meet the criteria for admission to the Hope VI mixed-income units.[77]

An Urban Institute study of Hope VI concluded that the average poverty rate in the census tracts containing those public housing occupants who moved to Hope VI projects was 27 percent, or less than one-half of the poverty rate (61 percent) of census tracts they moved from. The concentration of minorities was also less, decreasing from 88 to 68 percent.[78]

The Quality Housing and Work Responsibility Act

The Quality Housing and Work Responsibility Act of 1998[79] has provisions that correspond to those in Hope VI in that they enable local government public housing authorities to demolish distressed units; to replace them with lower-density developments; to deconcentrate poverty in the lower-density developments, and in existing public housing (a topic addressed by President Clinton in the message excerpted below); and to provide for the relocation of the displaced residents. As of 2004, some 165 public housing units have been slated for demolition under this 1998 statute.[80]

Vouchers give recipients some flexibility in determining whom they wish to live with. In Hope VI and the Quality Housing Act, the federal integrative effort turned inward to the public housing units themselves, seeking their substantial demolition and the economic diversification of units left standing. The Clinton administration barred criminals from eligibility for public housing (the "one strike" rule), and proposed integrative admission standards for those dwellings. The next excerpt outlines the standards that later became part of the federal administrative code[81] applicable to the bulk of public housing.

Proposed Rule to Deconcentrate Poverty and Promote Integration in Public Housing

Federal Register, Vol. 65, NO. 74, 20686 April 17, 2000

[20686] Public housing is a form of subsidized housing development that is typically developed and managed by local public housing agencies (rather than private or nonprofit landlords), with funding from HUD.

For decades, many of the Nation's cities and towns sited public housing developments in predominantly low-income, minority neighborhoods. Discriminatory local political processes thus concentrated a large share of the locality's most affordable, subsidized rental units in geographic areas that tended to be . . . older, more dilapidated, higher in poverty, less politically powerful, and more poorly supported by public services than other areas. It was hardly the dream that our Nation's founding fathers, or the framers of Federal housing policy in the last century, envisioned. And the results of discrimination in the siting of public housing have been all too predictable: opportunity denied, racial and economic isolation perpetuated, and a mountain of civil rights litigation. . . .

With the issuance of this revised rule, the Administration initiates another historic shift in the direction of housing policy and a significant strengthening of HUD's role as a promoter of opportunity and protector of civil rights. Fulfilling the aims and expectations outlined in the Quality Housing and Work Responsibility Act of 1998 (also known as the Public Housing Reform Act), this revised rule specifies what local public housing agencies must do, as part of the [local] Public Housing Agency Plans they submit to HUD in order to receive funding, to deconcentrate poverty and affirmatively further fair housing in the public housing program and to affirmatively further fair housing in the Section 8 voucher program.

No longer will an agency, whether by intent or by default, be able to [20687] concentrate relatively low-income families in some buildings and higher income families in other buildings. Under this revised rule, a local public housing agency will meet the first requirement—deconcentration—by bringing higher income tenants into relatively lower income buildings and lower income tenants into relatively higher income buildings. This will be accomplished by classifying buildings and prospective tenants according to their income levels and then making lease-up decisions . . . that gradually improve the income mix of each building under a public housing agency's management. In order to achieve deconcentration, an agency must skip particular families on its waiting list, as necessary. In addition, an agency may apply local admission preferences created to serve special, high-need groups: homeless persons, victims of domestic violence, and families with severe rent burden (greater than fifty percent of household income).

In addition, a public housing agency must meet the revised rule's second principal requirement by preparing and carrying out its Plan in ways that protect the civil rights of families served. First, each agency must carry out its Plan in conformity with Federal civil rights laws, including provisions of the Civil Rights Act of 1964 and the Fair Housing Act of 1968. Beyond the basic requirement of nondiscrimination, however, an agency should affirmatively further fair housing to reduce racial and national origin concentrations. As this revised rule indicates, HUD will take action to challenge civil rights certifications where it appears that a PHA [Public Housing Authority] Plan or its implementation does not reduce racial and ethnic concentrations and is perpetuating segregation or is, worse yet, creating new segregation. If HUD offers this challenge, the onus will be on the public housing agency to establish that it is providing the full range of housing opportunities to applicants and tenants or that it is implementing affirmative efforts. Affirmative efforts may include the marketing of geographic areas in which particular demographic groups typically do not reside, additional consultation and information for applicants, and provision of additional support services and amenities to a development. . . .

Resident Selection and the Unsteady State of Case Law on the Subject

Courts have authorized racially conscious, resident selection processes though Title VIII of the 1968 Fair Housing Act, on its face, precludes such except as a cure for a judicial determination of a previous intentional discrimination. The siting of federally subsidized housing for lower-income groups is important in this connection, as the Third Circuit Court of Appeals made clear in *Shannon v. HUD* (1970).[82] There, HUD was accused of failing to take steps to prevent the segregative impact of a publicly assisted, multiunit complex which that department had sponsored. The project would have supposedly increased the already high density of low-income African Americans in the area.[83] The circuit court ruled that the FHA required that HUD go beyond administering that act in a color-neutral fashion. Because of that act and Title VI of the 1964 Civil Rights Act, HUD could no longer

remain blind to the very real effect that racial concentration has had in the development of urban blight. Today such color-blindness is impermissible. Increase or maintenance of racial concentration is *prima facie* likely to lead to urban blight and is thus *prima facie* at variance with the national housing policy. . . . We hold . . . that the Agency [HUD] must utilize some institutionalized method whereby, in considering site selection or type selection, it has before it the relevant racial and socio-economic information necessary for compliance with its duties under the 1964 and 1968 Civil Rights Acts.[84]

Also, in *Otero v. New York City Housing Authority* (1973),[85] the Second Circuit applauded a housing authority racial-balancing policy limiting the number of black residents. The court said:

> The [New York City Housing] Authority is obligated to take affirmative steps to promote racial integration even though this may in some instances not operate to the immediate advantage of some non-white persons. . . . Action must be taken to fulfill, as much as possible, the goal of open, integrated residential housing patterns and to prevent the increase of segregation, in ghettos, of racial groups whose lack of opportunities the [FHA] Act was designed to combat. Senator Mondale . . . pointed out that the proposed law [Title VIII] was designed to replace the ghettos "by truly integrated and balanced living patterns." . . . We hold . . . that the Authority may limit the number of apartments to be made available to persons of white or non-white races, including minority groups, where it can [be] show[n] that such action is essential to promote a racially balanced community and to avoid concentrated racial pockets that will result in a segregated community.[86]

The 1973 *Otero* court ruled that the racial balancing involved in the case conformed with the Constitution's equal protection requirement as integration was a compelling governmental interest.[87] However, a First Circuit panel (*Raso v. Lago*)[88] held in 1998 that a racial-balancing plan adopted by HUD in Boston was not subject to the strict scrutiny applied in *Otero*. In Boston, a group of predominantly white residents (the "Old West Enders") had been removed to make way for urban renewal. Pursuant to Massachusetts law, the developer of new assisted housing in the West End gave first-tenancy preference to that dislocated group. HUD—conforming both to a consent decree it had agreed to in connection with its alleged discriminatory practices in Boston, and to its reading of the pro-integrative dictates of the FHA—sought to reduce the scope of the preference granted to the Old (predominantly white) West Enders. Under the new plan, half of the apartments were to be made available by lottery with no preference to the former residents of the area. The *Raso v. Lago* court agreed that HUD's effort was racially motivated in that it sought to promote integration rather than allotting the apartments to the predominantly white group. The court ruled, however, that since the HUD lottery plan was race-blind, there was no racial classification involved, and no reason to invoke strict scrutiny. HUD's consent decree and the FHA were sufficient to uphold the agency's program in this case.[89] The court explained itself thusly:

> The primary test is that any government action—regardless of benign intent—is suspect if it has been taken on the basis of a "racial classification"; in such cases, the classification must be justified by a compelling state interest and narrow tailoring. . . . The term [racial classification] normally refers to a governmental standard, preferentially favorable to one race or another, for the distribution of benefits. Yet under the plan adopted in this case, the apartments freed from statutory preference are made available to *all* applicants regardless of race.[90]

In short, the court maintained that the former West Enders were denied nothing because of their race. Is this correct? Did not the "Old West Enders" group lose its 100 percent preference under Massachusetts law because it was predominantly white, and because HUD wanted to advance integration? Was not this HUD policy an act of racial classification and thus subject to strict scrutiny?

In 1988, a Second Circuit panel ruled—in *U.S. v. Starrett City*[91]—against extending the *Otero v. New York City Housing Authority* precedent to cover a long-term quota scheme at the Starrett City housing complex. That complex is an enormous one, consisting of some 5,881 publicly subsidized apartments located in forty-six high-rise buildings. The management of the complex sought—and generally maintained—a racial balance of 64 percent white; 22 percent black; and 8 percent Hispanic. The goal was to avoid "tipping," that is, the population ratio that provokes white flight.[92]

The *Starrett* court found that race-conscious affirmative action did not necessarily violate federal statutory and constitutional provisions. However, a plan that involves racial distinctions must be temporary. White flight may be taken into account in the integration equation. But, "It cannot serve to justify attempts to maintain integration at Starrett City through inflexible racial quotas that are neither temporary nor used to remedy past racial discrimination or imbalance within the complex."[93] The court concluded enigmatically by saying:

> We do not intend to imply that race is always an inappropriate consideration under Title VIII in efforts to promote integrated housing. We hold only that Title VIII does not allow appellants to use rigid racial quotas of indefinite duration to maintain a fixed level of integration at Starrett City by restricting minority access to scarce and desirable rental accommodation otherwise available to them.[94]

Professor Schwemm, in his housing discrimination treatise, summarizes the unsteady law in this connection:

> [I]t is clear that some narrowly tailored form of race-conscious remedy might be appropriate for a public housing authority and other housing provider that has engaged in past discrimination against racial or national origin minorities. It is also possible that, even in the absence of such past discrimination, a housing provider might be able to adopt a plan to *enhance* opportunities for groups protected by the Fair Housing Act if its current residents include a disproportionately small percentage of such groups and its plan is narrowly tailored to remedy this imbalance. On the other hand, quotas like those imposed by Starrett City seem clearly unlawful, under the Fair Housing Act and also, if the entity adopting such a quota is a public housing authority or other governmental actor, under the equal protection clause. However, limited affirmative marketing activities designed to disseminate housing information to a more racially diverse audience than would otherwise receive it may well be consistent with the Fair Housing Act and other applicable laws.[95]

Affirmative Marketing/Special Mobility Programs

Increasingly, desegregation advocates focus on "affirmative marketing"/"special mobility" techniques that counsel prospective tenants, or home buyers, to seek residences in areas they would not ordinarily consider. African Americans are encouraged to consider white areas; whites are urged to look in minority-impacted or integrated places.[96] Housing-search counseling has been supplemented with such aid as help with moving expenses, landlord outreach, and postplacement advising.[97] Counseling of this nature has been challenged as deflecting information away from blacks to prevent segregation.[98] Deflection, on the other hand, has been countenanced as serving the compelling need for integration.[99]

The extensive counseling, landlord outreach, and other services feature of affirmative marketing/special mobility programs is not ordinarily associated with voucher undertakings as typically administered.[100] The most famous special mobility effort is one that came in the wake of *Hills v. Gautreaux* (1976)[101] where the Supreme Court upheld a district court remedial plan seeking the movement of African Americans to predominately white neighborhoods in the Chicago metropolitan area. This plan was imposed after a judicial determination that HUD had intentionally discriminated on racial grounds in the siting of its Chicago-area housing projects. Some seven thousand low-income families (volunteers from public housing or those on public housing waiting lists) were relocated to white areas after receiving the array of affirmative marketing counseling and assistance services, along with rental vouchers.[102]

HUD inaugurated its own rental voucher–supported affirmative marketing/special mobility program (called Moving to Opportunity [MTO]) in 1993. Unlike *Gautreaux*, which required the moving of blacks to white areas, MTO has focused on the economic integration of its 4,600 volunteers from public or voucher housing. They were to move to areas with a poverty rate of less than 10 percent irrespective of racial composition.[103]

In 2006, housing scholar Professor Alex Schwartz summarized the research on *Gautreaux*, MTO, and the Minneapolis affirmative marketing projects: special mobility–assisted families gained access to middle-class neighborhoods "to a greater extent than is usually achieved by vouchers alone"; and these neighborhoods were safer and provided better housing. However, special mobility/affirmative marketing did not "necessarily promote racial integration." *Gautreaux* required movement from black areas to white; MTO granted a choice, and most black MTO participants chose black areas. Further, the research "does not demonstrate that the change in residential environments made major improvements in employment, education, or health, at least in the short run."[104]

Special mobility/affirmative action raises the issue as to how this endeavor is to be scrutinized through the lens of the Equal Protection Clause. An interesting case is presented by *Walker v. City of Mesquite* (1999).[105] There a panel of the Fifth Circuit Court of Appeals determined that a race-conscious, site-selection court order was subject to strict scrutiny; while the "helping hand" of race-conscious affirmative marketing was not. To remedy the past discrimination perpetrated by the Dallas Housing Authority (DHA), the district court ordered that new public housing acquired by the DHA be located in predominantly white areas.[106] The appellate tribunal viewed this order as a racial classification which had to conform with the narrow-tailoring component of strict scrutiny. Narrow tailoring would not be satisfied "until less sweeping alternatives—particularly race neutral ones—have been considered . . . tried" and found wanting.[107] One less-sweeping alternative—affirmative marketing used with Section 8 vouchers—was also a part of the lower-court remedy. As explained by the court of appeals, this affirmative marketing endeavor included the "helping hand" of signing bonuses for landlords accepting Section 8 tenants. The appeals court concluded that affirmative marketing was to be tried and evaluated as a total remedy for the DHA's past discrimination before the race-conscious site selection order could be judged as narrowly tailored.[108] As in *Raso v. Lago*,[109] left precariously hanging is the question why race-conscious, affirmative marketing was not regarded as a racial classification and, thus, subject to strict scrutiny?

Fair Share/Inclusionary Zoning

To Charles Haar, in his book *Suburbs Under Siege* (1996),[110] the New Jersey Supreme Court offered a provocative new opportunity for suburban racial integration through its Mount Laurel "doctrine"—a doctrine much discussed by scholars.[111] By that doctrine, the New Jersey Supreme Court, in 1975, liberally read the state constitution's general welfare and equal protection provisions as requiring the state's municipalities to affirmatively make provision for low and moderate-income housing. This constitutional reading was meant to ensure that those local governments would assume a "fair share" of the regional need for such dwellings.[112] Later, the New Jersey legislature adopted provisions implementing the fair share requirement.[113] The Mount Laurel "fair share" doctrine,[114] to Haar, was meant to provide minorities the possibility of real estate ownership in the white suburbs along with "the web of goals it furthers—independence, dignity, civil peace, and democracy."[115] This was the doctrine's "singular achievement."[116]

Haar noted that the Mount Laurel doctrine enabled thousands of people to live in attractive suburban communities, but it was unclear to him how many of these were minorities.[117] Other scholars reported that minorities were not often Mount Laurel beneficiaries.[118] Haar did make clear that many minorities were priced out of the low and moderate-cost units,[119] and that Mount Laurel remedies were not tied to other social welfare services. He also concluded that "[w]ithout a full panoply of social effort—education, day care, job training—lower and upper income residents continue to feel estranged from one another, generating greater social distance even as geographical distance is reduced."[120]

The Institute on Race and Poverty at the University of Minnesota shared Haar's enthusiasm for "Fair Share," the central feature of which, to the institute, would be legislation requiring municipalities to "take affirmative actions" to help low and moderate-income people obtain decent "affordable housing," usually through some form of voluntary or mandated "inclusionary" zoning. The primary advantage of fair share policy is that—unlike Title VIII (The Fair Housing Act of 1968)—it targets the "systemic nature of segregation," rather than the culpability of identified exclusionary actors. Consequently, fair share provides a more systematic approach "to providing affordable housing" than does Title VIII.[121] The Institute on Race and Poverty proposed "affirmative goals (including race-based criteria) and timetables for the creation of affordable housing in suburban areas."[122] An example of this would have municipalities earmark a certain percentage of new developments for affordable housing, as well as conditioning upscale development on the construction of homes accessible to lower income groups.[123] However, at the close of the institute's report, the reader is informed that the Mount Laurel plan has had mixed results: "Since the mid-1980s close to 25,000 [low and moderate-income] units have been made available in New Jersey through constructed and rehabilitated housing. . . . Because Mount Laurel housing fails to take account of race, however, the new housing has mirrored segregated housing patterns. "[124]

The states have adopted a variety of fair share policies. New Hampshire requires its localities to provide reasonable opportunities for the siting of prefabricated homes which are popular with the non-rich. Every city in California is mandated to produce a long-term housing development program meant to meet pressing residential needs. Massachusetts fair share law takes the form of facilitating challenges to exclusionary zoning based on economic status.[125] Hundreds of localities—mainly in New Jersey, Massachusetts, and California—have adopted mandatory or incentive-based fair share/inclusionary zoning regulations. Through these incentive-based inclusionary devices, developers, in return for a benefit (usually greater density levels for their new construction) set aside a portion of their units (10 to 20 percent typically) for low and/or moderate income households for ten to thirty years. Low and/or moderate incomes are defined as a percentage (between 50 and 120 percent) of the area's median income.[126]

Fair share/inclusionary zoning endeavors—such as the above-described federal efforts at deconcentrating residential poverty—also have been prompted by the notion that economic integration could advance racial/ethnic integration.[127] While it is estimated that, as of 2006, some eighty to ninety thousand units of low and/or moderate-income dwellings have resulted from inclusionary zoning policies, scholarly data tell us that Mount Laurel's failure to racially integrate has been generally repeated in other fair-share locales.[128] An exception is Maryland's Montgomery County, which allocated 14 percent of its fair share units to public housing where 80 percent of the inhabitants are people of color. A lottery system was used to distribute the fair share units. As a result, that county has emerged as one of the nation's most economically and racially integrated communities.[129]

A number of residential integration advocates *have* urged that economic status is an insufficient basis for racial integration. What then should be the way? The lotteries of Montgomery County are lobbied for by some, as are the pro-integrative postures of Shaker Heights, Ohio, and Maplewood/ South Orange, New Jersey, to be outlined below. To encourage similar community efforts, housing scholar John Boger recommends the forceful policy of gradually reducing income tax deductions for property taxes in those communities that are laggard in the achievement of racial integration.[130]

Shaker Heights, Ohio, is one of but a few examples of suburban communities that have conducted sustained multifaceted efforts to racially integrate residences. A city-created commission for that purpose has banned For Sale signs on front lawns to impede "blockbusting"—panic selling prompted by fears of potential ghettoization. The city and the school district have also created a privately supported fund to offer low-interest mortgage loans of $3,000 and $6,000 to whites who move to districts that are more than 50 percent black.[131]

South Orange and Maplewood, New Jersey, are two cities that share a school district. With funding from the city governments, residents there organized both to publicize their communities as pleasant places with good schools, as well as to offer $10,000 low-interest mortgage loans to whites and people of color who move to neighborhoods where their race is under-represented. Racial integration has proceeded well in both cities. Whites and nonwhites purchased homes in all areas of both municipalities.[132]

Regulating Real Estate Advertising; Financing Assistance

Denial of mortgage financing to minorities ("redlining") has been a significant concern to civil rights reformers. An affirmative action mechanism was devised by Congress to mitigate this problem. The Community Reinvestment Act of 1977[133] requires federal bank regulators to evaluate whether banks covered by the statute have met the borrowing needs of the communities they serve. If banks do not measure up, their applications to serve as depositories for federal funds as well as applications for mergers and acquisitions may be denied. Community reformers have seized upon these periodic reviews to pressure banks to increase their lending to minorities. Under such pressure, banks have significantly increased their minority loans.[134]

The Community Reinvestment Act (CRA) has been charged with being at the core of the financial/banking ills that began plaguing the nation in 2008, a charge vigorously denied by the Federal Reserve. The Fed's message includes the insistence that the foreclosure rate for CRA mortgagees is lower than that experienced by higher-income groups[135] A paper published by the American Enterprise Institute, however, provides a forceful rebuttal. It points to the difficulty of determining how CRA borrowers have behaved because the data about that undertaking are thoroughly politicized and not to be trusted. The financial crisis of 2008 had many fathers: greedy bankers, predatory lending, foolish and irresponsible investors. Importantly, the federal CRA effort to stimulate home ownership by low and moderate-income people through very liberal lending policies encouraged the same lax underwriting for higher-income groups. And bank regulators could hardly reject loan requirements for richer people that were available to the less fortunate. These "easy credit" policies produced a host of baneful effects: the extraordinary increase in real estate values; the encouragement of foolish risk taking with the hope that home prices would continue to rise; the inevitable bursting of the "bubble," and the marked decline in home values, bringing in its wake mortgage obligations that far exceeded the equity held by the borrower. And this resulted in mortgagees walking away from their mortgage obligations, leaving the homes to be foreclosed. The rate of foreclosure was of sufficient magnitude to produce the banking "meltdowns" of 2008–09.[136]

Section 3604(c) of the Fair Housing Act[137] makes it unlawful "[t]o make, print, or publish, or cause to be made, printed, or published any notice, statement, or advertisement, with respect to the sale or rental of a dwelling that indicates any preference, limitation, or discrimination based on race, color, religion, sex, handicap, familial status, or national origin." Here appellate court case law accepts disparate-impact theory. Any housing-related communication—irrespective of the intent of the communicator—which indicates to an ordinary person any race-conscious housing preference, limitation, or discrimination is prohibited. It appears that § 3604(c) has silenced at least blatant racial/ethnic discriminatory advertising.[138]

Like Shaker Heights, a number of communities have limited real estate solicitation and For Sale sign practices in order to frustrate "blockbusting."[139] The For Sale sign and solicitation regulation undertaken by several governments in the Chicago area was examined in *South Suburban Housing Center v. Greater South Suburban Board of Realtors* (1991).[140] The solicitation regulation barred realtor entreaties to homeowners who indicated (by putting their names on a list distributed by the municipalities involved) that they did not want salespeople calling. The realtors argued in *South Suburban* that the solicitation bans were meant to keep whites from selling, thus discriminating against black home seekers in a fashion contrary to Title VIII.[141] The court rejected that argument, saying that there was no real evidence that the solicitation ban ordinances were intended to discriminate against African Americans. Nor would the bans have "a discernable discriminatory effect on the potential home buying public, even if it is predominantly black, since those who opted to be placed on the solicitation ban list were least likely to offer their homes for sale in the first place."[142]

The solicitation bans and the restrictions on the size, placement, and number of For Sale signs also came under First Amendment, "free speech" scrutiny. Both sets of restraints were judged as limits on commercial speech, allowable if they served a substantial government interest, and were no more extensive than necessary to serve that interest. Using this hybrid form of strict and intermediate scrutiny, the court rejected the realtors' arguments, finding that the solicitation ban was no more extensive than necessary to serve the important interest of privacy; while the substantial municipal value of environmental aesthetics was properly accommodated by sign regulations.[143]

Epilogue

Residential integration concerns continue to remain at the lower end of the affirmative action "totem pole."[144] There is sharp dispute among civil rights advocates over the merits of affirmative action for housing desegregation. Strenuous arguments can and have been made supportive of the ghetto's racial homogeneity: for example, that black political strength and talent is kept cohesive and strong, rather than dissipated through population dispersion.[145] Critics—such as the late, eminent sociologist E. Franklin Frazier[146]—insist, however, that a mainstay of ghetto cohesiveness is the selfish commitment of black political leaders to self-protection and aggrandizement. But there is much more behind integration reluctance. Pro-integration affirmative action in housing has been shackled to the "tipping" variable, a notion that an area will tip to segregation once the black population reaches a certain point. The estimates as to when this point is reached oscillate widely, but they generally hover around 20 percent. Conformity with the tipping standard translates into limits on black housing choice, and this helps to partially explain the pro-integration reluctance of civil rights groups and government. One must wonder whether white attitudes should govern the integration process. If the "tipping" thesis is correct, and followed, the large majority of African Americans will be restricted to the ghetto for the foreseeable future. But is the tipping thesis correct? Are not white attitudes mellowing? Whites have come to at least accept freedom of choice for minorities in employment, schooling, and voting. Is there hope for housing?

Progressive thinking has endorsed a variety of integration achievement and maintenance schemes. A number of these have been touched upon above, and they have relied heavily on economic integration as the pedestal for racial/integration. America's residential segregation remains impressive. Consequently, we are unable to contradict the views of a very leading student in the housing field:

> [F]ederal agencies, especially HUD, almost perfectly mirror the confusion, apathy, and shortsightedness of Congress, civil rights leaders, and the public. Ambiguity about the requirement or need to promote housing desegregation is echoed, and amplified, within the corridors of HUD, the Department of Justice, and the Office of Management and Budget. No federal agency is likely to develop a coherent, comprehensive desegregation strategy when it is whipsawed by Congress and budgetary pressures, and when its "natural" allies remain silent, confused, or antagonistic. Also, how does an agency begin systematic desegregation when there is judicial uncertainty about the legality of race-conscious tools needed to desegregate.[147]

We end by reemphasizing some of the key questions raised in this chapter: Is residential racial/ethnic integration a legitimate civil rights goal? Or should we insist only on freedom of access and egress? How much racial segregation is explained by economics; by personal preferences? To what extent is it necessary or appropriate to employ racial/ethnic preferences, or even undisguised quotas, in making decisions about access, rents, and financing? Are efforts to promote ethno-racial integration through socioeconomic integration sufficient? To what extent can housing integration policy appropriately regulate zoning and land use restrictions; advertising and marketing, including even For Sale signs; mortgage lending "redlining"; property insurance; and such real estate brokerage chicanery as "blockbusting?" How should the impact of residential segregation on school segregation be addressed by law? Should racial/ethnic-balancing occupancy limits be outlawed, or sanctioned? To pose the policy questions in the broadest terms, should government undertake to persuade whites to remain when minorities move into "their" neighborhoods; or to move into neighborhoods with substantial minority populations; or to persuade blacks and other minorities to move into predominantly or all-white neighborhoods; or to stabilize racially balanced neighborhoods in order to prevent resegregation?

Eight

Constitutional Underclasses and Affirmative Action

The Disabled, Older Workers, Homosexuals

Prologue

Challenging obstacles face those who attempt to master affirmative action law and policy. The literature of affirmative action makes little attempt to treat the subjects of employment, voting, education, and housing affirmative action in a comprehensive and integrated fashion. This volume attempts to both mitigate that deficiency, and to expand the scope of affirmative action analysis—as it should be—beyond its usual topics of race, gender, and ethnicity by addressing antidiscrimination measures affecting the disabled, senior workers, and homosexuals.

The Supreme Court has not granted the disabled, older workers, and homosexuals the same solicitude that body has afforded racial and ethnic minorities. Ethno-racial discriminatory treatment directed at minorities is subject to strict judicial scrutiny under equal protection review; while third-tier/mere rationality review is what is available when elders, gays, lesbians, and the disabled claim due process and equal protection violations (although homosexuals have clearly received a heightened form of third-tier analysis). The disparate-impact protection available to racial/ethnic groups under Title VII of the 1964 Civil Rights Act has been found by the High Court to be inapplicable to older workers under the 1967 Age Discrimination in Employment Act;[1] and that statute has been determined by the Court to have been inappropriately extended to state government employees.[2] The protection against gender discrimination in Title VII of the 1964 Civil Rights Act does not, according to lower federal courts, extend to sexual orientation harassment.[3] The Supreme Court has not overruled this view, but has concluded that homosexuals have a due process *full* right to engage in adult, consensual homosexual activity without indicating whether that full right is fundamental, mid, or lowest-tier,[4] and without changing the third-tier scrutiny to which discrimination against homosexuals has been subject in U.S. Supreme Court equal protection/due process jurisdprudence.

The Disability/Antidiscrimination Difference Canon

Some scholars have added to the burden of understanding affirmative action by adopting a mode of thought—a canon, if you will—that insists that the "reasonable accommodation" requirement for disabled people in disability law differs from the standards of other recent antidiscrimination statutes. Actually, the affirmative action components of the latter probably nurtured[5] and are surely comparable to the "reasonable accommodation" requirement in disability law. Let us first address this misleading canon. And here we will be guided by and elaborate upon a thesis presented by Professor Christine Jolls in her essay titled *Antidiscrimination and Accommodation*, 115 Harvard Law Review 642 (2001). The Jolls essay describes the canon and delineates its bibliography.

It is to be recalled that Title VII of the 1964 Civil Rights Act (1964 CRA) declared it an unlawful employment practice for an employer (of fifteen or more) to "fail or refuse to hire or to discharge any individual, or otherwise discriminate against any individual with respect to his compensation, terms, conditions, or privileges of employment because of such individual's race, color, sex, or national origin."[6] Among other things, moreover, employers and labor organizations were prohibited from discriminating "against any individual because of his race, color, religion, sex, or national origin in admission to, or employment in, any program established to provide apprenticeship or other training."[7]

By comparison, Title I of the 1990 Americans With Disabilities Act (ADA) declares[8] that "[n]o covered entity [of fifteen or more employees] shall discriminate against a qualified individual with a disability because of the disability of such individual in regard to job application procedures, the hiring, advancement, or discharge of employees, employee compensation, job training, and other terms, conditions, and privileges of employment." Further, covered entities are required to make "reasonable accommodations to the known physical or mental limitations of an otherwise qualified individual with a disability who is an applicant or employee, unless such covered entity can demonstrate that the accommodation would impose an undue hardship on the operation of the business of such covered entity." These accommodations could include: "adjustment or modification of examinations, training materials, or policies"; "modification of equipment"; "job restructuring, part-time work schedules, [and] reassignment to vacant positions."[9] Race/ethnic/gender affirmative action benefits are at least equally accommodationist. They involve outreach efforts; special training; public school integration; preferences in hiring, promotion, and university admissions; set-asides in government contracts; and mechanisms designed to increase minority voting and representation.

An entrenched canon of civil rights scholarship is the distinction between the above-cited employment accommodation requirement in the 1990 Americans With Disabilities Act (ADA) and the employment antidiscrimination mandate of the 1964 Civil Rights Act (1964 CRA). This same distinction is also applied by the canon to other civil rights antidiscrimination prohibitions not concerned with employment. In its essence, this canon regards the non-ADA measures as seeking—without any special help or compensation—equal treatment for those who are, in fact, equal. The ADA, on the other hand, requires, as noted, employers to reasonably accommodate the disabled unless doing so "would impose an undue hardship." According to the canon, the ADA seeks to "equalize the unequal" through reasonable accommodation. "Fundamentally," Professor Sherwin Rosen—an expounder of the canonic view—maintains:

> the ADA is not an antidiscrimination law. By forcing employers to pay for work site and other job accommodation that might allow workers with impairing conditions defined by law to compete on equal terms, it . . . [requires] firms to treat unequal people equally, thus discriminating in favor of the disabled. If not by imposing hiring preferences then by imposing greater expenditures to produce the same amount of work, it . . . [is] discriminatory.[10]

Because of its reasonable accommodation provision, Rosen viewed the ADA as a "social insurance" program, which is "best provided and monitored directly by the state through the tax system."[11] But Professor Rosen failed to explain why the 1964 CRA (and other recent civil rights measures) could not be deemed "social insurance" programs. Surely, the aim of their affirmative action dimensions (and their disparate-impact ideology) was to ensure—as do social insurance programs generally—that minorities and females obtain a fair share of the benefits society has to offer.

Also illustrative of the "accommodation is different from antidiscrimination" school is the advocacy of Professors Pamela Karlan and George Rutherglen[12] who insist that their comparison of ADA and "traditional" civil rights law was meant to "shed light on antidiscrimination law generally."[13] It fails to do that. To these writers, traditional civil rights law is governed by a "sameness" model, while the ADA

> embraces both a "sameness" and "difference" model of discrimination. Under the sameness model, discrimination occurs when individuals who are fundamentally the same are treated differ-

ently for illegitimate reasons. . . . A difference model, by contrast, assumes that individuals who possess the quality or trait at issue are different in a relevant respect from individuals who don't and that "treating [them] similarly can itself become a form of oppression." To paraphrase Justice Blackmun's comment in *Regents v. Bakke* (1978),[14] in the context of disabilities, a difference model requires that "[i]n order to go beyond [an individual's disability], we must first take account of [that disability]. There is no other way. And in order to treat some persons equally, we must treat them differently."[15]

The Blackmun *Bakke* opinion accepts the doctrine that race could be used as a factor in the admissions process to overcome the disadvantaged condition of minorities; and that the granting of such an advantage could conform with the dictates of both the Constitution's Equal Protection Clause, and the 1964 CRA. At the time of *Bakke*, the United States was already awash with affirmative action programs created under the banner of "traditional" civil rights laws, and designed to compensate minorities and females for the oppression they experienced in American history. And these affirmative action remedies treated protected racial/ethnic groups differently from the unprotected. In short, the "difference" model was very much fostered by the "traditional" civil rights laws and their administrative regulations.

Karlan and Rutherglen agree that sex, race, and ethnic affirmative action programs do conform with the "difference" model, but they argue that such affirmative action is quite different from the "reasonable accommodation" practices of the ADA. For one thing, race/gender/ethnic affirmative action changes selection procedures and not job *requirements* or job *environments*.[16] They provide not one whiff of evidence supporting this assertion, leaving the question of whether job standards were changed to accommodate affirmative action hires. Have not efficiency standards been affected by contract "set-asides" and preferential bidding practices for protected groups? Have grading procedures been changed to accommodate minorities in the "job" of higher education? The environment and standards of college sports have changed in the wake of the civil rights legal requirement that females share organized college athletics in a fashion that was proportional to their school populations.[17] Clearly, too, the substance of radio and TV broadcasting was meant to be changed by affording minorities preferences in obtaining FCC licenses—preferences pushed by the FCC to advance a statutory mandate for social/cultural/viewpoint diversification. In this connection, the Supreme Court determined that equal protection dictates of the Constitution were not violated.[18] Broadcast diversification is not an isolated phenomenon. The central rationale of current-day race/sex/ethnic affirmative action is the need to change workplace and educational environments through diversification. Social/cultural diversity in seemingly all things has become the new civil rights mantra!

Karlan and Rutherglen also assert that the ADA—when compared to traditional civil rights law—is *relational* and *sensitive*, in the sense that jobs are adjusted to the needs of the disabled individual. However, a great deal of sensitivity adjustment also occurs in the conduct of the affirmative action programs associated with traditional civil rights employment law. Thus, race/ethnic/gender sensitivity training has been commonplace in the workplaces of America. "Set-asides" have attentively allocated percentages of government contracts to minorities and females. Public contract bidding practices have been adjusted to give minorities an advantage.[19] The number of groups covered by affirmative action is so broad and has grown so extensively that this aspect of "sensitivity" has been challenged as overinclusive.[20] The Equal Employment Opportunity Commission (EEOC)—a major federal overseer of affirmative action in employment—has prompted widespread adoption of its guidelines, which require all "users" to maintain job inventory records by sex and the following race and ethnic groups: blacks (Negroes), American Indians (including Alaskan Natives), Asians (including Pacific Islanders), Hispanic (including persons of Mexican, Puerto Rican, Cuban, Central or South American, or other Spanish origin or culture regardless of race), whites (Caucasians) other than Hispanic.[21] The records are meant to be and have been an important generator of employment affirmative action by encouraging the granting of employment opportunities to "underutilized" minorities and women so that accusations of prohibited discrimination under the 1964 CRA will be avoided. (See 31–32.) All this should impress the observer as especially "relational and sensitive" to the needs of protected groups covered by the affirmative action dimensions of traditional civil rights laws.

Finally, Karlan and Rutherglen distinguish the ADA from Title VII by insisting that the latter's embrace of affirmative action is rooted in disparate-impact suits whereas ADA cases are propelled typically by disparate-treatment claims. As they properly point out, plaintiffs pursuing disparate-treatment remedies are required to prove that defendants are guilty of intentional discrimination. On the other hand, those pursuing disparate-impact remedies must show culturally systemic discrimination. And this is done usually by demonstrating that a protected group is statistically underrepresented. Karlan and Rutherglen, however, do not inform the reader that at the heart of the ADA was the view that the disabled were underrepresented, in large measure, because of cultural bias, and that "reasonable accommodation" was essential to the cure. In short, disparate-impact lives at the core of the ADA. Consider the congressional findings attached to the 1990 statute:

SEC. 2. FINDINGS AND PURPOSES

(a) Findings.—The Congress finds that—. . . .

(2) historically, society has tended to isolate and segregate individuals with disabilities, and, despite some improvements, such forms of discrimination against individuals with disabilities continue to be a serious and pervasive social problem;

(3) discrimination against individuals with disabilities persists in such critical areas as employment, housing, public accommodations, education, transportation, communication, recreation, institutionalization, health services, voting, and access to public services; . . .

(5) individuals with disabilities continually encounter various forms of discrimination, including outright intentional exclusion, the discriminatory effects of architectural, transportation, and communication barriers, overprotective rules and policies, failure to make modifications to existing facilities and practices, exclusionary qualification standards and criteria, segregation, and relegation to lesser services, programs, activities, benefits, jobs, or other opportunities;

(6) census data, national polls, and other studies have documented that people with disabilities, as a group, occupy an inferior status in our society, and are severely disadvantaged socially, vocationally, economically, and educationally; . . .

(b) Purpose.—It is the purpose of this Act—

(1) to provide a clear and comprehensive national mandate for the elimination of discrimination against individuals with disabilities. . . .[22]

Given the obvious overlap between ADA's reasonable accommodation requirement and affirmative action, one must wonder why the canon discussed herein has received such substantial scholarly support. Professor Samuel Bagenstos attempts to answer this question:[23]

Emphasizing the differences between antidiscrimination and ADA accommodationism, as the canon does, serves as a vehicle for advancing affirmative-action accommodations for minorities, and safeguarding exiting affirmative-action practices.

For critics of the ADA on the right, stressing the difference between accommodation and antidiscrimination strengthened their attack on the ADA—an attack which argues that free markets untrammeled by accommodationist restraints is best.

Traditional liberal critics of the ADA champion the canon to underscore their commitment to an antidiscrimination policy unembellished by affirmative action which they feel is insufficiently sensitive to its burdens on other social welfare programs and rights.

The ADA and Its Predecessors

American disability policy has been dominated by an income maintenance policy involving the transfer of government funds to the disabled, allowing them to purchase necessities of life. Income maintenance includes state workmen's compensation undertakings for injuries on the job; and the U.S. Social Security Administration's disability program for those so disabled that they can do no work. As originally conceived and implemented, these income maintenance efforts did not seek to overcome barriers limiting the social integration of the disabled.[24] As one leading scholar in the field put it: "From the 1920s to the 1970s, the theme of separation predominated in all the government's social welfare programs. Income-maintenance programs asked the handicapped to remove themselves from the labor force in order to receive benefits."[25]

Promoting the integration of the disabled into the workforce has been associated with vocational rehabilitation undertakings which have existed alongside social insurance. But—critics charge—participation in earlier manifestations of vocational training was a participation characterized by subordination and condescension, with the disabled seen and treated as supplicants needing the merciful, patronizing help of a superior caste of expert specialists.[26] Guided by the African American civil rights movement of the 1960s, disability rights activists insisted on governmental programs designed to achieve the full societal integration of the disabled as equal citizens by removing social mindset barriers that viewed the disabled as different—as abnormal, frightened people who were not full-fledged members of society and who were appropriately kept out of the mainstream.[27] Advocacy of this nature produced mature vocational rehabilitation operations in which enrollees are consulted about their treatment and must agree in writing to participate.[28]

Other efforts at battling discrimination against the disabled and promoting their independence and social integration included:[29]

> *Architectural Barriers Act of 1968*—Promulgated a broad-gauged requirement that buildings constructed or financed by the United States be usable by the physically disabled. [Pub L 90-480, 82 Stat 718, codified as amended at 42 USC, §§ 4151–4157 (2009)].
>
> *Individuals with Disabilities Education Act* **(1990)**—Provided a federal grant-in-aid, which allocated funds to states attempting to guarantee children with disabilities an adequate and appropriate education in the least restrictive setting. Each child was to receive an individualized plan suitable to the child's needs. [(Pub L 108-476; 118 Stat 2647, codified as amended at 20 USC §1400 *et seq* (2009)].
>
> *The Developmental Disabilities Assistance and Bill of Rights Act* **(1975)**—Provided federal grants to the states for the care and treatment of those with severe and long-term disabilities. Individualized plans must be developed for each covered person.[Pub L 94-103; 89 Stat 486, codified as amended at 42 USC § 1501 *et seq* (2009)].
>
> *The Air Carrier Access Act* **(1986)**—Barred air carriers from discriminating against people with disabilities. Carriers were to conform with regulations issued by the Department of Transportation. [Pub L 99-435; 100 Stat 1080, 49 USC § 41705 (2009)].
>
> *The Voting Accessibility for the Elderly and Handicapped Act* **(1984)**—Required voting places conducting federal elections be accessible to the disabled, and that voting aids (such as large-print ballots) be available to assist the handicapped. [(Pub L 98-435; 98 Stat 1678 codified at 42 USC §§ 1973ee, 1973ee-6 (2009)].
>
> *The Fair Housing Amendments Act* **(1988)**—Adds disability to the other prohibited grounds for discrimination (race, color, religion, national origin, sex) in the sale and rental of housing. Disabled persons are to be reasonably accommodated in policies and services so that they have an equal opportunity to enjoy their dwellings. Accessibility standards are required for the first floor of multi family units (or all floors where an elevator has been installed) available for occupancy after March 1991. These standards include the requirements that doors be wide enough to permit wheelchair passage; and that public/common areas be fully accessible to wheelchair users.

The requirements of this amendment were incorporated in the ADA. [(Pub L 100-430; 102 Stat 1619, codified at 42 USC § 3601 *et seq* (2009)].

The Rehabilitation Act of 1973 —Mandates, in Section 501, that federal agencies operate an affirmative action program to provide employment opportunities for the disabled, particularly the deaf, blind, mentally retarded, those with missing extremities, the paralyzed (complete or partial), and those with convulsive disorders. Administrative regulations require that reasonable accommodation be afforded the disabled in federal employment. Section 503 imposes an affirmative action requirement on federal contractors comparable to that imposed by Section 501 on federal agencies. Section 504 prohibits discrimination against otherwise qualified disabled individuals in programs receiving federal financial assistance. [(Pub L 93-112, 87 Stat 355, codified as amended at 29 USC, § 794 *et seq* (2009)].

The Americans with Disabilities Act-ADA **(1990)**—This statute was the most extensive federal law (fifty-two pages in *Statutes at Large*) meant to promote the civil rights theme of the disability rights movement: to socially integrate the disabled by ameliorating discriminatory practices affecting them, and by requiring the reasonable accommodation of the disabled. The titles of that statute of concern to this chapter were numbered I, II, and III. The findings by Congress stressed that the disabled had historically been subject to society's discriminatory treatment, making them, in the language of equal protection law, a "suspect class."[30] [(Pub L 101-336, 104 Stat 327, codified as amended at 42 USC, § 1210 *et seq* (2009)].

As we have noted, Title I of the ADA provides that no covered employers "shall discriminate against a qualified individual with a disability on the basis[31] of the disability of such individual in regard to"[32] employment opportunities. A qualified person with a disability is defined as "an individual with a disability who, with or without reasonable accommodation can perform the essential functions of the employment that such individual holds or desires."[33] Employers are required to reasonably accommodate the disabled by means that do not impose undue hardship on employers.[34] Included in the definition of those who are disabled are those with "a physical or mental impairment that substantially limits one or more of the major life activities of such an individual."[35]

The ADA also prohibits discrimination affecting the disabled in the provision of public services and public accommodations. State and local public services are covered by Title II, which states that "no qualified individual with a disability shall, by reason of such disability, be excluded from participation in or be denied the benefits of the services, programs or activities of public entities.[36] Title III prohibits discrimination "on the basis of disability in the full and equal enjoyment of the goods, services, facilities, privileges, advantages or accommodation of any place of public accommodation."[37] For the purposes of Titles II and III, the disabled are those with "a physical or mental impairment that substantially limits one or more of the major life activities of such an individual."[38]

Under Title II, a "qualified individual with a disability" is a person with a disability "who, with or without reasonable modification to rules, policies, practices, the removal of architectural, communication, or transportation barriers, or the provision of auxiliary aids and services, meets the essential eligibility requirements for the receipt of services or the participation in programs or activities provided by a public entity."[39] Under Department of Justice regulations, states and localities do not have to make modifications that involve fundamental alterations or impose undue fiscal or administrative burdens.[40] New construction or alteration cannot claim undue burden defenses.[41] Public accommodations must also reasonably modify those accommodations to cater to the disabled unless fundamental alterations would be the result.[42]

One should celebrate the changes wrought by these sections of the law for the disabled: augmented services for students; better access to transportation, streets, theatres, and restaurants. But as for the employment area (ADA's Title I), Professor Samuel Bagenstos reported in 2004 that the act had not resulted in significantly increased employment for the disabled. He also noted that some scholars feel that the act actually made job acquisition by the disabled more difficult. To him, job increases for the disabled will require more welfare services such as home health aid services to help prepare the disabled for work.[43]

The Courts and the ADA

Judging from the first decade of the ADA, plaintiffs in Title I (employment cases) typically have lost in lower federal courts as they have in Title II (public services) and Title III (public accommodations), although they were more successful in connection with Title II and III than in Title I controversies.[44] In the some 3,400 Title I cases brought in lower federal courts between 1992–2002, the defendants prevailed[45] at a rate of about 95 percent. In the public services (Title II) area, defendants prevailed[46] in some 53 percent of all the reported cases through 2001. In the 247 Title III cases, defendants prevailed[47] in 55 percent of the rulings.

The U.S. Supreme Court has impeded Title I suits by finding that the congressional effort to subject states to suit under Title I violated the Eleventh Amendment. In *University of Alabama v. Garrett* (2001),[48] the Court determined that Section 5 of the Fourteenth Amendment did not authorize the Congress to enable individuals to sue states for discrimination against the disabled in employment. Section 5 permits Congress to implement the due process and equal protection mandates of the Fourteenth Amendment. To defeat the Eleventh Amendment ban against suits directed at states by using Section 5 in the Fourteenth Amendment, Congress must show that state violation of the Fourteenth Amendment was gross enough to warrant the bypassing of the Eleventh Amendment's bar against private suits directed at state government. Congress had failed to demonstrate a marked pattern of employment discrimination affecting the disabled.[49] Further, the Court said, states in their employment practices must be merely rational—that is, a reasonable (average) person could *possibly* find government's action justifiable. States "could quite hardheadedly—and perhaps hardheartedly—hold to job qualification requirements which do not make allowances for the disabled."[50] "For example, whereas it would be entirely rational (and therefore constitutional) for a state employer to conserve scarce resources by hiring employees who are able to use existing facilities, the ADA requires employers to 'make existing facilities used by employees readily accessible to and usable by individuals with disabilities.' "[51] An excerpt from the *Garrett* majority and dissent follows:

The University of Alabama v. Patricia Garrett, et al., 531 U.S. 356 (2001)

[360] Chief Justice Rehnquist delivered the opinion of the Court.

We decide here whether employees of the State of Alabama may recover money damages by reason of the State's failure to comply with the provisions of Title I of the Americans with Disabilities Act of 1990. We hold that such suits are barred by the Eleventh Amendment. . . .

[363] The Eleventh Amendment provides: "The Judicial power of the United States shall not be construed to extend to any suit in law or equity, commenced or prosecuted against one of the United States by Citizens of another State, or by Citizens or Subjects of any Foreign State."

Although by its terms the Amendment applies only to suits against a State by citizens of another State, our cases have extended the Amendment's applicability to suits by citizens against their own States. . . .

We have recognized, however, that Congress may abrogate the States' Eleventh Amendment immunity when it both unequivocally intends to do so and "act[s] pursuant to a valid grant of constitutional authority." . . . The [364] first of these requirements is not in dispute here. . . . The question, then, is whether Congress acted within its constitutional authority. . . .

Congress may subject nonconsenting States to suit in federal court when it does so pursuant to a valid exercise of its § 5 [of the Fourteenth Amendment] power. . . .

[365] Section 1 of the Fourteenth Amendment provides, in relevant part: "No State shall make or enforce any law which shall abridge the privileges or immunities of citizens of the United States; nor shall any State deprive any person of life, liberty, or property, without due process of law; nor deny to any person within its jurisdiction the equal protection of the laws."

Section 5 of the Fourteenth Amendment grants Congress the power to enforce the substantive guarantees contained in § 1 by enacting "appropriate legislation." Congress is not limited to mere legislative repetition of this Court's constitutional jurisprudence. "Rather, Congress' power 'to enforce' the Amendment includes the authority both to remedy and to deter violation of rights guaranteed thereunder by prohibiting a somewhat broader swath of conduct, including that which is not itself forbidden by the Amendment's text."

City of Boerne [*v. Flores*] also confirmed, however, the long-settled principle that it is the responsibility of this Court, not Congress, to define the substance of constitutional guarantees. 521 U.S., at 519–524 (1997). Accordingly, § 5 legislation reaching beyond the scope of § 1's actual guarantees must exhibit "congruence and proportionality between the injury to be prevented or remedied and the means adopted to that end."

The first step in applying these now familiar principles is to identify with some precision the scope of the constitutional right at issue. Here, that inquiry requires us to examine the limitations § 1 of the Fourteenth Amendment places upon States' treatment of the disabled. . . . [W]e look to our prior decisions under the Equal Protection Clause dealing with this issue.

[366] In *Cleburne v. Cleburne Living Center, Inc.*, 473 U.S. 432, (1985), we considered an equal protection challenge to a city ordinance requiring a special use permit for the operation of a group home for the mentally retarded. The specific question before us was whether the Court of Appeals had erred by holding that mental retardation qualified as a "quasi-suspect" classification under our equal protection jurisprudence. We answered that question in the affirmative, concluding instead that such legislation incurs only the minimum "rational-basis" review applicable to general social and economic legislation. In a statement that today seems quite prescient, we explained that

"if the large and amorphous class of the mentally retarded were deemed quasi-suspect for the reasons given by the Court of Appeals, it would be difficult to find a principled way to distinguish a variety of other groups who have perhaps immutable disabilities setting them off from others, who cannot themselves mandate the desired legislative responses, and who can claim some degree of prejudice from at least part of the public at large. One need mention in this respect only the aging, the disabled, the mentally ill, and the infirm. We are reluctant to set out on that course, and we decline to do so."

Under rational-basis review, where a group possesses "distinguishing characteristics relevant to interests the State has the authority to implement," a State's decision [367] to act on the basis of those differences does not give rise to a constitutional violation. "Such a classification cannot run afoul of the Equal Protection Clause if there is a rational relationship between the disparity of treatment and some legitimate governmental purpose." Moreover, the State need not articulate its reasoning at the moment a particular decision is made. Rather, the burden is upon the challenging party to negative " 'any reasonably conceivable state of facts that could provide a rational basis for the classification.' " . . .
States are not required by the Fourteenth Amendment to make special accommodations for the disabled, so long as their actions toward such individuals are rational. They could quite hardheadedly—[368] and perhaps hardheartedly—hold to job-qualification

requirements which do not make allowance for the disabled. If special accommodations for the disabled are to be required, they have to come from positive law and not through the Equal Protection Clause.

Once we have determined the metes and bounds of the constitutional right in question, we examine whether Congress identified a history and pattern of unconstitutional employment discrimination by the States against the disabled. . . . Congress' § 5 authority is appropriately exercised only in response to state transgressions. . . . The legislative record of the ADA, however, simply fails to show that Congress did in fact identify a pattern of irrational state discrimination in employment against the disabled.

Respondents contend that the inquiry as to unconstitutional discrimination should extend not only to States themselves, but to units of local governments, such as cities and counties. All of these, they say, are "state actors" for [369] purposes of the Fourteenth Amendment. This is quite true, but the Eleventh Amendment does not extend its immunity to units of local government. These entities are subject to private claims for damages under the ADA without Congress' ever having to rely on § 5 of the Fourteenth Amendment to render them so. It would make no sense to consider constitutional violations on their part, as well as by the States themselves, when only the States are the beneficiaries of the Eleventh Amendment.

Congress made a general finding in the ADA that "historically, society has tended to isolate and segregate individuals with disabilities, and, despite some improvements, such forms of discrimination against individuals with disabilities continue to be a serious and pervasive social problem." The record assembled by Congress includes many instances to support such a finding. But the great majority of these incidents do not deal with the activities of States. . . .

[370] Several of these incidents undoubtedly evidence an unwillingness on the part of state officials to make the sort of accommodations for the disabled required by the ADA. Whether they were irrational under our decision in *Cleburne* is more debatable, particularly when the incident is described out of context. But even if it were to be determined that each incident upon fuller

examination showed unconstitutional action on the part of the State, these incidents taken together fall far short of even suggesting the pattern of unconstitutional discrimination on which § 5 legislation must be based. Congress, in enacting the ADA, found that "some 43,000,000 Americans have one or more physical or mental disabilities." In 1990, the States alone employed more than 4.5 million people. It is telling, we think, that given these large numbers, Congress assembled only such minimal evidence of unconstitutional state discrimination in employment against the disabled. . . .

[372] Even were it possible to squeeze out of these examples a pattern of unconstitutional discrimination by the States, the rights and remedies created by the ADA against the States would raise the same sort of concerns as to congruence and proportionality as were found in *City of Boerne, supra*. For example, whereas it would be entirely rational (and therefore constitutional) for a state employer to conserve scarce financial resources by hiring employees who are able to use existing facilities, the ADA requires employers to "mak[e] existing facilities used by employees readily accessible to and usable by individuals with disabilities." The ADA does except employers from the "reasonable accommodatio[n]" requirement where the employer "can demonstrate that the accommodation would impose an undue hardship on the operation of the business of such covered entity." However, even with this exception, the accommodation duty far exceeds what is constitutionally required in that it makes unlawful a range of alternative responses that would be reasonable but would fall short of imposing an "undue burden" upon the employer. The Act also makes it the employer's duty to prove that it would suffer such a burden, instead of requiring (as the Constitution does) that the complaining party negate reasonable bases for the employer's decision.

The ADA also forbids "utilizing standards, criteria, or methods of administration" that disparately impact the disabled, without regard to whether such conduct has a rational basis. Although disparate impact may be [373] relevant evidence of racial discrimination, such evidence alone is insufficient even where the Fourteenth Amendment subjects state action to strict scrutiny. ("Our cases have not embraced the proposition that a law or other official act, without regard to whether it reflects a racially discriminatory purpose, is unconstitutional *solely* because it has a racially disproportionate impact").

The ADA's constitutional shortcomings are apparent when the Act is compared to Congress' efforts in the Voting Rights Act of 1965 to respond to a serious pattern of constitutional violations. In *South Carolina v. Katzenbach*, 383 U.S. 301 (1966), we considered whether the Voting Rights Act was "appropriate" legislation to enforce the Fifteenth Amendment's protection against racial discrimination in voting. Concluding that it was a valid exercise of Congress' enforcement power under § 2 of the Fifteenth Amendment, we noted that "[b]efore enacting the measure, Congress explored with great care the problem of racial discrimination in voting."

In that Act, Congress documented a marked pattern of unconstitutional action by the States. State officials, Congress found, routinely applied voting tests in order to exclude African-American citizens from registering to vote. Congress also determined that litigation had proved ineffective and that there persisted an otherwise inexplicable 50-percentage-point gap in the registration of white and African-American voters in some States. Congress' response was to promulgate in the Voting Rights Act a detailed but limited remedial scheme designed to guarantee meaningful enforcement of the Fifteenth Amendment in those areas of the Nation where abundant evidence of States' systematic denial of those rights was identified. . . .

Justice Breyer, with whom Justice Stevens, Justice Souter, and Justice Ginsburg join, dissenting. . . .
[377] Section 5 . . . grants Congress the "power to enforce, by appropriate legislation," the Fourteenth Amendment's equal protection guarantee. As the Court recognizes, state discrimination in employment against persons with disabilities might " 'run afoul of the Equal Protection Clause' " where there is no " 'rational relationship between the disparity of treatment and some legitimate governmental purpose.' " . . . In my view, Congress reasonably could have concluded that the remedy before us constitutes an "appropriate" way to enforce this basic equal protection requirement. And that is all the Constitution requires.

The Court says that its primary problem with this statutory provision is one of legislative evidence. It says that "Congress assembled only . . . minimal evidence of unconstitutional state discrimination in employment." In fact, Congress compiled a vast legislative record documenting " 'massive, society-wide discrimination' " against persons with disabilities. . . . [378] As to employment, Congress found that "[t]wo-thirds of all disabled Americans between the age of 16 and 64 [were] not working at all," even though a large majority wanted to, and were able to, work productively. And Congress found that this discrimination flowed in significant part from "stereotypic assumptions" as well as "purposeful unequal treatment."

The powerful evidence of discriminatory treatment throughout society in general, including discrimination by private persons and local governments, implicates state governments as well, for state agencies form part of that same larger society. There is no particular reason to believe that they are immune from the "stereotypic assumptions" and pattern of "purposeful unequal treatment" that Congress found prevalent. The Court claims that it "make[s] no sense" to take into consideration constitutional violations committed by local governments. But the substantive obligation that the Equal Protection Clause creates applies to state and local governmental entities alike. Local governments often work closely with, and under the supervision of, state officials, and in general, state and local government employers are similarly situated. Nor is determining whether an apparently "local" entity is entitled to Eleventh Amendment immunity as simple as the majority suggests—it often requires a " 'detailed examination of the relevant provisions of [state] law.' "

[379] In any event, there is no need to rest solely upon evidence of discrimination by local governments or general societal discrimination. There are roughly 300 examples of discrimination by state governments themselves in the legislative record. I fail to see how this evidence "fall[s] far short of even suggesting the pattern of unconstitutional discrimination on which § 5 legislation must be based." . . .

As the Court notes, those who presented instances of discrimination rarely provided additional, independent evidence sufficient to prove in court that, in each instance, the discrimination they suffered lacked justification from a judicial standpoint. . . . Perhaps this explains the Court's view that there is "minimal evidence of unconstitutional state discrimination." But a legislature [380] is not a court of law. And Congress, unlike courts, must, and does, routinely draw general conclusions—for example, of likely motive or of likely relationship to legitimate need—from anecdotal and opinion-based evidence of this kind, particularly when the evidence lacks strong refutation. . . . In reviewing § 5 legislation, we have never required the sort of extensive investigation of each piece of evidence that the Court appears to contemplate. . . .

[384] Unlike courts, Congress can readily gather facts from across the Nation, assess the magnitude of a problem, and more easily find an appropriate remedy. . . . Unlike courts, Congress directly reflects public attitudes and beliefs, enabling Congress better to understand where, and to what extent, refusals to accommodate a disability amount to behavior that is callous or unreasonable to the point of lacking constitutional justification. Unlike judges, Members of Congress can directly obtain information from constituents who have firsthand experience with discrimination and related issues.

Moreover, unlike judges, Members of Congress are elected. When the Court has applied the majority's burden of proof rule, it has explained that we, *i.e.*, the courts, do not " 'sit as a super legislature to judge the wisdom or desirability of legislative policy determinations.' " . . . [385] Read with a reasonably favorable eye, the record indicates that state governments subjected those with disabilities to seriously adverse, disparate treatment. And Congress could have found, in a significant number of instances, that this treatment violated the substantive principles of justification—shorn of their judicial-restraint-related presumptions—that this Court recognized in *Cleburne*. . . .

The 2008 ADA Amendments

Supreme Court opinions perceived as ADA-restrictive prompted amendments to that act, although from a business-needs or laissez-faire point of view these same opinions could be conceptualized as helpful. For one, the Court allowed mitigating measures (e.g., assistive devices, auxiliary aids, medical therapies) to be taken into account when determining the existence of an ADA disability (See *Sutton v. United Airlines*, 1999).[52] One could then be found not ADA-disabled if medication corrected a situation, potentially leaving uncovered those suffering from epilepsy, diabetes, and mental illness.[53] In its 2008 ADA amendments (ADAAA), Congress criticized *Sutton* and its companion cases for narrowing the "broad scope of protection intended to be afforded by the ADA."[54] The ADA now reads that except for eyeglasses and contact lenses, "[t]he determination of whether an impairment substantially limits a major life activity [and may thus be considered ADA-disabling] shall be made without regard to the ameliorative effects of mitigating measures."[55]

Sutton limited ADA coverage in still another way. Under that statute, a claimant can seek relief if he or she is *regarded* as disabled by an employer who discriminates on that ground.[56] *Sutton* concluded that to prevail under the "regarded as disabled" provision, the plaintiff would have to demonstrate that the employer regarded the claimant as ineligible for a wide variety of related jobs, not merely a specific job.[57] Thus, the Suttons claimed that United Airlines violated the ADA by refusing jobs as "global pilots." But they did "not demonstrate that United Airlines would have refused them jobs as "regional pilots," or pilot instructors, and consequently failed to prevail on the "regarded as disabled basis."[58] The ADAAA rejected this approach to the "regarded as disabled" prong of the ADA,[59] and defined that prong as a perception of "physical or mental impairment whether or not the impairment limits or is perceived to limit a major life activity."[60] Employers are required to reasonably accommodate all the ADA-disabled, or those regarded as disabled, by means that do not "fundamentally" alter the "goods, services, facilities, privileges, advantages, or accommodations involved" in an undertaking.[61]

The ADAAA also chastised the Supreme Court's opinion in *Toyota of Kentucky v. Williams* (2002)[62] for requiring that the ADA "be interpreted strictly to create a demanding standard for qualifying as disabled."[63] *Toyota*, the ADAAA insists, "require[s] a greater degree of limitation than was intended by Congress."[64] These amendments direct ADA implementers to understand that the intent of Congress is that the determination of disability "should not demand extensive analysis,"[65] and that "[t]he definition of disability in this Act shall be construed in favor of broad coverage."[66]

Left untouched by the ADAAA was the bottom-line, business-protective thinking exhibited in the Supreme Court's acceptance of a "business-necessity" defense in ADA (Title I) *disparate-treatment* (intentional) cases, while restricting this defense to *disparate-impact* cases in Title VII (1964 CRA) cases where intent need not be proven. The business-necessity defense in disability employment controversies gives employers much strength in defeating claims under ADA Title I, and points to a guidepost in the law that business-necessity, intentional discrimination negatively affecting minorities is not rational, while similarly motivated discrimination directed at the disabled may be.[67]

The Supreme Court and Age Discrimination

The Equal Protection Clause

No Supreme Court majority emerged until 1989 that interpreted the Constitution's Equal Protection Clause as a potential barrier to affirmative action for protected racial and ethnic groups. In that year, the clause was interpreted as subjecting state racial classifications to strict judicial scrutiny, a scrutiny made applicable to federal racial classifications in 1995. (See 65–68.) In 1976 though, the High Court fashioned an Equal Protection Clause that allowed state government very broad discretion to practice age discrimination in its employment practices. Further, the reasoning of the Court nurtured the very age discrimination stereotypes which Congress attempted to weaken in the Age Discrimination Act (ADEA) of 1967.[68]

The extent to which the Court has adopted a laissez-faire attitude in its willingness to allow government employers to engage in age discrimination is graphically illustrated in *Massachusetts v. Murgia* (1976).[69] There, the Massachusetts requirement that its state police troopers retire at age fifty was upheld, even though between ages forty and fifty troopers were required to successfully pass annual mental and physical exams. The Court rejected the notion that mandatory retirement of a fifty-year-old who had passed the annual test with "flying colors" was arbitrary or irrational. The Court said:

> We need state only briefly our reasons for agreeing that strict scrutiny is not the proper test for determining whether the mandatory retirement provision denies appellee equal protection. *San Antonio School District v. Rodriguez* reaffirmed that equal protection analysis requires strict scrutiny of a legislative classification only when the classification impermissibly interferes with the exercise of a fundamental right or operates to the peculiar disadvantage of a suspect class. Mandatory retirement at age 50 under the Massachusetts statute involves neither situation.

> This Court's decisions give no support to the proposition that a right of governmental employment per se is fundamental. Accordingly, we have expressly stated that a standard less than strict scrutiny "has consistently been applied to state legislation restricting the availability of employment opportunities."

> Nor does the class of uniformed state police officers over 50 constitute a suspect class for purposes of equal protection analysis. *Rodriguez* observed that a suspect class is one "saddled with such disabilities, or subjected to such a history of purposeful unequal treatment, or relegated to such a position of political powerlessness as to command extraordinary protection from the majoritarian political process." While the treatment of the aged in this Nation has not been wholly free of discrimination, such persons, unlike, say, those who have been discriminated against on the basis of race or national origin, have not experienced a "history of purposeful unequal treatment" or been subjected to unique disabilities on the basis of stereotyped characteristics not truly indicative of their abilities.[70]

Absent the need to engage in strict scrutiny, the Court chose the "rational basis" standard for age discrimination under which legislation is presumed valid unless irrational. Though Murgia had passed his fitness test, mandatory retirement at fifty was deemed rational since—as the oversimplified judgment/stereotype has it—physical ability generally declines with age.[71]

Three years after *Murgia*, the Court in *Vance v. Bradley* (1979)[72] upheld the State Department's requirement of mandatory retirement at age sixty for Foreign Service officers. To the Court, this requirement advanced productivity by opening up promotional opportunities for younger employees and by spurring recruitment, and was not otherwise irrational because overseas duty requires physical fortitude which declines with age.[73] Justice Marshall found this reasoning nonsensical. "In the absence of any evidence," he said, "that employees aged 60 and over are less able, or that forced retirement does in fact boost productivity by enhancing recruitment and promotional opportunities, this proffered justification does not withstand analysis."[74]

Still again in 1991, the Court upheld the Missouri mandatory retirement age for most state judges at seventy. In its view, the people of that state, in a referendum, could rationally conclude that older judges more readily suffered mental decline than younger ones.[75] The Court went to repeat its third-tier, laissez-faire—leave public employer/employee relations alone—sentiment concerning age discrimination and the Equal Protection Clause:

> The Missouri mandatory retirement provision, like all legal classifications, is founded on a generalization. It is far from true that all judges suffer significant deterioration in performance at age 70. It is probably not true that most do. It may not be true at all. But a State " 'does not violate the Equal Protection Clause merely because the classifications made by its laws are imperfect.' " "In an equal protection case of this type . . . those challenging the . . . judgment [of the people] must convince the court that the . . . facts on which the classification is apparently based could not reasonably be conceived to be true by the . . . decisionmaker." The people of Missouri rationally could conclude that the threat of deterioration at age 70 is sufficiently great, and the alternatives for removal sufficiently inadequate, that they will require all judges to step aside at age 70. This classification does not violate the Equal Protection Clause.[76]

The Courts and the Age Discrimination in Employment Act

The Court's insensitivity to employment age discrimination in its Equal Protection Clause opinions is in the same family of things as its restrictive approach to the Age Discrimination in Employment Act, 1967—the ADEA.[77]

This "statutory short-leash" attitude was exhibited both in disparate-treatment and disparate-impact ADEA cases.

The ADEA (which now covers those forty or older and generally bars mandatory age retirement in employment) declared in its *Findings* that

> (1) in the face of rising productivity and affluence, older workers find themselves disadvantaged in their efforts to retain employment, and especially to regain employment when displaced from jobs; (2) the setting of arbitrary age limits regardless of potential for job performance has become a common practice . . . ; (3) the incidence of unemployment, especially long-term unemployment with resultant deterioration of skill, morale, and employer acceptability is, relative to the younger ages, high among older workers; their numbers are great and growing; and their employment problems grave [78]

Consequently, the Congress, in the ADEA, declared that: "It shall be unlawful for an employer (1) to fail or refuse to hire or discharge any individual or otherwise discriminate against any individual with respect to his compensation, terms, conditions, or privileges of employment, because of such individual's age. . . . [But] it shall not be unlawful for an employer . . . to take any action otherwise prohibited . . . where the differentiation is on reasonable factors other than age."[79]

In 1993, the Supreme Court increased the difficulty workers face in proving age discrimination disparate treatment. In such cases, employees may attempt to persuade a court that—more likely than not—the employer was motivated by the intent to engage in age discrimination. Or, more typically, the employee maintains that the employer's proffered reasons for negative action are mere fabrications—pretexts. At one time, the Supreme Court held that the judicial finding of employer pretext awarded victory to the worker. That Court view changed in *St Mary's Honor Center v. Hicks* (1993),[80] which held that juries *may* infer discriminatory intent on the part of employer once pretext is found, but they are not mandated to do so as previously required.[81]

Another impediment to success in age-related, disparate-treatment suits was created in *Hazen Paper v. Biggins* (1993).[82] Before that opinion, many federal courts found that the unfairness of age-correlated discrimination (such as laying off higher-paid employees who tended to be older) was the functional equivalent of the age discrimination barred in the ADEA.[83] Typical of this approach was an appellate opinion that noted that keeping older employees (who can be replaced with lower-cost younger ones) competed with such other values as profits and economic efficiency. "The ADEA," the appellate court opined, "represents a choice among these values. It stands for the proposition that this is a better country for its willingness to pay the costs for treating older employees fairly."[84] But proving that an employer's negative action correlates substantially with age is no longer enough. To gain a victory under the ADEA, as decided in *Hazen Paper v. Biggins,* employees must now prove that the employer was motivated by the age stereotype "that productivity and competence decline with old age."[85] Arguments of age-correlated unfairness are no longer sufficient,[86] as was reemphasized by the Court in *Smith v. Jackson* (2005)[87] excerpted below. And even if workers can prove, in a disparate-impact suit, that age-incompetence stereotypes guided a negative decision, employers can still prevail if they can prove that factors other than age discrimination would also have resulted in the negative employer decision.[88] Moreover, age-based stereotypes of incompetence can constitutionally be used by government to support mandatory retirement under the Equal Protection Clause. The ADEA provides no protection for state employees as it has been found inapplicable to state (not city) government for the same reason that the ADA is not applicable to states: Congress did not demonstrate that states discriminated against older workers in a substantial fashion.[89] Until 1993, U.S. appellate courts ruled that disparate-impact theory for age discrimination was authorized by the ADEA. This appellate solidarity was dissipated thereafter. In *Smith v. Jackson,* the Supreme Court held that disparate-impact theory, operative under Title VII of the 1964 Civil Rights Act for race/gender/ethnic discrimination, was also applicable under the ADEA. But, in an effort to satisfy both sides of the appellate divide, the Court determined that the scope of that theory was "narrower"[90] (to the point of negligibility, it is argued here) under the ADEA than under Title VII. An excerpt from the Court's opinion in *Smith v. Jackson* follows:

Smith v. City of Jackson, Mississippi, 544 U.S. 228 (2005)

Justice Stevens delivered the following opinion of the Court:

[230] Petitioners, police and public safety officers employed by the city of Jackson, Mississippi (hereinafter City), contend that salary increases received in 1999 violated the Age Discrimination in Employment Act of 1967 (ADEA) because they were less generous to officers over the age of 40 than to younger officers. Their suit raises the question whether the "disparate-impact" theory of recovery announced in *Griggs v. Duke Power Co.,* 401 U.S. 424 (1971), for cases brought under Title VII of the Civil Rights Act of 1964, is cognizable under the ADEA. Despite the age of the ADEA, it is a question that we have not yet addressed. [231]

On October 1, 1998, the City adopted a pay plan granting raises to all City employees. The stated purpose of the plan was to "attract and retain qualified people, provide incentive for performance, maintain competitiveness with other public sector agencies and ensure equitable compensation to all employees regardless of age, sex, race and/or disability." On May 1, 1999, a revision of the plan, which was motivated, at least in part, by the City's desire to bring the starting salaries of police officers up to the regional average, granted raises to all police officers and police dispatchers. Those who had less than five years of tenure received proportionately greater raises when compared to their former pay than those with more seniority. Although some officers over the age of 40 had less than five years of service, most of the older officers had more.

Petitioners are a group of older officers who filed suit under the ADEA claiming both that the City deliberately discriminated against them because of their age (the "disparate-treatment" claim) and that they were "adversely affected" by the plan because of their age (the "disparate-impact" claim). The District Court granted summary judgment to the City on both claims. The Court of Appeals . . . majority concluded that disparate-impact claims are categorically unavailable under the ADEA. Both the majority and the dissent assumed that the facts alleged by petitioners would entitle them to relief under the reasoning of *Griggs*.

[232] We granted the officers' petition for certiorari, and now hold that the ADEA does authorize recovery in "disparate-impact" cases comparable to *Griggs*. Because, however, we conclude that petitioners have not set forth a valid disparate-impact claim, we affirm.

During the deliberations that preceded the enactment of the Civil Rights Act of 1964, Congress considered and rejected proposed amendments that would have included older workers among the classes protected from employment discrimination. Congress did, however, request the Secretary of Labor to "make a full and complete study of the factors which might tend to result in discrimination in employment because of age and of the consequences of such discrimination on the economy and individuals affected." The Secretary's report, submitted in response to Congress' request, noted that there was little discrimination arising from dislike or intolerance of older people, but that "arbitrary" discrimination did result from certain age limits. Moreover, the report observed that discriminatory effects resulted from "[i]nstitutional arrangements that indirectly restrict the employment of older workers."

In response to that report Congress directed the Secretary to propose remedial legislation, and [233] then acted favorably on his proposal. As enacted in 1967, § 4(a)(2) of the ADEA, provided that it shall be unlawful for an employer "to limit, segregate, or classify his employees in any way which would deprive or tend to deprive any individual of employment opportunities or otherwise adversely affect his status as an employee, because of such individual's age. . . ." Except for substitution of the word "age" for the words "race, color, religion, sex, or national origin," the language of that provision in the ADEA is identical to that found in § 703(a)(2) of the Civil Rights Act of 1964 (Title VII). Other provisions of the ADEA also parallel the earlier statute. Unlike Title VII, however, § 4(f)(1) of the ADEA, 81 Stat. 603, contains language that significantly narrows its coverage by permitting any "otherwise prohibited" action "where the differentiation is based on reasonable factors other than age" (hereinafter RFOA provision). . . .

[240] Two textual differences between the ADEA and Title VII make it clear that even though both statutes authorize recovery on a disparate-impact theory, the scope of disparate-impact liability under ADEA is narrower than under Title VII. The first is the RFOA provision, which we have already identified. The second is the amendment to Title VII contained in the Civil Rights Act of 1991, 105 Stat. 1071. One of the purposes of that amendment was to modify the Court's holding in *Wards Cove Packing Co. v. Atonio,* 490 U.S. 642 (1989), a case in which we narrowly construed the employer's exposure to liability on a disparate-impact theory. While the relevant 1991 amendments expanded the coverage of Title VII, they did not amend the ADEA or speak to the subject of age discrimination. Hence, *Wards Cove's* pre-1991 interpretation of Title VII's identical language remains applicable to the ADEA.

Congress' decision to limit the coverage of the ADEA by including the RFOA provision is consistent with the fact that age, unlike race or other classifications protected by Title VII, not uncommonly has relevance to an individual's capacity to engage in certain types of employment. To be sure, Congress recognized that this is not always the case, and that society may perceive those differences to be larger or more consequential than they are in fact. However, as Secretary Wirtz noted in his report, "certain circumstances . . . unquestionably affect older workers more strongly, as a [241] group, than they do younger workers." Thus, it is not surprising that certain employment criteria that are routinely used may be reasonable despite their adverse impact on older workers as a group. Moreover, intentional discrimination on the basis of age has not occurred at the same levels as discrimination against those protected by Title VII. While the ADEA reflects Congress' intent to give older workers employment opportunities whenever possible, the RFOA provision reflects this historical difference.

Turning to the case before us, we initially note that petitioners have done little more than point out that the pay plan at issue is relatively less generous to older workers than to younger workers. They have not identified any specific test, requirement, or practice within the pay plan that has an adverse impact on older workers. As we held in *Wards Cove*, it is not enough to simply allege that there is a disparate impact on workers, or point to a generalized policy that leads to such an impact. Rather, the employee is " 'responsible for isolating and identifying the *specific* employment practices that are allegedly responsible for any observed statistical disparities.' " Petitioners have failed to do so. Their failure to identify the specific practice being challenged is the sort of omission that could "result in employers being potentially liable for 'the myriad of innocent causes that may lead to statistical imbalances. . . .' " In this case not only did petitioners thus err by failing to identify the relevant practice, but it is also clear from the record that the City's plan was based on reasonable factors other than age.

The plan divided each of five basic positions—police officer, master police officer, police sergeant, police lieutenant, and deputy police chief—into a series of steps and half-steps. The wage for each range was based on a survey of comparable communities in the Southeast. Employees were then assigned a step (or half-step) within their position that corresponded [242] to the lowest step that would still give the individual a 2% raise. Most of the officers were in the three lowest ranks; in each of those ranks there were officers under age 40 and officers over 40. In none did their age affect their compensation. The few officers in the two highest ranks are all over 40. Their raises, though higher in dollar amount than the raises given to junior officers, represented a smaller percentage of their salaries, which of course are higher than the salaries paid to their juniors. They are members of the class complaining of the "disparate impact" of the award.

Petitioners' evidence established two principal facts: First, almost two-thirds (66.2%) of the officers under 40 received raises of more than 10% while less than half (45.3%) of those over 40 did. Second, the average percentage increase for the entire class of officers with less than five years of tenure was somewhat higher than the percentage for those with more seniority. Because older officers tended to occupy more senior positions, on average they received smaller increases when measured as a percentage of their salary. The basic explanation for the differential was the City's perceived need to raise the salaries of junior officers to make them competitive with comparable positions in the market.

Thus, the disparate impact is attributable to the City's decision to give raises based on seniority and position. Reliance on seniority and rank is unquestionably reasonable given the City's goal of raising employees' salaries to match those in surrounding communities. In sum, we hold that the City's decision to grant a larger raise to lower echelon employees for the purpose of bringing salaries in line with that of surrounding police forces was a decision based on a "reasonable facto[r] other than age" that responded to the City's legitimate goal of retaining police officers.

[243] While there may have been other reasonable ways for the City to achieve its goals, the one selected was not unreasonable. Unlike the business necessity test, which asks whether there are other ways for the employer to achieve its goals that do not result in a disparate impact on a protected class, the reasonableness inquiry includes no such requirement.

Accordingly, while we do not agree with the Court of Appeals' holding that the disparate-impact theory of recovery is never available under the ADEA, we affirm its judgment.

In interpreting the ADEA, the Court—given the absence of a definition for the word *discrimination* in that statute—had a choice between the narrow and restrictive reading it gave the act, and one which would have prohibited employer age-related action commonly regarded as *unfair*. That it chose the former, along with its holding that freedom from age discrimination under

Equal Protection is a third-class right, reflects the relaxed view that age discrimination in employment is not particularly invidious.[91] Age, the *City of Jackson* majority said—flirting with the very stereotypical thinking it supposedly banned in *Hazen,* (see 278–79), "not uncommonly has relevance to an individual's capacity to engage in certain types of employment. . . . Moreover, intentional discrimination on the basis of age has not occurred at the same levels as discrimination against those protected by Title VII."[92]

In this downplaying of the role of negative employer discrimination, and in its age discrimination cases generally, there is a marked congruence between the thinking of the Supreme Court and the ideology of classical, laissez-faire economics. Thus, the Court, by adopting a business-rationality standard, and by giving employers broad freedom to exercise it, accepted as appropriate and acceptable the professed "profit-loss," "efficiency," "free-market," and "the employee can take it or leave it" commitments of the business world.

The Supreme Court's restricted view of age discrimination is not aligned well with the congressional *Findings* introducing the ADEA (see 278). These included the congressional conclusion that the problems associated with employment age discrimination were "grave."[93] Nor does the Court's view coincide with the sentiments of those in Congress who led in the creation of the ADEA and its expansion to those over sixty-five. That congressional attitude had it[94] that arbitrary age discrimination (like the difficulties competent older people have in finding and keeping jobs) was nothing short of tragic. Given this congressional sentiment, it could be well argued that Supreme Court age discrimination jurisprudence is tantamount to the "dissing" of Congress.

To support its age discrimination conclusions, the Supreme Court has been fond[95] of citing the report issued on age discrimination by the secretary of labor after Congress had requested the Department of Labor to obtain more information about that problem. Actually that report underscored the pathos of the age discrimination in employment problem:

> There is no harsher verdict in most men's lives than someone else's judgment that they are no longer worth their keep. It is then, when the answer at the hiring gate is "You're too old," that a man turns away . . . finding "nothing to look backward to with pride, nothing to look forward to with hope." If that verdict is fair on the facts, it can only be viewed as part of life's bruising mystery. But if that verdict is unfair, or unnecessary, it is part of man's inhumanity to man that can be and must be stopped. . . . The prevailing assumption is that people are created for jobs, not jobs for people. The difference between a great and a lesser society—particularly one which prides itself on being individual-oriented rather system-oriented—includes its readiness to review this assumption.[96]

Arguably, the Court in its ADEA interpretation should have been less relaxed about age discrimination in employment. An appropriate methodology, which seeks to balance profits/business needs and civilization's dictates of fairness might be to graft onto the ADEA and the Equal Protection Clause interpretations the requirement that, when employers prove that they have business-necessity grounds for engaging in age-correlated discrimination, they should also be required to show that less-harsh alternatives are unavailable. Unfortunately, this mode—impregnated in Title VII's disparate-impact theory—was rejected in *City of Jackson* in favor of a laissez-faire, flexible rationality scrutiny. Adoption of the "less-harsh alternative" approach would help reduce the chance that "reasonable factors other than age" are mere cover for ageist bias. In short, disparate-impact analysis would be allowed to do its job of helping both to correct socially rooted systemic deficiencies, and to cultivate proportional employment representation for seniors as it does for protected racial, ethnic groups, and females.

Taking a less-harsh approach was not the posture of the majority of the Court in its 2008–09 term. In a 2009 ADEA disparate-treatment case—*Gross v. FBL*[97]—the Supreme Court continued its laissez-faire approach to that statute. It ruled that to prevail in a disparate-treatment claim, a plaintiff had to prove by a preponderance of evidence "that age was the 'but-for' cause of the challenged employer decision," and not one of the motivating factors.[98] In Title VII disparate-treatment suits, if the plaintiff presents substantial evidence that race/ethnic/gender discrimination was *a* motivating factor, the burden of persuasion shifts to the employer to present evidence that the adverse action would have occurred irrespective of forbidden discrimination. Federal appellate courts have ruled that the burden-shifting process and its attendant consideration of motivating factors was applicable to the ADEA; and Justice Stevens's dissent in *Gross* argued that the reasoning in *Smith v. Jackson* accepted the burden-shifting/multiple motivation doctrine of Title VII.[99] The majority, however, insisted that a proper reading of the ADEA required that the whole burden of proving that age was the cause of the negative treatment rested with the plaintiff.[100] The *Gross v. FBL* rejection of the requirement that employers explain their adverse actions in disparate-treatment cases greatly limits employee capacity to challenge them. Reportedly, *Gross* was applauded by business and decried by advocates of senior workers.[101]

The Supreme Court and Homosexuals

Homosexuals have been the object of pronounced prejudice and discrimination. They cannot openly be members of the military; they can get married in only a limited number of states, although several other states recognize domestic partner unions approximating closely, or in part, the benefits and obligations associated with marriage. Gays are forbidden to adopt children or provide foster care services in most of the states. And if confronted with antigay bias in the private workplace, they are protected by no federal statute as are other minorities with histories of invidious discrimination. However, state and local antidiscrimination statutes provide a substantial number of gays with a variety of protective shields at their jobs, and in other areas.[102] And antihomosexual discrimination in federal employment has been barred since the 1970s.[103]

In the summer of 2008, the California Supreme Court determined that antigay animus was invidious, and consequently declared homosexual sexual orientation a "suspect classification," under the state's constitutional equal protection provision, triggering strict scrutiny review of California's single-sex marriage ban. The declared purpose of that decision was to foster the continuation of California's progress in repudiating "gay bashing," and to promote a state policy that regarded homosexuality as "simply one of the numerous variables of our common and diverse humanity."[104] Did California's popular-referendum, statutory ban on same-sex marriage pass the California Supreme Court's exercise of strict scrutiny? The answer by that court was a resounding "no." No compelling interest was served by the statutory marriage ban, making it unconstitutional. The same-sex marriage ban was not neces-sary to preserve the benefits and obligations of opposite-sex marriage; the lifting of the ban would not require religious practices to be changed; and the lifting of the ban would enable gays to exercise their fundamental right under the California Constitution to engage in the union of marriage.[105]

In the fall of 2008, a referendum changing California's constitution to bar same-sex marriage was adopted by the voters of that state. The Cali-fornia Supreme Court accepted as constitutional this popular repudiation of its previous holding, although it declared that same-sex marriages consum-mated in California between its decision of Summer 2008 and the popular referendum of the fall of that year remained lawful.[106]

The U.S. Supreme Court has not classified homosexuals as a suspect class. Consequently, this group remains protected by third-tier scrutiny when governmental action negatively affecting them is challenged. What arguably has been involved in two major cases of late—*Romer v. Evans* (1996)[107] and *Lawrence v. Texas* (2003)[108]—has been a "heightened" form of this limited scrutiny. In both of these, as Justice Scalia not unreasonably argued,[109] the Court found arbitrary and capricious (that is, the failure to pass third-tier scrutiny) efforts of state government to uphold customary and traditional sexual values.

Romer represented a dramatic departure from *Bowers v. Hardwick* (1986).[110] The Court in *Bowers* determined that the Georgia antisodomy statute was fully reasonable and constitutional, while rejecting the argument that societal values were inadequate supports of that measure.[111] What is more, the Court's answer to a central issue in the case—whether sodomy was a fundamental right—was an emphatic "no" as social and legal proscriptions against that activity had "ancient roots."[112] Only a decade after *Bowers*, the Court in *Romer* ruled that a popular referendum meant to uphold these proscriptions (by abolishing all Colorado gay antidiscrimination measures) was ruled "implausible."[113] In dissent, Justice Scalia could not understand how the Court could find Georgia's criminal action against homosexual practices in *Bowers* constitutional, and yet conclude that Colorado's referendum meant to remove legal protection for this same conduct unconstitutional.[114] The answer came in *Lawrence v. Texas* (2003),[115] which overruled *Bowers*, and determined that the Due Process Clause of the Fourteenth Amendment recognized consensual, private homosexual practices as a "full" right, and that the Texas antisodomy statute was irrational and unconstitutional. We now turn to an excerpt from that case.

Lawrence v. Texas, 539 U.S. 558 (2003)

[562] Justice KENNEDY delivered the opinion of the Court.

. . . Liberty presumes an autonomy of self that includes freedom of thought, belief, expression, and certain intimate conduct. The instant case involves liberty of the person both in its spatial and in its more transcendent dimensions.

The question before the Court is the validity of a Texas statute making it a crime for two persons of the same sex to engage in certain intimate sexual conduct. . . .

[564] We granted certiorari to consider . . . [w]hether petitioners' criminal convictions for adult consensual sexual intimacy in the home violate their vital interests in liberty and privacy protected by the Due Process Clause of the Fourteenth Amendment. . . .

The petitioners were adults at the time of the alleged offense. Their conduct was in private and consensual.

We conclude the case should be resolved by determining whether the petitioners were free as adults to engage in the private conduct in the exercise of their liberty under the Due Process Clause of the Fourteenth Amendment to the Constitution. For this inquiry we deem it necessary to reconsider the Court's holding in *Bowers* [*v. Hardwick* (1986)]. . . .

[566] The facts in *Bowers* had some similarities to the instant case. A police officer, whose right to enter seems not to have been in question, observed Hardwick, in his own bedroom, engaging in intimate sexual conduct with another adult male. The conduct was in violation of a Georgia statute making it a criminal offense to engage in sodomy. . . . Hardwick was not prosecuted, but he brought an action in federal court to declare the state statute invalid. He alleged he was a practicing homosexual and that the criminal prohibition violated rights guaranteed to him by the Constitution. The Court, in an opinion by Justice White, sustained the Georgia law. . . .

The Court began its substantive discussion in *Bowers* as follows: "The issue presented is whether the Federal Constitution confers a fundamental right upon homosexuals to engage in sodomy and hence invalidates the laws of the many States that still make such conduct illegal and have done so [567] for a very long time." That statement, we now conclude, discloses the Court's own failure to appreciate the extent of the liberty at stake. To say that the issue in *Bowers* was simply the right to engage in certain sexual conduct demeans the claim the individual put forward, just as it would demean a married couple were it to be said marriage is simply about the right to have sexual intercourse. The laws involved in *Bowers* and here are, to be sure, statutes that purport to do no more than prohibit a particular sexual act. Their penalties and purposes, though, have more far-reaching consequences, touching upon the most private human conduct, sexual behavior, and in the most private of places, the home. The statutes do seek to control a personal relationship that, whether or not entitled to formal recognition in the law, is within the liberty of persons to choose without being punished as criminals. . . .

It suffices for us to acknowledge that adults may choose to enter upon this relationship in the confines of their homes and their own private lives and still retain their dignity as free persons. When sexuality finds overt expression in intimate conduct with another person, the conduct can be but one element in a personal bond that is more enduring. The liberty protected by the Constitution allows homosexual persons the right to make this choice.

Having misapprehended the claim of liberty there presented to it, and thus stating the claim to be whether there is a fundamental right to engage in consensual sodomy, the *Bowers* Court said: "Proscriptions against that conduct have ancient roots." In academic writings, and in many of the scholarly *amicus* briefs filed to assist the Court in this case, there are fundamental criticisms of the historical premises relied upon by the majority and concurring opinions [568] in *Bowers*. We need not enter this debate in the attempt to reach a definitive historical judgment, but the following considerations counsel against adopting the definitive conclusions upon which *Bowers* placed such reliance.

At the outset it should be noted that there is no longstanding history in this country of laws directed at homosexual conduct as a distinct matter. Beginning in colonial times there were prohibitions of sodomy derived from the English criminal laws passed in the first instance by the Reformation Parliament of 1533. The English prohibition was understood to include relations between men and women as well as relations between men and men. Nineteenth-century commentators similarly read American sodomy, buggery, and crime-against-nature statutes as criminalizing certain relations between men and women and between men and men. The absence of legal prohibitions focusing on homosexual conduct may be explained in part by noting that according to some scholars the concept of the homosexual as a distinct category of person did not emerge until the late 19th century. . . . Thus early American sodomy laws were not directed at homosexuals as such but instead sought to prohibit nonprocreative sexual activity more generally. This does not suggest approval of [569–70] homosexual conduct. It does tend to show that this particular form of conduct was not thought of as a separate category from like conduct between heterosexual persons. . . .

It was not until the 1970's that any State singled out same-sex relations for criminal prosecution, and only nine States have done so. Post-*Bowers* even some of these States did not adhere to the policy of suppressing homosexual conduct. Over the course of the last decades, States with same-sex prohibitions have moved toward abolishing them.

[571] In summary, the historical grounds relied upon in *Bowers* are more complex than the majority opinion and the concurring opinion by Chief Justice Burger indicate. Their historical premises are not without doubt and, at the very least, are overstated.

It must be acknowledged, of course, that the Court in *Bowers* was making the broader point that for centuries there have been powerful voices to condemn homosexual conduct as immoral. The condemnation has been shaped by religious beliefs, conceptions of right and acceptable behavior, and respect for the traditional family. For many persons these are not trivial concerns but profound and deep convictions accepted as ethical and moral principles to which they aspire and which thus determine the course of their lives. These considerations do not answer the question before us, however. The issue is whether the majority may use the power of the State to enforce these views on the whole society through operation of the criminal law. "Our obligation is to define the liberty of all, not to mandate our own moral code." . . .

[W]e think that our laws and traditions in the past half century are of [572] most relevance here. These references show an emerging awareness that liberty gives substantial protection to adult persons in deciding how to conduct their private lives in matters pertaining to sex. . . .

This emerging recognition should have been apparent when *Bowers* was decided. In 1955 the American Law Institute promulgated the Model Penal Code and made clear that it did not recommend or provide for "criminal penalties for consensual sexual relations conducted in private." It justified its decision on three grounds: (1) The prohibitions undermined respect for the law by penalizing conduct many people engaged in; (2) the statutes regulated private conduct not harmful to others; and (3) the laws were arbitrarily enforced and thus invited the danger of blackmail. In 1961 Illinois changed its laws to conform to the Model Penal Code. Other States soon followed. . . . [573]

[T]he deficiencies in *Bowers* became even more apparent in the years following its announcement. The 25 States with laws prohibiting the relevant conduct referenced in the *Bowers* decision are reduced now to 13, of which 4 enforce their laws only against homosexual conduct. In those States where sodomy is still proscribed, whether for same-sex or heterosexual conduct, there is a pattern of nonenforcement with respect to consenting adults acting in private. The State of Texas admitted in 1994 that as of that date it had not prosecuted anyone under those circumstances.

Two principal cases decided after *Bowers* cast its holding into even more doubt. In *Planned Parenthood of Southeastern Pa. v. Casey*, 505 U.S. 833 (1992), the Court reaffirmed the substantive force of the liberty protected by the Due Process Clause. The *Casey* decision again confirmed [574] that our laws and tradition afford constitutional protection to personal decisions relating to marriage, procreation, contraception, family relationships, child rearing, and education. In explaining the respect the Constitution demands for the autonomy of the person in making these choices, we stated as follows:

"These matters, involving the most intimate and personal choices a person may make in a lifetime, choices central to personal dignity and autonomy, are central to the liberty protected by the Fourteenth Amendment. At the heart of liberty is the right to define one's own concept of existence, of meaning, of the universe, and of the mystery of human life. Beliefs about these matters could not define the attributes of personhood were they formed under compulsion of the State."

Persons in a homosexual relationship may seek autonomy for these purposes, just as heterosexual persons do. The decision in *Bowers* would deny them this right.

The second post-*Bowers* case of principal relevance is *Romer v. Evans*, (1996). There the Court struck down class-based legislation directed at homosexuals as a violation of the Equal Protection Clause. *Romer* invalidated an amendment to Colorado's Constitution which named as a solitary class persons who were homosexuals, lesbians, or bisexual either by "orientation, conduct, practices or relationships," and deprived them of protection under state antidiscrimination laws. We concluded that the provision was "born of animosity toward the class of persons affected" and further that it had no rational relation to a legitimate governmental purpose. . . .

[575] Equality of treatment and the due process right to demand respect for conduct protected by the substantive guarantee of liberty are linked in important respects, and a decision on the latter point advances both interests. If protected conduct is made criminal and the law which does so remains unexamined for its substantive validity, its stigma might remain even if it were not enforceable as drawn for equal protection reasons. When homosexual conduct is made criminal by the law of the State, that declaration in and of itself is an invitation to subject homosexual persons to discrimination both in the public and in the private spheres. The central holding of *Bowers* has been

brought in question by this case, and it should be addressed. Its continuance as precedent demeans the lives of homosexual persons. . . .

[577] The rationale of *Bowers* does not withstand careful analysis. In his dissenting opinion in *Bowers* Justice Stevens came to these conclusions:

"Our prior cases make two propositions abundantly clear. First, the fact that the governing majority in a State has traditionally viewed a particular practice as immoral is not a sufficient reason for upholding a law prohibiting the practice; neither history nor tradition could save a law prohibiting miscegenation from constitutional [578] attack. Second, individual decisions by married persons, concerning the intimacies of their physical relationship, even when not intended to produce offspring, are a form of 'liberty' protected by the Due Process Clause of the Fourteenth Amendment. Moreover, this protection extends to intimate choices by unmarried as well as married persons."

Justice Stevens' analysis, in our view, should have been controlling in *Bowers* and should control here.

Bowers was not correct when it was decided, and it is not correct today. It ought not to remain binding precedent. *Bowers v. Hardwick* should be and now is overruled.

The present case does not involve minors. It does not involve persons who might be injured or coerced or who are situated in relationships where consent might not easily be refused. It does not involve public conduct or prostitution. It does not involve whether the government must give formal recognition to any relationship that homosexual persons seek to enter. The case does involve two adults who, with full and mutual consent from each other, engaged in sexual practices common to a homosexual lifestyle. The petitioners are entitled to respect for their private lives. The State cannot demean their existence or control their destiny by making their private sexual conduct a crime. Their right to liberty under the Due Process Clause gives them the full right to engage in their conduct without intervention of the government. "It is a promise of the Constitution that there is a realm of personal liberty which the government may not enter." The Texas statute furthers no legitimate state interest which can justify its intrusion into the personal and private life of the individual. . . .

[586] Justice Scalia, with whom the Chief Justice and Justice Thomas join, dissenting.

. . . Most of . . . today's opinion has no relevance to its actual holding—that the Texas statute "furthers no legitimate state interest which can justify" its application to petitioners under rational-basis review. . . . Though there is discussion of "fundamental proposition[s]," and "fundamental decisions," nowhere does the Court's opinion declare that homosexual sodomy is a "fundamental right" under the Due Process Clause; nor does it subject the Texas law to the standard of review that would be appropriate (strict scrutiny) if homosexual sodomy *were* a "fundamental right." Thus, while overruling the *outcome* of *Bowers*, the Court leaves strangely untouched its central legal conclusion: "[R]espondent would have us announce . . . a fundamental right to engage in homosexual sodomy. This we are quite unwilling to do." Instead the Court simply describes petitioners' conduct as "an exercise of their liberty"—which it undoubtedly is—and proceeds to apply an unheard-of form of rational-basis review that will have far-reaching implications beyond this case. . . .

After discussing the history of antisodomy laws, the Court proclaims that, "it should be noted that there is no longstanding history in this country of laws directed at homosexual conduct as a distinct matter." [596] This observation in no way casts into doubt the "definitive [historical] conclusion," on which *Bowers* relied: that our Nation has a longstanding history of laws prohibiting *sodomy in general*—regardless of whether it was performed by same-sex or opposite-sex couples. . . .

[T]he Court . . . says: "[W]e think that our laws and traditions in the past half century are of most relevance here. These references show *an emerging awareness* that liberty gives substantial protection to adult persons in deciding how to conduct their private lives *in matters pertaining to sex*." (emphasis added) [598] Apart from the fact that such an "emerging awareness" does not establish a "fundamental right," the statement is factually false. States continue to prosecute all sorts of crimes by adults "in matters pertaining to sex": prostitution, adult incest, adultery, obscenity, and child pornography. Sodomy laws, too, have been enforced "in the past half century," in which there have been 134 reported cases involving prosecutions for consensual, adult, homosexual sodomy. In relying, for evidence of an "emerging recognition," upon the American Law Institute's 1955 recommendation not to criminalize " 'consensual sexual relations conducted in private,' " the Court ignores the fact that this recommendation was "a point of resistance in most of the states that considered adopting the Model Penal Code." . . .

[599] I turn now to the ground on which the Court squarely rests its holding: the contention that there is no rational basis for the law here under attack. This proposition is so out of accord with our jurisprudence—indeed, with the jurisprudence of *any* society we know—that it requires little discussion.

The Texas statute undeniably seeks to further the belief of its citizens that certain forms of sexual behavior are "immoral and unacceptable,"—the same interest furthered by criminal laws against fornication, bigamy, adultery, adult incest, bestiality, and obscenity. *Bowers* held that this *was* a legitimate state interest. The Court today reaches the opposite conclusion. The Texas statute, it says, "furthers *no legitimate state interest* which can justify its intrusion into the personal and private life of the individual,"(emphasis added). The Court embraces instead Justice Stevens' declaration in his *Bowers* dissent, that " 'the fact that the governing majority in a State has traditionally viewed a particular practice as immoral is not a sufficient reason for upholding a law prohibiting the practice.' " This effectively decrees the end of all morals legislation. If, as the Court asserts, the promotion of majoritarian sexual morality is not even a *legitimate* state interest, none of the above-mentioned laws can survive rational-basis review. . . . [602]

One of the most revealing statements in today's opinion is the Court's grim warning that the criminalization of homosexual conduct is "an invitation to subject homosexual persons to discrimination both in the public and in the private spheres." It is clear from this that the Court has taken sides in the culture war, departing from its role of assuring, as neutral observer, that the democratic rules of engagement are observed. Many Americans do not want persons who openly engage in homosexual conduct as partners in their business, as scoutmasters for their children, as teachers in their children's schools, or as boarders in their home. They view this as protecting themselves and their families from a lifestyle that they believe to be immoral and destructive.

The Court views it as "discrimination" which it is the function of our judgments to deter. So imbued is the Court with the law profession's anti-anti-homosexual culture, that it is seemingly unaware that the attitudes of that [603] culture are not obviously "mainstream"; that in most States what the Court calls "discrimination" against those who engage in homosexual acts is perfectly legal; that proposals to ban such "discrimination" under Title VII have repeatedly been rejected by Congress; that in some cases such "discrimination" is *mandated* by federal statute, see 10 U.S.C. § 654(b)(1) (mandating discharge from the Armed Forces of any service member who engages in or intends to engage in homosexual acts); and that in some cases such "discrimination" is a constitutional right, see *Boy Scouts of America v. Dale*, 530 U.S. 64 (2000).

Let me be clear that I have nothing against homosexuals, or any other group, promoting their agenda through normal democratic means. Social perceptions of sexual and other morality change over time, and every group has the right to persuade its fellow citizens that its view of such matters is the best. That homosexuals have achieved some success in that enterprise is attested to by the fact that Texas is one of the few remaining States that criminalize private, consensual homosexual acts. But persuading one's fellow citizens is one thing, and imposing one's views in the absence of democratic majority will is something else. I would no more *require* a State to criminalize homosexual acts—or, for that matter, display *any* moral disapprobation of them—than I would *forbid* it to do so. What Texas has chosen to do is well within the range of traditional democratic action, and its hand should not be stayed through the invention of a brand-new "constitutional right" by a Court that is impatient of democratic change. It is indeed true that "later generations can see that laws once thought necessary and proper in fact serve only to oppress"; and when that happens, later generations can repeal those laws. But it is the premise of our system that those judgments are to be made [604] by the people, and not imposed by a governing caste that knows best. . . .

At the end of its opinion—after having laid waste the foundations of our rational-basis jurisprudence—the Court says that the present case "does not involve whether the government must give formal recognition to any relationship that homosexual persons seek to enter." Do not believe it. More illuminating than this bald, unreasoned disclaimer is the progression of thought displayed by an earlier passage in the Court's opinion, which notes the constitutional protections afforded to "personal decisions relating to *marriage,* procreation, contraception, family relationships, child rearing, and education," and then declares that "[p]ersons in a homosexual relationship may seek autonomy for these purposes, just as heterosexual persons do." (emphasis added). Today's opinion dismantles the structure of constitutional law that has permitted a distinction to be made between heterosexual and homosexual unions, insofar as formal recognition in marriage is concerned. If moral disapprobation of homosexual conduct is "no legitimate state interest" for purposes of proscribing that conduct; and if, as the Court coos (casting aside all pretense of neutrality), "[w]hen [605] sexuality finds overt expression in intimate conduct with another person, the conduct can be but one element in a personal bond that is more enduring"; what justification could there possibly be for denying the benefits of marriage to homosexual couples. . . .

Affirmative Action and Homosexuals

There are those who see governmental acceptance of homosexual deviation from traditional values as governmental granting of special privileges or preferences. Such privileges afforded a systemically oppressed gay community a special consideration for the purpose of enhancing their status thus placing it in the same family of things as race/gender/ethnic affirmative action preferences. The notion that governmental acceptance of homosexual practices amounts to special privileges is scathingly rejected by the homosexual advocates who insist that their objective is "equal rights," not special privileges. The *Romer* majority agreed with this position. To that majority, the Colorado referendum which abolished gay-protective legislation did not "deprive gays special privileges; it impose[d] upon them a special disability—gays are forbidden the safeguards that others enjoy."[116]

There has been discussion among gays and lesbians as to the appropriateness of seeking affirmative action for homosexuals in the employment arena. A thoughtful review of the pros and cons was provided in a 1993 edition of the *Stanford Law and Policy Review.*[117] A summary of this review follows: Affirmative action would encourage "outing" and a more diverse workplace. Surveys indicate that those who get to know gays experience a reduction in negative stereotyping and become more tolerant and accepting of homosexuals. On the other hand, employment affirmative action would produce a hornet's nest of criticism, endangering existing antidiscrimination regulations. Many gays are content not to be assisted through affirmative action. Many "straights" will tolerate homosexual practices if practiced privately, but certainly do not wish to legitimatize it. Affirmative action will reinforce the notion that gays want special privileges, not equal rights. And supporters of race/ethnic/gender affirmative action see clear differences between their cause and gay rights.

Epilogue: The Constitutional Underclasses and the Critical Issues

The groups covered in this chapter—gays, senior workers, and the disabled—remain in the constitutional jurisprudence of the U.S. Supreme Court equal protection and due process underclasses. These groups are not "suspect classes" covered by strict scrutiny judicial review as are blacks and protected ethnic groups. Is this scheme of constitutional subordination appropriate? If the Court is to exercise this capacity to determine levels of judicial scrutiny, why is it allowed to do so with such ambiguity? How are we to define the prongs of strict scrutiny and mid-tier scrutiny? What is the meaning of such notions as compelling and important governmental interests; narrow tailoring and substantial relationship? What is the nature of the heightened mere-rationality scrutiny so evidently granted homosexuals in *Lawrence v. Texas*? The Supreme Court has imposed a typology of judicial review standards, but it has failed to define these standards with precision. It appears that we have a scheme of too much and too little judicial review in the equal protection/due process areas of civil rights, particularly where affirmative action is concerned. Can the ambiguity be reduced? Does the highly politicized affirmative action field admit of more precision? What might be an appropriate antidote to affirmative action ambiguity is a specialized court assigned the function of treating affirmative action questions—those mentioned here and others detailed in this volume. We return to this proposal in the next chapter.

Nine

Facing Affirmative Action's Future

Prologue

Here we return primarily to the central concern of this volume: race/gender/ethnic affirmative action. The day of reckoning for affirmative action in its ethno-racial and gender formulations is long overdue. Should race/ethnic/gender protected-group preference be retained as antidiscrimination policy?

The race/ethnic/gender affirmative action about which we quarrel most today started mainly as an "outreach" program meant to attract minority candidates for jobs, contract grants, and college admission. Thereafter, it was transformed into a far-reaching policy of applying race, ethnic, and gender preferences and other considerations in decisions about employment, government procurement of services and supplies, legislative districting, K-12 student attendance policies, English-language instruction, university admissions, and—in a limited and largely indirect fashion—housing. The transition was designed to improve the lot of historically disadvantaged minorities and women, but came at the cost of widespread, often legitimate, popular resentment. The question that readers now must ask is whether affirmative action has struck a reasonable balance between competing equities. Are its costs outweighed by its benefits; and, if not, what should be done?

The judgment will be exceedingly difficult. Unlike Reconstruction's abortive "emancipation" program, affirmative action cannot be written off as a failure to address the problem of American sexism and ethno-racial antagonism. All of affirmative action's many race, ethnic, and gender-based plans target discrimination, but they vary considerably in design and outcome. While they have made undeniable remedial inroads, there is profound disagreement—learned and otherwise—over the extent and the social costs of their impact. Separating heat from light in this controversy is at best a daunting task. To a great extent, moreover, affirmative action is still a work in progress.

In this closing chapter, we offer some comments and raise major issues about the materials that have been assembled in the preceding pages, including those which concern the disabled, senior workers, and the homosexual community. We hope that this will help our readers to draw their own conclusions. Initially we focus on the civil rights hierarchy established by the Supreme Court.

The Supreme Court's Civil Rights Hierarchy

This volume has described how the Supreme Court—through the adoption of disparate-impact theory—helped convert Title VII of the 1964 CRA into a race/ethnic/gender affirmative action statute. The Court, additionally, advanced affirmative action accommodationism in its *Swann v. Charlotte-Mecklenburg* (1971) conclusion[1] that the desegregation command in *Brown v. Board* (1954)[2] required racial integration in the public schools. Accepting, as it did in 2003,[3] the argument that student body diversity is a compelling government interest, the Court provided a constitutional platform supportive of preferential university admissions for minorities. And in the realm of voting rights, the Court found fully constitutional[4] the 1965 Voting Rights Act's abolition of literacy tests—a congressionally promulgated disparate-impact strategy meant to accommodate blacks and Hispanics by increasing their voting power in areas where it was disproportionately low.

While it has strongly supported race/ethnic/gender accommodation, the Court has limited the liberal potentialities for accommodating disabled and senior workers. In another central area of civil rights concern, consensual, adult homosexuality has recently received helpful constitutional support from the Court by being declared a *full right*.[5] However, consensual homosexuality in the Court's hierarchy of civil rights movements has not been elevated to "fundamental right" status. The *full right* afforded consensual adult homosexuality is not part of the traditional language of the Equal Protection and Due Process Clauses. The rights recognized by those clauses are traditionally titled: *fundamental, mid-tier,* and *third-tier*. To repeat the learning in this volume, at the constitutional level, the critical constitutional dispute affecting race/ethnic discrimination has been whether equal protection scrutiny of governmental action should be "mid-tier" or "strict."

Strict scrutiny is reserved for situations where government discrimination negatively affects a fundamental right or a suspect class. To pass strict judicial scrutiny requires a *compelling* government interest, and means to achieve that interest which are *narrowly tailored*. Where mid-tier rights are invaded, intermediate scrutiny is required—that is, a demonstration by government of an *important* interest and means that are *substantially related* to the achievement of that important interest. Constitutional law recognizes still another class of our rights, namely, third-class or lowest-tier. Judicial scrutiny related to this abundance of "rights" is guided by the doctrine of "mere rationality": governmental action affecting these rights is constitution-ally permissible unless irrational, defined as something unsupportable by "any reasonably conceivable state of facts."[6]

Despite the passions associated with the disabled rights cause, govern-ment actions taken affecting disabled workers are judicially subject only to third-tier scrutiny under the Equal Protection Clause. The disabled have not been deemed by the Supreme Court to be a *suspect class* or a *quasi-suspect class* (as Congress, in effect, deemed them to be) and thus entitled to higher judicial scrutiny. Unlike blacks, the disabled—in the eyes of the Supreme Court—have not been victims of that degree of animus which gives rise to suspect class status. States, as *University of Alabama v. Garrett* (2001)[7] makes clear, can rationally and constitutionally refuse to accommodate the disabled in state employment.[8] States, additionally, are not subject to the employment requirements of the Americans With Disabilities Act (ADA).[9] The Court also has taken a restrictive approach to the duties of private employers under the ADA. Congress, in ADA amendments, has attempted to overturn a number of these restraints, and in the process strenuously declared its opposition to major Court ADA opinions. (See 266–75.)

It is suggested that the restrictive approach that the Court has taken in connection with the ADA and employment was an outgrowth of the fear "that the doors of the courts will open too wide" if a more liberal ADA interpretation were taken.[10] Whatever the reason, the Supreme Court's busi-ness, laissez-faire approach in this area warrants noting. The Court has even permitted a business-necessity defense in disparate-treatment ADA cases—a defense that is not allowed in Title VII (of the 1964 CRA) controversies where intentional discrimination is charged.[11] Negative treatment of the disabled is permitted so long as it is "merely rational," but this defense is unavailable in cases involving negative racial and ethnic discrimination.[12] And the leeway given to employers in their treatment of the disabled has been broad. Consider the Court's determination in *Garrett* that states could be hardhearted and hardheaded in their employment practices affecting the disabled.[13] Moreover, the Court's definition of disability in both *Sutton v. United Airlines* (1999)[14] and *Toyota of Kentucky* (2002)[15] greatly reduced the opportunities for employees to seek relief under the ADA.

In the ADA, the disabled were blanketed with an affirmative action mandate from Congress requiring "reasonable accommodation" for them in employment, public accommodations, and public services. (See 265–66.) The changes wrought by these sections of the law for the disabled are worthy of celebration: augmented services for students; better access to transportation, streets, theatres, and restaurants. Observers, however, have argued that the restrictive approach to the ADA by the federal courts in connection with Title I (employment) has frustrated job opportunities for the disabled. To Professor Bagenstos though, the essential employment problem for the disabled is not court interpretation. He noted that the employment of the disabled has not improved since the inaugural of the 1990 ADA. If disability is defined as an impairment that limits a vital activity of life, the employment rate for the disabled declined from 49 percent in 1990 to 46.6 percent in 1996. What is the problem? To Bagenstos, critical to the unemployment of the disabled is the absence of social welfare services (e.g., home health aid) needed to move the disabled to work. He is well aware that social welfare services are viewed by disability advocates as patronizing, lacking in respect, and insufficiently sensitive to the dignity of the disabled. He urges the development of social welfare services that abandon these characteristics, but leaves the question open as how this is to be accomplished.[16]

Perhaps the employment problems of the disabled would be reduced (and their affirmative action benefits increased) if the Equal Protection Clause interpretation was changed to grant "suspect-class" status to that group. That status would conform with the ADA's congressional findings that the disabled have been subject to extraordinary societal discrimination. (See 262–63.) Congress in its 2008 ADA amendments attempted to reduce barriers to disability rights by directing that ADA interpretation foster broad coverage. For example, judges and administrators were ordered to generally eschew consideration of disease-amelioration devices and mitigating measures in determining who is to be considered disabled under the ADA. (See 274–75.) How ADA implementers respond to this amendment, as well the congressional insistence on broad coverage remains to be seen.

Should senior workers be awarded affirmative action benefits comparable to those given racial/ethnic minorities and females? The congressional findings appended to the Age Discrimination in Employment Act of 1967 (ADEA) described the discrimination affecting senior workers as "grave." A major vehicle supporting affirmative action for senior workers would be an ADEA interpretation affording them disparate-impact coverage. But the Supreme Court in *Smith v. Jackson* (2003) enabled employers to easily frustrate such coverage. (See 279*ff.*) Congress could overrule this example of latter-day laissez-faire adjudication, but the legislature cannot annul another barrier to the expansion of affirmative action benefits to senior workers, namely, that governmental discrimination affecting public employees is subject only to lowest-tier equal protection scrutiny.

One reason for the congressional passage of the Age Discrimination in Employment Act (ADEA) was to help older workers keep their jobs so that their expertise could bolster the economy.[17] The Supreme Court's treatment of the ADEA, by facilitating business "rationality" excuses, and rejecting the "fairness" interpretation of the ADEA has not advanced the objective of keeping older people at work. A sophisticated student of the ADEA—John Macnicol—has reported[18] that

ADEA plaintiffs have primarily been white males alleging
wrongful discharge or wrongful failure to promote. These
suits, where successful, may have undercut affirmative action
for minorities and females.

The ADEA has not been able to influence the trend of early male
retirement and the fall in the average age of male retirement.

Between 1960–1995, the average age of older worker movement
into economic inactivity fell from 66.5 to 63.6.

The rights of transsexuals have not been adjudicated by the High
Court. As we have seen, adult homosexuals have been granted a "full" right
under the "Due Process Clause" to engage in consensual sexual activity. The
implications of this "full" right straddle are yet to be spelled out, but a major
doctrine of the organized homosexual community rejects special privileges,
insisting only upon equal treatment. This emphasis is manifested in a recent
iteration of the Employment Nondiscrimination Act (ENDA) proposal which
failed of congressional passage in 2007. Was the fear that ENDA could be
converted into an affirmative action vehicle a reason for its congressional
defeat? The language of the proposed ENDA measure (presented below)
would make such a conversion difficult. Should homosexuals be granted
affirmative action benefits such as like those available to other persecuted
minorities? Transsexuals?

SEC. 4. EMPLOYMENT DISCRIMINATION PROHIBITED.

(a) Employer Practices—It shall be an unlawful employment
practice for an employer—

(1) to fail or refuse to hire or to discharge any individual, or
otherwise discriminate against any individual with respect to the
compensation, terms, conditions, or privileges of employment of
the individual, because of such individual's actual or perceived
sexual orientation; or

(2) to limit, segregate, or classify the employees or applicants for
employment of the employer in any way that would deprive or tend
to deprive any individual of employment or otherwise adversely
affect the status of the individual as an employee, because of such
individual's actual or perceived sexual orientation. . . .

(f) No Preferential Treatment or Quotas—Nothing in this Act shall be construed or interpreted to require or permit—

(1) any covered entity to grant preferential treatment to any individual or to any group because of the actual or perceived sexual orientation of such individual or group on account of an imbalance which may exist with respect to the total number or percentage of persons of any actual or perceived sexual orientation employed by any employer, referred or classified for employment by any employment agency or labor organization, admitted to membership or classified by any labor organization, or admitted to, or employed in, any apprenticeship or other training program, in comparison with the total number or percentage of persons of such actual or perceived sexual orientation in any community, State, section, or other area, or in the available work force in any community, State, section, or other area; or

(2) the adoption or implementation by a covered entity of a quota on the basis of actual or perceived sexual orientation.

(g) Disparate Impact—Only disparate treatment claims may be brought under this Act.[19]

Ethno-racial and Gender Affirmative Action as an Instrument of Equal Opportunity: Genesis, Variety, and Uncertainty

In returning to our primary topic, it should be noted that the friends of affirmative action would paraphrase Pascal and argue that if group race, ethnic, and gender-conscious programs did not exist, it would be necessary to invent them. To them, this is the simple lesson of the disparities existing in America's workplaces, its schoolhouses, voting booths, and neighborhoods. The civil rights revolution came into being because of intolerable inequities in jobs, education, housing, and civil rights affecting those we have come to protect under the affirmative action umbrella. The architects of affirmative action envisioned the end of discrimination as a stepping stone toward equalizing access to America's bounty. It was in the furtherance of this Rawlsian concept of social justice that they made fighting fire with fire—minority/female discrimination with minority/gender-based remedies—the cornerstone of antidiscrimination policy. We urge our readers to judge these remedies (with their abundance of preferences) in terms of success or failure as instruments of social policy—not as the workings of original sin, as some would have it.

We have also asked whether comparable remedies should be made available for gays, transsexuals, senior workers, and the disabled.

It should be noted that an important dimension of affirmative action's aspects is the diversity of its applications. Some prominent critics reduce the entire enterprise to a single outcome,[20] but this is a woeful misrepresentation. At the federal level alone, the national government constructed an impressively large inventory of race, ethnic, and gender-based programs, which differed widely in design and result.[21] These plans often contained explicitly preferential provisions, but are fundamentally distinguishable in at least the following respects:

> *Origin*: executive order, court order, statute, or administrative regulation;
> *Nature*: whether they mandate, or merely authorize consideration of race, ethnicity, or gender; whether they seek to promote ethno-racial access/integration directly (e.g., contractual set-asides), or indirectly (e.g., subsidizing the residential movement of poorer people to higher income areas to promote racial integration);
> *Tools*: whether they contemplate application of outreach efforts, preferences, goals, timetables, set-asides, quotas, or other forms of assistance;
> *Constituencies*: specifically defined minorities, and/or generalized references to minorities and females;
> *Benefits:* recruitment, training; employment, educational access, contracts and grants (including procurement set-asides), participation in federally assisted education and housing programs, voting rights; and
> *Collateral Effect:* degree of adverse impact, if any, on nonbeneficiaries.

The gist of remedial affirmative action is the versatile use of protected-group status to undo the lingering effects of past and present societal, historical discrimination—intentional or not—and to prevent its recurrence. In passing judgment, it is imperative to avoid confusion between its singularity of objective and multiplicity of application.

The federal affirmative action program necessarily reflects constant change in the society which it monitors and regulates. Changes in affirmative action policies are inevitable, and it faces alterations from hostile or supportive judges and state legislators. Moreover, it must deal with a growing number of serious operating challenges such as the revolutionary transformation of the economy; intractable black and Hispanic unemployment; demands for adoption of a nonremedial (diversity) rationale; changes in constituencies due to demographic shifts such as the "majoritarianization" of minorities as in California;[22] and the persistent claim of racial bias in the administration of the criminal justice system. Reasonable accommodation for the disabled represents a branch of affirmative action that is uncertain in its requirements and impact. Uncertainties also face the future of affirmative action—if any—for other groups (such as gays and transsexuals) historically subject to invidious discrimination.

Doubtless, affirmative action's future, like its past, will be a "stormy sea"—an uncertainty compounded by a constellation of unsettled legal questions and ideological claims. We now focus on central examples of these.

Central Legal Issues of Ethno-racial and Gender Affirmative Action

The Constitutional Questions

Strict scrutiny and nonremedial affirmative action

The standard of judicial review has been an overriding constitutional issue in affirmative action litigation. In the 1989 *Croson*[23] and 1995 *Adarand*[24] minority "set-aside" decisions, and the 1993 *Shaw v. Reno* majority-minority redistricting case, the Supreme Court's race-neutral majority seemed after long delay to lay this crucial question to eternal rest, holding, in opinions written by Justice O'Connor: All federal, state, and local racial/ethnic classifications, "benign" or otherwise, must be narrowly tailored to further a compelling interest; and absent proof of "specifically identified" past discrimination, preferences flowing from such classifications violate the equal protection clause.

This bedrock issue has not been settled after all. An unmistakable split has emerged among the circuit courts of appeal over whether strict scrutiny applies to facially neutral outreach/recruitment plans. These cases involve "affirmative action" as do the guidelines of the Office of Federal Contract Compliance Programs for administering Executive Order 11246 in connection with government contractors. These guidelines establish numerical goals and timetables for hiring and promoting minorities without requiring preferential hiring or treatment. Some circuits hold that such plans are not subject to strict scrutiny under *Adarand* because they do not unduly burden nonbeneficiaries.[25] Other circuits hold, to the contrary, that *Adarand*'s mandate must be applied literally, and that plans based on numerical hiring goals necessarily encourage quotas, even if they do not explicitly require preferential hiring.[26]

When the Supreme Court reviews this conflict, as one assumes that eventually it must, is it a foregone conclusion that the O'Connor version of strict scrutiny will be reaffirmed? In a 1996 redistricting opinion, the author herself wrote that strict scrutiny does not apply to "*all* cases of intentional creation of majority-minority districts."[27]

In chapter 6 above, we saw that antidilutive (majority-minority) voting districts are analytically indistinguishable from any of the other "benign" preferences which the Justice has viewed with such abhorrence in the past. Textually, then, O'Connor's dictum invites speculation. Did she change her position? Does it represent the view of the current Court? If yes, how would this view affect the Court's position regarding the cited conflict among the circuits regarding affirmative action outreach efforts?

The wise course would be to reconsider *Adarand*. Reconsideration would provide the Court with a vehicle for specifically determining the constitutional status of disparate-impact theory. This theory is a central conceptual basis of remedial affirmative action, with its emphasis on group rights and non-victim entitlements. However, as we saw in chapter 3, under the teaching of *Adarand*, strict scrutiny derives from the conviction that group rights are unconstitutional "in most circumstances."[28] Arguably, then, this decision *impliedly* holds that remedial affirmative action may inherently violate the Equal Protection Clause. Surely an issue of such keystone importance must not be left to implication. The Court must tell us what strict scrutiny prohibits, and in the process clarify what the standards of adjudication are, particularly in connection with the meaning of compelling government interest and narrow tailoring. It is also important to learn whether gays, lesbians, and transsexuals are to be considered a "suspect class" for equal protection and due process review—and if not, why not? The reader should also ponder the merit of the Court's insistence that senior workers and the disabled not be considered suspect classes. (See 267–77.)

Important, too, is the long-festering question of whether state government and its entities can be required to follow federal disparate-impact regulations generated by Title VI of the 1964 Civil Rights Act (such as those accepted by the Court in *Lau*[29] to help students with language problems) when the majority in *Bakke* determined that state government was prohibited by Title VI from engaging in disparate-treatment and not disparate-impact discrimination.[30] Additionally, the Equal Protection Clause has been interpreted, in *Washington v. Davis* (1976)[31] as prohibiting only state disparate treatment.

As we saw in chapter 3 (53–54), Justice Powell in his controlling *Bakke* opinion applied strict scrutiny in two different ways. First in rejecting the societal-discrimination—disparate-impact—defense, he held that remediation of specified past discrimination was a condition precedent of the disputed set-aside's constitutionality under the strict scrutiny test.[32] Second, in ruling on the nonremedial "diversity" defense, he also applied strict scrutiny analysis: student-body diversity was a "compelling interest," but the Davis set-aside was not "necessary" to further it—*not* because it failed to remedy past discrimination, but because it violated nonminority applicants' present equal protection rights.[33]

By thus decoupling strict scrutiny and disparate-impact mediation, Justice Powell set the table for the advocates of nonremedial diversity who have used the diversity rationale as a major weapon promoting affirmative action. However, this was more than three decades ago, and Justice Powell wrote only for himself. The Powell doctrine was called into question, and was the subject of another split in the circuits. On the authority of *Croson* and *Adarand*, a panel of the Fifth Circuit held that consideration of race for the nonremedial purpose of achieving student-body diversity can never be a "compelling interest," and that Justice Powell's view is not "binding precedent."[34] (See 145–46.) The First Circuit, on the other hand, specifically disagreed with the Fifth Circuit's pronouncement that the Powell doctrine is "dead." "[W]e assume . . . that *Bakke* remains good law and that some iterations of 'diversity' might be sufficiently compelling to justify race-conscious action."[35] In *Smith v. University of Washington Law School* (2000),[36] the Ninth Circuit upheld the preferential admissions program of that school, holding that the Powell opinion accepting diversity objectives under strict scrutiny was *implicitly* accepted by four additional justices.

Strange as it may seem, the Supreme Court never provided a majority opinion dealing directly with the relationship between strict scrutiny and nonremedial preference until 2003. In that year, the Court ended its disengagement with the issue and rendered a majority opinion in *Grutter v. Bollinger*,[37] which held that student-body diversity was a compelling government interest, and that the University of Michigan's law school preferential admissions program posited as one meant to acquire a "critical mass" of minority students was narrowly tailored. (See 146–61.) The Court now must tell us whether nonremedial affirmative action is applicable to other realms; whether color can be equated with cultural diversification; and, in other ways, what a constitutionally acceptable quest for diversity requires. Today, the Court should no longer have the option of disengagement in telling us how *Bakke* lives. The upshot is that the legal status of "diversity" is still very much up in the air. This at a time when its proponents' clamor is insistent,[38] and in the face of the claim that there is substantial evidence that it has been successfully applied in a number of different contexts.[39]

School integration and the historically black colleges and universities

A half-century has passed since *Brown*, but, due in large part to vacillation by the Supreme Court, it is not clear whether its integration mandate will—or should—ever be fulfilled. As we saw in chapter 4 (102–3), the Court has made a 180-degree turn during its stewardship of *Brown's* legacy—from uncompromising advocate of federally directed integration to proponent of local control. There may—or may not—be a causal relationship between this shift and the resurgence of segregation in our public schools. Whatever the case, a number of localities have pursued school integration through the nonremedial affirmative-action route. In *Parents Involved v. Seattle* (2007),[40] this effort failed. Still a majority of the Court accepted the diversity rationale as a basis for K-12 school integration, but failed to agree on how diversity was to be defined and implemented. (See 104–14.)

The High Court must, once and for all, determine the constitutional status of publicly funded black colleges in higher learning. In chapter 5 (at 170–78) we learned that the future of our Historically Black Colleges and Universities (HBCUs) remained an open question even after more than a generation of litigation, the Court—in *U.S. v. Fordice* (1992)[41]—held that the practices that gave rise to segregated higher education and the creation of Historically Black Colleges and Universities were to be eliminated. Various efforts have been undertaken in the states to implement *Fordice* through improved HBCU funding and by establishing higher admission standards to attract non-blacks. Both HBCUs and Traditionally White Institutions have agreed to seek "other race" students. But there has been extensive post-*Fordice* litigation over questions of its implementation, and the Supreme Court refused review. Meanwhile, the HBCUs remain very racially identifiable. In our view, the Supreme Court should not allow the *Fordice* case to become the Dickensian "endless lawsuit" in *Bleak House*, the *Jarndyce v. Jarndyce* of civil rights law.

Voting rights

For majority-minority districts, as with any derivative of disparate-impact affirmative action, *Adarand* is the Sword of Damocles. Is strict scrutiny, as mandated by *Shaw v. Reno*[42] and *Miller v. Johnson*,[43] the death warrant of race/ethnic-based redistricting? One surmises that every redistricting agency in the country will grapple with this question, while pondering the results of the 2010 decennial census. The *Shaw/Miller* standard of the 1990s called for strict scrutiny review of majority-minority legislative districts where race was the predominant factor in their creation. Whether the race predominance standard is capable of being applied is a lingering issue, as is the question of whether political gerrymandering is a defense in racial gerrymandering cases. Further, the Court has yet to determine what are constitutional and unconstitutional political gerrymanders. (See 210–21.)

Fair housing

In chapter 7 we noted that the Supreme Court has never passed either on the constitutionality of the Fair Housing Act of 1968, or on many of the standards that apply to its enforcement. It has even refused to decide the propriety of disparate-impact remediation under this housing statute. Of all the instances of judicial inaction that we have encountered, this is the most unfathomable. It is generally agreed that housing discrimination is our worst, most intractable civil rights problem, both of itself and as a source of collateral discrimination. The federal government has been hesitant in the use of direct affirmative action, racial/ethnic balancing techniques to root out systemic discrimination and promote integrated housing; and this is surely, in part, attributable to the lack of a clear signal from the Supreme Court. Under these circumstances, that the Court would deliberately distance itself from the field of action is difficult to understand.

Gender issues

The time has also come for the High Court to resolve the question of whether intermediate scrutiny is to remain the standard of equal protection review for gender discrimination, and if so, how the formulation of mid-tier scrutiny in *U.S. v. Virginia* is to be distinguished from strict scrutiny. (See 179–81.) It is to be recalled that in that case the Court held that gender discrimination met equal protection mandates if an "exceedingly persuasive justification"[44] could be found for it. How an "exceedingly persuasive justification" differs from strict scrutiny is unclear, as is the rationale for not applying the same equal protection standards to race, ethnic, *and* gender discrimination. That said, can gender proportionality in all phases of education, or gender segregation (e.g., separate male and female athletic teams) be constitutionally supported by an "exceedingly-persuasive justification under the Equal Protection Clause?"

Statutory Issues

We have noted (at 184–87) that the circuits have interpreted Title IX of the 1972 Education Act[45]—which bars sexual discrimination in education activities receiving federal financial aid—as requiring female/male proportionality in athletics funding and participation. Is gender proportionality required by the act in areas outside of athletics (e.g., engineering programs)? The Bush II administration both rejected the view that Title IX required proportionality in athletics participation, and proposed that female/male interest in sport be taken into account when judging conformity with the law. Should the Obama administration further the Bush policy?

The 1964 Civil Rights Act's Title VII case law—the core of equal-employment statutory jurisprudence—is a hodgepodge of irreconcilable interpretations, for example, the majority and dissenting opinions in the *Weber*[46] case. Even after a generation of judicial warfare, the battle still continues over whether the goal of antidiscrimination law is "equal treatment" or "equal results."

Congress helped foment this confusion by neglecting to establish the vocabulary of equal employment opportunity law. For example, neither Title VII nor its 1991 amendments offer a clue about what Congress meant by such key statutory terms as "equal opportunity," "discrimination," or "preferential treatment." By design or otherwise, policy making initially was almost totally delegated to the administrative bureaucracies and the judiciary, resulting, for better or for worse, first in affirmative action's extensive capture of the economy and now the looming possibility of its demise. In our view, Congress must reclaim responsibility for civil rights reform, by resolving all doubts about Title VII's meaning, and by formulating comprehensive guidelines for its enforcement.

At a minimum, the following are open questions:

1. Is it the purpose of "equal opportunity" to improve the socioeconomic status of minorities and women, or only to end invidious discrimination?

2. What is the meaning of "discriminate" in 42 USC § 2000e-2(a) (1) of Title VII?[47]

3. What is the meaning of "disparate impact" in section 105 of the 1991 amendments of Title VII codified at 42 USC 2000e-2(k) (1) (A)?

   Does it relate to "discriminate" in 42 USC § 2000e-2(a) (1)?

   Does it relate to "adversely affect . . . status" in 42 USC § 2000e-2(a) (2)?

   Was the inclusion of the concept of disparate impact in section 105 of the 1991 amended Title VII intended to ratify the holding in *Griggs v. Duke Power Co.*[48] that unjustified adverse group effects of facially neutral employment practices can violate Title VII?

4. What is the meaning of "business necessity" and "job related" in section 105 of the 1991 amendments codified at 42 USC § 2000e-2(k) (1) (A)?

   Which decisions of the Supreme Court govern the parties' burden of proof in the trial of disparate-impact cases?

   Does the Equal Employment Opportunity Commission's 80 percent rule [29 CFR 1607.4.D] apply to the sufficiency of statistical evidence in the trial of disparate-impact cases"? [See Appendix Two at 355–59, for excerpts from 29 CFR 1607.]

5. What is the meaning of "affirmative action" in section 116 of the 1991 amendments in the Civil Rights Act of that year, and codified at 42 USC § 1981, Construction of 1991 Amendments?

    How does it relate to "affirmative action" referred to in the 1964 Civil Rights Act, and codified under 42 USC § 2000e-5(g)?

    Which decisions of the Supreme Court govern the status of "affirmative action" under section 116 of the 1991 amendments codified at 42 USC § 1981, Construction of 1991 Amendments?

    Are the 1991 amendments intended to validate voluntary affirmative action through race, ethnic, and gender preferences in order to remedy the effects of societal discrimination and/ or preclude its recurrence? (The uncodified 1991 statutory amendments are found in Pub L 102-166, 105 Stat 1071.)

6. Does Title VII of the 1964 Civil Rights Act sanction affirmative action for nonremedial purposes?

7. What is the meaning of "preferential treatment" in 42 USC § 2000e-s 2(j) of Title VII? Does the title permit preferential treatment?

8. Should the 2009 Lilly Ledbetter amendments[49] to both Title VII and the Age Discrimination in Employment Act (ADEA) strengthen the application of disparate-impact theory in race/ethnic/gender and age discrimination cases? The Ledbetter amendments permitted plaintiffs charging disparate-treatment discrimination in employment to use alleged olden discriminatory treatment to prove violations of Title VII and the ADEA. (See 75–76.)

9. The rejection of the "racial essentialism" thesis (i.e., that members of minority groups think alike) in *LULAC v. Perry* (2006)[50] runs contrary to prevailing diversity theory where color is equated with culture. Should the *LULAC v. Perry* view prevail?

10. In a nation that is becoming a nation of minorities, how should the 1965 Voting Rights Act[51] be amended?

The Need for a Specialized Court

The difficulty of the questions we have outlined in this chapter and throughout the volume warrant careful judicial deliberation. However, after a generation of legalistic disputation, we yearn for greater firmness in the legal rights and wrongs of affirmative action. It is sobering to consider how many fundamental legal questions await closure. Statutory and constitutional clarity might be enhanced if Congress created a specialized tribunal charged with treating the affirmative action issues raised here. Congress has created special courts under both its Article I and Article III powers. Under Article I, Congress has established territorial and military courts; a Tax Court; the courts of the District of Columbia; the Court of Federal Claims; and the Court of Veterans Appeals. Additionally, there are thousands of administrative law judges who have been empowered by Article I. Those connected with the Social Security Administration alone have a caseload larger than all the Article III courts combined.[52] These Article I judges are not protected by the salary and tenure guarantees given Article III judges, and the Constitution could be read to limit the creation of judgeships to those who are covered by such protections. But this potential constitutional impediment has not stopped Congress from creating judges with limited tenure. Further, Congress has created specialized Article III courts: the Court of International Trade; and the Court of Appeals for the Federal Circuit which has jurisdiction over appeals stemming from claims against the federal government.[53]

Article I and Article III specialized-court creation is a function of congressional determination that specialization could further justice by facilitating clarification of rights and obligations connected with particular bodies of law.[54] Affirmative action issues are of such complexity and importance as to warrant judges who could give them their full-time attention.

While the writers hope otherwise, the Supreme Court's affirmative action clarification will probably proceed at a slow and incremental rate. The analytical problems involved are formidable, and there are fierce opinions on the matter, both in and outside the Court. The decisive moral question is how far "equality" can be stretched. How does the state resolve the inherent conflict between the citizenry's freedom of choice and its own moral duty to eradicate bias? Has government the legal right and moral duty to impose limits or require the expansion of minority and female rights as well as those of gays, the disabled, seniors, and transsexuals? There is no explicit guidance for the solution of these issues in the words of the Constitution. Given the absence of such guidance, the eye-crossing analytical problems, and the enormous political controversy, it should be recognized that affirmative action is a labyrinth in which even the most seasoned legal travelers easily lose their way. Consequently, those seeking a near-term, energetic High Court initiative for the adoption of specific and comprehensive standards in this area are likely to be disappointed. Those so affected will doubtless view the Court's moral authority as considerably deficient. On the other hand, a major Court historian—Robert McCloskey—praised the caution, deliberateness and incrementalism which the Court has historically exercised, theorizing that this operational mode was the Court's most efficient way to exercise its moral authority and promote justice and decency. He wrote:

> Surely the record teaches that no useful purpose is served when the judges seek all the hottest political caldrons of the moment and dive into the middle of them. . . . The Court's greatest successes have been achieved when it has operated near the margins rather that in the center of political controversy, when it has nudged and gently tugged the nation, instead of trying to rule. . . . [C]onsider the long campaign on behalf of laissez-faire from 1905 to 1934, with its pattern of concession to the principle of regulation, dotted here and there with a warning that the principle could be carried too far. . . . The Court ruled more in each case when it tried to rule less, and that paradox is one of the clearest morals to be drawn from its history.[55]

The congressional avoidance of statutory clarification is rooted in the difficult analytical and ideological problems that have limited the Supreme Court. Both the legislative and judicial schemes of problem avoidance have resulted in an enormous and very questionable allocation of rule-making power to the administrators. The elaborateness of the rules issued by the Equal Employment Opportunity Commission and the Office of Federal Contract Compliance Programs illustrates the problem. (See appendixes Two through Four at end of the volume, 355–73.) As David Schoenbrod saw it, lawmaking delegation impedes democracy because the administrators are largely unremovable by the electoral process. Further, legislators exercise their power without responsibility by unfairly deflecting criticism onto administrators, thus immunizing themselves against removal.[56] Lawmaking delegation to administrators is defended with notions that elected representatives have neither the time, nor the expertise to treat the details of complicated problems. Surely though, the representatives are, on the whole, as competent as the bureaucrats. And it is expected of them to make the time to confront problems that are central to the nation's welfare.

In setting out an agenda for the Supreme Court and the Congress, we have avoided taking any position on the merits, but have sought only to provide the reader with a bridge over the legal terrain that should be traversed before venturing onto the battlefield. There is an ideological terrain also, and major claims thereupon should be highlighted.

The Ideological Clash Regarding
Race/Gender/Ethnic Affirmative Action

The unremitting dispute that envelops affirmative action stems from the clash between two theories of equal opportunity.

Affirmative action exemplifies the principle that "society should do what it can to 'level the playing field' among individuals who compete for positions . . . so that all those with relevant potential will eventually be admissible to pools of . . . [competing] candidates."[57] In this version, "leveling" is achieved by honoring race, ethnicity, gender, age, disability, sexual orientation preferences and other aids in various arenas of competition.[58] The common underlying justification is the claimed need to compensate disadvantaged individuals for the legacy of past discrimination[59]—a justification typically embedded in diversity, nonremedial advocacy. Justice Ginsburg recognized this "hidden agenda" in her *Gratz v. Bollinger* dissent.[60] After being confronted with the University of Michigan's much-emphasized nonremedial, diversity argument supporting its preferential admission program, she paid no heed to it recognizing the underlying remedial motivation of the University. "The stain of generations of racial oppression" she wrote "is still visible . . . and the determination to hasten its removal remains vital. One can reasonably anticipate, therefore, that colleges and universities will seek to maintain their minority enrollment and the networks and opportunities thereby opened to minority graduates whether or not they can do so in full candor. . . ."[61]

Arrayed against this is the principle that "in the competition for positions . . . all individuals who possess the attributes relevant for . . . the duties of [a] position [should] be included in the pool of eligible candidates, and that an individual's possible occupancy of the position [should] be judged only with respect to those relevant attributes."[62] The corollary is that race, ethnicity, age, disability, or sexual orientation should not count for or against an individual's eligibility for a job, when they are not relevant for its duties.

Thus, preference versus merit. The voluminously chronicled debate over affirmative action boils down to an exchange of claims and counterclaims, attacks and defenses, by the advocates of these polar opposites.

To assist the reader in weighing this exchange, following is a synopsis of its main themes:

Affirmative action's proponents justify minority and gender-based measures as remedies for present effects of past discrimination; preventives of recurrence; and devices for securing crucially needed inclusion of diverse minorities in our highly competitive, demographically fluid economy. Color-blindness promotes exclusion; the merit principle is far more honored in the breach than in the observance. The claim of reverse discrimination is a myth.

The opposing camp maintains that affirmative action discriminates against innocent whites; compromises merit; benefits non-disadvantaged minorities; stigmatizes its beneficiaries; perpetuates racism; and promotes economic inefficiency.

Readers should evaluate these claims—as well as the legal/policy issues presented above, and throughout the volume—by consulting the earlier specialized chapters. To help the reader assemble expanded arguments on "both sides" (and thus build a bridge to judgment), we summarize below the writings of a sample of distinguished disputants, believing it appropriate for readers to reference them as they develop their own conclusions. We leave to the readers the exacting task of attempting to resolve the fierce disputes they will encounter, and sorting the broad areas of agreement. Although the disputants deal mainly with the bellwether black community, how the status of that community and the effect of affirmative action on it are perceived is critical to the future of affirmative action, as it has been to its past.

Prelude to Judgment: A Sampler of Distinguished Disputants

Christopher Edley's *Not All Black and White*[63] is a quixotic addition to the affirmative action literature. The book urges the necessity of race-conscious programs, but it is very much marked by queasy doubts about their validity. Truly, the issue is *not all black and white*!

Those who are committed to color-blind governmental policy are castigated by Edley because of their failure to grasp the immorality of their postures.[64] Edley maintains that a serious, widening "opportunity gap" exists between American whites and blacks, based on unacceptable racial disparities.[65] Race-conscious policies that go beyond color-blindness are justifiable as a critical element in a program for bringing about "morally equal opportunity," in the sense of a full and equal chance to develop and use one's talents.[66] While affirmative action has "moral costs" in terms of "consequences" for third parties, it may be justified by the benefits, provided that the need for race-based measures is minimized through consideration of race-neutral alternatives.[67] In Edley's view, this moral calculus is an integral element of the communal vision which Americans should share.[68]

Despite Edley's advocacy of race-consciousness, he stresses that "it is almost impossible . . . to separate the effects of pure *antidiscrimination* norms from the effects of *additional* measures commonly thought of as 'affirmative action.' "[69] The proper administration of affirmative action requires great sensitivity (as in considering race-neutral alternatives), lest the moral cost be too high. He wrote that "The value intensive choices . . . are tough ones, and Edley's maxim states that there are more tough jobs than there are good people to fill them . . . and we have a poor understanding of the extent to which we can mitigate—by regulation, training, or enforcement—the damage done when character fails."[70] Equally bemoaned by Edley is the hard reality that the affirmative action cost-benefit evaluations are, to him, impossible in this real world.[71]

Given the above misgivings, one must wonder why Edley is so committed to race-conscious affirmative action. *Croson* and *Adarand*'s requirement of strict scrutiny poses additional problems for Edley. The proof of discrimination required by strict scrutiny is most difficult to come by he tells us.[72] Many federal affirmative action programs were inaugurated without the strict-scrutiny, evidentiary analysis now required.[73] Importantly, he continued, racial "exclusion is not solely—or, today, even primarily—the result of present discrimination and racial animus. A large factor is the "birds of a feather" tendency to prefer people like oneself. "In hundreds of subtle ways, this tendency pervades American social and economic life, and the aggregate effect is to divide us, starving ourselves and our institutions of the benefits that come from having more diverse and inclusive communities."[74] Through this route, Edley comes to embrace "diversity theory" as an integral part of affirmative action.[75] It is a theory free from the constraints of strict scrutiny, but it is a theory that is viewed, along with other criticisms, as fostering social disunity.

Berkeley history professor David Hollinger regarded Justice Powell's diversity thesis in *Bakke* as a "tactic" meant to provide support for affirmative action. To Hollinger, the tactic of using color to predict culture was a marked departure from the affirmative action of the 1960s and 1970s. In those years, preferences were allocated on ethno-racial grounds not because color predicted culture, but because people of color were subject to invidious discriminatory treatment.[76] Powell, "struggling for a way to justify preferences in academic admissions for historically disadvantaged ethno-racial minorities, declared such preference potentially permissible, if their aim was to diversify the 'ideas and mores' of campuses."[77] This "alliance with affirmative action interrupted the demanding struggle to liberate culture from blood and soil in the interest of maximizing the opportunity of every individual to affiliate culturally as he or she might choose."[78] Nevertheless, those who promoted an appreciation for cultural diversity—the multicultural movement of growing importance starting in the 1960s—increasingly followed the Powell lead.[79] "Recognizing the expedient character of Powell's act, and of multiculturalism's use of color codes, may save us from mistaking tactic for truth."[80]

Hollinger is much concerned with the question of "[h]ow can a democratic society achieve political cohesion."[81] Helpful to cohesion, would be the maximization of opportunities for people to choose their own cultural identities, in contrast to governmental structuring identities as in affirmative action classifications. These classifications Hollinger finds harmful to cohesion.[82] In 1995, he expressed considerable concern about America's unity. "Americans have become too afraid of each other and too unwilling to take up the task of building a common future."[83] And in his 2005 edition of *Postethnic America*, Hollinger continued with the somber insistence that increasingly national solidarity was not advocated by our political leaders. His remedy is the espousal of a "historical narrative" which "emphasizes the liberal and cosmopolitan elements of the national self-image without denying the parts of American history that are not liberal and cosmopolitan."[84]

Peter Schuck shares Hollinger's concern with societal unity. To this end, Schuck objects to affirmative action privileges. These privileges do not achieve their economic goals. They separate Americans by reifying and ossifying anachronistic categories. Americans value diversity when they see it as natural and authentic—stemming from personal choice—and not something contrived, as government-designed, color-coded diversity is.[85]

On the other hand, political theorist Will Kymlicka argues that government granting of special privileges to groups helps national unification. After all, the objective of preferences, such as those characteristic of affirmative action, is to facilitate out-group participation in and enjoyment of the bounties of a larger America, thus solidifying societal adherence.[86]

Stephan and Abigail Thernstroms' *America in Black and White*[87] presents *Croson* and *Adarand* as a necessary correction for the disparate-impact corruption of Title VII,[88] but as treated by the Clinton Administration, "*Adarand* . . . had been a waste of the Supreme Court's breath."[89]

The Thernstroms not only present affirmative action in employment as legally perverse, but also as a fomenter of racial bitterness and conflict.[90] And all of this possibly for naught, because there are no grounds to believe that affirmative action improved the economic lot of blacks save perhaps in increasing the number of black professionals, such as doctors and lawyers. But professionals are a small portion of African America. That society, as a whole, has been making very strong economic advances since the 1940s. It is terribly wrong, the Thernstroms maintain, to view black economic gains as a function of disparate-impact remediation.[91] "The best generalization to make . . . is that the trends visible in the first period [1940–1970] continued in the second [post-1970] without notable change."[92]

Liberals will doubtless tend to dismiss the Thernstrom tome as mere acerbic, conservative scolding. This would be a mistake. The first segment of this large book provides an extensive history of African America from "Jim Crow" times. It would be difficult for anyone who reads the Thernstrom account of Jim Crow monstrosities and their moving treatment of Reverend King's undertaking not to become a greater champion of black civil rights. Further, the volume contains forceful argumentation, which students of affirmative action should grapple with. Major positions taken by the Thernstroms include the following:

> Affirmative action is rooted in the legal distortions of disparate-impact thinking, is counterproductive, and perpetuates racism.[93]

The status of blacks has "improved dramatically" over the last half-century "by just about every possible measure of social and economic achievement."[94] Much of the improvement antedated affirmative action.

"Hard-core" white racism is a thing of the past.[95] While racism has "obviously" not disappeared, "racial tolerance" is now the social "norm."[96]

Existing socioeconomic inequality "is less a function of white racism than of the racial gap in levels of educational achievement, the structure of the black family, and the rise in black crime."[97] The cure for this "serious" situation is adoption of "color-blind public policies," which embody "the sense that we are one nation—that we sink or swim together, that black poverty impoverishes us all, that black alienation eats at the nation's soul, and that black isolation simply cannot work."[98]

Continuation of affirmative action would necessarily heighten racial separation, and would "spell disaster in a nation with an ugly history of racial subordination and a continuing problem, albeit dramatically diminished, of racial intolerance."[99]

Inner-city black poverty—"the single most depressing fact about the state of black America today"[100]—has persisted since the 1970s notwithstanding affirmative action.[101]

While most black citizens are law-abiding, African Americans are "represented far out of proportion to their numbers"[102] in arrest, conviction, and incarceration for crime.[103] These disparities are not attributable to bias in the criminal justice system.[104] The evidence does not seem to support the charge that administration of the death penalty is racially biased.[105] The Thernstroms argue that "if the African-American crime rate suddenly dropped to the current level of the white crime rate, we would eliminate a major force that is driving blacks and whites apart and is destroying the fabric of black urban life."[106]

The evidence does not establish that the current level of racial discrimination in employment and contracting warrants continuation of affirmative action.[107] Notwithstanding the recent trend against affirmative action in the Supreme Court's rulings against employment/procurement, racial preferences face an uncertain future, since the Clinton administration and the civil rights groups attempted to nullify those rulings.[108]

A 2001 report produced by the Tomas Rivera Policy Institute called attention to a thriving and growing Hispanic middle class. Though concentrated among the U.S.-born, the Latino middle class (households with incomes of over $40,000) grew at a rate almost three times as high as non-Hispanic whites. They have experienced dramatic gains in earnings and education; and within educational levels, they enjoy economic opportunities roughly comparable to non-Hispanic whites.[109]

Critics are quick to challenge optimistic economic reports regarding minorities and females. The glaring recent growth in U.S. income inequality is a staple of this criticism. Princeton professor Douglas Massey, in his 2007 volume *Categorically Unequal: The American Stratification System*,[110] presents data showing that since the 1970s, households in the top 20 percent of the income-distribution ladder have experienced steady income gains. For example, the share of the nation's income going to the top 10 percent rose from 32.9 percent in 1980 to 43.9 percent in 2000.[111] Income rose modestly in the middle-income distribution range, but only because females entered the workforce in record numbers. Those in the lowest fifth showed little income growth as the upper fifth pulled dramatically away.[112] The black-white and Latino-white income gap actually rose in the period from $16,000 to $18,000.[113] Female/male income has become more equal but this is as much the result of male earnings stagnation as it is in the increase in female pay.[114]

To Senator Bernie Sanders, the "United States has, by far, the most unfair distribution of wealth and income of any major nation. The richest 1% of the population now owns as much wealth as the bottom 95% of all Americans combined."[115] The notion that the exponentially widening income gap is mitigated by the opportunity to move up the scale is, to one critic, a "conceit."[116] In 2004, the wealthiest country in the world tolerated an African American poverty rate of 26 percent; a 22 percent poverty rate for Hispanics, and 25 percent for American Indians—all more than twice the rate of the population as a whole.[117] Despite highly publicized exceptions, minority representation, at the turn of the new millennium, in senior management and executive positions, the professions, and academe remained as marginal as when Congress took note of it in the 1991 Civil Rights Act.[118]

Tom Wicker also provided a dramatically different account from that of the Thernstroms in *Tragic Failure*.[119] America's majority is not increasingly accepting blacks. It has for some time jettisoned the goal of an integrated America where blacks fully share in the nation's benefits. True, the African American middle class has grown, but the underclass of that minority has burgeoned at a much faster rate. In 1970, the underclass numbered some seven hundred thousand—one-half of 1 percent of the population. By 1980, there had been a virtual explosion, with the very poor numbering 2.5 million, or 1.37 percent of the entire population. The largest U.S. cities are now overwhelmed with a minority-underclass population packed into ghettos racked by crime, violence, family breakdown, school dropouts, drugs, and the like. The outlook is not a good one. Middle-class blacks and whites have fled the social turmoil of the inner city, and their absence augments the social disorientation of those areas.[120]

Professorial support for Wicker's journalistic account is to be found in William Julius Wilson's *When Work Disappears*,[121] a book that underscores the environmental forces shaping the new urban poor ghettos: the extraordinary decline in well-paying jobs requiring lesser skills; the increased educational requirements for better-paying jobs; racially restrictive mortgage practices, which have prevented middle-class blacks from purchasing homes in the ghetto areas, thus encouraging them to leave; the lowering of income levels required of those living in low-rent public housing, converting those homes to havens of the dispossessed; and the refusal of suburban areas to accept more low-rent public housing.[122]

Wilson's book helpfully reviews other efforts to describe the roots of the new urban poor. George Gilder's *Wealth and Poverty* (1981); and Charles Murray's *Losing Ground* (1984) argued that social welfare programs undercut self-reliance and increased joblessness. Richard Herrnstein and Charles Murray's *Bell Shaped Curve* insisted upon genetic inferiority as the cause. But Wilson notes that geneticists maintain that there is no clear line between genetic and such environmental influences that he concentrated upon.[123] Orlando Patterson put the case against genetic inferiority forcefully. He classified Arthur Jensen as the most "sophisticated defender" of that approach who "had very nearly thrown in the towel" with his concession that "'the genetic hypothesis will remain untested in any acceptably rigorous manner for some indeterminate length of time, most likely beyond the lifespan of any present-day scientists.' "[124]

Wilson is among our leading academic authorities on race and poverty. *When Work Disappears* is an authoritative, recent portrait of America's urban crisis:

> There are in every major metropolitan area, festering center-city ghettos, populated by blacks, assorted ethnic minorities, and low-income whites; mired in unemployment,[125] job displacement, declining real wages, family dysfunction, escalating medical and housing costs, scarcity of affordable child care facilities, sharp decline in quality of public education, crime, and drug trafficking; gripped by explosive intergroup tensions based on racial, class, cultural, and linguistic differences,[126] and exacerbated by "the poisonous racial rhetoric of certain highly visible spokespersons."[127]
>
> A "clear racial divide "exists between the central cities and the suburbs.[128]
>
> This crisis calls the efficacy of disparate-impact affirmative action and its compensatory remedy emphasis into serious question.

The problems originating in historical racism, Wilson flatly asserts, "cannot be solved through race-based remedies alone."[129] Based on analysis of voluminous data on income, employment, and educational attainment, he finds that affirmative action policies "based solely on . . . racial group membership"[130] have disproportionately benefited "the more advantaged members of minority groups"[131] in terms of college admissions and higher-paying jobs, but have not opened up "broad avenues of upward mobility for the masses of disadvantaged blacks."[132] Nevertheless, he argues that, as long as minorities are "underrepresented in higher-paying and desirable positions,"[133] disparate-impact affirmative action programs will be a necessity. These programs should recognize that the problems of the disadvantaged "are not always clearly related to previous racial discrimination,"[134] and should address the *environmental* factors that afflict the disadvantaged of all races, that is, those bearing on "economic class position or need."[135] At the same time, Wilson is keenly aware that affirmative action based solely on need would systematically exclude many middle-income blacks from desirable positions, since it would leave them at the mercy of "standard . . . measures of performance [which] are not sensitive to the cumulative effect of race."[136] Accordingly, he proposes "a comprehensive race-neutral initiative"[137] to address economic and social inequality, which would serve as "an extension of—not a replacement for—opportunity-enhancing programs that include race-based criteria to fight social inequality."[138] Such programs should employ flexible criteria of evaluation in college "admission, hiring, job promotion, and so on, and should be based on a broad definition of disadvantage that incorporates notions of both *need* and *race*."[139] Wilson's initiative would also include programs "that can accurately be described as purely race-neutral such as national health care, school reform, and job training based on need rather than race, that would strongly and positively impact racial minority groups but would benefit large segments of the dominant white population as well."[140]

To flesh out his vision, Wilson has put forward wide-ranging, specific proposals for educational reform and job training;[141] city-suburban integration and cooperation;[142] increases in minimum wage and health insurance coverage;[143] measures for surmounting the "spatial mismatch" between residence and job location, for example, increases in public transportation, and job referral facilities;[144] and last-resort public employment, and retraining, of displaced low-skilled workers.[145]

Wilson concludes with a plea for a new, broad-based political coalition to press for economic and social reform, and dissipate the "paralysis" that, in his view, has taken hold of national policy under both Republican and Democratic administrations.[146]

For reasons similar to those of Wilson, Wicker urges the maintenance of affirmative action, along with a major enlargement of race-neutral public works and educational programs. Wicker insists on the need for a new political party for these purposes. Only in this fashion can we counter the total disinterest by the major parties in the plight of the underclass.[147]

In his 2009 contribution to understanding the plight of low-income, inner-city blacks—titled *More Than Just Race*[148]—Wilson urged political leaders to champion policies that address the need to cure both the socioeconomic factors producing inner-city poverty, as well as the behavioral patterns and values that help fuel that impoverishment. The model communicator was Senator Obama in his March 18, 2008, speech on race and poverty, which called upon whites to realize that ghetto ills are rooted in slavery and racism, and to dedicate themselves to improving schools, implementing civil rights laws, and acquiring fairness in the criminal justice system. The senator concurrently highlighted the need for behavioral change in the inner city, namely, the reduction of violence and defeatism; fathers who spent more time with their children "reading to them, and teaching them . . . [that] they must always believe that they can write their own *destiny*."[149]

More Than Just Race teaches that we should research the behavioral values of inner-city dwellers and the relationship of those values to poverty. Little is known. The most "compelling evidence" in this connection comes from studies portraying the ghetto as suffering from widespread distrust, which interferes greatly with the networking helpful in the acquisition of gainful employment. Wilson also is impressed with the ethnographic studies presenting poor black, white, and Puerto Rican females as widely rejecting marriage because the males they are affiliated with are poor marriage prospects because of poor education, imprisonment, and joblessness. Still, these females wanted children, believing that life would be harsher without them, and believing (often unjustifiably) that they could provide for them economically.[150]

In what may be affirmative action's eleventh hour, Richard D. Kahlenberg's *The Remedy*[151] proposes to install race-neutral, class-based preferences in order to ensure genuine equality of opportunity for the economically disadvantaged of all groups. The preferences would apply in entry-level employment, education, and contracting. In this regime, the 1964 and 1991 Civil Rights Acts would remain in effect for the purpose of dealing with ongoing and future race, ethnic, and gender discrimination; but such preferences would be implemented only in the "very rare instances"[152] that conform strictly to the *Croson* and *Adarand* rulings.[153]

Kahlenberg has proposed the shift, not because he believes race has been overemphasized—in his words, "there are plenty of times when race *is* the issue"[154]—but mainly to redress the marginalization of the moral basis of class-based disadvantage. Class-based programs, he vehemently insists, must *supplant* today's protected-group programs, rather than merely *supplement* them.[155]

Kahlenberg's point of departure is the asserted failure of compensatory protected-group preferences to provide genuine equal opportunity, long-term color-blindness, benefits of integration, or even compensation for past discrimination.[156] The net result, in his view, has been overinclusion of *advantaged* minorities and underinclusion of their *disadvantaged* brethren—a very bad social imbalance which class-based affirmative action will help correct.[157]

The Remedy as a policy proposal suffers from a number of shortcomings. Its attack on racial preferences is unaccountably limited. It bypasses voting rights completely, and touches on housing segregation only in passing. Since "equal opportunity" in this "new regime" would be confined to "starting places," it would appear that Kahlenberg does not advocate social regulation of discrimination in *post*-hire employment (e.g., refusal to promote) or *post*-admission higher education (e.g., refusal to grant tenure). Indeed, Kahlenberg says that class-based preferences "would not be employed for promotions, since the idea is to provide disadvantaged young people with a chance to prove themselves, not to promote preferences as a way of life."[158] In Kahlenberg's Darwinian world, discrimination ceases to concern society after hire on the job or admission to college. But this position ignores the real world of discrimination.

Even Kahlenberg's commitment to the abolition of protected-group preference is far from clear as he would keep disparate-impact theory operative as insurance against current or future racial/ethnic/gender discrimination.[159] But the disparate-impact model of discrimination is central to racial, ethnic and gender affirmative action remediation! See, for example, *Griggs v. Duke Power* (1971),[160]—a decision that he specifically approved.[161] To retain it would seem to guarantee the preservation of preferences, rather than moderate their effects, or their extinction.

Kahlenberg's calculus in the implementation of class-based preferences would grant disproportionate benefits to poor blacks since their backgrounds are even more disadvantaged than poor whites.[162] Doubtless, such a mechanism would be seen as "stealth" affirmative action and duplicitous, hardly the attitudes promotive of the racial harmony Kahlenberg wants so much.[163]

Kahlenberg has not articulated a governing rationale for his *Remedy*. He steadfastly maintains that "the ultimate test of class-based affirmative action is whether it provides individual equality of *opportunity* . . . not equality of group *results*."[164] But, as he candidly acknowledges, this distinction is always lost in practice: "Inevitably, universities and employers do treat people as members of groups, for at some point the tradeoff between fairness and efficiency tips in favor of the latter."[165] Therefore, a policy oriented totally to class would be unenforceable,[166] and it is incumbent upon Kahlenberg to formulate a more realistic "ultimate test."

Given the above shortcomings, it is clear that if a case can be made for class preference, *The Remedy* does not do the job.

Have, then, the black and Hispanic communities progressed since the 1960s, or is the racial/economic gap in socioeconomic status wider than ever? Is racial tolerance the social norm in today's America, or are our cities hotbeds of racial animosity? Should affirmative action's ethnic/racial/gender special considerations and preferences be banished forever from our country, or should they be cleaned up and kept in place? Do we need a third party, or must we limp along with the two major parties we already have?

Such key writers as the Thernstroms, William Julius Wilson, Tom Wicker (grouping Wilson and Wicker for the moment), differ so radically that one wonders if they live in the same country. Still some broad areas of agreement are discernible:

Some minorities have progressed

But how far? And at what cost?

By the conventional econometric standards of income, occupation, educational achievement, and home ownership, at least one-third of our black population is "middle-class."[167] The Thernstroms claim that about one-third of all black families now live in "generally integrated" suburbs.[168] In Wicker's words: "Despite the difficulties and disappointments of desegregation, despite continuing prejudice and discrimination, numerous African-Americans (have) made economic progress that (compares) well with or (betters) that of whites moving up from poorer status into the middle class."[169] But the aftermath of this upward movement has been the "degradation of the ghetto, the communities . . . left behind."[170] As chronicled in Wilson's book, the last thirty-five years have witnessed the emergence of "a very poor, disproportionately African-American [underclass] living in drug-plagued, inner-city areas bereft of adequate job opportunities and hampered by inadequate public services."[171] The "lurid new visibility" of the ghetto underclass has largely obscured the growth of the black middle class.[172]

The Thernstroms are ambivalent. They note, and lament, the persistence of black poverty, yet hesitate to acknowledge its extent. According to Wilson, the disadvantaged African American population, particularly the ghetto poor, have regressed steadily since the early 1970s in terms of joblessness, concentrated poverty, family breakup, and receipt of welfare. By 1993, "the average poor black family . . . slipped further below the poverty level than in any year since the Census Bureau started collecting such data in 1967."[173] In Wicker's terse formulation, "as the black middle class expanded, the urban underclass grew even faster."[174] It strains belief that this situation could prevail in such a wealthy country, especially during a period of unprecedented economic growth. The Thernstroms, however, point to the fact that "a majority of blacks are not poor, and a majority of poor Americans are not black."[175] It is difficult to see what bearing such statistical nostrums, even if valid, can have on the fact that inner-city poverty is intensely concentrated within all our major cities, and has an "overwhelmingly racial cast."[176]

There has been a growth in the Hispanic middle class, but that growth has been concentrated among the U.S.-born.[177] To Douglas Massey, Hispanics as a whole have lost ground since the 1980s when tougher border/immigration controls impeded return migration resulting in the greater exploitation of illegals. Consequently, during the 1990s Hispanics—who traditionally held a middle economic position between blacks and whites—suffered income decline and impoverishment increases[178] "reaching levels comparable to those historically observed among African Americans."[179]

Massey paints a mixed picture for females. Female employment has become socially validated as of late, and most women now hold paying jobs. Growing male/female wage equalization is manifest. Well-educated, upper-class women have it better now in the employment arena than before, even though a "glass ceiling" keeps them from the highest positions.[180]

Uneducated, lower-class women are restricted to unskilled, low-mobility jobs and have become less attractive as marriage partners with the onset of effective contraception. Those who marry often face husbands with stagnant incomes not yet ready to assume more equal household and parenting duties.[181]

Racial/ethnic tensions persist

Beyond this, total disagreement prevails.

The Thernstroms contend that America has largely overcome its odious legacy of racism. The hard-core white variety is extinct. There have been "incidents" in recent years, but the level of racial animosity has been greatly exaggerated by politicians, including President Clinton, the "civil rights lobby," the academy, and most of the "mainstream media." In fact, racial tolerance is now the prevailing social norm. True, most African Americans do not believe this; but this is because they too often come in contact with the "wrong" kinds of whites, and have not yet developed an immunity to false racist innuendo ("psycho-facts"). In time, this too will pass. Racial attitudes are undergoing great change.[182] For instance, white opposition to affirmative action, fair housing, and "other racial questions," stems primarily from political ideology, unrelated to "gut feelings toward African Americans."[183] Also, white opposition to residential integration, once the norm, has declined rapidly in recent years;[184] "white attitudes would seem to allow for considerably more residential integration than is actually to be found in our cities today."[185]

The provocative writer and Berkeley professor John McWhorter can be placed in the same "racism has dramatically declined" camp as the Thernstroms. In his *Winning the Race* (2006), McWhorter highlights the popularity of Halle Berry among white children and the high positions gained by African Americans such as Colin Powell and Condoleezza Rice as evidence of racism's atrophy.[186] (Doubtless, he would have cited Barack

Obama's phenomenal appeal in this connection had it blossomed when he was writing his book.) The charge of racism by African Americans, in McWhorter's view, is a pestilence:

> Hovering ever in the background; it provides a standing excuse for mediocrity, teaching many blacks a visceral wariness of whites divorced from personal experience; it discourages promotions as blacks under its influence often cannot form the social bonds with white superiors and coworkers that partly determine who is moved upward. Lending a sense that school is the domain of The Man, it discourages black students from embracing knowledge for its own sake, and decreases even middle-class black students' test scores. It teaches other Americans that blacks consider themselves exempt from reason (i.e., are dumb and self-righteous). It keeps us from coming together—and does nothing to help black people move forward.[187]

The Thernstroms and McWhorter are simply not reading from the same page as Wilson, Wicker, and Edley. Wilson reports that racial antagonisms are rife in urban America. Relations among all our races, not just black and white, have soured. Ghetto joblessness, crime, and gang violence are perceived to spill over into other parts of our cities, resulting in "fierce class antagonisms" in the higher-income black communities located near the ghettos, and heightened antiblack racial animosity, among central-city and suburban whites, and especially among lower-income white ethnic and Latino groups who live near the black ghettos. In essence, a racial/ethnic struggle for power and privilege is being waged by have-nots in the central cities, and has flowed over into the rest of the metropolitan areas.[188] Wilson, writing in 2006, argued that while many still hoped for a residentially integrated America, his research maintains that urban areas would "remain divided culturally and racially" with "profound implications" for "racial and ethnic relations."[189]

Wicker's findings speak for themselves: American cities are hotbeds of racial animosities. Racial "incidents" in school buildings and college campuses are commonplace. Old hate groups have reemerged and new ones have formed. Worse, evidence of animosity toward or disdain for the other race can be found even among educated middle-class whites and African Americans.[190]

Edley offers the bleakest vision of all. America's attitudes and behavior about race are akin to "a deep . . . neurosis, a mental disorder or illness."[191] Our nation suffers from "a virulent strain of resistant racism, gut-pure and as simple as sin."[192] These racial tensions cannot be dissolved "by reason, by passion, or by experience."[193] The most we can hope for is an armistice, a "constructive peace."[194]

If, as reported by the Tomas Rivera Institute, U.S.-born Hispanics receive societal treatment roughly equal to that of non-Hispanic whites,[195] that surely is not the lot of Hispanic immigrants according to the way Douglas Massey sees the United States. They have been denigrated as unworthy inhabitants by academics (e.g., Samuel Huntington) and political pundits (e.g., Patrick Buchanan). The public's mind has been poisoned. Polls taken by the Pew Charitable Trust make clear that most Americans regard Latino immigrants as a national millstone "because they take our jobs, housing, and health care."[196] Most of the thirty-five million post-1935 legal immigrants who came to the United States were Hispanic. Many more Hispanic immigrants are undocumented, and they are the most despised.[197]

Orlando Patterson's *The Ordeal of Integration*[198] calls for an affirmative action compromise as to its length of operations. Patterson is a distinguished scholar of slavery and a maverick polemicist. The book is a "jihad" against "the dogmatic ethnic advocates and extremists"[199] of the Left and Right who are polluting reasoned discourse with poisoned evaluations of black America's condition, including the outrageous lie that the nation is wallowing in an intractable race crisis.[200]

In Patterson's opinion, our forty-year antidiscrimination program has been a great success in that (with carefully noted exceptions) it has moved our country "toward greater integration . . . not merely in neighborhoods, but in the economic, social, cultural, political, and moral life of the nation. . . . Afro-Americans, from a status of semiliterate social outcasts as late as the early fifties, have now become an integral part of American civilization and are so recognized both within the nation and outside it."[201]

To Patterson, the "two nations" and "racism forever" views are criminally perpetrated by the mass media (which thrives on ghetto carrion); pundits; and race leaders (whose punditry and brokerage roles are exalted by the perpetual-racism thesis); and by timorous liberal academics who remain politically correct in order to avoid "Tom" and "Oreo" and similar epithets.[202] Actually, black/white relations have never been better even though the races largely remain geographically separate.[203] Further, blacks are positive about their own situation. Survey research tells us that fewer than 40 percent of African Americans feel that they have been subject to discriminatory treatment, although most feel that blacks generally are mistreated.[204] For many, integration has been painful, if not traumatic, but African American progress—though far from complete—has been nothing short of "astonishing"; indeed, in many respects, "unparalleled," "amazing," even "extraordinary."[205]

Patterson's sanguine appraisal of black America's situation echoes the Thernstrom optimistic view,[206] even going one step farther in rhapsodizing the lot of the "vast majority" of blacks.[207] Like the Thernstroms, he fully acknowledges the dreadful problems of the urban underclass, but intimates that this situation may be improving.[208] And like them he fiercely denounces the "out-of-touch" nay-sayers and "pessimists."[209]

However, Patterson and the Thernstroms are directly at odds over the reasons for Afro-American upward mobility. Without a whiff of supporting social science data, Patterson argues that affirmative action has been "the single most important factor accounting for the rise of a significant Afro-American middle class."[210] As noted, the Thernstroms find it impossible to attribute special significance to affirmative action in the upward economic advance experienced by blacks since the 1940s.[211] They also maintained that preference/affirmative action is illegal, counterproductive, and perpetuates racism; therefore they demand its immediate abolition and restoration of traditional color-blindness, and other meritocratic values.[212] Patterson acknowledges that affirmative action condemned by the Thernstroms has flaws, but (as we discussed and critiqued at 23–24) he would nevertheless compromise and maintain protected-group preferences for the next fifteen years, phasing it out and ultimately replacing it with class-based preferences for the American-born poor.[213]

Patterson's position regarding affirmative action and integration is not an unqualified success. He has failed to define affirmative action. While it is reasonably clear that he equates affirmative action with preferences and disparate-impact remediation, such a matter should not be left to inference, particularly given Patterson's preoccupation with semantic rigor. Thus—to exorcise the demons misrepresenting the nature of America's social relationships—requires, Patterson insists, a change in our vocabulary. In his stern regime, terms such as *race*, *black*, *white*, *race relations*, and *racism* give way to *ethnic groups*, *Afro-Americans*, *Euro-Americans*, and *ethnocentrism* or *class prejudice*.[214]

Patterson is of two minds with respect to the success of integration. On the one hand, he proclaims its success, telling us that black/white relations have never been better.[215] Later, he ruefully notes that there is a strong trend toward voluntary resegregation on and off campuses,[216] which to him amounts to a "lamentable betrayal and abandonment of the once cherished goal of integration."[217]

Patterson's presentation is marked by an arresting and sometimes breathtaking eclecticism. His basic posture is light years away from "pessimists" such as Edley, Wilson, and Wicker. Yet his support[218] of a diversity rationale for affirmative action reads like Edley's brief[219] for the same; and his proposal for class-based affirmative action could have been written by Wilson or Wicker. He cannot abide dogma, but is not above a little himself, as witness his bald claim that ultimately integration must mean intermarriage.[220] All told, his book is a compelling example of the rich diversity in the equal rights debate, and a clarion call for further scholarly study.

Public opinion research can help sort out the quarrel over race perceptions. One of the most impressive recent works in this field is Donald R. Kinder and Lynn M. Sanders's *Divided by Color*.[221] The subject of this book is the basis of the views white and black Americans hold on matters of race. Of the authors' voluminous findings,[222] the most relevant are:

1. The most striking feature of public opinion on race is how emphatically black and white Americans disagree with each other. Race has been and remains our most difficult subject. In this area, unlike most others concerned with public policy, American opinion is tenaciously firm, consistent, and more difficult to alter.

2. Many whites support racial equality in principle, but are considerably less enthusiastic about policies for bringing the principle to life.

3. The differences between blacks and whites over equal opportunity, social welfare assistance to blacks, and affirmative action are "extraordinary." Overwhelming white majorities oppose affirmative action of the disparate-impact variety; overwhelming black majorities support it. However, of all antidiscrimination policies, affirmative action is the least popular among blacks and whites alike.

4. The most important, though not the only, determinant of white public opinion on race policy is racial resentment based on the stereotypical notion that blacks are "unwilling to try and too willing to take what they have not earned."[223] "Most whites believe that their racial group is more industrious, smarter, more loyal, less violent, and more self-reliant than blacks."[224]

5. Most black Americans support remedial affirmative action in principle, but feel that it has not yet been implemented in education and employment. Blacks continue to believe that they face discrimination in schooling and employment, among other areas.

6. Racial differences are not a "mask for class differences." Race, not class, divides contemporary American society over social policy.

7. Racial differences in American politics are more dramatic now than ever before.

8. The racial divide is deep, widening, and persistent. There is no reason to believe that it is about to become obsolete.

At pages 269–272 of their text, Kinder and Sanders address the body of "notable and in many ways admirable"[225] opinion research that tends to support the Thernstroms' views, including Paul Sniderman and Thomas Piazza's *The Scar of Race*,[226] cited by the Thernstroms as an "important book."[227] Under the heading "Whitewashing Prejudice," Kinder and Sanders squarely reject the central theme of these works, namely, that white racism is no longer (to cite Sniderman and Piazza) "the primary factor [in] the contemporary arguments over the politics of race."[228] Notwithstanding that "revolutionary changes" have taken place in white Americans' racial attitudes, they maintain that "resentments rooted in racial difference continue to shape American opinion powerfully."[229]

Readers skilled in reading scholarly tea leaves will draw their own conclusions. The Wilson-Wicker class-plus-race recipe seems to deserve serious consideration, but there are at least two drawbacks. First, as Kinder and Sanders have demonstrated, class is not an issue for most Americans. Second, there is little momentum for the creation of a new political coalition, or third party, dedicated to promoting class preferences for the poor.

Those who follow Kinder and Sanders will surely question the Thernstroms' position.[230] Moreover, in Randall Kennedy's *Race, Crime, and the Law*,[231] they will find ample grounds for skepticism about some of the Thernstroms' views on crime. This is a study of race discrimination in our criminal justice system. Kennedy's much-needed, ably researched and written treatise concerns itself with the legal dimensions in the area: for instance, the staggeringly disgraceful history of unequal application of the criminal law to African Americans; the use of race as a proxy for dangerousness; race and the death penalty; race and drug law; and race and the composition of juries.

Indisputably, blacks and crime is the most incendiary aspect of race relations in this country. Many whites instinctively associate blackness and crime, despite the fact that the majority of blacks are law-abiding. On the other hand, many blacks are consumed by cynicism, mistrust, and outrage over the police and the courts. Professor Kennedy has been widely acclaimed for his evenhandedness. He has declared a deep reluctance "to use racial criteria in efforts to redress racial disadvantage."[232] He insists upon a Constitution that "looks beyond looks." Color-blind administration of the criminal law is his essential remedy. Accordingly, he disapproves of race/ethnic-conscious jury member selection, an affirmative action focus that has received considerable scholarly and political support. Race/ethnic-consciousness in this connection takes on a variety of dimensions: selecting trial venues that would facilitate the selection of diverse juries; removing whites from a potential jury roll call to achieve racial balance; and the set-aside of a particular number of seats for minorities.[233]

Race/ethnic consciousness in jury selection is supported by notions that the presence of diverse minority attitudes would improve jury deliberations, making them more sensitive to minority conditions and less open to antiminority bias. Remedying the underrepresentation of minorities on juries would also increase minority civic participation and commitment. Kennedy found these sentiments substantial, but not controlling. For one, minority underrepresentation on juries could be ameliorated in a number of race-neutral ways such as relying on tax rolls for jury selectees (which are likely to contain more minorities than the oft-used voter registration rolls), increasing compensation for jury service, and prohibiting employer retaliation for jury service.[234] But race/ethnic selection would, in Kennedy's mind, be harmful by perpetuating the view that "Americans of different hues cannot hope to entrust themselves to the fair judgments of others [and] would therefore likely deepen racial distrust at the very moment it attempts to establish a hedge against racial misconduct."[235]

"Jury nullification" on racial grounds is also rejected by Kennedy. The nullification doctrine calls for jury repudiation of guilt where it is established beyond a reasonable doubt. Here, Kennedy focused on Professor Paul Butler's version of jury nullification as stated in *Racially Based Jury Nullification: Black Power in the Criminal Justice System*.[236] To Butler, white racism is the cause of much black criminality. The antidote is nullification by African American jurors for less serious nonviolent crimes performed by blacks. For more serious nonviolent crimes (such as perjury), black jurors should consider nullification if the benefits of black community rehabilitation of the guilty outweigh the costs to that community.[237]

Kennedy sees Butler's thinking as egregiously flawed. Black criminals, as a result of racism, are wrongly pictured by Butler as incapable of making moral choices, and thus are blameless. Ignored by Butler were the improvements in the operations of the criminal justice system, such as the sizeable increase in the number of black police officers and chiefs. Also ignored is the insistence in black communities for imposition of harsher criminal punishment rather than more lenient.[238] Most importantly, Butler supports the notion that jurors should treat their "own kind" better than others. Advancing this regrettable thesis "would demolish the moral framework upon which an effective and compelling" challenge to racial injustice must be structured.[239]

To Kennedy, racial disparities in the criminal justice system do not necessarily reflect racial bias, and he condemns "activists" for automatically citing statistical disparities as proof of police bias.[240] (The Thernstroms make the same point at pages 272–274 of *America in Black and White*.) He acknowledges frequent racial maltreatment of black suspects, defendants, and criminals, but stresses that "more burdensome now in the day-to-day lives of African Americans are private, violent criminals (typically black) who attack those most vulnerable without regard to racial identity"[241]—a judgment that earned him a commendation in the Thernstrom book.[242]

But there is another side to Kennedy, which the Thernstroms have not cited. While, as mentioned, he cautions against overplaying racial disparities, he is also fully aware that they often point directly to official racism. He demands an end to indiscriminate racial profiling/stop-and-search police techniques.[243] Importantly, he scathingly denounces the courts for rejecting statistical evidence of bias in capital cases. (See the notorious *McCleskey* case.)[244] It is fair to say that Professor Kennedy would not second the Thernstroms' opinion that the argument that racism infects our policing is essentially meritless.[245]

Princeton sociology professor Bruce Western cites racism as a partial factor in what he calls the "mass imprisonment" of poor black males.[246] At the turn of the new millennium, some 30 percent of non-college educated blacks[247] had been imprisoned by their early thirties, and the risk of incarceration for that cohort was about three times greater than it was twenty years earlier. Prison had become a common occurrence for that group.

Western attributes the mass imprisonment of poor black males in the last portion of the twentieth century to a number of causes: increased employment difficulties; the rejection of rehabilitative techniques as alternatives to jail time; the increased political demand for more "law and order." In part, the "law and order" mantra was prompted by a racist response to the civil rights protests and gains associated with the rights movement of the 1960s and 1970s. But the main drivers consisted of black male occupational marginality and family fragmentation rooted in mass imprisonment itself. Importantly, civil rights gains were substantially offset by the woeful expansion of black incarceration.[248]

Conclusion

In the federal regime of modern civil rights reform, race, ethnic, gender, and disability-based affirmative action has had an extraordinary career of ups and downs. To its friends, affirmative action has been regarded as an important element in the battle against the oppressiveness visited upon minorities, females, and the disabled—a battle that also requires much greater public attention to factors beyond invidious discrimination such as family planning, trade practices with low-wage countries, antitrust law, monetary policy, national full employment policy,[249] and the often complex problems of reasonable accommodation for the handicapped.

Affirmative action reduces to the application of special assistance (including preferences) in order to achieve proportional representation of minorities, females, and the disabled in the workplace and other spheres from which they have been discriminatorily excluded. While experiencing pendulum swings of approval and disapproval in the courts of law and public opinion, remedial preferences and other assistance have become embedded in our government apparatus as well as the corporate and educational establishments. From the beginning, affirmative action has been a creature of racial, ethnic, gender, and disability-group political activity. Even though it cannot and does not claim that it has brought about equal opportunity, its abolition would undoubtedly exacerbate tensions among its recipients. Presently, given the scarcity of jobs for all, affirmative action may be in danger of extinction at the hands of an increasingly unemployed and outraged citizenry. In what may well be affirmative action's eleventh hour, its advocates seek, so far with only limited success, judicial and popular approval of a nonremedial rationale of "diversity."

Nonetheless, there is no way of telling who will win the war we have tried to chronicle in these pages. It bears remembering that leading voices which may have the final say—the Congress and the judiciary—have not yet spoken clearly. Until they do, the outcome of the war will be unknown.

We end by referencing Steven Steinberg's *Turning Back*.[250] This volume is affirmative action's "Book of Lamentations." He gives credit to the "civil rights movement" and the remedial legislation of the 1960s for liberating African American citizens from "Jim Crow" official racism.[251] However, he passionately condemns the society for not "following through" on these advances by creating the conditions of economic and social equality thus far thwarted by white racism.[252] This, he states, has been the mission of affirmative action. However, not only are there "persistent and even widening gaps between blacks and whites in incomes and living standards,"[253] but there is an "ominous new trend to blame blacks for the ills that afflict American society."[254]

The country, Steinberg maintains, is at a "crossroads, still uncertain whether to take the road back to the benighted past, or to forge a new path . . . to a historical reconciliation between black and white citizens."[255] What will it take to resolve this dilemma, perhaps to "move history forward again?"[256] Steinberg's answer: " 'the mounting pressure' that emanates from those segments of black society that have little reason to acquiesce in the racial status quo. It has yet to be seen exactly what form resistance and protest will take."[257]

One fervently hopes that this Cassandra is mistaken. It may be that the "resistance" will be led by minority-group leaders who balance their racially and ethnically specific demands with a strong concern for all-group progress. Political scientist Zoltan Hajmal has demonstrated that such black mayors have reduced racial tension and won white support both for themselves and minority-assistance programs.[258] Hopefully, President Obama can replicate this experience for the nation as a whole. But one cannot suppress the gnawing sadness of the notion that if our economic ills deepen, suffering will be widespread. The response of both minority and majority, in growing hard times, will likely be fevered and passionate. Affirmative action offers itself as a convenient scapegoat for majority discontent. If one or more of affirmative action's group remedies are jettisoned in the near term, how will its successor, if any, come into being? And what will it be? We await the future with apprehension.

Appendix One

A Sampler of Federal Affirmative Action
Programs Explicitly Mandated
or Authorized by Statute or
Administrative Regulation

This sampler consists of verbatim excerpts from a number of sources: The material under the titles of *Equal Employment Opportunity*, *Federal Grant and Procurement Law; Aiding Minorities and Women-Owned Businesses* is from two reports issued by the Congressional Research Service as cited below. The information in these reports has been rearranged, and placed under some titles devised by the authors/editors of this volume. The abbreviation U.S.C.S. or U.S.C.A. therein has been changed to U.S.C. The writing under the title of *Military Recruiting and Integration* is from a report to President Clinton. Additionally, an *Authors' Note* (353–54) provides the authors' summary of the briefs submitted by retired military and Defense Department officials in connection with the *Grutter/Gratz* (2003)[1] and *Parents Involved v. Seattle* (2007)[2] cases. These briefs provide information about affirmative action policies in the military.

Equal Employment Opportunity

The evolution of federal law and policy regarding affirmative action in employment may be traced to a series of executive orders dating to the 1960s which prohibit discrimination and require affirmative action by contractors with the federal government.[3] The Office of Federal Contract Compliance Programs, an arm of the U.S. Department of Labor, currently enforces the E.O. (Executive Order) 11246, as amended, by means of a regulatory program requiring larger federal contractors, those with procurement or construction contracts in excess of $50,000, to make a "good faith effort" to attain "goals and timetables" to remedy underutilization of minorities and women.

Public and private employers with fifteen or more employees are also subject to a comprehensive code of equal employment opportunity regulation under Title VII of the 1964 Civil Rights Act.[4] Except as may be imposed by court order to remedy "egregious" violations of the law, or by consent decree to settle pending claims, however, there is no general statutory obligation on employers to adopt affirmative action measures. But the EEOC (Equal Employment Opportunity Commission) has issued guidelines to protect employers and unions from charges of "reverse discrimination" when they voluntarily take action to correct the effects of past discrimination.[5] Federal departments and agencies, by contrast, are required to periodically formulate affirmative action plans for their employees and a "minority recruitment program" to eliminate minority "underrepresentation" in specific federal job categories.

Section 717 of the 1972 Amendments to Title VII of the 1964 Civil Rights Act empowers the Equal Employment Opportunity Commission to enforce nondiscrimination policy in federal employment by "necessary and appropriate" rules, regulations, and orders and through "appropriate remedies, including reinstatement or hiring of employees, with or without back-pay."[6] Each federal department and agency, in turn, is required to prepare annually a "national and regional equal employment opportunity plan" for submission to the EEOC as part of "an affirmative program of equal employment opportunity for all . . . employees and applicants for employment."[7]

Section 717 was reinforced in 1978 when Congress enacted major federal civil service reforms including a mandate for immediate development of a "minority recruitment program" designed to eliminate "underrepresentation" of minority groups in specific federal job categories.[8] The EEOC and Office of Personnel Management have issued rules to guide implementation and monitoring of minority recruitment programs by individual federal agencies. Among various other specified requirements, each agency plan "must include annual specific determinations of underrepresentation for each group and must be accompanied by quantifiable indices by which progress toward eliminating under-representation can be measured."[9]

In addition, the following [are among the] statutes and regulations [that] relate to employment policies of the federal government or under federal grant and assistance programs. . . .

5 U.S.C. § 4313(5): Performance appraisal in the Senior Executive Services to take account of individuals' "meeting affirmative action goals, achievement of equal employment opportunity requirements, and compliance with merit principles . . ." . . . .

22 U.S.C. § 4141(b): Establishes the Foreign Service Internship Program "to promote the Foreign Service as a viable and rewarding career opportunity for qualified individuals who reflect the cultural and ethnic diversity of the United States. . . ."

42 U.S.C. § 282(h): The Secretary of HHS [Health and Human Services], and the National Institutes of Health, "shall, in conducting and supporting program for research, research training, recruitment, and other activities, provide for an increase in the number of women and individuals from disadvantaged backgrounds (including racial and ethnic minorities) in the fields of biomedical and behavioral research. . . ." . . .

Executive Order 13116 (2000): Requires Federal agencies to examine services and prepare a plan "to improve access to federally conducted and federally assisted programs and activities for persons who, as a result of national origin, are limited in their English proficiency." (See also Executive Order 50123.)

Executive Order 13171 (2000): The head of each executive department and agency shall establish and maintain a program for the recruitment and career development of Hispanics in Federal employment.

Federal Grant and Procurement Law; Aiding Minority and Women-Owned Businesses

Federal efforts to increase minority and female participation in contracting, federally assisted programs, and employment have been a major aspect of civil rights enforcement for more than three decades.[10] Congress and the Executive Branch have crafted a wide range of federal laws and regulations authorizing, either directly or by judicial or administrative interpretation, race or gender "conscious" strategies in relation to jobs, housing, education, voting rights, and governmental contracting. The historical model for federal laws and regulations establishing minority participation "goals" may be found in Executive Orders which since the early 1960's have imposed affirmative minority hiring and employment requirements on federally financed construction projects and in connection with other large federal contracts. Presently, Executive Order 11246, as administered by the Office of Federal Contract Compliance Programs (OFCCP), requires that all employers with federal contracts in excess of $50,000 must file written affirmative action plans with the government. These are to include minority and female hiring goals and timetables to which the contractor must commit its "good faith" efforts. Similar affirmative action measures relating to federal government employment were enacted as part of the Equal Employment Opportunity Act Amendment of 1972[11] and the 1978 Civil Service Reform Act.[12]

Affirmative action for minority entrepreneurs soon became a focus of efforts by the Small Business Administration (SBA) and other federal agencies to assist "socially and economically disadvantaged" small businesses under a variety of federal programs. Increasingly, an "affirmative action" model, in the form of participation "goals" or "set-asides" for members of racial or ethnic minorities, and businesses owned or controlled by these or other "disadvantaged" persons, found legislative expression in a wide range of federal programs.

The Small Business Act, as amended, provides the statutory prototype for a host of federal programs to increase minority and female participation as contractors or subcontractors on federally funded projects. First, the "Minority Small Business and Capital Ownership Development," or § 8(a) program authorizes the Small Business Administration (SBA) to enter into all kinds of construction, supply, and service contracts with other federal departments and agencies. The SBA acts as a prime contractor and then "subcontracts" the performance of these contracts to small business concerns owned and controlled by "socially and economically disadvantaged" individuals, Indian Tribes or Hawaiian Native Organizations.[13]

Applicants for § 8 (a) certification must demonstrate "socially disadvantaged" status or that they "have been subjected to racial or ethnic prejudice or cultural bias because of their identities as members of groups without regard to their individual qualities."[14] The Small Business Administration "presumes," absent contrary evidence, that small businesses owned and operated by members of certain groups—including Blacks, Hispanics, Native Americans, and Asian Pacific Americans—are socially disadvantaged.[15] Any individual not a member of one of these groups must prove "social disadvantage" by a "preponderance" of evidence in order to qualify for § 8(a) certification. The § 8(a) applicant must, in addition, show that "economic disadvantage" has diminished its capital and credit opportunities, thereby limiting its ability to compete with other firms in the open market.[16]

The "Minority Small Business Subcontracting Program" authorized by § 8(d) of the Small Business Act codified the presumption of disadvantaged status for minority group members that applied by SBA regulation under the § 8(a) program.[17] Prime contractors on major federal contracts are obliged by § 8(d) to maximize minority participation and to negotiate a "subcontracting plan" with the procuring agency which includes "percentage goals" for utilization of small socially and economically disadvantaged firms (SDBs). To implement this policy, a clause required for inclusion in each such prime contract states that "[t]he contractors shall presume that socially and economically disadvantaged individuals include Black Americans, Hispanic Americans, Native Americans, Asian Pacific Americans, and other minorities, or any other individual found to be disadvantaged by the Administration pursuant to § 8(a) . . ." Accordingly, SBA has discretion in designating a firm or individual as socially and economically disadvantaged for purposes of both the § 8(a) and § 8(d) programs in conformity with specified criteria.[18]

These obligations, first codified in 1978 as an amendment to the SBA, were augmented a decade later by the Business Opportunity Development Reform Act of 1988.[19] Congress there directed the president to set annual, government-wide procurement goals of at least 20 percent for small businesses and 5 percent for disadvantaged businesses, as defined by the SBA. Simultaneously, federal agencies were required to continue to adopt their own goals, compatible with the government-wide goals, in an effort to create "maximum practicable opportunity" for small disadvantaged businesses to sell their goods and services to the government. The goals may be waived where not practicable due to unavailability of disadvantaged business enterprises (DBEs) in the relevant area and other factors.[20] While the statutory definition of DBE includes a racial component, in terms of presumptive eligibility, it is not restricted to racial minorities but also includes persons subjected to "ethnic prejudice or cultural bias."[21] It also excludes businesses owned or controlled by persons who, regardless of race, are "not truly socially and/or economically disadvantaged."[22] Federal Acquisition Act amendments adopted in 1994 amended the 5 percent minority procurement goal, and the minority subcontracting requirements in § 8(d), to specifically include "small business concerns owned and controlled by women" in addition to "socially and economically disadvantaged individuals."[23]

In addition, Congress has frequently adopted "set-asides" or other forms of statutory preference for "socially and economically disadvantaged" firms and individuals, following the definitions of the Small Business Act, or by designating minority groups and women as part of specific grant or contract authorization programs. Thus, targeted funding, in various forms, and minority or disadvantaged business set-asides or preferences have been included in major authorization or appropriation measures for agriculture, communications, defense, education, public works, transportation, foreign relations, energy and water development, banking, scientific research and space exploration, and other purposes. Other federal laws appear to authorize some consideration of race or gender to enhance the participation of minorities and women in federal programs or employment but without directly mandating preferential goals or set-asides.

The following statutes, regulations, and executive orders governing federal contracts and grant programs are, to the extent possible, grouped according to agency and subject matter. . . .

Agriculture[24]

7 U.S.C. § 2279: "The Secretary of Agriculture shall carry out an outreach and technical assistance program to encourage and assist socially disadvantaged farmers and ranchers in owning and operating farms and ranches" and participating in agricultural programs." Socially disadvantaged is "a group whose members have been subjected to racial or ethnic prejudice because of their identity as members of a group without regard to their individual qualities" (§ 2279(e)). . . .

7 U.S.C. § 3241(a): The Secretary is authorized to make grants to "Hispanic-serving institutions for the purpose of promoting and strengthening the ability of Hispanic-serving institutions to carry out education, applied research, and related community development programs." . . .

7 C.F.R. § 272.4(b) (2004): Bilingual program information and certification, and interpreters must be provided in certain low income areas with specified percentages of non–English speaking minority households under Food Stamp and Food Distribution Program. . . .

7 C.F.R. § 1944.671(b) (2004): Equal Opportunity and outreach requirements applicable to FmHA Housing Preservation Grants program state that "[a]s a measure of compliance, the percentage of the individuals served by the HPG grantee should be in proportion to the percentages of the population of the service area by race/national origin." . . .

7 C.F.R. §§ 3403.1, 3403.2 (2004): USDA regulation implementing small business innovation grants program has as one of its goals to "foster and encourage the participation of socially and economically disadvantaged small business concerns and women owned small business concerns." For this purpose, minority groups specifically covered include "Black Americans, Hispanic Americans, Native Americans, Asian Pacific Americans, or Subcontinent Asian Americans," or any others designated by the SBA pursuant to § 8(a). . . .

Banking[25]

12 U.S.C. § 1441a(r-w): Provides for various incentives . . . to preserve and expand bank ownership by minorities and women; authorizes establishment of Resolution Trust Corporation guidelines to achieve parity in distribution of RTC contracts, and "reasonable goals" for subcontracting, to minority and women-owned businesses and firms. . . .

12 U.S.C. § 4520: The Federal National Mortgage Association and Federal Home Loan Mortgage Corporation shall establish a minority outreach program to ensure the inclusion of minorities and women in their contractual transactions.

12 C.F.R. § 4.63 (2003): Establishes Contracting Outreach Program for the Office of Comptroller of the Currency to "ensure that minority and women-owned businesses have the opportunity to participate, to the maximum extent possible, in contracts awarded by the OCC." "Minority means any African American, Native American, . . . Hispanic American, Asian-Pacific American, or Subcontinent-Asian American." Id. at § 462(b). . . .

Commerce. . . .[26]

15 U.S.C. § 7404: "The Director of the National Science Foundation shall establish a program to award grants to institutions (including minority serving

institutions) of higher education to establish or improve undergraduate and master's degree programs in computer and network security, to increase the number of students, including the number of students from groups historically underrepresented in these fields . . ."

Executive Order 11625 (1971): Directs the Secretary of Commerce "[w]ith the participation of other Federal departments and agencies . . . [t]o develop comprehensive plans and specific program goals for the minority enterprise program; establish regular performance monitoring and reporting systems to assure that goals are being achieved; and evaluate the impact of Federal support in achieving the objectives established by the order." *See also* Executive Order 12138 (Women-owned Business Enterprise Program). . . .

15 C.F.R. § 917.11(d) (2004): A "factor considered" in the approval of proposals under the Sea Grant Matched Funding Program "will be the potential of the proposed program to stimulate interest in marine related careers among those individuals; for example, minorities, women, and the handicapped whose previous background or training might not have generated such an interest."

15 C.F.R. § 2301.5 (2004): The National Telecommunications and Information Administration of the Department of Commerce, in administering the Public Telecommunications Facilities Program, "will give special consideration to applications that foster ownership and control of, operation of, and participation in public telecommunication entities by minorities and women." *See also* id. at §2301.17(b)(6). . . .

Communications[27]

47 U.S.C. § 309(i)(3)(A): "The [Federal Communications]Commission shall establish rules and procedures to ensure that, in the administration of any system of random selection . . . used for granting licenses or construction permits for any media of mass communications, significant preferences will be granted to applicants or groups of applicants, the grant to which of the license or permit would increase the diversification of ownership of the media of mass communications. To further diversify the ownership of media of mass communications, an additional significant preference shall be granted to any applicant controlled by a member or members of a minority group." For this purpose, "minority group" includes "Blacks, Hispanics, American Indians, Alaskan Natives, Asians, and Pacific Islanders." Id at §309(i)(4)(A).

47 U.S.C. § 309(j)(4)(D): In radio licensing proceedings, the Federal Communications Commission is directed to prescribe regulations to "ensure that small businesses, rural telephone companies, and businesses owned by members of minority groups and women are given the opportunity to participate in the provision of spectrum-based services and, for such

purposes, consider the use of tax certificates, bidding preferences, and other procedures."

47 U.S.C. § 396(a)(6): The Corporation for Public Broadcasting is directed to "encourage the development of programming . . . that addresses the needs of unserved and underserved audiences, particularly children and minorities." . . .

68 F.C.C. 2d 983 (1978): FCC "Distress Sale" Policy. Under this policy, existing licensees in jeopardy of having their licenses revoked or whose licenses have been designated for a renewal hearing are given the option of selling the license to a minority-owned or controlled firm for up to 75 percent of fair market value. The minority-assignee must meet the basic qualifications necessary to hold a license under FCC regulations and must be approved by the FCC before the transfer is consummated.

Defense[28]

10 U.S.C. § 2191: The Secretary shall take appropriate action to encourage applications for the National Defense Science and Engineering Graduate Fellowships from persons who are member of groups (minority groups, women, and disabled persons) which historically have been underrepresented in science and technology fields.

10 U.S.C. § 2193: The Secretary shall give priority to awarding grants for higher education in science and mathematics "in a manner likely to stimulate the interest of women and members of minority groups in pursuing scientific and engineering careers. The Secretary may consider the financial need of applicants in making awards."

10 U.S.C. § 2194: Defense laboratories shall ensure priority consideration to historically Black colleges and universities and other minority institutions in entering into education partnership agreements. . . .

10 U.S.C. § 2323: Establishes a goal of awarding 5 percent of the total value of Department of Defense, Coast Guard, and the National Aeronautics and Space Administration contracts and subcontracts to socially and economically disadvantaged individuals, historically black colleges and universities, and minority institutions, which includes Hispanic-serving institutions. This section is applicable to the Department of Defense during fiscal years 1987 through 2006. This section is applicable to the Coast Guard and the National Aeronautics and Space Administration during fiscal years 1995 through 2006. . . .

50 U.S.C. § 403: Requires the Director of Central Intelligence to carry out and report to Congress on a three-year pilot project to test and evaluate alternative, innovative methods to promote equality of intelligence community employment opportunities for women, minorities, and individu-

als with diverse ethnic and cultural backgrounds, skills, language proficiency, and expertise.

P.L. 108-106, 117 Stat. 1234, § 2217 (2003): "Requires activities carried out by the U.S. with respect to civilian governance of Afghanistan and Iraq to include advice from women's organizations, increase access of financial resources and assistance to women, and military and police force training to women." . . .

48 C.F.R. Part 219, § 219.000 (2003): DOD regulation implements "goal" in 10 U.S.C. 2323 to "[a]ward five percent of contract and subcontract dollars to small disadvantaged business (SDB) concerns, Historically black colleges and universities(HBCUs), and minority institutions (MIs)." Specific requirements include data collection and reporting (§ 219.202-5); eligibility criteria for program participation (§ 219.703); subcontracting plan goals for SDB concerns and institutions (§ 219.704); reviewing the subcontracting plan (§ 219.705-4); solicitation provisions and contract clauses (§ 219.708); and price evaluation adjustments for small disadvantaged business concerns as determined by the Commerce Department (§19.1101). See also 48 C.F.R. § 19.1202 (evaluation factors or subfactors for participation of SDB concerns); § 19.2003 (monetary incentives for subcontracting with SDB concerns); and § 252.219-7004) (small business and small disadvantaged business subcontracting plan on DOD contracts). . . .

Education[29]

20 U.S.C. § 1063b: Authorizes Education grants to specified postgraduate institutions "determined by the Secretary [of Education] to be making substantial contributions to the legal, medical, dental, veterinary, or other graduate education opportunities in mathematics, engineering, or the physical or natural sciences for Black Americans."

20 U.S.C. §§ 1070a-12; 1070a-13; 1070a-14; 1070-15; 1070-16: Authorizes Education grants under the Federal Trio Programs for various educational programs and services provided to individuals who are "underrepresented, disadvantaged, and/or students of limited English proficiency."

20 U.S.C. § 3916: Fifteen percent of National Science Foundation funds available for science and engineering education is to be allocated to faculty exchange and other programs involving higher educational institutions with "an enrollment which includes a substantial percentage of students who are members of a minority group, or who are economically or educationally disadvantaged and institutions which demonstrate a commitment to meet the special educational needs of students who are members of a minority group or are economically or educationally disadvantaged."

20 U.S.C. § 5205(d): No less than 10 percent of Eisenhower Exchange Fellowship Program funds "shall be available only for participation by individuals who are representative of United States minority populations." . . .

20 U.S.C. § 6662(c)(10): The Secretary is authorized to award grants to partnership (§ 6661(b)(1)) activities of the engineering, mathematics, science department of an institution of higher education and a high-need elementary and secondary school which include "training mathematics and science teachers and developing programs to encourage young women and other underrepresented individuals in mathematics and science careers to pursue post secondary degrees in majors leading to such careers." . . .

20 U.S.C. § 9579: Authorizes the Director of the Institute for Education Sciences to establish fellowships in "institutions of higher education (which may include . . . historically Black colleges and universities and other institutions of higher education with large numbers of minority students) that support graduate and postdoctoral study on site at the Institute or at the institution of higher education. . . . The Director shall ensure that women and minorities are actively recruited for participation."

42 U.S.C. § 1862d: At least 12 percent of amounts appropriated for the Academic Research Facilities Modernization Program shall be reserved for historically Black colleges and universities and other institutions which enroll a substantial percentage of Black American, Hispanic American, or Native American students. . . .

34 C.F.R. Parts 608, 609 (2003): "The Strengthening Historically Black Colleges and Universities Program [HBCU] provides grants to Historically Black Colleges and Universities to assist these institutions in establishing and strengthening their physical plants, academic resources and student services so that they may continue to participate in fulfilling the goal of equality of educational opportunity." . . .

Energy. . . .[30]

42 U.S.C. § 13556: Provides that "[t]o the extent practicable, the head of each agency shall provide that the obligation of not less than 10 percent of the total combined amounts obligated for contracts and subcontracts by each agency" under the Energy Policy Act of 1992 "shall be expended with" socially and economically disadvantaged individuals or women, historically Black colleges or universities, or college and universities with more than 20 percent Hispanic or Native American enrollment." . . .

10 C.F.R. Part 800 (2004): Sets forth DOE policies and procedures for the award and administration of loans to minority business enterprises. "The loans are to defray a percentage of the costs of obtaining DOE contracts and other agreements, including procurements, cooperative agreements, grants, loans, and loan guarantees. . . ." Id. at § 800.001. "Minority" refers to

"[a]n individual who is a citizen of the United States and who is a Negro, Puerto Rican, American Indian, Eskimo, Oriental, or Aleut, or is a Spanish speaking individual of Spanish descent. . . ." Id. at § 800.3. . . .

Environment[31]

P.L. 101-549, 104 Stat. 2399, 2708 (1990): "In providing for any research relating to requirements of the amendments made by the Clean Air Act Amendments of 1990 which uses funds of the Environmental Protection Agency [EPA], the Administrator of the [EPA] shall, to the extent practicable, require that not less than 10 percent of total Federal funding for such research will be made available to disadvantaged business concerns," defined to mean any concern with 51 percent of the stock owned by "Black Americans, Hispanic Americans, Native Americans, Asian Americans, Women or Disabled Americans."

40 C.F.R. § 1.25(d) (2003): EPA Office of Small and Disadvantaged Business Utilization "develops and implements a program to provide maximum utilization of women-owned business enterprises in all aspects of EPA contract work" and "develops programs to stimulate and improve involvement of small and minority business enterprises." . . .

Health and Housing[32]

42 U.S.C. § 3027(20): State plans for grant program on aging "shall provide assurances that special efforts will be made to provide technical assistance to minority providers of services."

42 C.F.R. § 52c.2 (2003): Minority Biomedical Research Support Program makes grants to higher educational institutions with 50 percent or other "significant proportion" of ethnic minority enrollment.

42 C.F.R. § 62.57(h) (2003): Among factors considered in making certain State loan repayment grants to State applicants is "[t]he extent to which special consideration will be extended to medically underserved areas with large minority populations." . . .

38 U.S.C. § 7303: Authorizes the Veteran's Administration to provide grants to medical research programs that conduct and support clinical research of women and minorities who are veterans. "The Secretary . . . shall foster and encourage the initiation and expansion of research relating to the health of veterans who are women." . . .

48 C.F.R. § 2426.101 (2003): States the policy of the Department of Housing and Urban Development "to foster and promote Minority Business Enterprise (MBE) participation in its procurement program, to the extent permitted by law and consistent with its primary mission." For this purpose, "minority" includes members of any group designated as "socially

disadvantaged" by the SBA under the § 8(a). *See also* 48 C.F.R. § 2452.219-70 (Small Business and Small Disadvantaged Business Subcontracting Plan to include percentage goals).

Interior[33]

16 U.S.C. § 1445c: The Secretary of the Department of Interior shall establish and administer through the National Ocean Service the Dr. Nancy Foster Scholarship Program to provide graduate education scholarships in oceanography, marine biology or maritime archeology particularly to women and members of minority groups. . . .

    43 C.F.R. § 27.6 (2003): Affirmative action plan requirements for recipient of financial assistance from the Department of Interior include "specific goals and specific timetables to which its efforts will be directed, to correct all deficiencies and thus to increase materially the participation of minorities and women in all aspects of its operation." . . .

Justice. . . .[34]

31 U.S.C. § 6701(f): Not less than 10 percent of the amount paid from the Local Government Fiscal Assistance Fund created by the Violent Crime Control Act shall be expended on contracts or subcontracts with socially and economically disadvantaged and women-owned small businesses, historically Black colleges and universities, and higher educational institutions with more than 20 percent Hispanic or Native-American student enrollment. . . .

    28 C.F.R. § 42.206 (c)(1) (2003): Recipients of Criminal Justice Improvement Act funds shall be selected for post-award compliance reviews in part on the basis of "[t]he relative disparity between the percentage of minorities, or women, in the relevant labor market, and the percentage of minorities, or women, employed by the recipient." . . .

Labor. . . .[35]

20 C.F.R. § 653.111 (a), (b)(3) (2003): State agencies participating in the administration of Services for Migrant and Seasonal Farmworkers, under the United States Employment Service, are to develop affirmative action plans which contain "a comparison between the characteristics of the staff and the workforce and determine if the composition of the local office staff(s) is representative of the racial and ethnic characteristics of the workforce in the local office service area(s)." "On a statewide basis, staff representative of the racial and ethnic characteristics in the work force shall be distributed in substantially the same proportion among (1) all 'job groups' . . . and (2) all offices in the plan(s)." . . .

29 C.F.R. § 95.44(b) (2002): All recipients of DOL grants and agreements awarded to institutions of higher education, hospitals, and other nonprofit organizations are to establish written procurement procedures to provide for "positive efforts . . . to utilize small businesses, minority-owned businesses, and women's business enterprises, whenever possible" and to ensure that such businesses "are utilized to the fullest extent practicable." . . .

State Department and Foreign Affairs[36]

22 U.S.C. § 2665a: "Priority consideration" for Foreign Service fellowships is given to the faculty of institutions of higher learning who teach in programs in international affairs which serve significant numbers of students who are from cultural and ethnic groups which are underrepresented in the Foreign Service."

22 U.S.C. § 4823: "The Secretary of State shall actively recruit women and members of minority groups" for special agent positions.

22 U.S.C. § 4852(d): Not less than 10 percent of the amount appropriated for diplomatic construction or designed projects each fiscal year shall be allocated to the extent practicable for contracts with American minority contractors.

22 U.S.C. § 4864(e): Not less than 10 percent of the amount of funds obligated for local guard contracts for Foreign Service buildings shall be allocated to the extent practicable for contracts with minority small business contractors.

22 U.S.C. § 4901(e): The Secretary shall actively recruit women and members of minority groups to receive fellowships for temporary service at United States missions abroad.

P.L. 103-306, 108 Stat. 1608, 1646 § 555 (1994): Provides for a 10 percent set-aside of the aggregate amount of certain appropriations to the Agency for International Development—the Development Assistance Fund, Population, Development Assistance, and the Development Fund for Africa—for socially and economically disadvantaged U.S. businesses and private voluntary organizations, historically black colleges and universities, and higher educational institutions with more than 40 percent Hispanic student enrollment. . . .

48 C.F.R. § 706.302-71 (2003): Agency for International Development (AID)requirement that "[e]xcept to the extent otherwise determined by the Administrator, not less than ten percent of amounts made available for development assistance and for assistance for famine recovery and development in Africa shall be used only for activities of disadvantaged enterprises." "Disadvantaged enterprise" means concerns owned and controlled by "socially and economically disadvantaged individuals," as defined by FAR (48 C.F.R. § 19001(b)) to be members of designated racial and ethnic minority groups,

"Historically Black Colleges and Universities," and "colleges and universities having a student body in which more than 40 percent of the students are Hispanic American." 48 C.F.R. § 726.7002. . . .

Transportation[37]

Transportation Equity Act for the 21st Century (TEA-21), P.L. 105-178, §1101(b), 112 Stat. 107 (1998). The U.S. Department of Transportation (DOT) established a minority and women's business enterprise (DBE) program for its highway, airport, and transit programs by regulation in 1980. The Surface Transportation Assistance Act of 1982 contained the first statutory DBE provision for federal highway and transit programs, requiring that at least 10 percent of the funds provided by the act be expended with small businesses owned and controlled by socially and economically disadvantaged individuals, unless the Secretary of Transportation determined otherwise. Nonminority women were not included as socially and economically disadvantaged individuals. The Surface Transportation and Relocation Assistance Act of 1987 continued and expanded the program to include nonminority women, thereby allowing states to use contracts with minority and women-owned businesses to meet their DBE goals. The Intermodal Surface Transportation Efficiency Act of 1991 and, most recently, §1101(b) of TEA-21 reauthorized the program, continuing the combined 10 percent provision for participation by minority-owned and nonminority women–owned DBEs.

49 U.S.C. § 47107(e)(1): Requires federally aided airport operators to ensure "to the maximum extent practicable" that at least 10 percent of contracts for consumer services to the public be placed with "small business concerns owned and controlled by a socially and economically disadvantaged individual." The statute incorporates the Small Business Act definition of that term "except that women are presumed to be socially and economically disadvantaged." (49 U.S.C. § 47113(a)(2)).

49 C.F.R. Part 26 (2003). In 1999, DOT substantially revised its regulations for DBE participation in federally assisted contracting administered by the department. Stricter eligibility requirements included a personal net worth cap of $750,000 on owners of disadvantaged firms (§26.67(a)(2)), and the program's goal-setting process was overhauled to place greater emphasis on race-neutral measures (e.g., outreach and technical assistance) to achieve a "level playing field"—that is, the level of DBE participation that would be expected in the absence of discrimination (§ 26.1). States and transit authorities, which formerly had to justify goals lower than the statutory 10 percent," now are required to base their DBE goals on demonstrable evidence of the relative number of "ready, willing, and able" DBEs available in local markets as compared to other qualified business entities (§ 26.45(b)). Such evidence may be drawn from DBE directories and Census Bureau data, bidders lists,

disparity studies, or the goal of another recipient (§ 26.45 (c)). The overall goal must then be adjusted to account for other factors affecting DBEs, such as capacity to perform work on DOT-assisted contracts (§ 26.45(d)). States and transit authorities must meet the maximum feasible portion of their overall DBE goals using race-neutral measures not focused exclusively upon DBEs (§ 26.51).While quotas are prohibited and set-asides are allowed only in the most extreme cases of discrimination (§ 26.43), states and transit authorities must use contract goals and other race conscious means to meet any otherwise unattainable portion of their overall goals. But a recipient will not be punished for failure to attain its overall goal provided that it can demonstrate "good faith efforts" (§ 26.53). Recipients are required to submit their overall DBE participation goals, including the methodology used to set goals and the projected use of race-neutral and race-conscious measures, to DOT for approval on an annual basis.

14 C.F.R. § 152.409 (2004): Grantees under federal Airport Aid Program must develop affirmative action plan comparing separately the percentage of minorities and women in various categories of the employer's workforce with the demographic makeup of the contiguous counties and implement "goals and timetables designed to eliminate obstacles to equal opportunities for women and minorities in recruitment and hiring." . . .

Military Recruiting and Integration[38]

Because minorities are overrepresented in the enlisted ranks and underrepresented in the officer corps, . . . the armed forces have focused recently on the officer "pipeline." The services employ a number of tools.

Goals and Timetables: The Navy and the Marine Corps, historically less successful than the other services in this arena, have responded in recent months by setting *explicit goals* to increase minority representation in the officer corps. Both services seek to ensure that, in terms of race and ethnicity, the group of officers commissioned in the year 2000 roughly reflects the overall population: 12 percent African American, 12 percent Hispanic, and 5 percent Asian. Department of the Navy officials point out that this represents a significantly more aggressive goal than had been the case, when the focus for comparison had been on college graduates; the more aggressive goal implies vigorous outreach and other efforts. . . . Moreover, the Navy and the Marine Corps have set specific year-by-year targets for meeting the 12/12/5 goal.

Outreach, Recruiting, and Training: All of the services target outreach and recruiting activities through ROTC, the service academies, and other channels. Also, the services have made *special, race-conscious (though not racially exclusive) efforts to recruit officer candidates.* For example, the Army operates a very successful "preparatory school" for students nominated to West Point whose academic readiness is thought to be marginal; the enrollees are disproportionately but nonexclusively minority.

Selection Procedures: All of the services emphasize racial and gender diversity in their promotion procedures. The Army, for example: instructs officer promotion boards to "be alert to the possibility of past personal or institutional discrimination—either intentional or inadvertent"; [and] sets as a *goal that promotion rates for each minority and gender group at least equal promotion rates for the overall eligible population.* . . . [I]f, for example, a selection board has a general guideline that 44 percent of eligible lieutenant colonels be promoted to colonel, the flexible goal is that promotions of minorities and women be at that same rate. . . . [The procedure] establishes [a] *"second look"* process under which the files for candidates from underrepresented groups who are not selected upon initial consideration are reconsidered with an eye toward identifying any past discrimination; and [the procedure] instructs members of a promotion board carefully so that the process does not force promotion boards to use quotas. . . .

Management Tools: These include performance standards, reporting requirements, and training and analytic capacity. Personnel evaluations include matters related to effectiveness in EO [Equal Opportunity] matters. [Department of Defense] DOD maintains the Defense Equal Opportunity Management Institute, which trains EO personnel, advises DOD on EO policy, and conducts related research. —DOD conducts various surveys and studies to monitor equal opportunity initiatives and the views of personnel. —Most important, DOD requires each service to maintain and review affirmative action plans and to complete an annual "Military Equal Opportunity Assessment" (MEOA). The MEOA reports whether various equal opportunity objectives were met and identifies problems such as harassment and discrimination.

The MEOA includes both data and narrative assessments of progress in ten areas. One of these is recruitment and accessions (i.e., commissioning of officers). Other areas include officer and enlisted promotion results, completion of officer and enlisted professional military education (e.g., the war colleges and noncommissioned officer academies), augmentation of officers into the Regular component, assignment to billets that are Service defined as career-enhancing and to commanding officer and deputy commanding officer billets, and over and under-representation of minorities or women in any military occupational category. In addition to these formal efforts, the Services support the efforts of nonprofit service organizations, such as the Air Force Cadet Officer Mentor Action Program, that strengthen professional and leadership development through mentorship, assist in the transition to military life, and support the establishing of networks.

Authors' Note: The Amicus Briefs of Retired Military Officers Supporting Diversity and Integration in the Military

A number of former high-ranking military officers submitted an amicus pro-diversity affirmative action brief in *Grutter/Gratz v. Bollinger* (2003).[39] (See 142–63.) Retired military and Defense Department officials also supported student-body diversity in a brief presented in connection with *Parents Involved v. Seattle.*(2007).[40] (See 104–14.)

In the *Grutter/Gratz* brief,[41] the retired officers highlighted the following affirmative action steps undertaken by the military:

> In conformity with the affirmative action programs of the Department of Defense, the service academies have been vigorous in their efforts to increase the number of women, black, Hispanic, and other minority officers.[42] The academies "use financial and tutorial assistance, as well as recruiting programs. . . . They also employ race as a factor in recruiting and admissions policies and decisions."[43] Officer candidates are trained in a racially diverse environment, providing them with "invaluable experience for their future command of our nation's highly diverse enlisted ranks."[44]
>
> In 1968, there were thirty African American cadets at West Point. The goal for the class of 2005 was a minority student body of 25 percent, including 8 percent African Americans (100 cadets); 6 percent Hispanic (70 cadets). In 2002, there were more than three hundred African American, and 150 Hispanic cadets at the Point. The minority-presence goals are based on the percentage of minorities in the nation's population; within college student bodies; and in the Army.[45] Minorities are "consistently" offered admission to West Point despite "lower academic predictor scores and lower academic, physical education and military grades."[46]
>
> The Naval Academy "aggressively recruits minorities," and " 'a higher percentage of minorities who did qualify were admitted to the Academy than their white counterparts.' "[47]
>
> Between 1991-1995, 18 percent of minority candidates qualified for admission to the Air Force Academy as compared with 28 percent of white applicants. But 76 percent of minority candidates were offered admission, as compared to 51 percent of white applicants. In that period admission scores for minorities were some 3,000 points and 3,200 for whites.[48]

The ROTC "employs an aggressive race-conscious admissions program"[49] to attract minority college students for the officer corps.

Retired officers and former Department of Defense officials supported diversity in K-12 education by noting that:[50]

Since WW II, the military has voluntarily engaged in efforts to integrate both its ranks and the education of its dependent children.[51]

Before *Brown v. The Board* (1954),[52] the Department of Defense (DOD) determined that a fully integrated military required an integrated education for the children of the armed forces. DOD schools were fully integrated by 1953. Where local governments refused to desegregate schools serving military dependents, DOD established its own desegregated classrooms.[53]

DOD schools are "among the most racially integrated of any in the country, and, not coincidentally, have the very highest levels of achievement for minority students."[54]

Along with the integration of its ranks, the military has integrated base housing since 1948.[55]

The military not only integrated hundreds of K-12 classrooms, it has also integrated university classes attended by military personnel.[56]

Appendix Two

Uniform Guidelines on
Employee Selection Procedures (1978)

29 CFR 1607 (2009)

Sec. 1607.1 Statement of Purpose

B. Purpose of guidelines. These guidelines incorporate a single set of principles which are designed to assist employers, labor organizations, employment agencies, and licensing and certification boards to comply with requirements of Federal law prohibiting employment practices which discriminate on grounds of race, color, religion, sex, and national origin. They are designed to provide a framework for determining the proper use of tests and other selection procedures. These guidelines do not require a user to conduct validity studies of selection procedures where no adverse impact results. However, all users are encouraged to use selection procedures which are valid, especially users operating under merit principles. . . .

Sec. 1607.2 Scope

C. Selection procedures. These guidelines apply only to selection procedures which are used as a basis for making employment decisions. For example, the use of recruiting procedures designed to attract members of a particular race, sex, or ethnic group, which were previously denied employment opportunities or which are currently underutilized, may be necessary to bring an employer into compliance with Federal law, and is frequently an essential element of any effective affirmative action program; but recruitment practices are not considered by these guidelines to be selection procedures. . . .

Sec. 1607. 3 Discrimination Defined: Relationship Between Use of Selection Procedures and Discrimination

A. Procedure having adverse impact constitutes discrimination unless justified. The use of any selection procedure which has an adverse impact [disparate impact] on the hiring, promotion, or other employment or membership opportunities of members of any race, sex, or ethnic group will be considered to be discriminatory and inconsistent with these guidelines, unless the procedure has been validated in accordance with these guidelines, or the provisions of section [1607.] 6 below are satisfied.

B. Consideration of suitable alternative selection procedures. Where two or more selection procedures are available which serve the user's legitimate interest in efficient and trustworthy workmanship, and which are substantially equally valid for a given purpose, the user should use the procedure which has been demonstrated to have the lesser adverse impact. . . .

Sec. 1607.4 Information on Impact

A. Records concerning impact. Each user should maintain and have available for inspection records or other information which will disclose the impact which its tests and other selection procedures have upon employment opportunities of persons by identifiable race, sex, or ethnic group as set forth in paragraph B of this section, in order to determine compliance with these guidelines. Where there are large numbers of applicants and procedures are administered frequently, such information may be retained on a sample basis, provided that the sample is appropriate in terms of the applicant population and adequate in size.

B. Applicable race, sex, and ethnic groups for record keeping. The records called for by this section are to be maintained by sex, and the following races and ethnic groups: Blacks (Negroes), American Indians (including Alaskan Natives), Asians (including Pacific Islanders), Hispanic (including persons of Mexican, Puerto Rican, Cuban, Central or South American, or other Spanish origin or culture regardless of race), whites (Caucasians) other than Hispanic. . . .

C. Evaluation of selection rates. The "bottom line." If the information called for by sections [1607.] 4 A and B above shows that the total selection process for a job has an adverse impact, the individual components of the selection process should be evaluated for adverse impact. If this information shows that the total selection process does not have an adverse impact, the Federal enforcement agencies, in the exercise of their administrative and prosecutorial discretion, in usual circumstances, will not expect a user to evaluate the individual components for adverse impact, or to validate such individual components, and will not take enforcement action based upon adverse impact of any component of that process, including the separate parts of a multipart selection procedure or any separate procedure that is used as an alternative method of selection. However, in the following circumstances the Federal enforcement agencies will expect a user to evaluate the individual components for adverse impact and may, where appropriate, take enforcement action with respect to the individual components:

(1) Where the selection procedure is a significant factor in the continuation of patterns of assignments of incumbent employees caused by prior discriminatory employment practices, (2) where the weight of court decisions or administrative interpretations hold that a specific procedure (such as height or weight requirements or no-arrest records) is not job related in the same or similar circumstances. In unusual circumstances, other than those listed in (1) and (2) of this paragraph, the Federal enforcement agencies may request a user to evaluate the individual components for adverse impact and may, where appropriate, take enforcement action with respect to the individual component.

D. Adverse impact and the "four-fifths rule." A selection rate for any race, sex, or ethnic group which is less than four-fifths (4/5) (or eighty percent) of the rate for the group with the highest rate will generally be regarded by the Federal enforcement agencies as evidence of adverse impact, while a greater than four-fifths rate will generally not be regarded by Federal enforcement agencies as evidence of adverse impact. Smaller differences in selection rate may nevertheless constitute adverse impact, where they are significant in both statistical and practical terms or where a user's actions have discouraged applicants disproportionately on grounds of race, sex, or ethnic group. Greater differences in selection rate may not constitute adverse impact where the differences are based on small numbers and are not statistically significant, or where special recruiting or other programs cause the pool of minority or female candidates to be atypical of the normal pool of applicants from that group. Where the user's evidence concerning the impact of a selection procedure indicates adverse impact but is based upon numbers which are too small to be reliable, evidence concerning the impact of the procedure over a longer period of time and/or evidence concerning the impact which the selection procedure had when used in the same manner in similar circumstances elsewhere may be considered in determining adverse impact. Where the user has not maintained data on adverse impact as required, . . . the Federal enforcement agencies may draw an inference of adverse impact of the selection process from the failure of the user to maintain such data, if the user has an underutilization of a group in the job category, as compared to the group's representation in the relevant labor market or, in the case of jobs filled from within, the applicable work force.

E. Consideration of user's equal employment opportunity posture. In carrying out their obligations, the Federal enforcement agencies will consider the general posture of the user with respect to equal employment opportunity for the job or group of jobs in question. Where a user has adopted an affirmative action program, the Federal enforcement agencies will consider the provisions of that program, including the goals and timetables which the user has adopted and the progress which the user has made in carrying out that program and in meeting the goals and timetables. While such affirmative action programs may in design and execution be race, color, sex, or ethnic conscious, selection procedures under such programs should be based upon the ability or relative ability to do the work.

Sec. 1607.5 General Standards for Validity Studies

A. Acceptable types of validity studies. For the purposes of satisfying these guidelines, users may rely upon criterion-related validity studies, content validity studies or construct validity studies. . . .

B. Criterion-related, content, and construct validity. Evidence of the validity of a test or other selection procedure by a criterion-related validity study should consist of empirical data demonstrating that the selection procedure is predictive of or significantly correlated with important elements of job performance. . . . Evidence of the validity of a test or other selection procedure by a content validity study should consist of data showing that the content of the selection procedure is representative of important aspects of performance on the job for which the candidates are to be evaluated. . . . Evidence of the validity of a test or other selection procedure through a construct validity study should consist of data showing that the procedure measures the degree to which candidates have identifiable characteristics which have been determined to be important in successful performance in the job for which the candidates are to be evaluated. . . .

C. Guidelines are consistent with professional standards. The provisions of these guidelines relating to validation of selection procedures are intended to be consistent with generally accepted professional standards for evaluating standardized tests and other selection procedures, such as those described in the Standards for Educational and Psychological Tests prepared by a joint committee of the American Psychological Association, the American Educational Research Association, and the National Council on Measurement in Education (American Psychological Association, Washington, DC, 1974) (hereinafter "A.P.A. Standards") and standard textbooks and journals in the field of personnel selection. . . .

Sec. 1607.6 Use of Selection Procedures Which Have Not Been Validated

A. Use of alternate selection procedures to eliminate adverse impact. A user may choose to utilize alternative selection procedures in order to eliminate adverse impact or as part of an affirmative action program. . . . Such alternative procedures should eliminate the adverse impact in the total selection process, should be lawful and should be as job related as possible.

B. Where validity studies cannot or need not be performed. There are circumstances in which a user cannot or need not utilize the validation techniques contemplated by these guidelines. In such circumstances, the user should utilize selection procedures which are as job related as possible and which will minimize or eliminate adverse impact as set forth below.

(1) Where informal or unscored procedures are used. When an informal or unscored selection procedure which has an adverse impact is utilized, the user should eliminate the adverse impact, or modify the procedure to one which is a formal, scored or quantified measure or combination of measures and then validate the procedure in accord with these guidelines, or otherwise justify continued use of the procedure in accord with Federal law.

(2) Where formal and scored procedures are used. When a formal and scored selection procedure is used which has an adverse impact, the validation techniques contemplated by these guidelines usually should be followed if technically feasible. Where the user cannot or need not follow the validation techniques anticipated by these guidelines, the user should either modify the procedure to eliminate adverse impact or otherwise justify continued use of the procedure in accord with Federal law.

Sec. 1607.7 Use of Other Validity Studies

A. Validity studies not conducted by the user. Users may, under certain circumstances, support the use of selection procedures by validity studies conducted by other users or conducted by test publishers or distributors and described in test manuals. While publishers of selection procedures have a professional obligation to provide evidence of validity which meets generally accepted professional standards . . . , users are cautioned that they are responsible for compliance with these guidelines. Accordingly, users seeking to obtain selection procedures from publishers and distributors should be careful to determine that, in the event the user becomes subject to the validity requirements of these guidelines, the necessary information to support validity has been determined and will be made available to the suser. . . .

Appendix Three

Affirmative Action Guidelines
of the Equal Employment
Opportunity Commission

29 CFR 1608 (2009)

Sec. 1608.1 Statement of Purpose

Need for Guidelines. Since the passage of title VII in 1964, many employers, labor organizations, and other persons subject to title VII have changed their employment practices and systems to improve employment opportunities for minorities and women, and this must continue. These changes have been undertaken either on the initiative of the employer, labor organization, or other person subject to title VII, or as a result of conciliation efforts under title VII, action under Executive Order 11246, as amended, or under other Federal, State, or local laws, or litigation. Many decisions taken pursuant to affirmative action plans or programs have been race, sex, or national origin conscious in order to achieve the Congressional purpose of providing equal employment opportunity. Occasionally, these actions have been challenged as inconsistent with title VII, because they took into account race, sex, or national origin. This is the so-called "reverse discrimination" claim. . . . The Commission believes that by the enactment of title VII Congress did not intend to expose those who comply with the Act to charges that they are violating the very statute they are seeking to implement. Such a result would immobilize or reduce the efforts of many who would otherwise take action to improve the opportunities of minorities and women without litigation, thus frustrating the Congressional intent to encourage voluntary action and increasing the prospect of title VII litigation. The Commission believes that it is now necessary to clarify and harmonize the principles of title VII in order to achieve these Congressional objectives and protect those employers, labor organizations, and other persons who comply with the principles of title VII. . . .

These Guidelines describe the circumstances in which persons subject to title VII may take or agree upon action to improve employment opportunities of minorities and women, and describe the kinds of actions they may take which are consistent with title VII. . . .

Sec. 1608. 2 Written Interpretation and Opinion

These Guidelines constitute "a written interpretation and opinion" of the Equal Employment Opportunity Commission as that term is used in section 713(b)(1) of title VII of the Civil Rights Act of 1964, as amended, 42 U.S.C. 2000e-12(b)(1), and Sec. 1601.33 of the Procedural Regulations of the Equal Employment Opportunity Commission (29 CFR 1601.30; 42 FR 55, 394 (October 14, 1977)). Section 713(b)(1) provides:

"In any action or proceeding based on any alleged unlawful employment practice, no person shall be subject to any liability or punishment for or on account of (1) the commission by such person of an unlawful employment practice if he pleads and proves that the act or omission complained of was in good faith, in conformity with, and in reliance on any written interpretation or opinion of the Commission. . . . Such a defense, if established, shall be a bar to the action or proceeding, notwithstanding that . . . after such act or omission, such interpretation or opinion is modified or rescinded or is determined by judicial authority to be invalid or of no legal effect. . . ."

Sec. 1608. 3 Circumstances Under Which Voluntary Affirmative Action is Appropriate

(a) **Adverse effect.** [disparate impact] Title VII prohibits practices, procedures, or policies which have an adverse impact unless they are justified by business necessity. In addition, title VII proscribes practices which "tend to deprive" persons of equal employment opportunities. Employers, labor organizations and other persons subject to title VII may take affirmative action based on an analysis which reveals facts constituting actual or potential adverse impact, if such adverse impact is likely to result from existing or contemplated practices.

(b) **Effects of prior discriminatory practices.** Employers, labor organizations, or other persons subject to title VII may also take affirmative action to correct the effects of prior discriminatory practices. The effects of prior discriminatory practices can be initially identified by a comparison between the employer's work force, or a part thereof, and an appropriate segment of the labor force.

(c) **Limited labor pool.** Because of historic restrictions by employers, labor organizations, and others, there are circumstances in which the available pool, particularly of qualified minorities and women, for employment or promotional opportunities is artificially limited. Employers, labor organizations, and other persons subject to title VII may, and are encouraged to take affirmative action in such circumstances, including, but not limited to, the following:

(1) Training plans and programs, including on-the-job training, which emphasize providing minorities and women with the opportunity, skill, and experience necessary to perform the functions of skilled trades, crafts, or professions; (2) Extensive and focused recruiting activity; (3) Elimination of the adverse impact caused by unvalidated selection criteria (see sections 3 and 6, Uniform Guidelines on Employee Selection Procedures (1978), 43 FR 30290; 38297; 38299 (August 25, 1978)); (4) Modification through collective bargaining where a labor organization represents employees, or unilaterally where one does not, of promotion and layoff procedures.

Sec. 1608.4 Establishing Affirmative Action Plans

An affirmative action plan or program under this section shall contain three elements: a reasonable self analysis; a reasonable basis for concluding action is appropriate; and reasonable action.

(a) **Reasonable self analysis.** The objective of a self analysis is to determine whether employment practices do, or tend to, exclude, disadvantage, restrict, or result in adverse impact or disparate treatment of previously excluded or restricted groups or leave uncorrected the effects of prior discrimination, and if so, to attempt to determine why. There is no mandatory method of conducting a self analysis. The employer may utilize techniques used in order to comply with Executive Order 11246, as amended, and its implementing regulations, including 41 CFR part 60-2 (known as Revised Order 4), or related orders issued by the Office of Federal Contract Compliance Programs or its authorized agencies, or may use an analysis similar to that required under other Federal, State, or local laws or regulations prohibiting employment discrimination. In conducting a self analysis, the employer, labor organization, or other person subject to title VII should be concerned with the effect on its employment practices of circumstances which may be the result of discrimination by other persons or institutions. See *Griggs v. Duke Power Co.*, 401 U.S. 424 (1971).

(b) **Reasonable basis.** If the self analysis shows that one or more employment practices: (1) Have or tend to have an adverse effect on employment opportunities of members of previously excluded groups, or groups whose employment or promotional opportunities have been artificially limited, (2) Leave uncorrected the effects of prior discrimination, or (3) Result in disparate treatment, the person making the self analysis has a reasonable basis for concluding that action is appropriate.

It is not necessary that the self analysis establish a violation of title VII. This reasonable basis exists without any admission or formal finding that the person has violated title VII, and without regard to whether there exists arguable defenses to a title VII action.

(c) Reasonable action. The action taken pursuant to an affirmative action plan or program must be reasonable in relation to the problems disclosed by the self analysis. Such reasonable action may include goals and timetables or other appropriate employment tools which recognize the race, sex, or national origin of applicants or employees. It may include the adoption of practices which will eliminate the actual or potential adverse impact, disparate treatment, or effect [of] past discrimination by providing opportunities for members of groups which have been excluded, regardless of whether the persons benefited were themselves the victims of prior policies or procedures which produced the adverse impact or disparate treatment or which perpetuated past discrimination. . . .

Affirmative action plans or programs may include, but are not limited to, those described in the Equal Employment Opportunity Coordinating Council "Policy Statement on Affirmative Action Programs for State and Local Government Agencies." . . . That statement reads, in relevant part:

When an employer has reason to believe that its selection procedures have . . . exclusionary effect, . . . it should initiate affirmative steps to remedy the situation. Such steps, which in design and execution may be race, color, sex or ethnic 'conscious,' include, but are not limited to, the following:

The establishment of a long term goal and short range, interim goals and timetables for the specific job classifications, all of which should take into account the availability of basically qualified persons in the relevant job market;

A recruitment program designed to attract qualified members of the group in question;

A systematic effort to organize work and re-design jobs in ways that provide opportunities for persons lacking 'journeyman' level knowledge or skills to enter and, with appropriate training, to progress in a career field;

Revamping selection instruments or procedures which have not yet been validated in order to reduce or eliminate exclusionary effects on particular groups in particular job classifications;

The initiation of measures designed to assure that members of the affected group who are qualified to perform the job are included within the pool of persons from which the selecting official makes the selection;

A systematic effort to provide career advancement training, both classroom and on-the-job, to employees locked into dead end jobs; and

The establishment of a system for regularly monitoring the effectiveness of the particular affirmative action program, and procedures for making timely adjustments in this program where effectiveness is not demonstrated.

(2) Standards of reasonable action. In considering the reasonableness of a particular affirmative action plan or program, the Commission will generally apply the following standards:

(i) The plan should be tailored to solve the problems which were identified in the self analysis, see Sec. 1608.4 (a), supra, and to ensure that employment systems operate fairly in the future, while avoiding unnecessary restrictions on opportunities for the workforce as a whole. The race, sex, and national origin conscious provisions of the plan or program should be maintained only so long as is necessary to achieve these objectives.

(ii) Goals and timetables should be reasonably related to such considerations as the effects of past discrimination, the need for prompt elimination of adverse impact or disparate treatment, the availability of basically qualified or qualifiable applicants, and the number of employment opportunities expected to be available. . . .

Appendix Four

Office of Federal Contract
Compliance Programs

Affirmative Action Programs[57]

41 CFR. 60 (2009)

Sec. 60-2.10 General Purpose and Contents of
Affirmative Action Programs

(a) Purpose. (1) An Affirmative action program is a management tool designed to ensure equal employment opportunity. A central premise underlying affirmative action is that, absent discrimination, over time a contractor's workforce, generally, will reflect the gender, racial and ethnic profile of the labor pools from which the contractor recruits and selects. . . . OFCCP has found that when an affirmative action program is approached from this perspective, as a powerful management tool, there is a positive correlation between the presence of affirmative action and the absence of discrimination.

(b) Contents of affirmative action programs. (1) An affirmative action program must include the following quantitative analyses: (i) Organizational profile—Sec. 60-2.11; (ii) Job group analysis—Sec. 60-2.12; (iii) Placement of incumbents in job groups—Sec. 60-2.13; (iv) Determining availability—Sec. 60-2.14; (v) Comparing incumbency to availability—Sec. 60-2.15; and (vi) Placement goals—Sec. 60-2.16. (2) In addition, an affirmative action program must include the following components specified in the Sec. 60-2.17 of this part: (i) Designation of responsibility for implementation; (ii) Identification of problem areas; (iii) Action-oriented programs; and (iv) Periodic internal audits.

(c) Documentation. Contractors must maintain and make available to OFCCP documentation of their compliance with Secs. 60-2.11 through 60-2.17.

Sec. 60-2.11 Organizational Profile

(a) Purpose. An organizational profile is a depiction of the staffing pattern within an establishment. It is one method contractors use to determine whether barriers to equal employment opportunity exist in their organizations. The profile provides an overview of the workforce at the establishment that may assist in identifying organizational units where women or minorities are underrepresented or concentrated. The contractor must use either the organizational display or the workforce analysis as its organizational profile:

(b) Organizational display. (1) An organizational display is a detailed graphical or tabular chart, text, spreadsheet or similar presentation of the contractor's organizational structure. The organizational display must identify each organizational unit in the establishment, and show the relationship of each organizational unit to the other organizational units in the establishment.

(2) An organizational unit is any component that is part of the contractor's corporate structure. In a more traditional organization, an organizational unit might be a department, division, section, branch, group or similar component. In a less traditional organization, an organizational unit might be a project team, job family, or similar component. The term includes an umbrella unit (such as a department) that contains a number of subordinate units, and it separately includes each of the subordinate units (such as sections or branches).

(3) For each organizational unit, the organizational display must indicate the following: (i) The name of the unit; (ii) The job title, gender, race, and ethnicity of the unit supervisor (if the unit has a supervisor); (iii) The total number of male and female incumbents; and (iv) the total number of male and female incumbents in each of the following groups: Blacks, Hispanics, Asians/Pacific Islanders, and American Indians/Alaskan Natives.

(c) Workforce analysis. (1) A workforce analysis is a listing of each job title as appears in applicable collective bargaining agreements or payroll records ranked from the lowest paid to the highest paid within each department or other similar organizational unit including departmental or unit supervision. (2) If there are separate work units or lines of progression within a department, a separate list must be provided for each such work unit, or line, including unit supervisors. For lines of progression there must be indicated the order of jobs in the line through which an employee could move to the top of the line. (3) Where there are no formal progression lines or usual promotional sequences, job titles should be listed by department, job families, or disciplines, in order of wage rates or salary ranges. (4) For each job title, the total number of incumbents, the total number of male and female incumbents, and the total number of male and female incumbents in each of the following groups must be given: Blacks, Hispanics, Asians/Pacific

Islanders, and American Indians/Alaskan Natives. The wage rate or salary range for each job title must be given. All job titles, including all managerial job titles, must be listed.

Sec. 60-2.12 Job Group Analysis

(a) Purpose: A job group analysis is a method of combining job titles within the contractor's establishment. This is the first step in the contractor's comparison of the representation of minorities and women in its workforce with the estimated availability of minorities and women qualified to be employed.

(b) In the job group analysis, jobs at the establishment with similar content, wage rates, and opportunities, must be combined to form job groups. Similarity of content refers to the duties and responsibilities of the job titles which make up the job group. Similarity of opportunities refers to training, transfers, promotions, pay, mobility, and other career enhancement opportunities offered by the jobs within the job group.

(c) The job group analysis must include a list of the job titles that comprise each job group. If . . . the job group analysis contains jobs that are located at another establishment, the job group analysis must be annotated to identify the actual location of those jobs. If the establishment at which the jobs actually are located maintains an affirmative action program, the job group analysis of that program must be annotated to identify the program in which the jobs are included.

(d) . . . [A]ll jobs located at an establishment must be reported in the job group analysis of that establishment.

(e) Smaller employers: If a contractor has a total workforce of fewer than 150 employees, the contractor may prepare a job group analysis that utilizes [Equal Employment Opportunity] EEO-1 categories as job groups. EEO-1 categories refers to the nine occupational groups used in the Standard Form 100, the Employer Information EEO-1 Survey: Officials and managers, professionals, technicians, sales, office and clerical, craft workers (skilled), operatives (semiskilled), laborers (unskilled), and service workers.

Sec. 60-2.13 Placement of Incumbents in Job Groups

The contractor must separately state the percentage of minorities and the percentage of women it employs in each job group established pursuant to Sec. 60-2.12.

Sec. 60-2.14 Determining Availability

(a) Purpose: Availability is an estimate of the number of qualified minorities or women available for employment in a given job group, expressed as a percentage of all qualified persons available for employment in the job group.

The purpose of the availability determination is to establish a benchmark against which the demographic composition of the contractor's incumbent workforce can be compared in order to determine whether barriers to equal employment opportunity may exist within particular job groups.

(b) The contractor must separately determine the availability of minorities and women for each job group.

(c) In determining availability, the contractor must consider at least the following factors: (1) The percentage of minorities or women with requisite skills in the reasonable recruitment area. The reasonable recruitment area is defined as the geographical area from which the contractor usually seeks or reasonably could seek workers to fill the positions in question. (2) The percentage of minorities or women among those promotable, transferable, and trainable within the contractor's organization. Trainable refers to those employees within the contractor's organization who could, with appropriate training which the contractor is reasonably able to provide, become promotable or transferable during the AAP [affirmative action programs] year.

(d) The contractor must use the most current and discrete statistical information available to derive availability figures. Examples of such information include census data, data from local job service offices, and data from colleges or other training institutions.

(e) The contractor may not draw its reasonable recruitment area in such a way as to have the effect of excluding minorities or women. For each job group, the reasonable recruitment area must be identified, with a brief explanation of the rationale for selection of that recruitment area.

(f) The contractor may not define the pool of promotable, transferable, and trainable employees in such a way as to have the effect of excluding minorities or women. For each job group, the pool of promotable, transferable, and trainable employees must be identified with a brief explanation of the rationale for the selection of that pool.

(g) Where a job group is composed of job titles with different availability rates, a composite availability figure for the job group must be calculated. The contractor must separately determine the availability for each job title within the job group and must determine the proportion of job group incumbents employed in each job title. The contractor must weight the availability for each job title by the proportion of job group incumbents employed in that job group. The sum of the weighted availability estimates for all job titles in the job group must be the composite availability for the job group.

Sec. 60-2.15 Comparing Incumbency to Availability

(a) The contractor must compare the percentage of minorities and women in each job group determined pursuant to Sec. 60-2.13 with the availability for those job groups determined pursuant to Sec. 60-2.14.

(b) When the percentage of minorities or women employed in a particular job group is less than would reasonably be expected given their availability percentage in that particular job group, the contractor must establish a placement goal in accordance with Sec. 60-2.16.

Sec. 60-2.16 Placement Goals

(a) Purpose: Placement goals serve as objectives or targets reasonably attainable by means of applying every good faith effort to make all aspects of the entire affirmative action program work. Placement goals also are used to measure progress toward achieving equal employment opportunity.

(b) A contractor's determination under Sec. 60-2.15 that a placement goal is required constitutes neither a finding nor an admission of discrimination.

(c) Where, pursuant to Sec. 60-2.15, a contractor is required to establish a placement goal for a particular job group, the contractor must establish a percentage annual placement goal at least equal to the availability figure derived for women or minorities, as appropriate, for that job group.

(d) The placement goal-setting process described above contemplates that contractors will, where required, establish a single goal for all minorities. In the event of a substantial disparity in the utilization of a particular minority group or in the utilization of men or women of a particular minority group, a contractor may be required to establish separate goals for those groups.

(e) In establishing placement goals, the following principles also apply:

(1) Placement goals may not be rigid and inflexible quotas, which must be met, nor are they to be considered as either a ceiling or a floor for the employment of particular groups. Quotas are expressly forbidden. (2) In all employment decisions, the contractor must make selections in a nondiscriminatory manner. Placement goals do not provide the contractor with a justification to extend a preference to any individual, select an individual, or adversely affect an individual's employment status, on the basis of that person's race, color, religion, sex, or national origin. (3) Placement goals do not create set-asides for specific groups, nor are they intended to achieve proportional representation or equal results. (4) Placement goals may not be used to supersede merit selection principles. Affirmative action programs prescribed by the regulations in this part do not require a contractor to hire a person who lacks qualifications to perform the job successfully, or hire a less qualified person in preference to a more qualified one. (f) A contractor extending a publicly announced preference for American Indians as is authorized in 41 CFR 60-1.5(a)(6) may reflect in its placement goals the permissive employment preference for American Indians living on or near an Indian reservation.

Sec. 60-2.17 Additional Required Elements of
Affirmative Action Programs

In addition to the elements required by Sec. 60-2.10 through Sec. 60-2.16, an
acceptable affirmative action program must include the following: (a) Designation of responsibility. The contractor must provide for the implementation of
equal employment opportunity and the affirmative action program by assigning
responsibility and accountability to an official of the organization. Depending
upon the size of the contractor, this may be the official's sole responsibility.
He or she must have the authority, resources, support of and access to top
management to ensure the effective implementation of the affirmative action
program. (b) Identification of problem areas. The contractor must perform
in-depth analyses of its total employment process to determine whether and
where impediments to equal employment opportunity exist. At a minimum
the contractor must evaluate: (1) The workforce by organizational unit and
job group to determine whether there are problems of minority or female
utilization (i.e., employment in the unit or group), or of minority or female
distribution (i.e., placement in the different jobs within the unit or group);
(2) personnel activity (applicant flow, hires, terminations, promotions, and
other personnel actions) to determine whether there are selection disparities; (3) compensation system(s) to determine whether there are gender-,
race-, or ethnicity-based disparities; (4) selection, recruitment, referral, and
other personnel procedures to determine whether they result in disparities
in the employment or advancement of minorities or women; and (5) any
other areas that might impact the success of the affirmative action program.
(c) Action-oriented programs. The contractor must develop and execute
action-oriented programs designed to correct any problem areas identified
pursuant to Sec. 60-2.17(b) and to attain established goals and objectives.
In order for these action-oriented programs to be effective, the contractor
must ensure that they consist of more than following the same procedures
which have previously produced inadequate results. Furthermore, a contractor
must demonstrate that it has made good faith efforts to remove identified
barriers, expand employment opportunities, and produce measurable results.
(d) Internal audit and reporting system. The contractor must develop and
implement an auditing system that periodically measures the effectiveness
of its total affirmative action program. The actions listed below are key to a
successful affirmative action program: (1) Monitor records of all personnel
activity, including referrals, placements, transfers, promotions, terminations,
and compensation, at all levels to ensure the nondiscriminatory policy is
carried out; (2) Require internal reporting on a scheduled basis as to the
degree to which equal employment opportunity and organizational objectives
are attained; (3) Review report results with all levels of management; and

(4) Advise top management of program effectiveness and submit recommendations to improve unsatisfactory performance. . . .

Sec. 60-2.31 Program Summary

The affirmative action program must be summarized and updated annually. The program summary must be prepared in a format which will be prescribed by the Deputy Assistant Secretary and published in the Federal Register as a notice before becoming effective. Contractors and subcontractors must submit the program summary to OFCCP each year on the anniversary date of the affirmative action program.

Sec. 60-2.32 Affirmative Action Records

The contractor must make available to the Office of Federal Contract Compliance Programs, upon request, records maintained pursuant to Sec. 60-1.12 of this chapter and written or otherwise documented portions of AAPs [affirmative action programs] maintained pursuant to Sec. 60-2.10 for such purposes as may be appropriate to the fulfillment of the agency's responsibilities under Executive Order 11246. . . .

Sec. 60-2.35 Compliance Status

No contractor's compliance status will be judged alone by whether it reaches its goals. The composition of the contractor's workforce (i.e., the employment of minorities or women at a percentage rate below, or above, the goal level) does not, by itself, serve as a basis to impose any of the sanctions authorized by Executive Order 11246 and the regulations in this chapter. Each contractor's compliance with its affirmative action obligations will be determined by reviewing the nature and extent of the contractor's good faith affirmative action activities as required under Sec. 60-2.17, and the appropriateness of those activities to identified equal employment opportunity problems. Each contractor's compliance with its nondiscrimination obligations will be determined by analysis of statistical data and other non-statistical information which would indicate whether employees and applicants are being treated without regard to their race, color, religion, sex, or national origin. . . .

Notes

Chapter One. Introduction

1. *Regents v. Bakke*, 438 U.S. 265, 284–285, 287, 281, 307–320 (1978).

2. See Peter Schuck, *Diversity in America: Keeping Government at a Safe Distance* 160–163 (The Belknap Press of Harvard U Press, 2003); Sanford Levinson, *Wrestling with Diversity* 16, 64 (Duke U Press, 2003).

3. In this book "discrimination" means invidious treatment (i.e., unfair or unjust) of people. "Societal (systemic) discrimination" means societally rooted invidious treatment of people due to group membership or affiliation. "Protected group" means the racial and ethnic (national origin/ancestral) and gender groups covered by antidiscrimination laws and regulations. "Minorities" are the racial and ethnic groups so covered. "Affirmative action" means the general policy for treating societal discrimination. There are many specific policies for implementing this general policy.

4. Disparate treatment of *individuals* remains a legitimate topic, but, in our view, a relatively noncontroversial antidiscrimination target, and we have accordingly paid little attention to it.

5. For analysis of compensation theory, see 41–42.

6. Title VII of the 1964 Civil Rights Act, Pub L 88-352, 78 Stat 241, codified, as amended, at 42 USC 2000e *et seq* (2009).

Chapter Two. The Roots of Affirmative Action

1. See Herman Belz, *Equality Transformed* 12–13 (Transaction, 1992) to this effect.

2. Eric Foner, *Reconstruction* 67 (Perennial/Harper and Row, 1989) (emphasis added).

3. During the final phase of the war, and for two years after it ended, federal policy for relations with the South was controlled by Johnson's so-called "Presidential Reconstruction" program. See Eric McKittrick, *Andrew Johnson and Reconstruction* (U of Chicago Press, 1960); Herman Belz, *A New Birth of Freedom* 35–50 (Greenwood, 1976). Congress' confrontation with the president over policy in 1865–67, including the famous impeachment, is one of the most fascinating chapters in our national history. See Foner, *Reconstruction* at chs 6–8 (cited in note 2).

4. Rogers M. Smith, *Legitimating Reconstruction*, 108 Yale L J 2039, 2064 (1999); John Hope Franklin, *Slavery and the Constitution* 61, 61–74 in Leonard W. Levy, Kenneth L. Karst, and Dennis J. Mahoney, eds, *Civil Rights and Equality* (Macmillan, 1986).

5. Eric Foner, *The Story of American Freedom* 75 (Norton, 1998).

6. Kenneth M. Stampp, *The Peculiar Institution* ch 2, 430 (Vintage/Random House, 1989); John Hope Franklin and Alfred A. Moss Jr., *From Slavery to Freedom* ch 8 (Knopf, 8th ed, 2000).

7. *Dred Scott v. Sandford*, 19 How (60 U.S.) 393, 404–406 (1857).

8. Harold M. Hyman, *Thirteenth Amendment (Framing)* 102,102–105; Kenneth L. Karst, *Thirteenth Amendment (Judicial Interpretation)* 106, 106–110; William I. Nelson, *Fourteenth Amendment (Framing)* 118, 118–124; Kenneth L. Karst, *Equal Protection of the Laws* 30, 30–43; Charles L. Black Jr., *State Action* 44, 44–57; William Gillette, *Fifteenth Amendment (Framing and Ratification)* 125, 125–128; Ward E. Y. Elliott, *Fifteenth Amendment (Judicial Interpretation)* 129, 129–131. All the aforementioned articles in Levy, Karst, and Mahoney, eds, *Civil Rights* (cited in note 4).

9. See Harold M. Hyman, *Civil Rights Act of 1866 (Framing)* 113, 113–114; Theodore Eisenberg, *Civil Rights Act of 1866 (Judicial Interpretation)* 115, 115–117 in Levy, Karst, and Mahoney, eds, *Civil Rights* (cited in note 4).

10. 1866 Civil Rights Act ch 31, §1, 14 Stat 27, codified at 42 USC § 1982 (2009).

11. Ch 28, 15 Stat 14 (1867).

12. Foner, *Reconstruction* at 276–280 (cited in note 2).

13. Eric Foner, *The Strange Career of the Reconstruction Amendments*, 108 Yale L J 2003, 2006 (1999).

14. Id at 2006.

15. Alfred W. Blumrosen, *Modern Law* 17 (U Wisconsin Press, 1993).

16. Michael Les Benedict, *Reconstruction* 381, 382 in Kermit Hall et al., eds, *The Oxford Companion to the Supreme Court of the United States* (Oxford U Press, 1992).

17. Pub L 88-352, 78 Stat 241, codified, as amended, generally at 42 USC § 1971 *et seq* (2009).

18. Codified at 42 USC § 2000a *et seq* (2009).

19. Codified at 42 USC § 2000d *et seq* (2009).

20. Codified,as amended, at 42 USC § 2000e *et seq* (2009).

21. Pub L 89-110, 79 Stat 437, codified, as amended, at 42 USC § 1973 *et seq* (2009).

22. Pub L 90-284; 82 Stat 83, codified, as amended, at 42 USC § 3601 *et seq* (2009).

23. Kenneth L. Karst, *Introduction* xi in Leonard W. Levy, Kenneth L. Karst, and Daniel L. Mahoney, eds, *Civil Rights and Equality* (Macmillan, 1986).

24. Eric Foner, *Reconstruction* 281–291, 602 (Perennial/Harper and Row, 1989); Kenneth Stampp, *The Era of Reconstruction* 165–174 (Vintage/Random House, 1965); John Hope Franklin, *Reconstruction After the Civil War* 109–112 (U Chicago Press, 1994); John Hope Franklin and Alfred A. Moss, *Story of Freedom* chs 12-13 (Knopf, 8th ed, 2000).

25. On the end of Reconstruction under the "compromise" of 1877, see Foner, *Reconstruction* at xxvii, 575–583 (cited above); Stampp, *Reconstruction* at 210 (cited

above); C. Vann Woodward, *Compromise of 1877* in Levy, Karst, and Mahoney, eds, *Civil Rights* at 161, 161–162 (cited in note 23).

26. Stampp, *Reconstruction* at 214 (cited in note 24). See Foner, *Reconstruction* at 602–603 (cited in note 24); Franklin, *Reconstruction* at 169–219 (cited in note 24).

27. Foner, *Reconstruction* at 277 (cited in note 24).

28. Id at 277.

29. For example, a proposed declaration that all persons are equal before the law failed. See Earl M. Maltz, *Civil Rights, Constitution, and Congress, 1863–1869* at 21–28 (U Kansas Press, 1990). As did a proposed federal guarantee of state-law voting rights. Id at 36–37, 46–47, 81, 141–145; Foner, *Reconstruction* at 257–261 (cited in note 24); Stampp, *Reconstruction* at 141–144 (cited in note 24).

30. Maltz, *Civil Rights and the Constitution* at 94 (cited above).

31. The Fourteenth Amendment was adopted in order to shore up the constitutionality of the 1866 Civil Rights Act, but it did not replicate the statute's unprecedented enumeration of substantive rights. Nor did it specifically refer to universal manhood suffrage, even though, as seen, Congress later made this the centerpiece of reunion. The amendment's deliberately broad language strongly suggests the belief that the principle of equal citizenship was compatible with states-rights dogma. See Kenneth L. Karst, *Equal Protection of the Laws* in Levy, Karst, and Mahoney, eds, *Civil Rights* at 33 (cited in note 23). By the same token, the Fifteenth Amendment's reference to the "right to vote" was not necessarily a claim of national origin. Compare the earlier Act of 1867, under which the all-important black franchise was to come into being not pursuant to a self-executing federal mandate, but through state constitutional amendments. See Maltz, *Civil Rights and the Constitution* at 37 (cited in note 29).

32. See Michael Les Benedict, *Constitutional History and Constitutional Theory*, 108 Yale L J 2011, 2026–2027 (1999).

33. Foner, *Reconstruction* at 258–259 (cited in note 24).

34. Benedict, 108 Yale L J at 2203 (cited in note 32).

35. Foner, *Reconstruction* at 277 (cited in note 24).

36. Id at 277.

37. Eric Foner, *Story of Freedom* 65 (Norton, 1998).

38. See Stampp, *Reconstruction* at 122–123 (cited in note 24).

39. Maltz, *Civil Rights and the Constitution* at 37 (cited in note 29).

40. See Foner, *Reconstruction* at 119–123, 587–601 (cited in note 24); Franklin, *Reconstruction* 127–128, 169, 203, 211–213. (cited in note 24); Keith J. Bybee, *Mistaken Identity* 14–16 (Princeton U Press, 1998).

41. In 1870 and 1871, Congress enacted a series of "Force Acts" authorizing armed intervention by the occupation force in order to protect black voters, but these measures were too little, too late. See Foner, *Reconstruction* at 119–123, 342–343, 442–444, 458–459, 558–563, 580–583 (cited in note 24); Stampp, *Reconstruction* at 200–219 (cited in note 24).

42. Foner, *Reconstruction* at 106 (cited in note 24).

43. Id at 103–104.

44. Stampp, *Reconstruction* at 126–133 (cited in note 24).

45. Foner, *Reconstruction* at 106 (cited in note 24).

46. Id at 1–6,156–159; Stampp, *Reconstruction* at 188 (cited in note 24).

47. Jay R. Mandle, *Not Slave, Not Free* ch 1 (Duke U Press, 1992).

48. Stampp, *Reconstruction* at 120 (cited in note 24). For an encyclopedic account of the slaves' occupational skills, see Eugene D. Genovese, *Roll Jordan Roll* 285–398 (Vintage/Random House, 1996). During Reconstruction, the great majority of skilled Southern craftsmen (former slaves) were routinely barred from off-plantation work in their trades on account of their race. See Mandle, *Not Slave, Not Free* at 21–24, 30–32 (cited in note 47).

49. Stampp, *Reconstruction* at 122 (cited in note 24).

50. Eric Foner, *Strange Career of the Reconstruction Amendments*, 108 Yale L J 2003, 2007 (1999).

51. Foner, *Story of Freedom* at 131–132 (cited in note 37).

52. Eric Foner, *Reconstruction* 604 (Perennial/Harper and Row, 1989).

53. See *United States v. Teamsters Union*, 431 U.S. 324, 349 ff (1977) for the Supreme Court's analysis of disparate treatment and disparate impact.

54. See Herman Belz, *Equality Transformed* (Transaction, 1991).

55. See Alfred W. Blumrosen, *Modern Law* (U Wisconsin Press, 1993).

56. 438 U.S. 265, 312, 314.

57. *Grutter v. Bollinger*, 539 U.S. 306, 323 (2003).

58. 438 U.S. 265, 313.

59. *Grutter v. Bollinger*, 539 U.S. at 331.

60. For an extended statement of the nonremedial rationale, see Christopher Edley Jr., *Not All Black and White* 9, 134, 121–141, 189–197 (Hill and Wang, 1996); Nicholas de B. Katzenbach and Burke Marshall, *Not Color Blind, Just Blind*, The New York Times Magazine 42 ff (February 22, 1998); Orlando Patterson, *The Ordeal of Integration* 157 (Civitas/Counterpoint, 1997).

61. *Grutter v. Bollinger*, 539 U.S. 306 (2003).

62. *Parents Involved v. Seattle & Meredith v. Jefferson County Board of Education*, 127 S. Ct. 2738 (2007).

63. Sanford Levinson, *Wrestling with Diversity* 16 (Duke U Press, 2003).

64. Id at 46.

65. Id at 22–53.

66. Id at 52.

67. Peter Schuck, *Diversity in America: Keeping Government at a Safe Distance* chps 1, 4, 7 and *passim* (The Belknap Press of Harvard U Press, 2003).

68. Eric Foner, *Strange Career of Reconstruction Amendments*, 108 Yale L J 2003, 2007 (1999).

69. See Foner, *Story of Freedom* at 131 (cited in note 37).

70. 163 U.S. 537. See Foner, 108 Yale L J at 2007 (cited in note 68), and see Foner, *Story of Freedom* at 133 (cited in note 37).

71. 163 U.S. 537, 544.

72. Id at 559.

73. 16 Wall. (83 U.S.) 36.

74. 92 U.S. 542, 555.

75. 92 U.S. 214, 216.

76. 100 U.S. 313.

77. 100 U.S. 303.

78. 109 U.S. 3.

79. See further commentary on these cases in Leonard W. Levy, Kenneth L. Karst, Dennis J. Mahoney, eds, *Civil Rights and Equality* 157–158, 163–167, 169–172, 173–176, 185–186 (Macmillan, 1986).

80. 347 U.S. 483. See Douglas Rae, *Equalities* 32–33, 41, 80, 103 (Harvard U Press, 1981).

81. Michael Les Benedict, *Constitutional History and Constitutional Theory*, 108 Yale L J 2011, 2033–2035 (1999).

82. Eric Foner, *Story of Freedom* 131–132 (Norton, 1998).

83. Id at 135.

84. Id at 185–193, 236–247.

85. Leon F. Litwack, *Trouble in Mind* 218–219 (Knopf, 1998).

86. *Gaston County v. U.S.*, 395 U.S. 285 (1969); and *Griggs v. Duke Power*, 401 U.S. 424 (1971).

87. John Hope Franklin and Alfred A. Moss, *From Slavery to Freedom* 515–521 (Knopf, 8th ed, 2000); Litwack, *Trouble in Mind* at 135, 314, 405, 430, 481–496 (cited in note 85). The modern phase of the Great Migration is described in Nicholas Lemann, *The Promised Land* (Knopf, 1991).

88. Jay R. Mandle, *Not Slave, Not Free* 72 (Duke U Press, 1992).

89. *Editor's Introduction* in Paul Burstein, ed, *Equal Employment Opportunity* ix, ix–xii (Aldine De Gruyter, 1994); Herbert Hill, *Black Labor* 5, 5–15, in aforementioned volume; Franklin and Moss, *From Slavery to Freedom* at 515–521 (cited in note 87); John Charles Boger, *Race and the American City* 3, 9 and ns 44–47 in John Charles Boger and Judith Welch Wegner, eds, *Race, Poverty, and American Cities* (U of North Carolina Press, 1996); Wegner, *Notes and Reflections*, in aforementioned volume 551, 551–557. It should be noted that the same pattern of urban decay has come to pass in the major metropolitan areas of the South.

90. See *Affirmative Action Review: Report to the President*, 7–8, 40–42 (July 19, 1995), submitted by George Stephanopoulos, Senior Adviser to the President and Christopher Edley Jr., Special Counsel to the President.

91. Peter Dreier, *America's Urban Crisis* in Boger and Wegner, *Race, Poverty, and American Cities* at 79, 102 (cited in note 89); Wegner, *Notes and Reflections* in aforementioned volume at 551–552.

92. Jay R. Mandle, *Not Slave, Not Free* at 32, 68 (cited in note 88).

93. Christina Hoff Sommers, *Who Stole Feminism?* 74–86 (Touchstone/Simon and Schuster, 1995).

94. Cited in Mary Becker, Cynthia Grant Bowman, and Morrison Torrey, eds, *Cases and Materials on Feminist Jurisprudence* 6 (West, 1994).

95. Id at 6.

96. William L. O'Neill, *feminism in America* 3–48 (Transaction Publishers, 2d ed, 1989); David Conway, *Free-Market Feminism* 1, 6–9 in David Conway, ed, *Free-Market Feminism* (IEA Health and Welfare Unit, 1998).

97. Eric Foner, *The Story of American Freedom* 112 (Norton, 1998).

98. O'Neill, *feminism in America* at 119–176 (cited in note 96).

99. Hugh Davis Graham, *Civil Rights and the Presidency* 48 (Oxford U Press, 1992).

100. O'Neill, *feminism in America* at 254–294 (cited in note 96).

101. Graham, *Civil Rights and the Presidency* at 48–50 (cited in note 99).

102. Id at 9.

103. Id.

104. Cited by David Conway, ed, *Free-Market Feminism* at 10–11 (cited in note 96).

105. *Editor's Introduction*, John David Skrentny, ed, *Affirmative Action*, 41 Am Behavioral Scientist 877, 881–883 (1998).

106. *Presumptions for Preferences*, 6 J of Policy History 439, 439–467 (1994) (L/S I); *Deconstructing the Affirmative Action Categories*, 41 Am Behavioral Scientist 913, 913–926 (1998) (L/S II); *Gross Presumptions*, 41 Santa Clara L Rev 103, 103–159 (2000) (L/S III).

107. For a summary of the federal MBE programs, see L/S III at 103 n 1; Also see Appendix One, 337–51.

108. Pub L 95-507: 92 Stat 1761, codified, as amended, at 15 USC 637 *et seq* (2009).

109. L/S I at 443 (cited in note 106). For a history of minority set-asides, see L/S III at 119–120 (cited in note 106); Herman Belz, *Equality Transformed* 195, 201, 296 n 46 (Transaction, 1992).

110. 13 CFR 124.103(b) (2009). Charles V. Dale and Cassandra Foley, *Survey of Federal Laws and Regulations Mandating Affirmative Action Goals, Set-asides or Other Preferences Based on Race, Gender, or Ethnicity* 21 (Congressional Research Service, September 7, 2004).

111. L/S I at 442 and L/S III at 110 (cited in note 106).

112. L/S III at 122–123 (cited in note 106).

113. Id at 129–130, 138–139, 157–159.

114. L/S I at 449 (cited in note 106).

115. See 15 USC 637(a)(5) (2009) (racial or ethnic bias); 15 USC 637(a) (6)(A) (2009). (income limits).

116. L/S III at 123, quoting from an SBA policy manual (cited in note 106).

117. Id at 107–108.

118. L/S II at 920–923; L/S III at 129–131, 156 (cited in note 106).

119. L/S III at 122, 129–130 (cited in note 106).

120. Id at 138–139.

121. Id at 146–147.

122. Id at 122–124.

123. Id at 106, 147.

124. L/S I at 442–444, 445–446. 461; L/S III at 135–136 (cited in note 106).

125. L/S I at 441 (cited in note 106).

126. L/S III at 104, 112, 119, 136–139, 158–159 (cited in note 106).

127. Id at 159.

128. Id at 110.

129. Hugh Davis Graham, *Unintended Consequences*, 41 Am Behavioral Scientist 898, 898–912 (1998); Hugh Davis Graham, *Collision Course: The Strange Convergence of Affirmative Action and Immigration Policy in America* 132 (New York: Oxford U Press, 2002).

130. 29 CFR §1607.4 B (2009).

131. Christopher Edley Jr., *Not All Black and White* 174 (Hill and Wang, 1996).

132. Id at 174.

133. Id at 176.

134. Id at 177.

135. Orlando Patterson, *Ordeal of Integration* 192–193 (Civitas/Counterpoint, 1997).

136. Id at 193.

137. Id at 10.

138. Id at 9–10.

139. Id at 148.

140. Id at 9, 148–156, 163.

141. Id at 148, 158–166.

142. Id at 192.

143. Id at 193.

144. Id at 193.

145. Id at 79–81.

146. Hugh Davis Graham, *Collision Course: The Strange Convergence of Affirmative Action and Immigration Policy in America* 129–132 (Oxford U Press, 2002).

147. Id at 133–143.

148. Id at 132.

149. Graham, 41 Am Behavioral Scientist at 898–912, 910 (cited in note 129).

150. Graham, *Collision Course* at 191–192 (cited in note 146).

151. Id at 157–160.

152. Graham, 41 Am Behavioral Scientist at 909 (cited in note 129).

153. *Producing Conflict: Immigration Management of Diversity in the Multiethnic Metropolis* 147, 147–167 in John D. Skrentny, ed., *Color Lines: Affirmative Action, Immigration, and Civil Rights Options for America* (U of Chicago Press, 2001).

154. Lichter and Waldinger, *Producing Conflict* in id at 161–164 (cited in above note).

155. Skrentny, ed., *Editor's Introduction* 13 in id (cited in note 153).

156. *The Racial and Ethnic Meaning Behind Black: Retailers' Hiring Practices in Inner-City Neighborhoods* at 168, 168–187 in id.

157. Graham, *Collision Course* at 193 (cited in note 146).

158. Id at 197.

159. *Reflections on Race, Hispanicity, and Ancestry in the U.S.* 318, 318–326 in Joel Perlmann and Mary C. Waters, *The New Race Question: How the Census Counts Multiracial Individuals* (Russell Sage Foundation, 2002).

160. Kim M. Williams, *Mark One or More: Civil Rights in Multiracial America* Appendix B (U of Michigan Press, 2005). In 2000, those specifying themselves as Asian had to check an Asian subcategory, namely, Asian Indian, Chinese, Filipino, Japanese, Korean, Vietnamese, Native Hawaiian, Guamanian or Chamorro, Samoan, or to print out the name of another Pacific Island. Id at Appendix B.

161. Joshua R. Goldstein and Ann J. Morning, *Back in the Box: The Dilemma of Using Multiple Race Data For Single Race Laws,* in Perlmann and Waters, *The New Race Question* at 119, 127 (cited in note 159). Where white was coupled with more

than one minority, the allocation depended on the circumstances: where disparate treatment was claimed, the allocation was made to the minority alleged to be the subject of discrimination. Where more than one minority group claimed discriminatory treatment, the allocation of population increases alternated among minority groups. Id at 127.

162. Graham, *Collision Course* at 193 (cited in note 146).

163. Goldstein and Morning, *Back in the Box*, in Perlmann and Waters, *The New Race Question* at 127 (cited in note 159).

164. Id at 127.

165. Peter Skerry, Multiracialism and the Administrative State at 327, 338 in id.

166. *Policy-Elite Perceptions and Social Movement Success: Understanding Variations in Group Inclusion in Affirmative Action*, 111 Am J of Sociology 1762, 1762–1815 (2006).

Chapter Three. The Career of Affirmative Action in Employment

1. On Booker T. Washington, see John Hope Franklin and Alfred A. Moss, *From Slavery to Freedom* 209–306 (Knopf, 8th ed, 2000).

2. Id at 353–354, 452–454; Diane Ravitch, *Troubled Crusade* 120–128 (Basic Books, 1983).

3. Hugh Davis Graham, *Civil Rights Era* 10 (Oxford U Press, 1990).

4. Id at 14–15.

5. Id at 15, 19, 95.

6. Jay R. Mandle, *Not Slave, Not Free* 95–97 (Duke U Press, 1992); Ravitch, *Troubled Crusade* at 138–141 (cited in note 2); John Charles Boger, *Race and the American City* 3, 6, 46 ns 19, 20 in John Charles Boger and Judith Welch Wegner, eds, *Race, Poverty, and American Cities* (U of North Carolina Press, 1996); Graham, *Civil Rights Era* at 74–76, 104–106, 405 ns 3, 4 (cited in note 3). For graphic accounts of the "nonviolent" civil disobedience struggle, see Taylor Branch, *Parting of Waters* (Simon and Schuster, 1988), and *Pillar of Fire* (Simon and Schuster, 1998); Southern Poverty Law Center, *Free at Last* (1989).

7. Executive Order (EO) 10925 (emphasis added). EO 10925 was superseded in 1965 by EO 11246, 3 CFR 1964–1965 Compilation at 339 n 2.

8. See Graham, *Civil Rights Era* at 95–99 (cited in note 3); Paul Burstein, *Discrimination, Jobs, and Politics* 9 (U of Chicago Press, 1998).

9. Id at 8.

10. Pub L 88-352, 78 Stat 241, codified, as amended, generally at 42 USC § 1971 *et seq* (2009).

11. 42 USC § 2000e *et seq* (2009).

12. See authorities collected in Theodore Eisenberg's *Antidiscrimination Legislation and Federal Protection of Civil Rights* 252, 253; 258, 262–263 in Leonard W. Levy, Kenneth L. Karst, and Dennis J. Mahoney, eds, *Civil Rights and Equality* (Macmillan, 1989).

13. Pub L 89-110, 79 Stat 437, codified as amended at 42 USC § 1973 *et seq* (2009).

14. Executive Order 11246 (cited in note 7).

15. John Andrew III, *Lyndon Johnson and the Great Society* 23 (Ivan Dee, 1998).

16. *Editor's Introduction* ix. ix–x, in Paul Burstein, ed, *Equal Employment Opportunity* (Aldine De Gruyter, 1994); David L. Rose, *Twenty-Five Years Later: Where Do We Stand on Equal Employment Law Enforcement*, 42 Vand L Rev 1121, 1132 (1989).

17. Theodore Eisenberg, *Civil Rights Act of 1964*, in Levy, Karst, and Mahoney, eds, *Civil Rights* at 235, 236 (cited in note 12).

18. Id at 235–236.

19. The statistical data presented to Congress on these inequities is summarized in Rose, 42 Vand L Rev at 1129–1132 (cited in note 16); Alfred W. Blumrosen, *Modern Law* 292 (U Wisconsin Press, 1993).

20. Pub L 88-352, 78 Stat 241, § 703(a)(1),(2), codified as amended at 42 USC § 2000e-2(a)(1),(2) (2009). Similar prohibitions apply to nonreferral for employment and exclusion from union membership. See Pub L 88-352, 78 Stat 241, § 703(b), (c), codified as amended at 42 USC § 2000-2(b),(c) (2009).

21. Pub L 88-352, 78 Stat 241, § 703(j), codified, as amended, at 42 USC § 2000e-2(j) (2009).

22. Pub L 88-352, 78 Stat 241 § 706(g), codified as amended at 42 USC § 2000e-5(g)(1) (2009).

23. See Alfred W. Blumrosen, *Modern Law* 47–49 (U of Wisconsin Press, 1993) for analysis of the so-called "Dirksen Compromise" that led to this odd result.

24. Id at 176.

25. Id at 174.

26. Id at 176.

27. Id at 242.

28. Id at 55.

29. Id at 69–70, 101–102.

30. Id at 110, 255, 351 n 2.

31. Id at 80–85, 115–117.

32. Id at 73–75, 80–85, 112–171, 255.

33. Id at 74.

34. David L. Rose, *Twenty-Years Later: Where Do We Stand on Equal Employment Law Enforcement*, 42 Vand L Rev 1121, 1135 (1989).

35. Blumrosen, *Modern Law* at 73–75 (cited in note 23).

36. Id at 65–66, 74, 114–116, 292–294, 382 n. 21, and Rose, 42 Vand L Rev at 1162–1166 (cited in note 34).

37. Id at 1136.

38. Hugh Davis Graham, *Civil Rights Era* 95, 189–204 (Oxford U Press, 1990).

39. 404 U.S. 424 (1971).

40. Graham, *Civil Rights Era* at 389 (cited in note 38).

41. The 1964 Civil Rights Act permitted employers "to give and act upon the results of any professionally developed ability test, provided that such test, its administration, or action upon the results is not designed, intended, or used to discriminate because of race, color, religion, sex or national origin." 42 USC § 2000e-2h (2009). The EEOC's 1966 testing guidelines interpreted "professionally developed

ability test" to mean "a test which fairly measures the knowledge or skills required by the particular job or class of jobs the applicant seeks, or which fairly affords the employer a chance to measure the applicant's ability to perform a particular job or class of jobs." See *Griggs*, 401 U.S. 424 at 431 n 9; Rose, 42 Vand L Rev at 1136 (cited in note 34). Appendices Two, Three and Four located in this volume (355*ff*) contain excerpts from the current guidelines regarding the use of employment tests and other selection procedures.

42. Alfred W. Blumrosen, *Modern Law* 96 (U of Wisconsin Press, 1993).

43. Id at 121.

44. David L. Rose, *Twenty-Five Years Later: Where Do We Stand on Equal Employment Law Enforcement*, 42 Vand L Rev 1121, 1132 (1989).

45. 29 CFR 1607.3 D (2009).

46. Id at 1607.5 C (2009).

47. Id.

48. 422 U.S. 405, 425 (1975).

49. 480 U.S. 616, 676–677.

50. *Ricci v. DeStefano*, Slip Opinion No. 07-1428, 20 (2009).

51. Id at 19–21 (Ginsburg dissent).

52. 29 CFR 1608 (2009).

53. 490 U.S. 642.

54. Slip Opinion No. 07-1428.

55. Blumrosen, *Modern Law* at 124–131 (cited in note 42); See Debra A. Millenson, *Whither Affirmative Action: The Future of Executive Order 11,246*, 29 U of Memphis L Rev 679, 687–691 (1999).

56. *Contractors Ass'n. of Eastern Pennsylvania v. Secretary of Labor*, 442 F 2d 159 (3d Cir), *cert den* 404 U.S. 854 (1971).

57. Hugh Davis Graham, *Voting Rights and the American Regulatory State* 177, 185 in Bernard Grofman and Chandler Davidson, eds, *Controversies in Minority Voting* (Brookings, 1991).

58. *Lutheran Church-Missouri Synod v. FCC*, 141 F 3d 344, 353–354 (D C Cir 1998).

59. Millenson, 29 U of Memphis L Rev at 681–684 (cited in note 55).

60. James T. Patterson, *Restless Giant: The United States from Watergate to Bush v. Gore* 27–28 (Oxford U Press, 2005).

61. Erin Kelly and Frank Dobbin, *How Affirmative Action Became Diversity Management*, 41 Am Behavioral Scientist, 960, 960–984 (1998).

62. Cynthia L. Estlund, *Putting Grutter to Work: Diversity, Integration, and Affirmative Action in the Workplace*, 26 Berkeley J Emp. & Lab L 1, 4 (2005).

63. Kelly and Dobbin, 41 Am Behavioral Scientist at 966–972 (cited in note 61).

64. Id at 966–969.

65. Peter Schuck, *Diversity in America: Keeping Government at a Safe Distance* 160–163 (The Belknap Press of Harvard U Press, 2003); Sanford Levinson, *Wrestling with Diversity* 161 (Duke U Press, 2003).

66. For a revealing account of the adoption of affirmative action as an instrument of crisis management, see John David Skrentny, *The Ironies of Affirmative Action* ch 4 (U of Chicago Press, 1996).

67. Hugh Davis Graham, *Civil Rights Era* 116–117, 456–457 (Oxford U Press, 1990).

68. Id at 120.

69. Id at 460.

70. Alfred W. Blumrosen, *Modern Law* 154 (U of Wisconsin Press, 1993).

71. Id at 153–155.

72. 42 USC 2000e-(5)(g)(1)(2009).

73. Ronald Fiscus, *The Constitutional Logic of Affirmative Action* xiii (Duke U Press, 1992).

74. Pub L 102-166, 105 Stat 1071, codified at 42 USC § 1981 (2009) and elsewhere in sections 2, 29 of 42 USC.

75. 490 U.S. 642.

76. 488 U.S. 469.

77. See Civil Rights Act of 1991, Pub L 102-166, 105 Stat 1071, codified in scattered sections of 2, 29, 42 USC. (2009).

78. Professor Eugene Volokh quoted in Schuck, *Diversity* at 162 (cited note 65).

79. See the *amicus* briefs supportive of the University of Michigan's preferential admissions program at issue in *Grutter v. Bollinger*, 539 U.S. 306 (2003) collected at the LexisNexis Academic Supreme Court briefs Web site covering that case.

80. See *Bolling v. Sharpe*, 347 U.S. 497 (1954).

81. 481 U.S. 469.

82. 515 U.S. 200.

83. 401 U.S. 424.

84. 422 U.S. 405, 425 (1975).

85. 443 U.S. 193.

86. Id at 200.

87. Id at 208.

88. Id at 201–203.

89. Id at 204.

90. Id at 205.

91. See above at 30 for text.

92. 443 U.S. at 206.

93. Id at 208–209.

94. Id at 254–255.

95. 476 U.S. 267.

96. Id at 280–281.

97. 467 U.S. 561.

98. For text of 703(j), see above at 30.

99. 467 U.S. at 581–583.

100. Candidate Reagan promised to abolish or drastically restrict race/ethnic/gender-based equal employment opportunity policies and practices. Due, however, to internal differences in his administration, and the fact that affirmative action was so deeply entrenched in the economy, President Reagan failed to bring about any permanent changes. His civil rights agenda was reduced to deliberate underenforcement by the EEOC, and pursuit of victims only/prior discrimination court rulings. See Herman Belz, *Equality Transformed* 181–207 (Transaction, 1992); Alfred W.

Blumrosen, *Modern Law* 267–269 (U Wisconsin Press, 1993); Robert Detlefsen, *Civil Rights under Reagan* (Inst. For Contemporary Studies, 1991); Steven Shull, *A Kinder and Gentler Racism?* 154 (M. E. Sharpe, 1993).

101. 478 U.S. 421.

102. For text, see 30–31.

103. 478 U.S. at 482.

104. The text is at 30. See Justice O'Connor's dissenting opinion, 478 U.S. at 495–496, on the distinction between "goals" and "quotas" under Title VII. In this connection, see Ronald Fiscus, *The Constitutional Logic of Affirmative Action* (Duke U Press, 1992).

105. 478 U.S. at 483.

106. Id at 479–481, 484.

107. Id at 475.

108. Id at 476.

109. Id at 476–477.

110. Id at 477–478.

111. Id at 479.

112. 478 U.S. 501.

113. Id at 508–509.

114. Hugh Davis Graham, *Civil Rights and the Presidency* 9–10; 107–111 (Oxford U Press, 1992).

115. Id at 111–116, 204.

116. William Henry Chafe, *The Paradox of Change: American Women in the 20th Century* 203 (Oxford U Press, 1991).

117. Cited in Mary Becker, Cynthia Grant Bowman, and Morrison Torrey, eds, *Cases and Materials on Feminist Jurisprudence* 24 (West, 1994). When first introduced to Congress in 1923, the first sentence of the proposed Equal Rights Amendment read: "Men and women shall have equal rights throughout the United States and in every place subject to its jurisdiction." Id at 22.

118. 480 U.S. 616.

119. 443 U.S. 193.

120. 480 U.S. 616, 631.

121. Id at 632, citing *Hazelwood School District v. United States*, 433 U.S. 299 (1977).

122. 480 U.S. 616, 632.

123. Id at 630, 633.

124. Id at 632.

125. Id at 663.

126. Id at 628, n 6.

127. Id at 635–636.

128. Id at 621–622.

129. Id at 636–637.

130. Id at 637.

131. Id at 637–638.

132. Id at 639–640.

133. Alfred W. Blumrosen, *Modern Law* 242–245, 261–262 (U Wisconsin Press, 1993).

134. Herman Belz, *Equality Transformed* 196–200 (Transaction, 1992); John David Skrentny, *Ironies of Affirmative Action* 141, 232 (U Chicago Press, 1996); Melvin I. Urofsky, *Affirmative Action on Trial* 20–22 (U Press Kansas, 1997). Also see appendices to this volume.

135. 443 U.S. 193, 219.

136. 480 U.S. 616, 658.

137. In his *Johnson* dissent, Justice Scalia called on the Court to overrule *Weber*. Id at 673.

138. 438 U.S. 265.

139. 42 USC § 2000d *et seq* (2009).

140. *Regents v. Bakke*, 438 U.S. 265, 306.

141. Id at 271–272.

142. Id at 411.

143. Id at 412.

144. Id at 421.

145. 42 USC § 2000d (2009).

146. *Regents v. Bakke*, 438 U.S. 265, 325–326.

147. Id at 328–340.

148. Id at 355–356.

149. Id at 357–358, 373–375.

150. Id at 359. The "intermediate scrutiny" test was established by the Court in *Craig v. Boren* 429 U.S.190 (1976) for adjudication of gender discrimination claims. See 179–82 and 184–87.

151. *Regents v. Bakke*, 438 U.S. 265, 362, 369–375.

152. Id at 272, 325–326.

153. Id at 271, 421.

154. For example, the decision serves as a primer on the meaning of "quota." The parties differed over whether the set-aside was a "racial quota" because white applicants could not compete for the reserved minority seats (Id at 288 and n 26), or merely a "goal" of minority representation, with neither a "floor" nor a "ceiling" on the total number of minority admittees. Id.

For Justice Powell, it was dispositive that white applicants were limited to competition for only 84 seats rather than the 100 open to minority applicants. In his view, since the limitation was racial on its face, it violated equal protection whether described as a quota or a goal. Id at 289–290 and n 27. Justice Powell also opined that an admissions program that gives appropriate individualized weight to "all pertinent elements of diversity," including race, in evaluating applications by disadvantaged minorities, would pass muster. Id at 317–318.

Justice Brennan held that although the set-aside excludes whites, it will not likely result in "harm comparable to that imposed on . . . minorities by racial segregation." The "purpose [of the set-asides] is to overcome the effects of segregation by bringing the races together," i.e., by reducing the number of white admittees in order to make room for "a reasonable percentage . . . of otherwise underrepresented qualified minority applicants." Id at 374 and n 58. The Davis plan does not discriminate against its purported beneficiaries: it does not establish a quota in the invidious sense of a ceiling on the number of minority admittees, or stigmatize them as inferior (id at 375–376); and there is no constitutional difference between setting aside a fixed number of seats for qualified minority applicants, and—as suggested by Justice Powell—using race as a "positive factor" in evaluating applications by disadvantaged minorities. In terms of result, these approaches are simply different ways of factoring racial preferences into the admission process. Exclusions of nonminority candidates under both are constitutionally equivalent. Id at 378–379, and see Justice Powell's rejoinder at 318–319.

155. Id at 287.

156. Id at 284–285.

157. Id at 287.

158. Id at 291.

159. Id at 305. On this point, Justice Powell wrote only for himself. However, his formulation provided the conceptual basis of the "strict scrutiny" test for affirmative action. See this chapter at 60–74.

160. Id at 307–310, and n 44.

161. Id at 311–315.

162. Id at 319–320.

163. Id at 316–318.

164. 448 U.S. 448.

165. Id at 475–480 (opinion of Burger, C.J.).

166. Id at 517–521.

167. George R. La Noue and James C. Sullivan, *Presumptions for Preferences*, 6 J of Policy History 439, 441 (1994).

168. 515 U.S. 200, 235.

169. 448 U.S. at 495–496.

170. 476 U.S. 267.

171. Id at 284.

172. Id at 274–278.

173. 480 U.S. 149.

174. Id at 185–186.

175. Id at 171–185.

176. Id at 184–185.

177. All of these decisions involved employment discrimination issues: *Wards Cove Packing Co. v. Atonio*, 490 U.S. 642 (1989); *Price Waterhouse v. Hopkins*, 490 U.S. 228 (1989); *Patterson v. McLean Credit Union*, 491 U.S. 164 (1989); *Lorance v. AT&T Technologies*, 490 U.S. 900 (1989); and *Martin v. Wilks*, 490 U.S. 755 (1989). For summaries of these decisions, see David A. Cathcart and Mark Snyderman, *The Civil Rights Act of 1991*, 8 Lab L J 849 (1992); Blumrosen, *Modern Law* at 424 n 6 (cited in note 133). The sixth decision was *City of Richmond v. J. A Croson Co.*, 488 U.S. 469 (1989), involving set-aside of municipal funds for the benefit of minority contractors.

178. 490 U.S. 642.

179. Id at 650.

180. Id.

181. Id at 648, citing *Watson v. Fort Worth Bank & Trust*, 487 U.S. 977 (1988).

182. *Wards Cove*, 490 U.S. 642, 655.

183. Id at 650–651.

184. Id at 651.

185. Id at 651 n 7.

186. Id at 652.

187. Id at 657.

188. Id.

189. Id at 659.

190. Id at 660–661.

191. *Note: The Civil Rights Act of 1991*, 106 Harv L. Rev. 1621, 1623–1624 (1993). See also *Developments in the Law*, 109 Harv L Rev 1568, 1579 (1996).

192. For a statement of this view, see Alfred W. Blumrosen, *Modern Law* 279–282 (U Wisconsin Press, 1993).

193. For a legislative history and analysis of the Act, see J. B. Franke, *The Civil Rights Act of 1991*, 17 S Illinois U L Rev 267, 267–298 (1993).

194. Pub L 102-166, 105 Stat 1071, codified in scattered sections of 2, 29, and 42 U.S.C. (2009).

195. See Blumrosen, *Modern Law* at 284–288 (cited in note 192).

196. 42 USC § 1981 note (2009).

197. Id at § 1981 note (2009).

198. 488 U.S. 469, 505, 507–508.

199. For a history of minority set-asides, beginning with their initiation by the Small Business Administration during the Great Society era, see Herman Belz, *Equality Transformed* 195, 201, 296 n 46 (Transaction, 1992).

200. *Richmond v. Croson*, 488 U.S. 469, 477–478.

201. Id at 478.

202. 497 U.S. 547.

203. Id at 600–601.

204. Id at 564–566.

205. 515 U.S. 200.

206. Id at 227.

207. Id at 237.

208. *Affirmative Action Review: Report to the President* (July 19, 1995), submitted by George Stephanopoulos, Senior Adviser to the President and Christopher Edley Jr., Special Counsel to the President.

209. *Remarks on Affirmative Action*, July 19, 1995, Published Papers and Addresses of President William J. Clinton 1112–1113 (Government Printing Office, 1995).

210. Walter Dellinger, *Memorandum to General Counsels Re Adarand* 1 (Office of Legal Counsel, U.S. Dept of Justice, June 28, 1995).

211. 515 U.S. 200, 237.

212. Dellinger, *Memorandum Re Adarand* at 5 (cited in note 210).

213. 515 U.S. at 227. The concurring opinions of Scalia, id at 239, and Thomas, id at 240 ff, virtually demand a flat constitutional ban. Scalia believes that "government can never have a 'compelling interest' in discrimination on the basis of race in order to 'make up' for past racial discrimination." This is the view that he had previously expressed in *Croson* (488 U.S. at 524), thereby eliciting a declaration of support in principle by Justice Kennedy (see 488 U.S. at 734 ff), and which, in effect, tracks Rehnquist's dissent in the *Weber* case (see 443 U.S. at 219 ff).

214. Jennifer L. Hochschild, *The Future of Affirmative Action*, 59 Ohio State L J 997, 1034 (1998).

215. 515 U.S. 200, 517.

216. 429 U.S. 190.

217. 518 U.S. 515.

218. Id at 531–534.

219. Michael K. Fauntroy, *Disadvataged Businesses: A Review of Federal Assistance* 4–5 (Congressional Research Service, January 14, 2002).

220. Id at 4–5.

221. John R. Schmidt, *Memorandum to General Counsels: Re Post-Adarand Guidance on Affirmative Action* 5 (U.S. Dept of Justice, Office of the Associate Attorney General, February 29, 1996).

222. Richard N. Appel, Alison L. Gray, and Nilufer Loy, *The 40ᵗʰ Anniversary of Title VII of the Civil Rights Act of 1964 Symposium: Affirmative Action in the Workplace, Forty Years Later*, 22 Hofstra Lab & Emp L J 549, 555 (2005).

223. Debra A. Millenson, *Whither Affirmative Action: The Future of Executive Order 11*, 246, 29 U of Memphis L Rev 679, 704 (1999).

224. Id at 696.

225. Walter Dellinger, *Memorandum to General Counsels Re Adarand* 1–2 (Office of Legal Counsel, U.S. Dept of Justice, June 28, 1995).

226. 488 U.S. at 500. Internal quote marks omitted.

227. Dellinger, *Memorandum Re Adarand* at 10 (cited in note 225).

228. Id at 11.See 488 U.S. at 501, 507.

229. 488 U.S. at 501.

230. Dellinger, *Memorandum Re Adarand* at 10 (cited in note 225).

231. U.S. Commission on Civil Rights, *Federal Procurement after Adarand* x (Government Printing Office, September 2005).

232. George La Noue, *To the Disadvantaged Go the Spoils* 91, 91–93, The Public Interest (January 2000).

233. Charles V. Dale, *Minority Contracting and Affirmative Action for Disadvantaged Small Businesses: Legal Issues* 21–22 (Congressional Research Service, February 24, 2006).

234. Derek M. Alphran, *Proving Discrimination after Croson and Adarand: "If It Walks Like a Duck,"* 37 USF L. Rev 887, 915 (2003).

235. Id at 915–916.

236. Dale, *Minority Contracting and Affirmative Action for Disadvantaged Small Businesses* at 21–22 (cited in note 233).

237. Id at 15–20.

238. 321 F3d 950 (10th Cir 2003).

239. Id at 970–972. Also see, Dale, *Minority Contracting and Affirmative Action for Disadvantaged Small Businesses* at 21 (cited in note 233).

240. *Concrete Works of Colorado v. Denver, cert* denied, 540 U.S. 1027 (2003).

241. 515 U.S. at 237–238 citing *Croson*, 488 U.S. at 507.

242. 539 U.S. at 339.

243. U.S. Commission on Civil Rights, *Federal Procurement after Adarand* at xi, 21 (cited in note 231).

244. Id at 81–83.

245. Id at 22–31.

246. Id at xi.

247. Id at 22–23.

248. Id at 31, 71–77.

249. Id at 24–25.

250. Id at 26.

251. Id at 17.

252. La Noue, *To the Disadvantaged Go the Spoils* at 94–95 (cited in note 232).

253. U.S. Civil Rights Commission, *Federal Procurement after Adarand* at 27 (cited in note 231).

254. See Erin Kelly and Frank Dobbin, *How Affirmative Action Became Diversity Management: Employer Reaction to Antidiscrimination Law*, 41 Am Behavioral Scientist 960, 971–972 (1998).

255. Richard D. Kahlenberg, *The Remedy* 27–41 (Basic Books, 1996).

256. Peter Wood, *Diversity: The Invention of a Concept* 117 (Encounter Books, 2003).

257. Id at 135.

258. Dellinger, *Memorandum Re Adarand* at 14 (cited in note 225).

259. 539 U.S. 306.

260. Id at 322.

261. Id at 325.

262. Id at 330.

263. Id at 322.

264. Id at 322.

265. Id at 349.

266. See Cynthia L. Estlund, *Putting Grutter to Work: Diversity, Integration, and Affirmative Action in the Workplace*, 26 Berkeley J Emp & Lab L 1, 1–38 (2005).

267. *Parents Involved v. Seattle*, 127 S. Ct. 2738.

268. Id.

269. 167 L. Ed. 2d 982.

270. Robert Pear, *House Passes 2 Measures on Job Bias*, The New York Times, natl ed, A13 (January 10, 2009).

271. Pub L 111-2.

272. See authorities collected at Samuel Issacharoff, Pamela S. Karlan, and Richard H. Pildes, eds, *The Law of Democracy* 435 (Foundation Press, 1998).

273. Michelle Adams, *The Last Wave of Affirmative Action*, 1998 Wisc L Rev 1395, 1398–1399.

274. Id at 1398–1399.

275. For example, see Walter Dellinger, *Memorandum to General Counsels Re Adarand* 10 (Office of Legal Counsel, U.S. Department of Justice, June 28, 1995).

276. Slip Opinion No. 07-1428 (2009).

277. Id at 20 (Opinion of the Court).

278. Id.

279. Id at 16 (Opinion of the Court).

280. Id at 28 (Opinion of the Court).

281. Id at 28 (Opinion of the Court).

282. Id at 22 (Opinion of the Court).

283. Id at 21 (Opinion of the Court).

284. Id at 26–34 (Opinion of the Court).

285. Id at 19 (Ginsburg dissent).

286. Id at 11 (Ginsburg dissent).

287. Id at 19 (Ginsburg dissent).

288. Id at 20 (Ginsburg dissent).

289. Id at 22 (Ginsburg dissent).

290. Id at 20 (Ginsburg dissent).

291. 401 U.S. 424, 426 (1971) (emphasis added).

292. Id at 430–431.

293. Paul Meier, Jerome Sacks, and Sandy L. Zabell, *What Happened in Hazelwood* 1, 2 in Morris DeGroot, Stephen E. Fienberg, and Joseph B. Kadane, eds, *Statistics and the Law* (Wiley, 1986) (emphasis added).

294. 401 U.S. at 429.

295. 433 U.S. 299.

296. Id at 312 n 17.

297. Id at 307–308.

298. Meier, Sacks, and Zabell, *What Happened in Hazelwood* at 3, 5, (emphasis added); Dolores A. Conway and Harry V. Roberts, *Regression Analysis in Employment Discrimination Cases* 107, 107–165; Robert F. Coulam and Stephen Fienberg, *The Use of Court-Appointed Statistical Experts* 305, 305–331 in DeGroot, Fienberg, Kadane, eds, *Statistics and the Law* (cited in note 293).

299. See material in Meier, Sacks, and Zabell, *What Happened in Hazelwood* in id at 24 (cited in note 293 above).

300. Id at 5.

301. Id at 4–5.

302. Id at 7.

303. Lawrence Tribe, *Trial by Mathematics: Precision and Ritual in the Legal Process*, 84 Harv L Rev 1329, 1329–1393 (1971).

304. "Expert" discussion on quantitative criteria can be found in Meier et al, *What Happened in Hazelwood* at 1–39; Stephen E. Fienberg, *Comment* 41. 41–46; Paul Meier et al, *Rejoinder* 47, 47–48; Conway and Roberts, *Regression Analysis in Employment Discrimination Cases* at 107–166 in DeGroot, Fienberg, and Kadane, eds, *Statistics and the Law* (cited in note 293).

305. John R. Schmidt, *Memorandum to General Counsels: Re Post-Adarand Guidance on Affirmative Action* 12 (U.S. Dept of Justice, Office of the Associate Attorney General, February 29, 1996).

306. Id at 16.

307. 539 U.S. 306, 379.

308. Id at 380–381.

309. Id at 383.

310. Id at 384–385.

311. Id at 383.

312. Id at 389.

313. Anne B. Fisher, *Business Likes to Hire by the Numbers*, Fortune 26 ff (September 16, 1985); Herman Belz, *Equality Transformed* 196–202 (Transaction, 1991).

314. U.S. Department of Commerce, *Statistical Abstract of the United States* 2007 Table 602.

315. Id at Table 608.

316. Id at Table 40.

317. Id at Table 682.

318. U.S. Department of Labor, Bureau of Labor Statistics, *Women in the Labor Force: A Databook* 1 (2006 Edition).

319. Id at 1.

320. Id.

321. Id.

322. *Editor's Preface*, in Suzanne W. Helburn, ed., *The Silent Crisis in Child Care* 563 Annals of the Am Academy of Political and Social Science, 8, 8–19 (May 1999).

323. Peggie R. Smith, *Laboring for Child Care: A Consideration of New Approaches to Represent Low-Income Service Workers*, 8 U Pa J. Lab. & Emp. L 583, 587 (2006).

324. John David Skrentny, *Policy-Elite Perceptions and Social Movement Success: Understanding Variations in Group Inclusion in Affirmative Action*, 111 Am J of Sociology 1762, 1777–1782 (2006).

325. William L. O'Neill, *feminism in America* 315 (Transaction, 2d rev ed 1989).

326. U.S. Department of Commerce, *Statistical Abstract of the United States, 2007*, Table 564.

327. Editor's *Preface*, at 8–19; John Morris, *Market Constraints on Child Care Quality* 130, 130–145; Mary Whitebook, *Child Care Workers* 146, 146–161 in Helburn, ed., *The Silent Crisis in Child Care* (cited in note 322); Smith, *Laboring for Child Care*, 8 U Pa J. Lab & Emp L at 587–589 (cited in note 323).

328. Julia Wrigley, *Hiring A Nanny* in Helburn, ed, *The Silent Crisis in Child Care* at 162, 173 (cited in note 322).

329. Editor's *Preface* in Helburn, ed, *The Silent Crisis in Child Care* at 8–19 (cited in note 322).

330. Godfrey Hodgson, *More Equal Than Others: America from Nixon to the New Century* 153 (Princeton U Press, 2004).

331. Fred Dvorak, *Women Slowly Break into the Boardroom, The Wall Street Journal* B3 (March 27, 2006).

332. Hodgson, *More Equal Than Others* at 151 (cited in note 330).

333. Id at 153.

334. Mary Becker, *Patriarchy and Inequality: Towards A Substantive Feminism*, 1999 U Chi Legal F 21, 21–86; Nicole Buonocore Porter, *Re-Defining Superwoman: An Essay on Overcoming the "Maternal Wall" in the Legal Workplace*, 13 Duke J Gender L & Pol'y 55.55-84 (2006).

335. George Rutherglen, *Employment Discrimination Law: Visions of Equality in Theory and Doctrine*, 2d ed, 114 (Foundation Press, 2007).

336. Heather S. Dixon, *National Daycare: A Necessary Precursor to Gender Equality with New Found Promise of Success*, 30 Colum Human Rights L Rev 561 (2005).

337. Harry J. Holzer and David Neumark, *Affirmative Action: What Do We Know?* 25 J of Policy Analysis and Management 463, 469 (2006).

338. Stephan and Abigail Thernstrom, *America in Black and White* 499–504, 533 (Simon and Schuster, 1997); Orlando Patterson, *The Ordeal of Integration* 81 (Civitas/Counterpoint, 1997).

339. Christopher Edley, *Not All Black and White* 42–46 (Hill and Wang, 1996).

340. Richard Epstein, *Forbidden Grounds: The Case against Employment Discrimination Laws* (Harvard U Press, 1992) (demands repeal of Title VII); Richard A. Posner, *The Efficiency and Efficacy of Title VII*, 136 U Penn L Rev 512, 512–521 (1987).

341. John J. Donohue, *Is Title VII Efficient?* 134 U of Penn L Rev 1411, 1411–1436 (1986).

342. Harry Holzer and David Neumark, *Assessing Affirmative Action*, 38 J of Economic Literature 483, 558 (September 2000).

343. George M. Fredrickson, *America's Caste System: Will It Change?* 68, 68–75 *The New York Review of Books* (October 23, 1997); Andrew Hacker, *Goodbye to Affirmative Action?* 21, 21–28 *The New York Review of Books* (July 11, 1996).

344. U.S. Department of Commerce, *Statistical Abstract of the United States, 1998*, Table 472; *Statistical Abstract of the United States, 2007*, Table 40.

345. Stephan and Abigail Thernstrom, *America in Black and White* 183–184 (Simon and Schuster, 1997).

346. Paul Burstein, Editor's *Introduction* to *Chapter IV* 129, 130 in Paul Burstein, ed, *Equal Employment Opportunity* (Aldine De Gruyter, 1994).

347. James P. Smith and Finis R. Welch, *Black Economic Progress after Myrdal* in id at 155, 178.

348. John J. Donohue and James Heckman, *Continuous Versus Episodic Change* in id at 183, 202.

349. Burstein, *Editor's Introduction* to *Chapter IV* in id at 130.

350. Harry Holzer and David Neumark, *Assessing Affirmative Action*, 38 J of Economic Literature 483, 558 (September 2000).

351. Id at 503–504, 558.

352. Id.

353. Id at 506–507.

354. Id at 512–513.

355. Id at 507.

356. Id at 544, 558.

357. Id at 558.

358. Id at 559–560.

359. Harry J. Holzer and David Neumark, *Affirmative Action: What Do We Know?* 25 J of Policy Analysis and Management 463, 472, 463–490 (2006).

360. Id at 484.

361. Id at 474.

362. For example, in Christopher Edley, *Not All Black and White* (Hill and Wang, 1996), the author concedes that affirmative action has had only "a modest positive effect on employment," but contends that we are *morally* obliged to continue it. Id at 51.

Chapter Four. Affirmative Action and the Primary and Secondary Schools

1. 163 U.S. 537.

2. Leonard W. Levy, *Plessy v. Ferguson* 173, 173–176 in Leonard W. Levy, Kenneth L. Karst, and Dennis J. Mahoney, eds, *Civil Rights and Equality* (Macmillan, 1989).

3. Kenneth L. Karst, *Separate But Equal Doctrine* in Levy, Karst, Mahoney, eds, *Civil Rights* at 185, 185–186 (cited above).

4. 5 Cush (Mass) 198.

5. Leonard W. Levy, *Roberts v. City of Boston* in Levy, Karst, and Mahoney, eds, *Civil Rights* at 80 (cited in note 2).

6. Kenneth L. Karst, *Segregation* in id at 169 (cited in note 2).

7. Diane Ravitch, *Troubled Crusade* 115 (Basic Books, 1983).

8. 109 U.S. 3.

9. *Buchanan v. Warley*, 245 U.S. 60 (1917).

10. *Guinn v. U.S.*, 238 U.S. 347 (1915).

11. *Nixon v. Herndon*, 273 U.S. 536 (1927); *Nixon v. Condon*, 286 U.S. 73 (1932).

12. 347 U.S. 483.

13. Kenneth L. Karst, *Separate But Equal*, in Levy, Karst, Mahoney, eds, *Civil Rights* at 185, 186 (cited in note 2).

14. Kenneth L. Karst, *Brown v. Board of Education (1954)* in id at 208, 212 (cited in note 2).

15. 349 U.S. 294.

16. Pub L 88-352, 78 Stat. 241, codified, as amended, at 42 U S C. 2000d *et seq* (2009).

17. *Green v. The Board*, 391 U.S. 430 (1968); *Alexander v. Holmes County*, 396 U.S. 19 (1969); *Swann v. Charlotte-Mecklenburg*, 402 U.S. 1 (1971).

18. James T. Patterson, *Brown v. Board of Education: A Civil Rights Milestone and Its Troubled Legacy* 207, 211 (Oxford U Press, 2001).

19. Ravitch, *Troubled Crusade* at 179 (cited in note 7).

20. 498 U.S. 237.

21. 515 U.S. 70.

22. Id at 120–121. Justice Thomas is strongly supported in this view by William H. Tucker, *The Science and Politics of Racial Research* ch 4 (U Illinois Press, 1994).

23. 127 S. Ct. 2738.

24. Steven Halpern, *On the Limits of Law* 167, 174, 270 (Johns Hopkins U Press, 1995).

25. (Urban Institute Press, 2006).

26. 413 U.S. 189.

27. Jack Greenberg, *Civil Rights* in Levy, Karst, Mahoney, eds, *Civil Rights* at 10 (cited in note 2).

28. Diane Ravitch, *Troubled Crusade* 177 (Basic Books, 1983).

29. 418 U.S. 717.

30. 127 S. Ct. 2738.

31. Id at 2792.

32. *Wessmann v. Gittens*, 160 F 3d 790, 798, 796–800 (1st Cir 1998).

33. 195 F 3d 698 (4th Cir 1999).

34. Id at 701.

35. 127 S. Ct. 2738.

36. *Missouri v. Jenkins*, 515 U.S. 70.

37. Gary Orfield, et al., *Dismantling Desegregation* 20–21 (New Press, 1996).

38. U.S. Department of Education, *The State of Charter Schools, Third Year Report, 1999* at 42.

39. United States Department of Commerce, *Statistical Abstract of the United States; 2007,* Table 226; Kevin Welner, *Vouchers Under the Radar,* District Administration 11 (December 2008).

40. Orfield et al., *Dismantling Desegregation* at 21, 25 (cited in note 37).

41. 402 U.S. 1 (1971).

42. *Keyes v. School District #1, Denver,* 413 U.S. 189 (1973).

43. Hugh Davis Graham, *Civil Rights Era* 366–375 (Oxford U Press, 1990).

44. K. B.Clark, *Effect of Prejudice and Discrimination on Personality Development* (Midcentury White House Conference on Children and Youth, 1950); Witmer and Kotinsky, *Personality in the Making* ch vi (1952); Deutscher and Chein, *The Psychological Effects of Enforced Segregation: A Survey of Social Science Opinion,* 26 J. Psychol. 259 (1948); Chein, *What Are the Psychological Effects of Segregation under Conditions of Equal Facilities?,* 3 Int. J. Opinion and Attitude Res. 229 (1949); Brameld, *Educational Costs, in Discrimination and National Welfare* 44–48 (MacIver, ed.,1949); Frazier, *The Negro in the United States* 674–681 (1949). See generally Myrdal, *An American Dilemma* (1944).

45. Ravitch, *Troubled Crusade* at 179 (cited in note 28).

46. The studies cited in *Brown I* have received harsh criticism. See, e.g., Yudof, *School Desegregation: Legal Realism, Reasoned Elaboration, and Social Science Research in the Supreme Court,* 42 Law & Contemp Prob 57, 70 (Autumn 1978); L. Graglia, *Disaster by Decree: The Supreme Court Decisions on Race and the Schools* 27–28 (1976). Moreover, there simply is no conclusive evidence that desegregation either has sparked a permanent jump in the achievement scores of black children, or has remedied any psychological feelings of inferiority black schoolchildren might have had. See, e.g., Bradley and Bradley, *The Academic Achievement of Black Students in Desegregated Schools,* 47 Rev. Educational Research 399 (1977); N. St. John, *School Desegregation: Outcomes for Children* (1975); Epps, *The Impact of School Desegregation on Aspirations, Self-Concepts, and Other Aspects of Personality,* 39 Law & Contemp Prob 300 (Spring 1975). Contra, Crain, and Mahard, *Desegregation and Black Achievement: A Review of the Research,* 42 Law & Contemp Prob 17 (Summer 1978); Crain and Mahard, *The Effect of Research Methodology on Desegregation-Achievement Studies: A Meta-Analysis,* 88 Am. J. of Sociology 839 (1983). Although the gap between black and white test scores has narrowed over the past two decades, it appears that this has resulted more from gains in the socioeconomic status of black families than from desegregation. See Armor, *Why Is Black Educational Achievement Rising?,* 108 The Public Interest 65, 77–79 (Summer 1992).

47. 349 U.S. 294.

48. Id at 300–301.

49. 42 USC 2000d *et seq* (2009).

50. 391 U.S. 430.

51. Id at 442.

52. *Alexander v. Holmes County Board of Education,* 396 U.S. 19, 20 (1969).

53. *Swann v. Charlotte-Mecklenberg,* 402 U.S. 1, 24 (1971).

54. David Armor, *Forced Justice* 158–160 (Oxford U Press, 1995).

55. Diane Ravitch, *Troubled Crusade* 176, 268,142–143, 162–165 (Basic Books, 1983).

56. *Keyes v. School District #1, Denver,* 413 U.S. 189 (1973).

57. Ravitch, *Troubled Crusade* at 177 (cited in note 55).

58. 418 U.S. 717.

59. Gary Orfield, et al., *Dismantling Desegregation* 12 (New Press, 1996).

60. *Parents Involved v. Seattle*, 127 S. Ct. 2738 at 2788–2791.

61. Id at 2791.

62. Id at 2792, 2793.

63. Id at 2788.

64. Id at 2814.

65. The authors' review of the Orfield, Halpern, and Armor books covered in this section is largely from our essay, *Affirmative Action and the Presidential Role in Modern Civil Rights Reform: A Sampler of Books of the 1990's*, 29 Presidential Studies Quarterly 175, 184–188 (1999). Center for the Study of the Presidency. It is reprinted here with the permission of Sage Publications.

66. Steven Halpern, *On the Limits of Law* (Johns Hopkins U Press, 1995).

67. Id at ix, x, 133, 303–304, ch 1.

68. Id at ch 7.

69. 42 U.S.C. § 2000d *et seq* (2009).

70. Halpern, *On the Limits of Law* at ch 4, 50–80, 81–136, 231–235 (cited in note 66).

71. Peter Schmidt, *Clinton Civil-Rights Agenda Cloudy*, Education Week 1, 15 (January 25, 1995).

72. Patrick J. McGuinn, *No Child Left Behind and the Transformation of Federal Education Policy, 1965–2005* 5–6 (U Kansas Press, 2006).

73. Gary Orfield, et al., *Dismantling Desegregation* (cited in note 59).

74. Id at 344.

75. Id at 12.

76. Id at ch 12.

77. Id at 346–348.

78. *Milliken v. Bradley*, 418 U.S. 717.

79. Orfield, *Dismantling Desegregation* at 10 (cited in note 59).

80. 433 U.S. 267 (1977).

81. 515 U.S. 70.

82. Orfield et al., *Dismantling Desegregation* at xxiii (cited in note 59).

83. Id at 21.

84. Id at chs 1–4.

85. Id at 14–16.

86. Hugh Davis Graham, *Civil Rights Era* 320–321 (Oxford U Press, 1990).

87. David Armor, *Forced Justice* (Oxford U Press, 1995).

88. Id at 158–160.

89. Diane Ravitch, *Troubled Crusade* 163 (Basic Books, 1983).

90. Christine H. Rossell, *The Fulfillment of Brown* 45, 47–48 in Richard Fossey, ed, *The Courts, and Equal Education*, in vol 15 of *Readings on Equal Education* (AMS Press, 1998).

91. Armor, *Forced Justice* at 76–98, 99–102, 174–188, 169–174 (cited in note 87).

92. Id at 172–188. Doubtless, the atrophy of "exposure" is also a function of mass minority immigration since the late 1960s, along with the high minority

fertility rate. In many big cities, the non-Hispanic white student body has declined so dramatically that—in Stephan Thernstrom's view—"it has become absurd to bus white kids all over the place in the quest for an elusive racial balance." Letter from Professor Stephan Thernstrom to the authors, July 3, 1999.

93. Armor, *Forced Justice* at 228–233 (cited in note 87).

94. Gary Orfield, et al., *Dismantling Desegregation* 82, 86 (New Press, 1996).

95. Stephan and Abigail Thernstrom, *No Excuses: Closing the Racial Gap in Learning* (Simon and Schuster (2003).

96. Id at 174–179.

97. Id at 187.

98. Id at 12–14.

99. Id at 2.

100. Id at 14.

101. Id at 274.

102. Id at 167.

103. Id at 217.

104. Id at 121–122.

105. Id at 83–84.

106. Id at 248–267.

107. Id at 313, n 4.

108. Michael Winerip, *What A Voucher Study Truly Showed and Why*, The New York Times, natl ed, A 27 (May 7, 2003).

109. Peter Edelman, Harry Holzer, and Paul Offner, *Reconnecting Disadvantaged Young Men* (Urban Institute Press, 2006).

110. Id at 1–9.

111. Id at 26.

112. Id at 13.

113. Id at 15.

114. Id at 19.

115. Id at chs 5, 6.

116. Id at ch 3.

117. Id at 70–71.

118. Id at 56.

119. Diane Ravitch, *Troubled Crusade* 268–274 (Basic Books, 1983).

120. Rachel F. Moran, *The Politics of Discretion: Federal Intervention in Bilingual Education*, 76 Cal Law Rev 1249, 1288 (1988).

121. U.S. Congress, House of Representatives, *Reforming Bilingual Education*, Hearing before the Subcommittee on Early Childhood, Youth, and Families, of the Committee on Education and the Workforce, 105th Congress, 2d Sess, 208–209 (April 30, 1998).

122. Ethan Bronner, *Bilingual Education Is Facing Its Demise in California*, The New York Times, natl ed, A1 (May 30, 1998).

123. Hearing before the Subcommittee on Early Childhood, Youth, and Families, 105th Congress, 2d Sess, at 209–211 (cited in note 121).

124. Id at 209.

125. Guadalupe San Miguel, *Contested Policy: The Rise and Fall of Bilingual Education in the United States, 1960–2008* 38 (U North Texas Press, 2004).

126. Cited by Moran, 76 Cal L Rev at 1302 (cited in note 120).

127. Hearing before the Subcommittee on Early Childhood, Youth and Families, 105th Congress, 2d Sess, at 2–7 (cited in note 121).

128. Study reviewed in Moran, 76 Cal L Rev at 1285 (cited in note 120).

129. Id at 1288.

130. Luis Rodriguez, *Discretion and Destruction: The Debate Over Language in California's Schools*, 4 Texas Forum on Liberties & Civil Rights 189, ns 244, 245 (Summer/Fall, 1999).

131. Cited by Moran, 76 Cal L Rev at 1266 (cited in note 120).

132. 414 U.S. 563.

133. Id at 566.

134. Id at 567–568. Only four years after *Lau*, a conflict between Title VI's administrative regulations and the statute itself emerged. In *Regents v. Bakke* 438 U.S. 265 (1978), a Court majority, deviating from the majority in *Lau*, interpreted Title VI as barring only intentional discrimination where state action was involved. This interpretation has been adhered to by the Court as have, curiously enough, Title VI's administrative regulations (affecting public programs) that prohibit disparate-impact discrimination where bad intent has not been shown to exist. This tension between the statute and its "subordinate" administrative regulations is yet to be resolved. However, in 2001, the Supreme Court determined that states could not be barred by federal statute from disparately impacting the disabled in state employment, as evidence of such impact was insufficient to prove state wrongdoing. *Alabama v. Garrett*, 531 U.S. 356, 372–373 (2001).

135. 414 U.S. at 565.

136. Rachel F. Moran, *The Politics of Discretion: Federal Intervention in Bilingual Education*, 76 Cal Law Rev 1249, 1280–1282 (1988).

137. Statement of James M. Littlejohn at U.S. Congress, House of Representatives, *Reforming Bilingual Education*, Hearing before the Subcommittee on Early Childhood, Youth, and Families, of the Committee on Education and the Workforce, 105th Congress, 2d Sess, 261 (April 30, 1998).

138. 648 F 2d 989 (5th Cir 1989).

139. Statement of James M. Littlejohn in Hearing before the Subcommittee on Early Childhood, Youth, and families, 105th Congress, 2d Sess, at 261 (cited in note 137).

140. Rachel F. Moran, *Bilingual Education As A Status Conflict*, 75 Cal L Rev 321, 332–333, 341–349 (1987).

141. California Secretary of State, *Proposition 227*, in California Ballot Pamphlet for the Primary Election, June 2, 1998 at 75–76.

142. Don Terry, *The Reply, It Turned Out, Was a Bilingual No*, The New York Times, natl ed, A10 (June 5, 1998).

143. Id.

144. Statement of Richard W. Riley, U.S. Secretary of Education, in U.S. Congress, House of Representatives, *Reforming Bilingual Education*, Hearing before the Subcommittee on Early Childhood, Youth, and Families, of the Committee on Education and the Workforce, 105th Congress, 2d Sess, 243–248 (April 30, 1998).

145. Meredith May, *Districts Give Final Say on Prop. 227*, The San Francisco Chronicle A15 (September 29, 1999).

146. Louis Shagun, *L.A. Schools Are Abusing Prop. 227, Report Says*, Los Angeles *Times* B3 (July 1, 1999).

147. Don Terry, *California Bilingual Teaching Lives On after Vote to Kill It*, The *New York Times*, natl ed, A1, A17 (October 3, 1998).

148. Christine Rossell, *Dismantling Bilingual Education, Implementing English Immersion: The California Initiative* i–iv (Public Policy Institute of California, 2002).

149. Lisa B. Ross, *Note: Learning the Language: An Examination of the Use of Voter Initiative to Make Language Education Policy*, 82 NYU L Rev 1510, 1511–1512 (2007). The language controversy in Arizona is extensively described in *Horne v. Flores*, 129 S. Ct. 2579 (2009).

150. Debra Vadero, *Delving Deep: Research Hones Focus on ELLs*, Education Week 22, 22–25 (January 8, 2009). Also see Lori Aratami, *Espanol, English Mingle in Md. Classroom*, The *Washington Post* C1 (November 12, 2006).

151. John Rhee, *Theories of Citizenship and Their Role in the Bilingual Education Debate*, 33 Colum J L & Soc Probs 33, 79 (1991).

152. *Diversity in America: Keeping Government at a Safe Distance* 121–122 (The Belknap Press of Harvard U Press, 2003).

153. Diane Ravitch, *Troubled Crusade* 228–266 (Basic Books, 1983).

154. Jodi Wilgoren, *2 Florida Schools Become Test Ground For Vouchers*, The *New York Times*, natl ed, A18 (March 14, 2000).

155. P L 107–110; 115 Stat 1425 (2002) codified at 20 USC § 6313 *et seq* (2009).

156. *No Child Left Behind and the Transformation of Federal Education Policy, 1965–2005*, 180–181, 196–202 (U Press of Kansas, 2006).

157. L. Scott Miller, *Promoting Academic Achievement Among Non-Asian Minorities* 47, 71, in Eugene L. Lowe, ed, *Promise and Dilemma* (Princeton U Press, 1997).

158. Id at 72–73.

Chapter Five. Affirmative Action in Higher Education

1. Pub L 92-318, 86 Stat 373, codified, as amended, at 20 USC § 1681 *et seq* (2009).

2. Diane Ravitch, *Troubled Crusade* 268 (Basic Books, 1983).

3. Gary Orfield, *Campus Resegregation and Its Alternatives* 1–6 in Gary Orfield and Edward Miller, eds, *Chilling Admissions* (Harvard Education Publishing Group, 1998).

4. 416 U.S. 312.

5. 438 U.S. 265.

6. Susan Welch and John Gruhl, *Affirmative Action and Minority Enrollments in Medical and Law Schools* 140 (U of Michigan Press, 1998).

7. 76 F3d 932.

8. Id at 944–946.

9. 539 U.S. 306.

10. 539 U.S. 244.

11. (U Michigan Press, 1998).

12. *Behind Bakke: Affirmative Action and the Supreme Court* (NYU Press, 1988).

13. Welch and Gruhl, *Affirmative Action and Minority Enrollments* at 140 (cited in note 6).

14. Id at 140–143.

15. Letter to authors, July 3, 1999.

16. U.S. Department of Education, National Center for Educational Statistics, *Status and Trends in the Education of Racial and Ethnic Minorities* (September 2007).

17. Letter to the authors, July 3, 1999.

18. 72 NYU L Rev 1 (April 1997).

19. Id at 50.

20. Id at 1–2.

21. *Diversity and Meritocracy in Legal Education: A Critical Evaluation of Linda F. Wightman's The Threat to Diversity in Legal Education*, 15 Constitutional Commentary 37, 39 (Spring 1998).

22. Id at 39.

23. Richard Kahlenberg, *The Remedy* 98–101(Basic Books, 1996).

24. K. Anthony Appiah and Amy Gutmann, *Color Conscious: The Political Morality of Race* 140–141 (Princeton U Press, 1996).

25. Id at 141 n 38.

26. Ronald Dworkin, *Affirming Affirmative Action*, New York Review of Books 91, 91–102 (October 22, 1998). The cited essay appears as chapter 11, *Affirmative Action: Does It Work?* in Dworkin's *Sovereign Virtue* (Harvard, 2000). See also chapter 12, *Affirmative Action: Is It Fair?*

27. William Bowen and Derek Bok, *The Shape of the River* (Princeton U Press, 1998).

28. These were Bryn Mawr, Duke, Princeton, Rice, Stanford, Swarthmore, Williams, Yale, Barnard, Columbia, Emory, Hamilton, Kenyon, Northwestern, Oberlin, Smith, Tufts, University of Pennsylvania, Vanderbilt, Washington University, Wellesley, Wesleyan, Denison, Miami University (Ohio), Pennsylvania State, Tulane, Michigan (Ann Arbor), and the University of North Carolina (Chapel Hill).

29. Ronald Dworkin, *New York Review of Books* at 91, 91–93 (October 22, 1998).

30. Id at 93, quoting original.

31. Id at 102.

32. Id at 94. To Dworkin, Bowen and Bok found that application of race-neutral admission policies would have substantially reduced the number of blacks actually admitted to the elite schools. In Dworkin's view, there is no basis for assuming that the black applicants who would have been rejected if race-neutral tests had been used were less qualified than those admitted, given the closeness of the average test scores for both groups. Therefore, "while abolishing affirmative action would very greatly decrease the number of blacks who attended selective schools, it would not much improve the average scores of those who did." Id at 94.

33. Id at 94–95.

34. Id at 95–96.

35. This is obviously a sore spot with many affirmative action supporters, but Dworkin reports that the overwhelming number of blacks canvassed by Bowen and Bok applauded their universities' race-sensitive policies. Id at 97–98.

36. Id at 98.

37. Id at 98–100.

38. Id at 100. Dworkin claims that current versions of affirmative action in university admissions do not use quotas or require decisions "simply by virtue of race." Id at 100.

39. Id at 100–101. Dworkin rejects the notion that it is impossible to distinguish between "invidious use of race to achieve results in themselves creditable from a so-called 'benign' use." Id at 100.

40. Id at 101.

41. Id at 94–95.

42. Stephan and Abigail Thernstrom, *America in Black and White* 393 (Simon and Schuster, 1997).

43. Id at ch 14.

44. Id.

45. Id at 409. Professor Thernstrom pointed out that the above-cited Dworkin 11% higher black dropout figure was an error. He wrote that Bowen and Bok "calculate two sorts of graduation rates (and their converse dropout rates). Appendix Table D.3.1 shows that the 1989 first-school dropout rate for blacks was 25.3[%] and for whites 14.2[%]. The overall dropout rate, including those who transferred and graduated elsewhere, was 20.8[%] for blacks, 6.3[%] for whites. In the former case, we do have a difference of 11 points, but that does not mean that the black rate was only 11 percent higher than that for whites; it was 78 percent higher!! 11 points higher would be correct." Letter to the authors, July 3, 1999.

46. *A Systemic Analysis of Affirmative Action in American Law Schools*, 57 Stan L Rev 367 (2004).

47. Id at 372.

48. Id at 371.

49. Id at 449–450.

50. Id at 371, 373–374, 479.

51. Id at 450.

52. Id at 373–374.

53. Id at 375, 378, 382–383, 480.

54. Id at 480.

55. Id at 406–409.

56. Id at 405

57. Id at 416.

58. Id at 478–479.

59. Id at 482.

60. Id at 477.

61. Id at 483.

62. John Hechinger, *Critics Assail Study of Race, Law Students, The Wall Street Journal* B1, B3 (January 5, 2004).

63. 57 Stan L Rev at 476 (cited in note 46).

64. Hechinger, *The Wall Street Journal* at B1, B3 (January 5, 2004, cited in note 62).

65. Harry Holzer and David Neumark, *Assessing Affirmative Action*, 38 J of Economic Literature 483, 483–568 (2000).

66. *Affirmative Action: What Do We Know?*, 25 J of Policy Analysis and Management 463, 463–490 (2006).

67. Holzer and Neumark, 38 J of Economic Literature at 558 (cited in note 65).

68. Id at 509.

69. Id at 510–512.

70. Id at 553, 558–559.

71. Id.

72. Id at 553, 559.

73. Id.

74. Holzer and Neumark, 25 J of Policy Analysis and Management at 483 (cited in note 66).

75. Id.

76. Id at 481.

77. Id at 482.

78. Id at 487.

79. Id at 480.

80. Id.

81. 505 U.S. 717.

82. *The Wall Street Journal* A11 (June 28, 2008).

83. Id.

84. *Racial Diversity Reconsidered,* The Public Interest 25–38 (Spring 2003).

85. Id at 29–30.

86. Id at 29–38.

87. 539 U.S. 306 (2003).

88. 539 U.S. 244 (2003).

89. 539 U.S. at 328.

90. Patricia Gurin, et al., *Defending Diversity: Affirmative Action at the University of Michigan* 99 (U Michigan Press, 2003).

91. Id at 173, 179.

92. 539 U.S. at 330.

93. Gurin, et al., *Defending Diversity* at 98 (cited in note 90).

94. Id at 115.

95. Id at 206, n 4.

96. Id at 117.

97. Id at 117–118.

98. Id at 119.

99. Id at 170.

100. Id at 131–132.

101. Id.

102. Id at 165.

103. Id at 175.

104. *The New York Times,* natl ed, Sect 4, p 7 (February 23, 2003).

105. Holman W. Jenkins Jr., *Why the Michigan Case Matters to Business, The Wall Street Journal* A15 (January 22, 2003).

106. *Consolidated Brief of Lt. General Julius W. Becton, Jr., et al,* 2003, LexisNexis Academic: 2003 Supreme Court Briefs 532 (February 19, 2003).

107. David Savage, *Justices Hear Affirmative Action Cases*, Los Angeles Times A17 (April 2, 2003).

108. Id at A17.

109. 38 F 3d 147 (4th Cir).

110. 78 F 3d 932, 952–955 (5th Cir).

111. 78 F3d 932 (5th Cir).

112. 233 F3d 1188 (9th Cir).

113. 78 F3d 932 (5th Cir, 1996).

114. Id at 945.

115. Id at 946.

116. Id at 947.

117. 233 F3d 1188.

118. Id at 1197–1200.

119. *Regents v. Bakke*, 438 U.S. 265, 324–325.

120. 122 F Supp 2d 811, 821 (E D Mich, Southern Div).

121. 539 U.S. 306, 325.

122. 122 F Supp 2d at 822–823.

123. Id at 823.

124. Id at 824–830.

125. 106 F Supp 2d 1362, 1371–1372 (S D Ga, Savannah Div).

126. *Grutter v. Bollinger*, 137 F Supp 2d 821, 849 (E D Mich Southern Div, 2001).

127. Id at 849, 869.

128. Id at 853.

129. Id at 851.

130. 539 U.S. 306, 348 ff.

131. 539 U.S. 386.

132. Id at 389–391.

133. 539 U.S. 244.

134. Id at 269–272.

135. Id at 271.

136. Id at 293–298.

137. 91 F 3d 1547 (3d Cir 1996).

138. *Brief for the United States as Amicus Curiae for Piscataway Township v. Taxman* in the Supreme Court of the United States, 1996, No. 96-679 at 8.

139. Id at 8–9.

140. 539 U.S. at 330.

141. Linda Chavez, *Colleges and Quotas*, The Wall Street Journal A21 (Feb 22, 2001).

142. James Traub, *The Class of Prop. 209*, The New York Times Magazine 8, 51 (May 12, 1999). Traub writes that "[t]he vast majority of four-year institutions admit all or almost all students who apply." Id. For support of this view, see Thomas J. Kane, *Misconceptions in the Debate over Affirmative Action in College Admissions* 18 in ary Orfield and Edward Miller, eds, *Chilling Admissions* (Harvard Education Publishing Group, 1998). Also see Stephan Thernstrom's comments above at 133 in this volume.

143. *Affirmative Action: What Do We Know?* 25 J of Policy Analysis and Management, 463, 475 (2006).

144. Id at 475.

145. Quoted by James Traub, *The New York Times Magazine* at 50 (cited in note 142).

146. *The Flawed Defense of Preferences, The Wall Street Journal,* A19 (October 23, 1998).

147. Eugene Y. Lowe Jr., *Incorporating Racial Diversity in Selective Higher Education* 3, 5 in Eugene Y. Lowe Jr., ed., *Promise and Dilemma: Perspectives on Racial Diversity and Higher Education* (Princeton U Press, 1999).

148. Wash Rev Code 49.60.400 (1999).

149. Nebr Const Art I § 30 (2009).

150. Mich Const Art I § 26 (2006).

151. Calif Const Art I § 31 (2009).

152. Holzer and Neumark, 25 J of Policy Analysis and Management at 477 (cited in note 143).

153. Ethan Bronner, *Minority Enrollment at the U. of California Will Dip in Fall, The New York Times,* natl ed, A20 (May 21, 1998).

154. Ward Connerly, *Why I'm Still Fighting Preferences in Florida, The Wall Street Journal* A26 (November 18, 1999); *Fla. Regents Endorse Plan to End Affirmative Action, Los Angeles Times* A26 (November 20, 1999).

155. Peter Schmidt, *Study Challenges Assumptions About Affirmative-Action Bans,* The Chronicle of Higher Education A20, A20-A21 (February 8, 2008).

156. Monica L. Rose, *Note: Proposal 2 and the Ban on Affirmative Action: An Uncertain Future for the University of Michigan in Its Quest for Diversity,* 17 B.U. Pub Int LJ 309, 320, 323 (Spring 2008).

157. Kimberly West Faulcon, *The River Runs Dry: When Title VI Trumps State Anti-Affirmative Action Laws,* 157 U Pa L Rev 1075, 1092 (2009).

158. 42 USC sect. 2000d *et seq* (2009).

159. Faulcon, 157 U Pa L Rev at 1122–1123 (cited in note 157).

160. 438 U.S. 265, 287, 411ff (1978).

161. *Colleges Will Just Disguise Racial Quotas, Los Angeles Times* B11 (June 30, 2003).

162. Greg Winter, *After Ruling, 3 Universities Maintain Diversity in Admissions, The New York Times,* natl ed, A22 (March 13, 2004).

163. Larry Gordon, *Action Delayed on SAT Subject Exams, Los Angeles Times* B1, B8 (July 17, 2008).

164. Susan Wilbur and Marguerite Bonous-Hammarth, *Testing a New Approach to Admission* 111, 114–115 in Gary Orfield and Edward Miller, eds, *Chilling Admissions* (Harvard Education Publishing Group, 1998).

165. Id at 116.

166. Id at 118.

167. Traub, *The New York Times Magazine* at 46 (cited in note 142).

168. Id at 46.

169. *Grutter v. Bollinger,* 137 F Supp 2d 821, 870 (E D Mich, Southern Div, 2001).

170. Ethan Bronner, *Minority Enrollments at U. of California Will Dip in Fall*, *The New York Times*, natl ed, A20 (May 21, 1998).

171. Samantha Levine, *Taking Action to Admit*, U.S. News & World Report 34, 34–36 (June 4, 2007).

172. Catherine Ivey, *Calif. Minority Admissions Top Level Reached in 1997*, *The Boston Globe* 2 (April 6, 2002).

173. Tessa McClellan, *U.C. California Welcomes Diverse Class for Fall 2008*, *Daily Bruin-UCLA* (April 15, 2008) (Accessed at LexisNexis Academic, News).

174. Holzer and Neumark, 25 J of Policy Analysis and Management at 476 (cited in note 143).

175. Id.

176. Peter Schmidt, *Researchers Accuse Selective Colleges of Giving Admissions Tests Too Much Weight*, The Chronicle of Higher Education A20, A20–A21 (May 9, 2008).

177. Amy Dockser Marcus, *New Weights Can Alter SAT Scores*, *The Wall Street Journal* B1, B8 (August 13, 1999).

178. Cited in Amy Dockser Marcus, *Colleges Back Recruiting Test For Minorities*, *The Wall Street Journal* B1, B4 (November 19, 1999).

179. Id at B1, B4.

180. Jeffrey Selingo, *Why Minority Recruiting Is Alive and Well in Texas*, The Chronicle of Higher Education A34, A34-A36 (November 19, 1999).

181. Cited in id at A34.

182. Id at A35.

183. 38 F 3d 147.

184. Scott Jaschik, *'No' On Black Scholarships; Supreme Court Won't Second-Guess Ruling Against Race-Exclusive Awards*, The Chronicle of Higher Education A 25, A 29 (June 2, 1995).

185. Scott Jaschik, *Education Dept. Sticks by Policy Upholding Minority Scholarships*, The Chronicle of Higher Education A28 (June 9, 1995).

186. Cited in id at A28.

187. Id.

188. Daniel Golden, *Colleges Cut Back Minority Programs After Court Ruling*, *The Wall Street Journal* A1, A2 (December 30, 2003).

189. U.S. Commission on Civil Rights, *The Black/White Colleges* 3–4 (Clearinghouse Publication 66, April, 1981).

190. Cited in id at 4 n 9.

191. Roland G. Fryer Jr. and Michael Greenstone, *The Causes and Consequences of Attending Historically Black Colleges and Universities*, Massachusetts Institute of Technology, Department of Economics, Working Paper, 07-12, 1 (April 9, 2007); Marybeth Gasman *et al.*, *Historically Black Colleges and Universities*, 93 Academe 69 (2007).

192. Abigail and Stephan Thernstrom, *Separation Anxiety*, *The Wall Street Journal* W13 (November 30, 2007).

193. Cited by Kenneth Jost, *Black Colleges: Do They Still Have An Important Role?* 13 CQ Researcher (December 12, 2003).

194. Id at 8.

195. Id at 9–11.

196. Adapted from id at 13–24.

197. 391 U.S. 430 (1968).

198. Kenyon D. Bunch and Grant B. Mindle, *Testing the Limits of Precedent: The Application of Green to the Desegregation of Higher Education*, 2 Seton Hall Constitutional Law J 541, 541–592 (1992).

199. Id passim.

200. Id passim.

201. 112 S. Ct. 2727.

202. Id at 2745.

203. Id at 2737.

204. Id.

205. Id at 2738–2742, 2742.

206. See Web site of U.S. Department of Education, Office for Civil Rights and its *Notice of Application of Supreme Court Decision*. (Accessed on August 1, 2008).

207. Sara Hebel, *Segregation's Legacy Still Troubles Campuses*, The Chronicle of Higher Education A24, A24-A27 (May 14, 2004).

208. See *Ayers v. Fordice*, 879 F Supp 1419 (N D Miss 1995); 111 F3d 1183 (5th Cir 1997), cert denied, 139 L. Ed.2d 768 (1998).

209. *Knight v. Alabama*, 900 F Supp 272 (N D Ala, 1995).

210. Southern Education Foundation, *Miles to Go: A Report on Black Students and Postsecondary Education in the South* 47–48 (Southern Education Foundation, 1998).

211. Eric Lichtblau, *Miss. To Pay $500 Million in Bias Case*, The Los Angeles Times A1, A17 (April 24, 2001).

212. Jeffrey Selingo, *Judge Tells Black Colleges in Mississippi to Use Aid to Recruit White Students*, The Chronicle of Higher Education A28 (June 30, 2000).

213. Sara Hebel, *A New Push to Integrate Public Black Colleges*, The Chronicle of Higher Education A21, A21-A22 (June 8, 2001); Marybeth Gassman, et al., *Historically Black Colleges and Universities*, Academe 69–78 (January/February, 2007).

214. Sara Hebel, *Desegregation Pacts Set in Maryland, Tennessee, and Louisiana*, The Chronicle of Higher Education A35 (January 5, 2001).

215. Southern Education Foundation, *Miles to Go* at xiv–xxxiii (cited in note 210).

216. 112 S. Ct. 2727, 2746.

217. Id at 2749.

218. Diane Ravitch, *Troubled Crusade* 179 (Basic Books, 1983).

219. 20 USC § 1681 *et seq* (2009).

220. *Editors' Historical Introduction*, in Mary Becker, Cynthia Grant Bowman, Morrison Torrey, eds, *Cases and Materials on Feminist Jurisprudence* 17, 23, 26 (West, 1994).

221. Id at 26.

222. See *U.S. v. Virginia*, 518 U.S. 515, 532 (1996).

223. *Goesaert v. Cleary*, 335 U.S. 464 (1948).

224. 404 U.S. 71.

225. Id at 27.

226. 411 U.S. 677.

227. 429 U.S. 190.

228. 518 U.S. 515.

229. Id at 531–534.

230. Id at 535–546.

231. See *Cohen v. Brown*, 101 F 3d 155, 183, and n 22 at 197 (1st Cir 1996) cert denied, 137 L Ed 2d 682 (1997).

232. 518 U.S. at 533 n 7.

233. Id at 553–557.

234. Tod Christopher Gurney, *Comment: The Aftermath of the Virginia Military Institute Decision*, 38 Santa Clara Law Review 1183, 1186–1194 (1998).

235. Id.

236. American Association of University Women Educational Foundation, *Separated by Sex: A Critical Look at Single-Sex Education for Girls* 1–10 (American Association of University Women Educational Foundation, 1998).

237. Elizabeth Veil, *Teaching to the Testosterone, The New York Times Magazine* 41 (March 7, 2008).

238. Id at 40.

239. Rosemary C. Salomone, *Single-Sex Programs: Resolving the Research Conundrum*, 108 Teachers College Record 778,791,794 (2006).

240. U.S. Department of Education, Press Release: *Secretary Spellings Announces More Choices in Single-Sex Education*, October 24, 2006.

241. 20 USC § 1681(a) *et seq* (2009).

242. U.S. Senate, *Hearing Before the Senate Subcommittee on Science, Technology, and Space*, 107th Cong, 2nd sess, 11–12 (October 3, 2002).

243. Id at 27.

244. Id at 30, 41.

245. Note: *Cheering on Women and Girls in Sports*, 110 Harv L Rev 1627, 1627–1644 (1997).

246. *New Arenas for Title IX?* 26 *NEA Today* (2008).

247. Deborah J. Anderson, John Jesse Cheslock, and Ronald G. Ehrenberg, *Gender Equity in Intercollegiate Athletics: Determinants of Title IX Compliance*, 77 J of Higher Education 225, 225–250 (March/April 2006).

248. Note: *Cheering on Women and Girls in Sports*, 110 Harv L Rev 1627, 1627–1644 (1997).

249. U.S. Congress, House of Representatives, *Hearing on Title IX of the Education Amendments of 1972* before the Subcommittee on Postsecondary Education, 104th Cong, 1st Sess, 78 (May 9, 1995).

250. Id at 79.

251. 101 F3d 155, 175–176 (1st Cir).

252. Id at 170–171, 174–176.

253. 20 USC § 1681 (b) (2009).

254. 101 F3d at 177.

255. Cited in 101 F3d at 166.

256. Id at 175–176, 178–181.

257. Id at 181.

258. 515 U.S. 200.

259. 101 F 3d at 182.

260. Id at 183–184 and n 22.

261. Id at 184.

262. Id at 175, 197–198.

263. Id at 196.

264. Id.

265. Id at 190–191, 197.

266. Id at 198.

267. Welsh Suggs, *Education Department Stands Pat on Title IX,* The Chronicle of Higher Education A35 (July 23, 2003).

268. Cited in id.

269. Sara Lipka, *Use of Interest Surveys for Title IX Compliance Is Debated before Civil Rights Commission,* The Chronicle of Higher Education 43 (May 25, 2007).

270. John J. Cheslock and Suzanne E. Eckes, *Statistical Evidence and Compliance with Title IX,* No. 138 New Directions for Institutional Research, 31, 43 (Summer 2008).

271. Eileen McDonagh and Laura Pappano, *Playing With the Boys: Why Separate Is Not Equal in Sports passim* (Oxford U Press, 2008).

272. 864 F 2d 881, 897–899 (1st Cir).

273. See *Meritor v. Vinson,* 477 U.S. 57 (1986); *Oncale v. Sundowner Offshore Services,* 118 S. Ct. 998, 1001(1998).

274. 526 U.S. 629, 651–652 (1999).

275. Foundation for Individual Rights in Education, *The State of Free Speech on our Nation's Campuses: Spotlight on Speech Codes* 10 (2007).

276. Id at 7.

277. Id at 11.

278. Cited in id at 11.

279. Daphne Patai, *Heterophobia* (Rowman and Littlefield, 1998).

280. Id at xxi, xv, 6, 12, 23, 24, 35,57, 158, 161, 207.

281. Stephen Shulhofer, *Unwanted Sex* 148, 169, 186, 272–273 (Harvard U Press, 1999).

Chapter Six. Affirmative Action and Political Representation of Minorities

1. Pub L 89-110, 79 Stat 437, codified, as amended, at 42 USC § 1973 *et seq* (2009).

2. *Reynolds v. Sims,* 377 U.S. 533, 538 (1964).

3. For an excellent account, see Alexander Keyssar, *The Right to Vote* (Basic Books, 2000).

4. Id at 256–266, 287; Chandler Davidson, *The Voting Rights Act* 7, 10–17 in Bernard Grofman and Chandler Davidson, eds, *Controversies in Minority Voting* (Brookings, 1992); Samuel Issacharoff, Pamela Karlan, and Richard H. Pildes, eds, *Editors' Introduction to Preclearance,* in *The Law of Democracy* at 285–286 (Foundation, 1998).

5. 383 U.S. 301, 308.

6. Id at 308–310.

7. 42 USC § 1973c(a) (2009) (emphasis added).

8. *Editors' Introduction on Changes Covered by Section 5*, in Issacharoff, Karlan, and Pildes, eds, *The Law of Democracy* at 285–286 (cited in note 4).

9. PL 109–246, 120 Stat 577.

10. Samuel Issacharoff, Pamela S. Karlan, and Richard Pildes, eds, *The Law of Democracy*, 3d ed, 487 (Foundation Press, 2007).

11. Pei-te Lien, *The Voting Rights Act and Its Implications for Three Nonblack Minorities* 129, 132 in Richard M. Valelly, ed, *The Voting Rights Act: Securing the Ballot* (Congressional Quarterly Press, 2006).

12. *Northwest Austin Municipal Utility District v. Holder*, Slip Opinion 08-322 at 16 (2009) (Opinion of the Court).

13. 42 USC § 1973b (2009).

14. David A. Bositis, *Impact of the 'Core' Voting Rights Act on Voting and Office Holding* in Valelly, ed., *The Voting Rights Act* at 113–127 (cited in note 11).

15. Lien, *The Voting Rights Act and Its Implications for Three Nonblack Minorities*, in id at 129–144.

16. PL 109-246; 120 Stat 577.

17. Lien, *The Voting Rights Act and Its Implications for Three Nonblack Minorities*, in Valelly, ed, *The Voting Rights Act* at 132 (cited in note 11).

18. Id at 140–143.

19. Id.

20. Id.

21. Keith J. Bybee, *Mistaken Identity* 28 (Princeton U Press, 1998).

22. David Lublin, *The Paradox of Representation* 22 (Princeton U Press, 1997).

23. Stephen J. Wayne, *The Road to the Whitehouse, 2008*, 8th ed., Epilogue, 17–20 (Wadsworth/Cengage, 2008).

24. Adam Nagourney et al., *Obama: Racial Barrier Falls in Decisive Victory, The New York Times*, natl ed, A1 (November 5, 2008).

25. Timothy Noah, *What We Didn't Overcome*, Slate, posted on November 10, 2008, http://www.slate.com/id/2204251/ (accessed on July 26, 2009).

26. For the statistics on this point, see Lublin, *Paradox of Representation* at 23–24 (cited in note 22); Laughlin McDonald, The *1982 Amendments* in Grofman and Davidson, eds, *Controversies in Minority Voting* at 66, 73–74 (cited in note 4).

27. Bybee, *Mistaken Identity* at 29 (cited in note 21).

28. Lublin, *Paradox of Representation* at 23–24 (cited in note 22).

29. Davidson, *The Voting Rights Act*, in Grofman and Davidson eds, *Controversies in Minority Voting* at 17–21 (cited in note 4); Bybee, *Mistaken Identity* at 18 (cited in note 21).

30. 347 U.S. 483.

31. See *Editors' Introduction to Changes Covered by Section 5*, in Issacharoff, Karlan, Pildes, eds, *The Law of Democracy* at 285–286 (cited in note 4).

32. For a full description, see Davidson, *The Voting Rights Act*, in Grofman and Davidson, eds, *Controversies in Minority Voting* at 25–29 (cited in note 4).

33. *South Carolina* v. *Katzenbach*, 383 U.S. 301, 334–335 (1966).

34. 393 U.S. 544.

35. Id at 555.

36. Timothy G. O'Rourke, *The 1982 Amendments*, in Grofman and Davidson, eds, *Controversies in Minority Voting* at 85,90 (cited in note 4).

37. 393 U.S. at 569.

38. *Reynolds* is located at 377 U.S. 533. It is referenced in *Allen* at 393 U.S. at 555–556.

39. David Lublin, *The Paradox of Representation* 5–6 (Princeton U Press, 1997).

40. Id at 6, 28–29.

41. Kathryn Abrams, *Raising Politics Up*, 63 NYU L Rev 449, 470–471 n 139 (1988).

42. Lublin, *The Paradox of Representation* at 6, 7, 28 (cited in note 39).

43. Id at 6, and *passim*.

44. 425 U.S. 130 (1976).

45. Id at 134–135.

46. Id at 136 (emphasis added).

47. Id at 137.

48. Id.

49. Id at 141.

50. Id at 142.

51. See, e.g., *City of Richmond v. United States*, 422 U.S. 358 (1973), upholding preclearance of an urban annexation plan that reduced the city's black population share by 10 percent but did not provide for carryover of its level of representation. The Court ruled that Section 5 did not mandate a carryover, but would be satisfied if the blacks' post-annexation "representation [were] reasonably equivalent to their political strength in the enlarged community." Id at 370.

52. Drew Days, *Section 5 Enforcement* 52, 56 in Bernard Grofman and Chandler Davidson, eds, *Controversies in Minority Voting* (Brookings, 1992).

53. Keith Bybee, *Mistaken Identity* 20–21; 41 n 40 (Princeton U Press, 1998) referring to the well-known contrarian view of Abigail Thernstrom.

54. This is not to say that Section 5 has become a dead letter. Under the VRA extension, it remains in effect. It furnished a major portion of DOJ's VRA-workload. Editors' *Notes and Questions on Section 5*, in Samuel Issacharoff, Pamela Karlan, and Richard Pildes 293–294 *The Law of Democracy* (Foundation, 1998).

55. *Focus on the Voting Rights Act—Section 5 of the Voting Rights Act, By Now a Murky Mess*, 5 Georgetown J L Pub Pol'y, 41, 54–55; 61–62 (Winter 2007).

56. *Fortson v. Dorsey*, 379 U.S. 433, 439 (1965) (emphasis added).

57. 403 U.S. 124 (1992).

58. Id at 133, 149.

59. 412 U.5. 755.

60. Id at 766, 769.

61. See *Zimmer v. McKeithen*, 485 F 2d 1297, 1395 (5th Cr 1975) listing the nine criteria of the "totality of the circumstances "test applied by the *White* majority. For analysis, see *Editors' Notes and Questions on Dilution*, in Issacharoff, Karlan, Pildes, eds *The Law of Democracy* at 383, 386 (cited in note 54).

62. 430 U.S. 144.

63. Id at 159–161.

64. Id at 161–162.

65. Id at 165.

66. Id.

67. Id at 186–187.

68. Thernstrom, 5 Georgetown J L Pub Pol'y at 56 (cited in note 55).

69. 528 U.S. 320.

70. Id at 328, 335.

71. 539 U.S. 461.

72. Id at 472–473.

73. Id at 479–482.

74. Thernstrom, 5 Georgetown J L & Pub Pol'y at 66 ff (cited in note 55).

75. Slip Opinion No. 08-322.

76. Id at 8, 9 (Opinion of the Court).

77. Id at 8 (Opinion of the Court).

78. Id at 10 ff (Opinion of the Court).

79. Id at 11, 16 (Opinion of the Court).

80. Id at 3 (Opinion of Justice Thomas).

81. Id at 3–4 (Opinion of Justice Thomas).

82. 446 U.S. 55.

83. *Thornburg v. Gingles*, 478 U.S. 30, 35 (1986).

84. In this view, *Bolden* unjustifiably abandoned the *White/Zimmer* standard, and imposed an unfair burden of proof on minority plaintiffs. See McDonald, *The 1982 Amendments,* in Grofman and Davidson, eds *Controversies in Minority Voting* at 68 (cited in note 52). For in-depth analysis, see *Editors' Notes and Questions on Bolden,* in Issacharoff, Karlan, Pildes, eds, *The Law of Democracy* at 405–407 (cited in note 54). It should be noted that, in *Rogers* v. *Lodge,* 458 U.S. 613 (1982), the Supreme Court held that discriminatory motive may be inferred from evidence of discriminatory results, thus, in the view of some authorities, mooting opposition to the *Bolden* ruling. See id at 408–409.

85. *Thornburg v. Gingles*, 478 U.S. 30, 35 (emphasis added).

86. Section 2(a), 42 USC § 1973 a (2009) (emphasis added).

87. Section 2(b), 42 USC § 1723b (2009).

88. See Thomas M. Boyd and Stephen J. Markman, *The 1982 Amendments* 412, 412–434, as excerpted in Samuel Issacharoff, Pamela Karlan, and Richard Pildes, eds, *The Law of Democracy* (Foundation, 1998), for a narrative summary and excerpts from the Senate Judiciary Committee Report on the 1982 Amendments.

89. 446 U.S. 55.

90. See Boyd and Markman, *The 1982 Amendments,* in Issacharoff, Karlan, and Pildes, eds, *The Law of Democracy* at 413, 426–428, 434 (cited in note 88).

91. Id at 427.

92. Id at 427–428. The Senate report regarding the amendment of Section 2 enumerated seven "typical factors"; and described two "additional factors" that have had "probative value" in some cases; and said that "other factors" will indicate "the alleged dilution" in some cases.

93. *Editors' Notes and Questions on the 1982 Amendments,* in Issacharoff, Karlan, Pildes, *The Law of Democracy* at 434 (cited in note 88).

94. *Johnson v. De Grandy*, 512 U.S. 997, 1007 (1994), quoting *Voinovich v. Quilter,* 507 U.S. 146, 153–154 (1993) (emphasis added).

95. See chapter 3 at 31–82; and chapter 4 at 92–119 in this volume.

96. Hugh Davis Graham, *Voting Rights* 177, 180–196 in Bernard Grofman and Chandler Davidson, eds, *Controversies in Minority Voting* (Brookings, 1992). Professor Graham maintained that VRA, like Title VII in EEO law, has moved beyond color-blind equality of treatment to institutionalized racial preference. But cf *Editors' Postscript* 300, 315 and n 36, in id, questioning whether the VRA benefit of undiluted voting strength "fits the usual model of affirmative action case law."

97. See Steven F. Lawson, *Running for Freedom* 154 (McGraw-Hill, 1996).

98. 478 U.S. 30.

99. *Editors' Notes and Questions on the 1982 Amendments*, in Issacharoff, Karlan, Pildes, eds, *The Law of Democracy* at 434 (cited in note 88).

100. *Thornburg v. Gingles*, 478 U.S. 30, 42, 80, 82.

101. Id at 48, and n 15, 49.

102. Id at 47.

103. Id at 50–51 (emphasis added).

104. *Editors' Notes and Questions on Gingles*, in Issacharoff, Karlan, Pildes, eds, *The Law of Democracy* at 464, 466 (cited in note 88).

105. See, e.g., *Johnson v. DeGrandy* (1994) rejecting "packing" claims by Hispanic residents of single-member, majority-minority districts in Dade County, Florida. Based on the plaintiffs' existing power to elect "their chosen representatives in substantial proportion to their percentage of the area's population," the Court held that they were not entitled, under Section 2, to a proportionate number of majority-minority districts in the area. 512 U.S. 997, 1008. For analysis, see *Editors' Notes on Section 2*, in Issacharoff, Karlan, Pildes, eds, *The Law of Democracy* at 499–500, 506–509 (cited in note 88).

106. David T. Canon, *Race, Redistricting, and Representation* 71–72 (U of Chicago Press, 1999).

107. *Thornburg v. Gingles*, 478 U.S. at 44, 49 n 17.

108. Alexander Keyssar, *The Right to Vote* 294–295 (Basic Books, 2000); Canon, *Race, Redistricting and Representation* at 70—73 (cited in note 106).

109. *Thornburg v. Gingles*, 478 U.S. at 50 n 17.

110. Keyssar, *The Right to Vote* at 294 (cited in note 108); David Lublin, *The Paradox of Representation* 30 (Princeton U Press, 1997).

111. *Thornburg v. Gingles*, 478 U.S. at 96.

112. 129 S. Ct. 1231.

113. 515 U.S. 900.

114. 512 U.S. 874.

115. Id at 892.

116. Samuel Isacharoff, Pamela Karlan, and Richard Pildes, *The Law of Democracy*, 3d ed, 789–790 (Thomson-West, 2007).

117. 126 S. Ct. 2594.

118. Id at 2614–2621.

119. 528 U.S. 320 (2000).

120. 539 U.S. 461 (2003).

121. 126 S. Ct. 2594 (2006).

122. Name now is *Easley v. Cromartie*. 149 L Ed 2d 430.

123. *Shaw v. Reno*, 509 U.S. 630 (1993); *Miller v. Johnson*, 515 U.S. 900 (1995). *Shaw v. Hunt*, 517 U.S. 899 (1996); *Bush v. Vera*, 517 U.S. 952 (1996).

124. *Editors' Notes and Questions on Reynolds v. Sims*, in Samuel Issacharoff, Pamela Karlan, and Richard Pildes, eds, 148 *The Law of Democracy* (Foundation, 1998).

125. Id.

126. *Davis v. Bandemer*, 478 U.S. 109, 164 (1986) (Powell concurring).

127. J. Morgan Kousser, *The Voting Rights Act*, in Grofman and Davidson, eds, *Controversies in Minority Voting* at 135, 144 (cited in note 96); Eric Foner, *Reconstruction* 590 (Perennial/Harper, 1989).

128. *Shaw v. Reno*, 509 U.S. 630, 670 (1993) (White dissenting).

129. See David Lublin, *The Paradox of Representation* 8, 30 (Princeton U Press, 1997); *Editors' Notes and Questions on Redistricting*, in Issacharoff, Karlan, and Pildes, eds, *The Law of Democracy* at 546, 566–567, 582–588 (cited in note 124).

130. Lublin, *The Paradox of Representation* at 10–12 (cited in note 129).

131. 509 U.S. 630.

132. Id at 633–636.

133. Lublin, *The Paradox of Representation* at 7 (cited in note 129).

134. 509 U.S. at 636–637; Lublin, *The Paradox of Representation at 7* (cited in note 129).

135. 509 U.S. at 642.

136. Id at 646–648.

137. 430 U.S. 144.

138. *Shaw v. Reno*, 509 U.S. at 651–653, 659–668, 670–673, 676–684, 685–686.

139. 509 U.S. 630.

140. 517 U.S. 899, 908–918.

141. 515 U.S. 900, 925–926.

142. 517 U.S. 952.

143. 515 U.S. 900 (1995).

144. 517 U.S. 952.

145. Id at 1000.

146. Id at 1060.

147. Id at 1062.

148. Id at 1070–1071.

149. Id at 1073–1074.

150. J. Gerald Hebert, *Redistricting in the Post-2000 Era*, 8 Geo Mason U L Rev 431, 437–438. 458, 475–476 (2000).

151. 149 L. Ed. 2d 430.

152. 517 U.S. 899.

153. *Hunt v. Cromartie*, 149 L. Ed. 2d 430.

154. Id at 445–446.

155. Id at 453.

156. Id at 444, 453 citing and quoting *Bush v. Vera*, 517 U.S. 952, 968 (1996) (O'Connor principal opinion): "If district lines merely correlate with race because, they are drawn on the basis of political affiliation, which correlates with race, there is no racial classification to justify."

157. 149 L. Ed. 2d at 453 (emphasis added).

158. *Hunt v. Cromartie*, 143 L. Ed. 2d 731, 732–733 (1999)(*Cromartie* I).

159. *Easley v. Cromartie*, 149 L. Ed. 2d 430 (2001) (*Cromartie* II) illustrates the potential dangers of a fact-specific approach. This decision must be seen as something of a judicial mutant, considering that it came into being only because of Justice O'Connor's as yet unexplained defection to the side of her former antagonists.

160. *Hunt v. Cromartie*, 143 L Ed 2d 731(*Cromartie* I) at n 7, citing *Davis v. Bandemer*, 478 U.S. 109.

161. Hebert, 8 Geo Mason L Rev at 437–438, 449–450 (cited in note 150).

162. 377 U.S. 533 (1964).

163. *Resolving the Dilemma of Representation*, 92 Calif L Rev 1589, 1612–1616, 1628–1629 (2004).

164. Id at 1610.

165. Id at 1606.

166. For illustrations of these concerns, see Matt A. Barreto, Gary M. Segura, and Nathan D. Woods, *The Mobilizing Effect of Majority-Minority Districts on Latino Turnout*, 98 Am Pol Sci Rev 65, 65–75 (2004); and Claudine Gay, *Legislating Without Constraints: The Effect of Minority Districting on Legislators' Responsiveness to Constituency Preferences*, 69 J of Politics 442, 442–456 (2007).

167. William L. O'Neill, *feminism in American History* ch 8 (Transaction, 2d revised ed, 1989).

168. *Afterword by Ellen Fitzpatrick* 326, 327 in Eleanor Flexner and Ellen Fitzpatrick, *Century of Struggle* (enlarged ed, Harvard U Press, 1996).

169. David Lauter, *Emily's List* 217, 217–218 in Alida Brill, ed, *A Rising Public Voice* (Feminist Press, 1995).

170. Kathleen A. Dolan, *Voting for Women: How the Public Evaluates Women Candidates* 46 (Westview Press, 2004).

171. Id at 50.

172. Id at 160.

173. Paul S. Herrnson, *Congressional Elections* 78 (CQ Press, 1998).

174. Center for American Women and Politics, Eagleton Institute of Politics, *Women in Elective Office 2009*, http://www.cawp. Rutgers.edu/ (accessed July 26, 2009).

175. Dolan, *Voting for Women* at 160 (cited in note 170).

176. Beth Reingold, *Representing Women* 1 (U North Carolina Press, 2000).

177. Id at 3–4.

178. Id at 251.

179. Id at 4.

180. Id at 6–7, 23.

181. Id at 240.

182. Susan Caroll, *Representing Women: Women in State Legislators as Agents of Policy-Related Change* 3, 17–18 in Susan Caroll, ed, *The Impact of Women in Public Office* (Indiana U Press, 2004).

183. Kathlene Lyn, *Words That Matter: Women's Voice and Institutional Bias in Public Policy Formation* at 22, 30–31 in id.

184. Dolan, *Voting for Women* at 16–17 (cited in note 170).

185. McDonald, *The 1982 Amendments* 74–75 in Bernard Grofman and Chandler Davidson, eds, *Controversies in Minority Voting* (Brookings, 1992); Bositis, *Impact of the 'Core' Voting Rights Act on Voting and Office Holding* 118–119 in Richard M.

Valelly, ed., *The Voting Rights Act: Securing the Ballot* (Congressional Quarterly Press, 2006); Lien, *The Voting Rights Act and Its Implications for Three Nonblack Minorities*, 142–143 in id.

186. McDonald, *The 1982 Amendments* in Grofman and Davidson, *Controversies in Minority Voting* at 82 (cited in note 185); Davidson, *The Voting Rights Act*, in Grofman and Davidson, eds, *Controversies in Minority Voting* at 46 (cited in note 185); Bositis, *Impact of the "Core" Voting Rights Act on Voting and Office Holding*, in Valelly, ed, *The Voting Rights Act: Securing the Ballot* at 118–119 (cited in note 185); Lien, *The Voting Rights Act and Its Implications for Three Nonblack Minorities*, in id at 142–143.

187. Lani Guinier, *Voting Rights* 283, 283–288, in Grofman and Davidson, eds, *Controversies in Minority Voting* (cited in note 185).

188. For representative statements, see Abigail Thernstrom, *Whose Votes Count?* (Harvard U Press, 1987); Timothy G. O'Rourke, *The 1982 Amendments*; Hugh Davis Graham, *Voting Rights*, in Grofman and Davidson, eds, *Controversies in Minority Voting* (cited in note 185).

189. Graham, *Voting Rights*, in id at 188.

190. Id at 189.

191. See Roger Clegg and Linda Chavez, *The Reauthorized Sections 5 and 203 of The Voting Rights Act of 1965: Bad Policy and Unconstiutional*, 5 Georgetown J L & Pub Pol'y, 561, 563 (2007).

192. Id at 563.

193. See, e.g., in Grofman and Davidson, eds, *Controversies in Minority Voting* (cited in note 185): Days, *Section 5 Enforcement* at 58–64; McDonald, *The 1982 Amendments* at 77–79; Kousser, *The Voting Rights Act* at 166–176. For reasonably evenhanded critiques, see Davidson, *The Voting Rights Act* at 7–51, and *Editors' Postscript* at 300, 300–317, in aforementioned volume. Also see Keith J. Bybee, *Mistaken Identity* ch 3 (Princeton U Press, 1998).

194. Pub L 109-246, 120 Stat 578, §2 (9).

195. J. Gerald Hebert, *Redistricting in the Post-2000 Era*, 8 Geo Mason U L Rev 431, 475 (2000).

196. In the decade of the 1990s, the country's growth rate was the greatest in our history. See Eric Schmitt, *U.S. Population Has Biggest 10-Year Rise Ever, The New York Times*, natl ed, A10 (April 3, 2001).

197. Eric Schmitt, *Whites in Minority in Largest Cities, the Census Shows, The New York Times*, natl ed, A1, A15 (April 30, 2001); Jim Yardley, *Non-Hispanic Whites May Soon Be a Minority in Texas, The New York Times*, late ed—final, 22 (March 25, 2001); Editorial, *America's Demographic Quilt, The New York Times*, natl ed, A14 (April 2, 2001); U.S. Bureau of the Census, Press Releases: May 1, 2008 (*Hispanic Population Surpasses 45 Million—Now 15 Percent of the Total)*-http://www.census.gov/Press-Release/www/releases/archives/population/011910.html; August 14, 2008; *An Older and More Diverse Nation by Midcentury*, http://www.census.gov/Press-Release/www/releases/archives/population/0012496.html (Accessed both on July 26, 2009).

198. U.S. Bureau of the Census, Press Release, May 1, 2008 (cited in above note).

199. Id, Press Release, August 14, 2008 (cited in note 197).

200. Todd S. Purdum. *California Census Confirms Whites Are In Minority, The New York Times*, natl ed, A1, A16 (March 30, 2001); U.S. Bureau of the Census, Press Release. May 1, 2008 (cited in note 197).

201. Editorial, *America's Demographic Quilt, The New York Times*, natl ed A14 (April 2, 2001).

202. See, for example, Melissa Williams, *Voice, Trust, and Memory* (Princeton U Press, 1998).

203. See, for example, Abigail Thernstrom, *Whose Votes Count?* (Harvard U Press, 1987).

204. See David Lublin, *The Paradox of Representation* 10–11 (Princeton U Press, 1997); Bositis, *Impact of the "Core" Voting Rights Act on Voting and Office Holding* 125 in Richard M. Valelly, ed., *The Voting Rights Act: Securing the Ballot* (Congressional Quarterly Press, 2006); Lien, *The Voting Rights Act and Its Implications for Three Nonblack Minorities* in id at 143.

205. 539 U.S. 461, 480–482.

206. Name is now *Easley v. Cromartie.* 149 L. Ed. 2d 430, 444, 453.

207. J. Gerald Hebert, *Redistricting in the Post-2000 Era*, 8 Geo Mason U L Rev 431, 437–438, 463–464 (2000) for description of a hypothetical "functional majority" district in which minority voters comprise 40 percent of the voting age population.

208. *Editors' Note Cumulative Voting* 722–726 in Samuel Issacharoff, Pamela S. Karlan, and Richard H. Pildes, eds, *The Law of Democracy* (Foundation, 1998); Davidson, *The Voting Rights Act* 48–51 in Bernard Grofman and Chandler Davidson, eds, *Controversies in Minority Voting* (Brookings, 1992); and McDonald, *The 1982 Amendments,*in id at 83–84.

209. Guinier, *Voting Rights*, in Grofman and Davidson, eds, *Controversies in Minority Voting* at 290–291 and n16 (cited in note 208). See *Editors' Note on Consociational Democracy*, in Issacharoff, Karlan, Pildes, eds, *The Law of Democracy* at 780–784 (cited in note 208).

210. 377 U.S. 533 (1964).

211. Name is now *Easley v. Cromartie.* 149 L. Ed2d 430.

212. 515 U.S. 900.

213. 478 U.S. 109.

214. Bruce Cain, *Voting Rights and Democratic Theory*, in Grofman and Davidson, eds, *Controversies in Minority Voting* at 262, 262–263 (cited in note 208).

215. Alexander Keyssar, *The Right to Vote* 290–291 (Basic Books, 2000).

216. David T. Canon, *Race, Redistricting, and Representation* 69–70 (U of Chicago Press, 1999).

217. *South Carolina v. Katzenbach*, 383 U.S. 301, 308, 337 (1966).

Chapter Seven. Affirmative Action and Fair Housing

1. Pub L 90-284, 82 Stat 73, codified as amended, at 42 USC § 3601 *et seq* (2009).

2. 42 USC § 1982 (2009).

3. The Institute on Race and Poverty, *Examining the Relationship between Housing, Education, and Persistent Segregation: Final Report, Part IV* at 1–2 (U of Minnesota Law School, 2000).

4. Margery Turner, *Limits on Housing and Neighborhood Choice: Discrimination, Segregation in U.S. Housing Markets*, 41 Ind L Rev 797, 807 (2008).

5. Id at 807–808.

6. James Kushner, *Urban Neighborhood Regeneration and the Phases of Community Evolution*, 41 Ind L Rev 575, 576 (2008).

7. Id at 589–590, 592.

8. Karl Taeuber, *Statement* 33 in Robert Schwemm, ed, *The Fair Housing Act After Twenty Years—A Conference* at 33 (Yale Law School, 1989).

9. Gary Orfield, et al., *Dismantling Desegregation* 304 (The New Press, 1996).

10. Id at 306; John O. Calmore, *Spatial Equality and the Kerner Commission* 309, 324–325 in John Charles Boger and Judith Welch Wegner, eds, *Race, Poverty, and American Cities* (U North Carolina Press, 1996).

11. Orfield, et al., *Dismantling Desegregation* at 304, 306 (cited in note 9).

12. As detailed by Eric Schmitt, *Analysis of Census Finds Segregation Along with Diversity, The New York Times*, natl ed, A15 (April 4, 2001). For segregation data prior to pre-2000 census, see Douglas S. Massey and Nancy A. Denton, *American Apartheid* (Harvard U Press, 1993).

13. As noted whites are less "isolated." Additionally, the Brookings Institution reports that census tracts with less than a 1 percent black population have decreased from 40 percent in 1960 to 23 percent in the last census, and that far fewer African Americans live in tracts that are 80 percent or more black. See Robin Fields, *Census Fuels Debate over Integration, Los Angeles Times* A 1, A 24 (June 24, 2001).

14. Robin Fields and Ray Herndon, *Segregation of a New Sort Takes Shape, Los Angeles Times* A1, A17 (July 5, 2001).

15. Eric Schmitt, *Segregation Growing Among U.S. Children, The New York Times*, natl ed, A 20 (May 6, 2001). Data for the article from the Mumford Center at SUNY-Albany.

16. Gary Orfield, *The Movement for Housing Integration* 18, 20–21, in John M.Goering, ed, *Housing Desegregation and Federal Policy* (U North Carolina Press, 1986).

17. John Charles Boger, *Race and the American City* 3, 8–9 in John Charles Boger and Judith Welch Wegner, eds, *Race, Poverty, and American Cities* (U North Carolina Press, 1996).

18. William Julius Wilson, *When Work Disappears* 11–17, 37–42 (Knopf, 1997).

19. Cited by Boger, *Race and the American City*, in Boger and Wegner, eds, *Race, Poverty, and American Cities* at 9 (cited in note 17).

20. See for example, Justice Breyer's dissent in *Parents Involved v. Seattle* 127 S. Ct. 2738, 2800 ff (2007).

21. Judith Welch Wegner, *Notes and Reflections* in Boger and Wegner, eds, *Race, Poverty, and American Cities* at 551–552 (cited in note 17).

22. *Statements* by James Kushner, John Payne, and Robert Schwemm 48, 52–54, 81–89, 106 in Robert Schwemm, ed, *The Fair Housing Act After Twenty Years—A*

Conference (Yale Law School, 1989); W. Dennis Keating, *The Suburban Racial Dilemma* 5 (Temple U Press, 1994).

23. *Statement* by Robert Ellickson 58–61 in Robert Schwemm, ed, *Fair Housing Act after Twenty Years—A Conference* (cited in note 22); Elizabeth Julian, *Fair Housing and Community Development: Time to Come Together*, 41 Ind L R 555, 557–561 (2008).

24. See Neil A. Lewis, *For Black Scholars Wedded to Prism of Race, New and Separate Goals*, *The New York Times*, natl ed, A14 (May 5, 1997); Wendy Brown-Scott, *Does Sound Educational Policy Support the Continued Existence of Historically Black Colleges?* 43 Emory L J 1, 1–81 (1994).

25. Michelle Adams, *Radical Integration*, 94 Calif L Rev 261, 266 (2006).

26. Douglas S. Massey and Nancy A. Denton, *American Apartheid* 212–216 (Harvard U Press, 1993).

27. See Peter Flemister, *Statement* 116–120 in Robert Schwemm, ed, *The Fair Housing Act After Twenty Years—A Conference* (Yale Law School, 1989).

28. Julian, 41 Ind L Rev at 557–561 (cited in note 23).

29. Florence Wagman Roisman, *Living Together: Ending Racial Discrimination and Segregation in Housing*, 41 Ind L Rev 507, 516–520 (2008).

30. Robert D. Putnam, *E Pluribus Unum: Diversity and Community in the Twenty-first Century*, 30 Scandinavian Political Studies 137, 137–174 (2007).

31. Id at 144–145.

32. Id at 137.

33. In 1988, the handicapped and families with children were added to the protected groups covered by the Fair Housing Act. Pub L 100-812, 102 Stat 1619-39 Codified, as amended, at 42 USC § 3604 (2009).

34. 42 USC § 3601 *et seq* (2009).

35. See citations collected at *U.S. v. Starrett City Associates*, 840 F2d 1096, 1100 (2d Cir 1988).

36. Paul Boudreaux, *An Individual Preference Approach to Suburban Racial Desegregation*, 27 Fordham Urban L J 533, 539–540 (1999).

37. Id at 533–534.

38. 42 USC §§ 3613, 3614 (2009).

39. *Mountain Side Mobile Estate Partnership v. HUD*, 56 F3d 1243 (10th Cir 1994); *Betsey v. Turtle Creek Associates*, 736 F2d 983 (4th Cir 1984); *Huntington Branch NAACP v. Town of Huntington*, 844 F2d 926 (2d Cir 1988); *United States v. City of Black Jack*, 508 F2d 1179 (8th Cir 1974).

40. Statements by Roberta Achtenberg, Assistant Secretary, HUD Office of Fair Housing and Equal Opportunity, and Deval Patrick, Assistant Attorney General—Civil Rights Division, U.S. Department of Justice in House of Representatives, Subcommittee on Civil and Constitutional Rights, Hearings on Fair Housing Issues, 103d Congress, 2nd Sess, 17–18, 72–74 (September 28 and 30, 1994).

41. Id at 61.

42. 245 U.S. 60.

43. 334 U.S. 1.

44. 392 U.S. 409.

45. Id at 439.

46. 840 F2d 1096 (2d Cir 1988), cert denied, 488 U.S. 946 (1988).

47. *Town of Huntington v. Huntington Branch, NAACP*, 488 U.S. 15 (1988).

48. *Hills v. Gautreaux*, 425 U.S. 284 (1976).

49. Douglas S. Massey and Nancy A. Denton, *American Apartheid* 199 (Harvard U Press, 1993).

50. Id at ch 7; W. Dennis Keating, *Suburban Racial Dilemma* 34–36 (Temple U Press, 1994).

51. *Editor's Concluding Remarks* 327, 330 in John M. Goering, ed, *Housing Desegregation and Federal Policy* (U North Carolina Press, 1986).

52. Michael Selmi, *Public vs. Private Enforcement of Civil Rights*, 45 UCLA Law Review 1401, 1422–1427 (1998).

53. Florence Wagman Roisman, *Keeping the Promise: Ending Racial Discrimination and Segregation in Federally Financed Housing*, 48 Howard L J, 913, 921 (2005).

54. Keating, *Suburban Racial Dilemma, part III* (cited in note 50); Charles M. Haar, *Suburbs under Siege* 15–29, 166 n 20, 246–248 (Princeton U Press, 1996).

55. Id at 6.

56. See statement by Deval Patrick, Assistant Attorney General—Civil Rights Division, Department of Justice, in *Hearings on Fair Housing* at the Subcommittee on Civil and Constitutional Rights at 73 (cited in note 40). In this testimony, the assistant attorney general noted that Justice focused primarily on the abolition of intentional discrimination in its fair housing pursuits.

57. *Special Message to Congress Proposing Legislation and Outlining Administration Actions to Deal with Federal Housing Policy*, September 19, 1973, Public Papers of Richard Nixon, 1973 at 807 (Government Printing Office, 1975).

58. Public housing can be appropriately divided into "family" and "elderly" units. The latter are inhabited by many whites, while the former are typically dominated by blacks. See Cara Hendrickson, *Racial Desegregation and Income Deconcentration in Public Housing*, 9 Georgetown J Poverty Law & Pol'y 35, 53 (2002).

59. *Special Message to Congress Proposing Legislation and Outlining Administration Actions to Deal with Federal Housing Policy*, September 19, 1973 at 807 (cited in note 57).

60. Id at 808.

61. R. Allen Hays, *The Federal Government and Urban Housing* 143–166 (State U New York Press, 1995).

62. Alex F. Schwartz, *Housing Policy in the United States* 151 (Routledge, 2006).

63. *Housing Segregation in Suburban America Since 1960* (Cambridge U Press, 2005), *passim*.

64. Id, 165.

65. *Statement About Federal Policies Relative to Equal Housing Opportunity*, June 11, 1971, Public Papers of Richard Nixon, 1971 at 730 (Government Printing Office, 1972).

66. Id at 731–733.

67. Rodney A. Smolla, *Integration Maintenance*, 1981 Duke U L J 891, 915–917 (1981).

68. Schwartz, *Housing Policy in the United State* at 102, 151 (cited in note 62).

69. Pub L 93-383, 88 Stat 633.

70. Id.

71. Pub L 105-276, 112 Stat 2510, codified in scattered sections of 42 USC (2009).

72. Schwartz, *Housing Policy in the United States* at 150–151 (cited in note 62). Local voucher administrators have been allowed to set acceptable rents from 90 to 110 percent (or higher in certain circumstances) of fair market rent. Id at 151.

73. Hays, *The Federal Government and Urban Housing* at 143–144 (cited in note 61).

74. Alex F. Schwartz, *Housing Policy in the United States* 160–163 (Routledge, 2006).

75. Pub L 102-389, Title II (1992), 106 Stat 1571, codified as amended at 42 USC 12747 (2009). Hope (the acronym for Housing Opportunities for People Everywhere) has experienced several changes, each marked with a different Roman numeral. Thus, Hope I, inaugurated during the first Bush administration, focused on enabling public housing dwellers to purchase their own residences.

76. Schwartz, *Housing Policy in the United States* at 117–123 (cited in note 74).

77. Id at 122–123.

78. Id at 163.

79. Pub L 105-276, 112 Stat 2510, codified in scattered sections of 42 USC (2009).

80. Schwartz, *Housing Policy in the United States* at 124 (cited in note 74).

81. 24 CFR § 903 (2009).

82. 436 F 2d 809 (3d Cir).

83. Id at 811–812.

84. Id at 820–821.

85. 484 F 2d 1122 (2d Cir).

86. Id at 1125, 1134, 1140 (1st Cir).

87. Id at 1133, 1136.

88. 135 F3d 11.

89. Id at 12–18.

90. Id at 16.

91. 840 F2d 1096 (2d Cir).

92. Id at 1098.

93. Id at 1102.

94. Id at 1103.

95. Robert G. Schwemm, *Housing Discrimination: Law and Litigation* ch 11A, 24–25 (Thomson-West, 2008).

96. Alexander Polikoff, *Sustainable Integration* 43, 44–45 in Goering, ed, *Housing Desegregation and Federal Policy* (cited in note 51).

97. The Institute on Race and Poverty, *Examining the Relationship between Housing, Education, and Persistent Segregation: Final Report, Part IV* at 7 (U of Minnesota Law School, 2000).

98. Smolla, 1981 Duke U L J 891 at 891–939 (cited in note 67); Robert W. Lake, *Unresolved Themes in the Evolution of Fair Housing* in Goering, ed, *Housing Desegregation and Federal Policy* at 313, 320–322 (cited in note 51).

99. Id at 320–322.

100. See Cara Hendrickson, *Racial Desegregation and Income Deconcentration, Public Housing,* 9 Georgetown J Poverty Law & Pol'y 35, 59 (2002).

101. 425 U.S. 284.

102. Alex F. Schwartz, *Housing Policy in the United States* 167 (Routledge, 2006).

103. Id at 172.

104. Id.

105. 169 F 3d 973.

106. Id at 981.

107. Id at 983.

108. Id.

109. 135 F3d 11 (1st Cir 1998).

110. (Princeton U Press, 1996).

111. For examples, see articles collected at 27 Seton Hall Law Review 1268–1471 (1997).

112. Charles Haar, *Suburbs under Siege* 15–29 (Princeton U Press, 1996)).

113. Peter Schuck, *Diversity in America: Keeping Government at a Safe Distance* 219–217 (The Belknap Press of Harvard U Press, 2003).

114. Doctrine name derived from opinion title: *Southern Burlington County N.A.A.C.P. v. Town of Mount Laurel,* 67 N.J. 151 (1975).

115. Haar, *Suburbs under Siege* at 10 (cited in note 112).

116. Id at 10.

117. Id at 190–191.

118. John M. Payne, *Statement,* in Robert Schwemm, ed, *The Fair Housing Act After Twenty Years—A Conference* at 84–85 (Yale Law School, 1989); John Charles Boger, *Mount Laurel at 21 Years,* 27 Seton Hall Law Review 1450, 1455 (1997).

119. Haar, *Suburbs under Siege* at 166 (cited in note 112).

120. Id at 243 n 112.

121. The Institute on Race and Poverty, *Examining the Relationship between Housing, Education, and Persistent Segregation: Final Report* 24, Part IV (U of Minnesota Law School, 2000).

122. Id at 4.

123. Id at 2–4.

124. Id at 34.

125. Id at 3.

126. Schwartz, *Housing Policy in the United States* at 192–197 (cited in note 102).

127. Douglas R. Porter, *The Promise and Practice of Exclusionary Zoning* 212, 213 in Anthony Downs, ed, *Growth Management and Affordable Housing: Do They Conflict?* (Brookings Institution, 2004).

128. Schwartz, *Housing Policy in the United States* at 192–197 (cited in note 102).

129. Myron Orfield, *Land Use and Housing Policies to Reduce Concentrated Poverty and Racial Segregation,* 33 Fordham Urb L J 877, 915–917 (2006).

130. Id at 914.

131. Id at 925–926.

132. Id at 926–928.

133. Pub L 95-128, Title VIII, 91 Stat 1147, § 2901, codified, as amended, at 12 USC sect 2901 *et seq* (2009).

134. Schwartz, *Housing Policy in the United States* at 242–243 (cited in note 102).

135. *The Community Reinvestment Act and the Recent Mortgage Crisis,* States News Service, December 3, 2008 (Accessed at Lexis Nexis Academic, News).

136. Peter J. Wallison, *Government Policies and Financial Crisis,* States News Service, December 3, 2008 (Accessed at Lexis Nexis Academic, News).

137. 42 USC § 3604 (c) (2009).

138. Schwemm, *Housing Discrimination: Law and Litigation* at chps 15–19 (cited in note 95).

139. W. Dennis Keating, *The Suburban Racial Dilemma* 200–210 (Temple U Press, 1994).

140. 935 F2d 868 (7th Cir).

141. Id at 887.

142. Id.

143. Id at 892–895.

144. Here, and throughout this chapter, the authors are particularly indebted both to Robert Lake's essay *Unresolved Themes in the Evolution of Fair Housing* and the writing of John M. Goering, editor of *Housing Desegregation and Federal Policy* (U North Carolina Press, 1986) where the Lake essay appears at 313–326.

145. Wilhelmina A. Leigh and James D. McGhee, *A Minority Perspective on Residential Integration* in Goering, ed, *Housing Desegregation and Federal Policy* at 31, 31–42 (cited above).

146. See his essay, *Human, All Too Human: The Negro's Vested Interest in Segregation* 283–291 in G. Franklin Edwards, ed, *E. Franklin Frazier: On Race Relations—Selected Writings* (U Chicago Press, 1968).

147. *Editor's Concluding Remarks,* in Goering, ed, *Housing Desegregation and Federal Policy* at 330–331.

Chapter Eight. Constitutional Underclasses and Affirmative Action

1. *Smith v. Jackson,* 544 U.S. 228 (2005).

2. *Kimel v. Florida,* 528 U.S. 62 (2000).

3. J. Bannin Jasiunas, *Note: Is ENDA the Answer? Can A "Separate but Equal" Federal Statute Adequately Protect Gays and Lesbians From Employment Discrimination?* 61 Ohio St L J 1529, 1539 (2000).

4. *Lawrence v. Texas,* 539 U.S. 558, 578 (2003).

5. Hugh Davis Graham, *Legacies of the 1960s: The American "Rights Revolution" in an Era of Divided Governance,* 10 J of Policy History, 267, 276 (1998).

6. Pub L 88-352, 78 Stat 241, § 703(a), codified at 42 USC, § 2000e-2(a) (2009).

7. Pub L 88-352, 78 Stat 241, § 703(d), codified at 42 USC, § 2000e-2(d) (2009).

8. Pub L 101-336, 104 Stat 327, § 102(a); § 102 (B) (5) (A), codified at 42 USC, § 12112 (a) and 12112(b) (5)(A) (2009).

9. Pub L 101-336, 104 Stat 327, § 101(9), codified at 42 USC, § 12111(9) (2009). Other ADA provisions prohibit discrimination against and reasonable accommodation for the disabled in public services and public accommodations. See Pub L 101-336, 104 Stat 327, § 201 codified at 42 USC § 12131 *et seq*, and § 12181 *et seq* (2009).

10. Sherwin Rosen, *Disability Accommodation and the Labor Market* 18, 21 in Carolyn L. Weaver, ed., *Disability and Work: Incentives, Rights, and Opportunities* (The AEI Press, 1991).

11. Id at 22.

12. Pamela Karlan and George Rutherglen, *Disabilities, Discrimination, and Reasonable Accommodation*, 46 Duke Law J 1, 1–72 (1996).

13. Id at 4.

14. 438 U.S. 265.

15. Karlan and Rutherglen, 46 Duke Law J at 10 (cited in note 12).

16. Id at 9.

17. See Pub L 92-318, 86 Stat 373, codified at 20 USC § 1681 (a) (2009) [Title IX of the Education Act of 1972]; Note: *Cheering on Women and Girls in Sports*, 110 Harv L Rev, 1627, 1627–1644 (1997); *Cohen v. Brown*, 101 F3d 155 (1st Cir 1996).

18. *Metro Broadcasting v. FCC*, 497 U.S. 547 (1990).

19. *Affirmative Action Review: Report to the President* 40–42, 55–63, submitted on July 19, 1995, by George Stephanopoulos, Senior Adviser to the President and Christopher Edley Jr., Special Counsel to the President.

20. George R. La Noue and John C. Sullivan, *Presumptions for Preferences: The Small Business Administration's Decisions on Groups Eligible for Affirmative Action*, 6 J of Policy History 439, 439–467 (1994); *Deconstructing the Affirmative Action Categories*, 41 Am Behavioral Scientist 913, 913–926 (1998); *Gross Presumptions: Determining Group Eligibility for Federal Procurement Preferences*, 41 Santa Clara L Rev 103, 103–159 (2000).

21. 29 CFR 1607.4B (2009).

22. Pub L 101-336, 104 Stat 327, § 2, codified at 42 USC, § 12101 (a) (b) (2009).

23. Samuel R. Bagenstos, *Rational Discrimination, Accommodation, and the Politics of (Disability) Civil Rights*, 89 Va L Rev 822, 825 (2003).

24. Edward Berkowitz, *Disabled Policy: America's Programs for the Handicapped* 184 (New York: Cambridge U Press, 1987).

25. Id.

26. Id.

27. James Leonard, *The Equality Trap: How Reliance on Traditional Civil Rights Concepts Has Rendered Title I of the ADA Ineffective*, 56 Case W. Reserve L Rev 1 (2004).

28. Berkowitz, *Disabled Policy* at 180 (cited in note 24).

29. Thumbnail descriptions of the disability statutes discussed from this point derived generally from Robert Burgdorf Jr., *Disability Discrimination in Employment Law* chps 1, 2 (The Bureau of National Affairs, 1995).

30. 42 USC, § 1210 (a) (2) and (3). For the language of these Findings, see 262–63.

31. "On the basis" of replaced "because" in the ADA amendments of 2008, Pub L 110-325.

32. 42 USC § 12112(a).

33. Id at § 12111(8).

34. Id at § 12112(b) (5)(A).

35. Id at § 12102 (2).

36. Id at §12132.

37. Id.

38. Id at § 12102 (2).

39. Id at § 12131.

40. 28 CFR 35.150 (a)(3) (2009).

41. Id at § 35.151(2009).

42. 42 USC § 12182 (b)(A)(ii).

43. Samuel Bagenstos, *The Future of Disability Law*, 114 Yale L J 1, 6 (2004).

44. Data on judicial responses regarding the ADA generally from Susan Gluck Mezey, *Disabling Interpretations: The Americans with Disabilities Act in Federal Courts*, chps 3, 4, 5 (U Pittsburgh Press, 2005).

45. That is, one of the parties prevailed on the merits, or the case was dismissed.

46. At the District court, defendants were coded as prevailing if their motions were granted; if they were victorious at trial; or if summary judgment was denied the plaintiff. At the appellate level, defendants were coded as prevailing if the plaintiff cases were defeated totally.

47. The coding procedure for Title III cases was the same as that described in the above footnote for Title II cases.

48. 531 U.S. 356.

49. Id at 369–372.

50. Id at 367–368.

51. Id at 372.

52. 527 U.S. 471.

53. Ann Bond Emrich, *ADA Amendments Take Effect January 1*, Grand Rapids Business Journal, 3ff (October 27, 2008) (Accessed at Lexis Nexis Academic, News).

54. Pub L 110-325, § 2(4).

55. Id at § 3(E)(i)(ii).

56. 42 USC § 12102(2)(C).

57. 527 U.S. at 490–491.

58. Id at 493.

59. Pub L 110-325, § 2(8)(3).

60. Id at § 3(3)(A). Excluded are transitory/minor impairments lasting, or expected to last six months or less. Id at § 3(3)(B).

61. Id at § 6(f).

62. 534 U.S. 184.

63. Pub L 110-325, § 2(8)(4).

64. Id at § 2(7).

65. Id at § 2(8)(5).

66. Id at § 3(4)(A).

67. Samuel R. Bagenstos, *The Supreme Court, The Americans with Disabilities Act, and Rational Discrimination*, 55 Ala L Rev 923, 934–949 (2004).

68. Pub L 90-202, 81 Stat 602, codified, as amended, at 29 USC § 621 *et seq* (2009).

69. 427 U.S. 307.

70. Id at 312–316. Internal citations and footnotes omitted.

71. Id at 312–316.

72. 440 U.S. 93.

73. Id at 98–106.

74. Id at 123–124.

75. *Gregory v. Ashcroft*, 501 U.S. 452, 471–473.

76. Id at 473.

77. Pub L 90-202, 81 Stat 602 § 2, codified at 29 USC § 621 (2009).

78. Id.

79. Id at § 4.

80. 509 U.S. 502.

81. Raymond F. Gregory, *Age Discrimination in the American Workplace: Old at a Young Age* 205–206 (Rutgers U Press, 2001).

82. 507 U.S. 604.

83. Gregory, *Age Discrimination* 210 (cited in note 81).

84. Id at 210 citing *Graefenhaim v. Pabst Brewing Co.*, 827 F2d 13 (7th Cir, 1987).

85. 507 U.S. 604, 610 (1993).

86. Gregory, *Age Discrimination* at 216 (cited in note 81).

87. 161 L. Ed. 2d 410.

88. Gregory, *Age Discrimination* at 155–162 (cited in note 81).

89. *Kimel v. Florida*, 528 U.S. 62 (2000).

90. 161 L. Ed. 2d 410, 414.

91. Howard Eglit, *Elders on Trial: Age and Ageism in the American Legal System* 15 (U Press of Florida, 2004).

92. *Smith v. Jackson*, 544 U.S. 228, 240–241.

93. Pub L 90-202, 81 Sat. 602 § 2 (1967).

94. See U.S. Equal Employment Opportunity Commission, Office of General Counsel—Trial Division, *Legislative History of the Age Discrimination in Employment Act*, 5–14, 51, 118, 147, 153, 156, 157, 213 (U.S. Government Printing Office, 1981).

95. See *Smith v. Jackson*, 544 U.S. 228 (2005); *Hazen Paper v. Biggins*, 507 U.S. 604, 610–611 (1993); *EEOC v. Wyoming* 460 U.S. 226, 231 (1983).

96. U.S. Secretary of Labor, *The Older American Worker: Age Discrimination in Employment* 1 (Government Printing Office, June 1965).

97. Slip Opinion No. 08-441.

98. Id at 9 (Opinion of the Court).

99. Id at 1 ff (Stevens dissenting).

100. Id at 9 (Opinion of the Court).

101. David Savage, *Age Bias Much Harder to Prove, Los Angeles Times* A1, A24 (June 19, 2009).

102. Susan Gluck Mezey, *Queers in Court: Gay Rights Law and Public Policy* 30 (Rowman and Littlefield, 2007).

103. Franklin E. Kameny, *Government v. Gays: The Sad Stories with Two Happy Endings—Civil Service Employment and Security Clearance* 188, 188–207 in John D'Emilio, William B. Turner, and Uruashi Vaid, eds, *Creating Change: Sexuality, Public Policy, and Civil Rights* (St. Martin's Press, 2000).

104. *In Re Marriage Cases*, 43 Cal 4th 757, 784, 821 (2008).

105. Id at 820, 854–855 (2008).

106. *Strauss v. Horton*, 2009 Cal. Lexis 4626.

107. 517 U.S. 620.

108. 539 U.S. 558.

109. 517 U.S. at 636; 539 U.S. at 599.

110. 478 U.S. 186.

111. Id at 196.

112. Id at 192, 191–194.

113. 517 U.S. at 626.

114. Id at 636.

115. 539 U.S. 558.

116. 517 U.S. at 631.

117. Jeffrey S. Byrne and Bruce Deming, *On the Prudence of Discussing Affirmative Action for Lesbians and Gay Men*, 5 Stan L & Pol'y Rev 177, 177–187 (1993).

Chapter Nine. Facing Affirmative Action's Future

1. 402 U.S. 1, 15.

2. 347 U.S. 483.

3. *Grutter v. Bollinger*, 539 U.S. 306, 328.

4. *South Carolina v. Katzenbach*, 383 U.S. 301, 325–326 (1966).

5. *Lawrence v. Texas*, 539 U.S. 558, 578 (2003).

6. *University of Alabama v. Garrett*, 531 U.S. 356, 367.

7. 531 U.S. 356.

8. Id at 367–368.

9. Id at 368–374. Unlike employment (covered by Title I of the ADA), states are required by Congress to accommodate the disabled in the provision of public services (Title II of the ADA). The Court reasoned that states have frequently violated the fundamental rights of the disabled by limiting public services such as permitting courtroom access to be difficult for the handicapped. *Tennessee v. Lane*, 158 L. Ed. 2d 820, 828–831 (2004).

10. Samuel Issacharoff and Justin Nelson, *Discrimination with a Difference: Can Employment Discrimination Law Accommodate the Americans with Disabilities Act?* 79 N.C. L Rev 307, 333 (2001).

11. Samuel R. Bagenstos, *The Supreme Court, the Americans with Disabilities Act, and Rational Discrimination*, 55 Ala L. Rev.923, 934–949 (2004).

12. Id.

13. *University of Alabama v. Garrett*, 531 U.S. at 367–368 (2001).

14. 527 U.S. 471.

15. 534 U.S. 184.

16. Samuel R. Bagenstos, *The Future of Disability Law*, 114 Yale L J 1, 1–83 (2004).

17. John Macnicol, *Age Discrimination: An Historical and Contemporary Analysis* 228 (Cambridge U Press, 2006).

18. Id at 255–262.

19. The language is from H.R. 3685 passed by the House of Representatives in 2007. A new ENDA was introduced in the House in summer of 2009, and contains protection for transsexuals. *Employment Non-Discrimination Act*, http://en.wikipedia. org./wiki/Employment Non_Discrimination_Act (accessed on July 28, 2009).

20. Witness the following remarks by Senator Orrin Hatch: "I want to emphasize that affirmative action means quotas or it means nothing. It means discrimination on the basis of race or sex. It does not mean remedial education [or] special programs for the disadvantaged. . . . It has nothing to do with equality of opportunity. . . . Affirmative action is about equality of results, statistically measured. . . . All distinctions [between quotas and "goals," "targets," and "timetables"] dissolve in practice." Orrin Hatch, *Loading the Economy*, in Paul Burstein, ed, *Equal Employment Opportunity* at 261, 262 (Aldine De Gruyter, 1994).

21. See appendixes 1 and 3 of this volume.

22. Todd S. Purdum, *Shift in Mix Alters the Face of California*, *The New York Times*, natl ed, A1 (July 4, 2000).

23. 488 U.S. 469.

24. 515 U.S. 200.

25. *Allen v. Alabama State Board*, 164 F3d 1347, 1353 (11th Cir 1999); *Duffy v. Wolle*, 123 F3d 1026, 1038–1039 (8th Cir 1997). See also *Raso v. Lago*, 135 F3d 11 (1st Cir 1998).

26. *Lutheran Church-Missouri Synod v. FCC*, 141 F3d 344, 351–353 (DC Cir 1998); *Monterey Mechanical Co. v. Wilson*, 125 F3d 702, 709–713 (9th Cir 1997).

27. *Bush v. Vera*, 517 U.S. 952, 958 (1996) (emphasis added).

28. *Adarand v. Peña*, 515 U.S. 200, 227 (1995).

29. 414 U.S. 563 (1974). See ch 4, note 134; and 166–67.

30. 438 U.S. 265, 287, 411ff (1978).

31. 426 U.S. 229.

32, 438 U.S. at 307–309.

33. Id at 311–312, 314–315, 319–320. Justice Powell held that diversity was a "compelling interest," but that the set-aside was not "necessary to promote this interest," hence unconstitutional under well-settled strict scrutiny principles. The "fatal flaw" in the set-aside was not a failure to prove that it was intended to remedy past discrimination, but rather "its disregard of" the white applicants' individual Fourteenth Amendment rights to compete for the reserved minority seats. Id at 314–315, 321.

34. *Hopwood v. Texas*, 78 F 3d 932, 944–946 (5th Cir 1996). The panel held, 2-1, that the state law school violated equal protection by applying lower LSAT and grade requirements for minority applicants. See also *Lutheran Church I*, 141 F3d at

351–355, where a panel of the DC Circuit rejected the FCC's claim that it had a compelling interest in fostering racial diversity by requiring broadcast licensees to establish numerical minority-hiring goals.

35. *Wessmann v. Gittens*, 160 F3d 790, 796 (1st Cir 1998). See also *Eisenberg v. Montgomery*, 19 F Supp 2d 449 (SD Md) refusing to follow *Hopwood*.

36. 233 F3d 1188. Also see *Gratz v. Bollinger*, 122 F Supp 2d 811 (E D Mich Southern Div 2000).

37. 539 U.S. 306.

38. See Christopher Edley Jr., *Not All Black and White* 126–141 (Hill and Wang, 1996) for a comprehensive statement of the pros and cons of nonremedial preference in education and employment. Also see, Nicholas deB. Katzenbach and Burke Marshall Sunday, *Not Color Blind; Just Blind, The New York Times Magazine*, 42 ff (February 22, 1998).

39. E.g., law enforcement, prison administration, firefighting, education, broadcasting, health care, and corporate administration. See *Wessmann v. Gittens*, 160 F3d at 795–798. Authorities on diversity successes are collected at Walter Dellinger, *Memorandum to General Counsels Re Adarand*, Office of Legal Counsel, U.S. Department of Justice 14–19 (June 28, 1995).

40. 127 S. Ct. 2738.

41. 505 U.S. 717.

42. 509 U.S. 630 (1993).

43. 515 U.S. 900 (1996).

44. *U.S. v. Virginia*, 518 U.S. 515, 531 (1996).

45. Pub L 92-318, 86 Stat 373 codified, as amended, at 20 USC § 1681 (2009).

46. 443 U.S. 193 (1978).

47. The statutory and regulation reference source in this section on Statutory Issues is the Government Printing Office's Web site: *GPO Access* http://www.gpoaccess.gov which provided the U.S. Code updated to July 2009.

48. 401 U.S. 424 (1971).

49. Pub L 111-2.

50. 126 S. Ct. 2594.

51. 42 USC 1973 *et seq.*

52. Richard H. Fallon Jr., Daniel J. Meltzer, and David Shapiro, *Hart and Wechsler's The Federal Courts and the Federal System*, 5th ed, 43–47 (Foundation Press/Thomson-West, 2003).

53. Id at 41–43.

54. Paul Bator, *Symposium: The Constitution as Architecture: Legislative and Administrative Courts Under Article III*, 65 Ind L J, 233, 233–235 (1990).

55. Robert G. McCloskey, *The American Supreme Court* 212–213 (2d ed., revised by Sanford Levinson, U Chicago Press, 1994).

56. David Schoenbrod, *Power Without Responsibility* 3–21 (Yale U Press, 1993).

57. John E. Roemer, *Equality of Opportunity* 1 (Harvard U Press, 1998).

58. Id at 108.

59. Some theorists propose the alternative rationale of "distributive justice," under which disadvantaged persons, *regardless of race, gender, or ethnic affiliation*, are entitled

to whatever they would have gained proportionally absent invidious discrimination. See Ronald J. Fiscus, *The Constitutional Logic of Affirmative Action* 8–14 (Duke, 1992).

60. 539 U.S. 244 (2003).

61. Id at 304.

62. Roemer, *Equality of Opportunity* at 1 (cited in note 57).

63. Christopher Edley Jr. *Not All Black and White* (Hill and Wang, 1996).

64. Id at 84–106.

65. Id at 42–46, 122.

66. Id at 16–17, 21–24, 44–52, ch 4.

67. Id at 83, 121.

68. Id at ch 10.

69. Id at 50.

70. Id at 204.

71. Id at 140.

72. Id at 78.

73. Id at 67.

74. Id at 125.

75. Id at 123–141.

76. David A. Hollinger, *Postethnic America: Beyond Multiculturalism*, 10th Anniversary Edition 181–182 (Basic Books, 2005).

77. Id at 182.

78. Id at 187.

79. Id at 186.

80. Id at 187.

81. Id at xii.

82. Id at 236–237.

83. Id at 157.

84. Id at 216.

85. Peter Schuck, *Diversity in America: Keeping Government at a Safe Distance* 521 (The Belknap Press of Harvard U Press, 2003).

86. *Multicultural Citizenship* 67–68 (Oxford U Press, 1995).

87. Stephan and Abigail Thernstrom, *America in Black and White* (Simon and Schuster, 1997).

88. Id at 424–426.

89. Id at 459.

90. Id at 459–461.

91. Id at 184–189.

92. Id at 188.

93. Id at 537–539.

94. Id at 533.

95. Id at 499–501, 661 ns 34–40.

96. Id at 501–504.

97. Id at 534.

98. Id at 540.

99. Id at 539.

100. Id at 234.

101. Id at 234–235.

102. Id at 264.

103. Id at 259, 264.

104. Id at 271–279.

105. Id at 274–277.

106. Id at 285.

107. Id at 443–449.

108. Id at 460–461.

109. Frank D. Bean et al., *The Latino Middle Class: Myth, Reality and Potential* 3–4 (Tomas Rivera Policy Institute, 2001).

110. *Categorically Unequal: The American Stratification System* (Russell Sage Foundation, 2007).

111. Id at 35.

112. Id at 49.

113. Id at 49.

114. Id at 50.

115. Congressman Bernie Sanders, *Falling Behind in Boom Times*, *The Boston Globe* A15 (February 12, 2000).

116. Michael M. Weinstein, *America's Rags to Riches Myth*, *The New York Times*, natl ed, A 30 (February 18, 2000).

117. U.S. Department of Commerce, *Statistical Abstract of the U.S.: 2007*, Table 40 (Government Printing Office, 2006).

118. Debra A. Millenson, *Whither Affirmative Action*, 29 Memphis L Rev 704, 731–738 (1999); *Affirmative Action Review: Report to the President* chps 3 and 4 (July 19, 1995) submitted by George Stephanopoulos, Senior Adviser to the President, and Christoper Edley Jr., Special Counsel to the President.

119. Tom Wicker, *Tragic Failure* (Morrow, 1996).

120. Id at 126–127.

121. William Julius Wilson, *When Work Disappears* (Knopf, 1997).

122. Id at 3–55.

123. Id at xv–xviii; 172–182.

124. *Taking Culture Seriously: A Framework and Afro-American Illustration* 202, 206 in Lawrence E. Harrison and Samuel P. Huntington, eds, *Culture Matters: How Values Shape Human Progress* (Basic Books, 2000).

125. A Wilson central finding is, "For the first time in the twentieth century most adults in many inner-city ghetto neighborhoods are not working in a typical week." Wilson, *When Work Disappears* at xiii (cited in note 121).

126. Id at xxi–xxii, 183–192.

127. Id at 192.

128. Id at 186.

129. Id at 193.

130. Id at 197.

131. Id.

132. Id.

133. Id at 198.

134. Id.

135. Id.

136. Id.

137. Id at 205.
138. Id.
139. Id.
140. Id.
141. Id at 210–217.
142. Id at 218–220.
143. Id at 221–223.
144. Id at 223–224.
145. Id at 226–235.
146. Id at 235–238.
147. Tom Wicker, *Tragic Failure* 83, 62–73 (Morrow, 1996).
148. William Julius Wilson, *More Than Just Race: Being Black and Poor in the Inner City* (W.W. Norton, 2009).
149. Id at 141–143.
150. Id at 108–128, 147–152.
151. Richard D. Kahlenberg, *The Remedy* (Basic Books, 1996).
152. Id at 152.
153. Id at 83, 100–101, 124, 151–152. In the Kahlenberg scheme, even where the *Croson* standard for racial preferences is met, the employer or university would be subject to class-based affirmative action requirements. Id at 151–152.
154. Id at 186.
155. Id at 186, 203, 317 n 112, 151, 287 ns 158–162, 164–165.
156. Id at 80. For Kahlenberg's support of this claim, see id at 42–76.
157. Id at 44.
158. Id at 144.
159. Id at 156–160.
160. 404 U.S. 424.
161. Kahlenberg, *The Remedy* at 31, 159 (cited in note 151). See further, Alfred Blumrosen, *Modern Law* 254 (U Wisconsin Press, 1993): "the *Griggs* principle of 'adverse impact' . . . require(s) that an employer be 'race conscious.' The disparate impact concept requires an analysis of the effect of a selection procedure on race. . . . *It is impossible to analyze adverse impact without being race conscious.*" (Emphasis added.)
162. Kahlenberg, *The Remedy*, at 166–171 (cited in note 151).
163. Id at 64–74.
164. Id at 171.
165. Id at 177.
166. Id.
167. Stephan and Abigail Thernstrom, *America in Black and White* 16, 18, 81–82, 191–199 (Simon and Schuster, 1997); William Julius Wilson, *When Work Disappears* 193 (Knopf, 1997); Tom Wicker, *Tragic Failure* xi, 19, 57, 155 (Morrow, 1996).
168. Thernstrom and Thernstrom, *America in Black and White* at 211–219 (cited above). In *Grand Illusion, The New York Review of Books* 26, 27–28 (June 11, 1998), Andrew Hacker argues that the number should be higher, given the threefold increase in the number of black families earning more than $75,000, and that the claim that the suburbs are generally integrated is simply not true. He faults the Thernstroms for failing to observe that a "depressing number" of "mainly black" suburbs "are just a few steps from slums." Id at 28.

169. Wicker, *Tragic Failure* at 157 (cited in note 167).

170. Id.

171. John Charles Boger, *Race and the American City* 3, 41, in John Charles Boger and Judith Welch Wegner, eds, *Race, Poverty, and American Cities* (The U North Carolina Press, 1996).

172. Wicker, *Tragic Failure* at 157 (cited in note 167).

173. William Julius Wilson, *When Work Disappears* 194–195 (Knopf, 1997).

174. Wicker, *Tragic Failure* at xi (cited in note 167).

175. Thernstrom and Thernstrom, *America in Black and White* at 232 (cited in note 167).

176. Boger, *Race and the American City*, in Boger and Wegner eds, *Race, Poverty, and American Cities* at 41 (cited in note 171).

177. Frank D. Bean et al., *The Latino Middle Class: Myth, Reality and Potential* 3–4 (Tomas Rivera Policy Institute, 2001).

178. *Categorically Unequal: The American Stratification System* 246–247 (Russell Sage Foundation, 2007).

179. Id at 247.

180. Id at 248–249.

181. Id at 249.

182. Thernstrom and Thernstrom, *America in Black and White* at 501–505, 507–508, 519–528 (cited in note 167).

183. Id at 500, 499–501.

184. Id at 219–221.

185. Id at 224.

186. John McWhorter, *Winning the Race: Behind the Crisis in Black America* 376–391 (Gotham Books, 2006).

187. Id at 385.

188. Wilson, *When Work Disappears* at 119–120, 183, 186–187 (cited in note 173).

189. William Julius Wilson and Richard P. Taub, *There Goes the Neighborhood: Racial, Ethnic, and Class Tensions in Four Chicago Neighborhoods and Their Meaning for America* 161 (Alfred A. Knopf, 2006).

190. Tom Wicker, *Tragic Failure* 188 (Morrow, 1996).

191. Christopher Edley Jr., *Not All Black and White* 47 (Hill and Wang, 1996).

192. Id at 50.

193. Id at 209.

194. Id. Other versions of the Doomsday scenario can be found in Derrick Bell, *Faces at the Bottom of the Well* (Basic Books, 1992) and Andrew Hacker, *Two Nations* (Scribner's, 1992). On Bell and Hacker in this connection, see Wilson, *When Work Disappears* at 183 (cited in note 173).

195. Frank D. Bean et al., *The Latino Middle Class: Myth, Reality and Potential* 3–4 (Tomas Rivera Policy Institute, 2001).

196. Massey, *Categorically Unequal* at 148. (Cited in note 178.)

197. Id at 148–150.

198. Orlando Patterson, *The Ordeal of Integration* (Civitas/Counterpoint, 1997).

199. Id at ix.

200. Id at 2–5, 177–181.

201. Id at 81.

202. Id at 48.

203. Id at 43–48.

204. Id at 57–58.

205. Id at 15, 16, 18, 21.

206. Stephan and Abigail Thernstrom, *America in Black and White* 207 n 18 (Simon and Schuster, 1997).

207. Patterson, *Ordeal of Integration* at ix, 5, 15–21, 48, 82–85 (cited in note 198).

208. Id at 28–42.

209. Id at 48–50, 77–81.

210. Id at 147.

211. Stephan and Abigail Thernstrom, *America in Black and White* at 533 (cited in note 206).

212. Id at 539.

213. Orlando Patterson, *Ordeal of Integration* 192–193 (Civitas/Counterpoint, 1997).

214. Id at 173.

215. Id at 42–48.

216. Id at 157.

217. Id.

218. Id.

219. Christopher Edley Jr., *Not All Black and White* 9, 134, 141, 189 (Hill and Wang, 1996).

220. Patterson, *Ordeal of Integration* at 193–198 (cited in note 213).

221. Donald R. Kinder and Lynn Sanders, *Divided by Color* (U Chicago Press, 1996).

222. Id at 6–8, 11, 13–14, 31–34, 25–27, 68, 85–86, 90–91.

223. Id at 124.

224. Id at 191.

225. Id at 269.

226. Paul Sniderman and Thomas Piazza, *The Scar of Race* (Harvard U Press, 1993).

227. Stephan and Abigail Thernstrom, *America in Black and White* 500 ff (Simon and Schuster, 1997).

228. Donald R. Kinder and Lynn Sanders, *Divided by Color* 271 (U of Chicago Press, 1996).

229. Id at 272.

230. In *Grand Illusion, The New York Review of Books* 26, 28 (June 11, 1998), Andrew Hacker addresses the question of "how to account for the persistence of racial subordination . . . the feelings of most black Americans that white Americans continue to judge them unjustly." Id at 28. He disputes opinion research indicating that white opposition to affirmative action is based on principle, not aversion to the blacks who may benefit. In his view, whites, when interviewed, always try to convey a compassionate, unprejudiced, not necessarily truthful image. Id at 28.

231. Randall Kennedy, *Race, Crime, and the Law* (Pantheon Books, 1997).

232. Id at 231.

233. Id at 238–240.

234. Id at 240–241.

235. Id at 245.

236. 105 Yale Law J 677 (1995).

237. Kennedy, *Race, Crime, and the Law* at 296–297 (cited in note 231).

238. Id at 300–306.

239. Id at 310.

240. Id at 9–10, 238–252.

241. Id at 19.

242. Stephan and Abigail Thernstrom, *America in Black and White* 274 (Simon and Schuster, 1997).

243. Kennedy, *Race, Crime, and the Law* at 5–7, chs 4, 8 (cited in note 231).

244. *McCleskey v. Kemp*, 481 U.S. 279 (1987). In this case a black defendant was condemned to death by a Georgia court for killing a white man. On appeal, he contended that the sentence was unconstitutionally predicated on his race and that of his victim. As proof, he presented a professional statistical study which, after controlling for some 230 variables, concluded that the odds of being condemned to death in Georgia were 4.3 times greater for defendants who killed whites than for those who killed blacks. The Supreme Court, 5-4, rejected the appeal, on the ground that the requisite inference of *intentional* discrimination directed at the defendant *individually* could not be drawn from the *group* data in the study.

245. For the Thernstrom view as to bias, see *America in Black and White* at 268–279 (cited in note 242).

246. Bruce Western, *Punishment and Inequality in America* 194 (Russell Sage Foundation, 2006).

247. Id at 31.

248. Id at ch 3 and 189–198.

249. Alfred W. Blumrosen, *Modern Law* 326 (U Wisconsin Press, 1993).

250. Stephen Steinberg, *Turning Back* (Beacon Press, 1995).

251. Id at 164.

252. Id at 179–220.

253. Id at 212.

254. Id at 213.

255. Id at 218.

256. Id at 219.

257. Id.

258. Zoltan L. Hajnal, *Changing White Attitudes toward Black Political Leadership* 159–162 (Cambridge U Press, 2007).

Appendices

1. 539 U.S. 306; 539 U.S. 244 (2003).

2. 127 S. Ct. 2738.

3. Up to Executive Order 13116 (2000), the material in this section is from Congressional Research Service, *Compilation and Overview of Federal Laws and Regulations Establishing Affirmative Action Goals or Other Preference Based on Race,*

Gender, or Ethnicity: A Report to Senator Robert Dole at 27–29 (February 17, 1995). The aforementioned cited data is replicated in Charles V. Dale and Cassandra Foley, *Survey of Federal Laws and Regulations Mandating Affirmative Action Goals, Set-asides or Other Preferences Based on Race, Gender, or Ethnicity* at 26–28 (Congressional Research Service, September 7, 2004) which is also the source of the information from Executive Order 13116 under this subtitle.

4. 42 U.S.C. § 2000e *et seq.*

5. 29 C. F. R. Part 1608 (the guidelines state the EEOC's position that when employers voluntarily undertake in good faith to remedy past discrimination by race- or gender-conscious affirmative action means, the agency will not find them liable for reverse discrimination).

6. 42 U.S.C. § 2000e-16(b).

7. 42 U.S.C. § 2000e-16(b)(1).

8. 5 U.S.C. § 7201.

9. 5 C.F.R. 720.205(b) (1991).

10. Material here until the subtopic titled **Agriculture** is from Charles V. Dale and Cassandra Foley, *Survey of Federal Laws and Regulations Mandating Affirmative Action Goals, Set-asides or Other Preferences Based on Race, Gender, or Ethnicity* 2–5 (Congressional Research Service, September 7, 2004).

11. 42 U.S.C. § 2000e-16(b).

12. 5 U.S.C. § 7201.

13. 15 U.S.C. § 637(a).

14. 15 U.S.C. § 637(a) (5).

15. 13 CFR § 124.105(b).

16. The statute, 15 U.S.C. § 637(a)(6)(A), defines economic disadvantage in terms of: socially disadvantaged individuals whose ability to compete in the free enterprise system has been impaired due to diminished capital and credit opportunities as compared to others who are not socially disadvantaged, and such diminished opportunities have precluded or are likely to preclude such individuals from successfully competing in the open market.

17. 15 U.S.C. § 637(a).

18. 15 U.S.C. § 637(d). Criteria set forth in the regulations permit an administrative determination of socially disadvantaged status to be predicated on "clear and convincing evidence" that an applicant has "personally suffered" disadvantage of a "chronic and substantial" nature as the result of any of a variety of causes, including "long term residence in an environment isolated from the mainstream of American society," with a negative impact "on his or her entry into the business world."13 C.F.R. § 124.105(c).

19. P.L. 100-656, § 502, 102 Stat. 3887, codified at 15 U.S.C. § 644(g) (1).

20. See e.g., 49 C.F.R. §§ 23.64(e), 23.65 (setting forth waiver criteria for the Department of Transportation).

21. 15 U.S.C. § 637(a)(5).

22. See 49 C.F.R. Pt. 23, Subpt. D, App. C.

23. P.L. 103-355, 108 Stat. 3243, 3374, § 7106 (1994).

24. Material on this topic from Charles V. Dale and Cassandra Foley, *Survey of Federal Laws and Regulations Mandating Affirmative Action Goals, Set-asides or*

Other Preferences Based on Race, Gender, or Ethnicity at 6–7 (Congressional Research Service, September 7, 2004).

25. Material on this topic from id at 8–9.

26. Material on this topic from id at 9–10.

27. Material on this topic from id at 10–11.

28. Material on topic from id at 11–13.

29. Material on topic from id at 13–16.

30. Material on topic from id at 15.

31. Material on topic from id at 12.

32. Material on topic from Charles V. Dale and Cassandra Foley, *Survey of Federal Laws and Regulations Mandating Affirmative Action Goals, Set-asides or Other Preferences Based on Race, Gender, or Ethnicity* 17–18, 25 (Congressional Research Service, September 7, 2004).

33. Material on topic from id at 18–19.

34. Material on topic from id at 19.

35. Material on topic from id.

36. Material on topic from id at 22–23.

37. Material on topic from id at 19–20.

38. Material on the military up to **Authors' Note** from George Stephanopoulos, Senior Adviser to the President and Christopher Edley Jr., Special Counsel to the President, *Affirmative Action Review: Report to the President* 41–42 (July 19, 1995).

39. 539 U.S. 306; 539 U.S. 244.

40. 127 S. Ct. 2738.

41. Information and quotes from *Consolidated brief of Lt. General Julius W. Becton, Jr. et al.*, 2003 U.S. Supreme Court Briefs 532 (LexisNexis Academic, February 19, 2003).

42. Id at 16.

43. Id at 12.

44. Id at 12–13.

45. Id at 31–33.

46. Id at 33.

47. Id at 33, 35.

48. Id at 37–38.

49. Id at 42.

50. *Brief for Hon. Clifford L. Alexander et. al. As Amici in Support of Respondents, Parents Involved v. Seattle*, U.S. Supreme Court. Briefs (2006 Westlaw Campus Research, 2922651).

51. Id at 6.

52. 347 U.S. 483.

53. U.S. Supreme Court Briefs at 6–15 (cited in note 50).

54. Id at 5.

55. Id at 9.

56. Id at 10.

57. Authors' note: This document applies to larger service and supply contractors.

Selected Bibliography

Abrams, Kathryn. " 'Raising Politics Up': Minority Political Participation and Section 2 of The Voting Rights Act." *New York University Law Review* 63 (1988): 449–531.

Adams, Michelle. "The Last Wave of Affirmative Action." *Wisconsin Law Review* (1998): 1395–1463.

———. "Radical Integration." *California Law Review* 94 (2006): 261–311.

Affirmative Action Review: Report to the President. Submitted by Presidential Advisors George Stephanopoulos and Christopher Edley Jr., July 19, 1995.

Age Discrimination in Employment Act. Pub L 90-202, 81 Stat 602, codified as amended at 29 USC § 621*et seq* (2009).

Alexander, Clifford, et al. *Consolidated Brief Favoring School Integration in Case of Parents Involved v. Seattle.* Westlaw Campus Research: 2006 U.S. Supreme Court Briefs, 2922651.

Alphran, Derek M. "Proving Discrimination after *Croson* and *Adarand*: 'If it Walks Like a Duck.' " *University of San Francisco Law Review* 37 (2003): 887–969.

American Association of University Women Educational Foundation. *Separated by Sex: A Critical Look at Single-Sex Education for Girls.* Washington, DC: American Association of University Women Educational Foundation, 1998.

Americans With Disabilities Act. Pub L 101-336, 104 Stat 327, codified as amended, at 42 USC § 12101 *et seq* (2009).

Anderson, Deborah J., John Jesse Cheslock, and Ronald G. Ehrenberg. "Gender Equity in Intercollegiate Athletics: Determinants of Title IX Compliance." *The Journal of Higher Education* 77 (March/April 2006): 225–250.

Andrew III, John A. *Lyndon Johnson and the Great Society.* Chicago: Ivan R. Dee, 1998.

Appel, Richard N., Alison L. Gray, and Nilufer Loy. "The 40th Anniversary of Title VII of the Civil Rights Act of 1964 Symposium: Affirmative Action in the Workplace, Forty Years Later." *Hofstra Labor & Employment Law Journal* 22 (2005): 549–574.

Appiah, K. Anthony, and Amy Gutmann. *Color Conscious: The Political Morality of Race.* Princeton: Princeton University Press, 1996.

Armor, David J. *Forced Justice: School Desegregation and the Law.* New York: Oxford University Press, 1995.

Bagenstos, Samuel R. "Rational Discrimination, Accommodation, and the Politics of (Disability) Civil Rights." *Virginia Law Review* 89 (2003): 822–933.

————. "The Future of Disability Law." *Yale Law Journal* 114 (2004): 1–83.

————. "The Supreme Court, The Americans with Disabilities Act, and Rational Discrimination." *Alabama Law Review* 55 (2004): 923–949.

Barreto, Matt A., Gary M. Segura, and Nathan D. Woods. "The Mobilizing Effect of Majority-Minority Districts on Latino Turnout." *American Political Science Review* 98 (2004): 65–75.

Bator, Paul. "Symposium: The Constitution as Architecture: Legislative and Administrative Courts under Article III." *Indiana Law Journal* 65 (1990): 233–275.

Bean, Frank D. et al. *The Latino Middle Class: Myth, Reality and Potential.* Claremont, CA: Tomas Rivera Policy Institute, 2001.

Becker, Mary, Cynthia Grant Bowman, and Morrison Torrey, eds. *Cases and Materials on Feminist Jurisprudence.* St. Paul: West, 1994.

Becker, Mary. "Patriarchy and Inequality: Towards a Substantive Feminism." *University of Chicago Legal Forum* 1999: 21–86.

Becton, Lt. General Julius W. Jr., et al. *Consolidated Brief in Support of University of Michigan Diversity Admissions.* LexisNexis Academic: 2003 U.S. Supreme. Court. Briefs, February 19, 2003.

Bell, Derrick. *Faces at the Bottom of the Well: The Permanence of Racism.* New York: Basic Books, 1992.

Belz, Herman. *Equality Transformed: A Quarter Century of Affirmative Action.* New Brunswick: Transaction, 1991.

Benedict, Michael Les. "Reconstruction, Federalism, and Economic Rights." In *The Oxford Companion to the Supreme Court of the United States,* edited by Kermit L. Hall, et al. 381-389 New York: Oxford University Press, 1992.

Berkowitz, Edward. *Disabled Policy: America's Programs for the Handicapped.* New York: Cambridge University Press, 1987.

Blumrosen, Alfred W. *Modern Law.* Madison: University of Wisconsin Press, 1993.

Bobo, Lawrence. "Race, Interests, and Beliefs about Affirmative Action: Unanswered Questions and New Directions." *American Behavioral Scientist* 41, no. 7 (April 1998): 985–1003.

Boger, John C., and Judith Welch Wegner, eds. *Race, Poverty, and American Cities.* Chapel Hill: The University of North Carolina Press, 1996.

Boger, John C. "Mount Laurel at 21 Years: Reflections on the Power of Courts and Legislatures to Shape Social Change." *Seton Hall Law Review* 27 (1997): 1450–1470.

Bositis, David A. Impact of the "Core" Voting Rights Act on Voting and Office Holding. In *The Voting Rights Act: Securing the Ballot,* edited by Richard M. Valelly, 113–127 Washington, DC: Congressional Quarterly Press, 2006.

Boudreaux, Paul. "An Individual Preference Approach to Suburban Racial Desegregation." *Fordham Urban Law Journal* 27 (1999): 533–563.

Bowen, William, and Derek Bok. *The Shape of the River: Long-Term Consequences of Considering Race in College and University Admissions.* Princeton: Princeton University Press, 1998.

Boyd, Thomas M., and Stephen J. Markman. "The 1982 Amendments to the Voting Rights Act: A Legislative History." *Washington and Lee Law Review* 40 (1983): 1347-1428.

Branch, Taylor. *Parting the Waters: America in the King Years, 1954–63.* New York: Simon and Schuster, 1988.

———. *Pillar of Fire: America in the King Years, 1963–65.* New York: Simon and Schuster, 1998.

Brill, Alida, ed. *A Rising Public Voice: Women in Politics Worldwide.* New York: The Feminist Press, 1995.

Brown-Scott, Wendy. "Race Consciousness in Higher Education: Does Sound Education Policy Support the Continued Existence of Historically Black Colleges?" *Emory Law Journal* 43 (1994): 1–81.

Bunch, Kenyon, and Grant B. Mindle. "Testing the Limits of Precedent: The Application of *Green* to the Desegregation of Higher Education." *Constitutional Law Journal* 2 (1992): 541–592.

Burgdorf, Robert Jr. *Disability Discrimination in Employment Law.* Washington, DC: The Bureau of National Affairs, 1995.

Burstein, Paul, ed. *Equal Employment Opportunity: Labor Market Discrimination and Public Policy.* Hawthorne, NY: Aldine De Gruyter, 1994.

Burstein, Paul. *Discrimination, Jobs, and Politics: The Struggle For Equal Employment Opportunity in the United States Since the New Deal.* Chicago: University of Chicago Press, 1998.

Bybee, Keith J. *Mistaken Identity: The Supreme Court and the Politics of Minority Representation.* Princeton: Princeton University Press, 1998.

Byrne, Jeffrey S., and Bruce Deming. "On the Prudence of Discussing Affirmative Action for Lesbians and Gay Men." *Stanford Law & Policy Review* 5 (1993): 177–187.

California Secretary of State. "Proposition 209: Prohibition Against Discrimination or Preferential Treatment by State and Other Public Entities. Initiative Constitutional Amendment." *California Ballot Pamphlet, General Election,* November 5, 1996 at 94.

———. "Proposition 227: English Language in Public Schools. Initiative Statute." *California Ballot Pamphlet, Primary Election,* June 2, 1998 at 75–76.

Canon, David T. *Race, Redistricting, and Representation: The Unintended Consequence of Black Majority Districts.* Chicago: University of Chicago Press, 1999.

Caroll, Susan. *Representing Women: Women in State Legislatures as Agents of Policy-Related Change.* In *The Impact of Women In Public Office,* edited by Susan Caroll, 3-21 Bloomington: Indiana University Press, 2004.

Center for American Women and Politics, Eagleton Institute of Politics, *Women in Elective Office 2009,* http://www.cawp. Rutgers.edu/ (accessed July 26, 2009).

Chafe, William Henry. *The Paradox of Change: American Women in the 20th Century.* New York: Oxford University Press, 1991.

"[Note:] Cheering on Women and Girls in Sports: Using Title IX to Fight Gender Oppression." *Harvard Law Review* 110 (May, 1997): 1627–1644.

Cheslock, John J., and Suzanne E. Eckes. "Statistical Evidence and Compliance with Title IX." *New Directions for Institutional Research,* no. 138 (Summer, 2008): 31–45.

Civil Rights Act of 1964, Pub L 88-352, 78 Stat 241, codified, as amended, generally at 42 USC § 1971 *et seq* (2009).

Civil Rights Act of 1965, Pub L 89-110, 79 Stat 437, codified as amended, at 42 USC § 1973 *et seq* (2009).

Civil Rights Act of 1968, Pub L 90-284, 82 Stat 73, codified as amended, at 42 USC § 3601 *et seq* (2009).

Civil Rights Act of 1991, Pub L 102-166, 105 Stat 1071, codified in scattered sections of 2, 29, and 42 USC (1999).

"[Note:] The Civil Rights Act of 1991 and Less Discriminatory Alternatives in Disparate Impact Litigation." *Harvard Law Review* 106 (1993): 1621–1638.

Clinton, William J. "Remarks on Affirmative Action, July 19, 1995." *Published Papers of William J. Clinton, 1995.* Washington, DC: Government Printing Office, 1995.

"The Community Reinvestment Act and the Recent Mortgage Crisis." *States News Service,* December 3, 2008 (Accessed at Lexis Nexis Academic, News).

Congressional Research Service American Law Division. *Compilation and Overview of Federal Laws and Regulations Establishing Affirmative Action Goals or Other Preferences Based on Race, Gender, or Ethnicity.* February 17, 1995. Washington, DC: The Library of Congress, 1995.

Conway, David, ed. *Free-Market Feminism.* London: IEA Health & Welfare Unit, 1998.

Dale, Charles V. *Minority Contracting and Affirmative Action for Disadvantaged Small Businesses.* Washington, DC: Congressional Research Service, February 24, 2006.

Dale, Charles V., and Cassandra Foley. *Survey of Federal Laws and Regulations Mandating Affirmative Action Goals, Set-asides or Other Preferences Based on Race, Gender, or Ethnicity.* Congressional Research Service, September 7, 2004.

DeGroot, Morris, Stephen E. Fienburg, and Joseph B. Kadane, eds. *Statistics and the Law.* New York: John Wiley, 1996.

Dellinger, Walter. *Memorandum to General Counsels Re Adarand,* Washington, DC: Department of Justice, Office of Legal Counsel, June 28, 1995.

Detlefsen, Robert R. *Civil Rights Under Reagan.* San Francisco: Institute for Contemporary Studies, 1991.

"Developments in the Law—Employment Discrimination." *Harvard Law Review* 109 (1996): 1579–1692.

Dixon, Heather S. "National Daycare: A Necessary Precursor to Gender Equality With New Found Promise of Success." *Columbia Human Rights Law Review* 30 (2005): 561–661.

Dolan, Kathleen A. *Voting for Women: How the Public Evaluates Women Candidates.* Boulder, COL: Westview, 2004.

Drake, W. Avon, and Robert D. Holsworth. *Affirmative Action and the Stalled Quest for Black Progress.* Urbana: University of Illinois Press, 1996.

Dworkin, Ronald. "Affirming Affirmative Action." *The New York Review of Books,* October 22, 1988: 91–102.

Edelman, Peter, Harry Holzer, and Paul Offner. *Reconnecting Disadvantaged Young Men.* Washington, DC: Urban Institute Press, 2006.

Edley Jr., Christopher. *Not All Black and White: Affirmative Action and American Values.* New York: Hill and Wang, 1996.

Edwards, Franklin, ed. *E. Franklin Frazier: On Race Relations—Selected Writings.* Chicago: University of Chicago Press, 1968.

Eglit, Howard. *Elders on Trial: Age and Ageism in the American Legal System.* Gainesville: University Press of Florida, 2004.

Epp, Charles. *The Rights Revolution: Lawyers, Activists, and Supreme Courts in Comparative Perspective.* Chicago: University of Chicago Press, 1998.

Epstein, Richard. *Forbidden Grounds: The Case against Employment Discrimination Laws.* Cambridge: Harvard University Press, 1992.

Estlund, Cynthia L. "Putting *Grutter* to Work: Diversity, Integration and Affirmative Action in the Workplace." *Berkeley Journal of Employment and Labor Law* 26 (2005): 1–38.

Fallon, Richard H. Jr., Daniel J. Meltzer, and David Shapiro, eds. *Hart and Wechsler's The Federal Courts and the Federal System,* 5th ed. New York: Foundation Press/Thomson-West, 2003.

Faulcon, Kimberly West. "The River Runs Dry: When Title VI Trumps State Anti-Affirmative Action Laws." *University of Pennsylvania Law Review* 157 (2009): 1075–1160.

Fauntroy, Michael K. *Disadvantaged Businesses: A Review of Federal Assistance.* Washington, DC: Congressional Research Service, January 14, 2002.

Fiscus, Ronald J. *The Constitutional Logic of Affirmative Action.* Edited by Stephen J. Wasby. Durham, NC: Duke University Press, 1992.

Fisher, Anne B. "Businessmen Like to Hire by the Numbers." *Fortune,* September 16, 1985: 28–30.

Flexner, Eleanor, and Ellen Fitzpatrick. *Century of Struggle: The Woman's Rights Movement in the United States.* Cambridge: Harvard University Press, expanded edition, 1996.

Foner, Eric. *Reconstruction: America's Unfinished Revolution.* New York: Harper and Row, 1988.

———. *The Story of American Freedom.* New York: Norton, 1998.

_____. "The Strange Career of the Reconstruction Amendments." 108 *Yale LJ* (1999): 2003–2009.

Fossey, Richard, ed. *Readings on Equal Education, Race, the Courts, and Equal Education: The Limits of the Law.* Vol.15. New York: AMS Press, 1998.

Foundation for Individual Rights in Education. *The State of Free Speech on our Nation's Campuses: Spotlight on Speech Codes.* (2007).

Franke, J. B. "The Civil Rights Act of 1991." *Southern Illinois University Law Journal* 17 (1993): 267–298.

Franklin, John Hope. *Reconstruction After the Civil War.* Chicago: University of Chicago Press, 1994.

Franklin, John Hope, and Arnold J. Moss Jr. *From Slavery to Freedom: A History of African Americans: 8th ed.* New York: McGraw-Hill, 2000.

Fredrickson, George M. "America's Caste System: Will It Change?" *The New York Review of Books,* October 23, 1997: 68–75.

Gay, Claudine. "Legislating Without Constraints: The Effect of Minority Districting on Legislators' Responsiveness to Constituency Preferences." *The Journal of Politics* 69 (2007): 442–456.

Genovese, Eugene. *Roll, Jordan, Roll: The World the Slaves Made*. New York: Vintage Books, 1996.

Glazer, Nathan. *Affirmative Discrimination: Ethnic Inequality and Public Policy*. Cambridge: Harvard University Press, 1975.

———. *We are All Multiculturalists Now*. Cambridge: Harvard University Press, 1977.

———. "Reflections on Race, Hispanicity, and Ancestry in the U.S." In *The New Race Question: How the Census Counts Multiracial Individuals*, edited by Joel Perlmann and Mary C. Waters, 318–324. New York: Russell Sage Foundation, 2002.

Goering, John, ed. *Housing Desegregation and Federal Policy*. Chapel Hill: University of North Carolina Press, 1986.

———, Helene Stebbins, and Michael Siewert. *Report to Congress: Promoting Housing Choice in HUD's Rental Assistance Programs*. Washington, DC: U.S. Department of Housing and Urban Development, Office of Policy Development and Research, 1995.

Goldstein, Joshua R., and Ann J. Morning, "Back in the Box: The Dilemma of Using Multiple Race Data for Single Race Laws." In *The New Race Question: How the Census Counts Multiracial Individuals*, edited by Joel Perlmann and Mary Waters, 119–136. New York: Russell Sage Foundation, 2002.

Graham, Hugh Davis. *The Civil Rights Era: Origins and Development of National Policy, 1960–1972*. New York: Oxford University Press, 1990.

———. *Civil Rights and the Presidency: Race and Gender in American Politics, 1960–1972*. New York: Oxford University Press, 1992.

———. "Unintended Consequences: The Convergence of Affirmative Action and Immigration Policy." *American Behavioral Scientist* 41, no. 7 (April 1998): 898–911.

———. *Collision Course: The Strange Convergence of Affirmative Action and Immigration Policy in America*. New York: Oxford University Press, 2002.

———. "Legacies of the 1960s: The American 'Rights Revolution' in an Era of Divided Governance." *Journal of Policy History* 10 (1998): 267–288.

Gregory, Raymond F. *Age Discrimination in the American Workplace: Old at a Young Age*. New Brunswick, NJ: Rutgers University Press, 2001.

Grofman, Bernard, and Chandler Davidson, eds. *Controversies in Minority Voting: The Voting Rights Act in Perspective*. Washington, DC: The Brookings Institution, 1992.

Gurin, Patricia, et al. *Defending Diversity: Affirmative Action at the University of Michigan*. Ann Arbor: University of Michigan Press, 2003.

Gurney, Todd Christopher. "Comment: The Aftermath of the Virginia Military Institute Decision: Will Single-Gender Education Survive?" *Santa Clara Law Review* 38 (1998): 1183–1222.

Haar, Charles. *Suburbs under Siege: Race, Space, and Audacious Judges*. Princeton: Princeton University Press, 1996.

Hacker, Andrew. *Two Nations: Black and White, Separate, Hostile, Unequal*. New York: Scribner's, 1992.

———. "Goodbye to Affirmative Action?" *The New York Review of Books*, July 11, 1996: 21–28.

————. "Grand Illusion." *The New York Review of Books*, June 11, 1998: 26–29.

Hajnal, Zoltan L. *Changing White Attitudes toward Black Political Leadership.* Cambridge: Cambridge University Press, 2007.

Halpern, Stephen C. *On the Limits of Law: The Ironic Legacy of Title VI of the 1964 Civil Rights Act.* Baltimore: Johns Hopkins University Press, 1995.

Harrison, Lawrence E., and Samuel P. Huntington, eds. *Culture Matters: How Values Shape Human Progress.* New York: Basic Books, 2000.

Hays, R. Allen. *The Federal Government and Urban Housing.* Albany: State University of New York Press, 1995.

Hebert, J. Gerald. "Redistricting in the Post-2000 Era." *George Mason Law Review* 8 (2000): 431–476.

Helburn, Suzanne W., ed. "The Silent Crisis in Child Care." *The Annals of the American Academy of Political and Social Science* 563 (May 1999).

Hendrickson, Cara. "Racial Desegregation and Income Deconcentration in Public Housing." 9 *Georgetown Journal on Poverty Law and Policy* 9 (2002): 35–38.

Herrnson, Paul S. *Congressional Elections: Campaigning at Home in Washington.* 2nd ed. Washington, DC: Congressional Quarterly, 1998.

Hill, Herbert, and James E. Jones Jr., eds. *Race in America: The Struggle for Equality.* Madison: University of Wisconsin Press, 1993.

Hochschild, Jennifer L. "The Future of Affirmative Action." *Ohio State Law Journal* 59 (1998): 997-1037.

Hodgson, Godfrey. *More Equal Than Others: America from Nixon to the New Century.* Princeton: Princeton University Press, 2004.

Hollinger, David A. *Post-Ethnic America: Beyond Multiculturalism*, 10th Anniversary Edition. New York: Basic Books, 2005.

Holzer, Harry, and David Neumark. "Assessing Affirmative Action." *Journal of Economic Literature.* 38 (September 2000): 483–568.

————. "Affirmative Action: What Do We Know?" *Journal of Policy Analysis and Management* 25 (2006): 463–490.

Institute on Race and Poverty. *Examining the Relationship between Housing, Education, and Persistent Segregation: Final Report, Part IV.* University of Minnesota Law School (2000): 1–33.

Issacharoff, Samuel, Pamela S. Karlan, and Richard H. Pildes, eds. *The Law of Democracy: Legal Structure of the Political Process.* Westbury, NY: The Foundation Press, 1998.

————. *The Law of Democracy,*3d ed. New York: Foundation Press, 2007.

Jaschik, Scott. "Education Dept Sticks by Policy Upholding Minority Scholarships." *Chronicle of Higher Education*, June 9, 1995: A 28.

Jasiunas, J. Bannin. "Note: Is ENDA the Answer? Can A 'Separate but Equal' Federal Statute Adequately Protect Gays and Lesbians From Employment Discrimination?" *Ohio State Law Journal* 61(2000): 1529–1557.

Jolls, Christine. "Antidiscrimination and Accommodation." *Harvard Law Review* 115(2001): 642–699.

Jost, Kenneth. "Black Colleges: Do They Still Have An Important Role?" *CQ Researcher* 13 (December 12, 2003): 1047–1054.

Julian, Elizabeth. "Fair Housing and Community Development: Time to Come Together." *Indiana Law Review* 41(2008): 555–574.

Kahlenberg, Richard D. *The Remedy: Class, Race, and Affirmative Action.* New York: Basic Books, 1996.

Kameny, Franklin E. *Government v. Gays: The Sad Stories With Two Happy Ending—Civil Service Employment and Security Clearance.* In *Creating Change: Sexuality, Public Policy, and Civil Rights,* edited by John D'Emilio, William B. Turner, and Uruashi Vaid, 188–207. New York: St. Martin's, 2000.

Karlan, Pamela, and George Rutherglen. "Disabilities, Discrimination, and Reasonable Accommodation." *Duke Law Journal* 46 (1996): 1–72.

Katzenbach, Nicholas de B., and Burke Marshall, "Not Color Blind, Just Blind." *The New York Times Magazine,* February 22, 1998: 42 ff.

Keating, W. Dennis. *The Suburban Racial Dilemma: Housing and Neighborhoods.* Philadelphia: Temple University Press, 1994.

Kelly, Erin, and Frank Dobbin. "How Affirmative Action Became Diversity Management: Employer Reaction to Antidiscrimination Law." *American Behavioral Scientist* 41, no. 7 (April,1998): 960–984.

Kennedy, Randall. *Race, Crime, and the Law.* New York: Pantheon, 1997.

Keyssar, Alexander. *The Right to Vote: The Contested History of Democracy in the United States.* New York: Basic Books, 2000.

Kinder, Donald R., and Lynn M. Sanders. *Divided by Color: Racial Politics and Democratic Ideals.* Chicago: University of Chicago Press, 1996.

Koppelman, Andrew, *Antidiscrimination Law and Social Equality.* New Haven: Yale University Press, 1996.

Kushner, James. "Urban Neighborhood Regeneration and the Phases of Community Evolution." 41 *Indiana Law Review* (2008): 575–603.

Kymlicka, Will. *Multicultural Citizenship.* Oxford: Oxford University Press, 1995.

Lamb, Charles. *Housing Segregation in Suburban America Since 1960.* New York: Cambridge University Press, 2005.

La Noue, George R., and John C. Sullivan. "Gross Presumptions: Determining Group Eligibility for Federal Procurement Preferences." *Santa Clara Law Review* 41 (2000): 103–159.

———. "Deconstructing the Affirmative Action Categories." *American Behavioral Scientist* 41, no. 7 (April, 1998): 913–926.

———. "Presumptions for Preferences: The Small Business Administration's Decisions on Groups Entitled to Affirmative Action." *Journal of Policy History* 6 (1994): 439–467.

Lawson, Steven F. *Running for Freedom: Civil Rights and Black Politics in America Since 1941.* New York: McGraw-Hill, 1996.

Lee, Jennifer. *The Racial and Ethnic Meaning Behind Black: Retailers' Hiring Practices in Inner-City Neighborhoods.* In *Color Lines: Affirmative Action, Immigration, and Civil Rights Options for America,* edited by John David Skrentny, 168-187. Chicago: University of Chicago Press, 2001.

Lemann, Nicholas. *The Promised Land: The Great Black Migration and How It Changed America.* New York: Knopf, 1991.

———. *The Big Test: The Secret History of the American Meritocracy.* New York: Farrar, Strauss and Giroux, 1999.

Leonard, James. "The Equality Trap: How Reliance on Traditional Civil Rights Concepts Has Rendered Title I of the ADA Ineffective." *Case Western Reserve Law Review* 56 (2004): 1–63.

Levine, Samantha. "Taking Action to Admit." *U.S. News & World Report*, June 4, 2007: 34–36.

Levinson, Sanford. *Wrestling with Diversity*. Durham, NC: Duke University Press, 2003.

Levy, Leonard W., Kenneth Karst, and Dennis J. Mahoney, eds. *Civil Rights and Equality*. New York: Macmillan, 1989.

Lichter, Michael and Roger Waldinger. "Producing Conflict: Immigration Management of Diversity in the Multiethnic Metropolis." In *Color Lines: Affirmative Action, Immigration, and Civil Rights Options for America*, edited by John David Skrentny, 147–167. Chicago: University of Chicago Press, 2001.

Lien, Pei-te. *The Voting Rights Act and Its Implications for Three Nonblack Minorities*. In *The Voting Rights Act: Securing the Ballot*, edited by Richard M. Valelly. Washington, DC: Congressional Quarterly Press, 2006.

Litwack, Leon F. *Trouble in Mind: Black Southerners in the Age of Jim Crow*. New York: Knopf, 1998.

———. *North of Slavery: The Negro in the Free States, 1790–1860*. Chicago: University of Chicago Press, 1961.

Lowe Jr., Eugene Y., ed. *Promise and Dilemma: Perspectives on Racial Diversity and Higher Education*. Princeton: Princeton University Press, 1999.

Lublin, David. *The Paradox of Representation: Racial Gerrymandering and Minority Interests in Congress*. Princeton: Princeton University Press, 1997.

Lyn, Kathlene. *Words That Matter: Women's Voice and Institutional Bias in Public Policy Formation*. In *The Impact of Women in Public Office*, edited by Susan Caroll. Bloomington: Indiana University Press, 2004.

Macnicol, John. *Age Discrimination: An Historical and Contemporary Analysis*. Cambridge: Cambridge University Press, 2006.

Maltz, Earl M. *Civil Rights, the Constitution, and Congress, 1863–1869*. Lawrence, KS: University Press of Kansas, 1990.

———, "Thirteenth Amendment." In the *Oxford Companion to the Supreme Court of the United States*, edited by Kermit L. Hall, et al. 869–870 New York: Oxford University Press, 1992.

Mandle, Jay R. *Not Slave, Not Free: The African American Economic Experience*. Durham: Duke University Press, 1992.

Massey, Douglas S. *Categorically Unequal: The American Stratification System*. New York: Russell Sage Foundation, 2007.

———, and Nancy A. Denton. *American Apartheid: Segregation and the Making of the Underclass*. Cambridge: Harvard University Press, 1993.

McCloskey, Robert G. *The American Supreme Court*. Chicago: University of Chicago Press, 1994 (2d ed, revised by Sanford Levinson).

McDonagh, Eileen, and Laura Pappano. *Playing With the Boys: Why Separate Is Not Equal in Sports*. New York: Oxford University Press, 2008.

McGuinn, Patrick J. *No Child Left behind and the Transformation of Federal Education Policy, 1965–2005*. Lawrence: University of Kansas Press, 2006.

McWhorter, John. *Winning the Race: Behind the Crisis in Black America*. New York: Gotham Books, 2006.

Mezey, Susan Gluck. *Disabling Interpretations: The Americans with Disabilities Act in Federal Courts*. Pittsburgh: University of Pittsburgh Press, 2005.

———. *Queers in Court: Gay Rights Law and Public Policy*. Lanham, MD: Rowman and Littlefield, 2007.

Millenson, Debra A. "Whither Affirmative Action: The Future of Executive Order 11,246." *University of Memphis Law Review* 29 (1999): 679–737.

Moran, Rachel F. "The Politics of Discretion: Federal Intervention in Bilingual Education." *California Law Review* 76 (December 1988): 1249–1352.

———. "Bilingual Education as a Status Conflict." *California Law Review* 75 (January 1987): 321–362.

Nixon, Richard M. "Special Message to Congress Proposing Legislation and Outlining Administration Actions to Deal with Federal Housing Policy, September 19, 1973." *Public Papers of Richard Nixon, 1973*. Washington, DC: Government Printing Office, 1975.

———. "Statement About Federal Policies Relative to Equal Housing Opportunity, June 11, 1971." *Public Papers of Richard Nixon, 1971*. Washington, DC: Government Printing Office, 1972.

Nussbaum, Martha C. *Sex and Social Justice*. New York: Oxford University, Press, 1999.

O'Neill, William L. *feminism in America: A History*. 2nd ed. New Brunswick, NJ: Transaction Publishers, 1989.

Orfield, Gary et al. *Dismantling Desegregation: The Quiet Reversal of Brown v. Board of Education*. New York: The New Press, 1996.

Orfield, Gary, and Edward Miller, eds. *Chilling Admissions: The Affirmative Action Crisis and the Search for Alternatives*. Cambridge: Harvard Education Publishing Group, 1998.

Orfield, Myron. "Land Use and Housing Policies to Reduce Concentrated Poverty and Racial Segregation." *Fordham Urban Law Journal* 33 (2006): 877–936.

Patai, Daphne. *Heterophobia: Sexual Harassment and the Future of Feminism*. Lanham, MD: Rowman and Littlefield, 1998.

Patterson, James T. *Restless Giant: The United States from Watergate to Bush v. Gore*. New York: Oxford University Press, 2005.

———. *Brown v. Board of Education: A Civil Rights Milestone and Its Troubled Legacy*. New York: Oxford University Press, 2001.

Patterson, Orlando. *The Ordeal of Integration: Progress and Resentment in America's "Racial" Crisis*. Washington, DC: Civitas/Counterpoint, 1997.

Porter, Douglas R. *The Promise and Practice of Exclusionary Zoning*. In *Growth Management and Affordable Housing: Do They Conflict?*, edited by Anthony Downs. Washington, DC: Brookings Institution, 2004.

Porter, Nicole Buonocore. "Re-Defining Superwoman: An Essay on Overcoming the 'Maternal Wall' in the Legal Workplace." *Duke Journal of Gender Law & Policy* 13 (2006): 55–84.

Posner, Richard A. "The Efficiency and Efficacy of Title VII." 136 *University of Pennsylvania Law Review* (1987): 512–521.

Putnam, Robert D. "E Pluribus Unum: Diversity and Community in the Twenty-first Century." *Scandinavian Political Studies* 30 (2007): 137–174.

Rae, Douglas. *Equalities*. Cambridge: Harvard University Press, 1981.

Ravitch, Diane. *The Troubled Crusade*. New York: Basic Books, 1983.

Reingold, Beth. *Representing Women: Sex, Gender, and Legislative Behavior in Arizona and California.* Chapel Hill: University of North Carolina Press, 2000.

Rhee, John. "Theories of Citizenship and Their Role in the Bilingual Education Debate." *Columbia Journal of Law & Social Problems* 33 (1991): 33–83.

Roemer, John E. *Equality of Opportunity.* Cambridge: Harvard University Press, 1998.

Roisman, Florence Wagman. "Long Overdue." *Cityscape* 4, no. 3 (1999): 171–196.

———. "Keeping the Promise: Ending Racial Discrimination and Segregation in Federally Financed Housing." *Howard Law Journal* 48 (2005): 913–935.

———. "Living Together: Ending Racial Discrimination and Segregation in Housing." *Indiana Law Review* 41 (2008): 507–520.

Rose, David. "Twenty-Five Years Later: Where Do We Stand on Equal Employment Opportunity Law Enforcement?" *Vanderbilt Law Review* 42 (1989): 1121–1139.

Rose, Monica L. "Note: Proposal 2 and the Ban on Affirmative Action: An Uncertain Future for the University of Michigan in Its Quest for Diversity." *Boston University Public International Law Journal* 17 (2008): 309–337.

Rosen, Sherwin. *Disability Accommodation and the Labor Market.* In *Disability and Work: Incentives, Rights, and Opportunities*, edited by Carolyn L. Weaver, 18–30. Washington, DC: The AEI Press, 1991.

Ross, Lisa B. "Note: Learning the Language: An Examination of the Use of Voter Initiative to Make Language Education Policy." *New York University Law Review* 82 (2007): 1510–1546.

Rossell, Christine. *Dismantling Bilingual Education Implementing English Immersion: The California Initiative.* San Francisco: Public Policy Institute of California, 2002.

Rothman, Stanley, Seymour Martin Lipset, and Neil Nevitte. "Racial Diversity Reconsidered." The Public Interest (Spring 2003): 25–38.

Rutherglen, George. *Employment Discrimination Law: Visions of Equality in Theory and Doctrine*, 2d ed. New York: Foundation Press, 2007.

Salomone, Rosemary. "Single-Sex Programs: Resolving the Research Conundrum." *Teachers College Record* 108 (2006): 778–802.

Sander, Richard. "A Systemic Analysis of Affirmative Action in American Law Schools." *Stanford Law Review* 57 (2004): 367–483.

San Miguel, Guadalupe. *Contested Policy: The Rise and Fall of Bilingual Education in the United States, 1960–2008.* Denton, TX: University of North Texas Press, 2004.

Schmidt, John R. *Memorandum to General Counsels Re Post-Adarand Guidance on Affirmative Action.* February 29, 1996. Department of Justice, Office of the Associate Attorney General, 1996.

Schmidt, Peter. "America's Universities Are Living a Diversity Lie." *The Wall Street Journal,* June 28, 2008: A11.

Schoenbrod, David. *Power Without Responsibility: How Congress Abuses the People Through Delegation.* New Haven: Yale University Press, 1993.

Schuck, Peter. *Diversity in America: Keeping Government at a Safe Distance.* Cambridge: The Belknap Press of Harvard University Press, 2003.

Schulhofer, Stephen J. *Unwanted Sex: The Culture of Intimidation and the Failure of Law*. Cambridge: Harvard University Press, 1999.

Schwartz, Alex F. *Housing Policy in the United States*. New York: Routledge, 2006.

Schwartz, Bernard. *Behind Bakke: Affirmative Action and the Supreme Court*. New York: New York University Press, 1988.

Schwemm, Robert G., ed. *The Fair Housing Act After Twenty Years: A Conference at Yale Law School, March 1988*. New Haven: Yale Law School, 1989.

Schwemm, Robert. *Housing Discrimination: Law and Litigation*. St. Paul: Thomson-West, 2008.

Selingo, Jeffrey. "Why Minority Recruiting Is Alive and Well in Texas." *Chronicle of Higher Education*, November 19, 1999: A34–36.

Selmi, Michael. "Public v. Private Enforcement of Civil Rights: The Case of Housing and Employment." *U.C.L.A. Law Review* 45 (1998): 1401–1459.

Shull, Steven A. *A Kinder, Gentler Racism—The Reagan-Bush Civil Rights Legacy*. Armonk, NY: M. E. Sharpe, 1993.

Skerry, Peter. "Multiculturalism in the Administrative State." In *The New Race Question: How the Census Counts Multiracial Individuals*, edited by Joel Perlmann and Mary Waters, 327–339. New York: Russell Sage Foundation, 2002.

Skrentny, John David. *Ironies of Affirmative Action: Politics, Culture, and Justice in America*. Chicago: University of Chicago Press, 1996.

———. *Editor's Introduction*. In *Color Lines: Affirmative Action, Immigration, and Civil Rights Options for America*, edited by John David Skrentny, 1–28. Chicago: University of Chicago Press, 2001.

———."Policy-Elite Perceptions and Social Movement Success: Understanding Variations in Group Inclusion in Affirmative Action." *American Journal of Sociology* 111 (2006): 1762–1815.

Smith, Peggie R. "Laboring for Child Care: A Consideration of New Approaches to Represent Low-Income Service Workers." *University of Pennsylvania Journal of Labor & Employment Law* 8 (2006): 583–621.

Smith, Rogers. "Legitimating Reconstruction: The Limits of Legalism." *Yale Law Journal* 108 (1999): 2039–2075.

Smolla, Rodney A. "Integration Maintenance: The Unconstitutionality of Benign Programs that Discourage Black Entry to Prevent White Flight." *Duke University Law Journal* (1981): 891–939.

Sommers, Christina Hoff. *Who Stole Feminism?: How Women Have Betrayed Women*. New York: Touchstone-Simon and Schuster, 1995.

Southern Education Foundation. *Miles to Go: Report on Black Students and Postsecondary Education in the South*. Atlanta: Southern Education Foundation, 1998.

Southern Poverty Law Center. *Free at Last*. Atlanta: Southern Education Foundation, 1989.

Stampp, Kenneth M. *The Era of Reconstruction, 1865–1877*. New York: Vintage Books, 1965.

Stanfield, Rochelle. "The Split Society." *The National Journal*, April 2, 1994: 762–767.

Steinberg, Stephen. *Turning Back: The Retreat from Racial Justice in American Thought and Policy*. Boston: Beacon Press, 1995.

"Symposium: Moments of Change: Transformation in American Constitutionalism." *Yale Law Journal* 108 (June 1999): 1917–2449.

"The Community Reinvestment Act and the Recent Mortgage Crisis." *States News Service*, December 3, 2008 (Accessed at Lexis Nexis Academic, News).

Thernstrom, Abigail. *Whose Votes Count?—Affirmative Action and Minority Voting Rights.* Cambridge: Harvard University Press, 1987.

———. "The Flawed Defense of Preferences." *The Wall Street Journal*, October 23, 1998: A19.

———. "Separation Anxiety." *The Wall Street Journal*, November 30, 2007: W13.

———. "Focus on the Voting Rights Act—Section 5 of the Voting Rights Act, By Now a Murky Mess." *Georgetown Journal of Law and Public Policy* 5 (2007): 41–77.

Thernstrom, Stephan, and Abigail Thernstrom. *America in Black and White, One Nation Indivisible: Race in Modern America.* New York: Simon and Schuster, 1997.

Thernstrom, Stephan "Diversity and Meritocracy in Legal Education: A Critical Evaluation of Linda F. Wrightman's 'The Threat to Diversity in Legal Education.' " *Constitutional Commentary* 15 (Spring 1998): 11–43.

Title IX of the Education Act of 1972, Pub L 92-318, 86 Stat 373, 20 USC § 1681 (2009).

Traub, James. "The Class of Prop. 209." *The New York Times Magazine*, May 12, 1999: 44ff.

Tribe, Lawrence. "Trial by Mathematics: Precision and Ritual in the Legal Process." *Harvard Law Review* 84 (1971): 1329–1393.

Tucker, William H. *The Science and Politics of Racial Research.* Urbana: University of Illinois Press, 1994.

Turner, Margery. "Limits on Housing and Neighborhood Choice: Discrimination, Segregation in U.S Housing Markets." *Indiana Law Review* 41 (2008): 797–816.

United States Commission on Civil Rights. *The Black/White Colleges: Dismantling the Dual System of Higher Education.* Washington, DC: Clearinghouse Publication 66, 1981.

———. *Federal Procurement After Adarand.* Washington, DC: U.S. Government Printing Office, September 2005.

United States Department of Education. *The State of Charter Schools, Third Year Report, 1999.* Washington DC: U.S. Government Printing Office, 1999.

United States Equal Employment Opportunity Commission. Affirmative Action Guidelines of the Equal Employment Opportunity Commission. 29 CFR 1608, 2009.

United States Equal Employment Opportunity Commission, Office of General Counsel—Trial Division. *Legislative History of the Age Discrimination in Employment.* Washington, DC: U.S. Government Printing Office, 1981.

United States Office of Federal Contract Compliance Programs. *Affirmative Action Programs.* 41 CFR 60, 2009.

U.S. Congress. House. Committee on Economic and Education Opportunities. *Hearings on Title IX of the Education Amendments of 1972 before the Subcommittee on Postsecondary Education, Training, and Life-Long Learning.* 104th Cong., 1st sess., May 9, 1995.

U.S. Congress. House. Committee on Education and the Workforce. *Hearing on Reforming Bilingual Education before the Subcommittee on Early Childhood, Youth, and Families.* 105th Cong., 2nd sess., April 30, 1998.

U.S. Congress. House. Committee on the Judiciary, *Hearings on Fair Housing Issues before the Subcommittee on Civil and Constitutional Rights.* 103d Cong., 2nd sess., September 28, 30, 1994.

U.S. Secretary of Labor. *The Older American Worker: Age Discrimination in Employment.* Washington, DC: Government Printing Office, June 1965.

U.S. Senate, *Hearing on Women in Science and Technology Before the Senate Subcommittee on Science, Technology, and Space.* 107th Cong., 2nd sess., October 3, 2002. Washington: DC: U.S. Government Printing Office, 2005.

U.S. *Uniform Guidelines on Employee Selection Procedures* (1978). 29 CFR 1607, 2009.

Urofsky, Melvin I. *Affirmative Action on Trial: Sex Discrimination in Johnson v. Santa Clara.* Lawrence: University Press of Kansas, 1997.

Veil, Elizabeth. "Teaching to the Testosterone." *The New York Times Magazine*, March 7, 2008: 41ff.

Wallison, Peter J. "Government Policies and Financial Crisis." *States News Service*, December. 3, 2008 (Accessed at LexisNexis Academic, News).

Wayne, Stephen J. *The Road to the White House, 2008*, 8th ed.: *Epilogue.* Boston: Wadsworth/Cengage, 2008.

Welch, Susan, and John Gruhl. *Affirmative Action and Minority Enrollments in Medical and Law Schools.* Ann Arbor: University of Michigan Press, 1998.

Western, Bruce. *Punishment and Inequality in America.* New York: Russell Sage Foundation, 2006.

Wicker, Tom. *Tragic Failure: Racial Integration in America.* New York: William Morrow, 1996.

Williams, Kim M. *Mark One or More: Civil Rights in Multiracial America.* Ann Arbor: University of Michigan Press, 2005.

Williams, Melissa S. *Voice, Trust, and Memory: Marginalized Groups and the Failings of Liberal Representation.* Princeton: Princeton University Press, 1998.

Wilson, James Q. *Bureaucracy: What Government Agencies Do and Why They Do It.* New York: Basic Books, 1989.

Wilson, William Julius. *When Work Disappears: The World of the New Urban Poor.* New York: Knopf, 1997.

———. *More Than Just Race: Being Black and Poor in the Inner City.* New York: W. W. Norton, 2009.

Wilson, William Julius, and Richard P. Taub. *There Goes the Neighborhood: Racial, Ethnic, and Class Tensions in Four Chicago Neighborhoods and Their Meaning for America.* New York: Knopf, 2006.

Wood, Peter. *Diversity: The Invention of a Concept.* San Francisco: Encounter Books, 2003.

Wrightman, Linda F. "Threat to Diversity in Legal Education." *New York Law Review* 72 (1997): 1–53.

List and Index of Selected Cases

The page numbers in bold italics refer to extended case excerpts
and/or related commentary.

Topical Index

To assist the reader, brief descriptions of central administrative regulations, laws, and judicial opinions are provided herein. Page references to the aforementioned include extended excerpts and related commentary. The Affirmative Action main entry is a cross-reference for all the other main entries. Main entries are in bold.

459

Index of Selected Names